D0919496

The Use of Psychological Testing for Treatment Planning and Outcomes Assessment

Third Edition

Volume 2 Instruments for Children and Adolescents

The Use of Psychological Testing for Treatment Planning and Outcomes Assessment

Third Edition

Volume 2 Instruments for Children and Adolescents

Edited by

Mark E. Maruish
Southcross Consulting

New York London

Senior Consulting Editor: Susan Milmoe
Editorial Assistant: Kristen Depken
Cover Design: Kathryn Houghtaling Lacey
Textbook Production Manager: Paul Smolenski
Full-Service Compositor: TechBooks
Text and Cover Printer: Hamilton Printing Company

This book was typeset in 10/12 pt. Palatino, Italic, Bold, and Bold Italic. The heads were typeset in Palatino and Berling, Bold, Italics, and Bold Italics.

Lawrence Erlbaum Associates, Inc., Publishers
10 Industrial Avenue
Mahwah, New Jersey 07430
www.erlbaum.com

First Published by Lawrence Erlbaum Associates, Inc., Publishers
10 Industrial Avenue
Mahwah, New Jersey 07430

Reprinted 2010 by Psychology Press

Library of Congress Cataloging-in-Publication Data

The use of psychological testing for treatment planning and outcomes assessment / edited by Mark E. Maruish.—3rd ed.
p. cm.
Includes bibliographical references and index.
Volume 1: ISBN 0-8058-4329-9 (casebound : alk. paper) – Volume 2: ISBN 0-8058-4330-2 (casebound : alk. paper) – Volume 3: ISBN 0-8058-4331-0 (casebound : alk. paper)
1. Psychological tests. 2. Mental illness—Diagnosis. 3. Mental illness—Treatment—Evaluation. 4. Psychiatric rating scales. 5. Outcome assessment (Medical care) I. Maruish, Mark E. (Mark Edward)

RC473.P79U83 2004
616.89'075–dc22 2003025432

For my family

Contents

Preface

Like other medical and behavioral health care services, the practice of test-based psychological assessment has not entered the era of managed care unscathed. Limitations placed on total moneys allotted for psychological services have had an impact on the practice of psychological testing. However, for those skilled in its use, psychological testing's ability to help quickly identify psychological problems, plan and monitor treatment, and document treatment effectiveness presents many potentially rewarding opportunities during a time when health care organizations must (a) provide problem-focused, time-limited treatment; (b) demonstrate the effectiveness of treatment to payers and patients; and (c) implement quality improvement initiatives.

With the opportunity at hand, it is now up to those with skill and training in psychological assessment to make the most of this opportunity to contribute to (and benefit from) efforts to control health care costs. However, this may not be as simple a task as it would appear. Many trained professionals are likely to have only limited knowledge of how to use test results for planning, monitoring, and assessing the outcomes of psychological interventions. Consequently, although the basic skills are there, many well-trained clinicians—and graduate students as well—need to develop or expand their testing knowledge and skills so as to be better able to apply them for such purposes. This need served as the impetus for the development of the first two editions of this book, and the development of this third edition of the work attests to its continued presence.

In developing the contents of this and the previous editions of this work, it was decided that the most informative and useful approach would be one in which aspects of broad topical areas are addressed separately. The first area has to do with general issues and recommendations to be considered in the use of psychological testing for treatment planning and outcomes assessment in today's behavioral health care environment. The second and third areas address issues related to the use of specific psychological tests and scales for these same purposes, one dealing with child and adolescent instruments, the other dealing with adult instruments. The fourth area concerns the future of psychological testing, including future developments in this area. For the current edition, issues related to future developments have been incorporated into the general considerations section. Because of increased content and a desire to better meet the needs of individual practitioners, each of the three sections is now printed in a separate volume.

Volume 1 of this third edition represents an update and extension of the first and fourth parts of the second edition. It is devoted to general considerations that pertain to the need for and use of psychological testing for treatment planning and outcome assessment. The introductory chapter provides an overview of the status of the health care delivery system today and the ways in which testing can contribute to making the system more cost-effective. Three chapters are devoted to issues related to treatment planning, whereas five chapters focus on issues related to outcomes assessment. The first of the planning chapters deals with the use of psychological tests for screening purposes in various clinical settings. Screening can serve as the first step in the treatment planning process; for this reason, it is a topic that warrants the reader's attention. The second of these chapters presents a discussion of the research suggesting how testing may be used as a predictor of differential response to treatment and its outcome. Each of these chapters represents updated versions of the original work. The next chapter deals with treatment planning within Prochaska's Transtheoretical Model—a widely accepted and researched approach that takes the patient's stage of readiness to change into consideration in developing and revising treatment plans.

The five chapters on the use of testing for outcomes assessment are complementary. The first provides an overview of the use of testing for outcomes assessment purposes, discussing some of the history of outcomes assessment, its current status, its measures and methods, individualizing outcome assessment, the distinction between clinically and statistically significant differences in outcomes assessment, and some outcomes-related issues that merit further research. The next four chapters expand on the groundwork laid in this chapter. The first of these four presents an updated discussion of a set of specific guidelines that can be valuable to clinicians in their selection of psychological measures for assessing treatment outcomes. These same criteria also are generally applicable to the selection of instruments for treatment planning purposes. Two chapters provide a discussion of statistical procedures and research design issues related to the measurement of treatment progress and outcomes with psychological tests. One chapter specifically addresses the analysis of individual patient data; the other deals with the analysis of group data. As noted in the previous editions of this work, knowledge and skills in these areas are particularly important and needed by clinicians wishing to establish and maintain an effective treatment evaluation process within their particular setting. The other outcomes-related chapter presents a discussion of considerations relevant to the design, implementation, and maintenance of outcomes management programs in behavioral health care settings.

Volume 1 also includes a chapter addressing a frequently neglected topic in discussions of outcomes assessment, that is, ethical considerations related to outcomes assessment. The volume concludes with a future-oriented chapter, written to discuss predictions and recommendations related to the use of psychological assessment for treatment planning and outcomes assessment.

Volumes 2 and 3 address the use of specific psychological instruments for treatment planning and outcome assessment purposes. Volume 2 deals with child and adolescent instruments, with one chapter devoted to a review of the research related to the conceptualization of quality of life (QOL) as is applies to children and how it has evolved over the years. The purpose of this chapter is to present a foundation for the future development of useful measures of child QOL—something that currently appears to be in short supply. Volume 3 focuses on instruments that are exclusively or primarily intended for use with adult populations.

Instruments considered as potential chapter topics for Volumes 1 and 3 were evaluated against several selection criteria, including the popularity of the instrument among clinicians; recognition of its psychometric integrity in professional publications; in the case of recently released instruments, the potential for the instrument to become widely accepted and used; the perceived usefulness of the instrument for treatment planning and outcomes assessment purposes; and the availability of a recognized expert on the instrument (preferably its author) to contribute a chapter to this book. In the end, the instrument-specific chapters selected for inclusion were those judged most likely to be of the greatest interest and utility to the majority of the book's intended audience.

Each of the chapters in the second edition had previously met these selection criteria; thus, Volumes 2 and 3 consist of updated or completely revised versions of the instrumentation chapters that appeared in the first edition. Both volumes also contain several new chapters discussing instruments that were not included in the second edition for one reason or another (e.g., was not developed at the time, has only recently gained wide acceptance for outcomes assessment purposes). Indeed, recognition of the potential utility of each of these instruments for treatment planning or evaluation served as one impetus for revising the second edition of this work.

A decision regarding the specific content of each of the chapters in Volumes 2 and 3 was not easy to arrive at. However, in the end, the contributors were asked to address those issues and questions that are of the greatest concern or relevancy for practicing clinicians. Generally, these fall into three important areas: (1) What the instrument does and how it was developed; (2) how one should use this instrument for treatment planning and monitoring; and (3) how it should be used to assess treatment outcomes. Guidelines were provided to assist the contributors in addressing each of these areas. Many of the contributors adhered strictly to these guidelines; others modified the contents of their chapter to reflect and emphasize what they judged to be important to the reader to know about the instrument when using the it for planning, monitoring, or outcome assessment purposes. Some may consider the chapters in Volumes 2 and 3 to be the "meat" of this revised work, because they provide "how to" instructions for tools that are commonly found in the clinician's armamentarium of assessment instruments. In fact, these chapters are no more or less important than those found in Volume 1. They are only extensions and are of limited value outside of the context of the chapters in Volume 1.

As was the case with the previous two editions, the third edition of *The Use of Psychological Testing for Treatment Planning and Evaluation* is not intended to be a definitive work on the topic. However, it is hoped that the reader will find its chapters useful in better understanding general and test-specific considerations and approaches related to treatment planning and outcomes assessment, and in effectively applying them in his or her daily practice. It also is hoped that it will stimulate further endeavors in investigating the application of psychological testing for these purposes.

—Mark E. Maruish
Minneapolis, MN

List of Contributors

Brian V. Abbott
Texas A&M University
College Station, TX

Thomas M. Achenbach
University of Vermont
Burlington, VT

Ross B. Andelman
Contra Costa Children's Mental Health Services
Concord, CA

Robert P. Archer
Eastern Virginia Medical School
Norfolk, VA

C. Clifford Attkisson
University of California
San Francisco, CA

Steven E. Bailley
University of Texas–Houston Health Sciences Center
Houston, TX

Thomas Beers
Kaiser Permanente San Diego Chemical Dependency Program
San Diego, CA

Albert J. Belanger
Harvard Medical School
Boston, MA

Larry E. Beutler
University of California
Santa Barbara, CA

Phillip J. Brantley
Pennington Biomedical Research Center
Baton Rouge, LA

Gary M. Burlingame
Brigham Young University
Provo, UT

James N. Butcher
University of Minnesota
Minneapolis, MN

David L. Carlston
Ohio University
Athens, OH

Antonio Cepeda-Benito
Texas A&M University
College Station, TX

Dianne L. Chambless
University of Pennsylvania
Philadelphia, PA

James A. Ciarlo
University of Denver
Denver, CO

Paul D. Cleary
Harvard Medical School
Boston, MA

James R. Clopton
Texas Tech University
Lubbock, TX

John D. Cone
Alliant International University
San Diego, CA

C. Keith Conners
Duke University School of Medicine
Durham, NC

Jonathan C. Cox
Brigham Young University
Provo, UT

William J. Culpepper
University of Maryland
Baltimore, MD

Constance J. Dahlberg
Alliant International University
San Diego, CA

Allen S. Daniels
Alliance Behavioral Care, University of Cincinnati
Cincinnati, OH

Edwin de Beurs
Leiden University Medical Center
Leiden, The Netherlands

Leonard R. Derogatis
Johns Hopkins University School of Medicine
Baltimore, MD

Kathy Dowell
Ohio University
Athens, OH

Gareth R. Dutton
Louisiana State University
Baton Rouge, LA

William W. Eaton
Johns Hopkins University, Bloomberg School of Public Health
Baltimore, MD

Susan V. Eisen
Center for Health Quality, Outcomes, and Economic Research, Edith Nourse Rogers Veterans Hospital
Boston, MA

Jeffery N. Epstein
Duke University School of Medicine
Durham, NC

Alex Espadas
University of Texas–Houston Health Sciences Center
Houston, TX

Laura E. Evison
Johns Hopkins University School of Medicine
Baltimore, MD

Kya Fawley
Northwestern University
Evanston, IL

Maureen Fitzpatrick
Johns Hopkins University School of Medicine
Baltimore, MD

Jenny Fleming
University of California
Santa Barbara, CA

Michael B. Frisch
Baylor University
Waco, TX

Anthony B. Gerard
Western Psychological Services
Los Angeles, CA

Sona Gevorkian
Massachusetts General Hospital
Boston, MA

David H. Gleaves
Texas A&M University
College Station, TX

Pamela Greenberg
American Managed Behavioral Healthcare Association
Washington, DC

Roger L. Greene
Pacific Graduate School of Psychology
Palo Alto, CA

Thomas K. Greenfield
University of California and Public Health Institute Berkeley
San Francisco, CA

Ann T. Gregersen
Brigham Young University
Provo, UT

Grant R. Grissom
Polaris Health Directions
Langhorne, PA

Seth D. Grossman
Institute for Advanced Studies in Personology
Coral Gables, FL

Kurt Hahlweg
Technical University of Braunschweig
Braunschweig, Germany

Steven R. Hahn
Albert Einstein College of Medicine
New York, NY

Ashley E. Hanson
University of Alabama
Tuscaloosa, AL

Nancy M. Hatcher
University of Georgia
Athens, GA

Derek Hatfield
Ohio University
Athens, OH

Eric J. Hawkins
Brigham Young University
Provo, UT

Jena Helgerson
Northwestern University
Evanston, IL

Kay Hodges
Eastern Michigan University
Ann Arbor, MI

Elizabeth A. Irvin
Services Research Group, Inc. and Simmons College, Graduate School of Social Work
Boston, MA

Gary Jeager
Kaiser Permanente Harbor City Chemical Dependency Program
Harbor City, CA

R. W. Kamphaus
University of Georgia
Athens, GA

Jennifer M. Karpe
University of Alabama
Tuscaloosa, AL

Sangwon Kim
University of Georgia
Athens, GA

Kenneth A. Kobak
Dean Foundation for Health Research and Education
Madison, WI

Scott H. Kollins
Duke University School of Medicine
Durham, NC

Steven Stein
Multi-Health Systems, Inc.
Toronto, ON, Canada

Randy Stinchfield
University of Minnesota
Minneapolis, MN

Sumner J. Sydeman
Northern Arizona University
Flagstaff, AZ

Elana Sydney
Albert Einstein College of Medicine
New York, NY

Hani Talebi
University of California
Santa Barbara, CA

Manuel J. Tejeda
Barry University
Miami Shores, FL

Allen Tien
MDLogix, Inc.
Towson, MD

John E. Ware, Jr.
QualityMetric Inc. and Tufts University Medical School
Lincoln, RI

Dana Aron Weiner
Northwestern University
Evanston, IL

Irving B. Weiner
University of South Florida
Tampa, FL

M. Gawain Wells
Brigham Young University
Provo, UT

Douglas L. Welsh
University of Alabama
Tuscaloosa, AL

Janet B. W. Williams
New York State Psychiatric Institute
New York, NY

Kimberly A. Wilson
Stanford University Medical School
Palo Alto, CA

Ken C. Winters
University of Minnesota
Minneapolis, MN

Stephen E. Wong
Florida International University
Miami, FL

Karen B. Wood
Louisiana State University
Baton Rouge, LA

Michele Ybarra
Johns Hopkins University, Bloomberg School of Public Health
Baltimore, MD

The Use of Psychological Testing for Treatment Planning and Outcomes Assessment

Third Edition

Volume 2 Instruments for Children and Adolescents

1

Use of the Children's Depression Inventory

Gill Sitarenios and Steven Stein
Multi-Health Systems, Inc.

CHILDHOOD DEPRESSION

From a clinical perspective, a syndrome is a characteristic constellation of psychopathologic symptoms and signs. A depressive syndrome typically encompasses a negative dysphoric mood and complaints such as a sense of worthlessness or hopelessness, preoccupation with death or suicide, difficulties in concentration or making decisions, disturbance in patterns of sleep and food intake, and reduced energy. A disorder is a particular syndrome that has been shown to have the characteristics of a diagnosable condition. That is, it has a recognizable pattern of onset and course, clear negative consequences with respect to the individual's functioning, distinct biologic or related correlates, an association with known etiologic or risk factors, and a course that may be altered in predictable ways by various treatments.

Major depressive disorder and dysthymic disorder are two forms of depressive disorder that affect children as well as adults. Episodes of major depression in childhood last about 10 months on average and may have psychotic or melancholic features associated with them (Kovacs, Obrosky, Gatsonis, & Richards, 1997). Major depression often is comorbid with other disorders, most commonly with disorders of anxiety and conduct (Kovacs, Gatsonis, Paulauskas, & Richards, 1989; Puig-Antich, 1982; Strober & Carlson, 1982). Major depression in childhood is associated with a high rate of recovery; there is, however, a very high risk of episode recurrence, and an increased risk for the development of other related disorders (Kovacs, 1996a, 1996b; Kovacs et al., 1989; Strober & Carlson, 1982). Compared with major depression, dysthymic disorder is milder and possibly less impairing. However, dysthymia usually lasts longer than major depression, with an average duration of about 3 and a half years or longer (Kovacs et al., 1997). Like major depression, dysthymia has a high rate of eventual recovery. Dysthymia is associated with a high rate of comorbid psychiatric disorders and increases the risk for major depression and other related conditions (Kovacs, Akiskal, Gatsonis, & Parrone, 1994; Kovacs et al., 1997).

Weiss et al. (1991) noted that depression in childhood, which was once thought to be rare or nonexistent, is now the subject of much clinical and research activity and is currently recognized by almost all authoritative sources (e.g., *The Diagnostic and Statistical Manual of Mental Disorders*, American Psychiatric Association, 1994). In fact, estimates of prevalence rates of depressive disorders in children have been found to be quite high (e.g., see Kashani et al., 1981), and some clinicians have diagnosed them as early as preschool age (e.g., Kashani & Carlson, 1985). The pattern of symptoms seen in childhood depression is similar to that seen in adults with similar affective, cognitive, behavioral, and somatic complaints (Kaslow, Rehm, & Siegel, 1984), and there appears to be little variability in the associated features of the disorder across the life span (Kovacs, 1996a). Depressive disorders can disrupt the functioning of children and adolescents in a number of areas—most notably in school—and cause significant developmental delays. Moreover, children who have depressive disorders may have trouble "catching up" in development (Kovacs & Goldston, 1991, p. 389).

ASSESSMENT OF DEPRESSION USING SELF-REPORT

Assessment of depression can focus on (a) the early identification of the extent and severity of depressive symptoms, (b) the diagnosis of depression and associated disorders, and (c) the monitoring the effectiveness of interventions.

Self-rated inventories have long been a part of the assessment of depressive symptoms in adults (e.g., Beck Depression Inventory; Beck, 1967). Such inventories typically are easy to administer, inexpensive, and readily analyzable. Because they quantify the severity of the depressive syndrome, they have been used for descriptive purposes, to assess treatment outcomes, to test research hypotheses, and to select research subjects. However, because self-rated inventories do not assess the temporal features, the onset, the course, or the contributing factors of the syndrome being examined, they cannot yield diagnostic information.

For children, self-report inventories nonetheless provide especially useful information in that many features of depression are internal and are not easily identified by informants such as parents or teachers. Moreover, according to psychological models, children's self-perceptions are of predictive value in their own right (Kovacs, 1992; Saylor, Finch, Baskin, Furey, & Kelly, 1984).

The Children's Depression Inventory (CDI) has been one of the most widely used and cited inventories of depression. According to a recent report by Fristad, Emery, and Beck (1997), the CDI was used in over 75% of the studies with children in which self-report depression inventories were employed.

The initial version of the CDI was developed in 1977. Formal publication of the instrument in 1992 increased its accessibility. This chapter provides a timely opportunity to summarize the research history and usage of the CDI since its inception 25 years ago and since its publication about a decade ago. The CDI, as well as its various versions, associated manuals, and scoring forms are described in the first part of this chapter. Current research and theory related to the CDI are also highlighted. The CDI manual (Kovacs, 1992) includes an annotated bibliography of about 150 related research studies up to the end of 1991. At least 200 additional articles pertaining to the CDI had been published by 1997 (Fristad et al., 1997).

Other goals of this chapter are to examine current use of the CDI, distinguish proper from improper use of the instrument, and address questions frequently asked by practitioners. The CDI can be helpful in the early identification of symptoms and in the monitoring of treatment effectiveness. The CDI also can play a role in the diagnostic process, but, as already noted, *it should not be used alone* to diagnose a depressive disorder. Finally, this chapter describes the ongoing development of the CDI, including anticipated accessories, future research directions, and extended applications.

SUMMARY OF THE DEVELOPMENT OF THE CDI

The Beck Depression Inventory (Beck, 1967), a clinically based, 21-item, self-rated symptom scale for adults, was the starting point for the development of a paper-and-pencil tool that would be appropriate for children. The research literature supported the decision to use an "adult" scale as the model, given that there appeared to be much overlap between the salient manifestations of depressive disorders in juveniles and in adults (Kovacs & Beck, 1977). Scale construction proceeded in four phases.

Phase I

The first version of the children's inventory (dated March 1975) was derived with the help of a group of 10- to 15-year-old "normal" youths and similar-aged children from an urban inpatient and partial hospitalization program. After the purpose of the scale revision project was explained individually to each child, he or she was asked for advice on how the items could be worded to make them "clear to kids." In this phase of scale construction, the Beck item pertaining to sexual interest was replaced by an item on loneliness, but the content and format of 20 items of the adult scale were essentially retained. However, five "Appendix" items, adapted from Albert and Beck (1975), were added; these concerned school and peer functioning. Piloting yielded further semantic changes.

Phase II

Data from normal youths and children who were under psychiatric-psychological care were used along with a semantic and conceptual item analysis to produce a second major revision (dated February 1976) that also included a new item on self-blame. This version of the inventory was administered to thirty-nine 8- to 13-year-old children who were consecutively admitted to a child guidance center's hospitalization units, twenty "normal" 8- to 13-year-olds with no history of psychiatric contacts, and one hundred and twenty-seven 10- to 13-year-old fifth- and sixth-grade students in the Toronto public school system.

The resultant data were analyzed according to standard psychometric principles, and the findings were used to derive a completely new version of the scale. Two of the original 21 items (shame and weight loss) and two of the appendix items (family fights and self-blame) were replaced by four new items that had face validity and appeared age appropriate (e.g., feeling unloved).

The CDI item-choice distributions in these samples also revealed that the items could be recast into a three-choice format: one choice reflects "normalcy," the middle choice pertains to definite although not disabling symptom severity, and the other response option reflects a clinically significant complaint. In order to prevent response bias, approximately 50% the items (randomly selected) were worded so that the first response choice suggested the most pathology, and the response choice order was reversed for the remaining items.

Phase III

The newly modified version of the CDI (dated May 1977) was again pilot-tested and sent to colleagues for a critique. A cover page was added with revised instructions and a sample item. Based on the results of pilot-testing, the items were further refined and reworded in order to improve face validity and comprehensibility.

TABLE 1.1
Authorized CDI Translations

Afrikaans	Japanese
Dutch	Lithuanian
French (European)	Norwegian
French (Canadian)	Polish
German	Russian
Greek	Spanish
Hebrew	Swedish
Icelandic	Turkish
Italian	Ukrainian

Phase IV

One minor change preceded preparation of the final version of the CDI (dated August 1979). The score values were eliminated from the inventory, and scoring templates were developed.

Current Work

Since the initial development of the CDI, additional psychometric analyses have been conducted. Based on these analyses, five factors have been identified and are fully described in the CDI manual (Kovacs, 1992). A short form of the CDI has been derived as well, and software has been developed for online administration, scoring, and reporting. The instrument is now available in several foreign languages. A listing of available translations appears in Table 1.1.

OVERVIEW OF THE CDI

The CDI is appropriate for children and adolescents aged 7 to 17 years. The instrument quantifies a range of depressive symptoms, including disturbed mood, problems in hedonic capacity and vegetative functions, low self-evaluation, hopelessness, and difficulties in interpersonal behaviors. Several items pertain to the consequences of depression with respect to contexts that are specifically relevant to children (e.g., school). Each of the 27 CDI items consists of three choices, keyed 0 (absence of a symptom), 1 (mild symptom), or 2 (definite symptom), with higher scores indicating increasing severity. The total scale score can range from 0 to54.

In addition to the total score, the CDI also yields scores for five factors or subscales: Negative Mood, Interpersonal Problems, Ineffectiveness, Anhedonia, and Negative Self-Esteem. Although author-approved definitions of these subscales have been available to users for some time, the definitions have not been widely published (although they are given in the recent *Software User's Manual*; Kovacs, 1995). Therefore, these definitions are provided in Table 1.2.

Reliability

Psychometric information on reliability is directly related to the proper use and interpretation of an instrument. The reliability of the CDI has been examined in terms of internal consistency, test-retest reliability, and standard error.

TABLE 1.2
Definitions of the Subscales of the CDI

Scale	*Definition*
Negative Mood	This subscale reflects feeling sad, feeling like crying, worrying about "bad things," being bothered or upset by things, and being unable to make up one's mind
Interpersonal Problems	This subscale reflects problems and difficulties in interactions with people, including trouble getting along with people, social avoidance, and social isolation
Ineffectiveness	This subscale reflects negative evaluation of one's ability and school performance
Anhedonia	This subscale reflects "endogenous depression," including impaired ability to experience pleasure, loss of energy, problems with sleeping and appetite, and a sense of isolation
Negative Self-Esteem	This subscale reflects low self-esteem, self-dislike, feelings of being unloved, and a tendency to have thoughts of suicide

TABLE 1.3
Estimates of Internal Consistency of the CDI and the Five CDI Factors

Scale	*Internal Consistency (Cronbach's Alpha)*
Total CDI	Alphas ranging from .71 to .89 (Kovacs, 1992)
Negative Mood	Normative sample: .62; Canadian sample: .65
Interpersonal Problems	Normative sample: .59; Canadian sample: .60
Ineffectiveness	Normative sample: .63; Canadian sample: .59
Anhedonia	Normative sample: .66; Canadian sample: .64
Negative Self-Esteem	Normative sample: .68; Canadian sample: .66

Internal Consistency. Internal consistency refers to the fact that all items on the given instrument consistently measure the same dimension. Kovacs (1992) summarized several research studies that reported alpha reliability statistics for the CDI. Alpha coefficients from .60 to .70 are usually taken to indicate satisfactory reliability (DeVellis, 1991), .70 to .80 indicate good reliability, and .80 to .95 indicate excellent reliability. The majority of the studies reported total score alpha values over .80, and all of the values were greater than .70. For instance, Kovacs (1985) found the total score coefficient alpha to be .86 for a heterogeneous, psychiatric referred sample of children, .71 for a pediatric-medical outpatient group, and .87 for a large sample of public school students ($N = 860$).

Although the internal consistency of the CDI total score has often been reported, data on alpha coefficients for the five factor scores have been less available. Therefore, the internal consistency of the five subscales was assessed using two large data sets: the CDI normative sample of 1,266 children and an independent sample of 894 Canadian children. The reliability values obtained are shown in Table 1.3, along with a summary of alpha values previously reported for the CDI total score.

Although the reliability for the five subscales is not as high as for the CDI total score, the findings for the subscales are satisfactory. Furthermore, the alpha values obtained from the two samples are very similar.

Test-Retest Reliability. The CDI is completed based on the respondent's feelings, moods, and functioning during the 2-week period just prior to the test administration. Thus, rather than measuring traits, which are less changeable over time, the inventory measures state symptoms. Because the CDI measures a state rather than a trait, the retest interval for assessing reliability should be short (2 to 4 weeks). In the research reviewed by Kovacs (1992), studies done with normal youths and psychiatric inpatients using such short intervals (Finch, Saylor, Edwards, & McIntosh, 1987; Kaslow et al., 1984; Meyer, Dyck, & Petrinack, 1989; Nelson & Politano, 1990; Saylor, Finch, Spirito, & Bennett, 1984; Wierzbicki, 1987) found test-retest correlations between .56 to .87 (an outlier of .38 was obtained in one study), and the median test-retest correlation was .75. Thus, the CDI has acceptable short-term stability.

Standard Error. Two types of standard error (Lord & Novick, 1968) are most relevant to the CDI: standard error of measurement (SEM_1) and standard error of prediction (SEM_2). SEM_1 is calculated using Cronbach's alpha and represents the standard deviation of *observed* scores if the true score is held constant. This means that, if parallel forms are used to assess the same individual at the same time, about 68% of the scores would fall within a 1 SEM_1 unit of the score obtained on the CDI scale and about 95% of the scores would fall within 1.96 SEM_1 units.

SEM_2 has particular relevance because it has an intimate connection to outcomes assessment. SEM_2 is calculated using the test-retest coefficient and represents the standard deviation of *predicted* scores if the obtained score is held constant. That is, if 100 individuals were reassessed on the CDI, about 68% of the retest scores would fall within 1 SEM_2 unit of the predicted scores and about 95% of the retest scores would fall within 1.96 SEM_2 units of the predicted scores.Thus, the SEM_2 value is one way of assessing how much CDI scores can be expected to change due to random fluctuation. Any change in CDI scores that substantially exceeds the expected random fluctuation is most likely attributable to a significant change in the status of the individual's symptoms.

The absolute value for SEM_1 or SEM_2 varies according to both the estimate of reliability and the estimate of the population standard deviation used in the calculation. The above noted SEM_1 value was calculated based on the median Cronbach alpha for the CDI total score, shown in Table 1.3, and SEM_2 values were derived using the median 2- to 4-week test-retest reliability estimate for the CDI total score. The resultant values for standard error of measurement are presented in Table 1.4.

TABLE 1.4
Standard Error Values for the CDI Total Score

Gender (Age Group)	*Standard Error of Measurement* (SEM_1)	*Standard Error of Prediction* (SEM_2)
Boys (overall)	2.9	3.8
Boys (7–12)	2.8	3.7
Boys (13–17)	3.1	4.2
Girls (overall)	2.6	3.5
Girls (7–12)	2.7	3.6
Girls (13–17)	2.4	3.2
Overall	2.7	3.7

Validity

The validity of an instrument is evaluated by estimating the extent to which it correctly measures the construct or constructs that it purports to assess. Constructs cannot be directly observed, so validity is assessed through empirical means. Specifically, construct validity is assessed through its correlation with other scales purported to measure the same construct, by its correlation with scales purported to measure related constructs, or by its correlation with independent ratings of behavior. Other aspects of validation include factor analyses examining the scale's subscale structure (factorial validity) and its ability to predict appropriate behaviors (predictive validity). Thus, the validity of a test rests on accumulated evidence from a number of studies using various methodologies (Campbell & Fiske, 1959).

The CDI has been utilized in hundreds of clinical and experimental research studies, and its validity has been well established using a variety of techniques. Overall, the weight of the evidence indicates that the inventory assesses important constructs that have strong explanatory and predictive utility in the characterization of depressive symptoms in children and adolescents. Table 1.5 lists some of the research related to different aspects of validity. Also, see Barreto (1994) for a brief review of validity information and Saylor, Finch, Baskin, et al. (1984) and Saylor, Finch, Spirito, et al. (1984), who used the multitrait, multimethod approach to assess the construct validity of the CDI. Further validation data pertinent to specific uses of the CDI are presented later in this chapter (see the section entitled "Use of the CDI for Clinical Purposes").

META-ANALYSIS OF THE CDI

Twenge and Nolen-Hoeksema (2002) conducted a within-scale meta-analysis using the CDI to examine children and adolescents with depressive symptoms. The studies included were examined in terms of age, gender, birth cohort, race, and class differences. Whereas a traditional meta-analysis computes an effect size for each study, a within-scale meta-analysis utilizes the sample means. A within-scale meta-analysis was used because it allows for generalization over many domains, gathering data that were collected at many different locations and times. The authors argued that this form of analysis is the best method for examining individual differences in CDI scores. They recognized that the chosen analytic method is limited to examining only one measure but asserted that the focus on the CDI was well justified because it is the most frequently used scale measuring depressive symptoms of children. Research studies were located using the Web of Science Citation Index, the Science Citation Index, and the Arts and Humanities Citation Index. Several criteria were used to select studies for inclusion. First, samples had to be from the United States or Canada. Second, each study had to include at least 15 subjects. Third, retained samples could not consist of psychiatric patients, delinquents, hospital patients, people diagnosed with any particular disease, or any other group singled out for maladjustment. Fourth, the samples had to be unselected groups (e.g., not specifically high or low depression groups and not groups that would be extremely high or low on any measure that might be correlated with the CDI). Fifth, the CDI mean scores had to be included in the research report.

In total, 310 data sets were included in the meta-analysis, representing 61,424 children (29,637 boys and 31,787 girls) between the ages of 8 and 16.

TABLE 1.5
Studies Containing Information Relevant to the Validity of the CDI

Reference	*Salient Measures or Methodology*
Construct Validity	
CDI compared with other measures of childhood depression	
Bodiford, Eisenstadt, Johnson, & Bradlyn, 1988	CBCL
Hammen et al., 1987	"
Hepperlin, Stewart, & Rey, 1990	"
Lam, 2000	"
Weiss & Weisz, 1988	"
Wolfe et al., 1987	"
Worchel et al., 1990	"
Nieminen & Matson, 1989	RADS
Shain, Naylor, & Alesi, 1990	RADS, Hamilton
Faulstich, Carey, Ruggiero, Enyart, & Gresham, 1986	CESD
Felner, Rowlison, Raley, & Evans, 1988	"
Weissman, Orvaschel, & Padian, 1980	CESD and SAS
Bartell & Reynolds, 1986	CDS
Haley, Fine, Marriage, Moretti, & Freeman, 1985	CDS and others
Rotundo & Hensley, 1985	CDS
Seligman et al., 1984	BDI
Lipovsky, Finch, & Belter, 1989	MMPI–D
Asarnow & Carlson, 1985	DSRS
CDI compared with measures of related constructs	
Eason, Finch, Brasted, & Saylor, 1985	Anxiety (RCMAS)
Felner, Rowlison, Raley, & Evans, 1988	"
Kovacs, 1985	"
Norvell, Brophy, & Finch, 1985	"
Ollendick & Yule, 1990	"
Blumberg & Izard, 1986	Anxiety (STAI)
Wolfe et al., 1987	
Allen & Tarnowski, 1989	Self-concept (Piers-Harris)
Elliott & Tarnowski, 1990	"
Knight, Hensley, & Waters, 1988	"
Kovacs, 1985	"
McCauley, Mitchell, Burke, & Moss, 1988	"
Rotundo & Hensley, 1985	"
Saylor, Finch, Baskin, Furey, & Kelly, 1984	"
Saylor, Finch, Spirito, & Bennett, 1984	"
Kaslow, Rehm, & Siegel, 1984	Self-esteem (Coopersmith)
Kovacs, 1985	"
Reynolds, Anderson, & Bartell, 1985	"
Kazdin, French, Unis, & Esveldt-Dawson, 1983	Self-esteem (Self-Esteem Inventory)
Bodiford, Eisenstadt, Johnson, & Bradlyn, 1988	Attributional style (CASQ)
Curry & Craighead, 1990	"
Gladstone & Kaslow, 1995	"
Hammen, Adrian, & Hiroto, 1988	"
Kuttner, Delamater, & Santiago, 1989	"
McCauley, Mitchell, Burke, & Moss, 1988	"
Nolen-Hoeksema, Girgus, & Seligman, 1986	"
Elliott & Tarnowski, 1990	Hopelessness (Hopelessness Scale)
Kazdin, French, Unis, & Esveldt-Dawson, 1983	"
Kazdin, French, Unis, Esveldt-Dawson, & Sherick, 1983	"
McCauley, Mitchell, Burke, & Moss, 1988	"
Spirito, Overholser, & Hart, 1991	"
Fauber, Forehand, Long, Burke, & Faust, 1987	Perceived Competence Scale
Weissman, Orvaschel, & Padian, 1980	Social Adjustment Scale

(Continued)

TABLE 1.5
(*Continued*)

Reference	*Salient Measures or Methodology*
CDI compared with behavioral measures/observations of depressive behavior/symptoms	
Blumberg & Izard, 1986	Parent/teacher rating/observation
Huddleston & Rust, 1994	"
Ines & Sacco, 1992	"
Renouf & Kovacs, 1994	"
Reynolds, Anderson, & Bartell, 1985	"
Sacco & Graves, 1985	"
Shah & Morgan, 1996	"
Slotkin, Forehand, Fauber, McCombs, & Long, 1988	"
Breen & Weinberger, 1995	Therapist/staff ratings
Stocker, 1994	Perceptions of relationships/adjustment
Hodges, 1990	Interview findings
Saylor, Finch, Baskin, Furey, & Kelly, 1984	Peer reports
Factorial Validity	
Carey, Faulstich, Gresham, Ruggiero, & Enyart, 1987	
Helsel & Matson, 1984	
Kovacs, 1992	
Lam, 2000	
Saylor, Finch, Spirito, & Bennett, 1984	
Weiss & Weisz, 1988	
Weiss et al., 1991	
Predictive Validity	
Devine, Kempton, & Forehand, 1994	Longitudinal procedure used
DuBois, Felner, Bartels, & Silverman, 1995	"
Mattison, Handford, Kales, Goodman, & McLaughlin, 1990	"
Reinherz, Frost, & Pakiz, 1991	"
Marciano & Kazdin, 1994	Statistical prediction procedure used
Slotkin, Forehand, Fauber, McCombs, & Long, 1988	"

Means and Standard Deviations Relative to the Existing CDI Norms

The norms used in the current version of the CDI are based on a sample of 1,266 children that are described in detail in the CDI manual (Kovacs, 1992) and in a report by Finch, Saylor, and Edwards (1985). Although the means and standard deviations provided in Twenge and Nolen-Hoeksema's (2002) meta-analysis do not constitute CDI norms, the large samples based on unselected, nonclinical groups makes for an intriguing comparison. The meta-analysis mean values and CDI normative values are shown comparatively in Table 1.6. For girls, the means and standard deviations from the existing CDI norms match up extremely well with the values from the meta-analysis. For boys, however, the CDI norms are notably higher than the values obtained in the meta-analysis. The upcoming CDI restandardization will provide the information needed to determine if these differences require changes in the male CDI norms.

Age and Gender Differences

For boys, there was no relationship between age and depression scores, although the mean for 12-year-old boys was considerably higher than the mean observed for boys of other ages. It is possible that this "spike" in the data might reflect the difficulties

TABLE 1.6
Boys' and Girls' Scores and Standard Deviations by Age on the Children's Depression Inventory

Source	*Age/Sex*	M	SD
Meta-analysis	8–12/boys	8.5–9.9	7.2–7.9
CDI existing norms	7–12/boys	10.8	7.4
Meta-analysis	13–16/boys	8.7–9.1	6.4–7.1
CDI existing norms	13–17/boys	11.4	8.3
Meta-analysis	8–12/girls	8.4–9.4	7.0–7.7
CDI existing norms	7–12/girls	9.0	7.1
Meta-analysis	13–16/girls	9.1–10.5	6.7–7.3
CDI existing norms	13–17/girls	9.7	6.3

in coping with the onset of puberty occurring at about that age. For girls between 8 to 13 years of age, CDI scores and age, again, were unrelated. Also, as with the boys, 12-year-olds yielded the highest score in the 8–13 age bracket. Unlike boys, however, 14- to 16-year-old girls scored considerably higher (range: 10.1–10.5) than younger girls (range: 8.4–9.4).

In terms of gender differences, for children up to 12 years of age, Twenge and Nolen-Hoeksema (2002) observed no significant differences between boys and girls. For 13- to 16-year-olds, however, the scores for girls were significantly higher. The *DSM–IV* (1994, p. 341) notes that Major Depressive Disorder is twice as common in adolescent females as in adolescent males. Although the *DSM–IV* notation pertains to those clinically diagnosed, the meta-analytic finding of greater depressive symptoms in unselected, nonclinical females is certainly consistent with the *DSM–IV* in this regard.

Socioeconomic Status (SES)

All samples included in the meta-analysis were coded as either lower class, lower to middle class, middle class, or middle to upper class. There were no significant correlations with values ranging from $r = .03$ to $r = .06$. This result indicates that depression is unrelated to SES in unselected, nonclinical samples.

Race/Ethnicity

Only studies in which 90% or more of the sample were from one racial/ethnic background were used for comparison. Sufficient data were available to perform meaningful comparisons between Whites, Blacks, and Hispanics. In total, 109 mixed-sex samples were used. Although there were no significant differences between Whites and Blacks, Hispanics scored significantly higher than both these groups, producing substantial effect sizes ($d = 0.62$ in relation to Whites and $d = 1.31$ in relation to Blacks). The authors noted that the high scores for Hispanics are consistent with some other research findings but indicated that further research is required to fully explain and interpret the results.

CDI Short Form

The 10-item CDI Short Form was developed to enable more rapid and economical assessment of depressive symptoms than the long form. The CDI Short Form can be used when a quick screening measure is desired or when the examiner's time with the child is limited. The short form takes 5 to 10 minutes to administer, about half the time it takes to administer the long version. However, the long and short forms generally provide comparable results. That is, the correlation between the CDI total score and the CDI Short Form total score was $r = .89$ (Kovacs, 1992).

ADMINISTRATION OF THE CDI

Reading Level

Past computations of the reading level for the CDI have produced different grade readability estimates (Berndt, Schwartz, & Kaiser, 1983; Kazdin & Petti, 1982). A first-grade reading level for the CDI is most frequently cited (e.g., Kovacs, 1992). Variable assessments of the instrument's reading level probably reflect the use of different reading level formulas. The Dale-Chall formula (Dale & Chall, 1948) has been found to be the most valid and accurate of the nine commonly utilized readability formulas (e.g., Harrison, 1980). It is based on semantic (word) difficulty and syntactic (sentence) difficulty.

Usually, two 100-word samples are taken to calculate the reading level using the Dale-Chall formula (Chall & Dale, 1995). However, to provide greater accuracy, the computation reported here used all of the CDI items. In accordance with the Dale-Chall standard procedure for determining reading level, the number of complete sentences were counted and divided into the number of words to determine average sentence length (WDS/SEN). Next, the "unfamiliar" words (UFMWDS) were counted. A word is considered unfamiliar if it does not appear on a list of 3,000 "familiar" words compiled by Edgar Dale (revised in 1983). Familiar words are known by at least 80% of children in the fourth grade. Consideration of the number of familiar and unfamiliar words in a sample of text increases the accuracy of the reading level assessment. The grade level was determined using the following formula:

$$\text{Grade} = (0.1579 \times \text{PERCENT UFMWDS}) + (0.0496 \times \text{WDS/SEN}) + 3.6365$$

The Dale-Chall procedure produced a Grade 3 reading level for the CDI, suggesting that the often cited Grade 1 reading level for the CDI is not definitive. Administrators and practitioners should not assume that all younger children will be able to understand the language on the inventory. For 7- and 8-year-olds and children with reading difficulties, it is recommended (Kovacs, 1992) that the administrator read aloud the instructions and the CDI items while the child reads along on his or her own form.

Administration Methods

One way to administer the CDI is to allow children to indicate their responses on a special Quikscore form (Kovacs, 1992). The Quikscore form is self-contained and includes all materials needed to score and profile the CDI. Conversion to *T*-scores is automatically made in the Quikscore form. The CDI also can be computer administered and scored using an IBM-compatible microcomputer (Kovacs, 1995).

Regardless of which option or format is chosen, the administrator should make sure that the child carefully reads the instructions and fully understands the inventory. As already noted, for younger children or those with reading difficulties, it may be necessary to read the instructions and the items aloud while the child reads along on his or her own form or the computer screen. After reading each item, the child selects one of the three response options provided. A child may say that none of the choices in a given item really applies to him or her. In such a case, the child should be instructed to select the item choice that fits him or her *best*.

Although the CDI is most often administered on an individual basis, group administration is permitted (e.g., Friedman & Butler, 1979; Saylor, Finch, Baskin, Saylor, et al., 1984). Additionally, with nonclinical populations, some test administrators have considered inclusion of the suicide item to be inappropriate; in such instances, it may be preferable to use the CDI Short Form, which does not include this item.

APPLICABLE POPULATIONS

In interpreting clinically significant patterns of total scale and factor scores on the CDI, it is important to consider the background of the child, including his or her socioeconomic status, country of origin, and ethnicity. The norms presented in the main manual for the CDI (Kovacs, 1992) are based on a select sample of North American children. The validity of the instrument for other groups of children is suggested by research studies with different populations. In general, this body of research, cited in Tables 1.7 and 1.8, shows very widespread applicability of the CDI.

Table 1.7 lists research citations in connection with the use of the CDI with children from different cultures and from different countries. The CDI research includes data on children who were African American, Mexican American, North American, Irish, Italian, Spanish, Chinese (from Hong Kong), Dutch, German, American Indian, Australian, Egyptian, Japanese, Brazilian, Icelandic, Croatian, and French. These references should be consulted to aid in the interpretation of CDI results regarding those populations. Tables 1.1 and 1.7 cite some of the translated versions of the CDI that have been developed or used in research.

Table 1.8 lists some of the research on the CDI with children in special circumstances. Data have been obtained from samples of children from families of low socioeconomic status, urban and rural children, children in public housing situations, and children with mental retardation or learning/intellectual disabilities. A large amount of data was also collected from samples of children who have experienced emotional problems in some form. This would include children who have experienced trauma related to a familial suicide or cancer and children who have witnessed alcohol and substance abuse (e.g., marijuana use) or have been affected by it prenatally. More invasive experiences include sexual or physical abuse of boys and girls and war. The CDI has been also used with children going through the tribulations of parental divorce and children who have insulin-dependent diabetes mellitus.

APPROACHES TO CDI INTERPRETATION

The manner in which CDI results are used or interpreted is generally a function of the setting in which the instrument is administered and the ostensible reason for the administration. Consequently, the interpretative focus can be on the specific responses of a given child to each individual item on the total CDI *T*-score or individual CDI factor *T*-scores, each of which "rank" the child in comparison to "normal" age- and gender-matched peers.

TABLE 1.7
Research Reports on the Use of CDI with Children of Different Ethnic and National Backgrounds

Reference	*Notes*
Abdel-Khalek, 1993	$N = 2{,}558^a$, Arabic version
Abdel-Khalek, 1996	$N = 1{,}981$, Arabic version, Kuwaiti students
Arnarson, Smari, Einarsdottir, & Jonasdottir, 1994	$N = 436$, Icelandic version
Bahls, 2002	$N = 463$, Brazilian sample
Canals, Henneberg, Fernandez-Ballart, & Domenech, 1995	$N = 534$, Spanish sample
Chan, 1997	$N = 621$, Hong Kong
Chartier & Lassen, 1994	$N = 792^a$, North American sample
M. Donnelly, 1995	$N = 887$, Northern Ireland sample
DuRant, Getts, Cadenhead, Emans, & Woods, 1995	$N = 225$, African American sample
Dyer, 1995	$N = 33$, American Indian sample
Fitzpatrick, 1993	$N = 221$, African American sample
Frias, Mestre, del Barrio, & Garcia-Ros, 1992	$N = 1{,}286$, Spanish sample
Frigerio, Pesenti, Molteni, Snider, & Battaglia, 2001	$N = 284$, Italian sample
Ghareeb & Beshai, 1989	$N = 2{,}029^a$, Arabic version
Goldstein, Paul, & Sanfilippo-Cohn, 1985	$N = 85$, African American sample
Gouveia, Barbosa, de Almeida, & de Andrade-Gaiao, 1995	$N = 305$, Brazilian version
Houghton, O'Connell, & O'Flaherty, 1998	$N = 1090^a$, Irish sample
Koizumi, 1991	$N = 1{,}090^a$, Japanese version
Lobert, 1989, 1990	$N = 128$, German version
Mestre, Frias, & Garcia-Ros, 1992	$N = 952^a$, Spanish sample
Oy, 1991	$N = 432$, Turkish sample
Reicher & Rossman, 1991	$N = 658$, German version
Reinhard, Bowi, & Rulcovius, 1990	$N = 84$, German version
Rybolt, 1995	$N = 91$, Mexican American and Caucasian
Saint-Laurent, 1990	$N = 470$, French version
Sakurai, 1991	$N = 237$, Japanese version
Spence & Milne, 1987	$N = 386^a$, Australian sample
Steinsmeier-Pelster, Schurmann, & Duda, 1991	$N = 918$, German version
Steinsmeier-Pelster, Schurmann, & Urhahne, 1991	$N = 319$, German sample
Timbremont & Braet, 2001	$N = 663$, Dutch version
Worchel et al., 1990	$N = 135$, Hispanic sample
Yu & Li, 2000	$N = 1645^a$, Chinese sample
Zivcic, 1993	$N = 480$, Croatian version

[a] Sample sufficient to be considered normative data for this group.

Determining the Validity of the Results

Regardless of the interpretive focus, CDI results need to be examined in the context of potential threats to validity. One approach is to determine the *quality* of the completed inventory. Another approach is to examine the inconsistency index.

Procedural Issues. The following issues should be kept in mind in assessing the quality of the completed CDI:

1. Has the inventory been filled in properly? Missing items will invalidate the total score. Although the administrator may prorate a missing item (e.g., by taking the average score on all remaining items and assigning that value to the missing item), subsequent interpretation must take any missing items into account.

TABLE 1.8
Research Reports on the Use of CDI with Special Groups

Reference	*Notes*
Benavidez & Matson, 1993	$N = 25$, mentally retarded children
Davis, 1996	$N = 120$, gifted children
T. F. Donnelly, 1995	$N = 61$, sexually abused children
Drucker & Greco-Vigorito, 2002	$N = 202$, children of substance abusers
DuRant, Getts, Cadenhead, Emans, & Woods, 1995	$N = 225$, public housing
Finkelstein, 1996	$N = 111$, learning disabled population
Gillick, 1997	$N = 20$, intrafamilial child abuse
Goldstein, Paul, & Sanfilippo, 1985	$N = 85$, learning disabled children
Gray, 1999	$N = 626$, prenatal substance exposure
Kovacs, Iyengar, Stewart, Obrosky, & Marsh, 1990	$N = 95$, diabetes mellitus
Lanktree, & Briere, 1995	$N = 105$, sexually abused children
Linna et al., 1999	$N = 6{,}000$, intellectual disability
Llabre & Hadi, 1997	$N = 151$, children assessed after war
Meins, 1993	$N = 798$, mentally retarded adults
Mestre, Frias, & Garcia-Ros, 1992	$N = 25$, mentally retarded children
Nelson, Politano, Finch, Wendel, & Mayhall, 1987	$N = 535$, emotionally disturbed children
Oy, 1991	$N = 432$, different socioeconomic status
Pfeffer, Karus, Siegel, & Jiang, 2000	$N = 80$, parental death from cancer/suicide
Polaino-Lorente & del-Pozo-Armentia, 1992	$N = 30$, familial cancer
Politano, Nelson, Evans, Sorenson, & Zeman, 1985	$N = 551$, emotionally disturbed children
Pons-Salvador & del Barrio, 1993	$N = 193$, parental divorce
Preiss, 1998	$N = 307$, children assessed after war
Rick, 1999	$N = 25$, sexually abused boys
Saylor, Finch, Spirito, & Bennett, 1984	$N = 154$, emotional-behavioral problems
Siegel, Karus, & Raveis, 1996	$N = 97$, familial cancer

2. Is there an apparent response bias? Response bias may be operating if a child *consistently* checks the first option on each item, the middle option, or the last option. Random checking of options, which may be inferred by the detection of apparently contradictory answers to similar items, may represent biased responding as well. Such patterns invalidate the CDI total score.

3. Are there any suggestions of lack of truthfulness? In a clinical setting that involves testing a child who has been referred, this possibility is indicated if the child "denies" every symptom or endorses the most severe option of every, or almost every, item. In such instances, inquiring into the child's expectations regarding the evaluation may be more informative than focusing on the CDI score itself.

4. Is the testing environment appropriate for psychological examination? As with all forms of psychological assessment, the CDI should be completed in a setting that is free from distraction, affords the child the requisite privacy, and is reasonably comfortable. An unsuitable testing environment is likely to threaten the validity of the child's responses and must be considered in score interpretation.

The Inconsistency Index. Children may exaggerate or misrepresent symptoms in some circumstances. As a result, some self-rated instruments include special items or scales to identify distorted responses (e.g., Beitchman, 1996; Reynolds & Richmond, 1985). Alternatively, for some instruments (e.g., MMPI–2 VRIN, and TRIN scales [Butcher, Dahlstrom, Graham, Tellegen, & Kaemmer, 1989]; MASC Inconsistency Index [March, 1997]), an inconsistency index has been developed that does not usually require special items. Inconsistency indexes are based on the premise that the most similar items, or the most highly correlated items, on a measure elicit similar (although not necessarily identical) responses. As determined by statistical procedures, if there is a large discrepancy in the responses for several correlated item pairs, then inconsistent and possibly invalid responding must be considered.

An inconsistency index exists for the CDI. Each of the five scales on the CDI (i.e., Negative Mood, Interpersonal Problems, Ineffectiveness, Anhedonia, and Negative Self-Esteem) contains sets of items that are highly correlated with one another. If a pair of items is highly correlated, then a child whose response is indicative of a symptom for one item of the pair should give a response indicative of a symptom for the other item of the pair. Although such consistency is generally expected, some inconsistency can and will occur to a limited extent, the magnitude of which can be assessed through the CDI Inconsistency Index (Kovacs, 1995). This index is generated based on a computer algorithm taking into account the factor loadings of items. For the Negative Mood Scale, the highly correlated item set used to measure consistency comprises Items 1, 8, 10, and 11; for Interpresonal Problems, the set consists of Items 5, 26, and 27; for Ineffectiveness, the set consists of Items 15, 23, and 24; for Anhedonia, the set consists of Items 16, 19, 20, and 22; and for Negative Self Esteem, the set consists of Items 7, 9, 14, and 25.

In the normative sample for the CDI, only 89 children out of 1,266 (6.9%) scored greater than or equal to 7 on the inconsistency index. And only 36 out of 1,266 (2.8%) scored greater than or equal to 9. Based on these data, the results from the inconsistency index are assessed as follows: If the index is less than 7, then the responses are considered sufficiently consistent. If the index is greater than or equal to 7 but less than 9, then the responses are considered somewhat inconsistent. If the index is greater than or equal to 9, then the responses are considered very inconsistent.

A high inconsistency index score should not be interpreted to mean that the CDI results should be disregarded. Inconsistent responding can occur for a variety of reasons, including an inability on the part of the child to concentrate on the task or understand the instructions. Such considerations must be part of interpreting the inconsistency index for a respondent.

Interpretive Steps

Interpretation of CDI results in the context of community-based or epidemiological studies are straightforward in so far as they usually employ clinically validated cutoff scores or normative *T*-scores to define "caseness." Thus, such cases will not be discussed in this chapter. Likewise, when the CDI is used as a screening instrument, a priori defined raw cutoff scores (or *T*-scores) are generally employed, with no need for specific interpretation. Because most questions regarding CDI score interpretation arise in the context of *clinical assessment* and for clinical purposes such as planning interventions or evaluations, pertinent information on these aspects of CDI use are now described in detail.

Interpretation of Total Scores and Factor Scores as T-*Scores.* Normative data tables are incorporated into the Profile Form for the CDI. The normative data tables utilize *T*-scores, which are standardized to have a mean or average of 50 and a standard deviation of 10. The normative tables automatically compare the child being assessed to children in the normative sample of the same gender and age and allow each component in the profile to be compared to every other. *T*-scores above 65 are generally

TABLE 1.9
Interpretive Guidelines for CDI *T*-Scores

T-*Score*	*Interpretation of Overall Symptoms/Complaints*[a]
Above 70	Very much above average
66 to 70	Much above average
61 to 65	Above average
56 to 60	Slightly above average
45 to 55	Average
40 to 44	Slightly below average
35 to 39	Below average
30 to 34	Much below average
Below 30	Very much below average

[a] Compared to children of similar age and gender in the normative sample.

considered clinically significant when the child being studied is from a "high base-rate" group, such as children in a clinical setting. When the child is believed to be from a "low base-rate" group, such as children without identified behavioral problems, a much higher cutoff, for example, a *T*-score of 70 or 75, should be used for inferring clinical problems. High scores suggest a problem and low scores indicate the absence of the problem.

It should be noted that the *T*-scores used with the CDI are linear *T*-scores. Linear *T*-scores do not transform the actual distributions of the variables, and hence, though each variable has been transformed to have a mean of 50 and a standard deviation of 10, the distributions of the scale scores do not change. Variables that are not normally distributed in the raw data will continue to be nonnormally distributed after the transformation.

As a rule of thumb, *T*-scores for the CDI can be interpreted using the guidelines in Table 1.9. These interpretations reflect how an individual child's score compares to those of children of the same age range and gender from the normative sample. Note, however, that the suggested adjectives are guidelines and that there is no reason to believe that a perceptible psychological difference is associated with the difference, for instance, between a *T*-score of 55 and a *T*-score of 56. *Therefore, these guidelines should not be used as absolute rules.*

For many clinical tests, it is common practice to interpret the overall profile based on the most elevated test scores. In such a case, a clinically elevated test score (in the metric of *T*-scores) would be defined as above 65. If, for a given set of scores, no test scores are above a *T*-score of 65, the profile is usually considered to be "normal." A profile in which a single *T*-score is elevated above 65 is usually considered to have a "one-point" code and is referred to by the single elevated scale. In general, given the high correlations of the factors of the CDI, such profiles should be relatively rare and, when encountered, may be viewed as only moderate evidence of a problem. When two or more subscale scores are clinically elevated, the profile is usually categorized by the two factors that are the highest and is called a "two-point code." Although two-point codes have not usually been employed with the CDI, some clinical practitioners may find it useful to use them. Experience with inventories such as the MMPI and the Personality Inventory for Children (PIC) indicates that two-point codes tend to be useful and robust ways of categorizing clinically meaningful patterns of behavior (Lachar & Gdowski, 1979).

In general, therefore, thoughtful examination of the CDI subscale profile should be more informative than consideration of only the total score. The CDI subscale *T*-score profile can be used to indicate specific areas of vulnerability as well as areas of strength. For example, from a clinical perspective, elevated *T*-scores on the Anhedonia factor or the Ineffectiveness factor may be particularly important. Because the Anhedonia factor contains items traditionally associated with "endogenous" depression, a child with a high *T*-score on this factor may be at particular risk for a serious depressive episode. A high score on the Ineffectiveness factor may indicate notable functional impairment, which may warrant additional interventions for a particular child. Concomitantly, in interpreting the CDI profile, a child who has elevated *T*-scores on both of these scales may be of greater clinical concern than a child who has an elevated score on the Anhedonia factor but an average score on the Ineffectiveness factor. In the former case, the child may be evidencing both functional impairment and troublesome depressive symptoms, whereas in the latter case, the troublesome depressive symptoms (area of vulnerability) are somewhat counteracted by child's having maintained reasonable functioning (area of strength).

Examination of the Total Raw Score and Item Response Pattern. A practitioner conducting a clinical assessment may decide to focus on the raw CDI score and individual item responses. For example, a total CDI score of 20 may result if a child endorses only 10 items but each to its most severe degree. Alternatively, a child may receive a score of 20 by endorsing up to 20 items but each to a mild degree. Examination of the number of items and the options for the items that contributed to the total CDI score can provide useful information about the extent and severity of the child's complaints and symptoms.

The examiner also may find it helpful to group the items endorsed by a child into phenomenologically meaningful categories. This approach can provide an additional perspective on the nature of the child's complaints. For example, if most or all endorsed CDI items pertain to physical and neurovegetative symptoms (somatic complaints, problems with sleep, appetite, and energy), a pediatric examination may be warranted. If all items with symptomatic responses relate to school or peer problems, a closer examination of those aspects of the child's life may be in order.

Examination of Individual Item Responses. By studying the individual responses of a child to the CDI items, the examiner may form hypotheses about the range and type of the child's difficulties. Furthermore, in conjunction with other information, item analysis can help to determine if the child is at particular risk for serious depression, even in the absence of a highly elevated total score.

For example, endorsements of the most severe options on Item 1 (sadness), Item 4 (anhedonia), and Item 10 (crying) are indicative of pervasive despondent mood. In so far as the presence of such a mood state has been shown to represent an early phase of depression, a child with such responses may warrant ongoing monitoring. Similarly, research evidence has suggested that children who are isolated may be at risk for a variety of adjustment problems. Thus, even if the total CDI score is low, a child who endorses both Item 20 (loneliness) and Item 22 (lack of friends) may be at risk for subsequent difficulties and could benefit from monitoring.

Unlike many other inventories, specific items on the CDI have not been designated as "critical." *All* of the items have been preselected by the author and validated by numerous investigators. *All* of the items are pertinent to the syndrome of depression in the juvenile years. However, the question pertaining to suicidal thoughts (Item 9) may be particularly important for screening children in clinical settings or identifying those at risk. Endorsement of this item should prompt the examiner to conduct a detailed clinical assessment to determine the frequency and severity of suicidal ideation, whether it involves a specific contemplated method, and whether the child has ever attempted suicide. The information obtained should facilitate the planning of strategies for management or treatment.

Integrate the CDI Scores With All Other Information About the Child. The examiner should observe the child directly and the CDI results should be integrated with other test scores and with information about the child's background, family history, and school adjustment. Interviews with the child, parent, and perhaps teachers should be conducted. Consideration of such diverse information sources should result in a more valid conclusion regarding the child's problems and strengths and the extent to which depression may be undermining his or her functioning.

Determination of Appropriate Intervention Strategy for the Child. Based on all sources of information, the examiner should decide what kinds of feedback are appropriate and ethical for the parents and how to make that information available, how and when a report should be filed, and who should have access to the information. A treatment plan should be developed jointly with the parents or an appropriate referral should be made.

The results of the CDI can be particularly useful in determining suitable interventions for the child and in selecting treatment targets. As already noted, CDI factor scores and responses to items can identify problems or areas of concern. For example, a child with an elevated score on the Interpersonal Problems factor may benefit from social-skills training, modeling, or targeted group intervention as a way to treat his or her depression. A child with an elevated score on the Ineffectiveness factor may benefit from remedial help as well as behavior modification. A very high score on the Negative Mood factor may indicate consideration of referral for antidepressant pharmacotherapy. If a child has a particularly high score on the Negative Self-Esteem factor, the intervention may focus on improving self-image and building confidence. In a similar vein, endorsement of items such as "I never have fun at school" and "I have to push myself all the time to do my schoolwork" would suggest that the treatment have a school-based component.

USE OF THE CDI FOR CLINICAL PURPOSES

Standards for Educational and Psychological Testing, developed through the collaboration of the American Psychological Association (1985) and the Association of Test Publishers, emphasizes the need to validate a measure with respect to each of its proposed purposes or uses. Therefore, in the following sections, validation information is integrated with descriptions of the main uses of the CDI.

Screening for Depression

The CDI is recommended as a screening tool and has been widely used for this purpose (e.g., Aronen & Soininen, 2000; Bahls, 2002; Canals, Henneberg, Fernandez-Ballart, & Domenech, 1995; Congleton, 1996; Fristad, Weller, Weller, Teare, & Preskorn, 1988; Garvin, Leber, & Kalter, 1991; Jacobs, 1990; Kazdin, Colbus, & Rodgers, 1986;

TABLE 1.10
Research Showing Differences on the CDI Between Depressed and Nondepressed Children

Armsden, McCauley, Greenberg, Burke, & Mitchell, 1990
Carey, Faulstich, Gresham, Ruggiero, & Enyart, 1987
Craighead, Curry, & Ilardi, 1995
Fine, Moretti, Haley, & Marriage, 1985
Fristad, Weller, Weller, Teare, & Preskorn, 1988
Hodges, 1990
Hodges & Craighead, 1990
Jensen, Bloedau, Degroot, Ussery, & Davis, 1990
Kazdin, Esveldt-Dawson, Unis, & Rancurello, 1983
Kazdin, Rodgers, & Colbus, 1986
Knight, Hensley, & Waters, 1988
Kovacs, 1985
Lipovsky, Finch, & Belter, 1989
Liss, Phares, & Liljequist, 2001
Lobovits & Handal, 1985
Marriage, Fine, Moretti, & Haley, 1986
McCauley, Mitchell, Burke, & Moss, 1988
Moretti, Fine, Haley, & Marriage, 1985
Rotundo & Hensley, 1985
Saylor, Finch, Spirito, & Bennett, 1984
Spirito, Overholser, & Hart, 1991
Stark, Kaslow, & Laurent, 1993
Worchel, Nolan, & Willson, 1987

Krane, 1996; Lobovits & Handal, 1985; Polaino-Lorente & Domenech, 1993; Rybolt, 1995; Stavrakaki, Williams, Walker, Roberts, & Kotsopoulos, 1991; Timbremont & Braet, 2001). As a screening tool, the CDI can serve to identify children who are "at risk" for a depressive disorder and may require further assessment with a more complex test battery (including behavioral observations, interviews, other psychological testing, etc.). The validity of the use of the CDI for this purpose largely depends on the ability of the inventory to differentiate children identified with depressive disorders from those who have not been identified with a depressive disorder. Many research studies have shown that the CDI effectively differentiates between depressed and nondepressed children. Some of this supporting literature is listed in Table 1.10.

The validity of the CDI as a screening tool also has been examined in terms of sensitivity and specificity. *Sensitivity* refers to the percentage of diagnosable depressed children who are correctly classified by the test, *specificity* to the percentage of nondepressed children who are correctly classified. For example, Craighead, Curry, and Ilardi (1995) reported that the five CDI factor scores classified participants as depressed versus not depressed with a high degree of accuracy. Using the CDI total score cutoff of 17 as the classification criterion, these investigators also found a sensitivity of 80% and a specificity of 84%.

When the CDI is used for screening purposes, a specific cutoff is usually selected, and children scoring above the cutoff are identified as those at risk. Different cutoff values may be used depending on the relative importance of sensitivity and specificity in a particular screening situation (Kovacs, 1992). In general, raising the cutoff value decreases sensitivity while it increases specificity. Lowering the cutoff value has the opposite effect: It increases sensitivity and decreases specificity.

High cutoff scores are more appropriate than low ones when it is important to minimize false positives, that is, nondepressed children falsely identified as at risk for depression. As noted, however, with high cut-off scores, the false-negative rate is increased; that is, many individuals who fall below the cutoff but are actually depressed will not be identified as at risk. Low cutoff scores are preferred when it is important to minimize false negatives, that is, depressed children wrongly identified as not at risk. However, the use of a low cutoff score will result in a higher false-positive rate; that is, more nondepressed individuals will be identified as at risk.

When the CDI is used as a general population–based screen, Kovacs (1992) recommended the raw score of 20 as a cutoff.[1] An example of a situation where the CDI can be used as a general screen with this cutoff score is in a school system in which routine testing is conducted on a large segment of the student population. On the other hand, for screening in clinical settings, a lower cutoff is appropriate because the base rate of depression can be expected to be higher. In the research literature (e.g., Garvin et al., 1991; Kazdin et al., 1986; Lobovits & Handal, 1985), cutoff scores as low as 12 or 13 have been proposed for clinical contexts.

Use as an Aid in the Diagnostic Process

Although the CDI can serve as an aid in the diagnostic process, it cannot by itself yield a diagnosis. As already noted, a psychiatric diagnosis of major depression or dysthymia requires that certain inclusion and exclusion diagnostic criteria be met, that the constellation of symptoms and signs be present for a particular duration, and that they should be associated with distress or functional impairment (American Psychiatric Association, 1980, 1985, 1994). The necessary information can only be obtained through a detailed clinical diagnostic interview. Regrettably, current usage of the CDI has not been satisfactory in this regard. An assessment by Fristad et al. (1997) found that 44% of the studies that used the CDI alone referred to high CDI scorers as "depressed" without providing a clear cautionary statement.

After a referred child has been administered the CDI, the results can be used in various ways to facilitate the process of diagnosis. If the clinical interview has confirmed the presence of a depressive disorder, the child's CDI score can serve as an indicator of the overall *severity* of his or her current symptoms. For example, a youngster whose CDI score is 28 is clearly more severely depressed than a comparably aged child whose CDI score is 16.

The CDI results also can be useful in reaching a diagnosis in cases where, subsequent to having interviewed the parents about the child, the clinician is unable to conduct a full face-to-face clinical assessment of the referred child. In such a case, information from the CDI may clarify aspects of the data provided by the parents because the test items and the *DSM* criteria for depression overlap. Ponterotto, Pace, and Kavan (1989), who reviewed the most commonly used depression measures, noted that the CDI was the only measure that had items pertaining to each of the

[1] Matthey and Petrovski (2002) rightly critique the text and tables presented in the CDI manual, for these do poorly explicate the measure's value as a screening tool. Further to their credit, these authors (as is done here) identify myriad articles in support of the CDI as a screening tool. Inexplicably, however, Matthey and Petovski then ignore all of this research in their conclusions, which, as they state, are made "on the basis of the data reported in the manual" (p. 148). The conclusions presented here and in the CDI manual reflect a more appropriate appraisal based on all of the existing literature on the CDI.

TABLE 1.11
Correspondence of CDI Items to DSM–IV Symptom Criteria for Major Depression

DSM–IV *Criterion*	*Related CDI Item and the Most Symptomatic Response*
1. Depressed mood	Item 1: "I am sad all the time." Item 2: "Nothing will ever work out for me." Item 10: "I feel like crying every day." Item 20: "I feel alone all of the time."
2. Markedly diminished interest or pleasure	Item 4: "Nothing is fun at all."
3. Significant weight loss or decreased appetite nearly every day	Item 18: "Most days I do not feel like eating."
4. Insomnia or hypersomnia	Item 16: "I have trouble sleeping every night."
5. Psychomotor agitation or retardation	Item 15: "I have to push myself all the time to do my schoolwork."
6. Fatigue or loss of energy nearly every day	Item 17: "I am tired all the time."
7. Feelings of worthlessness or excessive guilt nearly every day	Item 3: "I do everything wrong. Item 7: "I hate myself." Item 8: "All bad things are my fault." Item 25: "Nobody really loves me."
8. Diminished ability to think or concentrate or indecisiveness	Item 13: "I cannot make up my mind about things."
9. Recurrent thoughts of death, suicidal ideation, or suicide attempt	Item 9: "I want to kill myself."

DSM–III–R symptom criteria for major depression. The criteria for major depression essentially have remained the same in the *DSM–III*, *DSM–III–R*, and *DSM–IV*. Table 1.11 shows the correspondence between the nine criterion symptoms and specific CDI items.

Alternatively, the child's responses on the CDI can be used as starting points for probes in the clinical interview. The evaluator may note which particular CDI items were endorsed, then, citing to the child his or her item responses, the evaluator can ask the child during the interview to provide further information or elaborate on those responses.

USE OF THE CDI FOR TREATMENT MONITORING AND OUTCOMES ASSESSMENT

Because the CDI yields a quantified rating, the instrument is appropriate for monitoring levels of depressive symptoms during and at the end of treatment. For example, the CDI has been used to assess the effects of group therapy (e.g., Congleton, 1996; Garvin et al., 1991; Simmer-Dvonch, 1999), social training (e.g., Milne & Spence, 1987), pharmacotherapy (e.g., Preskorn, Weller, Hughes, Weller, & Bolte, 1987), cognitive-behavioral family therapy (e.g., Asarnow, Scott, & Mintz, 2002), and preventive intervention (e.g., Garvin et al., 1991). The application of the CDI in clinical practice or treatment monitoring entails several issues or considerations; these are described in the following sections.

Evaluation Against NIMH Criteria

The National Institute of Mental Health (NIMH) has specified 11 criteria for evaluating outcome measures (Ciarlo, Brown, Edwards, Kiresuk, & Newman, 1986; Newman, Ciarlo, & Carpenter, 1999). The CDI rates favorably with respect to these criteria, each of which is indicated below by means of italics.

The CDI has been highly useful with various populations and in different settings. As described earlier, it has been validated with the key *target groups* of nonreferred children as well as clinically depressed children. It has also been used with various other populations. As emphasized throughout this chapter, proper use of the CDI involves its integration with information from *multiple informants* and sources in order to make diagnostic and treament decisions. An amendment to the CDI, currently in progress, includes the development of parallel forms that can be completed by parents and teachers. Preliminary versions of the CDI–Parent version (CDI–P: Kovacs, 1997a) and CDI–Teacher version (CDI–T: Kovacs, 1997b) are being pilot-tested and standardized. The complementary Emotional Regulation Scales (Kovacs, in press) are also being developed and directly link to treatment planning.

It has been demonstrated that the CDI has a high degree of *utility in the area of clinical services and is compatible with a variety of clinical theories and practices*. Its results can easily be translated so as to be appropriate and useful in clinical treatment strategies. The CDI also can be used to evaluate the effectiveness of such treatment strategies. The CDI adheres to the NIMH criterion that an outcome measure be useful in *identifying relevant changes in the client during the process of treatment*—changes that can act as "behavioral markers of progress or risk level" (Newman, Ciarlo, & Carpenter, 1999, p. 160). Several strategies for assessing the significance of changes in CDI scores during treatment are described in this chapter.

The *psychometric strengths* of the CDI are well established and documented by an abundance of research publications. *Normative data*, described in the CDI manual (Kovacs, 1992), provide clinicians with benchmarks that act as *objective referents* to be used in interpreting test results. The norms in the manual are based on a North American sample, but data from many other countries are also available. Furthermore, in accordance with stipulations of the American Psychological Association and the Association of Test Publishers, the CDI has been validated for each of its proposed uses.

From a pragmatic perspective, the CDI is *simple and easy to use*; manuals and materials are available to facilitate proper administration, scoring, and interpretation. In addition, the CDI is extremely *cost-efficient*, and its results are both easy to relay and *readily comprehensible* by nonprofessional audiences.

For all of the above reasons, the CDI is well deserving of the worldwide attention it has received as both a research and a clinical tool in a wide range of contexts. And its adherence to NIMH standards for assessment instruments also supports its suitability for monitoring treatment and assessing outcomes.

Establish Baseline Severity of Symptoms

If feasible and appropriate, the CDI should be administered twice at baseline. The resultant two scores can be averaged to yield an index of initial symptom severity. This procedure, also known as multiple baseline assessment, has been recommended by Milich, Roberts, Loney, and Caputo (1980), Conners (1997), and Nelson and Politano (1990), particularly for studies designed to evaluate treatment outcomes. Repeated administration of a scale can produce a declines in scores influenced by methodological artifacts such as statistical regression to the mean, placebo response to the initial assessment, or spontaneous improvement (Finch et al., 1987; Kaslow et al., 1984; Meyer et al., 1989). Therefore, a multiple baseline (rather than a single baseline) assessment is usually considered to yield a more valid index of symptom severity at the beginning of treatment.

Determine a Treatment Goal

The goals of treatment can include an a priori defined decrement in overall symptom severity, the absence of depressive symptoms, and improvements in specific areas of the child's functioning. Changes in the total CDI score can be interpreted as reflecting changes in the severity of the child's depressive symptoms. If CDI item responses scored "2" are initially selected as treatment targets, the clinician's goal may include the lessening or elimination of these particular complaints. Additionally, change (or lack of change) in factor scores may help pinpoint areas of functioning in which therapy has had the most (or least) impact.

Determine Frequency of CDI Administration During Treatment

Practical considerations are likely to affect how often the CDI can be readministered during treatment. Such considerations may include the time interval between sessions with the child as well as the burden of other assessments to which the child may be subjected. In general, a 2-week test-retest interval may be most appropriate (Kovacs, 1992), and the time required for any given test battery (including the CDI) should not exceed 20 minutes or so, particularly with younger patients. If possible, the instrument should be administered at about the same time of day each time and in the same location in order to control extraneous variables that might impact the responses.

Assess the Statistical/Clinical Significance of Changes in CDI Scores

CDI scores for the same respondent are likely to vary with repeated administration owing to random fluctuation in responses. Therefore, it is important to define the magnitude of change in CDI scores that is to be considered significant.

On a purely descriptive level, significant improvement can be defined in terms of a desired change in responses to selected CDI items. For example, if one treatment target is to improve the child's sleep, then a change on Item 16 from "I have trouble sleeping every night" to "I have trouble sleeping many nights" or "I sleep pretty well" may be considered clinically meaningful. As Conners (1994) noted:

> Clinically . . . it is always useful in assessing change to . . . circle three to five items that . . . are the most crucial problem areas. Then, regardless of changes in factor scores, it is possible to examine particular target symptoms or behaviors for evidence of a treatment effect. Obviously, one must be mindful of the possibility of interpreting random fluctuations as real change, but this is precisely the reason for not relying on a single outcome measure. (p. 569)

From a clinical perspective, *T*-score changes of five or more points on the CDI subscales also may be considered to be indicative of significant change (e.g., Conners, 1994). This approach, which is suggested as a rough guideline, has the advantage of ease of application, and it is useful in most instances.

Other methods, including the procedure described in Jacobsen and Truax (1991), address "significant change" with reference to statistical criteria (for a review, see Speer

& Greenbaum, 1995). The Jacobson-Truax method involves obtaining the difference between the baseline raw score and the raw score obtained during or after treatment, which is then divided by the standard error of the differences. This formula utilizes an appropriate reliability value for the test instrument; this value can be a test-retest, Cronbach's alpha, or split-half reliability value.

A repeated measures *t*-test represents an alternative statistical method of estimating significant change in scores. The responses from the baseline CDI administration are paired with the responses from the administration during or after treatment. The repeated measures *t*-test procedure is produced automatically by the CDI software program (Kovacs, 1995), and thus information regarding the significance of change in CDI scores is readily accessible.

Decide on the Effects of Treatment

In general, downward trends in CDI scores are likely to indicate that treatment is progressing in a proper direction. If CDI scores rise or fluctuate unpredictably from one administration to the next, a full clinical reassessment is warranted to verify the child's psychiatric status and reevaluate the appropriateness of the intervention. Treatment studies of adults have shown that most of the improvement in symptom status occurs by the eighth treatment session (Howard, Kopta, Krause, & Orlinsky, 1986). Thus, after one or two months of treatment, there should be an observable reduction in the child's depressive symptoms, although full remission would not yet be evident.

Decisions about the effects of treatment with a depressed child should not depend solely on the CDI. For example, one research study found a tendency among children to deny symptoms and to respond defensively (Joiner, Schmidt, & Schmidt, 1996). Such findings reinforce the need to corroborate self-report information prior to making decisions about the effects of treatment.

A HYPOTHETICAL CASE STUDY

A hypothetical case study is now provided (using elements of actual clinical cases) to illustrate some of the aforementioned principles in the use of the CDI. This case study includes screening, treatment planning, treatment monitoring, and outcomes assessment components.

Tamara is a 9-year-old girl who has been living with her mother. Tamara's mother had contacted the clinic because of concern regarding her daughter's behavior. The mother described Tamara as being overly sensitive and emotionally labile and prone to extreme emotional outbursts. During some of these outbursts, Tamara screamed, cried, and voiced concern that her mother would leave her. The CDI was first administered to Tamara after the initial contacts with the mother. The first administration yielded a CDI total raw score of 34, which is well above established cutoff points for identifying children who are at risk.

In the 3-year period before the initial assessment, Tamara experienced several major negative life events, including a fire in the family home that resulted in the death of Tamara's older brother and the destruction of all of the family's personal belongings and the subsequent disappearance of her natural father.

A psychiatric interview with the mother revealed symptoms for Tamara that dated back to the disappearance of her natural father. At the time of his disappearance,

Tamara had developed considerable sadness, crying, negative self-esteem, and guilt. She also had difficulty sleeping. After the fire, she additionally developed nightmares. Tamara started to experience occasional thoughts of wanting to die as well as difficulty with concentration. The latter symptom was verified by her school records and declining school grades.

In a psychiatric interview with Tamara, it became clear that she was aware of what was upsetting her and talked about her fear of being apart from her mother. She spoke of her long-standing sadness, difficulty with concentration, difficulty in sleeping, and feeling like a burden to others. She also believed that nothing would change in her life. She admitted to not wanting to go to school because of how the other children were treating her.

Based on the information obtained during these detailed psychiatric interviews, it was determined that Tamara met psychiatric diagnostic criteria for dysthymic disorder (American Psychiatric Association, 1994). She also had a diagnosable anxiety disorder. By examining her CDI factor scores, it became apparent that negative affect, ineffectiveness, and anhedonia were more problematic for her than behavior problems or low self-esteem. The Ineffectiveness score was relatively elevated and was consistent with her recent school problems.

The combining of information from the CDI with the developmental history and clinical information resulted in the development of an intervention plan. Before treatment began, a second administration of the CDI was conducted in order to strengthen the accuracy of the baseline and corroborate other clinical observations. Recommendations for individual and concomitant parent-child therapy sessions were made, and treatment began approximately 1 month after the initial evaluation.

Over the next few months of the intervention program, important improvements were noted. A third administration of the CDI was done, and it appeared that the symptoms had been reduced to an acceptable level. On the third administration, Tamara's total CDI raw score had dropped to 11. The CDI software program was used to generate a comparison between the posttreatment administration and the baseline scores, and the large change was determined to be statistically significant. A full clinical evaluation at that point suggested that Tamara had recovered from her depression and anxiety. Periodic follow-up checks were done to make sure that Tamara had maintained the gains from the therapeutic intervention. Six months after discontinuing intervention, a follow-up (fourth) administration of the CDI was given, and although the scores had increased slightly compared with the third administration, Tamara continued to show reasonably benign levels of depressive symptoms.

Figure 1.1 shows portions of the report produced by the CDI software, which includes a graph of the four CDI administrations and a statistical assessment of the magnitude of the change that occurred over administrations. There was no significant difference between the two baseline administrations, but after treatment Tamara's scores were significantly lower than both of the baseline results. These findings strongly suggest that the treatment was effective in dealing with Tamara's depression.

NEW DEVELOPMENTS

Parent and Teacher Versions of the CDI

Youth self-report provides a valuable means of gathering information about depressive symptoms. Ideally, however, assessments from apporpriate observers should

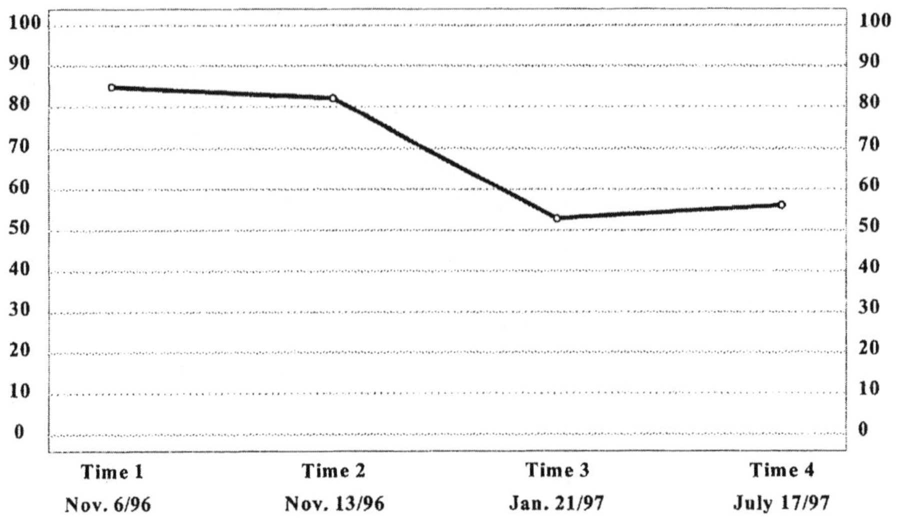

Time 1 (Nov. 6/96) vs. Time 2 (Nov. 13/96)
Total CDI score at Time 1 = 85, total CDI score at Time 2 = 82.
There was a drop in the CDI total score. Although this drop may reflect improvement between the two administrations, the statistics shown below indicate that the change was small and may reflect random fluctuation as opposed to significant change.
Statistical analysis: $t = 1.00$, $df = 26$, not statistically significant.

Time 2 (Nov. 13/96) vs. Time 3 (Jan. 21/97)
Total CDI score at Time 2 = 82, total CDI score at Time 3 = 53.
There was a substantial decline in the CDI total score, indicating improvement between the two administrations. The statistics indicate that this improvement was statistically significant.
Statistical analysis: $t = 5.05$, $df = 26$, $p < .05$.

Time 3 (Jan. 21/97) vs. Time 4 (July 17/97)
Total CDI score at Time 3 = 53, total CDI score at Time 4 = 56.
There was an increase in the CDI total score. Although this change may reflect a worsening condition between the two administrations, the statistics indicate that the change was small and may reflect random fluctuation as opposed to significant change.
Statistical analysis: $t = -1.44$, $df = 26$, not statistically significant.

Raw Scores

	Time 1 11/6/96	Time 2 11/13/96	Time 3 1/21/97	Time 4 7/17/97
Q#1	2	2	0	0
Q#2	1	1	1	1
Q#3	1	1	1	1
Q#4	2	2	1	1
Q#5	0	0	0	0
Q#6	2	1	0	1
Q#7	0	0	0	0
Q#8	1	1	0	1
Q#9	2	2	0	0
Q#10	1	2	0	0
Q#11	2	2	1	1
Q#12	1	1	0	0
Q#13	1	1	1	1
Q#14	1	1	1	1
Q#15	2	2	1	1
Q#16	2	2	0	0
Q#17	2	2	0	0
Q#18	1	0	0	0
Q#19	0	0	0	0
Q#20	2	1	1	1
Q#21	2	2	1	1
Q#22	1	1	1	1
Q#23	2	2	0	0
Q#24	1	1	1	1
Q#25	1	1	0	0
Q#26	1	1	0	0
Q#27	0	0	0	0

Fig 1.1 Portions of sample report from CDI software (based on hypothetical case example).

supplement the self-assessment. Specifically, parent and teacher versions of the CDI would be of great value. The *DSM–IV* emphasizes the importance of "multirater" assessments, and other measures have effectively created child, parent, and teacher versions (e.g., Conners Rating Scales Revised; Conners, 1997).

Parent and teacher versions of the CDI have, in fact, appeared sporadically in the literature (e.g., Cole, Hoffman, Tram, & Maxwell, 2000; Cole, Martin, Peeke, Truglio, & Seroczynski, 1998; Fristad, Weller, Weller, Teare, & Preskorn, 1991; Hoffman, Cole, Martin, Tram, & Seroczynski, 2000; Slotkin, Forehand, Fauber, McCombs, & Long, 1988; Wierzbicki, 1987). Use of these versions has been problematic since they are idiosyncratic, lack proper norms, and often have insufficient reliability and validity. To correct this problem, standard parent and teacher versions of the CDI have been created by Kovacs (1997a, 1997b). The CDI–P consists of 17 items, and the CDI–T consists of 12 items. The items were selected to correspond to items on the self-report version but were rephrased for administration to parents and teachers. Only items that maximize validity when answered by parents and teachers as respondents were retained.

A significant amount of research has been conducted with these standardized versions of the parent and teacher forms (Kovacs, 1997a, 1997b), and some of the preliminary results are provided here. For the parent form, 467 (205 women and 262 men) completed forms have been compiled from nonclinical sites, with 167 (49 women and 118 men) clinical cases also collected. For the teacher form, 583 (266 women and 317 men) completed sets of responses were compiled from nonclinical sites, and 114 (32 women and 82 men) clinical cases were obtained. The ethnic breakdown of the samples was approximately 80% white, 7% Hispanic, 4% Asian, 6% black, and 3% other.

In terms of reliability, total scores for both the parent and teacher forms were evaluated using Cronbach's alpha statistic. For the parent form, the overall alpha was .90, with alphas of .90 and .87 for the nonclinical and clinical groups, respectively. For the teacher form, the alpha was .89 for the overall combined sample as well as for the nonclinical and clinical samples treated separately. The values obtained suggest excellent internal reliability for the total scores for the parent and teacher forms of the CDI.

In another set of analyses, ANCOVAs were conducted to see if the CDI–P and CDI–T could differentiate between nonclinical and clinical cases. Gender and age (covariate) were controlled in the analysis. The CDI–P total score significantly differentiated nonclinical from clinical cases ($F_{1,629} = 31.6$, $p < .001$), and the CDI–T was also successful in this regard ($F_{1,692} = 44.2$, $p < .001$). These analyses provide evidence of the validity of the teacher and parent versions of the CDI and show that they successfully discriminate between nonclinical and clinical cases.

Finally, further analyses were done comparing the parent, teacher, and self-report versions. The CDI–P and CDI–T correlated at $r = .55$ ($n = 193$, $p < .001$), the CDI–P and CDI–self correlated at $r = .45$ ($n = 188$, $p < .001$), and the CDI-T and CDI-self correlated at $r = .52$ ($n = 140$, $p < .001$). This range of correlations suggests comparability among the measures and some overlap in the observers. At the same time, the correlations indicate sufficient variation among parents, teachers, and youths to highlight the importance of capturing the ratings of all three sources. By examining and comparing the information provided from the three informants, clinicians can explore discrepancies for more accurate assessments.[2] For example, if the parent and teacher

[2] Preliminary data comparing mothers' and fathers' ratings on the CDI–P indicate that fathers reported more depressive symptoms than mothers (Total: $M_F = 13.89$, $M_m = 12.32$, $p < .05$; Emotional Problems: $M_F = 4.94$, $M_m = 4.51$, not significant; Behavioral Problems: $M_F = 4.10$, $M_m = 3.62$, $p < .10$).

disagree, then the clinician should explore both perspectives to resolve the difference. If the child and teacher indicate that there is depressed mood but the parent does not, he or she might be denying the problem or underestimating its importance. The clinician may have to work through the parent's mindset to facilitate the appropriate intervention. If, on the other hand, the results from different informants are comparable, showing that everyone agrees on the assessment, the clinician will likely have greater confidence in his or her conclusions and actions, and the intervention could become easier to carry out.

Emotional Regulation Scales (ERS)

The CDI can play a valuable role in identifying depressive symptoms and offer insights into the nature of the symptoms via its subscales and items. The ERS scales (Kovacs, in press) are linked to the CDI but generate clinical information about the strategies individuals use to contend with emotions and emotional situations. Thus, they provide a mechanism that relates directly to clinical understanding and treatment of depressed pateints.

The scales were specifically designed to assess frequency of utilization (rated on a 3-point scale: "not true of me," "sometimes true of me," "many times true of me") of various emotion-regulatory strategies in response to situations that evoke sadness, fear, anger, or happiness. The items sample strategies from four emotion-regulatory domains: physical/biologic, behavioral, cognitive, and social-interpersonal. The items are classified into four sets: behavioral (25 items), cognitive (21 items), social-interpersonal (15 items), and physical (5 items), each set with both positive and negative items. Two additional items that reflect overall competence at regulating emotion were classified as "not domain specific." For each of the four sets of items, two scores are computed. "Frequency" scores for each domain reflect the frequency with which strategies in the given domain are used regardless of whether they are positive/adaptive or negative/maladaptive. "Skill" scores reflect the skill with which the individual uses strategies in the given domain, that is, the degree to which the individual uses positive/adaptive strategies and avoids negative/maladaptive strategies. A Frequency subscale indicates how typically the respondent uses the given strategy (regardless of whether it is adaptive or not). Skill subscale items are scored in the direction of increasing adaptive strategy. There are three versions of the ERS: for youth self-report, for parent report, and for adult self-report.

CONCLUSION

Given the high prevalence of depressive disorders in children and adolescents and their likely disruption of functioning in a number of areas, the development of assessment tools designed for this population is of utmost important. The Children's Depression Inventory (CDI) was developed to address this need, and it has since become one of the most widely used and cited inventories of depression. This chapter described the various versions of the CDI and current research and theory related to the CDI. It examined the current use of this instrument, distinguished proper use from improper use, and presented answers to questions frequently asked by practitioners. It also addressed the research history, administration, psychometric properties, and interpretation of the CDI.

The CDI, which is appropriate for children and adolescents aged 7 to 17, quantifies a range of depressive symptoms, including disturbed mood, problems in hedonic capacity and vegetative functions, low self-esteem, hopelessness, and difficulties in interpersonal behaviors. It is useful for the early identification of symptoms and for monitoring treatment effectiveness. It can also play a role in the diagnostic process as part of a larger assessment battery. Psychometric strengths of the CDI have been well established. Reliability, examined in terms of internal consistency, test-retest reliability, and standard error, has been found to range from satisfactory to excellent. The CDI has been used in many clinical studies and experimental research studies and has proved capable of assessing important constructs that have strong explanatory and predictive utility in characterizing depressive symptoms in children and adolescents.

The CDI has also been found to be useful with various populations and in different settings. Amendments to the CDI are currently being developed; these include parallel versions to be completed by teachers and parents. The complementary Emotional Regulation Scales, which are currently being developed, are directly linked to treatment planning. For all of the above reasons, as well as for its simplicity and ease of use and its adherence to NIMH standards for assessement instruments, the CDI is well deserving of its worldwide use in research and clinical settings.

ACKNOWLEDGMENTS

The authors wish to express their appreciation to Maria Kovacs, Ph.D., Lila Elkhadem, B.A., Jagruti Parmar, M.A., Joanne Morrison, B.A., and Karen Hirscheimer, M.A. for their contributions to this chapter.

REFERENCES

Abdel-Khalek, A. M. (1993). The construction and validation of the Arabic Children's Depression Inventory. *European Journal of Psychological Assessment, 9*, 41–50.

Abdel-Khalek, A. M. (1996). Factorial structure of the Arabic Children's Depression Inventory among Kuwaiti subjects. *Psychological Reports, 78*, 963–967.

Albert, N., & Beck, A. T. (1975). Incidence of depression in early adolescence: A preliminary study. *Journal of Youth and Adolescence, 4*, 301–307.

Allen, D. M., & Tarnowski, K. J. (1989). Depressive characteristics of physically abused children. *Journal of Abnormal Child Psychology, 17*, 1–11.

American Psychiatric Association. (1980). *Diagnostic and statistical manual of mental disorders* (3rd ed.). Washington, DC: Author.

American Psychiatric Association. (1985). *Diagnostic and statistical manual of mental disorders* (3rd ed., revised). Washington, DC: Author.

American Psychiatric Association. (1994). *Diagnostic and statistical manual of mental disorders* (4th ed.). Washington, DC: Author.

American Psychological Association. (1985). *Standards for educational and psychological testing*. Washington, DC: Author.

Armsden, G. C., McCauley, E., Greenberg, M. T., Burke, P. M., & Mitchell, J. R. (1990). Parent and peer attachment in early adolescent depression. *Journal of Abnormal Child Psychology, 18*, 683–697.

Arnarson, E. O., Smari, J., Einarsdottir, H., & Jonasdottir, E. (1994). The prevalence of depressive symptoms in pre-adolescent school children in Iceland. *Scandinavian Journal of Behaviour Therapy, 23*, 121–130.

Aronen, E. T., & Soininen, M. (2000). Childhood depressive symptoms predict psychiatric problems in young adults. *Canadian Journal of Psychiatry, 45*, 465–470.

Asarnow, J. R., & Carlson, G. A. (1985). Depression Self-Rating Scale: Utility with child psychiatric inpatients. *Journal of Consulting and Clinical Psychology, 53*, 491–499.

Asarnow, J. R., Scott, C. V., & Mintz, J. (2002). A combined cognitive-behavioral family education intervention for depression in children: A treatment development study. *Cognitive Therapy and Research, 26*, 221–229.

Bahls, S. (2002). Epidemiology of depressive symptoms in adolescents of a public school in Curitiba, Brazil. *Revista Brasileira de Psiquiatria, 24,* 63–67.

Barreto, S. J. (1994). Understanding the Children's Depression Inventory (CDI): A critical review. *Child Assessment News, 3,* 3–5.

Bartell, N. P., & Reynolds, W. M. (1986). Depression and self-esteem in academically gifted and nongifted children: A comparison study. *Journal of School Psychology, 24,* 55–61.

Beck, A. T. (1967). *Depression: Clinical, experimental, and theoretical aspects.* New York, NY: Harper & Row.

Beitchman, J. H. (1996). *Feelings, Attitudes, and Behaviors Scale for Children (FAB–C).* Toronto: Multi-Health Systems Inc.

Benavidez, D. A., & Matson, J. L. (1993). Assessment of depression in mentally retarded adolescents. *Research in Developmental Disabilities, 14,* 179–188.

Berndt, D. J., Schwartz, S., & Kaiser, C. F. (1983). Readability of self-report depression inventories. *Journal of Consulting and Clinical Psychology, 51,* 627–628.

Blumberg, S. H., & Izard, C. E. (1986). Discriminating patterns of emotions in 10- and 11-year-old children's anxiety and depression. *Journal of Personality and Social Psychology, 51,* 852–857.

Bodiford, C. A., Eisenstadt, T. H., Johnson, J. H., & Bradlyn, A. S. (1988). Comparison of learned helpless cognitions and behavior in children with high and low scores on the Children's Depression Inventory. *Journal of Clinical Child Psychology, 17,* 152–158.

Breen, M. P., & Weinberger, D. A. (1995). Regulation of depressive affect and interpersonal behavior among children requiring residential or day treatment. *Development and Psychopathology, 7,* 529–541.

Butcher, J. N., Dahlstrom, W. G., Graham, J. R., Tellegen, A. M., & Kaemmer, B. (1989). *Minnesota Multiphasic Personality Inventory–2 (MMPI–2): Manual for administration and scoring.* Minneapolis, MN: University of Minnesota Press.

Campbell, D., & Fiske, D. (1959). Convergent and discriminant validation by the multitrait-multimethod matrix. *Psychological Bulletin, 56,* 81–105.

Canals, J., Henneberg, C., Fernandez-Ballart, J., & Domenech, E. (1995). A longitudinal study of depression in an urban Spanish pubertal population. *European Child and Adolescent Psychiatry, 4,* 102–111.

Carey, M. P., Faulstich, M. E., Gresham, F. M., Ruggiero, L., & Enyart, P. (1987). Children's Depression Inventory: Construct and discriminant validity across clinical and nonreferred (control) populations. *Journal of Consulting and Clinical Psychology, 55,* 755–761.

Chall, J. S., and Dale, E. (1995). *Readability revisited: The new Dale-Chall readability formula.* Cambridge, MA: Brookline Books.

Chan, D. W. (1997). Depressive symptoms and perceived competence among Chinese secondary school students in Hong Kong. *Journal of Youth and Adolescence, 26,* 303–319.

Chartier, G. M., & Lassen, M. K. (1994). Adolescent depression: Children's Depression Inventory norms, suicidal ideation, and (weak) gender effects. *Adolescence, 29,* 859–864.

Ciarlo, J. A., Brown, T. R., Edwards, D. W., Kiresuk, T. J., & Newman, F. L. (1986). *Assessing mental health treatment outcome measurement techniques* (DHHS Pub. No. [ADM] 86-1301). Washington, DC: U.S. Government Printing Office.

Cole, D. A., Hoffman, K. B., Tram, J. M., & Maxwell, S. E. (2000). Structural differences in parent and child reports of children's symptoms of depression and anxiety. *Psychological Assessment, 12,* 174–185.

Cole, D. A., Martin, J. M., Peeke, J., Truglio, R., & Seroczynski, A. D. (1998). A longitudinal look at the relation between depression and anxiety in children and adolescents. *Journal of Counseling and Clinical Psychology, 66,* 451–460.

Congleton, A. B. (1996). The effect of a cognitive-behavioral group intervention on the locus of control, attributional style, and depressive symptoms of middle school students. *Dissertation Abstracts International. Section A: The Humanities and Social Sciences,* 56(9-A), 3507.

Conners, C. K. (1994). Conners' Rating Scales. In M. E. Maruish (Ed.), *The use of psychological testing for treatment planning and outcomes assessment* (pp. 550–578). Hillsdale, NJ: Lawrence Erlbaum Associates.

Conners, C. K. (1997). *Conners' Rating Scales–Revised: Technical manual.* Toronto: Multi-Health Systems Inc.

Craighead, W. E., Curry, J. F., & Ilardi, S. S. (1995). Relationship of Children's Depression Inventory factors to major depression among adolescents. *Psychological Assessment, 7,* 171–176.

Curry, J. F., & Craighead, W. E. (1990). Attributional style and self-reported depression among adolescent inpatients. *Child and Family Behavior Therapy, 12,* 89–93.

Dale, E., & Chall, J. S. (1948). *A formula for predicting readability.* Columbia, OH: Ohio State University Bureau of Educational Research. Research reprinted from *Educational Research Bulletin, 27,* 11–20, 37–54.

Davis, S. (1996). A study of depression and self-esteem in moderately gifted and nongifted children. *Dissertation Abstracts International. Section A: The Humanities and Social Sciences, 56*(10-A), 3886.

DeVellis, R. F. (1991). *Scale development: Theory and applications.* Newbury Park, CA: Sage.

Devine, D., Kempton, T., & Forehand, R. (1994). Adolescent depressed mood and young adult functioning: A longitudinal study. *Journal of Abnormal Child Psychology, 22*, 629–640.

Donnelly, M. (1995). Depression among adolescents in Northern Ireland. *Adolescence, 30*, 339–350.

Donnelly, T. F. (1995). Effects of parental reaction on depression, anxiety, and self-esteem in sexually abused children. *Dissertation Abstracts International. Section B: The Sciences and Engineering, 56*(5-B), 2896.

Drucker, P. M., & Greco-Vigorito, C. (2002). An exploratory factor analysis of Children's Depression Inventory scores in young children of substance abusers. *Psychological Reports, 91*, 131–141.

DuBois, D. L., Felner, R. D., Bartels, C. L., & Silverman, M. M. (1995). Stability of self-reported depressive symptoms in a community sample of children and adolescents. *Journal of Clinical Child Psychology, 24*, 386–396.

DuRant, R. H., Getts, A., Cadenhead, C., Emans, S. J., & Woods, E. R. (1995). Exposure to violence and victimization and depression, hopelessness, and purpose in life among adolescents living in and around public housing. *Journal of Developmental and Behavioral Pediatrics, 16*, 233–237.

Dyer, L. C. (1995). Assessing depression in American Indian children. *Dissertation Abstracts International. Section B: The Sciences and Engineering, 55*(11-B), 5064.

Eason, L. J., Finch, A. J., Jr., Brasted, W., & Saylor, C. F. (1985). The assessment of depression and anxiety in hospitalized pediatric patients. *Child Psychiatry and Human Development, 16*, 57–64.

Elliott, D. J., & Tarnowski, K. J. (1990). Depressive characteristics of sexually abused children. *Child Psychiatry and Human Development, 21*, 37–48.

Fauber, R., Forehand, R., Long, N., Burke, M., & Faust, J. (1987). The relationship of young adolescent Children's Depression Inventory (CDI) scores to their social and cognitive functioning. *Journal of Psychopathology and Behavioral Assessment, 9*, 161–172.

Faulstich, M. E., Carey, M. P., Ruggiero, L., Enyart, P., & Gresham, F. (1986). Assessment of depression in childhood and adolescence: An evaluation of the Center for Epidemiological Studies Depression Scale for Children (CES–DC). *American Journal of Psychiatry, 143*, 1024–1027.

Felner, R. D., Rowlison, R. T., Raley, P. A., & Evans, E. (1988). Depression in children and adolescents: A comparative analysis of the utility and construct validity of two assessment measures. *Journal of Consulting and Clinical Psychology, 56*, 769–772.

Finch, A. J., Saylor, C. F., & Edwards, G. L. (1985). Children's Depression Inventory: Sex and grade norms for normal children. *Journal of Consulting and Clinical Psychology, 53*, 424–425.

Finch, A. J., Saylor, C. F., Edwards, G. L., &, McIntosh, J. A. (1987). Children's Depression Inventory: Reliability over repeated administrations. *Journal of Consulting and Clinical Psychology, 16*, 339–341.

Fine, S., Moretti, M., Haley, G., & Marriage, K. (1985). Affective disorders in children and adolescents: The dysthymic disorder dilemma. *Canadian Journal of Psychiatry, 30*, 173–177.

Finkelstein, R. (1996). Depression and loneliness in the early adolescent, learning-disabled population. *Dissertation Abstracts International. Section A: The Humanities and Social Sciences, 56*(12-A), 4703.

Fitzpatrick, K. M. (1993). Exposure to violence and presence of depression among low-income, African-American youth. *Journal of Consulting and Clinical Psychology, 61*, 528–531.

Frias, D., Mestre, V., del Barrio, V., & Garcia-Ros, R. (1992). Estructura familiar y depresion infantil [Family structure and childhood depression]. *Anuario-de-Psicologia, 52*, 121–131.

Friedman, R. J., & Butler, L. F. (1979). *Development and evaluation of a test battery to assess childhood depression*. Final report to Health and Welfare, Canada, for Project #606-1533-44. Ottawa: Health and Welfare Canada.

Frigerio, A., Pesenti. S., Molteni, M., Snider, J., & Battaglia, M. (2001). Depressive symptoms as measured by the CDI in a population of northern Italian children. *European Psychiatry, 16*(1), 33–37.

Fristad, M. A., Emery, B. L., & Beck, S. J. (1997). Use and abuse of the Children's Depression Inventory. *Journal of Consulting and Clinical Psychology, 65*, 699–702.

Fristad, M. A., Weller, E. B., Weller, R. A., Teare, M., & Preskorn, S. H. (1988). Self-report vs. biological markers in assessment of childhood depression. *Journal of Affective Disorders, 15*, 339–345.

Fristad, M. A., Weller, E. B., Weller, R. A., Teare, M., & Preskorn, S. H. (1991). Comparisons of the parent and child versions of the Children's Depression Inventory (CDI). *Annals of Clinical Psychiatry, 3*, 341–346.

Garvin, V., Leber, D., & Kalter, N. (1991). Children of divorce: Predictors of change following preventive intervention. *American Journal of Orthopsychiatry, 61*, 438–447.

Ghareeb, G. A., & Beshai, J. A. (1989). Arabic version of the Children's Depression Inventory: Reliability and validity. *Journal of Clinical Child Psychology, 18*, 323–326.

Gillick, T. A. (1997). Depression in adolescent female victims of intrafamilial child sexual abuse. *Dissertation Abstracts International. Section B: The Sciences and Engineering, 57*(7-B), 4706.

Gladstone, T. R. G., & Kaslow, N. J. (1995). Depression and attributions in children and adolescents: A meta-analytic review. *Journal of Abnormal Child Psychology, 23*, 597–606.

Goldstein, D., Paul, G. G., & Sanfilippo-Cohn, S. (1985). Depression and achievement in subgroups of children with learning disabilities. *Journal of Applied Developmental Psychology, 6*, 263–275.

Gouveia, V. V., Barbosa, G. A., de Almeida, H. J. F., & de Andrade-Gaiao, A. (1995). Inventario de depressao infantil-CDI: Estudo de adptacao com escolares de Joao Pessoa [Children's Depression Inventory–CDI: Adaptation study with students of Joao Pessoa]. *Jornal Brasileiro de Psiquiatria, 44*, 345–349.

Gray, K. (1999). Prenatal substance exposure and childhood depressive symptoms. *Dissertation Abstracts International. Section B: The Sciences and Engineering, 60*(4-B), 1524.

Haley, G. M. T., Fine, S., Marriage, K., Moretti, M. M., & Freeman, R. J. (1985). Cognitive bias and depression in psychiatrically disturbed children and adolescents. *Journal of Consulting and Clinical Psychology, 53*, 535–537.

Hammen, C., Adrian, C., Gordon, D., Burge, D., Jaenicke, C., & Hiroto, D. (1987). Children of depressed mothers: Maternal strain and symptom predictors of dysfunction. *Journal of Abnormal Psychology, 96*, 190–198.

Hammen, C., Adrian, C., & Hiroto, D. (1988). A longitudinal test of the attributional vulnerability model in children at risk for depression. *British Journal of Clinical Psychology, 27*, 37–46.

Harrison, C. (1980). *Readability in the classroom.* Cambridge: Cambridge University Press.

Helsel, W. J., & Matson, J. L. (1984). The assessment of depression in children: The internal structure of the Child Depression Inventory (CDI). *Behaviour Research and Therapy, 22*, 289–298.

Hepperlin, C. M., Stewart, G. W., & Rey, J. M. (1990). Extraction of depression scores in adolescents from a general-purpose behaviour checklist. *Journal of Affective Disorders, 18*, 105–112.

Hodges, K. (1990). Depression and anxiety in children: A comparison of self-report questionnaires to clinical interview. *Psychological Assessment, 2*, 376–381.

Hodges, K., & Craighead, W. E. (1990). Relationship of Children's Depression Inventory factors to diagnosed depression. *Psychological Assessment, 2*, 489–492.

Hoffman, K. B., Cole, D. A., Martin, J. M., Tram, J., & Seroczynski, A. D. (2000). Are the discrepancies between self- and others' appraisals of competence predictive or reflective of depressive symptoms in children and adolescents: A longitudinal study. Part II. *Journal of Abnormal Psychology, 109*, 651–662.

Houghton, S., O'Connell, M., & O'Flaherty, A. (1998). The use of the Children's Depression Inventory in an Irish context. *Irish Journal of Psychology, 19*, 313–331.

Howard, K. I., Kopta, S. M., Krause, M. S., & Orlinsky, D. E. (1986). The dose-effect relationship in psychotherapy. *American Psychologist, 41*, 159–164.

Huddleston, E. N., & Rust, J. O. (1994). A comparison of child and parent ratings of depression and anxiety in clinically referred children. *Research Communications in Psychology, Psychiatry and Behavior, 19*, 101–112.

Ines, T. M., & Sacco, W. P. (1992). Factors related to correspondence between teacher ratings of elementry student depression and student self-ratings. *Journal of Consulting and Clinical Psychology, 60*, 140–142.

Jacobs, M. L. (1990). Diagnosis of depression in school-aged exceptional family member children: The Children's Depression Inventory as a screening tool. *Dissertation Abstracts International. 50*(9-B), 4205–4206.

Jacobson, N. S., & Truax, P. (1991). Clinical significance: A statistical approach to defining meaningful change in psychotherapy research. *Journal of Consulting and Clinical Psychology, 59*, 12–19.

Jensen, P. S., Bloedau, L., Degroot, J., Ussery, T., & Davis, H. (1990). Children at risk: I. Risk factors and child symptomatology. *Journal of the American Academy of Child and Adolescent Psychiatry, 29*, 51–59.

Joiner, T. E., Schmidt, K. L., & Schmidt, N. B. (1996). Low-end specificity of childhood measures of emotional distress: Differential effects for depression and anxiety. *Journal of Personality Assessment, 67*, 258–271.

Kashani, J. H., & Carlson, G. A. (1985). Major depressive disorder in a preschooler. *Journal of the American Academy of Child Psychiatry, 24*, 490–494.

Kashani, J. H., Husain, A., Shekim, W. O., Hodges, K. K., Cytryn, L., & McKnew, D. H. (1981). Current perspective on childhood depression: An overview. *American Journal of Psychiatry, 138*, 143–153.

Kaslow, N. J., Rehm, L. P., & Siegel, A. W. (1984). Social-cognitive and cognitive correlates of depression in children. *Journal of Abnormal Child Psychology, 12*, 605–620.

Kazdin, A. E., Colbus, D., & Rodgers, A. (1986). Assessment of depression and diagnosis of depressive disorder among psychiatrically disturbed children. *Journal of Abnormal Child Psychology, 14*, 499–515.

Kazdin, A. E., Esveldt-Dawson, K., Unis, A. S., & Rancurello, M. D. (1983). Child and parent evaluations of depression and aggression in psychiatric inpatient children. *Journal of Abnormal Child Psychology, 11*, 401–413.

Kazdin, A. E., French, N. H., Unis, A. S., & Esveldt-Dawson, K. (1983). Assessment of childhood depression: Correspondence of child and parent ratings. *Journal of the American Academy of Child Psychiatry, 22*, 157–164.

Kazdin, A. E., French, N. H., Unis, A. S., Esveldt-Dawson, K., & Sherick, R. B. (1983). Hopelessness, depression, and suicidal intent among psychiatrically disturbed inpatient children. *Journal of Consulting and Clinical Psychology, 51*, 504–510.

Kazdin, A. E., & Petti, T. A. (1982). Self-report and interview measures of childhood and adolescent depression. *Journal of Child Psychology and Psychiatry, 23*, 437–457.

Kazdin, A. E., Rodgers, A., & Colbus, D. (1986). The Hopelessness Scale for Children: Psychometric characteristics and concurrent validity. *Journal of Consulting and Clinical Psychology, 54*, 241–245.

Knight, D., Hensley, V. R., & Waters, B. (1998). Validation of the Children's Depression Scale and the Children's Depression Inventory in a prepubertal sample. *Journal of Child Psychology and Psychiatry, 29*, 853–863.

Koizumi, S. (1991). The standardization of Children's Depression Inventory. *Syoni Hoken Kenkyu (The Journal of Child Health), 50*, 717–721.

Kovacs, M. (1985). The Children's Depression Inventory. *Psychopharmacology Bulletin, 21*, 995–998.

Kovacs, M. (1992). *The Children's Depression Inventory (CDI) manual*. Toronto: Multi-Health Systems Inc.

Kovacs, M. (1995). *The Children's Depression Inventory (CDI) software manual*. Toronto: Multi-Health Systems Inc.

Kovacs, M. (1996a). Presentation and course of major depressive disorder during childhood and later years of the life span. *Journal of the American Academy of Child and Adolescent Psychiatry, 35*, 705–715.

Kovacs, M. (1996b). The course of childhood-onset depressive disorders. *Psychiatric Annals, 26*, 326–330.

Kovacs, M. (1997a). *The Children's Depression Inventory Parent Version (CDI–P)*. Toronto: Multi-Health Systems Inc.

Kovacs, M. (1997b). *The Children's Depression Inventory Teacher Version (CDI–T)*. Toronto: Multi-Health Systems Inc.

Kovacs, M. (in press). *Emotional Regulation Scales (ERS)*. Toronto: Multi-Health Systems Inc.

Kovacs, M., Akiskal, H. S., Gatsonis, C., & Parrone, P. L. (1994). Childhood onset dysthymic disorder: Clinical features and prospective naturalistic outcome. *Archives of General Psychiatry, 51*, 365–374.

Kovacs, M., & Beck, A. T. (1977). An empirical-clinical approach toward a definition of childhood depression. In J. G. Shulterbrandt & A. Raskin (Eds.), *Depression in childhood: Diagnosis, treatment, and conceptual models* (pp. 1–25). New York: Raven Press.

Kovacs, M., Gatsonis, C., Paulauskas, S. L., & Richards, C. (1989). Depressive disorders in childhood: IV. A longitudinal study of comorbidity with and risk for anxiety disorders. *Archives of General Psychiatry, 46*, 776–782.

Kovacs, M., & Goldston, D. (1991). Cognitive and social cognitive development of depressed children and adolescents. *Journal of the American Academy of Child and Adolescent Psychiatry, 30*, 388–392.

Kovacs, M., Iyengar, S., Stewart, J., Obrosky, S., & Marsh, J. (1990). Psychological functioning of children with insulin-dependent diabetes mellitus: A longitudinal study. *Journal of the American Academy of Child and Adolescent Psychiatry, 30*, 388–392.

Kovacs, M., Obrosky, S., Gatsonis, C., & Richards, C. (1997). First-episode major depressive and dysthymic disorder in childhood: Clinical and sociodemographic factors in recovery. *Journal of the American Academy of Child and Adolescent Psychiatry, 36*, 777–784.

Krane, N. J. (1996). A comparative study of effortful information processing in subclinically depressed and nondepressed elementary school children. *Dissertation Abstracts International. Section A: The Humanities and Social Sciences, 56*(11-A), 4326.

Kuttner, M. J., Delamater, A. M., & Santiago, J. V. (1989). Learned helplessness in diabetic youths. *Journal of Pediatric Psychology, 15*, 581–594.

Lachar, D., & Gdowski, C. L. (1979). *Actuarial assessment of child and adolescent personality: An interpretive guide for the Personality Inventory for Children Profile*. Los Angeles: Western Psychological Services.

Lam, K. N. (2000). An etic-emic approach to validation of the Chinese version of the Children's Depression Inventory. *Dissertation Abstracts International. Section B: The Sciences and Engineering, 60*(11-B), 5780.

Lanktree, C. B., & Briere, J. (1995). Outcome of therapy for sexually abused children: A repeated measures study. *Child Abuse and Neglect, 19*, 1145–1155.

Linna, S., Moilanen, I., Ebeling, H., Piha, J., Kumpulainen, K., Tamminen, T., et al. (1999). Psychiatric symptoms in children with intellectual disability. *European Child and Adolescent Psychiatry, 8*, 77–82.

Lipovsky, J. A., Finch, A. J., & Belter, R. W. (1989). Assessment of depression in adolescents: Objective and projective measures. *Journal of Personality Assessment, 53*, 449–458.

Liss, H., Phares, V., & Liljequist, L. (2001). Symptom endorsement differences on the Children's Depression Inventory with children and adolescents on an inpatient unit. *Journal of Personality Assessment, 76*, 396–411.

Llabre, M. M., & Hadi, F. (1997). Social support and psychological distress in Kuwaiti boys and girls exposed to the Gulf crisis. *Journal of Clinical Child Psychology, 26*, 247–255.

Lobert, W. (1989). Untersuchung von Merkmalen depressiver Verstimmung in der Pubertat mit dem Kinder-Depressions-Inventar nach Kovacs [Investigation of symptoms of depressive moodiness during puberty with the Children's Depression Inventory according to Kovacs]. *Zeitschrift fur Kinder und Jugendpsychiatrie, 17,* 194–201.

Lobert, W. (1990). Untersuchung zur Struktur der depressiven Verstimmung in der Pubertat mit dem GCDI (German Children's Depression Inventory) [Investigation of the structure of depressive moodiness during puberty with the GCDI (German Children's Depression Inventory)]. *Zeitschrift fur Kinder und Jugendpsychiatrie, 18,* 18–22.

Lobovits, D. A., & Handal, P. J. (1985). Childhood depression: Prevalence using DSM–III criteria and validity of parent and child depression scales. *Journal of Pediatric Psychology, 10,* 45–54.

Lord, F. M., & Novick, M. R. (1968). *Statistical theories of mental test scores.* Reading, MA: Addison-Wesley.

March, J. S. (1997). *The Multidimensional Anxiety Scale for Children (MASC).* Toronto: Multi-Health Systems Inc.

Marciano, P. L., & Kazdin, A. E. (1994). Self-esteem, depression, hopelessness, and suicidal intent among psychiatrically disturbed inpatient children. *Journal of Clinical Child Psychology, 23,* 151–160.

Marriage, K., Fine, S., Moretti, M., & Haley, G. (1986). Relationship between depression and conduct disorder in children and adolescents. *Journal of the American Academy of Child Psychiatry, 25,* 687–691.

Matthey, S., & Petrovski, P. (2002). The Children's Depression Inventory: Error in cutoff scores for screening purposes. *Psychological Assessment, 41,* 146–149.

Mattison, R. E., Handford, H. A., Kales, H. C., Goodman, A. L., & McLaughlin, R. E. (1990). Four-year predictive value of the Children's Depression Inventory. *Psychological Assessment, 2,* 169–174.

McCauley, E., Mitchell, J. R., Burke, P., & Moss S. (1988). Cognitive attributes of depression in children and adolescents. *Journal of Consulting and Clinical Psychology, 56,* 903–908.

Meins, W. (1993). Assessment of depression in mentally retarded adults: Reliability and validity of the Children's Depression Inventory (CDI). *Research in Developmental Disabilities, 14,* 299–312.

Mestre, V., Frias, D., & Garcia-Ros, R. (1992). Propiedades psicomettricas del Children's Depression Inventory (CDI) en poblacion adolescente: Fiabilidad y validez [Psychometric properties of the Children's Depression Inventory (CDI) in the adolescent population: Reliability and validity]. *Psicologica, 13,* 149–159.

Meyer, N. E., Dyck, D. G., & Petrinack, R. J. (1989). Cognitive appraisal and attributional correlates of depressive symptoms in children. *Journal of Abnormal Child Psychology, 17,* 325–336.

Milich, R., Roberts, M. A., Loney, J., & Caputo, J. (1980). Differentiating practice effects and statistical regression on the Conners' Hyperkinesis Index. *Journal of Abnormal Psychology, 8,* 549–552.

Milne, J., & Spence, S. H. (1987). Training social perception skills with primary school children: A cautionary note. *Behavioural Psychotherapy, 15,* 144–157.

Moretti, M. M., Fine, S., Haley, G., & Marriage, K. (1985). Childhood and adolescent depression: Child-report versus parent-report information. *Journal of the American Academy of Child Psychiatry, 24,* 298–302.

Nelson, W. M., & Politano, P. D. (1990). Children's Depression Inventory: Stability over repeated administrations in psychiatric inpatient children. *Journal of Clinical Child Psychiatry, 19,* 254–256.

Nelson, W. M., Politano, P. M., Finch, A. J., Wendel, N., & Mayhall, C. (1987). Children's Depression Inventory: Normative data and utility with emotionally disturbed children. *Journal of the American Academy of Child and Adolescent Psychiatry, 26,* 43–48.

Newman, F. L., Ciarlo, J. A., & Carpenter, D. (1999). Guidelines for selecting psychological instruments for treatment planning and outcome assessment. In M. E. Maruish (Ed.), *The use of psychological testing for treatment planning and outcomes assessment* (2nd ed., pp. 153–170). Hillsdale, NJ: Lawrence Erlbaum Associates.

Nieminen, G. S., & Matson, J. L. (1989). Depressive problems in conduct-disordered adolescents. *Journal of School Psychology, 27,* 175–188.

Nolen-Hoeksema, S., Girgus, J. S., & Seligman, M. E. P. (1986). Learned helplessness in children: A longitudinal study of depression, achievement, and explanatory style. *Journal of Personality and Social Psychology, 51,* 435–442.

Norvell, N., Brophy, C., & Finch, A. J. (1985). The relationship of anxiety to childhood depression. *Journal of Personality Assessment, 49,* 150–153.

Ollendick, T. H., & Yule, W. (1990). Depression in British and American children and its relation to anxiety and fear. *Journal of Consulting and Clinical Psychology, 58,* 126–129.

Oy, B. (1991). Children's Depression Inventory: A study of reliability and validity. *Turk Psikiyatri Dergisi, 2,* 132–136.

Pfeffer, C., Karus, D., Siegal, K., & Jiang, H. (2000). Child survivors of parental death from cancer or suicide: Depressive and behavioral outcomes. *Psycho-Oncology, 9,* 1–10.

Polaino-Lorente, A., & del-Pozo-Armentia, A. (1992). Modification de la depresion mediante un programa de intervencion psicopedagogica en ninos cancerosos no hospitalizados [Modification of depression through a psychopedagogic intervention program in childhood cancer hospitalization]. *Analisis y Modificacion de Conducta, 18,* 493–503.

Polaino-Lorente, A., & Domenech, E. (1993). Prevalence of childhood depression: Results of the first study in Spain. *Journal of Child Psychology and Psychiatry and Allied Disciplines, 34,* 1007–1017.

Politano, P. M., Nelson, W. M., Evans, H. E., Sorenson, S. B., & Zeman, D. J. (1985). Factor analytic evaluation of differences between Black and Caucasian emotionally disturbed children on the Children's Depression Inventory. *Journal of Psychopathology and Behavioral Assessment, 8,* 1–7.

Pons-Salvador, G., & del Barrio, V. (1993). Depresion infantil y divorcio [Child depression and divorce]. *Avances en Psicologia Clinica Latinoamericana, 11,* 95–106.

Ponterotto, J. G., Pace, T. M., & Kavan, M. G. (1989). A counselor's guide to the assessment of depression. *Journal of Counseling and Development, 67,* 301–309.

Preiss, M. (1998). Hloubka depresivity v sebeposuzovaci skale CDI u deti po valce v Bosne [Depression depth in self-rating scale CDI in children after the war in Bosnia]. *Ceskoslovenska Psychologie, 42,* 558–564.

Preskorn, S. H., Weller, E. B., Hughes, C. W., Weller, R. A., & Bolte, K. (1987). Depression in prepubertal children: Dexamethasone nonsupression predicts differential response to imipramine vs. placebo. *Psychopharmacology Bulletin, 23,* 128–133.

Puig-Antich, J. (1982). Major depression and conduct disorder in prepuberty. *Journal of the American Academy of Child Psychiatry, 21,* 118–128.

Reicher, H., & Rossmann, P. (1991). Zu den psychometrischen Eigenschaften einer deutschen Version des Children's Depression Inventory [The psychometric properties of a German version of the Children's Depression Inventory]. *Diagnostica, 37,* 236–251.

Reinhard, H. G., Bowi, U., & Rulcovius, G. (1990). Stabilitat, Reliabilitat und Faktorenstruktur einer deutschen Fassung des Children's Depression Inventory [Reliability, stability, and factor structure of a German version of the Children's Depression Inventory]. *Zeitschrift fur Kinder und Jugendpsychiatrie, 18,* 185–191.

Reinherz, H. Z., Frost, A. K., & Pakiz, B. (1991). Changing faces: Correlates of depressive symptoms in late adolescence. *Family and Community Health, 14,* 52–63.

Renouf, A. G., & Kovacs, M. (1994). Concordance between mothers' reports and children's self-reports of depressive symptoms: A longitudinal study. *Journal of the American Academy of Child and Adolescent Psychiatry, 33,* 208–216.

Reynolds, C. R., & Richmond, B. O. (1985). *Revised Children's Manifest Anxiety Scale manual.* Los Angeles: Western Psychological Services.

Reynolds, W. M., Anderson, G., & Bartell, N. (1985). Measuring depression in children: A multimethod assessment investigation. *Journal of Abnormal Child Psychology, 13,* 513–526.

Rick, S. (1999). Coping behaviors of sexually abused boys as related to levels of depression and hopelessness. (child sexual abuse). *Dissertation Abstracts International. Section B: The Sciences and Engineering, 60*(4-B), 1535.

Rotundo, N., & Hensley, V. R. (1985). The Children's Depression Scale. A study of its validity. *Journal of Child Psychology and Psychiatry, 26,* 917–927.

Rybolt, Y. (1995). Assessment of depression in school-age children: A cross-cultural comparison of Mexican American and Caucasian students. *Dissertation Abstracts International. Section A: The Humanities and Social Sciences, 56*(1-A), 0146.

Sacco, W. P., & Graves, D. J. (1985). Correspondence between teacher ratings of childhood depression and child self-ratings. *Journal of Clinical Child Psychology, 14,* 353–355.

Saint-Laurent, L. (1990). Psychometric study of Kovac's Children's Depression Inventory with a French-speaking sample. *Canadian Journal of Behavioural Science, 22,* 377–384.

Sakurai, S. (1991). The relation between depression and causal attributional style in Japanese children. *Japanese Journal of Health Psychology, 4,* 23–30.

Saylor, C. F., Finch, A. J., Jr., Baskin, C. H., Furey, W., & Kelly, M. M. (1984). Construct validity for measures of childhood depression: Application of multitrait–multimethod methodology. *Journal of Consulting and Clinical Psychology, 52,* 977–985.

Saylor, C. F., Finch, A. J., Jr., Baskin, C. H., Saylor, C. B., Darnell, G., & Furey, W. (1984). Children's Depression Inventory: Investigation of procedures and correlates. *Journal of the American Academy of Child Psychiatry, 23,* 626–628.

Saylor, C. F., Finch, A. J., Jr., Spirito, A., & Bennett, B. (1984). The Children's Depression Inventory: A systematic evaluation of psychometric properties. *Journal of Consulting and Clinical Psychology, 52,* 955–967.

Seligman, M. E. P., Peterson, C., Kaslow, N. J., Tanenbaum, R. L., Alloy, L. B., & Abramson, L. Y. (1984). Attributional style and depressive symptoms among children. *Journal of Abnormal Psychology, 93*, 235–238.

Shain, B. N., Naylor, M., & Alessi, N. (1990). Comparison of self-rated and clinician-rated measures of depression in adolescents. *American Journal of Psychiatry, 147*, 793–795.

Shah, F., & Morgan, S. B. (1996). Teacher's ratings of social competence of children with high versus low levels of depressive symptoms. *Journal of School Psychology, 34*, 337–349.

Siegel, K., Karus, D., & Raveis, V. H. (1996). Adjustment of children facing the death of a parent due to cancer. *Journal of the American Academy of Child and Adolescent Psychiatry, 35*, 442–450.

Simmer-Dvonch, L. M. (1999). Development and evaluation of a group treatment for sexually abused male adolescents. *Dissertation Abstracts International. Section B: The Science and Engineering, 59*(7-B), 3715.

Slotkin, J., Forehand, R., Fauber, R., McCombs, A., & Long, N. (1988). Parent-completed and adolescent-completed CDIs: Relationship to adolescent social and cognitive functioning. *Journal of Abnormal Child Psychology, 16*, 207–217.

Speer, D. C., & Greenbaum, P. E. (1995). Five methods for computing significant individual client change and improvement rates: Support for an individual growth curve approach. *Journal of Consulting and Clinical Psychology, 63*, 1044–1048.

Spence, S. H., & Milne, J. (1987). The Children's Depression Inventory: Norms and factor analysis from an Australian school population. *Australian Psychologist, 22*, 345–351.

Spirito, A., Overholser, J., & Hart, K. (1991). Cognitive characteristics of adolescent suicide attempters. *Journal of the American Academy of Child and Adolescent Psychiatry, 30*, 604–608.

Stark, K. D., Kaslow, N. J., & Laurent, J. (1993). The assessment of depression in children: Are we assessing depression or the broad-band construct of negative affectivity? *Journal of Emotional and Behavioral Disorders, 1*, 149–154.

Stavrakaki, C., Williams, E. C., Walker, S., Roberts, N., & Kotsopoulos, S. (1991). Pilot study of anxiety and depression in prepubertal children. *Canadian Journal of Psychiatry, 36*, 332–338.

Stiensmeier-Pelster, J., Schurmann, M., & Duda, K. (1991). Das Depressionsinventar fur Kinder und Jugendliche (DIKJ): Untersuchungen zu seinen psychometrischen Eigenschaften [The psychometric properties of the German version of the Children's Depression Inventory]. *Diagnostica, 37*, 149–159.

Stiensmeier-Pelster, J., Schurmann, M., & Urhahne, D. (1991). Das Depressionsinventar fur Kinder und Jugendliche (DIKJ): Einsetzbarkeit in der Primarstufe [The Depression Inventory for Children and Adolescents (DICA): Its applicability on the elementary school level]. *Zeitschrift fur Entwicklungspsychologie und Padagogische Psychologie, 23*, 171–176.

Stocker, C. M. (1994). Children's perceptions of relationships with siblings, friends, and mothers: Compensatory processes and links with adjustment. *Journal of Child Psychology and Psychiatry and Allied Disciplines, 35*, 1447–1459.

Strober, S., & Carlson, G. (1982). Bipolar illness in adolescents with major depression: Clinical, genetic, and psychopharmacologic predictors in a three- to four-year prospective follow-up investigation. *Archives of General Psychiatry, 39*, 549–555.

Timbremont, B., & Braet, C. (2001). Psychometric assessment of the Dutch version of the Children's Depression Inventory. *Gedragstherapie, 34*, 229–242.

Twenge, J., & Nolen-Hoeksema, S. (2002). Age, gender, race, socioeconomic status, and birth cohort differences on the Children's Depression Inventory: A meta-analysis. *Journal of Abnormal Psychology, 4*, 578–588.

Weiss, B., & Weisz, J. R. (1988). Factor structure of self-reported depression: Clinic-referred children versus adolescents. *Journal of Abnormal Psychology, 97*, 492–495.

Wierzbicki, M. (1987). A parent form of the Children's Depression: Reliability and validity in non-clinical populations. *Journal of Clinical Psychology, 43*, 390–397.

Weiss, B., Weisz, J. R., Politano, M., Carey, M., Nelson, W. M., & Finch, A. J. (1991). Developmental differences in the factor structure of the Children's Depression Inventory. *Psychological Assessment: A Journal of Consulting and Clinical Psychology, 3*, 38–45.

Weissman, M. M., Orvaschel, H., & Padian, N. (1980). Children's symptom and social functioning self-report scales: Comparison of mothers' and children's reports. *Journal of Nervous and Mental Disease, 168*, 736–740.

Wolfe, V. V., Finch, A. J., Jr., Saylor, C., Blount, R. L., Pallmeyer, T. P., & Carek, D. J. (1987). Negative affectivity in children: A multitrait-multimethod investigation. *Journal of Consulting and Clinical Psychology, 55*, 245–250.

Worchel, F. F., Hughes, J. N., Hall, B. M., Stanton, S. B., Stanton, H., & Little, V. Z. (1990). Evaluation of subclinical depression in children using self-, peer-, and teacher-report measures. *Journal of Abnormal Child Psychology, 18*, 271–282.

Worchel, F., Nolan, B., & Willson, V. (1987). New perspectives on child and adolescent depression. *Journal of School Psychology, 25*, 411–414.

Yu, D., & Li, Xu. (2000). Preliminary use of the Children's Depression Inventory (CDI) in China. *Chinese Mental Health Journal, 14*, 225–227.

Zivcic, I. (1993). Emotional reactions of children to war stress in Croatia. *Journal of the American Academy of Child and Adolescent Psychiatry, 32*, 709–713.

2

The Multidimensional Anxiety Scale for Children (MASC)

John S. March
Duke University Medical Center

James D. A. Parker
Trent University

Presumably because pathological anxiety is associated with significant suffering, disruption in normal psychosocial and academic development and family functioning, and increased utilization of medical services, "worry" is among the more common causes of referral to children's mental health care providers (Black, 1995; Simon, Ormel, Von Korff, & Barlow, 1995). Unfortunately, the population prevalence of childhood-onset fears, the structure of anxiety symptoms in the general pediatric population, and the relative importance of specific anxiety dimensions within gender, ethnic, or cultural groupings across time have, until recently, remained unclear (March & Albano, 1998). This is in part because of a lack of acceptable measurement tools (Costello & Angold, 1995; Greenhill, Pine, March, Birmaher, & Riddle, 1998; March & Albano, 1998).

Ideally, instruments intended to assess anxiety in pediatric patients should (a) provide reliable and valid ascertainment of symptoms across multiple symptom domains; (b) discriminate symptom clusters; (c) differentiate normal from pathological anxiety both qualitatively and quantitatively; (d) incorporate and reconcile multiple observations, such as parent and child ratings; and (e) be sensitive to treatment-induced change in symptoms. Other factors that may influence instrument selection include the reasons for the assessment—screening, diagnosis, or monitoring treatment outcome, for example—as well as time required for administration, level of training necessary to administer and/or interpret the instrument, reading level, and cost. Finally, with increasing emphasis on multidisciplinary approaches to assessment and treatment, assessment tools must facilitate communication, not only among clinicians but also between clinicians and regulatory bodies, such as utilization review committees within managed care environments.

Though currently available instruments fall well short of these goals, a complex matrix of tools for assessing normal and pathological fears is now available (Greenhill et al., 1998; March & Albano, 1998). In this chapter, we describe one such instrument, the Multidimensional Anxiety Scale for Children (MASC), which was designed to address the multidimensional assessment of anxiety in children and adolescents in a psychometrically rigorous fashion (March, 1998; March, Parker, Sullivan, Stallings, & Conners, 1997). Excellent reviews of pediatric anxiety disorders in general (March, 1995; Ollendick & King, 1994) and assessment issues in particular (Greenhill et al., 1998) are available.

BACKGROUND

Instruments designed specifically to address anxiety in children and adolescents are required for several reasons. First, children appear to undergo a developmentally sanctioned progression in anxiety symptoms (Keller et al., 1992; Last, Strauss, & Francis, 1987). Second, their day-to-day environments differ from those most typically experienced by adults so that the presentation of anxiety also differs, as in "school phobia." Third, to differentiate normal from pathological anxiety, gender and age norms are necessary. Finally, some fears may be viewed as adaptive protective; only when anxiety is excessive or the context is developmentally inappropriate does anxiety becomes clinically significant (Marks, 1987). Other fears, such those seen in obsessive-compulsive disorder, are developmentally inappropriate under many if not all circumstances (Leonard, Goldberger, Rapoport, Cheslow, & Swedo, 1990). Thus clinicians and researchers interested in childhood anxiety disorders face the challenging task of differentiating pathological anxiety from fears occurring as a part of normal developmental processes . The DSM–III–R (American Psychiatric Association, 1987) addressed this nosological conundrum by introducing a subclass of anxiety disorders of childhood and adolescence. The *DSM–IV* (American Psychiatric Association, 1994) both refines these constructs and establishes a greater degree of continuity—developmental and nosological—with the adult anxiety disorders. The *DSM* taxonomy in essence reflects an expert consensus regarding the actual clustering of anxiety in pediatric samples. Though empirical support for the *DSM* "factor structure" in some cases is questionable (e.g., generalized anxiety), for other constructs it is more robust (e.g., separation or social anxiety; March et al., 1997).

Some anxiety symptoms, such as refusing to attend school in the patient with panic disorder and agoraphobia, are readily observable; other symptoms are open only to child introspection and thus to child self-report. For this and other reasons, self-report measures of anxiety, which provide an opportunity for children to reveal their internal or "hidden" experiences, have found wide application in both clinical and research settings. Typically, self-report measures use a Likert scale format in which a child is asked to rate each questionnaire using either a frequency or intensity format. For example, a child might be asked to rate "I feel tense" on a four-point frequency scale that ranges from almost never to often. Self-report measures are easy to administer, require a minimum of clinician time, and economically capture a wide range of important anxiety dimensions from the child's point of view. Taken together these features make self-report measures ideally suited to gathering data prior to the initial evaluation, as self-report measures used in this fashion increase clinician efficiency by facilitating accurate assessment of the prior probability that a particular child will or will not have symptoms within a specific symptom domain.

For the most part, available self-report rating scales for assessing pediatric anxiety have until now represented age-downward extensions of adult measures that fail to capture or adequately operationalize important dimensions of anxiety in young persons (March & Albano, 1998). Three commonly cited instruments have been in use for over 20 years. The Fear Survey Schedule for Children–Revised (FSSC–R) focuses primarily on phobic symptoms, including fear of failure and criticism, fear of the unknown, fear of injury and small animals, fear of danger and death, and medical fears (Ollendick, 1983). The Revised Children's Manifest Anxiety Scale (RCMAS) provides three factors: physiological manifestations of anxiety, worry and oversensitivity, and

TABLE 2.1
Anxiety Rating Scales

	MASC	*RCMAS*	*FSSC-R*	*STAIC*
Broad conceptualization	Yes	Yes	No	Yes
Specific dimensions	Yes	Partial	Phobias	No
Matches *DSM-IIV*	Yes	No	No	No
Reliable	Yes	Yes	Yes	Trait scale
Convergent validity	Yes	Yes	Yes	Yes
Divergent validity	Yes	No	No	No

fear/concentration (Reynolds & Richmond, 1979). However, the presence of mood, attentional, impulsivity, and peer interaction items on the RCMAS clearly confound other diagnoses, such as ADHD and major depression (Perrin & Last, 1992). Another widely used measure, the State–Trait Anxiety Inventory for Children (STAIC; Spielberger, Gorsuch, & Luchene, 1976), consists of two independent 20-item inventories that assess anxiety symptoms from a variety of domains but do not exhaustively cover the symptom constellations represented in *DSM–IV*. The State scale purports to assess present-state and situation-linked anxiety; the Trait scale addresses temporally stable anxiety across situations. Numerous authors have questioned the validity of the state-trait distinction (Kendall, Finch, Auerbach, Hooke, & Mikulka, 1976) and the nature of item selection for the STAIC (Finch, Kendall, & Montgomery, 1976; Perrin & Last, 1992). Table 2.1 contrasts these older measures with the MASC with respect to construct validity, applicability to *DSM–IV*, reliability, and convergent and divergent validity. Thus, the MASC was developed within the context of broad agreement by clinicians and researchers that new instruments were necessary if the field of pediatric anxiety disorders was to progress scientifically (see, e.g., Jensen, Salzberg, Richters, & Watanabe, 1993; March & Albano, 1996).

OVERVIEW OF THE MASC

The MASC is a 39-item Likert-style self-report measure developed to index a wide range of anxiety symptoms in elementary, junior high, and high school age youngsters (8 to 19 years old). As shown in Table 2.2, the MASC has four main factors, three of which can be further divided into two subfactors. Taken together, these factors and

TABLE 2.2
MASC Factors and Subfactors

Physical Symptoms
Tense
Somatic
Social Anxiety
Humiliation Fears
Performance Fears
Harm Avoidance
Perfectionism
Anxious Coping
Separation Anxiety

subfactors capture the central constructs of pediatric anxiety as they emerge in both population and clinical samples.

Procedures for developing and psychometrically validating a new rating scale are complex and time consuming (Cicchetti, 1994). In developing the MASC, the following sequence was used:

- An exhaustive review of available rating scales, diagnostic interviews, and the *DSM–IV* generated over 400 potential items.
- A *Q*-sort procedure was used to divide these items into cognitive, emotional, physical, and behavioral categories.
- A data reduction procedure generated a 41-item scale representing the four conceptual domains.
- A pilot study of over 1,000 elementary, junior high, and senior high school students was conducted in a school-based community sample.
- Based on results from the pilot study, which yielded a five-factor solution, a 104-item scale (with approximately 20 items per factor) was again piloted in a school-based sample.
- Principle components factor analyses of data from this population survey provided the current MASC factor structure, which shows excellent internal reliability without excessive redundancy in item content.
- Based on further clinical and research experience using the scale with children and adolescents aged 5–18, 39 items were retained for the final version of the MASC.
- Confirmatory factor analyses in clinical and community populations and in a large sample of ADHD children replicated the MASC factor structure.
- Parent-child and parent-parent concordance was low to moderate, depending on the domain of symptomatology being assessed; this finding indicated the clinical usefulness of the MASC as a child self-report measure.
- Convergent and divergent validity of the MASC with respect to parent ratings of externalizing behavior and internalizing symptoms was shown to be high.
- Test-retest reliability (stability over time) has been demonstrated in clinical and epidemiological samples.
- The MASC has been shown to be treatment sensitive.
- The MASC in now in wide use in industry- and foundation-funded studies of pediatric anxiety disorders and studies funded by the National Institute of Mental Health (NIMH),

The theoretical background, initial construction, validation, reliability, and norming of the MASC are extensively discussed in the MASC manual (March, 1998).

DEVELOPMENT OF THE MASC

Preliminary Studies

Although work to date on the taxonomy of anxiety in children and adolescents provides limited support for the *DSM–IV* anxiety clusters (see, e.g., Silverman & Eisen, 1992), some have suggested that a broader conceptualization is necessary (March & Albano, 1998; Ollendick & King, 1994; Ollendick, Matson, & Helsel, 1985). In contrast to scales that assess a specific *DSM–IV* anxiety construct (see, e.g., Beidel, Turner, & Morris, 1994), the MASC was developed to assess a wide spectrum of common anxiety symptoms in children across the elementary, junior high, and senior high school age range. Thus, when beginning the item selection procedure, we elected not to assume anything about the normative clustering of pediatric anxiety symptoms other than to hypothesize that specific descriptors should, on theoretical grounds (Marks, 1987), fall within emotional, cognitive, physical, and behavioral symptom domains.

The actual procedure followed several steps. First, available self-report anxiety scales covering general and specific symptom domains as well as the *DSM–III–R* criterion items were reviewed. Each of the over 400 resulting items/questions from these measures was then placed on a 3″ × 5″ card and sorted by two expert clinicians into four symptom domains: cognitive, physical, emotional, and behavioral. Cognitive items were defined as ascertaining a thought, urge, or image, which could be specific, as in a fear of dogs, or general, as in "worry." Physical items were characterized by physiological indicators, such as nausea or a racing heart. Emotional items were defined as ascertaining a subjective feeling, such as fear, or a subjective sensation, such as tension. Behavioral items was defined as ascertaining operant mechanisms of anxiety reduction through approach behaviors, such as reassurance seeking, or avoidance behaviors, such as avoiding public speaking. Disagreements were resolved by forced consensus judgment.

Second, the item pools were reduced by (a) retaining items that were easy to understand, covered the desired age range, and closely reflected one and only one of the four chosen anxiety dimensions and (b) eliminating duplicates and rewording.

Third, a *Q*-sort procedure was used to enhance item-content validity. Expert clinicians, members of an anxiety disorders support group, and lay nonexperts classified 60 items (15 per group) into the four selected domains.

Fourth, based on their comments and the pattern of misclassification, a 41-item, four-point Likert scale—having approximately 10 items per hypothesized symptom domain—was developed and piloted in a population sample of 1,066 fourth- through eighth-grade students. A three-point Likert version was not entertained because of the possibility of excessive midpoint responding—one of the drawbacks, for example, of the RCMAS.

Results from this preliminary study suggested a five-factor solution, which only partially conformed to the hypothesized four-domain model of anxiety: Somatic/Autonomic Arousal (14 items), Fears and Worries (7 items), Social Fears (10 items), Behavioral Avoidance/Approach (6 items), and Separation Anxiety (4 items). The uneven distribution of the items, which attenuated the internal reliability of the smaller factors, coupled with the lack of precision in the model, indicated the need for further scale development.

Based on the results from the first study, additional items (from the initial pool) were added to the five factors to bring each up to a total item pool of approximately 20 items. The resultant 104-item questionnaire was then administered to a population sample of 374 third- through twelfth-grade students. One classroom from each school was chosen at random for each grade; subjects thus were evenly split between Grades 4 to 12. Elementary school students were tested in their usual classroom, junior high school students in their homeroom. Questionnaires were read aloud to students, who had the opportunity to ask questions about individual items but not to seek clarification about how they should respond. Like the earlier questionnaire, this questionnaire also used a four-point Likert scale in which respondents were asked to rate each question as

"Never," "Sometimes," "Rarely," and "Always true about me." Students with reading disabilities were given extra time or reading support as needed. Teachers provided demographic information.

Factor Structure

With these data in hand, we then conducted a series of exploratory principal components factor analyses (using Varimax rotation) on the total sample. A robust four-factor solution emerged: Physical Symptoms, Social Anxiety, Separation Anxiety, and Harm Avoidance (March, 1998; March et al., 1997). All four factors had 9 items except the first, which had 10 items. Specifying a conventional Eigenvalue of 1.0 as the PCA entry criterion generated additional factors. In contrast to the reported factor structure, where between-factor overlap proved minimal at the item level, these smaller factors explained little additional variance and contained items that tended to load across multiple factors.

Each major factor was then subjected to a principal components factor analysis (again using Varimax rotation). Three of the four main factors—all except the Separation Anxiety factor—produced a clear two-factor solution using an Eigenvalue of 1.0 as the entry. Physical Symptoms factored into Tense/Restless and Somatic/Autonomic subfactors, harm Avoidance factored into Perfectionism and Anxious Coping, Social Anxiety factored into Humiliation/Rejection Fears and Performance Anxiety, and the Separation Anxiety factor was found to be unidimensional. In all cases, the first listed subfactor carried the majority of the variance (March et al., 1997).

A large body of literature suggests that anxieties of all sorts are more common in females than males (Benjamin, Costello, & Warren, 1990) and that some symptoms, for example, separation anxiety, vary with age (Francis, Last, & Strauss, 1987). To establish between-group differences for age or gender when using a self-report questionnaire, it is crucial to first establish that the factor structures are identical. To this purpose, a multisample confirmatory factor analysis was conducted using the EQS (Bentler, 1995) statistical program to test whether the four-factor model for the 39 MASC items was equivalent for males and females. All factor loadings were constrained to be equal for males and females, as were the correlations between the four MASC factors. Multiple goodness-of-fit indicators revealed that the four-factor model fit well in both sexes. The nonnormed fit index (*NNFI*; Bentler & Bonnett, 1980) was 0.913, the comparative fit index (*CFI*; Bentler, 1988) was 0.916, and the incremental fit index (*IFI*; Bolen, 1989) was 0.917. The magnitude of the three indexes (above 0.90, as suggested by Bentler, 1995) suggests that the model had excellent fit to the data regardless of gender.

A multisample confirmatory factor analysis was also conducted to test whether the four-factor model was equivalent for younger and older students. The sample was separated into two age groups: 12 years and under (n = 159) and 13 years and over (n = 211). As suggested by Weiss et al. (1991) on theoretical grounds, this age cutoff approximates the move from concrete to formal operations in the context of emerging puberty. Multiple goodness-of-fit indicators revealed that the four-factor model fit well in both age groups: $NNFI = .976$, $CFI = .977$, and $IFI = .978$. Thus, we concluded that the MASC factor structure is invariant across age and gender.

Confirmatory Factor Analyses

Having established the factor structure of the MASC, we then sought to replicate the factor structure in two groups of subjects: a second large school-based sample of 2,698 children and adolescents and a clinical sample of 390 children and adolescents. As before, multiple goodness-of-fit indices were used to evaluate the fit of the data to the measurement model. In both nonclinical and clinical samples, the four-factor model for the 39-item MASC met the criteria standards for adequacy of fit (Bentler, 1988). Parameter estimates for the relationships were statistically significant. Thus, the data had good fit to the MASC model. Confirmatory factor analyses for the four-factor MASC model also have been conducted in a large sample of (mostly nonanxious) young children with ADHD, and these too demonstrated adequacy of fit of the data and thus the extraordinary robustness of the MASC factor structure (March et al., 1999). The overall conclusion to be gained from the confirmatory factor analyses is that the MASC factor structure replicates nicely across diverse samples of children and adolescents.

Reliability

Reliability in psychometric terms has several meanings. Internal reliability represents consistency between items within a group of items composing a discrete factor (Cronbach, 1970). Test-retest reliability represents consistency in a set of scores by the same rater (single-case intraclass correlation coefficient [ICC]) or set of raters (mean ICC) over time (Shrout & Fleiss, 1979). Test-retest reliability varies with the conditions under which the test is administered, practice or memory effects, true change in the variable(s) of interest, plus an instability component due to measurement error attributable to the instrument itself. Without adequate reliability, it is not possible to determine whether differences in scores between individuals or within subject over time are due to "true" differences or to "chance" error.

Internal Reliability. Using a cutoff of 0.6 (below which internal consistency is suspect), total sample α-reliabilities, which range from .6 to .85, are acceptable for all main factors and subfactors for the 39-item MASC (March et al., 1997). Internal reliability for the MASC total score is 0.9. Furthermore, α-reliabilities for the MASC total score are generally comparable for males (.85) and females (.87). Very high reliability coefficients (above .9) indicate excessive redundancy at the item level. Inspection of item content shows individual items within a factor or subfactor to be face valid for the measured construct but not redundant with respect to item content.

Test-Retest Reliability. In a clinical population of children and adolescents with a mixture of anxiety disorders and/or ADHD (March et al., 1997), we examined the test-retest reliability of the MASC at 3 weeks and 3 months using the intraclass correlation coefficient (ICC) calculated according to procedures outlined by Shrout and Fleiss (1979). Mean ICCs for the MASC total score were .785 at 3 weeks and .933 at three months, indicating satisfactory to excellent test-retest reliability (March et al., 1997). Similarly, mean ICCs for all factors and subfactors save the Harm Avoidance factor fell in the satisfactory to excellent range at 3 weeks; all factors and subfactors proved satisfactory to excellent at 3 months (March et al., 1997). Mean ICCs for the MASC–10 (an empirically derived short form) and an anxiety disorders index ranged from .64 to .89, again indicating satisfactory to excellent stability. More recently, we examined the test-retest reliability of the MASC in a school-based sample of children and adolescents (March & Sullivan, 1999). For both single-case and mean ICCs, the MASC exhibited satisfactory to excellent stability across all factors and subfactors. Importantly, reliability was good to excellent for both genders, for younger and older children, and for Caucasian and African American youths. Satisfactory test-retest reliability also was demonstrated for the MASC–10 and for an anxiety disorders index with high discriminant validity. Thus, the MASC (uniquely at this point) can be said to demonstrate excellent test-retest reliability in both clinical and epidemiological samples.

Validity

Correlational Analysis. The factor structure of the MASC also is unique among extant scales in its subdivision of main factors into subfactors that nevertheless explain a meaningful proportion of the variance (March et al., 1997). With the exception of Perfectionism, which shows a weaker relationship to Physical Symptoms in females than in males, the pattern of shared variance as indicated by correlational analysis is similar for males and females. Importantly, although almost all correlations are significant at a Bonferroni-corrected alpha level of .05 or lower, the absolute magnitude of the shared variance is in the low to moderate range for most pairs. This suggests that the MASC is indeed measuring separate dimensions of anxiety, even at the subfactor level, which in turn should make it ideally suited to discriminate patterns of anxiety in subgroups of children with anxiety disorders.

Convergent and Divergent Validity. For the MASC to be useful clinically, the MASC factors would share greater variance with measures in the same symptom domain (convergent validity) than in different domains (divergent validity). In a test of this hypothesis in a clinical sample of children and adolescents with a variety of internalizing and externalizing disorders, we hypothesized that the MASC would be strongly correlated with a measure of anxiety (RCMAS), less so with a measure of depression (CDI), and not all correlated with a measure of disruptive behavior (ASQ–P). In all instances, the results went in the predicted direction, implying that the MASC is a specific indicator of pediatric anxiety symptomatology. Notably, the MASC performed significantly better than either the RCMAS or the CDI in this regard (March et al., 1997).

More recently, Muris examined the correlation between the MASC and another new anxiety rating scale, the Screen for Child Anxiety Related Emotional Disorders (SCARED), which was by design keyed to the *DSM–IV* view of anxiety disorders in youths (Birmaher et al., 1997). Not surprisingly, given the specificity for anxiety of both scales and also their differences in factor structure, the overall correlation between the sales was .72, with correlations between subtests ranging between .35 and .63 (Muris, Gadet, Moulaert, & Merckelbach, 1998). In an extension of these findings, Muris, Merckelbach, Ollendick, King, and Bogie (2002) extended these findings, comparing the psychometrics of three older scales, the RCMAS, STAIC, and FSSC–R, with the psychometrics three newer scales, the MASC, the SCARED, and the Spence Children's Anxiety Scale (SCAS; Spencė, 1997) in a large sample of normal adolescents ($N = 521$). In general, internal consistency was superior for the new scales. Reflecing their common origin in the *DSM–IV*, the SCARED and the SCAS were more strongly associated with each other than either scale was with the MASC, though all correlations were significant. Not surprisingly, subscales intended to measure specific categories of anxiety symptoms proved more strongly associated, with the MASC Harm Avoidance scale showing unique variance.

Predictive Validity. Using the Anxiety Disorders Interview Schedule for Children (ADIS–C) as the reference standard (Silverman & Albano, 1996), Deirker et al. (2001) recently examined the level of diagnostic and discriminative accuracy of three dimensional rating scales for detecting anxiety and depressive disorders in a school-based survey of ninth-grade youths. They concluded that MASC scores were most strongly associated with individual anxiety disorders, particularly among females, and successfully discriminated diagnosed depressed youths from anxious youths. In contrast, the RCMAS was not successful in discriminating anxiety and depression.

Similarly, Wood, Piacentini, Bergman, McCracken, and Barrios (2002) examined the concurrent validity of the ADIS diagnoses of social phobia, separation anxiety disorder (SAD), generalized anxiety disorder (GAD), and panic disorder diagnoses using the MASC as the reference standard. They identified little relationship between MASC scores and GAD diagnoses (though they did not examine the relevant subfactors), but they did notice a strong convergence between ADIS diagnoses and the empirically derived MASC social phobia, separation, and panic symptom constellations.

Discriminant Validity. Discriminant validity has been a persistent problem for older scales, such as the RCMAS. For example, Perrin and colleagues showed that the RCMAS and the STAIC differentiated children with *DSM–III–R* anxiety and attention deficit disorders from normals but not from each other, whereas the FSSC–R was ineffective at discriminating between any grouping (Perrin & Last, 1992). We examined the discriminant validity of the four central scales from the MASC by using discriminant function analysis to predict group membership in patients with anxiety disorders versus normal controls. Two groups of children and adolescents were used in the present analysis. The first group consisted of children and adolescents who met *DSM–IV* criteria for an anxiety disorder other than obsessive-compulsive disorder. The second group (nonclinical) consisted of children and adolescents randomly selected from a large pool of subjects with normative data on the MASC and matched with the clinical sample on the basis of age and sex. A discriminant function analysis was performed using the four MASC subscales as predictors of membership in two groups (clinical vs. nonclinical). Discriminant function scores from this analysis were used to classify subjects into clinical or nonclinical groups. A variety of diagnostic efficiency statistics were calculated from these classification results: The sensitivity was 90%, the specificity was 84%, the positive predictive power was 85%, the negative predictive power was 89%, the false-positive rate was 16%, the false-negative rate was 11%, kappa was 0.74, and the overall correct classification rate was 87%. Interestingly, in the study by Muris and colleagues (2002), correlations among anxiety questionnaires were generally higher than those between anxiety scales and a measure of depression, with the MASC total score showing slightly better discriminant validity than other scales, again perhaps because of the included Harm Avoidance factor.

Females Are More Anxious Than Males. The literature consistently shows that, across ages and disorders, girls show more anxiety than boys (March, 1995; March & Sullivan, 1999). As expected, females show more anxiety than males in Bonferroni-corrected planned contrasts between item-mean scores for males and females on the 39-item MASC. These differences are significant at the $p < .001$ level, though the absolute magnitude of each difference is typically low.

MASC Anxiety Index

To further highlight discriminant validity for both normal and psychopathological controls, we also developed an anxiety index. Two groups of children and adolescents were used to develop the anxiety index for the MASC. The first group consisted of 40 children and adolescents (24 males and 16 females) who met *DSM–IV* clinical criteria for an anxiety disorder other than obsessive-compulsive disorder. The mean age for males was 11.96 years ($SD = 2.07$), and it was 10.88 years ($SD = 2.80$) for females. The second group (nonclinical) consisted of 40 children and adolescents randomly selected from a large pool of subjects with normative data on the MASC and matched with the clinical sample on the basis of age and sex.

Having defined a sample of subjects with and without anxiety disorders, we then identified items from the MASC that appeared to discriminate between clinical and nonclinical groups. Based on a series of *t*-test analyses, 15 items were identified as significantly discriminating between the two groups. A direct discriminant function analysis was performed using the 15 items as predictors of membership in the two groups. Items with the lowest standardized discriminant function coefficients (coefficients below .25) were dropped from the item pool, and the analysis was repeated until the only items remaining had coefficients above .25. Discriminant function scores from the 10 items identified in this analysis were then used to classify the 80 children and adolescents into clinical and nonclinical groups. As before, a variety of diagnostic efficiency statistics were calculated from these classification results: The sensitivity was 95%, the specificity was 95%, the positive predictive power was 95%, the negative predictive power was 95%, the false-positive rate was 5%, the false-negative rate was 5%, kappa was .90, and the overall correct classification rate was 95%. Cross-validation in an identically derived sample produced similar results.

Having established that the anxiety index discriminates anxiety disordered and normal children and adolescents, we wished to establish similar discriminant validity between children and adolescents with an anxiety disorder and those with a *DSM–IV* diagnosis of attention deficit/hyperactivity disorder (ADHD). As pointed out by Perrin and Last (1992), this is psychometrically a much more difficult problem than discriminating between subjects with and without clinical symptoms. Two groups of children and adolescents were used in the analysis: one that met *DSM–IV* criteria for an anxiety disorder other than obsessive-compulsive disorder, and one that met *DSM–IV* criteria for ADHD and was matched with the anxiety disorder group on the basis of age and sex. A direct discriminant function analysis was performed using the MASC anxiety index. Discriminant function scores were then used to classify the 140 children and adolescents into anxiety or ADHD groups. The following diagnostic efficiency statistics were calculated from these classification results: The sensitivity was 75%, the specificity was 67%, the positive predictive power was 73%, the negative predictive power was 69%, the false-positive rate was 33%, the false-negative rate was 25%, kappa was 0.42, and the overall correct classification rate was 71%. Though not as robustly as in the anxiety:normal comparison, the anxiety index nevertheless shows a quite acceptable ability to discriminate children with an anxiety disorder and children with ADHD.

Parent-Child and Parent-Parent Concordance

In general, parent-child and parent-parent concordance is low for internalizing symptoms, especially for domains that are relatively less observable by parents (see, e.g.,

Jensen et al., 1988, 1993). In considering this issue, it is important to keep clear the distinction between concordance (e.g., agreement at a single point in time) and reliability (stability of agreement over time irrespective of concordance), for it is at least theoretically possible that parent reports would show low concordance and high reliability or the converse. In a preliminary study in which we asked fathers and mothers to complete MASC ratings of their child's symptoms, we hypothesized that fathers would be less concordant than mothers with respect to their children's MASC scores and that parent-child agreement would be poor (March et al., 1997). As predicted, parent-child concordance was poor to fair, depending on the nature of the symptom domain being ascertained. Fathers proved less likely than mothers to identify anxiety symptoms in their offspring. Both parents were much more likely to identify anxiety symptoms, such as social avoidance, that are readily observable and stable over time.

TREATMENT PLANNING AND MONITORING TREATMENT OUTCOMES

The task of the mental health practitioner using the MASC is to understand the presenting symptoms in the context of constraints to normal development. The practitioner must also devise a treatment program that ameliorates those constraints so that the youngster can resume a normal developmental trajectory to the extent possible. For most children with anxiety disorders, this requires a careful multimodal evaluation and some combination of cognitive-behavioral, psychopharmacological, and, in many cases, behavioral or pedagogic academic interventions (March, 2002). In our experience, leaving out one or more legs of this three-legged stool is a common cause of so-called treatment resistance. Because few practitioners possess all the essential skills, and because reimbursement schedules increasingly constrain practice patterns, such complex assessment and treatment regimens are best delivered within a multidisciplinary "team" milieu using efficient diagnostic assessment tools such as the MASC and other dimensional rating scales.

The Initial Evaluation

It goes without saying that a thorough diagnostic assessment, including a clinical interview and a multimethod and multi-informant empirical evaluation, is essential to generating a comprehensive treatment plan. In the Program for Child and Adolescent Anxiety Disorders at Duke University Medical Center, the evaluation begins with the initial telephone contact and proceeds through previsit data gathering and a clinical interview before concluding with a feedback and treatment-planning session. To speed and concentrate the evaluation process, we gather a sizable amount of data prior to the patient's initial visit, and we use the same evaluation methods for every child seen within the subspecialty clinic. In addition to requesting psychiatric/psychological, neuropsychological, hospitalization, and school records, we ask patients and family members to complete a packet of materials designed to assess important domains of psychopathology in the context of the patient's presenting concerns. In addition to information about our clinic, these materials include rating scales that screen for the major internalizing and externalizing symptom constellations and the Conners/March Developmental Questionnaire (CMDQ; Conners & March, 1996). Table 2.3 lists the rating scales we typically obtain from the child and the parent or teacher; Table 2.4 summarizes the information obtained in the CMDQ.

TABLE 2.3
Rating Scales

Rating Scale	*Type of Information*
Conners Parent Rating Scale	Parent-rated general psychopathology
Conners Teacher Rating Scale	Teacher-rated general psychopathology
Multidimensional Anxiety Scale for Children (MASC)	Self-reported anxiety
Leyton Obsessional Inventory	Self-reported OCD
Child and Adolescent Trauma Survey	Self-reported stressors and PTSD symptoms
Children's Depression Inventory	Self-reported depression

Each patient and family complete an extensive clinical evaluation (lasting 1 and a half hours) by a child psychiatrist or psychologist. The overall goal is to move from the presenting complaint through a *DSM–IV* five-axis diagnosis to an ideographic portrayal of the problems besetting the patient. This initial visit includes a clinical interview of the child and his or her parents covering Axes I–V of *DSM–IV*; a review of findings from the rating scale data, the CMDQ, school records, and previous mental health treatment records; a formal mental status examination; and, in some cases, a specialized neurodevelopmental evaluation. By carefully examining the MASC in advance of seeing the patient, we adjust the assessing clinician's "prior probabilities" relative to the major domains of anxiety (Weinstein & Fineberg, 1980). By examining the other scales, we estimate the likelihood of complicating comorbidities. This allows the clinician to set up a diagnostic hierarchy—comprising a primary diagnosis (or primary diagnoses), rule-out diagnoses, and unlikely diagnoses—to guide the clinical interview.

Ideally, a structured interview, such as the Anxiety Disorders Interview Schedule for Children (ADIS; Silverman & Eisen, 1992), should be part of every diagnostic assessment. Unfortunately, we currently lack the staffing resources to complete an ADIS, which requires separate interviews of child and one parent, for every clinical patient. Thus, the development of reliable, valid, and cost-effective instruments, such as the MASC, that can be used in combination with other assessment tools, such as the Conners scales, in lieu of structured interviews is of considerable interest to us. Because the clinician has reviewed the child's MASC responses at the item level

TABLE 2.4
Conners/March Developmental Questionnaire

Information	*Specific Type of Information*
Demographics	Age, gender, race, school grade, socioeconomic status
History of presenting problem	Narrative summary by parent
Previous treatment providers	List of providers and addresses
Treatment history	Type and adequacy of drug and psychotherapy trials
Birth and pregnancy history	Pre- and perinatal risk factors
Early developmental history	Temperament and developmental milestones
School history/learning problems	Pedagogic and behavioral school experience
Peer relationships	Number and quality of friendships
Family psychiatric history	Multigenerational family history of mental illness
Family medical history	Heritable medical illnesses
Patient medical history	General medical history

in advance of seeing the child, the clinician more easily and empathetically gather information about the anxiety symptoms besetting the patient. This strategy both speeds the interview and builds trust between the clinician and the patient, which in turn facilitates treatment planning.

Following a careful discussion of our diagnostic impression, we then make recommendations in each of the following categories: (1) additional assessment procedures, when required; (2) cognitive-behavioral psychotherapies; (3) pharmacotherapies; (4) behavioral and/or pedagogic academic interventions, when necessary; and (5) level of care, including expected time to response and setting in which care can reasonably be delivered. Unlike less formal evaluations that lead to interventions that concentrate more heavily on historical (narrative) approaches, we attempt to implement interventions that present a logically consistent and compelling relationship between the disorder, the treatment, and the specified outcome. In particular, we attempt to keep the various treatment targets ("the nails") distinct with respect to the various treatment interventions ("the hammers") so that aspects of the symptom picture that are likely to require or respond to a psychosocial rather than a psychopharmacological intervention are kept clear insofar as is possible. This method allow us to review in detail the indications, risks, and benefits of proposed and alternative treatments, after which parents and patient generally chose a treatment protocol usually consisting of cognitive-behavioral therapy alone or in combination with an appropriate medication intervention (March, 2002). Such a procedure is consistent with medical evaluation procedures across medical specialties and meets goals for guideline-based practice in managed care (Lenhart & March, 1996).

General Interpretive Considerations

Having described a general framework for approaching the anxious child or adolescent, we are now ready to consider the administration, scoring, and interpretation of the MASC. This involves the following steps:

- Consider whether the child's responses are valid indicators of the measured constructs.
- Review the item scores.
- Review the total score and the factor and subfactor scores.
- Look for patterns in the factor scores that might suggest a diagnosis.
- Place the data in the context of all the other information available about the child.

Are the Child's Responses Valid? Before proceeding with the actual interpretation of the MASC, the clinician must consider threats to the validity of the information contained in the MASC. Though self-report measures, such as the MASC, directly ascertain a subject's anxiety level across multiple behavioral/symptomatic domains, MASC scores are subject to a variety of biases (La & Silverman, 1993; Weissman, Orvaschel, & Padian, 1980). For example, some children tend to underestimate or underreport anxiety in the service of presenting a favorable evaluation of themselves (Silverman, 1987). Some children overreport anxiety in order to minimize enforced exposure to phobic stimuli; others do exactly the opposite (underreport symptoms) for exactly the same reason. Gender and cultural differences also may influence reporting. For example, girls are generally more willing to endorse fearfulness than boys (Ollendick et al., 1985). A child's ability to read and to understand the questionnaire items directly influences the validity of responses. When help is necessary to read the questions, the expectations of the child regarding the adult helper may set up a response bias that in turn may influence the validity of the data obtained. Though the MASC shows excellent test-retest reliability as well as divergent, convergent, and predictive validity, these and other factors may lead to poor test-retest reliability and suspect validity in a particular case. Thus, it is important to ask about the circumstances in which the child completed the questionnaire and whether the child had difficulty in interpreting or understanding particular questions.

The Inconsistency Index. To further aid in interpreting the validity of the child's responses, the MASC includes an empirically derived inconsistency index (March, 1998). The inconsistency index uses summed difference scores on items that are expected to be highly intercorrelated. Using a *T*-score distribution derived from the normal sample, it is possible to establish cutoff scores beyond which valid responding is questionable. Low scores indicate valid responding; scores above an age- and gender-adjusted cutoff suggest that the MASC should be interpreted cautiously.

Interpreting Item Responses. The first step in interpreting the results from the MASC is to examine individual item responses. Each MASC factor has approximately 10 items; each subfactor contains approximately half that many. Perusing the "Often" or "Always" responses can make it apparent which categories of anxiety are problematic for the patient. For example, a child may endorse many symptoms in the social anxiety category but few indicating separation anxiety, keying the interviewer to think first of social phobia. Alternatively, a youngster who appears tense, has mild to moderate worries from many categories, and scores high in perfectionism and anxious coping may be showing signs of generalized anxiety disorder. It is also informative to examine items that receive a "Never" response, as these often flag symptom domains that are not important or reflect developmental considerations. For example, adolescents generally do not sleep with a light on; when they do, it may indicate significant panic symptomatology.

Conversely, when perusing individual items, it is important to look for consistency in the pattern of responses and not overinterpret any individual response with respect to predictive power for a *DSM–IV* disorder. In this context, the MASC contains no "critical items," that is, items that are weighted as more important than other items. Importantly, symptoms at the item level may be important indicators of ideographic treatment targets (i.e., targets defined at the point at which treatment is tailored for the individual child). For example, a child with separation anxiety disorder and palpitations will be approached differently in cognitive-behavioral psychotherapy than another child who has the same diagnosis but for whom dizziness is the most prominent somatic/autonomic symptom. To habituate the somatic/autonomic cue, the first child will be made to climb stairs; the other will undergo a regimen of spinning until dizziness no longer initiates the panic cascade (Carter & Barlow, 1993). The MASC makes it easy to pinpoint several of the more important somatic/autonomic symptoms, which in turn allows the clinician to efficiently and empathetically direct the clinical interview. Item review permits a similar approach to many other important signs and symptoms that may be present and allows the clinician to pay relatively less attention to symptoms than have not been endorsed.

Interpreting the Total Score and Individual Factor Scores. As noted, interpretation of the factor scores for the MASC requires that the reader have a general understanding of the nature of anxiety in pediatric patients. Given such an understanding, the MASC is easy to interpret based on an analysis of where a particular child or group of children fall with respect to MASC population norms. High *T*-scores represent a problem; lower scores suggest the absence of these particular symptoms or set of symptoms. For example, a child with a *T*-score above 70 on the Social Anxiety factor is likely to have significant concerns regarding self-presentation and may meet *DSM–IV* diagnostic criteria for social phobia. When using this strategy—for example, using *T*-score norms to compare a child's report of symptoms to population norms—it is important to check at the outset that the population norms are those of an appropriate comparison group. For the MASC, normative comparisons are presented by gender and age for a normal population sample.

Configural Interpretation. When interpreting the MASC, the clinician will wish to examine the pattern of elevation in *T*-scores in addition to considering individual *T*-score elevations. Where no *T*-score is above 65, the MASC results are not indicative of clinically elevated anxiety symptoms. When one *T*-score is above 65, the evidence of such symptoms is marginal. Indeed, the greater the number of factors and subfactors that show clinically relevant elevations, the greater the likelihood that the MASC scores indicate a problem in the moderate to severe range. Additionally, elevations in the Social Anxiety and Separation Anxiety factors are often accompanied by elevations in the Physical Symptoms and Anxious Coping factors. Thus, when the Social Anxiety or Separation Anxiety score is elevated, it is useful to examine the Physical Symptoms and Anxious Coping factors, subfactors, and items to better understand the child's total symptom picture.

A Step-by-Step Interpretive Strategy. The following steps represent a typical sequence for interpreting the MASC.

Is the MASC a valid representation of anxiety for this particular child? Given an understanding of the child's motivation to complete the scale, the impact of other comorbidities on his or her ability to complete the scale accurately and/or with bias, the setting in which the MASC was administered, and the purpose for which the results will be used, the clinician must make a judgment regarding the validity of the MASC data. As a first step, inspection of the validity index provides an estimate of whether the child's pattern of item responses is both internally consistent and consistent with the response patterns shown by other children of the same age, gender, and race. If it is not, then the results may or may not be valid, depending on other information available to the clinician. Motivational issues include the child's desire to avoid treatment by inflating symptoms ("It is too hard; where's the magic pill?") or minimizing symptoms ("I don't need it"). Concern about self-presentation—for example, the need to look perfect in the eyes of valued adults—may introduce a systematic response bias, especially if the child knows that a parent will see the results. This is a particularly significant issue when a parent is required to help the child read and/or understand the scale items. Not surprisingly, it is also important to consider whether response biases associated with the child's gender and/or cultural background might influences the child's report of symptoms. Where norms by age, gender, and race are available, these biases are controlled to some extent. However, regional and cultural differences may extend even to the neighborhood level, which requires a level of molecular analysis not possible in a manualized format.

Finally, the MASC can be used as both a clinical and epidemiological instrument. In a clinical setting, MASC *T*-score elevations will be less likely to be associated with a false-positive result because the prior probability of clinically significant anxiety symptomatology is already elevated in the population. In epidemiological surveys, the investigator will need to individualize the *T*-score cutoff to optimize the percentages of false positives and false negatives depending on whether the purpose is to capture all positive cases (lower cutoff), eliminate false-positive cases (screen), or balance the two (trap; Costello & Angold, 1988). Conventionally, receiver operating curve (ROC) analyses have been used for this purpose (Weinstein & Fineberg, 1980).

What is the overall level of anxiety symptomatology? The MASC total score represents a measure of the overall level of anxiety. Norms are given for population and clinical samples by age and gender, which allows the clinician to refine his or her estimate of whether the MASC total score is elevated into the clinical range. *T*-scores above 65 likely represent clinically significant symptoms in a "high base rate" group, such as a mental health clinic or a population study of posttraumatic stress disorder after a natural disaster. Conversely, the clinician may wish to use a higher criterion score (e.g., a *T*-score of 70 or even 75) in a "low base rate" group, such as a population of children without identified behavior problems, for inferring clinical problems.

Are all scales elevated or is there a pattern that suggests a specific anxiety disorder? Many children show elevations in all scales; other show selective elevation of specific domains of anxiety. Examining the MASC factor and subfactor scores allows the clinician to identify problem areas as well as areas in which the child does not appear to be clinically symptomatic. In many cases, the pattern may correspond to a diagnostic grouping. For example, a child with separation anxiety disorder will likely show elevations in the Physical Symptoms factor (especially the Somatic/Autonomic subfactor), the Harm Avoidance factor (especially the Anxious Coping subfactor), and the Separation Anxiety factor. Similary, a child with social anxiety disorder will show elevations on the Social Anxiety factor (the clinician could then determine the type, generalized social anxiety versus the less common performance-only subtype, by examining the relevant subfactors). Finally, disorders not formally represented on the MASC factor structure can still be identified by perusing the relevant factors or subfactors (e.g., Somatic/Autonomic for panic and Tense/Restless and Perfectionism for GAD).

What item responses are elevated? Having obtained a good sense of the child's global level of anxiety and which MASC factors and subfactors appear problematic, the clinician can now scan the individual items for those that are or are not particularly problematic. Particular items are very useful in helping the clinician devise pertinent questions during the clinical interview and select targets for treatment. For example, a child with heart rate accelerations that are panicogenic will require habituation to this particular cue; a child with dizziness but not heart rate triggers will be approached differently when constructing an ideographic exposure hierarchy.

Integrate information from the MASC with other information. Using available information from other rating scales, parent and child interviews, and teacher reports and data from other mental health professionals, the clinician can now interpret the MASC scores with respect to validity and clinical significance.

Use the MASC for treatment planning. In the final step, taking all sources of information into consideration, including the MASC, the clinician defines a set of recommendations for additional assessments, psychosocial treatment(s), possible use of medication and/or pedagogic or behavioral interventions at school. In addition to deciding on a treatment plan tailored to the needs of the child, the clinician will need to decide how best to make of the MASC data in discussing the child's problems with the child, the family, and the school. Additionally, the MASC format lends itself nicely to report generation, but whether anyone should have access to a report—and if so, who and when—is for the clinician and family to decide.

Use of the MASC in Monitoring Treatment Outcomes

Considerable attention has been placed on the problem of measurement error in assessing treatment outcomes (see, e.g., Hsu, 1995; Jacobson & Revenstorf, 1988). Because the MASC provides a reliable and valid estimate of the "true score" variance associated with the measured construct(s), it is an excellent candidate measure to be used as the dependent variable (or as a mediator or moderator variable) in treatment outcome studies (March & Curry, 1998).

Because of its robust psychometric profile and the lack of satisfactory alternatives, the MASC is in wide use in industry-, foundation-, and NIMH-funded treatment outcome studies despite the fact that it is a relatively new scale. Though relatively new (and treatment trials take a long time to complete), the MASC already has been shown to be treatment sensitive in studies of social phobia (Compton et al., 2001), GAD (Rynn, Siqueland, & Rickels, 2001), and posttraumatic stress disorder (March, Amaya-Jackson, Murry, & Schulte, 1998). In a pioneering multisite study of children and adolescents with generalized anxiety, separation anxiety, or social anxiety disorders, singly or in combination, the MASC (along with other anxiety-dependent measures) proved to be change sensitive (RUPP, 2001).

With respect to change in the individual child in treatment, though the most robust criteria for response to a clinical therapeutic intervention is movement from the clinical range (e.g., a *T*-score above 60 to 65) into the normal range, the MASC is stable enough that a half standard deviation *T*-score change of 5 (if clinically supportable) represents meaningful change.

EVALUATION OF THE MASC AGAINST NIMH CRITERIA FOR OUTCOMES MEASURES

In an update of criteria for screening selection, treatment planning, and/or evaluating the outcomes of treatment developed by a panel of experts convened by the National Institute of Mental Health, Newman and Ciarlo (1994) proposed five groupings by which a measure should be judged: (1) applications of the measure, (2) methods and procedures, (3) psychometric features, (4) cost considerations, and (5) utility considerations (Newman & Ciarlo, 1994). Though these main groupings and the criteria subsumed under them are not orthogonal, they represent the main concerns of clinicians and researchers in judging to the usefulness of assessment measures.

Applications

As a general pediatric anxiety measure, the MASC clearly meets Criterion 1: first, that it be relevant to the target group to which is it being applied, and second, that it be independent of any treatment provided. In particular, an argument can be made that the MASC is the only scale that accurately represents the factor structure of anxiety in the pediatric population irrespective of age (8–18), gender, or race. At the factor and/or subfactor level, the MASC taps constructs that represent the *DSM–IV* constructs of social anxiety, separation anxiety, panic, and generalized anxiety. Additionally, the MASC targets anxiety-reinforcing coping behaviors, which by themselves are often targets for treatment. At the item level, each MASC item is face valid for the constructs represented, thereby encouraging agreement between provider and patient on the selection of target symptoms for treatment. The MASC is sensitive to treatment-induced change and has been chosen as a predictive and as a dependent measure in a wide variety of NIMH-funded comparative studies and industry-funded treatment outcome studies.

Methods and Procedures

With a clearly written manual and straightforward forms and scoring procedures, the MASC also meets Criterion 2: that it use simple, teachable methods. In particular, the MASC items, subfactors, and factors are all face valid for the constructs they represent, making it very easy to interpret MASC scores at the item or factor level. Similarly, the MASC is easy to administer and score, whether computer-scored scanable forms or pen-and-paper QuickScore forms are used. In addition, the MASC manual provides a review of anxiety disorders in children and adolescents, instructions for administering and interpreting the MASC, normative data (by three age groupings and by gender) and documentation of psychometric adequacy for both clinical and research applications.

Its use of objective referents—the reason it meets Criterion 3—is a particular strength of the MASC. Before publishing the MASC, we (a) replicated the factor structure in both clinical and population samples and across age and gender; (b) established an anxiety disorder index with high discriminant validity for normal and ADHD samples; (c) documented stability over time in both clinical and population samples; (d) developed a validity index to provide an estimate of valid versus invalid responding; and (e) provided normative data in a large population sample of children and adolescents to allow clinicians, researchers, and utilization reviewers to establish extent of deviance (need for treatment) and determine when a patient has returned to the normal range (signifying the end of treatment). No other pediatric anxiety scale provides these assurances of robust psychometric properties.

Additionally, the MASC scales, subscales, and items are specifically designed to provide important information regarding treatment planning and outcome monitoring. For example, a child with excessive motor tension is a candidate for relaxation training; absent such a complaint, this intervention may not be necessary. The MASC Tense/Restless subfactor provides this information. Anecdotally, patients report that the detailed symptom review inherent in the MASC factor structure often indicates to the child that the clinician is interested in and understands those behavioral/symptomatic indicators that are disturbing to the child. In this fashion, the MASC facilitates communication between provider and patient, ultimately identifying unique targets (e.g., suffocation anxiety) for ad hoc treatment interventions as implemented in empirically validated treatment packages (Barlow, 1997).

With respect to Criterion 4—the use of multiple respondents—children and adolescents typically are much better reporters of internalizing symptoms than their parents (Faraone, Biederman, & Milberger, 1995; Jensen et al., 1988). In our initial study of the MASC, parent-child agreement was poor to fair even in a sample of clinically ill children who might been expected to show readily observable symptoms. Criterion 4 therefore may be less applicable to the assessment of pediatric anxiety disorders than, to the assessment of disruptive behavior disorders, for example. For this reason, the SCAS, like the MASC, does not include a parent version, though the SCARED does (providing a multi-informant view even absent strong correlations). Following this lead, future versions of the MASC likely will capture parent-reported anxiety as well.

Lastly, Criterion 5, the use of process-identifying outcome measures, is of critical importance for understanding the mechanisms by which treatment works and for disseminating new treatments. Though not a stated goal, the MASC is unique among general pediatric anxiety scales in including an Harm Avoidance factor, which in turn is subdivided into Perfectionism and Anxious Coping subfactors. To the extent that anxiety-reinforcing coping strategies are modified by treatment, a reduction in scores on the Anxious Coping factor may be construed as reflecting corollary therapy processes (e.g., in single-case designs aimed specifically at component analyses).

Psychometric Features

With the exception of cross-cultural documentation, where the RCMAS clearly shows important strengths (see, e.g., Ollendick & Yule, 1990; Yang, Ollendick, Dong, & Xia, 1995), the MASC shows more robust psychometric properties than older scales, such as the RCMAS, FSSC–R or STAIC, but less than the newer instruments, such as the SCARED or SCAS. Importantly, the MASC, unlike other extant scales that purport to assess the full range of pediatric anxiety symptoms (Perrin & Last, 1992), unquestionably measures anxiety (e.g., the MASC exhibits a high level of discriminant validity). Given excellent test-retest and robust population norms as well as unique features, such as the anxiety index, validity index, and Harm Avoidance factor, the MASC appears to be an appropriate instrument for identifying sufficient deviance/impairment to warrant consideration for use in psychopathology and treatment outcome studies, epidemiological screening, and diagnosis and treatment at the single-patient level.

Cost Considerations

Criterion 7, low cost, is unfortunately not a strength of the MASC, which is only available commercially through MultiHealth Systems, Toronto, Canada. Nevertheless, given efficiencies in the diagnostic process and validity considerations, the MASC likely is cost-effective for its intended purpose, though empirical data supporting this assertion are as yet lacking. Furthermore, the MASC is available at reduced cost for researchers interested in using the MASC in research protocols. Indeed, we explicitly support the use of the MASC in research and feed data from research protocols back into MASC psychometric studies. Research collaboration for this purpose is invited.

Utility Considerations

Criterion 8 (understanding by nonprofessional audiences), Criterion 9 (easy feedback and uncomplicated interpretation), and Criterion 10 (utility in clinical services) have been addressed previously.

Its compatibility with clinical theories and practices is an important strength of the MASC. As already pointed out, the MASC was developed in an atheoretical fashion to represent the factor structure of anxiety in the population rather than to conform to a particular theory of the genesis of anxiety or any anxiety subtype. Hence, the MASC fits well with a variety of theories and practices where the objective is to ascertain anxiety symptoms and not specifically to represent a particular theoretical perspective. In this regard, the MASC should minimize measurement error across divergent treatment interventions, making it especially suitable for comparative treatment outcome studies that include both medication and psychosocial treatment arms (Arnold, 1993; Jensen, 1993).

CASE STUDY

Ann is a 7-year-old Caucasian girl from a two-parent, lower middle class family. About 1 month before coming to the clinic, she began to experience stomachaches at school. Many other children were sick with a stomach virus at the time so Ann's symptoms did not arouse unusual concerns. After a visit to the pediatrician, which failed to turn up anything unusual, Ann soon went back to school. Unfortunately, although the other children were back to normal, Ann continued to have stomachaches and began to experience other sick feelings, such as dizziness. After several more days of this, she began to resist going to school as she felt better at home. Ann's mother, who was on the shy side and was generally sympathetic to and protective of Ann, partly because Ann reminded her of herself when she was a child, let Ann stay home. In contrast, Ann's father got rather angry when Ann repeatedly wanted to stay home. Over Mom's objections, he insisted that Ann go to school, which she did, though crying all the way. Midmorning she experienced her first full panic attack, actually throwing up in class. Her mother came to school to take Ann to the pediatrician, who again found nothing wrong. Ann by this time had become clingy, refused to stray far from home, and repeatedly expressed fears that something might happen to her parents, particularly her mother, who she worried might not be able to help her when she felt sick and scared. By the time she presented to me on the advice of her pediatrician, Ann had been out of school for 2 weeks. By this point, Ann and her family were "at war" over whether Ann was sick or just being oppositional.

As for the family history, Ann's mother suffered from panic disorder and social phobia, and her father exhibited a subclinical affective disorder. Ann was generally healthy, and neither she nor other family members were under any unusual stress.

Step 1: Is the MASC a valid representation of anxiety for this particular child? Ann filled out the MASC with her mother, who had to read but not explain the questions. Like most anxious kids, Ann knew from her own experiences what the questions meant. Clinically, it appeared that the mother's bias, like Ann's, was toward endorsing rather than minimizing symptoms, though only for symptoms that actually were present. Given the presenting complaint and a normal MASC validity index, it appeared that the MASC represented a valid index of Ann's symptoms.

Step 2: What is the overall level of anxiety symptomatology? Ann's MASC total *T*-score was mildly elevated at 65, reflecting the fact that not all anxiety domains were problematic and that even within symptomatic domains not all symptoms were equally problematic.

Step 3: Are all scales elevated or is there a pattern that suggests a specific anxiety disorder? As might be expected, her *T*-scores for Separation Anxiety were markedly elevated ($T = 80$), as were the *T*-scores for Anxious Coping ($T = 74$) and Somatic/Autonomic Symptoms ($T = 68$). Conversely, the *T*-scores for the other factors and subfactors were only marginally elevated or not elevated at all. Clinical questioning later revealed that the elevation in humiliation fears related to her fears about the effects of separation anxiety symptoms on her relationships at school.

Step 4: What item responses are elevated? Consistent with her history, Ann's dizziness and gastrointestinal symptoms were maximally elevated; conversely, she endorsed little in the way cardiac symptoms. Unlike many children with separation anxiety, Ann did not endorse a fear of sleeping away from home, perhaps because her fears had not had time to generalize beyond the school setting.

Step 5: Integrate information from the MASC with other information. The Conners Parent and Teacher Rating Scales suggested problems with disruptive behaviors at school and home plus elevated anxiety/shyness. The Children's Depression Inventory suggested problems with ineffectiveness, but there were no other indicators of depression. Taken together, the family history, clinical picture, and testing data all pointed to a diagnosis of separation anxiety disorder.

Step 6: Taking all sources of information into consideration, including the MASC, define a set of recommendations for additional assessments, psychosocial treatment(s), possible use of medication, and/or pedagogic or behavioral interventions at school. No additional assessments seemed necessary. Treatment began with CBT, with the possibility of later addition of a medication if Ann was not rapidly responsive to the CBT. To encourage a graded return to school, school personnel were closely involved in the CBT intervention.

CONCLUSION

To summarize, the MASC (a) provides reliable and valid ascertainment of anxiety symptoms across all major symptom domains as they exist in young persons aged 8 to 18; (b) discriminates between symptom clusters within anxiety groupings and between anxiety and other psychopathological groupings; (c) evaluates severity against age and gender norms; (d) provides information from the most important rater, the child or adolescent; and (e) indexes treatment-induced symptom change. With the increasing emphasis on multidisciplinary assessment and treatment strategies, the MASC should facilitate communication not only among clinicians but also between clinicians and regulatory bodies, such as utilization review committees. Finally, in a world where research advances increasingly drive differential therapeutics within a medical model, it is critical that mental health providers develop rapid and efficient tools for defining targets for medication and psychosocial treatment.

Perhaps because of insufficient time, lack of training, methodological constraints, or cost considerations, clinical practice as a rule cannot include a semistructured interview incorporating information from multiple informants (Reich & Earls, 1987). This lack often leads to missed diagnoses and ineffective treatment planning (Costello et al., 1988). In addition, clinicians under managed care will increasingly rely on practice guidelines, which in turn require systematic assessment tools (Barlow, 1994). Self-report measures like the MASC represent a time-efficient way to capture information about a wide variety of anxiety symptoms. In the Pediatric Anxiety Disorders Program at Duke, all new patients and their parents are asked to complete a comprehensive developmental questionnaire, the MASC, the Children's Depression Inventory, and the Conners Parent and Teacher Rating Scales before their first visit (March, Mulle, Stallings, Erhardt, & Conners, 1995). Reviewing the resulting information in advance of seeing the patient dramatically increases the efficiency of the clinical diagnostic interview by establishing a set of prior probabilities for specific diagnoses (Weinstein & Fineberg, 1980). The clinician is thereby freed to allocate more time to devising a comprehensive tailored treatment plan where the hammers (the treatments) accurately match the nails (the targets). Scales like the MASC, which shows increasingly strong and clinically relevant psychometric properties, will drive this process forward, much to the benefit of our anxious pediatric patients.

REFERENCES

American Psychiatric Association. (1987). *Diagnostic and statistical manual of mental disorders* (3rd ed., revised). Washington, DC: Author.

American Psychiatric Association. (1994). *Diagnostic and Statistical Manual of Mental Disorders* (4 ed.). Washington, DC: Author.

Arnold, L. (1993). Design and methodology issues for clinical treatment trials in children and adolescents. *Psychopharmacology Bulletin, 29*, 3–4.

Barlow, D. H. (1994). Psychological interventions in the era of managed competition. *Clinical Psychology: Science and Practice, 1*, 109–122.

Barlow, D. H. (1997). Cognitive-behavioral therapy for panic disorder: Current status. *Journal of Clinical Psychiatry, 58*(Suppl 2), 32–36; discussion 36–37.

Beidel, D., Turner, S., & Morris, T. (1994). *The SPAI-C: A new child self-report inventory for children.* Paper presented at the annual meeting of the Anxiety Disorders of America, Santa Monica, CA.

Benjamin, R. S., Costello, E. J., & Warren, M. (1990). Anxiety disorders in a pediatric sample. *Journal of Anxiety Disorders, 4*, 293–316.

Bentler, P. (1988). Comparative fit indexes in structural models. *Psychological Bulletin, 107*, 238–246.

Bentler, P. (1995). *EQS structural equations program manual.* Encino, CA: Multivariate Software, Inc.

Bentler, P., & Bonnett, D. (1980). Significance test and goodness of fit in the analysis of covariance structures. *Psychological Bulletin, 88*, 588–606.

Birmaher, B., Khetarpal, S., Brent, D., Cully, M., Balach, L., Kaufman, J., et al. (1997). The Screen for Child Anxiety Related Emotional Disorders (SCARED): Scale construction and psychometric characteristics. *Journal of the American Academy of Child and Adolescent Psychiatry, 36*(4), 545–553.

Black, B. (1995). Anxiety disorders in children and adolescents. *Current Opinion in Pediatrics, 7*, 387–391.

Bolen, K. (1989). A new incremental fit index for general structural equation models. *Sociological Methods and Research, 17*, 303–316.

Carter, M. M., & Barlow, D. H. (1993). *Interoceptive exposure in the treatment of panic disorder* (Vol. 12). Sarasota, FL: Professional Resource Press.

Cronbach, L. (1970). *Essentials of psychological testing* (3rd ed.). New York: Harper Row.

Cicchetti, D. V. (1994). Guidelines, criteria, and rules of thumb for evaluating normed and standardized assessment instruments in psychology. *Psychological Assessment, 6*, 284–290.

Compton, S. N., Grant, P. J., Chrisman, A. K., Gammon, P. J., Brown, V. L., & March, J. S. (2001). Sertraline in children and adolescents with social anxiety disorder: An open trial. *Journal of the American Academy of Child and Adolescent Psychiatry, 40*, 564–571.

Conners, C., & March, J. (1996). *The Conners/March Developmental Questionnaire.* Toronto: MultiHealth Systems, Inc.

Costello, E., & Angold, A. (1988). Scales to assess child and adolescent depression: Checklists, screens, and nets. *Journal of the American Academy of Child and Adolescent Psychiatry, 27*, 357–363.

Costello, E. J., & Angold, A. (1995). Epidemiology. In J. March (Ed.), *Anxiety disorders in children and adolescents* (pp. 109–124). New York: Guilford.

Costello, E. J., Edelbrock, C., Costello, A. J., Dulcan, M. K., Burns, B. J., & Brent, D. (1988). Psychopathology in pediatric primary care: The new hidden morbidity. *Pediatrics, 82*(3, Pt. 2), 415–424.

Dierker, L. C., Albano, A. M., Clarke, G. N., Heimberg, R. G., Kendall, P. C., Merikangas, K. R., et al. (2001). Screening for anxiety and depression in early adolescence. *Journal of the American Academy of Child and Adolescent Psychiatry, 40*, 929–936.

Finch, A. J., Jr., Kendall, P. C., & Montgomery, L. E. (1976). Qualitative difference in the experience of state-trait anxiety in emotionally disturbed and normal children. *Journal of Personality Assessment, 40*, 522–530.

Francis, G., Last, C. G., & Strauss, C. C. (1987). Expression of separation anxiety disorder: The roles of age and gender. *Child Psychiatry and Human Development, 18*(2), 82–89.

Greenhill, L. L., Pine, D., March, J., Birmaher, B., & Riddle, M. (1998). Assessment issues in treatment research of pediatric anxiety disorders: What is working, what is not working, what is missing, and what needs improvement. *Psychopharmacology Bulletin, 34*, 155–164.

Hsu, L. M. (1995). Regression toward the mean associated with measurement error and the identification of improvement and deterioration in psychotherapy. *Journal of Consulting and Clinical Psychology, 63,* 141–144.

Jacobson, N. S., & Revenstorf, D. (1988). Statistics for assessing the clinical significance of psychotherapy techniques: Issues, problems, and new developments. *Behavioral Assessment, 10,* 133–145.

Jensen, P. S. (1993). Development and implementation of multimodal and combined treatment studies in children and adolescents: NIMH perspectives. *Psychopharmacology Bulletin, 29,* 19–26.

Jensen, P. S., Salzberg, A. D., Richters, J. E., & Watanabe, H. K. (1993). Scales, diagnoses, and child psychopathology: I. CBCL and DISC relationships. *Journal of the American Academy of Child and Adolescent Psychiatry, 32,* 397–406.

Jensen, P. S., Traylor, J., Xenakis, S. N., & Davis, H. (1988). Child psychopathology rating scales and interrater agreement: I. Parents' gender and psychiatric symptoms. *Journal of the American Academy of Child and Adolescent Psychiatry, 27,* 442–450.

Keller, M. B., Lavori, P. W., Wunder, J., Beardslee, W. R., Schwartz, C. E., & Roth, J. (1992). Chronic course of anxiety disorders in children and adolescents. *Journal of the American Academy of Child and Adolescent Psychiatry, 31,* 595–599.

Kendall, P. C., Finch, A. J., Jr., Auerbach, S. M., Hooke, J. F., & Mikulka, P. J. (1976). The State-Trait Anxiety Inventory: A systematic evaluation. *Journal of Consulting and Clinical Psychology, 44,* 406–412.

La, G. A., & Silverman, W. K. (1993). Parent reports of child behavior problems: Bias in participation. *Journal of Abnormal Child Psychology, 21,* 89–101.

Last, C. G., Strauss, C. C., & Francis, G. (1987). Comorbidity among childhood anxiety disorders. *Journal of Nervous and Mental Disease, 175,* 726–730.

Lenhart, L., & March, J. (1996). Treatment of psychiatric disroders in children and adolescents. In B. Levin & J. Petrilla (Eds.), *Mental health services: A public health perspective* (pp. 211–233). New York: Oxford University Press.

Leonard, H. L., Goldberger, E. L., Rapoport, J. L., Cheslow, D. L., & Swedo, S. E. (1990). Childhood rituals: Normal development or obsessive-compulsive symptoms? *Journal of the American Academy of Child and Adolescent Psychiatry, 29,* 17–23.

March, J. (1995). *Anxiety disorders in children and adolescents.* New York: Guilford.

March, J. (1998). *Manual for the Multidimensional Anxiety Scale for Children (MASC).* Toronto: MultiHealth Systems.

March, J. S. (2002). Combining medication and psychosocial treatments: An evidence-based medicine approach. *International Review of Psychiatry, 14,* 155–163.

March, J., & Albano, A. (1996). Assessment of anxiety in children and adolescents. *Review of Psychiatry, 15,* 405–427.

March, J. S., & Albano, A. M. (1998). New developments in assessing pediatric anxiety disorders. *Advances in Clinical Child Psychology, 20,* 213–241.

March, J., Amaya-Jackson, L., Murry, M., & Schulte, A. (1998). Cognitive-behavioral psychotherapy for children and adolescents with post-traumatic stress disorder following a single incident stressor. *Journal of the American Academy of Child and Adolescent Psychiatry, 37,* 585–593.

March, J., Conners, C., Arnold, E., Epstein, J., Parker, J., Hinswaw, S., et al. (1999). The Multidimensional Anxiety Scale for Children (MASC): Confirmatory factor analysis in a pediatric ADHD sample. *Journal of Attention Disorders, 3,* 85–89.

March, J. S., & Curry, J. F. (1998). Predicting the outcome of treatment. *Journal of Abnormal Child Psychology, 26,* 39–51.

March, J., Mulle, K., Stallings, P., Erhardt, D., & Conners, C. (1995). Organizing an anxiety disorders clinic. In J. March (Ed.), *Anxiety disorders in children and adolesents* (pp. 420–435). New York: Guilford.

March, J., Parker, J., Sullivan, K., Stallings, P., & Conners, C. (1997). The Multidimensional Anxiety Scale for Children (MASC): Factor structure, reliability and validity. *Journal of the American Academy of Child and Adolescent Psychiatry, 36,* 554–565.

March, J. S., & Sullivan, K. (1999). Test-retest reliability of the Multidimensional Anxiety Scale for Children. *Journal of Anxiety Disorders, 13,* 349–358.

Marks, I. (1987). *Fears, phobias, and rituals.* New York: Oxford Unversity Press.

Muris, P., Gadet, B., Moulaert, V., & Merckelbach, H. (1998). Correlations between two Multidimensional Anxiety Scales for Children. *Perceptual and Motor Skills, 87*(1), 269–270.

Muris, P., Merckelbach, H., Ollendick, T., King, N., & Bogie, N. (2002). Three traditional and three new childhood anxiety questionnaires: Their reliability and validity in a normal adolescent sample. *Behavior Research and Therapy, 40,* 753–772.

Newman, F. L., & Ciarlo, J. A. (1994). Criteria for selecting psychological instruments for treatment outcome assessment. In M. Maruish (Ed.), *The use of psychological testing for treatment planning and outcomes assessment* (pp. 98–110). Hillsdale, NJ: Lawrence Erlbaum Associates.

Ollendick, T. H. (1983). Reliability and validity of the Revised Fear Surgery Schedule for Children (FSSC-R). *Behavior Research and Therapy, 21,* 685–692.

Ollendick, T. H., & King, N. J. (1994). Fears and their level of interference in adolescents. *Behavior Research and Therapy, 32,* 635–638.

Ollendick, T. H., Matson, J. L., & Helsel, W. J. (1985). Fears in children and adolescents: normative data. *Behavior Research and Therapy, 23*(4), 465–467.

Ollendick, T. H., & Yule, W. (1990). Depression in British and American children and its relation to anxiety and fear. *Journal of Consulting and Clinical Psychology, 58,* 126–129.

Perrin, S., & Last, C. G. (1992). Do childhood anxiety measures measure anxiety? *Journal of Abnormal Child Psychology, 20,* 567–578.

Reich, W., & Earls, F. (1987). Rules for making psychiatric diagnoses in children on the basis of multiple sources of information: Preliminary strategies. *Journal of Abnormal Child Psychology, 15,* 601–616.

Reynolds, C. R., & Richmond, B. O. (1979). Factor structure and construct validity of "What I Think and Feel": The Revised Children's Manifest Anxiety Scale. *Journal of Personality Assessment, 43,* 281–283.

RUPP. (2001). Fluvoxamine for the treatment of anxiety disorders in children and adolescents. *New England Journal of Medicine, 344,* 1279–1285.

Rynn, M. A., Siqueland, L., & Rickels, K. (2001). Placebo-controlled trial of sertraline in the treatment of children with generalized anxiety disorder. *American Journal of Psychiatry, 158,* 2008–2014.

Shrout, P., & Fleiss, J. (1979). Intraclass correlations: Uses in assessing rater reliability. *Psychological Bulletin, 86,* 420–428.

Silverman, W. K. (1987). Childhood anxiety disorders: Diagnostic issues, empirical support, and future research. *Journal of Child and Adolescent Psychotherapy, 4,* 121–126.

Silverman, W., & Albano, A. (1996). *The Anxiety Disorders Interview Schedule for DSM–IV, child and parent versions.* San Antonio, TX: The Psychological Corporation.

Silverman, W. K., & Eisen, A. R. (1992). Age differences in the reliability of parent and child reports of child anxious symptomatology using a structured interview. *Journal of the American Academy of Child and Adolescent Psychiatry, 31,* 117–124.

Simon, G., Ormel, J., Von Korff, M., & Barlow, W. (1995). Health care costs associated with depressive and anxiety disorders in primary care. *American Journal of Psychiatry, 152,* 352–357.

Spence, S. H. (1997). Structure of anxiety symptoms among children: A confirmatory factor-analytic study. *Journal of Abnormal Psychology, 106,* 280–297.

Spielberger, C., Gorsuch, R., & Luchene, R. (1976). *Manual for the State-Trait Anxiety Inventory.* Palo Alto, CA: Consulting Psychologists Press.

Weinstein, M., & Fineberg, H. (1980). *Clinical decision analysis.* Philadelphia: Saunders.

Weiss, B., Weisz, J., Politane, M., Carey, M., Nelson, W., & Finch, A. (1991). Developmental differences in the factor structure of the Children's Depression Inventory. *Psychological Assessment, 3,* 38–45.

Weissman, M. M., Orvaschel, H., & Padian, N. (1980). Children's symptom and social functioning self-report scales. Comparison of mothers' and children's reports. *Journal of Nervous and Mental Disease, 168,* 736–740.

Wood, J. J., Piacentini, J. C., Bergman, R. L., McCracken, J., & Barrios, V. (2002). Concurrent validity of the anxiety disorders section of the Anxiety Disorders Interview Schedule for *DSM–IV*: Child and parent versions. *Journal of Clinical Child and Adolescent Psychology, 31,* 335–342.

Yang, B., Ollendick, T. H., Dong, Q., & Xia, Y. (1995). Only children and children with siblings in the People's Republic of China: Levels of fear, anxiety, and depression. *Child Development, 66,* 1301–1311.

3

Characteristics and Applications of the Revised Children's Manifest Anxiety Scale (RCMAS)

Anthony B. Gerard
Western Psychological Services

Cecil R. Reynolds
Texas A&M University

The Revised Children's Manifest Anxiety Scale (RCMAS; Reynolds & Richmond, 1985) assesses both the degree and quality of anxiety experienced by children and adolescents. Based on the original Children's Manifest Anxiety Scale (CMAS; Castaneda, McCandless, & Palermo, 1956), the RCMAS is a relatively brief instrument suitable for group or individual administration in both clinical and educational settings. It is suitable for children from the early elementary years through high school, and it has norms for ages 5 through 19. The work that led to the development of the RCMAS, as well as subsequent experience with the instrument, has shown it to be a valid, useful indicator of anxiety. Because it can be administered to groups, it is highly suitable for use in school contexts. Although administration of the RCMAS can only form part of a thorough clinical evaluation of a child's anxiety, the strategies employed in its development render the RCMAS an effective aid in guiding the diagnosis and treatment of children's anxiety.

The RCMAS permits the clinician to meet Koppitz's (1982) first basic rule for the use of personality tests with children: Use the simplest test first. Koppitz found the RCMAS to be especially useful early in the evaluation process because it provides fodder for follow-up in the process of diagnosis and treatment. In the days of managed care, use of the RCMAS certainly makes sense in any screening for childhood psychopathology.

OVERVIEW

The RCMAS is a 37-item instrument subtitled "What I Think and Feel." Each of the items embodies a description of feelings and actions that, in turn, reflect an aspect of anxiety. For that reason, all of the items are positively keyed, and scoring consists in a count of "Yes" responses. Yielding a total score, three empirically derived subscale scores (Physiological Anxiety, Worry/Oversensitivity, and Social Concerns/Concentration), and a lie scale score, the RCMAS is suitable for assessing anxiety in children and adolescents from 6 to 19 years old. The item content of the RCMAS subscales is presented in Table 3.1.

TABLE 3.1
Item Content of the Four Subscales

I. Physiological Anxiety (10 items)	*II. Worry/Oversensitivity (11 items)*	*III. Social Concerns/ Concentration (7 items)*	*Lie (L) (9 items)*
1. I have trouble making up my mind. 5. Often I have trouble getting my breath. 9. I get mad easily. 13. It is hard for me to get to sleep at night. 17. Often I feel sick in the stomach. 19. My hands feel sweaty. 21. I am tired a lot. 25. I have bad dreams. 29. I wake up scared some of the time. 33. I wiggle in my seat a lot.	2. I get nervous when things do not go the right way for me. 6. I worry a lot of the time. 7. I am afraid of a lot of things. 10. I worry about what my parents will say to me. 14. I worry about what about me. 18. My feelings get hurt easily. 22. I worry about what is going to happen. 26. My feelings get hurt easily when I am fussed at. 30. I worry when I go to bed at night. 34. I am nervous. 37. I often worry about something bad happening to me.	3. Others seem to do things easier than I can. 11. I feel that others do not like the way I do things. 15. I feel alone even when there are people with me. 23. Other people are happier than I. 27. I feel someone will tell me I do things the wrong way. 31. It is hard for me to keep my mind on my schoolwork. 35. A lot of people are against me.	4. I like everyone I know. 8. I am always kind. 12. I always have good manners. 16. I am always good. 20. I am always nice to everyone. 24. I tell the truth every single time. 28. I never get angry. 32. I never say things I shouldn't. 36. I never lie.

Because it is both brief and specific, it is useful as both a screener and an assessment instrument. The RCMAS is the product of an intensive development effort, including research specifically aimed at the construction of a new instrument, and is based a great deal of prior work on the measurement of anxiety. The research that led to the development of the RCMAS, both the standardization and validation studies, was informed by the goal of producing an instrument that is powerful and flexible but also brief. As a result, the RCMAS is not only psychometrically sound but also meets many of the sometimes contradictory demands of measuring a phenomenon as variable and widespread as anxiety. Witt, Heffer, and Pfeiffer (1990), who noted that the RCMAS "appears to be a reliable and valid measure of general anxiety" (p. 384), suggested that the RCMAS assesses the two primary modes of expression of anxiety, physiological and cognitive. The RCMAS appears to be a more reliable measure of anxiety than are omnibus, multidimensional personality scales (Moran, 1990).

DEVELOPMENT

The RCMAS addresses many of the limitations of the original CMAS. Although the CMAS had been used successfully for some time—and perhaps because of clinicians' extensive experience with it—over the years a number of criticisms were leveled at it. Teachers described some of the items as too difficult for younger children and poor readers. Some of the items, researchers and clinicians recognized, failed to meet the criteria usually applied to test items (Flanagan, Peters, & Conry, 1969). As research on the anxiety of children progressed, it also became clear that the CMAS did not measure some important aspects of anxiety or did not measure them thoroughly enough. In addition, users wanted an instrument that would be a valid measure of anxiety in children across a much wider age range. The development of the RCMAS was an effort to make a popular instrument better by addressing these issues (Reynolds & Richmond, 1978).

As described more completely in the manual for the RCMAS (Reynolds & Richmond, 1985), instrument development included a number of goals that, if they could be met, would result in an instrument that was easy to use, psychometrically sophisticated, and clinically useful. The first objective was to create a measure of children's anxiety that was suitable for group administration, which requires an instrument that has relatively few items and can be administered in a short time. To meet objections about CMAS items, the items in the new instrument had to be clear and easy to read. The norms were conceived as addressing a broad range of contexts, demanding not only a large-scale standardization study but one that took into account the manifestation of anxiety among diverse groups of children. To the extent possible, the development studies were designed to determine whether manifest anxiety is best conceived as unidimensional or multidimensional. Within the limits imposed by the construction of a practical instrument that teachers, researchers, and clinicians could actually use, development goals required that the measure as a whole satisfy contemporary psychometric standards.

A new version of the CMAS suitable for standardization research was constructed with these goals in mind. Some of the wording of the items was altered so that they would be easier to read and understand, with the effect of improving the items, expanding the potential age range of the original instrument, and giving the instrument greater currency. Every effort was made to ensure that items could be read at a third-grade level. New items generated by a panel of experienced teachers and clinicians were also included. This larger research instrument, which contained 73 items, was administered to 329 children representing the entire age range of the proposed instrument (Grades 1 through 12).

Using the resulting data, the items themselves were subjected to a rigorous item analysis. All items with a probability of endorsement less than .3 or greater than .7 were eliminated; also, if the biserial correlation of an item with the total score was less than .4, it was eliminated. After these criteria were applied, 37 items remained, 28 anxiety items and 9 lie items. The KR20 reliability estimates for the Total Anxiety score computed on the development sample and on a cross-validation sample of 167 children were in the .8 range. The low correlation between the Total Anxiety and Lie scores was expected and desired.

The new instrument contains five fewer items than did the original scale but has reliabilities on the same order as those reported for the CMAS. The presence of fewer items almost automatically reduces the time of administration, rendering the instrument more attractive as a screener than was its predecessor. In spite of the improvement in length, the new instrument retains 25 of the 28 anxiety items from the CMAS. Consistent with the results of previous studies (Bledsoe, 1973; Castaneda et al., 1956) and confirmed in even larger, more recent samples (Reynolds & Kamphaus, 1992), the girls received higher Total Anxiety scores than did the boys, suggesting the need for separate norms; consistent differences appeared between the scores of Black and White participants, again suggesting the need for separate norms. Nevertheless, with some qualifications discussed in the RCMAS manual (Reynolds & Richmond, 1985), the scale behaved similarly regardless of age, ethnicity, and gender.

Factor analytic procedures were used to develop the RCMAS subscales. The purpose of these procedures was twofold. First, factor analytic techniques address questions about the unidimensionality or multidimensionality of anxiety. Second, the factors that have consistently emerged from a series of studies were used to establish a scale structure. For this reason, the current RCMAS embodies a rigorously derived theoretical model of manifest anxiety in children that has been tested against the results of an extensive series of studies.

Factor analyses of the RCMAS have consistently yielded remarkably similar results. An early factor analysis of the CMAS yielded three factors labeled Worry/Oversensitivity, Physiological, and Concentration (Finch, Kendall, & Montgomery, 1974). When Reynolds and Richmond (1978) examined the factor structure of the RCMAS using the original development sample, they also retained a three-factor varimax solution as the most statistically and psychologically sound reflection of the instruments's performance. Ultimately, they applied essentially the same labels as those used by Finch et al. (1974). Subsequent factor analytic studies yielded results consistent with those of earlier studies. For example, a study by Reynolds and Paget (1981) employing the data from the RCMAS standardization sample (described in the following section) yielded a five-factor solution consisting of three anxiety factors and two lie factors. A factor analytic study by Paget and Reynolds (1984) using data obtained from 106 learning-disabled students had similar results, as did a study by Reynolds and Scholwinski (1985) using results obtained from a large group of gifted students. Factor analytic evidence obtained from RCMAS results and extended to a more comprehensive description of children's manifest anxiety suggests the presence of a strong general anxiety factor (A_g), represented by the Total Anxiety score of the RCMAS, and three more specific anxiety factors, represented by the anxiety subscales of the RCMAS.

Based on multiple large sample studies and expert review of the content by the authors and others (e.g., Finch et al., 1974), anxiety in children is represented within the RCMAS as a multidimensional construct. That both anxiety and the overall symptom presentation of children with various psychopathological disorders may be multidimensional has long been recognized (American Psychiatric Association, 1994). Therefore, the description of anxiety on which the RCMAS is based fits closely with the diagnostic and treatment process as a whole. Different children may present with different patterns of symptoms of anxiety, and different symptoms may respond differently to treatment. The RCMAS is designed, through the presence of a general anxiety factor, to allow the clinician to assess and monitor overall anxiety levels and to permit monitoring of selective changes in symptom patterns through tracking of changes in subscale scores across successive administrations. The RCMAS subscales also assist in differentiating between anxiety as a disorder (indicated when the Total Anxiety score is elevated) and anxiety as a symptom of other disorders (indicated when one or two subscales are elevated but the Total Anxiety score remains below 70*T*). If anxiety is present as a symptom of another disorder such as depression, the RCMAS can be useful in identifying symptoms and in monitoring their responsiveness to treatment.

STANDARDIZATION

The large, diverse standardization sample for the RCMAS included approximately 5,000 children from 6 to 19 years old, half of whom were female and half male; roughly 10% of those tested were black. The participants came from all regions of the United States and were drawn from rural, suburban, and urban areas. In addition to the norms based on this large sample, group data reported in the RCMAS manual (Reynolds & Richmond, 1985) for 97 kindergarten children may be used as norms for this younger age group. The testing procedures used to collect these data employed the same instructions that presently accompany the RCMAS. All of the data were collected through group administration, with the items being read to the younger children.

Standard score distributions for the RCMAS Total Anxiety scale, the three specific anxiety scales, and the lie scale were derived through normalized transformation of the raw score distributions using the method of rolling weighted averages. Some slight smoothing of the score distributions was necessary. For each scale, there are separate norms for boys and girls at each age from 6 to 16 as well as separate gender-by-ethnicity (Black and White) norms for each age. Scores for participants aged 17 to 19 were collapsed to form a single normative group for each gender and for Blacks and Whites of each gender. Total Anxiety is expressed as a *T*-score with a mean of 50 and a standard deviation of 10; the scaled scores for the subscales have a mean of 10 and a standard deviation of 3. See the RCMAS manual (Reynolds & Richmond, 1985) for a detailed description of the standardization study.

PSYCHOMETRICS

Reliability

Two aspects of an instrument's reliability are usually of interest: the accuracy of scores at the time of assessment and the stability of scores over time. The first of these is largely a function of the internal consistency of the scale as a whole and of its subscales. Test-retest reliability, as measured by the Pearson correlation between two sets of scores collected from the same individuals, is the principal indicator of temporal stability.

The statistic typically used to estimate internal consistency is the coefficient alpha (Cronbach, 1951), and it is generally agreed that the coefficient alpha for a psychological scale should be at least .70 (Nunnally, 1978). Across all age and ethnicity groups as well as across samples, alpha coefficients for the Total Anxiety score of the RCMAS are, with few exceptions, in the .80 range. For the Physiological Anxiety subscale and the Social Concerns/Concentration subscale, however, the alpha coefficients are typically in the .60 or .70 range and are occasionally below .60. Reliability estimates for the Worry/Oversensitivity and Lie subscales are typically in the .70 or .80 range. The reliability of RCMAS scores has also been demonstrated to be equivalent for children with disabilities (Paget & Reynolds 1984). Although the internal consistency coefficients of some subscales fall below Nunnally's criterion, such reliability estimates are typical of children's personality measures.

Reynolds (1981) reported a test-retest reliability coefficient of .68 for the Total Anxiety score after an interval of 9 months. The temporal stability of the instrument is therefore relatively high given the time between testings and the temporal stability of personality measures in general and personality measures for children in particular.

Validity

The RCMAS rests on a sound empirical foundation, which is described in detail in the test manual (Reynolds & Richmond, 1985). A substantial proportion of the validity evidence for the RCMAS comes from the results of the factor analyses that determined the instrument's scale structure. These results suggest that RCMAS results are constant across a range of subject variables, including gender, ethnicity, and IQ. In addition, a series of studies comparing children's RCMAS scores with their scores on the State–Trait Anxiety Inventory for Children (STAIC; Spielberger, 1973) demonstrated that RCMAS scores are highly correlated with scores on the Trait subscale and essentially uncorrelated with scores on the State subscale (Reynolds, 1980, 1982, 1985). These results comport with the conception of the RCMAS as a measure of *manifest anxiety*, conceived as an enduring response to stress.

Validity research on the RCMAS is voluminous. The original journal article reporting the development of the RCMAS (Reynolds & Richmond, 1978) is the most frequently cited article ever published in the *Journal of Abnormal Psychology*, and the article was reprinted in the 25th anniversary issue of the journal. In implicit acknowledgment of the extensive data supporting the RCMAS as a valid measure of chronic, manifest anxiety, the RCMAS is commonly used in studies validating other instruments (e.g., Carey, Lubin, & Brewer, 1992; Kaslow, Stark, Pritz, Livingston, & Tsai, 1992; Kearney & Silverman, 1993).

CROSS-CULTURAL APPLICATIONS

Because cultural influences on the willingness to report affect can be quite strong (Moran, 1990), it is necessary to assess how easily a measure of affect traverses ethnic and gender boundaries. Unlike the vast majority of personality scales available, the RCMAS has been examined extensively for its cross-cultural validity as well as for ethnicity and gender bias. There is surprisingly little empirical work designed to detect cultural bias in personality tests or their individual items (Reynolds, Lowe, & Saenz, in press), and the RCMAS is one of a very few personality scales for which cross-cultural and cross-gender bias has been examined (Moran, 1990). In a review of cross-cultural assessment using personality scales, Dana (1993) concluded that most comparative studies across cultural groups have used inadequate statistics, selected samples inappropriately, and failed to provide an adequate basis for cross-cultural application of most measures of affect or personality. The RCMAS is an exception, having a foundation in several studies of ethnic and gender bias, which are reviewed in the RCMAS manual (Reynolds & Richmond, 1985).

Unlike most studies of the cross-cultural application of personality tests, which usually focus on mean score differences among groups, studies of the cross-cultural application of the RCMAS have focused on validity across gender and ethnicity. RCMAS item bias was evaluated empirically by Reynolds, Plake, and Harding (1983), who found that the RCMAS does contain some potentially biased items. Individuals from different ethnic backgrounds and of different genders but with equivalent levels of anxiety respond differently to some items on the RCMAS. The effect was, however, acceptably small, the race-by-item and gender-by-item interaction terms both being associated with an effect sizes of less than 1% cumulatively across all of the items, which suggests little if any bias of clinical significance. The direction of the bias was found to be balanced across groups as well.

Comparative factor analysis across groups is another method of examining cross-cultural equivalence of tests that is viewed as quite important in determining whether test-takers of various backgrounds perceive and respond to a given item based on a common latent cognitive structure (Dana, 1993; Reynolds et al., in press). Reynolds and Paget (1981) examined the factor structure of the RCMAS across ethnicity and gender for a large sample of Blacks and Whites from 5 to 19 years old. The high coefficients of congruence that were obtained demonstrate the equivalence of the factor structure across groups. Examination of the internal consistency of the scales across groups revealed that young Black females (below age 11) responded less reliably than other groups to these anxiety items, but this finding has not been replicated. Considerably more detail regarding these various results may be found in the RCMAS manual (Reynolds & Richmond, 1985).

Few, if any, personality scales have been scrutinized cross-culturally as carefully as the RCMAS. It is now in use in more than 16 countries representing myriad cultures. Because of its emphasis on sound psychometric principles in its early development and on the universal construct of trait anxiety, it has proven to be useful in many contexts. At this stage, clinicians should be relatively comfortable in applying RCMAS results to the diagnosis of minority group members in the United States and to monitoring the effects of treatment on minority group members. Clinicians in other countries are also likely to find local literature addressing cross-cultural applications of the RCMAS.

INTERPRETIVE STRATEGY

A child experiencing high stress at home or in school is likely to reveal this stress in responses to the RCMAS items. The results may indicate the means for ameliorating fearful or stressful reactions through identifying the sources of anxiety. Not only do the Total Anxiety score and the scores on the anxiety subscales suggest the character of the child's anxiety, but responses to individual items may indicate specific areas of concern. Although the RCMAS can be a powerful tool for identifying and classifying anxiety, interpretation of RCMAS results, particularly those indicating the presence of significant anxiety, must always be informed by clinical experience.

Determining the validity of RCMAS results requires both the application of clinical insight and attention to the form of the child's responses. Administration of the instrument constitutes part of the larger evaluation process because it affords the opportunity to observe the child's willingness to answer the items carefully and honestly. Obvious resistance to taking the test or a marked inability to record self-perceptions deserve particular attention. Because few children have trouble completing the RCMAS, failure to complete it according to instructions signals a problem. Resistance to reporting symptoms is most often accompanied by elevated Lie scale scores, but children who resist even completing the scale require additional investigation. First, one must determine whether the child can read the questions and may be resisting out of fear or embarassment. If the RCMAS or another objective questionaire is the first task facing a child, the examiner may wish to move to something perhaps less threatening, like a simple projective drawing. Continued resistance may require long-term efforts to establish a relationship with a troubled, cautious child before the child is comfortable relating feelings and cognitions to the clinician. In some instances, of course, a child clearly suffering from anxiety does not receive high RCMAS scores.

Even in those instances when the scores themselves do not contribute to an accurate assessment of the child's level of anxiety, the pattern of responding may provide other clinically useful information, signaling difficulties with concentration, reading problems, or defiance. The Lie subscale, in addition to providing a check on the validity of the child's responses, functions as a measure of "faking good," defensiveness manifesting as the need to provide socially desirable responses, which can sometimes point to a distorted view of self and others.

The raw Total Anxiety score varies from 0 to 28. The first task in the interpretation of an RCMAS protocol is to determine how deviant the Total Score is. In general, scores falling at least one standard deviation from the mean (60*T* or greater) are of clinical interest, and those falling two standard deviations or more from the mean (70*T* or greater) are clearly deviant and may indicate significant pathology. As discussed under the heading "Item Analysis" later in this chapter, it is important to note which items the child endorses because the individual pattern of item endorsement may point to problems that are not indicated by the pattern of subscale scores.

Each of the three factor-based subscales reflects a different aspect of anxiety. A high score on the Physiological Anxiety subscale suggests that the child is experiencing a number of the physiological signs of anxiety, such as stomach pains and sweaty hands. A high score on the Worry/Oversensitivity subscale is a sign that the child internalizes the experience of anxiety. Because this often means that the child feels overwhelmed, it is important for him or her to develop ways of relieving anxiety through discussing feelings and of coping through reaching out to others. A high score on the Social Concerns/Concentration subscale suggests that the child feels unable to live up to the expectations of parents and other important figures. The feeling of not being as capable as others can generate a level of anxiety that makes it difficult to concentrate on school work or other responsibilities.

Responses to individual RCMAS items can yield information or suggest clinical hypotheses about the origin and nature of a child's anxiety. There are no norms for individual items. Because the items reflect aspects of anxiety, however, examination of individual items can help in determining the extent and character of the child's anxiety. In addition, it may be possible to discuss each endorsed item with the child, not only giving the clinician more information regarding the child's distress but giving the child practice in exploring and expressing emotion. Such discussions about RCMAS items can, therefore, serve both assessment and treatment goals.

TREATMENT PLANNING WITH THE RCMAS

Paradoxically, as industrialization and social modernization improve the latitude action for many individuals, the number of decisions and the pressures to keep pace provide the perfect atmosphere to elevate anxiety levels. Relatively low levels of anxiety can facilitate performance, but chronic anxiety ultimately reduces an individual's effectiveness and can adversely affect both mental and physical health. Anxiety is the most frequent indicator of mental health problems, and anxiety may form the basis of depression. In a wide range of psychotherapeutic settings, the first task of the psychologist, psychiatrist, or counselor is to alleviate the symptoms of anxiety, permitting the client to function more easily and effectively.

Anxiety is unique among the psychopathologies in that it may be either a symptom or a disorder. Research results, review of the *DSM–IV*, and clinical experience with patients all show clearly, moreover, that anxiety and depression are related constructs but can and should be differentiated (Crowley & Emerson, 1996; Ialongo, Edelsohn, Werthamer-Larsson, Crockett, & Kellam, 1996; Reynolds & Kamphaus, 1992). It is, of course, common for children with a diagnosis of depression to display significant symptoms of anxiety. The RCMAS is useful across a range of clinical contexts in part because its results comport well with the *DSM–IV* criteria for generalized anxiety disorder (GAD) (Tracy, Charpita, Douban, & Barlow, 1997), but it is detailed enough in its assessment approach to address anxiety as a symptom of other disorders. The specificity of the RCMAS helps clinicians to distinguish the two problems and thus both address them in treatment planning and monitor the breadth of the child's symptom patterns in response to interventions (Crowley & Emerson, 1996).

Unfortunately, vulnerability to the stresses of society is not confined to adults. Many children experience anxiety in response to the pressure placed on them in a world that demands ever more decisions and ever higher performance. Naturally, school represents the most common source of stress for children; they worry about their academic progress, and they grow apprehensive with the approach of each test. Relationships with peers and family members also stimulate anxiety in children. Younger children become involved in negative interactions on the playground or with their siblings; adolescents face the prospect of relationships with members of the opposite sex, a realm full of worries even for a relatively well adjusted child. Problems with one or both parents can produce debilitating anxiety and perpetuate negative self-talk, putting a child or adolescent on a downward spiral of increasing anxiety (Ronan & Kendall, 1997).

For these reasons, information about the character and extent of a child's anxiety is important for the clinician, teacher, or parent. It can also be of great value to the child, assuming that it is presented in a manner consistent with his or her level of development. Anxiety appears to result inevitably from the complexities of life as it is now constituted. Therefore, efforts to reduce anxiety can be seen as part of a lifelong project that can begin with an understanding gained in childhood or early adolescence. Such an approach requires a source of organized information about the individual's anxiety, information that can be gained, in part, from examination of the RCMAS profile.

Objective measures of anxiety play an essential role in identifying a child's problems. The teacher, parent, or mental health professional may not be fully aware of the complex interrelationship of emotion, stress, and performance in a child's life. A structured description of each child's level of anxiety can help a teacher gauge the overall level of anxiety in the classroom, which can help in predicting which children will need intervention. By the same token, parents armed with fairly precise information about a child's level of anxiety may be in a better position to help a child cope with anxiety-provoking circumstances. A counselor, social worker, or psychologist can, of course, make use of objective data about a child's anxiety in treating an array of difficulties.

In addition, structured and specific information about anxiety presented directly to the client may support efforts to cope with the pressures of growing up. Because children usually cannot recognize either the extent or antecedents of anxious feelings, they naturally cannot discover effective strategies for overcoming those feelings or their possible effects. For example, a child typically cannot figure out that anxieties rooted in family relationships have caused his or her grades to fall. A closer look at a family conflict, including the stresses within it as well as the emotional and physical reactions to those stresses, can help him or her to develop better means of adapting and coping.

The design of the RCMAS facilitates its use in planning and monitoring treatment. The RCMAS has been used in many research studies since it attained more or less its current form during the late 1970s. Prior to that, more than 100 research articles using the CMAS appeared as part of the effort to define accurately the nature of manifest anxiety in children and its relationship to a number of cognitive, affective, and achievement variables, and well over 100 papers using the RCMAS have appeared since the 1978 revision. The development of the RCMAS proceeded from the assumption that a scale used to identify the symptoms of anxiety must facilitate the detection of relationships between anxiety and other disorders as well as between anxiety and external factors.

Interpretive Strategies and Treatment Planning

By providing insight into the child's feelings across situations, the RCMAS can illuminate the process of treatment planning. Because of the prevalence of anxiety and its relationship to depression, the evaluation of a child's anxiety level is crucial to the larger process of assessment. The choice of treatment modality depends on information about the overall level of anxiety and on the type and pattern of anxiety symptoms. As a relatively brief instrument, the RCMAS lends itself to use in screening for anxiety in the classroom. Therefore, RCMAS results can easily be used to guide the design of programs for preventing or ameliorating anxiety among groups of children.

The development of the RCMAS focused on ensuring that individual items correspond closely to symptoms associated with anxiety. For that reason, the child's endorsement of a given item or group of items points directly to his or her symptomatology. This information is available for use in counseling sessions to generate discussion, identify causes of anxiety-related symptoms, and construct efforts to alleviate those symptoms. Furthermore, because the RCMAS items embody anxiety symptoms, including anxiety-driven attitudes and behaviors, attention to the items the client has endorsed can support the selection of a treatment modality.

The Total Anxiety score, the pattern of RCMAS subscale scores, and the individual items all provide information useful in treatment planning. Among other things, the overall level of anxiety predicts the degree of dysfunction quite well. The pattern of scale scores, if it is consistent with other test scores and with additional information about the client, can reveal the contours of the client's experience of anxiety. The RCMAS items themselves provide clues to the child's condition, and they can be incorporated into the treatment process.

Total Anxiety. The Total Anxiety score indicates the breadth of symptomatology and the best assessment of the presence of GAD. Treatment approaches such as cognitive behavior modifications (CBM) or perhaps play therapy with younger children may be appropriate. This score is sensitive to treatment effects as well and should decline over time.

Physiological Anxiety. The score on the Physiological Anxiety scale is important to both diagnosis and treatment planning, because physiological symptoms are central to the experience of anxiety. Most of the items on this scale correspond closely to the symptoms of chronic overarousal: sleep problems, nightmares, irritability, indecisiveness, and restlessness. Although all of the items ultimately imply a negative physical response to stress, a few items, those referring to sweaty palms, breathlessness, and nausea, correspond to the more immediate aspect of anxious arousal. Learning-disabled children, along with children who have experienced trauma, tend to have elevated scores on this scale as well.

Those with high scores on this scale are experiencing the signs of physical tension and the accompanying autonomic arousal. For that reason, it may be necessary to select a form of treatment that more or less directly reduces the level of tension. Some types of strenuous physical exercise, such as running or swimming, may help in achieving this goal. On the other hand, training in progressive relaxation, for example, may be used to reduce the overall level of tension and may also form a part of treatment for specific anxieties such as test anxiety. Biofeedback is often chosen for individuals with these symptoms.

Worry/Oversensitivity. Items on the Worry/Oversensitivity scale either contain the word worry or mention the experience of fear, nervousness, and excitability. A high score on this scale indicates strong reactions to environmental pressures. Because this often means that the child feels overwhelmed by external events and internal pressures, it is important for him or her to develop ways of relieving anxiety through discussing feelings and of coping through reaching out to others.

Social Concerns/Concentration. Items on this subscale tend to reflect concern about the self in interaction with others and also concern about problems with concentration. A good assessment of social skills and other measures of interpersonal relations, available in the Behavior Assessment System for Children (Reynolds & Kamphaus, 1992), would be an excellent follow-up to elevations on this scale. In addition to CBM, social skill development and practice in role-playing might also be useful. Negative self-talk is a significant problem for those children who are overly concerned that they are not as good, effective, or capable as others.

Item Analysis and PTSD. Individual item responses maybe of particular importance in children suspected of having posttraumatic stress disorder (PTSD). Although hypervigilance, a key organic symptom of PTSD, is associated with general increases in anxiety levels, more specific symptoms may appear. A content analysis of items in comparison with the *DSM–IV* criteria for a diagnosis of PTSD suggests the following critical items, some or all of which may be PTSD related:

Item 6: I worry a lot of the time.
Item 13: It is hard for me to get to sleep at night.
Item 22: I worry about what is going to happen.
Item 25: I have bad dreams.
Item 29: I wake up scared some of the time.
Item 30: I worry when I go to bed at night.
Item 37: I often worry about something bad happening to me.

This list is not exhaustive by any means but represents symptoms associated with PTSD in a wide variety of cases. Although multiple approaches to the appraisal of PTSD and the monitoring of its resolution in treatment are necessary, endorsement of select RCMAS items does predict abuse, particularly sexual abuse (Spaccarelli & Fuchs, 1997). As these symptoms resolve, treatment may be seen to progress.

CASE STUDIES

The following vignettes, based on real cases, are designed to demonstrate the application of RCMAS results. The instrument is a highly versatile component of any assessment battery for children and adolescents. Recently, a similar tool, the Adult Manifest Anxiety Scale (AMAS; Reynolds, Richmond, & Lowe, 2001), has been developed for use with adults and adolescents.

Case 1: Distractibility and Parental Neglect

In some cases, ruling out anxiety can prove of value in arriving at an accurate assessment and choosing an appropriate treatment. A lack of concentration and a tendency to act out can result from anxiety, but they may also reflect other problems, including, of course, conditions that affect attentional mechanisms. Furthermore, it is important to see past a child's presenting symptoms to the possibility of problems within the family.

John, who is eight, is in the third grade. His parents brought him to a counseling center because of his problems at school. John's teacher describes his behavior as immature and inattentive. He looks around the schoolroom and out the window frequently and talks to other children during lessons. Not only does this behavior interfere with his own learning, but it disrupts learning and discipline in the classroom as a whole.

On the surface, there do not seem to be large problems in John's family. His mother, who is a native of an Asian country, has two children by a previous marriage. She met his father while he was overseas in the military, and they have lived in the United States for 6 years. Both parents were college students, and all three children live with them. They have few problems with John at home, although they notice that he rarely stays with any task for very long. He gets along well with his older brother and sister.

His achievement and IQ test scores suggest that John is of average ability. On the Wechsler Intelligence Scale for Children (WISC–III; Wechsler, 1991), he obtained a Verbal IQ of 99 and a Performance IQ of 94, resulting in a FSIQ of 96. His performance on the Human Figure Drawing Test (Mitchell, Trent, & McArthur, 1993) indicates a mental age of 8-0, and his performance on the Bender-Gestalt Test (Clawson, 1962) indicates a developmental age of 7-6 to 8-0. His achievement scores on the Norris Educational Achievement Test (NEAT; Switzer & Gruber, 1992) were adequate for his age: 107 on Reading, 107 on Spelling, 101 on Arithmetic, and 3.6 as his grade level.

John's behavior during the testing session was characterized by the psychologist as initially cooperative and polite. As the session went on, however, John began to exhibit avoidance behaviors, such as saying that he was tired, bored, or hungry. During testing, he got up and walked around the room and asked questions, which necessitated bringing him back on task several times. At the end, he appeared to miss a few items deliberately to shorten the time. Therefore, his achievement and IQ test results may not reflect his full ability.

John's RCMAS scores suggest average or below-average levels of anxiety but also a response bias. John obtained a scaled score of 17 on the Lie scale. His Total Anxiety score, however, was only 46, and he had scaled scores of 11, 6, and 11, respectively, on the Physiological Anxiety, Worry/Oversensitivity, and Social Concerns/Concentration subscales. Of the 11 anxiety items he did endorse, 6 were on the Physiological Anxiety subscale, 4 were on the Social Concerns/Concentration scale, and only 1 was a Worry/Oversensitivity item. Although he does not appear to suffer from anxiety, John's Lie score suggests the need to present himself in a socially desirable light, and the pattern of his scores is consistent with the presenting problem.

In conference, the parents recognized that their involvement in their own activities had left them with little time for John and the other children. Consequently, they were not aware of John's distractibility and immature behavior. Because his mother was especially busy with studying, household chores, and adapting to a new society, she spent practically no time with John individually.

John's immature behavior has not given him the social rewards he needs. Until the crisis precipitated by his teacher's report, it did not help him gain the attention of his parents. The defensiveness he displayed in his RCMAS responses implies that he views himself as perfect in order to compensate for the experience of rejection. Not only does he feel neglected by his parents, but his peers tend to avoid him because of his acting out. He needs help to find his way out of this vicious cycle. The parents have thus decided to restructure their daily routines, allowing more time to interact with John and his siblings, and they also intend to plan more family activities.

Although the elevations of his RCMAS scores do not indicate problems with anxiety, the pattern of scores is consistent with the possibility that John has difficulties with arousal and attention. He will receive assistance in developing better on-task behavior and in asking for help in a responsible way. It is assumed that if these changes prove insufficient, John will be evaluated for ADHD.

Case 2: Acting-out Adolescent

Jeannie, a 17-year-old girl in residence at a group home for emotionally disturbed adolescents, has had serious academic, emotional, and social problems since she was in the 8th grade. She has managed to complete the 10th grade, but her problems persist. Those problems began to appear around the time her brother was born and her interest in boys emerged. Prior to that, she had been a good student, earning As and Bs, and an outstanding athlete. The previous year she had been an all-star pitcher in the local American Girl softball league, and she was expected to make the varsity on her high school softball team as a freshman; she also excelled in several track and field events.

Her father was always proud of Jeannie's talent and of her willingness to work in order to succeed on the field. Ever since her special abilities began to appear, when she was in elementary school, the relationship between father and daughter had increasingly revolved around her participation in sports and his role as her coach. When she started dating and stopped participating in sports, her father objected strongly, and a serious rift quickly developed between them. At the same time, and perhaps out of disappointment with his daughter, the father began to focus on his infant son. Feeling shut out herself, Jeannie let her grades slip, became promiscuous, started smoking cigarettes, and began abusing drugs and alcohol. When he discovered a pack of cigarettes and a bag of marijuana in her room, her father threw Jeannie out of the house, claiming that she had betrayed everything he had taught her.

Jeannie moved in with her mother's sister, who lives in the same town, promising to "cool her jets." Soon, however, she stopped coming home at night and had all but dropped out of school. When she had a falling out with her aunt, with whom she had always been close, the family decided that Jeannie had to enter the group home, which is in another town about an hour's drive away.

Apparently, Jeannie is of roughly average intellectual ability. She obtained a Full Scale IQ of 94 on the Wechsler Adult Intelligence Scale–Revised (WAIS–R; Wechsler, 1981); her Performance IQ was slightly elevated but not significantly higher than her Verbal IQ. Her scores on the NEAT were 102 for Arithmetic, 119 for Reading, and 98 for Spelling. Although she made no errors on the Bender-Gestalt, she did have several erasures and made second attempts at some drawings.

Jeannie's performance on projective instruments was revealing. Her responses on a sentence completion task and the Thematic Apperception Test (TAT; Murray, 1943) revealed a strong attachment to her father and a need for his acceptance. She was frightened and depressed because he no longer wanted her in the home. Quite dependent, with a poor self-concept and a marked inability to envision solutions to her problems, she expected others to solve her problems for her. Her descriptions of her own previous behavior alternately reflected strong feelings of guilt and a deep sense of rejection.

Jeannie's RCMAS scores comport closely with the rest of the symptom picture. She had a Total Anxiety *T*-score of 74 (99th percentile) and Physiological Anxiety, Worry/Oversensitivity, and Social Concerns/Concentration subscale scores of 19, 16, and 14, respectively; her Lie scale score was 9. Clearly, she was experiencing high levels of anxiety. When interviewed, she reported feeling so "nervous and upset" that she found it nearly impossible to cope with any kind of stress, especially those related to her family situation, and she also reported feeling overcome by worries about her future. Her pleasant world of acceptance, success, and love had deteriorated rapidly over the previous two years. She was afraid and saw herself as unable to deal with her situation.

In the context of her history and her other test scores, the pattern of Jeannie's RCMAS scores guided the approach to treatment. Most of the RCMAS items she endorsed fell on the Physiological Anxiety and Worry/Oversensitivity scales. Although Jeannie's overall anxiety is high, according to her self-description in interviews she suffers most from the physical elements of nervous arousal, from badly hurt feelings, and from her fears about the future. Therefore, the intervention was organized around three goals. First, it was deemed important to find ways for her to relax by releasing pent-up energy. Second, efforts were made to eliminate some of the external sources of stress from her life. Third, she needed to confront the feelings of hurt and rejection, perhaps as a first step in reconciling with her father.

The means to address the physiological component of her anxiety were already a large part of her life. Jeannie was encouraged to reacquaint herself with athletics, but with a difference. Instead of focusing on competition, which was too reminiscent of the difficulties that brought her to treatment, she focused on conditioning, including weight training and aerobic exercise. Eventually her huge competitive spirit could not be denied, and she enrolled in a kung fu course, which had the dual benefit of bringing her back into competition and helping her develop greater self-confidence.

To reduce her fears about the future, Jeannie must acquire some skills and education. She is already a year behind in school. Therefore, she receives additional tutoring to help ensure that she will progress at an acceptable pace in her academic work. Because she already has had the experience of succeeding in school, she simply needs to rediscover the skills and strategies that she used before she entered high school. It is hoped that as she does succeed in her schoolwork, her self-image will improve.

The most difficult part of the treatment will involve healing the hurt Jeannie has sustained in the destructive conflict with her father. Clearly, she needs to differentiate her own contribution to her difficulties from her father's overly harsh reaction to the changes in her, which were partly a consequence of her entry into adolescence. For a child like her, so dependent on the good opinion of others, particularly her father, the more or less sudden withdrawal of affection she experienced was devastating. Jeannie often describes what happened as her father having lost interest in her because she was just a girl and he finally had a son. Interviews with the father indicate that he recognizes that he did not handle the situation with appropriate sensitivity. He is still very angry at his daughter, but he may be ready to reconcile if, as he says, "she stops using drugs and sleeping around." For her part, Jeannie must acquire a more realistic view of her father and her family and better control over the angry impulses that lie at the root of her acting out. She is receiving training in both impulse control and assertiveness.

Case 3: Academic Underachiever

Chuck, aged 14, was in the eighth grade at the time of this evaluation. His father is a high school mathematics teacher, and his mother is a nurse. He has one brother, who is 10. He was referred by his parents for counseling because of his poor academic progress. Unable or unwilling to concentrate on his schoolwork, Chuck usually does not do his homework and seems uninterested in academic achievement.

The parents, who have always valued good grades, reported having tried everything to encourage Chuck to do better. Although they punished him, praised him, and helped him with his homework, he remained unmotivated. They grew concerned that they were punishing him too much and that the conflict over Chuck's grades had become the most significant feature of family interaction. In addition, the younger brother began to resent the situation because Chuck receives more attention than he does.

His test results suggest that Chuck's academic achievement does not match his ability. On the WISC–III, Chuck obtained a Verbal IQ of 100 and a Performance IQ of 128, resulting a FSIQ of 113, which is in the high average range. On the other hand, his performance on the WRAT–3 was poor. He is functioning at the 9th percentile in Arithmetic, the 18th in Spelling, and 42nd in Reading, all scores lower than his ability would predict. He reports an interest in science and art but indicates that school is usually boring.

Chuck's RCMAS scores suggest that he is highly anxious. His Total Anxiety score of 75 (at the 99th percentile) reflects his responding in the scale-positive direction on all but five of the anxiety items. Not surprisingly, therefore, his scores on the anxiety subscales are also high: 15 on Physiological Anxiety, 16 on Worry/Oversensitivity, and 16 on Social Concerns/Concentration. His Lie scale score was 9.

Chuck is an extremely anxious youngster with anxiety severe enough to interfere with his concentration and with his ability to develop better social and interpersonal skills. He realizes that his poor grades form the subject of many family conflicts. He expresses concern that he does not have any friends, and he believes that his parents, as well as his peers, dislike him. Chuck is unhappy and sees no solution to his problems. His relatively low verbal ability may reflect his inability to verbalize his feelings of frustration and anxiety.

The RCMAS subscale scores he received suggest that Chuck's anxiety affects him in many ways. Nevertheless, his Social Concerns/Concentration score of 16 represents endorsement of every item on that scale. For that reason, and because the presenting problem was his inability to concentrate, the initial two-pronged intervention will focus on this aspect of his anxiety. He will receive help recognizing the feelings of anxiety he experiences in social situations. At the same time, an attempt will be made to restructure his perceptions of others and of his relationships with them.

The items on the Social Concerns/Concentration scale became the basis of discussions about the realities of social interaction and about the accuracy of Chuck's ideas about people and situations. For example, Item 11 is "I feel that others do not like the way I do things" and Item 27 is "I feel someone will tell me I do things the wrong way." Chuck was asked to examine whether others usually disapprove of his actions or see him as incompetent. Item 3 is "Others seem to do things easier than I can." Chuck is being helped to see that some people are indeed better than he is at some things but that this is not a reflection on him and does not in itself cause others to see him as incompetent or unattractive. Chuck's grades have improved. In addition, he recently asked a girl to go with him to a dance, and she accepted.

REFERENCES

American Psychiatric Association. (1994). *Diagnostic and statistical manual of mental disorders* (4th ed.). Washington, DC: Author.

Bledsoe, J. (1973). Sex and grade differences in children's manifest anxiety. *Psychological Reports, 32,* 285–286.

Boehnkem, K., Silbereisen, R. K., Reynolds, C. R., & Richmond, B. O. (1986). What I Think and Feel: German experience with the revised form of the Children's Manifest Anxiety Scale. *Personality and Individual Differences, 7,* 553–560.

Carey, M. P., Lubin, B. & Brewer, D. H. (1992). Measuring dysphoric mood in pre-adolescents and adolescents: The Youth Depression Adjective Checklist (Y–DACL). *Journal of Clinical Child Psychology, 21,* 331–338.

Castaneda, A., McCandless, B., & Palermo, D. (1956). The children's form of the Manifest Anxiety Scale. *Child Development, 27,* 317–326.

Clawson, A. (1962). *The Bender Visual Motor–Gestalt Test for Children.* Los Angeles: Western Psychological Services.

Cronbach, L. (1951). Coefficient alpha and the internal structure of tests. *Psychometrika, 16,* 297–334.

Crowley, S. L., & Emerson, E. N. (1996). Discriminant validity of self-reported anxiety and depression in children: Negative affectivity or independent constructs? *Journal of Clinical Child Psychology, 25,* 139–146.

Dana, R. H. (1993). *Multicultural assessment perspectives for professional psychology.* Boston: Allyn & Bacon.

DuBois, D. L., Felner, R. D., Bartels, C. L., & Silverman, M. M. (1995). Stability of self-reported depressive symptoms in a community sample of children and adolescents. *Journal of Clinical Child Psychology, 24,* 386–396.

Finch, A., Kendall, P., & Mongomery, L. (1974). Multidimensionality of anxiety in children: Factor structure of the Children's Manifest Anxiety Scale. *Journal of Abnormal Child Psychology, 2,* 331–336.

Flanagan, P., Peters, C., & Conry, J. (1969). Item analysis of the Children's Manifest Anxiety Scale with the retarded. *Journal of Educational Research, 62,* 472–477.

Ialongo, N., Edelson, G., Werthamer-Larson, L., Crockett, L., & Kellam, S. (1996). Social and cognitive impairment in first grade children with anxious and depressive symptoms. *Journal of Clinical Child Psychology, 25,* 15–24.

Kaslow, N. J., Stark, K. D., Printz, B., Livingston, R., & Tsai, S. L. (1992). Cognitive Triad Inventory for Children: Development and Relation to depression and anxiety. *Journal of Clinical Child Psychology,* 21, 339–347.

Kearney, C. A., & Silverman, W. K. (1993). Measuring the function of school refusal behavior: The School Refusal Assessment Scale. *Journal of Clinical Child Psychology, 22,* 85–96.

Kirk, R. (1968). *Experimental design: Procedure for the behavioral sciences.* Belmont, CA: Brooks/Cole.

Koppitz, E. M. (1982). Personality assessment in the schools. In C. R. Reynolds & T. B. Gutkin (Eds.), *The handbook of school psychology* (pp. 273–295). New York: Wiley.

Mitchell, J., Trent, R., & McArthur, R. (1993). *Human Figure Drawing Test.* Los Angeles: Western Psychological Services.

Moran, M. P. (1990). The problem of cultural bias in personality assessment. In C. R. Reynolds & R. W. Kamphaus (Eds.), *Handbook of psychological and educational assessment of children: Vol. 2. Personality, behavior, and context* (pp. 524–545). New York: Guilford.

Murray, H. (1943). *Thematic apperception test manual.* Cambridge, MA: Harvard University Press.

Nunnally, J. (1978). *Psychometric theory.* New York: McGraw-Hill.

Paget, K. D., & Reynolds, C. R. (1984). Dimensions, levels, and reliabilities on the Revised Children's Manifest Anxiety Scale with learning disabled children. *Journal of Learning Disabilities, 17,* 137–141.

Pela, O. A., & Reynolds, C. R. (1982). Cross-cultural application of the Revised Children's Manifest Anxiety Scale: Normative and reliability data for Nigerian primary school children. *Psychological Reports, 51,* 1135–1138.

Rabian, B., Peterson, R. A., Richters, J., & Jensen, P. S. (1993). Anxiety sensitivity among anxious children. *Journal of Clinical Child Psychology, 22,* 441–446.

Reynolds, C. R. (1980). Concurrent validity of What I Think and Feel: The Revised Children's Manifest Anxiety Scale. *Journal of Consulting and Clinical Psychology, 48,* 774–775.

Reynolds, C. R. (1981). Long-term stability of scores on the Revised Children's Manifest Anxiety Scale. *Perceptual and Motor Skills, 53,* 702.

Reynolds, C. R. (1982). Convergent and divergent validity of the Revised Children's Manifest Anxiety Scale. *Educational and Psychological Measurement, 42,* 1205–1212.

Reynolds, C. R. (1985). Multitrait validation of the Revised Children's Manifest Anxiety Scale for children of high intelligence. *Psychological Reports, 56,* 402.

Reynolds, C. R. (in press). Need we measure anxiety separately for males and females? *Journal of Personality Assessment.*

Reynolds, C. R., & Kamphaus, R. W. (1992). *Behavior Assessment System for Children.* Circle Pines, MN: American Guidance Service.

Reynolds, C. R., Lowe, P. L., & Saenz, A. (in press). The problem of bias in psychological assessment. In C. R. Reynolds & T. B. Gutkin (Eds.), *The handbook of school psychology* (3rd ed.). New York: Wiley.

Reynolds, C. R., & Paget, K. D. (1981). Factor analysis for the Revised Children's Manifest Anxiety Scale for Blacks, Whites, males, and females with a national normative sample. *Journal of Consulting and Clinical Psychology, 49,* 349–352.

Reynolds, C. R., Plake, B. S., & Harding, R. E. (1983). Item bias in the assessment of children's anxiety: Race and sex interaction on items of the Revised Children's Manifest Anxiety Scale. *Journal of Psychoeducational Assessment, 1,* 135–142.

Reynolds, C. R., & Richmond, B. (1978). What I Think and Feel: A revised measure of children's manifest anxiety. *Journal of Abnormal Child Psychology, 6,* 271–280.

Reynolds, C. R., & Richmond, B. (1985). *Revised Children's Manifest Anxiety Scale.* Los Angeles: Western Psychological Services.

Reynolds, C. R., Richmond, B., & Lowe, P. L. (2001). *Adult Manifest Anxiety Scale.* Los Angeles: Western Psychological Services.

Ronan, K. R., & Kendall, P. C. (1997). Self-talk in distressed youth: States of mind and content specificity. *Journal of Clinical Child Psychology, 26,* 330–337.

Spaccarelli, S., & Fuchs, F. (1997). Variability of symptom expression among sexually abused girls: Developing multivariate models. *Journal of Clinical Child Psychology, 26,* 24–35.

Spielberger, C. (1973). Preliminary manual for the State–Trait Anxiety Inventory for Children ("How I Feel Questionnaire"). Palo Alto, CA: Consulting Psychologists Press.

Switzer, J., & Gruber, C. (1992). *Norris Educational Achievement Test.* Los Angeles: Western Psychological Services.

Tracy, S. A., Chorpita, B. F., Douban, J., & Barlow, D. H. (1997). Empirical evaluation of DSM–IV generalized anxiety disorder criteria in children and adolescents. *Journal of Clinical Child Psychology, 26,* 404–414.

Wechsler, D. (1981). *Wechsler Adult Intelligence Scale–Revised.* San Antonio, TX: Psychological Corporation.

Wechsler, D. (1991). *Wechsler Intelligence Scale for Children* (3rd ed.). San Antonio, TX: Psychological Corporation.

Witt, J. C., Heffer, R. W., & Pfeifer, J. (1990). Structures rating scales: A review of self-report and informant rating processes, procedures, and issues. In C. R. Reynolds & R. W. Kamphaus (Eds.), *Handbook of psychological and educational assessment of children: Vol. 2. Personality, behavior, and context* (pp. 364–394). New York: Guilford.

4

Overview and Update on the Minnesota Multiphasic Personality Inventory–Adolescent (MMPI–A)

Robert P. Archer
Eastern Virginia Medical School

The purpose of this chapter is to review the Minnesota Multiphasic Personality Inventory–Adolescent (MMPI–A), a revision of the original MMPI specifically designed for use with teenagers. As with the MMPI–2, the MMPI–A was developed by building on the most useful and productive aspects of the original test instrument. Thus, for example, the original MMPI basic clinical scales were retained in the MMPI–A. The MMPI–A, however, also represents an attempt to improve on several aspects of the original test instrument in relation to adolescent assessment. These changes include a 16% reduction in the total length of the item pool, revision of 70 items to simplify or improve wording, the collection of new national norms representing diverse geographic and ethnic groups, and the development of several new scales specifically related to adolescent development and psychopathology. Since the publication of the MMPI–A in 1992, there has been a steady flow of publications on this instrument, estimated to total more than 50 studies by 2000 (Archer & Krishnamurthy, 2002). This chapter reviews the development and structure of the MMPI–A and provides an updated summary of the research literature on this instrument.

OVERVIEW

Summary of Development

The MMPI Adolescent Project Committee, created in 1989 by the University of Minnesota Press, consisted of James N. Butcher, Auke Tellegen, Beverly Kaemmer, and Robert P. Archer. This committee was appointed to guide the development of an adolescent form of the MMPI and to provide recommendations concerning normative criteria, item and scale selection, and profile construction to be incorporated in the adolescent form. The committee, wishing to maintain continuity between the original MMPI and the MMPI–A, sought to preserve the standard or basic MMPI scales. Scale *F* was substantially modified, however, to improve its psychometric performance with adolescents, and scales *Mf* and *Si* were shortened to reduce the total item pool of the instrument.

The MMPI basic clinical scales were developed by Hathaway and McKinley using a *criterion keying method*. Items were selected for scale membership based on the

TABLE 4.1
Overview of the MMPI–A Scales and Subscales

Basic Profile Scales (17 scales)
Validity Scales (7)
VRIN (Variable Response Inconsistency)
TRIN (True Response Inconsistency)
F_1
F_2
F (Frequency)
L (Lie)
K (Defensiveness)
Clinical Scales (10)
1/Hs (Hypochondriasis)
2/D (Depression)
3/Hy (Hysteria)
4/Pd (Psychopathic Deviate)
5/Mf (Masculinity-Femininity)
6/Pa (Paranoia)
7/Pt (Psychasthenia)
8/Sc (Schizophrenia)
9/Ma (Mania)
0/Si (Social Introversion)
Content and Supplementary Scales (21 scales)
Content Scales (15)
A-anx (Anxiety)
A-obs (Obsessiveness)
A-dep (Depression)
A-hea (Health Concerns)
A-aln (Alienation)
A-biz (Bizarre Mentation)
A-ang (Anger)
A-cyn (Cynicism)
A-con (Conduct Problems)
A-lse (Low Self-Esteem)
A-las (Low Aspirations)
A-sod (Social Discomfort)
A-fam (Family Problems)
A-sch (School Problems)
A-trt (Negative Treatment Indicators)
Supplementary Scales (6)
MAC-R (MacAndrew Alcoholism–Revised)
ACK (Alcohol/Drug Problem Acknowledgment)
PRO (Alcohol/Drug Problem Potential)
IMM (Immaturity)
A (Anxiety)
R (Repression)
Harris-Lingoes and Si Subscales (31 Subscales)
Harris-Lingoes Subscales (28)
D_1 (Subjective Depression)
D_2 (Psychomotor Retardation)
D_3 (Physical Malfunctioning)
D_4 (Mental Dullness)
D_5 (Brooding)
Hy_1 (Denial of Social Anxiety)
Hy_2 (Need for Affection)
Hy_3 (Lassitude-Malaise)
Hy_4 (Somatic Complaints)
Hy_5 (Inhibition of Aggression)

(Continued)

TABLE 4.1
(Continued)

Pd_1 (Familial Discord)
Pd_2 (Authority Problems)
Pd_3 (Social Imperturbability)
Pd_4 (Social Alienation)
Pd_5 (Self-Alienation)
Pa_1 (Persecutory Ideas)
Pa_2 (Poignancy)
Pa_3 (Naivete)
Sc_1 (Social Alienation)
Sc_2 (Emotional Alienation)
Sc_3 (Lack of Ego Mastery, Cognitive)
Sc_4 (Lack of Ego Mastery, Conative)
Sc_5 (Lack of Ego Mastery, Defective Inhibition)
Sc_6 (Bizarre Sensory Experiences)
Ma_1 (Amorality)
Ma_2 (Psychomotor Acceleration)
Ma_3 (Imperturbability)
Ma_4 (Ego Inflation)
Si Subscales (3)
Si_1 (Shyness/Self-Consciousness)
Si_2 (Social Avoidance)
Si_3 (Alienation–Self and Others)

Note. From *MMPI–A: Assessing adolescent psychopathology* (2nd ed., pp. 54–55), by R. P. Archer, 1997, Mahwah, NJ: Lawrence Erlbaum Associates. Copyright 1997 by Lawrence Erlbaum Associates. Reprinted with permission.

occurrence of item response frequencies that differentiated between a criterion group manifesting a specific diagnosis or characteristic and a comparison group (the Minnesota adult normal sample) thought not to manifest the trait or characteristic under study. Indeed, the original MMPI is widely cited (e.g., Anastasi, 1982) as an outstanding example of this method of test construction. In addition to the basic clinical scales, the MMPI–A contains four new validity scales presented within the Basic Scale Profile, 15 content scales, six supplementary scales, 28 Harris-Lingoes, and three *Si* subscales. Table 4.1 provides an overview of the scale structure of the MMPI–A, with scales organized into three broad headings corresponding to the three MMPI–A profile sheets.

The new validity scales in the basic scale profile include the F_1 and F_2 subscales, each containing a 33-item subset of the 66-item MMPI–A *F* scale. These items were selected based on a criterion that the item was endorsed in the deviant direction by no more than 20% of males and females in the MMPI–A normative sample. The MMPI–A validity scales also include the Variable Response Inconsistency (*VRIN*) scale and the True Response Inconsistency (*TRIN*) scale, consistency measures developed using a methodology very similar to that employed in the development of the MMPI–2 counterparts of these measures. The order of appearance of validity scales on the basic scale profile, from left to right, is as follows: *VRIN*, *TRIN*, F_1, F_2, F, L, and K. The 15 MMPI–A content scales heavily overlap with both the MMPI–2 content scales (Butcher, Dahlstrom, Graham, Tellegen, & Kaemmer, 1989) and with the Wiggins Scales (Wiggins, 1966, 1969) created for use with the original MMPI.

The MMPI–A content scales were developed based on a combination of rational and statistical criteria as described in the MMPI–A manual (Butcher et al., 1992) and by Williams, Butcher, Ben-Porath, and Graham (1992) in a book specifically focused on the MMPI–A content scales.

The six supplementary scales for the MMPI–A include the continuation, in modified form, of three scales used with the original form of the MMPI. These scales are slightly shortened versions of Welsh's (1956) Anxiety (*A*) and Repression (*R*) scales, and a revision of the MacAndrew Alcoholism Scale (MacAndrew, 1965), the MacAndrew Alcoholism Scale–Revised (*MAC–R*). In addition, three supplementary scales were developed for the MMPI–A: the Immaturity (*IMM*) scale, the Alcohol/Drug Problem Acknowledgment (*ACK*) scale, and the Alcohol/Drug Problem Potential (*PRO*) scale.

The Harris-Lingoes content scales (Harris & Lingoes, 1955) developed for the original MMPI were carried over to the MMPI–A, with a few item deletions resulting from modifications of the item pool within the basic scales. The *Si* subscales are identical to the MMPI–2 *Si* subscales and are presented on the same MMPI–A profile sheet as the Harris-Lingoes subscales.

In addition to the 58 items deleted from the original standard scales of the MMPI (88% of these items occurring in relation to *F*, *Mf*, or *Si*), 69 items were modified from their appearance in the original test form. Archer and Gordon (1994) and Williams, Ben-Porath, and Hevern (1994) examined the equivalency of the revised form of these items in adolescent samples. The findings from these studies indicated that the items rewritten for the MMPI–A resulted in response frequencies similar to those of the original versions of these items.

The final version of the MMPI–A is a 478-item, true-false objective measure of psychopathology. Scoring for the instrument is accomplished through hand-scoring templates or by computer programs available through organizations licensed to score the MMPI–A by the University of Minnesota Press. The scoring of the MMPI–A continues the MMPI tradition of using a simple summation of items endorsed in the critical direction for a particular scale, without the use of differential weighting formulas for items. It should be noted, however, that the scoring formula for the *TRIN* scale, described in the test manual (Butcher et al., 1992), is more complex than that of other scales because the endorsement of certain item pairs may result in a *subtraction* from the total raw score value and because *TRIN* scale *T*-score values must be 50 or above.

MMPI–A Norms

The MMPI–A normative data were collected in eight states, seven of which also provided normative data for the MMPI–2. Adolescent normative subjects were generally solicited by mail from the student rosters of junior and senior high schools in preselected areas, and subjects were tested in group sessions usually conducted within school settings. Adolescents in all sites except New York were paid for their participation in the MMPI–A normative data collection, with subjects receiving $10 to $15 at the time of the their completion of the testing materials. New York subjects participated without reimbursement as part of school activities. In total, approximately 2,500 adolescents were evaluated in data collection procedures in California, Minnesota, New York, North Carolina, Ohio, Pennsylvania, Virginia, and Washington State.

A variety of exclusion criteria were applied to the collected data to create the final normative set. Subjects were excluded who did not complete all data collection measures, left more than 35 items unanswered on MMPI Form TX, or produced a raw score value of more than 25 on the *F* scale (using the original item pool for this scale). Subjects below 14 years of age or above 18 also were excluded from the normative sample.

The final MMPI–A norms were based on 805 male and 815 female respondents. The ethnic backgrounds of these subjects reflected a reasonably balanced sample, with approximately 76% of the data collected from White adolescents and roughly 12% from Black adolescents. The remaining 12% came from adolescents representing several ethnic groups, including Hispanic and Native American groups. The MMPI–A normative sample ethnic distribution appears reasonably consistent with U.S. Census figures, and several data collection sites were selected to increase the number of respondents from diverse ethnic backgrounds (Butcher et al., 1992).

Data presented in the MMPI–A manual (Butcher et al., 1992) summarize parental educational levels as reported by adolescents in the normative sample. These data show that the parents of the MMPI–A normative sample overrepresented the higher educational levels in comparison with the 1980 U.S. Census and clearly constitute a well-educated group (Archer, 1997). Approximately 50% of fathers and 40% of mothers of adolescents who participated in the MMPI–A normative sample had obtained an educational level equal to or greater than a baccalaureate degree. In comparison, the 1980 U.S. Census indicates that only 20% of males and 13% of females reported comparable educational levels. This degree of overrepresentation of better educated individuals in the MMPI–A sample is very similar to the educational bias found for the MMPI–2 adult normative sample (Archer, 1992b) and could be subject to some of the same debates focused on this issue in relation to the MMPI–2. Archer (1997) speculated that this type of educational and occupational bias is related to the use of unselected volunteer subjects in normative data collection, for such volunteers tend to come from better educated components of the society. Additional descriptive data concerning the MMPI–A normative sample, including adolescents' grade levels, parental occupational levels, and adolescents' living situations, are reported in the MMPI–A test manual (Butcher et al., 1992). Further, cross-national normative studies of the MMPI–A have been undertaken in Mexico (Negy, Leal-Puente, Trainor, & Carlson, 1997) and in Hong Kong with a Chinese translation of the MMPI–A (Cheung & Ho, 1997). A Spanish version of the MMPI–A is currently available, with a related validation study reported by Scott, Butcher, Young, and Gomez (2002), and several other translation projects are in progress (Archer & Krishnamurthy, 2002).

The MMPI–A norms are based on adolescents between the ages of 14 and 18 inclusive. The mean age for male adolescents in the MMPI–A normative sample is 15.5 years (*SD* = 1.17 years), and the mean age for females is 15.6 years (*SD* = 1.16 years). The age 18 adolescent group overlaps the 18-year-old subsample of the MMPI–2 norms, which means that an 18-year-old respondent could potentially be evaluated with either the MMPI–A or the MMPI–2. In this regard, the MMPI–A manual recommends the following criterion for determining the form most appropriate to evaluate the 18-year-old:

> A suggested guideline would be to use the MMPI–A for those 18-year-olds in high school and the MMPI–2 for those in college, working, or otherwise living a more independent adult life-style. The MMPI–A, not the MMPI–2, should always be used for those 17 years and younger, regardless of whether they are in school. (Butcher et al., 1992, p. 23)

In the application of this guideline, however, it is quite possible to encounter an occasional adolescent for whom the selection of the most appropriate form is difficult or ambiguous. For example, an 18-year-old single mother with a 6-month-old infant who is in her senior year in high school but living with her parents presents a considerable challenge in terms of identifying the most appropriate MMPI form for use with this individual. In such cases, an important question arises concerning what effects, if any, the selection of the MMPI–A versus the MMPI–2 might have on the resulting *T*-score profile. Shaevel and Archer (1996) examined the effects of scoring 18-year-old respondents on the MMPI–2 and the MMPI–A and found that substantial differences can occur in *T*-score elevations. Specifically, these authors reported that 18-year-olds scored on MMPI–2 norms generally produced lower validity scale values and higher clinical scale values than the same adolescents scored on MMPI–A norms. This broad pattern of differences is also generally consistent with findings from Gumbiner's (1997) study of a sample of 43 college students administered the MMPI–2 and MMPI–A and also consistent with Osberg and Poland's (2002) comparison of the MMPI–2 and MMPI–A used with 18-year-olds. Differences in the Shaevel and Archer (1996) study ranged as high as 15 *T*-score points and resulted in different single-scale and two-point profile configurations in 34% of the cases examined. Shaevel and Archer concluded that, for those relatively rare assessment cases in which the selection of the MMPI–A versus the MMPI–2 is a relatively difficult decision for the 18-year-old respondent, a reasonable practice would be to score the respondent on both the MMPI–A and MMPI–2 norms in order to permit the clinician to assess the effects of instrument selection on profile characteristics.

The lower end of the age range for the MMPI–A normative sample was 14. Preliminary data analyses were interpreted by MMPI–A Adolescent Project Committee members as indicating that 12- and 13-year-old subjects tended to produce substantially different normative values than those in the 14- to 18-year-old group; consequently, there were concerns regarding the usefulness of MMPI–A data produced by adolescents under age 14. The MMPI–A manual notes that the instrument can be used cautiously with 12- and 13-year-old respondents with an awareness of the higher rate of administration difficulties found in this population. Archer (1997) provided a set of MMPI–A adolescent norms for 13-year-old boys and girls. He based norms on linear *T*-score conversions and used the same exclusion criterion employed for the 14- to 18-year-old MMPI norms developed for the test instrument. In general, preliminary studies (Archer, 1997) appear to indicate that MMPI–A norms based on this 13-year-old sample tend to produce lower *T*-score values on most clinical scales in comparison with the 14- to 18-year-old MMPI–A norms applied to identical raw score values. Janus, deGroot, and Toepfer (1998) examined the effects of scoring with standard MMPI–A norms versus the 13-year-old norm set and concluded that the use of the 13-year-old norms resulted in a significantly higher percentage of cases falling in the clinical range for the *Hs* basic scale and the *A-dep* content scale. The 13-year-old norm set was created to promote research with this age group and to provide the clinician with the potential to evaluate a 12- or 13-year-old adolescent who meets all administration criteria on this specialized norm set *in conjunction with* the standard MMPI–A norms. Such a comparison would allow the clinician to refine interpretive comments based on the use of the standard MMPI–A norms by taking into account elevation differences found for the 13-year-old norm set. The profile interpretation, however, should be primarily based on the standard MMPI–A norms. The MMPI–A should not be employed with adolescents below the age of 12, and the 12- and 13-year-old age group will contain many adolescents unable to successfully read and comprehend the MMPI–A item pool.

For many years a sixth-grade reading level was generally accepted as the basic requirement for MMPI administration. The MMPI–2 manual (Butcher et al., 1989) indicates an eighth-grade reading level is required for successful MMPI–2 administration. Archer (1997) noted that over 80% of the MMPI–A item pool can be accurately read and comprehended by adolescents reading at the seventh-grade reading level. Archer and Krishnamurthy (2002) also reviewed a variety of methods of evaluating reading comprehension on the MMPI–A, including the use of total test administration time, *VRIN* scale values, and the random MMPI–A profile configuration expected for the basic scales and the content and supplementary scales.

Dahlstrom, Archer, Hopkins, Jackson, and Dahlstrom (1994) evaluated the reading difficulty of the MMPI, MMPI–2, and MMPI–A using various indices of reading difficulty. One important finding derived from this study was that the instructions provided in the MMPI test booklets tended to be somewhat more difficult to read than the items contained in the inventories. Therefore, clinicians should ensure that the instructions are fully understood by the respondents. It is often appropriate to ask the test taker to read the instructions aloud and explain their meaning in order to ensure adequate comprehension.

Dahlstrom et al. (1994) found that on average all three forms of the MMPI had approximately a 6th-grade level of difficulty. The MMPI–A test instructions and items were slightly easier to read than the MMPI–2 or the original form of the MMPI; however, the total differences tended to be relatively small. If the most difficult 10% of items were excluded, the remaining 90% of items on all three versions of the MMPI had on average a 5th-grade level of difficulty. The authors also reported that approximately 6% of the MMPI–A items required a 10th-grade reading level or better. On average, the most difficult items appeared on Scale 9, whereas the easiest items tended to be presented within the item pool of Scale 5. Dahlstrom et al. cautioned that the number of years of education completed is often an unreliable index of an individual's reading competence.

The MMPI–A, like the MMPI–2, employs both linear *T*-score and uniform *T*-score transformation procedures within its collection of scales. This is in contrast to the original adult norms and the adolescent norms developed by Marks and Briggs (1972) for the original form of the MMPI, which were exclusively based on linear transformations of raw scores into *T*-score values. The MMPI–A retained the use of linear *T*-score transformations for all validity scales and for MMPI–A basic scales 5 and 0. Additionally, linear *T*-score transformations were employed for all 6 MMPI–A supplementary scales and for all scales appearing on the Harris-Lingoes and *Si* subscales profile sheet. In contrast, 8 of the clinical scales on the MMPI–A basic scale profile (1, 2, 3, 4, 6, 7, 8, and 9) and all of the 15 content scales employ uniform *T*-score transformations. These latter two scale groupings were selected for uniform *T*-score transformations because these clinical scales produced similar score distributions and because scales within each set (i.e., the basic and content scales) were developed using similar construction strategies. The rationale and methods involved in uniform *T*-score transformations are discussed extensively in the MMPI–A manual (Butcher et al., 1992). In general, uniform *T*-score transformations produce *T*-score values that essentially represent the average linear *T*-score found for the scales employed in the composite distributions for the basic scales and the content scales analyzed separately by gender. The *T*-score values obtained by uniform *T*-score transformations are quite similar to those that would be obtained from linear *T*-score conversions for a given scale. The purpose of the uniform *T*-score procedure is to produce *T*-score values with equivalent percentile value meanings across scales for a given *T*-score. This procedure, however, also maintains the underlying positive skew in the distribution of scores from these measures; thus, uniform *T*-scores do not convert to percentile values that would be expected if scores were normally distributed (e.g., a uniform *T*-score value of 50 does not convert to the 50th percentile on the MMPI–A but rather to the 55th percentile).

Most of the differences found between the Marks and Briggs (1972) norms for the original form of the MMPI and the MMPI–A norms are not attributable to the issue of uniform versus linear *T*-score transformation procedures. Rather, these *T*-score differences result from the substantial differences in the raw score means and standard deviations produced by the two normative groups on most basic scales. The overall effect of these differences, as will be discussed later, is that MMPI–A *T*-score values for a given raw score tend to be lower than those produced by the Marks and Briggs traditional norms. Appendix G of the MMPI–A manual and Appendix E of Archer (1997) provide *T*-score conversion tables to permit estimates of the Marks and Briggs normative values that would be produced for a given MMPI–A basic scale raw score value. This allows the clinician to evaluate the similarity between the profile that would have been produced on the original MMPI by the adolescent's item responses and the profile obtained on the MMPI–A. The issue of similarity is relevant to the degree to which the research literature developed for the original MMPI may be generalized for use in the interpretation of MMPI–A findings for a specific adolescent.

Basic Validity and Reliability Information

The MMPI–A manual (Butcher et al., 1992) provides information concerning the test-retest reliability, internal consistency, and factor structure of the MMPI–A scales. The test-retest correlations for the MMPI–A basic scales range from $r = .49$ for F_1 to $r = .84$ for *Si* and are very similar to the test-retest correlations found for the MMPI–2 basic scales. Stein, McClinton, and Graham (1998) evaluated the long-term (1-year) test-retest stability of the MMPI–A scales and reported basic clinical scale values ranging from $r = .51$ for *Pa* to $r = .75$ for *Si*. Test-retest correlations for the content scales ranged from $r = .40$ for *A-trt* to $r = .73$ for *A-sch*. The typical standard error of measurement for the basic scales is estimated to be two to three raw score points (Butcher et al., 1992). The internal consistency of the MMPI–A scales, as represented in coefficient alpha values, ranges from low to moderate values found for scales such as *Mf* ($r = .43$) and *Pa* ($r = .57$) to high ($r \geq .80$) values found for many of the content scales and the *IMM* scale. These latter scales were constructed using methods designed to produce high internal consistency values. The factor analytic findings for the MMPI–A are reasonably consistent with prior factor analytic findings reported in adolescent populations for the original MMPI (Archer, 1984; Archer & Klinefelter, 1991).

Validity data from normal and clinical samples of adolescents are also presented in the MMPI–A manual. In addition to MMPI Form TX, the MMPI–A normative sample was administered a 16-item biographical information form and a 74-item life stress events questionnaire. These forms served as external correlate sources to evaluate the concurrent validity of the MMPI–A. The MMPI–A manual also reports validity findings for a clinical sample of 420 boys and 293 girls between the ages of 14 and 18 receiving psychological services in Minnesota. In addition, Archer (1997) provides MMPI–A scale correlate data from a sample of 128 adolescent inpatients collected in Virginia.

Several studies have examined the psychometric characteristics or correlates of specific aspects of the MMPI–A. Imhof and Archer (1997) examined the concurrent validity of the Immaturity (*IMM*) scale based on a residential treatment sample of 66 adolescents aged 13 through 18 years. The MMPI–A *IMM* scale was developed to provide an objective measure of ego development or maturation. Participants were administered the MMPI–A, the Defining Issues Test (DIT), a short form of the Washington University Sentence Completion Test (WUSCT), the Extended Objective Measure of Ego Identity Status–Second Revision (EOM–EIS–2), and standardized measures of intelligence and reading ability. The results of this study provided evidence of the concurrent validity of the *IMM* scale, and a number of *IMM* correlate descriptors were reported. Meaningful *IMM* scale correlates and characteristics have also been reported by Milne and Greenway (1999) and Zinn, McCumber, and Dahlstrom (1999).

Archer and Jacobson (1993) examined the endorsement frequency of the Koss and Butcher (1973) and Lachar and Wrobel (1979) critical items resulting from administrations of the MMPI–A to normal and clinical adolescent samples and compared these results to MMPI–2 findings for adults. The data showed that adolescents in both normal and clinical samples endorse critical items with a higher frequency than do normal adults. Further, significant differences were uniformly found between the endorsement frequencies for normative versus clinical subjects for the MMPI–2 samples, whereas similar comparisons for the MMPI–A samples typically showed that adolescents in clinical settings did not endorse critical items more frequently than normal adolescents. These findings indicate the difficulties in constructing critical item lists for adolescents based on the type of empirical methodology used with adults, in which items are selected based on endorsement frequency differences found between comparison groups. Despite these challenges, however, Forbey and Ben-Porath (1998) recently identified a set of 82 critical items covering 15 content groups, including Aggression, Eating Problems, and Substance Use/Abuse. Items were selected based on a combination of response frequency comparisons in the normal and clinical adolescent samples as well as the application of expert judgment criteria. The Forbey and Ben-Porath MMPI–A critical item set merits focused research to evaluate the effectiveness and appropriate uses of these items.

Finally, Alperin, Archer, and Coates (1996) attempted to derive age-appropriate *K*-weights for the MMPI–A to determine the degree to which the use of this procedure could improve test accuracy in the classification of participants into normal and clinical groups. Discriminant function analyses were performed to determine the *K*-weight that, when combined with basic scale raw score values, optimally predicted normal versus clinical status for each of the eight basic clinical scales. Hit rate analyses were utilized to assess the degree to which *K*-corrected *T*-scores resulted in improvements in classification accuracy in contrast to standard MMPI–A non-*K*-corrected norms. The findings indicate that the adoption of a *K*-correction procedure for the MMPI–A does not result in systematic improvements in test accuracy, and they do not support the clinical use of a *K*-correction factor for interpreting MMPI–A protocols.

Basic Interpretive Strategy

Several guides have been provided for the interpretation of the MMPI–A, including extensive discussion in the test manual (Butcher et al., 1992) and recommendations by Archer (1997), Archer and Krishnamurthy (2002), Butcher and Williams (2000), and Williams et al. (1992). Table 4.2 provides a brief overview of the interpretive approach offered by Archer (1997).

The first two steps presented in this model emphasize the importance of considering the setting where the MMPI–A is administered and the history and background information available for the adolescent. As reviewed in Archer (1997), the original form of the MMPI has been used for research and clinical purposes with adolescents in a variety of settings, including public and private schools, medical groups, alcohol and drug treatment settings, correctional and juvenile delinquency programs, and outpatient and inpatient psychiatric settings. It is always important, in order to

TABLE 4.2
Steps in MMPI–A Profile Interpretation

1. Setting in which the MMPI–A is administered
   a. Clinical/psychological/psychiatric
   b. School/academic evaluation
   c. Medical
   d. Neuropsychological
   e. Forensic
   f. Alcohol/drug treatment
2. History and background of patient
   a. Cooperativeness/motivation for treatment or evaluation
   b. Cognitive ability
   c. History of psychological adjustment
   d. History of stress factors
   e. History of academic performance
   f. History of interpersonal relationships
   g. Family history and characteristics
3. Validity
   a. Omissions
   b. Consistency of responses
   c. Accuracy of responses
4. Codetype (provides main features of interpretation)
   a. Degree of match with prototype
      (1) Degree of elevation
      (2) Degree of definition
      (3) Caldwell A-B-C-D Paradigm for multiple high-points
   b. Low-point scales
   c. Note elevation of scales 2 (*D*) and 7 (*Pt*)
5. Supplementary scales (supplement and confirm interpretation)
   a. Factor 1 and Factor 2 issues
      (1) Welsh *A* and *R*
   b. Substance abuse scales
      (1) *MAC-R* and *PRO*
      (2) *ACK*
   c. Psychological maturation
      (1) *IMM* scale
6. Content scales
   a. Supplement, refine, and confirm basic scale data
   b. Interpersonal functioning (*A-fam*, *A-cyn*, *A-aln*), treatment recommendations (*A-trt*), and academic difficulties (*A-sch* and *A-las*)
   c. Consider effects of overreporting/underreporting
7. Review of Harris-Lingoes subscales and the Forbey and Ben-Porath critical items
   a. Items endorsed can assist in understanding reasons for elevation of basic scales
8. Structural Summary (factor approach)
   a. Identify factor dimensions most relevant in describing the adolescent's psychopathology
   b. Use to confirm and refine traditional interpretation
   c. Consider effects of overreporting/underreporting on factor patterns

Note. From *MMPI–A: Assessing Adolescent Psychopathology* (2nd ed., p. 272), by R. P. Archer, 1997, Mahwah, NJ: Lawrence Erlbaum Associates. Copyright 1997 by Lawrence Erlbaum Associates. Reprinted with permission.

increase the accuracy and utility of inferences derived from the MMPI–A, to combine MMPI–A test data with the results of other psychological tests and with demographic, psychosocial history, and psychiatric history information collected in individual and family interviews.

The third step noted in Table 4.2 involves the evaluation of the technical validity of the MMPI–A profile. This process begins with a review of the number of items omitted in the response process. The recommendation is that the profile be viewed as invalid if more than 30 item omissions have occurred in the response record. Validity assessment continues with an evaluation of the degree to which the adolescent responded in a consistent manner (e.g., *VRIN* and *TRIN* scale scores) and in an accurate manner (the *F*, *L*, and *K* configural pattern) using the validity assessment model proposed by Greene (1989, 2000). In this model, a distinction is made between *response consistency*, defined as the extent to which the respondent endorses items in a reliable pattern, and *response accuracy*, defined as the degree to which the respondent has overreported or underreported symptomatology. Response consistency may be viewed as a necessary but not a sufficient condition for technical validity. The tendency to overreport or underreport symptomatology, in turn, may be seen as relatively independent of the respondent's actual level of symptomatology (Greene, 1989, 2000).

The fourth step in MMPI–A interpretation involves the review of the basic scale clinical profile. This review should examine the degree to which one or more basic scales manifest clinical-range elevations and the relative magnitude of these elevations. In general, the greater the magnitude of an adolescent's *T*-score on a particular basic scale, the more likely the respondent is accurately described by the correlates typically associated with elevations on that scale. In addition, the degree of correspondence between the profile configuration and the existing two-point codetype literature should be examined. In this regard, the degree of definition manifested by an adolescent's two-point code also should be evaluated, with the two-point codetype defined by the degree of *T*-score elevation difference between the second and third highest elevations within the clinical profile. The greater the degree of definition for the two-point code, the more likely the descriptive statements associated with that codetype are accurate for a particular adolescent. If an adolescent's MMPI–A profile does not display clearly elevated and defined two-point code characteristics, the profile may be interpreted by an approach emphasizing individual scale descriptors (Archer, 1997; Butcher et al., 1992). Basic individual scale descriptors have been established based on the empirical literature for the original instrument in adolescent samples and for the MMPI–A summarized in the test manual (Butcher et al., 1992). In the case of an MMPI–A basic scale profile that displays clinical-range elevations on more than two clinical scales, the A-B-C-D paradigm developed by Alex Caldwell (1976) also may be employed for profile interpretation purposes. This latter approach emphasizes the common descriptor characteristics generated from multiple two-point configurations. For example, a 2-4-7 codetype would be broken into two-point codes and interpreted based on common descriptors found for the 2-4, 2-7, and 4-7 codetypes.

The two-point codetype correlate literature rests on the work of Marks, Seeman, and Haller (1974), and this literature has been summarized and extended by Archer (1997) for the MMPI–A. In this regard, Janus, Tolbert, Calestro, and Toepfer (1996) investigated the accuracy of MMPI–A codetype narratives in a sample of 134 adolescent psychiatric inpatients. The single and two-point codetype narratives generated for each patient from two sets of adolescent norms and one set of adult norms were blindly rated along various accuracy dimensions by inpatient treatment staff. Results indicated that the MMPI–A produced higher accuracy ratings when codetype narratives were based on either the original set of adolescent norms developed by Marks and Briggs (1972) or standard MMPI–A adolescent norms than when adult *K*-corrected norms were used to generate codetype narratives. The study by Janus et al. (1996) is an important initial step in establishing the clinical utility of codetype interpretation with the MMPI–A.

A review of the MMPI–A supplementary and content scales is involved in Steps 5 and 6. Supplementary scales *A* and *R* provide overall estimates of the adolescent's degree of maladjustment and the use of repression as a primary defense mechanism, respectively. Extensive substance abuse screening information is available through the combined use of the supplementary scales *MAC–R*, *ACK*, and *PRO*. In particular, the adolescent's willingness to acknowledge substance abuse problems is reflected in *ACK* scale scores, and the adolescent's similarity to teenagers with known substance abuse problems is assessed through responses to the *MAC–R* and *PRO* scales. The supplementary *IMM* scale also allows for an assessment of the adolescent's maturational level as related to cognitive processes, ability to engage meaningfully in interpersonal relationships, and degree of egocentricity and frustration tolerance (Archer, Pancoast, & Gordon, 1994).

The 15 content scales provide valuable information for refining and augmenting the interpretation of the basic scales (Williams et al., 1992). For example, scores from *A-anx* may be helpful in refining the interpretation of basic scale 7, scale *A-biz* may be useful in clarifying the interpretation of scale 8, and scales such as *A-con* and *A-fam* may be useful in refining the interpretation of MMPI basic scale 4. Further, scales such as *A-trt* may be useful in evaluating the adolescent's readiness to engage in a therapy process, particularly when used in conjunction with scales *L* and *K*. Content scales such as *A-fam*, *A-cyn*, and *A-aln* provide valuable information about the adolescent's interpersonal functioning, and scales such as *A-sch* and *A-las* provide important information about possible problems in the academic environment. In evaluating the findings from the content scales, it is important to consider the effects of overreporting and underreporting on profile accuracy because the content scales consist primarily of obvious and face valid items (Archer, 1997). Thus, the content scales can easily be biased by the adolescent's attempt to underreport or overreport symptomatology. Further, Sherwood, Ben-Porath, and Williams (1997) recently developed a total of 31 subscales to facilitate interpretation of 13 of the 15 content scales (the authors were unable to identify meaningful item clusters for *A-anx* and *A-obs*). These MMPI–A content component scales should prove useful in refining the meaning of content scale elevations by allowing for more specific descriptors for these elevations.

In the seventh stage of profile analysis, the clinician may wish to further consider and evaluate the content of the adolescent's MMPI–A responses. This may entail a selective review of the Harris-Lingoes and *Si* subscales and may also include a cautious review of responses to the MMPI–A critical items list developed by Forbey and Ben-Porath (1998). In reviewing critical items, it should be remembered that responses to any individual MMPI–A items are inherently unreliable and that normal adolescents tend to endorse critical items with a relatively high frequency. Archer (1997) and Archer and Krishnamurthy (2002) offered guidelines for the interpretation of content subscales, and as previously noted Sherwood et al. (1997) presented potentially useful content component scales.

In the final (eighth) stage of profile analysis, the interpreter may wish to use the MMPI–A Structural Summary form to organize MMPI–A scale data in a manner that identifies the most salient dimensions of the adolescent's current functioning. The first seven steps of the interpretive approach provide correlates and inferences concerning the adolescent's behaviors based on an organization of scales into traditional categories such as validity scales, basic clinical scales, content and supplementary scales, and Harris-Lingoes and *Si* subscales. The Structural Summary approach promotes a comprehensive assessment of the adolescent's functioning, deemphasizing the largely arbitrary distinction between categories of scales. The use of this approach serves to remind the clinician that data derived from the MMPI–A scales are highly intercorrelated and reflective of broad underlying dimensions of psychological functioning.

The interpretive guidelines for the Structural Summary form involve the following two propositions:

1. The higher the percentage of scales and subscales within a factor that produce critical values, the greater the role of that factor or dimension in providing a comprehensive description of the adolescent.
2. A majority of the scales or subscales associated with the particular factor must reach critical values ($T \geq 60$ or $T \leq 40$ depending on the scale or subscale) before the interpreter emphasizes that dimension as salient in describing the adolescent's personality characteristics.

The first section of the Structural Summary organizes information relevant to the evaluation of the validity of the MMPI–A along three dimensions, which include the number of item omissions, indices related to response consistency, and indices of response accuracy. The remainder of the Structural Summary presents groupings of MMPI–A scales and subscales organized around the eight factors identified by Archer, Belevich, and Elkins (1994) in the MMPI–A normative sample and replicated by Archer and Krishnamurthy (1997b) in a clinical sample of 358 adolescents and by Archer, Bolinskey, Morton, and Farris (2002) in a male sample of adolescents in juvenile detention. Within each factor, scales and subscales are grouped logically within the traditional categories of basic scales, content scales, and supplementary scales. Within each of these groupings, scales are presented in descending order from those measures that have the highest correlation with a particular factor (i.e., those scales and subscales serving as the most effective markers) to those scales that show progressively lower correlations with the total factor. With very few exceptions, the scales and subscales presented in the Structural Summary produce correlations of .60 and above or −.60 and below with their assigned factor. The Structural Summary also presents spaces at the bottom of each factor grouping to derive the total number (or percentage) of scales that show critical values for a specific factor.

The underlying purpose of the MMPI–A Structural Summary is to help the clinician parsimoniously organize the myriad data provided by the MMPI–A to assist in identifying the most salient dimensions to be utilized in describing the adolescent's personality functioning. Archer and Krishnamurthy (1994) provided a description of the empirical correlates of the MMPI–A Structural Summary factors based on an investigation of the 1,620 adolescents in the MMPI–A normative sample and an inpatient sample of 122 adolescent respondents. A comprehensive presentation of all external correlates of the Structural Summary factors is provided in the *MMPI–A Casebook* by Archer, Krishnamurthy, and Jacobson (1994), and a narrative summary of these correlates is provided in Table 4.3. Krishnamurthy and Archer (1999) examined the

TABLE 4.3
Description of the MMPI–A Structural Summary Factors

Factor	*Description*
General Maladjustment (23 scales or subscales)	This factor is associated with substantial emotional distress and maladjustment. Adolescents who score high on this dimension experience significant problems in adjustment at home and school and feel different from other teenagers. They are likely to be self-conscious, socially withdrawn, timid, unpopular, dependent on adults, ruminative, subject to sudden mood changes, and to feel sad or depressed. They are viewed as less competent in social activities and as avoiding competitive situations with peers. These adolescents are more likely than other teenagers to report symptoms of tiredness or fatigue, sleep difficulties, and suicidal thoughts, and to be referred for counseling and/or psychotherapy. Academic problems including low marks and course failures are common, and they are likely to be referred for counseling or psychotherapy.
Immaturity (15 scales or subscales)	The Immaturity dimension reflects attitudes and behaviors involving egocentricity and self-centeredness, limited self-awareness and insight, poor judgment and impulse control, and disturbed interpersonal relationships. Adolescents who obtain high scores on this factor often have problems in the school setting involving disobedience, suspensions, and histories of poor school performance. Their interpersonal relationships are marked by cruelty, bullying, and threats, and they often associate with peers who get in trouble. These adolescents act without thinking and display little remorse for their actions. Familial relationships are frequently strained, with an increased occurrence of arguments with parents. Their family lives are also often marked by instability that may include parental separation or divorce. High-scoring boys are more likely to exhibit hyperactive and immature behaviors whereas girls are prone to display aggressive and delinquent conduct.
Disinhibition/ Excitatory Potential (12 scales or subscales)	High scores in this dimension involve attitudes and behaviors related to disinhibition and poor impulse control. Adolescents who score high on this factor display significant impulsivity, disciplinary problems, and conflicts with parents and peers. They are perceived as boastful, excessively talkative, unusually loud, and attention-seeking. They display increased levels of heterosexual interest and require frequent supervision in peer contacts. High-scoring adolescents typically have histories of poor school work and failing grades, truancy, disciplinary actions including suspensions, school drop-out, and violations of social norms in the home, school, and social environment. Their interpersonal relationships tend to be dominant and aggressive, and they quickly become negative or resistant with authority figures. These adolescents are likely to engage in alcohol/drug use or abuse. Their behavioral problems include stealing, lying, cheating, obscene language, verbal abuse, fighting, serious disagreements with parents, and running away from home. In general, they may be expected to use externalization as a primary defense mechanism.
Social Discomfort (8 scales or subscales)	Adolescents who elevate the scales involved in this dimension are likely to feel withdrawn, self-conscious, and uncertain in social situations, and display a variety of internalizing behaviors. They are frequently bossed or dominated by peers and tend to be fringe participants in social activities. These adolescents are typically perfectionistic and avoid competition with peers. They are viewed by others as fearful, timid, passive or docile, and acting young for their age. They may present complaints of tiredness, apathy, loneliness, suicidal ideation, and somatic complaints. These adolescents have a low probability of acting-out behaviors including disobedience, alcohol or drug use, stealing, or behavioral problems in school.

(Continued)

TABLE 4.3
(Continued)

Factor	*Description*
Health Concerns (6 scales or subscales)	Adolescents who obtain high scores on the Health Concerns dimension are seen by others as dependent, socially isolated, shy, sad, and unhappy. They are prone to tire quickly and have relatively low levels of endurance. They may display a history of weight loss and report sleep difficulties, crying spells, suicidal ideation, and academic problems. A history of sexual abuse may be present. High-scoring boys are likely to be viewed as exhibiting schizoid withdrawal whereas high-scoring girls are primarily seen as somatizers. These adolescents typically display lower levels of social competence in the school setting. They are unlikely to be involved in antisocial behaviors or have histories of arrests.
Naivete (5 scales or subscales)	High scores on the Naivete factor are produced by adolescents who tend to deny the presence of hostile or negative impulses and present themselves in a trusting, optimistic, and socially conforming manner. They may be described as less likely to be involved in impulsive, argumentative, or socially inappropriate behaviors, and are more often seen as presenting in an age-appropriate manner. They have a low probability of experiencing internalizing symptoms such as nervousness, fearfulness, nightmares, and feelings of worthlessness, or of acting-out and provocative behaviors including lying or cheating, disobedience, and obscene language.
Familial Alienation (4 scales or subscales)	Adolescents who score high on scales or subscales related to this dimension are more likely to be seen by their parents as hostile, delinquent, or aggressive, and as utilizing externalizing defenses. They are also viewed as being loud, verbally abusive, threatening, and disobedient at home. These adolescents tend to have poor parental relationships involving frequent and serious conflicts with their parents. Presenting problems in psychiatric settings may include histories of running away from home, sexual abuse, and alcohol/drug use. In addition to family conflicts, high-scoring adolescents are also more likely to have disciplinary problems at school resulting in suspensions and probationary actions.
Psychoticism (4 scales or subscales)	Adolescents who produce elevations on the Psychoticism factor are more likely to be seen by others as obsessive, socially disengaged, and disliked by peers. They may feel that others are out to get them, and are more likely to be teased and rejected by their peer group. Sudden mood changes and poorly modulated expressions of anger are likely. They may also exhibit disordered behaviors including cruelty to animals, property destruction, and fighting, and are likely to have histories of poor academic achievement.

Note. From *MMPI–A Casebook* (pp. 17–18), by R. P. Archer, R. Krishnamurthy, and J. M. Jacobson, 1994, Odessa, FL: Psychological Assessment Resources. Copyright 1994 by Psychological Assessment Resources, Inc. Reprinted with permission.

efficacy of two methods of Structural Summary interpretation and reported that simply counting the number of scales and subscales elevated within a particular factor dimension was roughly as effective as computing the mean *T*-score value for each dimension. This finding has recently been replicated in independent research by Pogge, Stokes, McGrath, Bilginer, and DeLuca (2002) in a sample of 632 adolescent psychiatric inpatients. Therefore, this "checkmark" method is recommended as a quick and effective way of determining if a particular factor is salient in the psychological description of an adolescent.

Computer-Based Test Interpretation (CBTI)

There are several computer-based test interpretation (CBTI) packages that are currently available for the MMPI–A. These include the revised MMPI–A CBTI report developed by Archer (1992a, 1996) and an MMPI–A CBTI report developed by James N. Butcher and Carolyn L. Williams (1992). Both CBTI products are based on combinations of expert judgment and actuarial data. Archer (1997), Archer and Krishnamurthy (2002), and Butcher (1987) provide guidelines for the evaluation and assessment of CBTI products, including the relative advantages and disadvantages associated with this approach. It should be emphasized that the use of a CBTI product in the interpretation of the MMPI–A (or any other assessment instrument) does not reduce the clinicians' responsibility for the accuracy of their interpretation of the individual patient's profile.

USE OF THE MMPI–A IN TREATMENT PLANNING

General Treatment Planning Issues

Archer, Maruish, Imhof, and Piotrowski (1991) surveyed 165 clinicians who routinely evaluated teenage clients and asked respondents who used the original form of the MMPI to indicate its primary advantages and disadvantages. The results indicate that its advantages were its usefulness in treatment planning, including the accuracy of interpretive statements generated from profile information; the comprehensiveness of the measures of psychopathology assessed by the instrument; and the extensive research literature available to assist in the interpretation process. The major disadvantages were the length of the item pool and administration time required, the outdated aspects of the adolescent norms, the instrument's reading requirements, and the inclusion of inappropriate or outdated items.

The developers of the MMPI–A attempted to address most of these problem areas by reducing the instrument's length, providing contemporary norms, and revising many items to simplify wording and increase the appropriateness of item content. A recent clinician survey by Archer and Newsom (2000) found that the MMPI–A has quickly become the most widely used objective personality assessment instrument for adolescents. Nevertheless, the MMPI–A manifests many of the same advantages and disadvantages as the original instrument.

Despite potential improvements in the MMPI–A, the revised instrument requires substantial patience on the part of the adolescent to deal with the lengthy item pool and demands a level of literacy that renders administration problematic with many adolescents. It is also important to recognize that the MMPI–A, like the original MMPI, is designed as a measure of psychopathology rather than an assessment instrument appropriate for the evaluation of normal-range personality dimensions. Thus, the information drawn from the MMPI–A has limited value for identifying adaptive functioning characteristics or nonpathological dimensions beyond masculinity-femininity (*Mf*), social introversion-extroversion (*Si*), and possibly some of the content domain of the Immaturity (*IMM*) scale. Additionally, as discussed in Archer (1997) and Archer and Krishnamurthy (2002), both the MMPI and the MMPI–A are best used as measures for determining the individual's current level of functioning in relationship to standardized measures of psychopathology. Moreover, the MMPI–A, like its predecessor, does not generally yield data useful for making long-range predictions of personality functioning due to the instability manifested in adolescents' psychopathology and the consequent instability of test findings over extended periods (e.g., Hathaway & Monachesi, 1963).

Research Findings and Clinical Applications

Most clinicians see the development of an accurate and comprehensive diagnosis as central to the design of an effective intervention or treatment plan. A substantial literature therefore relates several diagnostic groupings or issues to relatively specific MMPI profile patterns. As noted in the MMPI–A manual (Butcher et al., 1992), the original version of the MMPI was used to examine a variety of diagnostic issues among adolescents, including behavioral problems, borderline personality disorder, depressed mood, eating disorders, homicidal behavior, aggression, incest and sexual abuse, sleeping problems, medical and neurological problems, schizophrenia, and suicide. The earliest research application of the MMPI with adolescents centered on the usefulness of this instrument for identifying groups of delinquent adolescents (Capwell, 1945a, 1945b). In a research study begun in 1947, Hathaway and Monachesi (1963) examined its ability to predict the onset of delinquent behaviors in Minnesota samples involving approximately 15,000 adolescents. In their research findings, these authors reported modest relationships between adolescents' original MMPI profiles and the later onset of delinquent behaviors. Hathaway and Monachesi found that elevations on scales 4, 8, and 9, singly or in combination, were associated with higher rates of delinquent behavior, and they labeled these three scales *excitatory* scales. Hathaway and Monachesi also noted much instability in the elevation pattern in adolescents' profiles when ninth-graders were reevaluated during their senior year in high school. They did observe, however, that adolescents who produced marked elevations during the ninth-grade assessment were more likely to show relative stability on those scales when reevaluated three years later.

The relationship between MMPI data and clinicians' diagnostic judgments has been examined in several studies within adolescent samples. Archer and Gordon (1988) investigated the relationship between scale 2 and scale 8 elevations and the occurrence of clinical diagnoses related to depression and schizophrenia in a sample of 134 adolescent inpatients. The authors found little evidence of a meaningful relationship between scale 2 elevations and clinicians' use of depression-related diagnoses. However, they did report that scale 8 elevation was an effective and sensitive indicator of schizophrenic diagnoses. Employing the criterion that *T*-score values equal to or above 75 on scale 8, used to identify schizophrenia in this study, resulted in an overall classification accuracy rate of 0.76. This level of performance is comparable to findings reported for scale 8 in adult populations (e.g., Hathaway, 1956).

An investigation by Archer and Krishnamurthy (1997a) extended the earlier Archer and Gordon research by examining the extent to which combining indices from the MMPI–A and the revised Rorschach Comprehensive System (Exner, 1986) furnishes incremental validity in terms of improved diagnostic prediction. The predictive accuracy of selected MMPI–A and Rorschach variables conceptually related to diagnoses of depression and conduct disorder were compared in a clinical sample of 152 adolescents. Results of these analyses revealed some significant differences between diagnostic groups on several MMPI–A scales and one significant difference on the Rorschach involving the *Vista* variable. Stepwise discriminant function analyses resulted in two MMPI–A scales and two Rorschach variables that collectively accounted for a small proportion of variance in the diagnosis of depression and three MMPI–A scales that accounted for a significant component of variance in the conduct disorder diagnosis. Classification accuracy results indicated that the hit rate for the depression diagnosis did not improve using an optimal linear combination of these four variables over the .68 hit rates produced by single use of either the MMPI–A Depression content scale (*A-dep*) or scale 2. For the conduct disorder diagnosis, the optimal linear combination of the MMPI–A Conduct Problems (*A-con*), Cynicism (*A-cyn*), and *IMM* scales served as the best predictor, and no Rorschach variables contributed significantly to classification accuracy. These results replicated the findings of Archer and Gordon (1988) in indicating that the combined use of MMPI–A and Rorschach variables does not appear to produce incremental increases in accuracy of diagnostic classification.

Johnson, Archer, Sheaffer, and Miller (1992) investigated the relationships between characteristics of MMPI and Millon Adolescent Personality Inventory (MAPI) profiles and psychiatric diagnoses in a sample of 199 adolescent inpatients and outpatients. The results indicated low levels of congruence between MMPI-derived diagnoses and clinician judgments. This finding is consistent with those typically obtained by researchers in adult populations employing broad diagnostic groups (e.g., Hedlund, Won Cho, & Wood, 1977; Moreland, 1983; Pancoast, Archer, & Gordon, 1988). The results of these studies underscore the need for caution in using the MMPI, or any other personality measure used in isolation, to arrive at definitive psychiatric diagnoses for patients. Graham (2000) noted that the poor correspondence traditionally found between MMPI results and psychiatric diagnoses may be a result of the high degree of intercorrelation between standard MMPI scales as well as the unreliability of specific diagnostic groups employed by Hathaway and McKinley in the original MMPI. These findings also likely reflect the well-established problems in reliability that appear to be inherent in the psychiatric nosology embodied in the *Diagnostic and Statistic Manual* (DSM) series.

MMPI–A Scales Related to Treatment Planning

The MMPI–A includes a variety of scales relevant to a number of treatment-planning issues. For example, research by Archer, White, and Orvin (1979) associated higher scores on validity scales *L* and *K* with longer treatment durations for hospitalized adolescents. Elevations on Welsh's Repression (*R*) scale, and the Negative Treatment Indicators (*A-trt*) content scale also appear to be relevant to evaluating the adolescent's readiness and capacity to engage in the treatment process. Basic scale measures, including scales 2 and 7, and the supplementary scale Anxiety (*A*) have direct relevance for estimating the degree of affective distress experienced by the adolescent. The degree of distress is also illuminated by the content scales Anxiety (*A-anx*), Obsessiveness (*A-obs*), and Depression (*A-dep*). Impulse and behavioral control issues, as noted in the discussion of excitatory scales, are related to elevations on the basic scales 4, 8, and 9. They are also related to findings from supplementary scale *IMM* and content scales such as Conduct Disorder (*A-con*), Anger (*A-ang*), and Cynicism (*A-cyn*). Potential problems can be identified in a number of specific life areas using the MMPI–A, including the academic environment (*A-sch, A-las*) and the family environment (*A-fam*). Some recent MMPI–A research has also focused on the issue of suicidal ideation and suicidal risk factors. Archer and Slesinger (1999), for example, evaluated basic scale profiles related to endorsement of the three MMPI–A items (items 177, 283, and 399) reflecting the presence of suicidal ideation. Kopper, Osman, Osman, and Hoffman (1998) found that scores from MMPI–A basic scales *D*, *Pd*, and *Ma* significantly contributed to the prediction of self-reported suicide risk for both boys and girls on the Suicide Probability Scale. Further, the inclusion of scores from selected MMPI–A

Harris-Lingoes and content scales provided increased accuracy in the prediction of suicide probability beyond the levels obtained solely from the basic clinical scales.

Also of note are the relative contributions of the *MAC–R, ACK,* and *PRO* scales to screening and evaluation of substance abuse problems among teenagers. A number of more recent studies have examined the relationship between scores on the MMPI–A and delinquency or substance abuse behaviors. Toyer and Weed (1998), for example, found that higher scores on the *MAC-R, A-con, A-sch, Pd,* and *IMM* characterized a sample of juvenile offenders, and Gallucci (1997) found scores on the *MAC-R, D, Pd, Ma, Hy, PRO,* and *ACK* useful in categorizing 180 adolescent substance abusers into groups varying in behavioral undercontrol. Micucci (2002) reported that the *ACK, MAC-R,* and *PRO* were effective in identifying substance abusers and particularly nonabusers across gender and ethnic backgrounds, with the greatest accuracy associated with codetypes that include scales 1, 2, 3, 5 and 0. In addition, Marks et al. (1974) noted an association between several two-point codetypes, including 2-4/4-2 and 4-9/9-4, and the occurrence of abuse or alcohol problems. Archer and Klinefelter (1992) demonstrated that, in a sample of 1,347 adolescents in clinical settings, certain MMPI codetypes, particularly those involving elevations on scale 4 or scale 9, are much more likely to be associated with elevations on the *MAC* scale.

As noted by Archer (1987, 1997) and by Archer and Krishnamurthy (2002), the MMPI has proved to be a very useful tool in treatment planning for adolescents for over 40 years. It is likely that the MMPI–A will also be valuable, particularly as more information becomes available concerning the correlate patterns for the new MMPI–A scales. McNulty, Harkness, Ben-Porath, and Williams (1997), for example, recently developed a set of MMPI–A-based PSY-5 scales that measure the constructs of Aggressiveness, Psychoticism, Constraint, Negative Emotionality/Neuroticism, and Positive Emotionality/Extraversion. Although more research is needed on the MMPI–A PSY–5 scales to determine the clinical usefulness of these measures, the initial findings provide evidence of promising psychometric properties and correlation patterns in both normal and clinical settings. Handel, Arnau, Archer, and Bolinskey (2002) recently reported independent psychometric data for the MMPI–A PSY-5 scales and also described a set of scale-level facets or subscales they developed for these measures.

Integration of MMPI–A Results With Other Evaluation Data for Prediction of Therapeutic Outcome

Findings from the MMPI–A should be routinely integrated with results from other test instruments and with clinical interview, family assessment, and psychosocial history data in developing diagnostic and treatment recommendations. Gallucci (1990) reviewed the literature related to the combination of MMPI results with data from other instruments, including the Wechsler Intelligence Scales, the Rorschach, and the Millon Inventory, used in adult populations. Archer and Krishnamurthy (1993b) reviewed the literature derived from 37 studies that reported interrelationships between MMPI and Rorschach variables in adult populations. This body of literature indicated, with impressive consistency, generally limited or minimal relationships between the MMPI and the Rorschach. Archer and Krishnamurthy (1993a) also examined the empirical findings related to the relationships between Rorschach and MMPI variables in seven studies conducted with adolescent samples and found consistently modest or nonsignificant relationships between the two instruments in this population as well.

Krishnamurthy, Archer, and House (1996) conducted an empirical investigation of the relationship between carefully selected MMPI–A and Rorschach variables in a clinical sample of 152 adolescents based on a priori hypotheses focused on specific construct areas. The constructs examined included anxiety, depression, somatic concern, defensiveness, bizarre thinking, self-image, and impulse control, and the research produced hypotheses that involved a total of 28 MMPI–A scales and 43 Rorschach variables. Once again, the results consistently indicated very limited associations between conceptually related MMPI–A and Rorschach variables. The authors observed that a logical conclusion from this body of literature is that variables receiving similar labels on the MMPI–A and Rorschach, such as the Rorschach *DEPI* variable and scale 2 of the MMPI–A, actually measure different constructs, or at least markedly different components of the same broad construct. Perhaps most troubling, these authors observed that a matrix comprising MMPI–A and Rorschach variables would not display significant evidence of convergent validity in terms of the patterns of intercorrelations that might be expected given the theoretical constructs attributed to these variables. Krishnamurthy et al. (1996) cautioned that scores on sets of similarly labeled variables across the Rorschach and the MMPI–A should not necessarily be viewed as confirming or disconfirming the data provided by either instrument. In cases where the Rorschach and the MMPI–A would lead to contradictory clinical inferences, Archer and Krishnamurthy (1993a) recommended that the clinician place particular emphasis on the use of additional sources of data, including individual and family interview data and psychosocial history findings, in reaching interpretive conclusions.

In addition to the clinical interview of the adolescent, the assessment of parental perceptions concerning the adolescent's functioning is very important. Several instruments, including the Child Behavior Checklist–Revised (CBCL; Achenbach & Edelbrock, 1983), provide a standardized format to collect this type of information. Archer (1987, 1997) and Williams (1986) also stress the importance of MMPI assessment of the parents of adolescents being evaluated to generate a greater understanding of possible family dynamics and influences that may shape or distort parental perceptions of their child's functioning. Archer (1987) noted the following:

> The current literature supports the involvement of parents of psychiatrically disturbed children in psychiatric treatment efforts. Perhaps the clearest finding from this literature is that the parents of psychiatrically disturbed children typically display substantial features of psychological distress and maladjustment. This conclusion is particularly marked for the parents of children in inpatient treatment settings. Therefore the involvement of parents in treatment programs that are responsive to the psychological features of the parents, as well as the symptomatology of the adolescent patient, appears to have firm empirical grounds. Clearly, such a treatment involvement does not require a causal assumption of a parental role in the etiology of the child's disorder. These treatment efforts may be more parsimoniously based upon the recognition of the marked degree of psychological pain and disturbance commonly reported among parents of children experiencing deviant psychological development. (p. 178)

Provision of MMPI–A Feedback

Archer (1997) and Archer and Krishnamurthy (2002) noted that the provision of MMPI–A feedback to the adolescent is an important factor in increasing the adolescent's motivation to cooperate with testing procedures. MMPI test feedback has been a central issue in several texts (Butcher, 1990; Finn, 1996; Lewak, Marks, & Nelson, 1990). Also, a computer software package has been developed by Marks and Lewak (1991) to assist the clinician in providing MMPI test feedback to adolescent clients, and a feedback manual was recently developed by Finn (1996).

MMPI–A feedback provided to an adolescent should begin with an explanation of the test instrument, including the ways MMPI–A data are used to generate hypotheses concerning personality characteristics. The adolescent should be encouraged to interact with the psychologist during the feedback session. The adolescent's input into the feedback process allows the psychologist an opportunity to appraise the adolescent's reaction to and acceptance of various features of the test findings. It is usually much easier for the adolescent to accept test feedback when the findings are presented individually instead of within the framework of a family therapy session. Many clinicians probably underestimate the extent of information that an adolescent is capable of usefully assimilating, particularly if technical jargon is avoided and language and concepts understandable to the adolescent are used.

Areas of Limitations or Potential Problems in MMPI–A Use

Several limitations or potential problems can arise when the MMPI–A is used for treatment-planning purposes. Issues similar to those regarding the generalizability of the literature from the MMPI to the MMPI–2 with adults have been raised concerning the applicability of adolescent research findings based on the original version of the MMPI. The two-point codetype congruence rates between the MMPI and MMPI–A for adolescents in the normative sample were 67.8% for males and 55.8% for females, and they were 69.5% for males and 67.2% for females in a clinical sample (Butcher et al., 1992). With the use of a five-point codetype definition requirement, the congruence rates increased to 95.2% for males and 81.8% for females in the normative sample and to 95.4% for males and 94.4% for females in the clinical sample (Butcher et al., 1992). These data are very similar to the two-point codetype congruence rates between the MMPI and MMPI–2 for normal and clinical samples of adults (Butcher et al., 1989).

Another difficulty is that there are 15 content scales, 3 supplementary scales, 3 *Si* subscales, and 4 new validity scales on the MMPI–A that do not have counterparts in the original version of the MMPI. These scales will require ongoing validity studies to establish their correlate meanings in clinical populations. As more clinical correlate data are firmly established, the interpretation of these scales should become less tentative and provisional. For instance, Arita and Baer (1998) recently reported correlate patterns for the MMPI–A content scales *A-anx, A-dep, A-hea, A-aln, A-ang, A-con,* and *A-sod* in a sample of 62 adolescent inpatients. The correlations between these selected MMPI–A scales and measures of convergent and divergent constructs provided substantial support for the validity of these scales. Further, McCarthy and Archer (1998) examined the factor structure of the MMPI–A content scales in the normative sample and a clinical adolescent sample and found evidence of two salient factors (labeled General Maladjustment and Externalizing Tendencies) that accounted for content scale variance.

It has been noted that the MMPI–A requires a substantial amount of cognitive maturation and reading ability for successful administration, and the revision of the test instrument has not substantially changed these requirements. Adolescents must still have the capacity and motivation to complete a relatively long and demanding test instrument. As with the original version of the MMPI, use of short forms is not recommended as a standard method of attempting to reduce the requirements of the MMPI–A for the adolescent respondent. Butcher and Hostetler (1990) defined short forms as "sets of scales that have been decreased in length from the standard MMPI form. An MMPI short form is a group of items that is thought to be a valid substitute for the full scale score even though it might contain only four or five items from the original scale" (p. 12).

Archer, Tirrell, and Elkins (2001) recently developed an MMPI–A short form based on the administration of the first 150 items of the test, and it illustrates the uses and limitations of short form approaches. This short form demonstrates usefulness in determining whether an adolescent is experiencing clinical levels of psychopathology, primarily in those rare instances when testing with the full length instrument is not possible. However, the basic scale profiles produced by this and other short forms often significantly differ from those produced in full-length administrations. Short forms, therefore, have limited interpretive accuracy when used to address issues beyond determining gross presence or absence of psychopathology.

Short form administrations may be contrasted with *abbreviated* administrations in which a clinician elects to administer the first 350 items of the MMPI–A. This administration approach will result in the item endorsements necessary to score the basic clinical scales. An abbreviated administration will *not*, however, provide sufficient information to score the content scales, several of the supplementary scales, or the validity scales *VRIN*, *TRIN*, F, and F_2. If an abbreviated administration increases the motivation or cooperation of an adolescent, this option may be used, but the clinician must understand what data can be gathered and what scales and measurement areas cannot be addressed.

A final area of potential limitation related to the MMPI–A is associated with the relatively low magnitude of MMPI–A basic scale elevations that are likely to occur with this revised instrument. As noted by Archer (1987), normal range mean profiles for adolescent populations were often found on the original form of the MMPI, leading to the recommendation by Ehrenworth and Archer (1985) that *T*-score values of 65 or above be used for clinical-range elevations when employing adolescent norms. Archer, Pancoast, and Klinefelter (1989) found that the use of a clinical scale *T*-score value of 65 or above (rather than 70) to define clinical levels of psychopathology resulted in increases in sensitivity in identifying profiles produced by normal adolescents versus adolescents receiving treatment in outpatient and inpatient settings. The MMPI–A produces even lower mean *T*-score values for adolescent clinical samples than those found using the original form of the MMPI with the Marks and Briggs (1972) adolescent norms (Archer, 1997).

The MMPI Adolescent Project Committee recognized that the revised test instrument would often produce lower *T*-score values for adolescents than the original test instrument. This observation led to the development of the "gray zone" or "shaded zone" on the MMPI–A profile sheets. Specifically, the use of a single "black line" value to delineate the demarcation point between normal and clinical range scores was abandoned in favor of the creation of a *range* of scores that serves as a transition area between normal- and clinical-range elevations. On the MMPI–A, this zone is placed in the range of *T*-score values from 60 to 65 for every MMPI–A scale regardless of whether linear or uniform *T*-score procedures were used for that particular scale. A central question requiring further study relates to the sensitivity and specificity of the MMPI–A instrument in identifying psychopathology in adolescents. Substantial research data are needed to determine whether the MMPI–A may be subject to increased problems in the accurate detection of psychopathology (sensitivity) because of the reduction of *T*-score values. This issue is directly related to two questions: how often a normal adolescent will produce *T*-score values within normal ranges on the MMPI basic scales and how often adolescents experiencing significant psychopathology will produce one or more significant elevations on the MMPI–A basic scales. Although more research is needed to fully resolve this issue, Alperin et al. (1996)

provided data on the relative efficacy of applying a T-score value of 60 or above versus 65 or above as the criterion for defining MMPI–A clinical-range elevations when using the standard MMPI–A norms in the normative sample of 1,620 adolescents and a clinical sample of 122 adolescent inpatients. In this investigation, the $T \geq 65$ criterion produced an overall hit rate of 70% accurate identification, in contrast to a 57% hit rate with the $T \geq 60$ criterion, and the former criterion also produced a more effective balance between test sensitivity (71%) and specificity (70%). These results appear consistent with the statement in the MMPI–A manual that "a clinically significant elevation is defined as an MMPI–A T-score ≥ 65" (Butcher et al., 1992, p. 43). Fontaine, Archer, Elkins, and Johansen (2001) recently replicated and expanded this research by comparing classification accuracy rates for normal and clinical adolescents using the $T \geq 60$ and $T \geq 65$ criteria with two different base rates (20% and 50%) for the occurrence of psychopathology. Across clinical base rates, the T-score criterion of 65 or above resulted in higher accuracy levels while also minimizing misclassification of both clinical and normal cases. To further explore the possible causes of the high frequency of within-normal-limits basic scale profiles for adolescents in clinical settings, Archer, Handel, and Lynch (2001) compared the item endorsement frequencies for the MMPI–A normative sample with frequencies found in two adolescent clinical samples. The results showed that the MMPI–A contains numerous items that do not receive a higher rate of endorsement in clinical samples. Furthermore, the MMPI–A basic and content scales generally show a much higher percentage of these "ineffective" items than do corresponding scales of the MMPI–2 as evaluated in normal and clinical samples of adults. The authors concluded that the markedly high rate of endorsement of MMPI–A items in the normative sample, rather than being an unusual characteristic of adolescent clinical samples, probably serves to reduce MMPI–A item effectiveness and also accounts for the high rate of within-normal-limits MMPI–A profiles found for adolescents in treatment settings.

USE OF THE MMPI–A FOR TREATMENT MONITORING AND OUTCOMES ASSESSMENT

General Issues

The focus thus far has been on using the MMPI–A to evaluate and describe an adolescent's level of functioning in relation to standardized measures of psychopathology. The MMPI–A also may be used in repeated administrations to assess change in functioning over time. This use of the MMPI–A is particularly important because many aspects of psychopathology manifested by adolescents during this developmental stage are subject to rapid change. When the MMPI–A is administered at various points in the treatment process, it can provide the clinician with a sensitive index of therapeutic progress. Further, when the MMPI–A is administered at the conclusion of treatment, it can provide a comprehensive assessment of the psychological changes that occurred as a result of the intervention process.

Evaluation Against Criteria for Outcome Measures

Although many aspects of the MMPI–A contain new features that will require extensive investigation, it is possible to offer some speculations concerning the ability of the MMPI–A to meet the criteria for outcome assessment measures formulated by Ciarlo, Edwards, Kiresuk, Newman, and Brown (1981) and discussed earlier in this chapter.

It is likely, for example, that the MMPI–A will have substantially more relevance to the assessment of adolescent psychopathology than the original MMPI because of the inclusion in the revised instrument of items and scales specifically targeted at this population. Thus, the MMPI–A retains the benefits of the original MMPI in the assessment of a wide range of psychopathological conditions and extends the applicability of the instrument to the adolescent age group in a manner consistent with the Ciarlo et al.'s Criterion 1, namely, that the instrument be relevant to the target group. In addition to meeting Criterion 1, the MMPI–A would appear to hold special utility by meeting the 6th criterion, which concerns the psychometric strength of the instrument, and the 10th criterion, which concerns the usefulness of the instrument in clinical services. More is probably known about the psychometric properties of the original version of the MMPI than any other widely used psychopathology-related assessment instrument. For example, Butcher (1987) estimated that over 10,000 articles and books have documented the use of the MMPI, and Butcher and Owen (1978) estimated that 84% of all research conducted in the personality inventory domain has centered on the MMPI. Archer (1997) provided approximately 400 references relevant to the use of the MMPI and MMPI–A with adolescents, and the MMPI–A manual provides extensive information on the reliability and validity of the revised instrument (Butcher et al., 1992). The MMPI and MMPI–A are also particularly strong in the area of the assessment findings related to the provision of clinical services. The MMPI–A, when used as an outcome assessment measure, can provide extensive clinical information helpful to both the treatment team and the patient.

Finally, it might also be noted that the MMPI and MMPI–A have a particular strength in reference to the last criterion listed by Ciarlo et al. (1981), Criterion 11, regarding compatibility with clinical theories and practices. Although the original MMPI and to a lesser extent the MMPI–A were developed in an atheoretical and empirical fashion, these instruments are clearly compatible with a very wide range of theories of psychopathology, from the behavioral to the psychoanalytic. This compatibility with a broad range of clinical orientations and theories is probably one of the most important factors in the widespread popularity of this instrument for the assessment of both adults and adolescents. Balanced against these areas of strength are possible weaknesses of the MMPI–A in meeting other of the criteria developed by Ciarlo et al. (1981), including that an instrument should have a simple, teachable methodology (Criterion 2), be employable with multiple respondents (Criterion 4), meet criteria related to cost factors (Criterion 7), be understandable by non professional audiences (Criterion 8), and have simple feedback and interpretation processes (Criterion 9). It could also be noted that these criteria are likely to be particularly valued in a managed health care environment. It should be acknowledged that the MMPI–A is a complicated, extensive test instrument that requires substantial time on the part of the adolescent to respond to the lengthy item pool and also requires extensive training and expertise on the part of the psychologist to ensure accurate interpretation.

Research Findings

Systematic and controlled treatment outcome studies are relatively limited for the MMPI–A. However, much treatment outcome research information is available on the MMPI basic and special scales in adult populations. For example, Barron (1953) developed the Ego Strength scale by identifying items that separated the response patterns of 17 neurotic patients judged to have clearly improved after 6 months of psychotherapy versus 16 neurotic patients judged unimproved over the same time interval. Because of the largely contradictory results of studies examining the usefulness of the Ego Strength scale, however, this measure was not retained by the MMPI Adolescent Project Committee for the MMPI–A. In contrast, a revised form of the MacAndrew Alcoholism Scale (*MAC-R*) was retained in the MMPI–A. Individuals' scores on the *MAC-R* scale appear to remain relatively stable across time (Archer, 1987, 1997). For example, *MAC* scale scores in alcoholics remained elevated following treatment in studies by Gallucci, Kay, and Thornby (1989) and others. In addition to the *MAC-R* scale, Welsh's Anxiety (*A*) and Repression (*R*) scales were carried over from the original MMPI to the MMPI–A. Welsh (1956) created the Anxiety and Repression scales to measure the first two factors of the MMPI. The particular usefulness of the *A* and *R* scales in the assessment of treatment outcomes may be directly related to their relationship to the factor structure of the MMPI.

Welsh found that the first factor of the MMPI had high positive loadings on MMPI basic scales 7 and 8 and a negative loading on scale *K*. This factor was originally labeled General Maladjustment (Tyler, 1951) and subsequently labeled Anxiety by Welsh (1956). It has also been identified in factor analyses of adolescents' basic scale values on the MMPI (Archer, 1984; Archer & Klinefelter, 1991) and the MMPI–A (Butcher et al., 1992). Thus, the MMPI–A Welsh's *A* scale served as a "marker" for first factor variance in the test instrument. In the MMPI–A normative sample, the *A* scale was highly intercorrelated with several other MMPI–A measures, including basic scales *K* ($r = -.72$), *Pt* ($r = .89$), and *Sc* ($r = .76$) and content scales *A-anx* ($r = .83$), *A-obs* ($r = .82$), and *A-dep* ($r = .80$). Thus, *T*-score values on *all* of these measures except scale *K* (which is negatively correlated to the first factor) tend to be lower when an adolescent reports lower reevaluation levels of emotional distress and maladjustment as a result of successful treatment efforts.

Welsh's second factor, although less clearly defined than the first factor, tends to be related to elevations on scale *3* and negatively related to elevations on scale *9*. Welsh labeled this factor Repression, and this factor has also been identified in factor analytic studies of adolescents using the original version of the MMPI (Archer, 1984; Archer & Klinefelter, 1991) and the MMPI–A (Butcher et al., 1992). The Repression scale is most highly intercorrelated with scales *L* ($r = .44$), *K* ($r = .45$), and *Ma* ($r = -.43$) in the MMPI–A normative sample. All 33 items in the MMPI–A *R* scale are scored in the false direction, and involve the denial of symptomatology, particularly aggressive or hostile feelings, and the expression of disinterest in sensation-seeking activities. As a component of this dimension, scale *K* is highly and negatively intercorrelated with several MMPI–A scales, including content scales *A-anx* ($r = -.59$), *A-obs* ($r = -.67$), *A-ang* ($r = -.62$), and *A-cyn* ($r = -.70$) and supplementary scale *A* ($r = -.72$). This pattern implies that MMPI–A test-retest administrations may often show a pattern where reduction of factor 1 symptomatology will be associated with increased elevations on factor 2–related scales such as Repression and particularly the *K* scale. This pattern may be related to the observation that the *K* scale, in its use in adult populations, has often been seen as an indicator of psychological health rather than a measure of defensiveness exclusively. An understanding of the interrelationships between factor 1 and factor 2 patterns in the MMPI–A will assist in interpreting individual change in test-retest MMPI–A administrations by providing a conceptual organization for the changes shown on the individual scale level.

Clinical Applications

Butcher and Tellegen (1978) and Ullmann and Wiggins (1962) reported that 80% to 85% of the items on the original MMPI were worded in a manner that related to trait personality features or biographical information that should not change on retest.

This estimate leaves approximately 15% to 20% of the original item pool to provide information on changes in psychological characteristics. If only 15% of the original 550 items were capable of indicating state changes, however, there would still be a pool of approximately 83 items capable of reflecting changes in psychological functioning.

Several studies have been conducted on the stability of high-point, two-point, and even three-point codetypes for the original MMPI, and this literature has been reviewed by Graham (2000). Among his conclusions, Graham noted that codetypes are likely to be more stable when the primary scales are more elevated and when there is a greater degree of elevation of the primary scales in relationship to other scales in the profile (i.e., when the codetype is well defined). Graham also noted that, although codetypes may change from one administration to another, they are likely to remain within the same broad diagnostic grouping. Pancoast et al. (1988) examined the congruence rate between discharge diagnoses rendered by psychiatrists and the admission and discharge MMPI-derived diagnoses from four diagnostic classification systems developed for the MMPI. The four classification systems included a simple high-point code based on the most elevated clinical scale in the profile, Henrichs' (1964, 1966) revision of the rules propounded by Meehl and Dahlstrom (1960), the Goldberg equation (Goldberg, 1965), and the system developed by Lachar (1974). This study indicated a modest hit rate of 24% to 34% for MMPI-derived diagnoses (across the various classification systems) and psychiatric diagnoses. Further, the stability of MMPI-based diagnoses from admission to discharge ranged from 48% to 51% depending on the classification system employed. Thus, there appeared to be little difference in the accuracy or the stability of profiles related to the complexity of the system used for diagnostic classification purposes.

Of the several factors that may affect the evaluation of change on the MMPI–A, perhaps the most important issue relates to the concept of the standard error of measurement. As previously noted, the MMPI–A manual reports that the standard error of measurement for the MMPI–A basic scales is approximately two to three raw score points or four to six T-score points (Butcher et al., 1992). This standard error of measurement estimate indicates that, if an individual were to retake the MMPI–A within a very brief period of time and without having undergone any change in emotion or psychopathology, we would expect the *T*-score values on the basic scales to fall within a range of plus or minus approximately five *T*-score points roughly 68% of the time. The standard error of measurement range for the MMPI–A places practical limits on the interpretation of small *T*-score differences in evaluating the degree of change shown by an individual's original and readministration scores on the MMPI–A. As noted in the MMPI–A manual, this standard error of measurement also has implications for codetype interpretation. For example, a *2-4-8* codetype, with all three scales having *T*-score values of 70, would be arbitrarily placed within a two-point code category (i.e., 2-4) but could be markedly different from a clearly defined *2-4* profile type with a substantial *T*-score difference between the second and third most elevated scales.

Use With Other Evaluation Data

As previously noted, findings from the MMPI–A should be routinely integrated with information about the adolescent from other sources, particularly those that provide other perspectives on the adolescent's functioning, including reports and ratings provided by teachers, parents, and treatment team members. These external sources of information provide very valuable and unique data that can supplement the types of information the adolescent can provide using the MMPI–A self-report format.

Provision of MMPI–A Feedback Regarding Assessment Findings

As previously noted, the provision of MMPI feedback has become a central issue in discussions of this instrument (Butcher, 1990; Finn, 1996; Lewak et al., 1990). Unfortunately, these discussions usually concern the use of the instrument for treatment planning rather than as a treatment outcome assessment measure. Nevertheless, it is clear that the MMPI and the MMPI–A can provide valuable information when used in a feedback process to document the adolescent's change over time as a result of participation in the treatment process. Used within this format, the initial testing provides a baseline against which later MMPI administrations can be compared in order to evaluate the degree of change in personality and psychopathology patterns over the course of treatment. The review of such test findings provides the adolescent and the therapist with an important opportunity to explore the extent of agreement between the therapist, the adolescent, and the test findings concerning the amount and nature of the change that has been experienced.

A readministering of the MMPI–A to evaluate treatment process or treatment outcome will usually not be resisted by the adolescent if he or she will receive feedback on the test findings and thus has a "stake" in such testing (Archer & Krishnamurthy, 2002). As previously noted, adolescents are capable of receiving and understanding a great deal of information about the MMPI–A. In addition to avoiding technical jargon, however, the therapist should avoid the use of feedback sessions as a means of "confronting" reluctant or resistant adolescents concerning their lack of treatment progress. Although such confrontations might be indicated for a particular adolescent, using the MMPI–A to provide grounds for a confrontation may reduce the adolescent's willingness to accurately report on this instrument in future evaluations.

Limitations and Potential Problems in MMPI–A Use

As previously noted, the greatest single problem in evaluating change on the MMPI is related to the overemphasis of small *T*-score shifts that represent changes less than the standard error of measurement on the test (i.e., five *T*-score points). In addition, the MMPI interpreter is often left with the challenge of determining whether an adolescent's improvement as reflected in MMPI–A *T*-score reductions on clinical scales represents actual positive changes in psychological functioning or the adolescent's use of a defensive response set in an attempt to minimize the report of psychopathology during the test readministration. One of the aspects of the MMPI–A that is relatively unique and substantially helps in this differentiation task is the presence of extensive validity scale information about the adolescent's approach to the response process. Using the original version of the MMPI, Herkov, Archer, and Gordon (1991) examined the relative efficacy of the traditional validity scales and the Wiener-Harmon Subtle-Obvious subscales in identifying fake-bad and fake-good response sets among adolescents. This study involved 403 adolescents from a nonpatient adolescent group who were administered the MMPI under standard conditions, a nonpatient group instructed to "fake bad," and a psychiatric inpatient group instructed to "fake good." The results of this study indicated that elevations on scale *L* were a highly sensitive indicator of adolescents' attempts to fake good and that elevations on scale *F* were quite sensitive in identifying adolescents attempting to overreport symptomatology on the test instrument. The utility of MMPI–A validity scales in detecting underreporting of symptoms was investigated by Baer, Ballenger, and Kroll (1998). The authors found that the MMPI–A *L* and *K* scales were effective in discriminating adolescents instructed to create an impression of excellent psychological adjustment from clinical and community sample counterparts taking the MMPI–A under standard instructions. Rogers, Hinds, and Sewell (1996) investigated attempts to overreport psychopathology among adolescent offenders and found that $F\text{-}K > 20$ was effective in identifying efforts to feign psychopathology. Several MMPI–A studies have also focused on the detection of random responding. Baer, Ballenger, Berry, and Wetter (1997), for example, found that increasing amounts of random responding was reliably reflected in increasing scores on MMPI–A scales F_1, F_2, F, and *VRIN*. Baer, Kroll, Rinaldo, and Ballenger (1999) investigated the utility of MMPI–A validity scales in detecting random responding and overreporting in samples of clinical and normal adolescents. The results demonstrated that the *VRIN* and *F* scales were sensitive indicators of random responding, and the *F* and the *F-K* index appeared useful in identifying overreported adolescent profiles. Archer and Elkins (1999) also found MMPI–A validity scales *F* and *VRIN* particularly effective in detecting entirely random profiles from those standardly collected in clinical settings, but Archer, Handel, Lynch, and Elkins (2002) found that MMPI–A validity scales, including F_1 and F_2 difference measures, were more limited in detecting partially random responding, particularly random responding involving less than half of the item pool. In general, this literature supports the use of the MMPI–A validity scales for determining the consistency and accuracy of the adolescents' reports of change in symptomatology across MMPI–A administrations.

CLINICAL CASE EXAMPLE

Examples of MMPI–A interpretation principles can be found in the test manual (Butcher et al., 1992) as well as in Archer (1997), Archer and Krishnamurthy (2002), Archer, Krishnamurthy, et al. (1994), and Butcher and Williams (2000). The following clinical case example was selected from Archer (1997) to illustrate the use of the MMPI–A for the purposes of personality description and treatment planning.

Deborah, a 17-year-old White female adolescent, was admitted to an acute inpatient unit in a psychiatric hospital. This patient had a history of antisocial behaviors and legal violations that included loitering, petty larceny, vagrancy, possession of drugs, and possession of drugs with intent to distribute. Her psychiatric symptomatology at the time of hospitalization included anger, hostility, and depression. Upon her admission, the treatment team's *DSM–III–R* diagnoses for this patient included dysthymic disorder (300.40), conduct disorder, undifferentiated type (312.90), and psychoactive substance abuse (305.90). She had an extensive history of abuse of alcohol and other substances, including hallucinogens, marijuana, cocaine, and barbiturates. Immediately prior to hospitalization, Deborah required emergency hospitalization for an unintentional drug overdose from her use of a combination of Valium and cocaine.

This adolescent was an only child from an upper-class family. Deborah's father was an executive vice president for a multi-national corporation, and his job responsibilities resulted in multiple relocations of the family to a variety of Western European countries. Approximately one year prior to the patient's current psychiatric admission, she had been arrested by British authorities for the possession and sale of narcotics. Deborah's parents reported a long history of difficulty controlling their daughter's behavior and indicated that she had an extensive history of school truancy and episodes of running away from home. Her parents also indicated their suspicions that she might engage in prostitution to support and maintain her drug use. Deborah's academic records indicated a history of underachievement, with grades in the average to below-average range.

The administration of the Wechsler Adult Intelligence Scale–Revised (WAIS–R) produced a Verbal IQ score of 110, a Performance IQ score of 124, and a Full Scale IQ score of 116. The Child Behavior Checklist (CBCL), developed by Achenbach and Edelbrock (1983), was administered to Deborah's mother; the results showed elevations on the Delinquent and Hyperactive scales. Staff ratings on the Devereux Adolescent Behavior (DAB) rating scale, developed by Spivack, Haimes, and Spotts (1967), showed elevations on the Unethical and Defiant/Resistant behavior factors.

Deborah's MMPI–A basic scale profile is shown in Fig. 4.1. This profile displays *T*-score values based on MMPI–A norms (Butcher et al., 1992) and on the norms developed by Marks and Briggs (1972) for the original version of the MMPI, which can be found in Appendix G of the MMPI–A manual (Butcher et al., 1992). The third step of the interpretive model presented in Table 4.2 involves the evaluation of the technical validity of the MMPI–A profile. This step is undertaken by reviewing the scales and raw score values appearing on the left side of the basic scale profile sheet. We might begin by noting that Deborah omitted only one item on the Cannot-Say scale, a value clearly within acceptable limits for profile interpretation. The response consistency measures *VRIN* ($T = 43$) and *TRIN* ($T = 54$) also produced values within acceptable limits for valid profile interpretation. Also note that there is relatively little difference between the *T*-score elevations on scales F_1 ($T = 66$) and F_2 ($T = 53$), providing evidence that Deborah did not respond to the latter part of the test booklet in a random manner. The validity scale configuration produced by MMPI–A scales *F*, *L*, and *K* are also within acceptable limits and consistent with there being a meaningful and useful interpretation of MMPI–A clinical scale findings.

The fourth step shown in Table 4.2 involves reviewing the basic scale clinical profile. Deborah's basic scale profile is a well-defined *4-9* codetype. The term definition, as applied to two-point codetypes, refers to the degree of *T*-score difference between the second most elevated (scale *9*) and third most elevated (scale *8*) clinical scales. The *4-9* codetype is very commonly found among adolescents in clinical settings on both the original version of the MMPI and the MMPI–A (Archer, 1987; 1997). In Marks et al.'s (1974) description of two-point codetypes, the *4-9* code was found for adolescents who were described as defiant, impulsive, disobedient, and school truant. Marks et al. also noted that these adolescents were likely to be runaways and were often described by their parents as difficult to control. The chief defense mechanism of the *4-9/9-4* adolescent was acting out, and therapists described these adolescents as resentful of authority, insecure, socially extroverted, and capable of initially arousing liking in others. Marks et al. referred to these adolescents as "disobedient beauties" and provided descriptors, including seductive, provocative, and handsome (p. 221). The clinical correlate data for the *4-9/9-4* codetype indicate individuals with this MMPI pattern are often in trouble with their environment because of antisocial behaviors. In the adult literature, individuals with this codetype often receive a diagnosis of antisocial personality disorder and are described as selfish, impulsive, and self-indulgent. As noted in our model for profile interpretation, it is often useful to review values for scales *2* and *7* to assess the overall degree of affective distress. Deborah's scores on these measures are markedly low for an adolescent recently admitted to inpatient treatment and are equivalent to those found for the MMPI–A normative population.

MMPI-A

Minnesota Multiphasic Personality Inventory— ADOLESCENT™

Profile for Basic Scales

James N. Butcher, Carolyn L. Williams, John R. Graham, Robert P. Archer, Auke Tellegen, Yossef S. Ben-Porath, and Beverly Kaemmer
S. R. Hathaway and J. C. McKinley

Name Deborah

Address

Grade Level 12th Date Tested / /

Setting Age 17

Referred By

Scorer's Initials

FEMALE

Ts	VRIN	TRIN (TrF TrT)	F_1	F_2	F	L	K	Hs 1	D 2	Hy 3	Pd 4	Mf 5	Pa 6	Pt 7	Sc 8	Ma 9	Si 0	Ts
Raw Score	2	10	8	6	14	2	9	5	18	19	33	30	12	14	28	30	21	

? Raw Score 1

LEGEND

- Ts T score
- VRIN Variable Response Inconsistency
- TRIN True Response Inconsistency
- F_1 Infrequency 1
- F_2 Infrequency 2
- F Infrequency
- L Lie
- K Defensiveness
- Hs Hypochondriasis
- D Depression
- Hy Conversion Hysteria
- Pd Psychopathic Deviate
- Mf Masculinity-Femininity
- Pa Paranoia
- Pt Psychasthenia
- Sc Schizophrenia
- Ma Hypomania
- Si Social Introversion
- ? Cannot Say

●—● MMPI-A

■- - ■ MMPI

PRINTED WITH AGRI-BASE INK
ABCD9876543

NATIONAL COMPUTER SYSTEMS
25000

This adolescent's lack of emotional or affective distress is a negative prognostic indicator for Deborah and may reflect an absence of the necessary motivation (i.e., emotional distress) to engage in the therapeutic change process.

Steps 5 and 6 in the profile interpretation process involve a review of the content and supplementary scales, as presented in Fig. 4.2. Consistent with the absence of affective distress reflected in the basic scale profile, Deborah's score on Welsh's *A* scale ($T = 51$) suggests little distress or discomfort at the time of her MMPI–A assessment. Further, her score on Welsh's *R* scale ($T = 46$) reinforces the findings from her *4-9/9-4* codetype in suggesting that acting out, rather than repression, is her primary defense mechanism. A review of Deborah's supplementary scale scores also provides a number of interesting observations related to potential substance abuse problems. This adolescent's raw score value of 30 on the *MAC-R* would lead to her classification as a probable substance abuser, a finding that is also consistent with her elevated scores on the *PRO* scale ($T = 84$) and her psychosocial history. Additionally, research by Archer, Gordon, Anderson, and Giannetti (1989) has indicated that adolescents with elevated *MAC* scores are much more likely to receive diagnoses related to conduct disorder. In contrast, Deborah's scores are within normal limits on the *ACK* scale ($T = 56$), a measure of her willingness to acknowledge or discuss alcohol or drug use symptoms and problems. Thus, Deborah may have many more problems in the area of drugs and alcohol than she will admit in a clinical interview. Finally, Deborah also shows a marginal elevation on the *IMM* scale, a measure of deficits and problems in the area of ego maturation, self-awareness, and the ability to form meaningful and nonexploitive relationships with others. Archer, Pancoast, et al. (1994) found that female adolescents with an elevation on the *IMM* scale have poor relationships with their parents and frequently have a history of school truancy.

Deborah's content scale profile, consistent with her low score on the Welsh's *A* scale, produced normal-range values on measures of affective distress and internal symptoms. This is reflected in her normal-range values on scales *A-anx*, *A-obs*, *A-dep*, *A-hea*, and *A-biz*. Deborah is likely to have marked difficulty in interpersonal functioning, reflected in her substantial elevation on the *A-fam* scale, which indicates the presence of family conflict and discord, and further reflected in an elevated content component *A-fam1* (Familial Discord) scale *T*-score of 78 as well as marginal elevations on *A-ang* and *A-cyn* ($55 \geq T \leq 60$). Deborah also shows a marginal elevation on the *A-con* scale, indicative of problem behaviors involving unlawful actions or attitudes and behaviors that violate societal standards. Our understanding of Deborah's score on the *A-trt* content scale is facilitated by a review of the content component scales for this dimension, and her relatively higher score ($T = 75$) on the *A-trt1* subscale (Low Motivation) suggests that Deborah is apathetic, is unmotivated, or feels hopeless about making significant changes in her life situation. Her *A-trt* scale value underscores that Deborah is likely to present substantial initial barriers to the treatment process, a common phenomenon among conduct-disordered adolescent patients. Finally, it can be noted that Deborah's *A-sch* score is quite elevated and accurately reflects her extensive

FIG. 4.1. MMPI–A basic scale profile sheet for clinical case example (Deborah). J. N. Butcher, C. L. Williams, J. R. Graham, R. P. Archer, A. Tellegen, Y. S. Ben-Porath, and B. Kaemmer. MMPI–A Profile forms: Minnesota Multiphasic Personality Inventory™ (MMPI–A)™ (Basic Scales; Content and Supplementary Scales; and Harris-Lingoes and Si Subscales) Copyright © the Regents of the University of Minnesota 1942, 1943 (renewed 1970), 1992. Reproduced by permission of the University of Minnesota Press. All rights reserved. "Minnesota Multiphasic Personality Inventory-Adolescent" and "MMPI–A" are trademarks owned by the University of Minnesota.

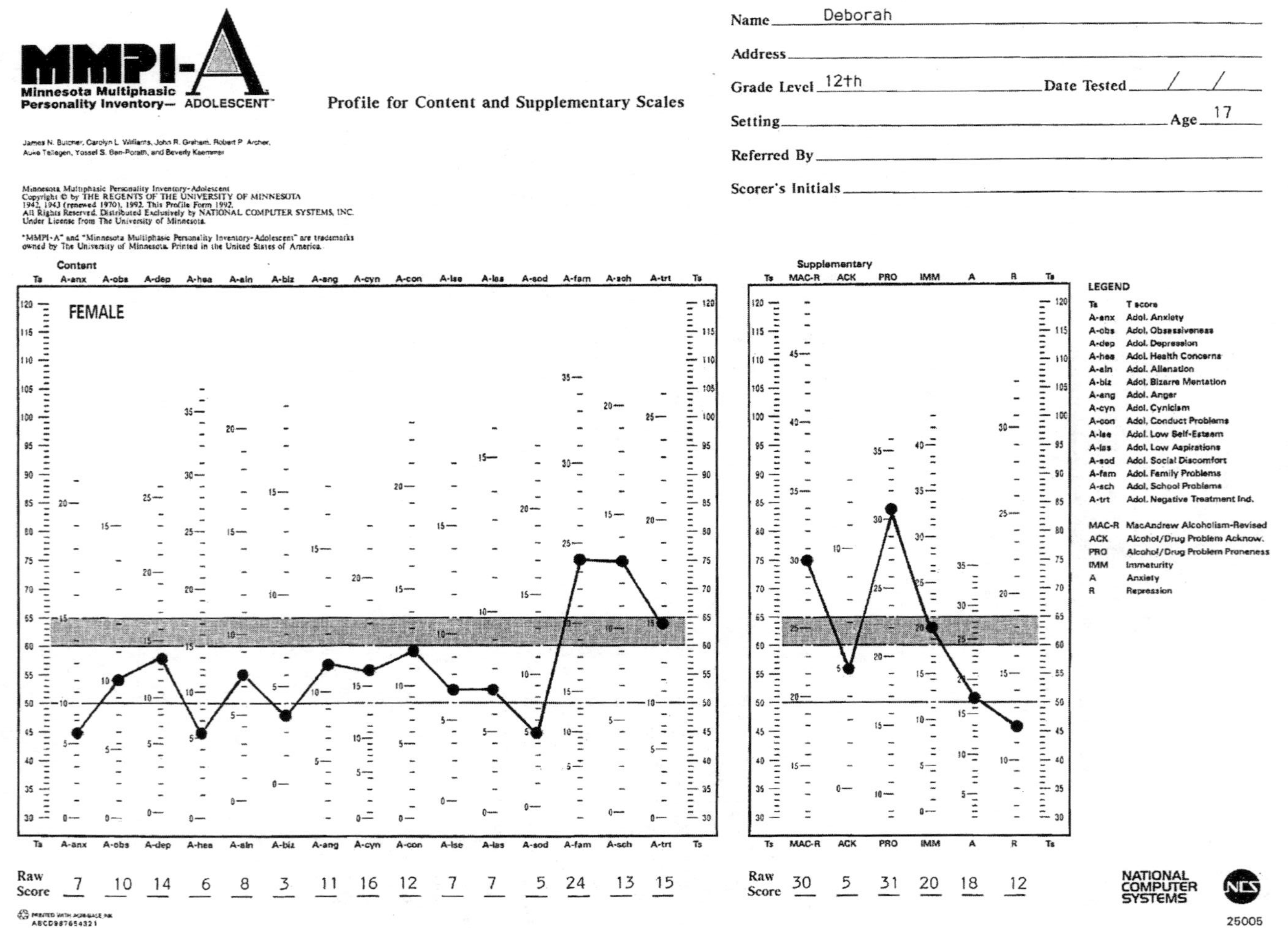

FIG. 4.2. MMPI–A content and supplementary scale profile for clinical case example (Deborah). J. N. Butcher, C. L. Williams, J. R. Graham, R. P. Archer, A. Tellegen, Y. S. Ben-Porath, and B. Kaemmer, 1992, Minneapolis, MN: Regents of the University of Minnesota. Copyright 1992 by the Regents of the University of Minnesota. Reprinted with permission.

MMPI-A
Minnesota Multiphasic Personality Inventory— ADOLESCENT™

Profile for Harris-Lingoes and Si Subscales

James N. Butcher, Carolyn L. Williams, John R. Graham, Robert P. Archer, Auke Tellegen, Yossef S. Ben-Porath, and Beverly Kaemmer
S. R. Hathaway and J. C. McKinley

Name Deborah
Address
Grade Level 12th Date Tested / /
Setting Age 17
Referred By
Scorer's Initials

Harris-Lingoes | Si

FEMALE

	D₁	D₂	D₃	D₄	D₅	Hy₁	Hy₂	Hy₃	Hy₄	Hy₅	Pd₁	Pd₂	Pd₃	Pd₄	Pd₅	Pa₁	Pa₂	Pa₃	Sc₁	Sc₂	Sc₃	Sc₄	Sc₅	Sc₆	Ma₁	Ma₂	Ma₃	Ma₄	Si₁	Si₂	Si₃
Raw Score	10	8	2	7	4	6	5	5	1	0	9	8	6	12	9	8	1	3	11	4	1	7	4	2	6	8	6	7	5	0	5

PRINTED WITH AGRI-BASE INK
BCD987654321

LEGEND

Ts T score
D₁ Subjective Depression
D₂ Psychom. Retardation
D₃ Phys. Malfunctioning
D₄ Mental Dullness
D₅ Brooding
Hy₁ Den. of Soc. Anxiety
Hy₂ Need for Affection
Hy₃ Lassitude-Malaise
Hy₄ Somatic Complaints
Hy₅ Inhib. of Aggression
Pd₁ Familial Discord
Pd₂ Authority Problems
Pd₃ Soc. Imperturbability
Pd₄ Social Alienation
Pd₅ Self-Alienation
Pa₁ Persecutory Ideas
Pa₂ Poignancy
Pa₃ Naivete
Sc₁ Social Alienation
Sc₂ Emotional Alienation
Sc₃ Lack of Ego Mast./Cog.
Sc₄ Lack of Ego Mast./Con.
Sc₅ Lack of Ego Mast./Def. Inh.
Sc₆ Bizarre Sensory Experiences
Ma₁ Amorality
Ma₂ Psychom. Acceleration
Ma₃ Imperturbability
Ma₄ Ego Inflation

Si₁ Shyness/Self-Conscious.
Si₂ Social Avoidance
Si₃ Alienation-Self/Others

Product Number 25009

problems in the academic environment. These problems have included substantial school truancy; repeated suspensions and disciplinary actions, reflected in the elevation on the *A-sch1* (School Conduct Problems) content component scale; and her marginal academic performance given her intellectual potential, reflected by the marked elevation of the *A-sch2* (Negative Attitudes) component scale.

The next step in the MMPI–A profile interpretation process presented in Table 4.2 involves looking at the Harris-Lingoes subscales and the MMPI–A critical item set developed by Forbey and Ben-Porath (1998). A review of the Harris-Lingoes subscales for basic scale 4 (see Fig. 4.3) shows marked elevations on Pd_1 (Familial Discord) and Pd_2 (Authority Problems). These scores indicate that Deborah is likely to perceive her home environment as unsupportive, conflictual, and controlling and critical (Pd_1); that she is likely to harbor substantial resentment of authority, possibly reflected in a history of academic or legal difficulties (Pd_2); and that she is likely to feel misunderstood, alienated, isolated, and unhappy (Pd_4). Deborah's scale 9 elevation is related to Harris-Lingoes subscale elevations on Ma_1 (Amorality) and Ma_3 (Imperturbability). Adolescents with such scores might be described as relating to others in an opportunistic, manipulative, and selfish manner (Ma_1), and they tend to operate independently, seek out excitement, and deny social anxiety (Ma_4). Deborah's item endorsement pattern on the Forbey and Ben-Porath (1998) critical items indicates endorsement of few items related to depression or anxiety; the majority of the critical items endorsed are related to adjustment problems in the areas of school (e.g., Items 80, 101, and 380), conduct (e.g., Items 249, 345, 440, and 460), and family problems (e.g., Items 365 and 405).

Figures 4.4 and 4.5 present the MMPI–A Structural Summary data for Deborah using the "check mark" system to designate the scales and subscales producing critical-range values. Of the eight factor dimensions included in the MMPI–A Structural Summary, Deborah produced critical-range values on the Familial Alienation (Factor 7) dimension. As noted in the correlate study by Archer, Krishnamurthy, et al. (1994), adolescents who produce elevations on a majority of the scales or subscales of this dimension are likely to utilize externalizing defenses and to be seen as delinquent, aggressive, or hostile. Empirical findings have related elevations on this dimension to the occurrence of frequent and serious parental conflicts and to significant disciplinary problems in the academic environment. Further, histories of alcohol and drug abuse are related to elevations on Familial Alienation. Congruent with our prior interpretation of this profile, Deborah produced few critical-range elevations on the General Maladjustment dimension, indicating that she experienced little generalized emotional distress at the time of the MMPI–A assessment.

Overall, the MMPI–A findings for Deborah suggest that she is an adolescent with significant conduct disorder and substance abuse problems. The use of both individual and family therapy appears indicated for this adolescent, and substance abuse treatment is also critical for her recovery. Deborah presents some very substantial treatment challenges, however, including the absence of affective distress and her low motivation to engage in the treatment process. Although Deborah might be expected to show substantial progress in settings in which extensive control could be exerted

---

FIG. 4.3. MMPI–A profile for Harris-Lingoes and Si subscales for clinical case example (Deborah). J. N. Butcher, C. L. Williams, J. R. Graham, R. P. Archer, A. Tellegen, Y. S. Ben-Porath, and B. Kaemmer, MMPI–A Profile forms: Minnesota Multiphasic Personality Inventory™ (MMPI–A)™ (Basic Scales; Content and Supplementary Scales; and Harris-Lingoes and Si Subscales) Copyright © the Regents of the University of Minnesota 1942, 1943 (renewed 1970), 1992. Reproduced by permission of the University of Minnesota Press. All rights reserved. "Minnesota Multiphasic Personality Inventory–Adolescent" and "MMPI–A" are trademarks owned by the University of Minnesota.

MMPI-A Structural Summary

Robert P. Archer and Radhika Krishnamurthy

Name: Deborah
Date:
Age: 17
Grade: 12th
Gender: Female
School:

Test-Taking Attitudes

1. Omissions (raw score total)

1 ? (Cannot Say scale)

2. Consistency (T-score values)

43 VRIN

54T TRIN

66 F_1 vs. 53 F_2

3. Accuracy (check if condition present)

Overreport

____ F scale *T* score ≥ 90

____ All clinical scales except 5 and 0 ≥ 60

Underreport

____ High L ($T \geq 65$)

____ High K ($T \geq 65$)

____ All clinical scales except 5 and 0 < 60

Factor Groupings
(enter *T*-score data)

1. General Maladjustment

____ Welsh's A
____ Scale 7
____ Scale 8
____ Scale 2
✓ Scale 4
____ D_1 (Subjective Depression)
____ D_4 (Mental Dullness)
____ D_5 (Brooding)
____ Hy_3 (Lassitude-Malaise)
✓ Sc_1 (Social Alienation)
____ Sc_2 (Emotional Alienation)
____ Sc_3 (Lack of Ego Mastery – Cognitive)
✓ Sc_4 (Lack of Ego Mastery – Conative)
____ Si_3 (Alienation)
✓ Pd_4 (Social Alienation)
✓ Pd_5 (Self-Alienation)
____ Pa_2 (Poignancy)
____ A-dep
____ A-anx
____ A-lse
____ A-aln
____ A-obs
✓ A-trt

6 /23 Number of scales with $T \geq 60$

2. Immaturity

✓ IMM
____ Scale F
____ Scale 8
____ Scale 6
____ ACK
✓ MAC-R
✓ Pa_1 (Persecutory Ideas)
____ Sc_2 (Emotional Alienation)
____ Sc_6 (Bizarre Sensory Experiences)
✓ A-sch
____ A-biz
____ A-aln
____ A-con
✓ A-fam
✓ A-trt

6 /15 Number of scales with $T \geq 60$

FIG. 4.4. MMPI–A Structural Summary for clinical case example (Deborah). Reproduced by special permission of Psychological Assessment Resources, Inc., from the MMPI–A Interpretive System by Robert P. Archer, PhD, Copyright 1992, 1995, 2000. Further reproduction is prohibited without permission from PAR, Inc.

3. Disinhibition/Excitatory Potential

- ✓ Scale 9
- ____ Ma_2 (Psychomotor Acceleration)
- ✓ Ma_4 (Ego Inflation)
- ____ Sc_5 (Lack of Ego Mastery, Defective Inhibition)
- ____ D_2 (Psychomotor Retardation) (low score)*
- ____ Welsh's R (low score)*
- ____ Scale K (low score)*
- ____ Scale L (low score)*
- ____ A-ang
- ____ A-cyn
- ____ A-con
- ✓ MAC-R

3 /12 Number of scales with $T \geq 60$ or ≤ 40 for scales with asterisk

4. Social Discomfort

- ____ Scale 0
- ____ Si_1 (Shyness/Self-Consciousness)
- ____ Hy_1 (Denial of Social Anxiety) (low score)*
- ____ Pd_3 (Social Imperturbability) (low score)*
- ____ Ma_3 (Imperturbability) (low scores)*
- ____ A-sod
- ____ A-lse
- ____ Scale 7

0 /8 Number of scales with $T \geq 60$ or $T \leq 40$ for scales with asterisk

5. Health Concerns

- ____ Scale 1
- ____ Scale 3
- ____ A-hea
- ____ Hy_4 (Somatic Complaints)
- ____ Hy_3 (Lassitude-Malaise)
- ____ D_3 (Physical Malfunctioning)

0 /6 Number of scales with $T \geq 60$

6. Naivete

- ____ A-cyn (low score)*
- ____ Pa_3 (Naivete)
- ____ Hy_2 (Need for Affection)
- ____ Si_3 (Alienation–Self and Others) (low score)*
- ____ Scale K

0 /5 Number of scales with $T \geq 60$ or $T \leq 40$ for scales with asterisk

7. Familial Alienation

- ✓ Pd_1 (Familial Discord)
- ✓ A-fam
- ✓ Scale 4
- ✓ PRO

4 /4 Number of scales with $T \geq 60$

8. Psychoticism

- ✓ Pa_1 (Persecutory Ideas)
- ____ Scale 6
- ____ A-biz
- ____ Sc_6 (Bizarre Sensory Experiences)

1 /4 Number of scales with $T \geq 60$

Note. The presentation of scales under each factor label is generally organized in a descending order from the best to the least effective marker. Within this overall approach, scales are grouped logically in terms of basic clinical scales, Harris-Lingoes and *Si* subscales, and content scales. The majority of scales included in this summary sheet were correlated ≥ .60 or ≤ –.60 with the relevant factor for the MMPI-A normative sample.

PAR Psychological Assessment Resources, Inc.
P.O. Box 998/Odessa, Florida 33556/Toll-Free 1-800-331-TEST

9 8 7 6 5 4 3 2 1 Reorder #RO-2698 Printed in the U.S.A.
This form is printed in blue ink on white paper. Any other version is unauthorized.

FIG. 4.5. MMPI–A Structural Summary for clinical case example (Deborah). Reproduced by special permission of Psychological Assessment Resources, Inc., from the MMPI–A Interpretive System by Robert P. Archer, PhD, Copyright 1992, 1995, 2000. Further reproduction is prohibited without permission from PAR, Inc.

over her use of acting out as a primary defense mechanism, the central issue in the treatment of this adolescent is whether the changes could be maintained in less structured treatment settings or through the use of outpatient interventions.

Deborah was discharged to outpatient care following 27 days of intensive inpatient treatment. One of the recommendations was to initiate individual, family, and group psychotherapy sessions. Deborah's prognosis at the conclusion of inpatient treatment was rated as guarded by treatment staff, who believed that she continued to manifest a low tolerance for frustration, interpersonal manipulativeness, and a relative absence of guilt or remorse concerning her antisocial behaviors. Within 6 months of her discharge from inpatient treatment, Deborah dropped out of high school and resumed involvement in drug use and distribution. Deborah was arrested on multiple counts of possession and distribution of drugs approximately 18 months following her discharge from the inpatient treatment unit.

Unfortunately, negative treatment outcomes for the *4-9/9-4* codetype are common among both adolescents and adults. Marks and Seeman (1963) reported that adult psychiatric patients admitted with a *4-9/9-4* profile also tended to produce the same codetype at discharge. Lachar (1974) reported that 80% of adult patients with an admission codetype of *4-9* were rated as unimproved at the time of discharge from treatment. Given that Deborah was only 17 years old at the time of her MMPI–A evaluation, it would be inappropriate to assume that her characteristics had the same stability as might be expected for a 30-year-old adult with similar profile features. It does seem probable, however, that had a discharge profile been obtained for this adolescent, it would have remained a *4-9* configural pattern. The consistency of the *4-9* profile through an admission, discharge, and readmission process is presented in a clinical case example for the original MMPI by Archer (1987). The MMPI–A admission characteristics exhibited by Deborah underscore the treatment challenges and difficulties that are likely to be encountered in cases like hers.

CONCLUSION

This chapter has provided an overview of the MMPI–A, including a description of the development of the test instrument and the MMPI–A normative sample. A number of recommendations were offered for the clinical use of the MMPI–A in treatment planning, and directions for future research were also noted. For example, there is a need for additional codetype congruency studies comparing the original version of the MMPI and the MMPI–A to determine the generalizability of findings from the original to the revised instrument. Additional external validity studies also will prove useful in establishing the correlate meanings for MMPI–A measures, particularly those recently created for this instrument, including the PSY–5 scales and content component scales. Research also should be focused on increasing the sensitivity and specificity of the MMPI–A in the detection of adolescents with and without histories of psychiatric symptomatology, including efforts to modify the item membership of the basic scales to evaluate the effects on hit rates.

Finally, this chapter reviewed the use of the MMPI–A for treatment outcome evaluation. Areas of relative strengths and weaknesses were noted, and emphasis was placed on interpreting change related to the factor structure of the instrument and validity scale findings. Future research should include controlled treatment outcome studies in which the test instrument is used in a test-retest format to assess psychological change as a function of psychotherapy.

REFERENCES

Achenbach, T. M., & Edelbrock, C. (1983). *Manual for the Child Behavior Checklist and Revised Child Behavior Checklist*. Burlington, VT: University of Vermont, Department of Psychiatry.

Alperin, J. J., Archer, R. P., & Coates, G. D. (1996). Development and effects of an MMPI–A *K*-correction procedure. *Journal of Personality Assessment, 67*, 155–168.

Anastasi, A. (1982). *Psychological testing* (5th ed.). New York: MacMillan.

Archer, R. P. (1984). Use of the MMPI with adolescents: A review of salient issues. *Clinical Psychology Review, 4*, 241–251.

Archer, R. P. (1987). *Using the MMPI with adolescents*. Hillsdale, NJ: Lawrence Erlbaum Associates.

Archer, R. P. (1992a). *MMPI–A interpretive system* [Computer software]. Odessa, FL: Psychological Assessment Resources, Inc.

Archer, R. P. (1992b). Review of the Minnesota Multiphasic Personality Inventory–2 (MMPI–2). In *The tenth mental measurements yearbook* (pp. 558–562). Lincoln, NE: Buros Institute of Mental Measurements.

Archer, R. P. (1996). *MMPI–A interpretive system* [Computer software]. Odessa, FL: Psychological Assessment Resources, Inc.

Archer, R. P. (1997). *MMPI–A: Assessing adolescent psychopathology* (2nd ed.). Mahwah, NJ: Lawrence Erlbaum Associates.

Archer, R. P., Belevich, J. K. S., & Elkins, D. E. (1994). Item-level and scale-level factor structures of the MMPI–A. *Journal of Personality Assessment, 62*, 332–345.

Archer, R. P., Bolinskey, P. K., Morton, T. L., & Farris, K. L. (2002). A factor structure for the MMPI–A: Replication with male delinquents. *Assessment, 9*, 319–326.

Archer, R. P., & Elkins, D. E. (1999). Identification of random responding on the MMPI–A. *Journal of Personality Assessment, 73*, 407–421.

Archer, R. P., & Gordon, R. A. (1988). MMPI and Rorschach indices of schizophrenic and depressive diagnoses among adolescent inpatients. *Journal of Personality Assessment, 52*, 276–287.

Archer, R. P., & Gordon, R. A. (1994). Psychometric stability of MMPI–A item modifications. *Journal of Personality Assessment, 62*, 416–426.

Archer, R. P., Gordon, R. A., Anderson, G. L., & Giannetti, R. A. (1989). MMPI special scale correlates for adolescent inpatients. *Journal of Personality Assessment, 52*, 707–721.

Archer, R. P., Handel, R. W., & Lynch, K. D. (2001). The effectiveness of MMPI–A items in discriminating between normative and clinical samples. *Journal of Personality Assessment, 77*, 420–435.

Archer, R. P., Handel, R. W., Lynch, K. D., & Elkins, D. E. (2002). MMPI–A validity scale uses and limitations in detecting varying levels of random responding. *Journal of Personality Assessment, 78*, 417–431.

Archer, R. P., & Jacobson, J. M. (1993). Are critical items "critical" for the MMPI–A? *Journal of Personality Assessment, 61*, 547–556.

Archer, R. P., & Klinefelter, D. (1991). MMPI factor analytic findings for adolescents: Item- and scale-level factor structures. *Journal of Personality Assessment, 57*, 356–367.

Archer, R. P., & Klinefelter, D. (1992). Relationships between MMPI codetypes and MAC scale elevations in adolescent psychiatric samples. *Journal of Personality Assessment, 58*, 149–159.

Archer, R. P., & Krishnamurthy, R. (1993a). Combining the Rorschach and MMPI in the assessment of adolescents. *Journal of Personality Assessment, 60*, 132–140.

Archer, R. P., & Krishnamurthy, R. (1993b). A review of MMPI and Rorschach interrelationships in adult samples. *Journal of Personality Assessment, 61*, 277–293.

Archer, R. P., & Krishnamurthy, R. (1994). A structural summary approach for the MMPI–A: Development and empirical correlates. *Journal of Personality Assessment, 63*, 554–573.

Archer, R. P., & Krishnamurthy, R. (1997a). MMPI–A and Rorschach indices related to depression and conduct disorder: An evaluation of the incremental validity hypothesis. *Journal of Personality Assessment, 69*, 517–533.

Archer, R. P., & Krishnamurthy, R. (1997b). MMPI–A scale-level factor structure: Replication in a clinical sample. *Assessment, 4*, 337–349.

Archer, R. P., & Krishnamurthy, R. (2002). *Essentials of MMPI–A assessment*. New York: Wiley.

Archer, R. P., Krishnamurthy, R., & Jacobson, J. M. (1994). *MMPI–A casebook*. Odessa, FL: Psychological Assessment Resources, Inc.

Archer, R. P., Maruish, M., Imhof, E. A., & Piotrowski, C. (1991). Psychological test usage with adolescent clients: 1990 survey findings. *Professional Psychology: Research and Practice, 22*, 247–252.

Archer, R. P., & Newsom, C. R. (2000). Psychological test usage with adolescent clients: Survey update. *Assessment, 7*, 227–236.

Archer, R. P., Pancoast, D. L., & Gordon, R. A. (1994). The development of the MMPI–A Immaturity (IMM) scale: Findings for normal and clinical samples. *Journal of Personality Assessment, 62,* 145–156.

Archer, R. P., Pancoast, D. L., & Klinefelter, D. (1989). A comparison of MMPI code types produced by traditional and recent adolescent norms. *Psychological Assessment: A Journal of Consulting and Clinical Psychology, 1,* 23–29.

Archer, R. P., & Slesinger, D. (1999). MMPI–A patterns related to the endorsement of suicidal ideation. *Assessment, 6,* 51–59.

Archer, R. P., Tirrell, C., & Elkins, D. E. (2001). Evaluation of an MMPI–A short form: Implications for adaptive testing. *Journal of Personality Assessment, 76,* 76–89.

Archer, R. P., White, J. L., & Orvin, G. H. (1979). MMPI characteristics and correlates among adolescent psychiatric inpatients. *Journal of Clinical Psychology, 35,* 498–504.

Arita, A. A., & Baer, R. A. (1998). Validity of selected MMPI–A content scales. *Psychological Assessment, 10,* 59–63.

Baer, R. A., Ballenger, J., Berry, D. T. R., & Wetter, M. W. (1997). Detection of random responding on the MMPI–A. *Journal of Personality Assessment, 68,* 139–151.

Baer, R. A., Ballenger, J., & Kroll, L. S. (1998). Detection of underreporting on the MMPI–A in clinical and community samples. *Journal of Personality Assessment, 71,* 98–113.

Baer, R. A., Kroll, L. S., Rinaldo, J., & Ballenger, J. (1999). Detecting and discriminating between random responding and overreporting on the MMPI–A. *Journal of Personality Assessment, 72,* 308–320.

Barron, F. (1953). An Ego-Strength scale which predicts response to psychotherapy. *Journal of Consulting Psychology, 17,* 327–333.

Butcher, J. N. (1987). *Computerized psychological assessment: A practitioner's guide.* New York: Basic Books.

Butcher, J. N. (1990). *MMPI–2 in psychological treatment.* New York: Oxford University Press.

Butcher, J. N., Dahlstrom, W. G., Graham, J. R., Tellegen, A., & Kaemmer, B. (1989). *Minnesota Multiphasic Personality Inventory–2 (MMPI–2): Manual for administration and scoring.* Minneapolis, MN: University of Minnesota Press.

Butcher, J. N., & Hostetler, K. (1990). Abbreviating MMPI item administration: What can be learned from the MMPI for the MMPI–2? *Psychological Assessment: A Journal of Consulting and Clinical Psychology, 2,* 12–21.

Butcher, J. N., & Owen, P. L. (1978). Objective personality inventories: Recent research and some contemporary issues. In B. Wolman (Ed.), *Clinical diagnoses of mental disorders* (pp. 475–546). New York: Plenum.

Butcher, J. N., & Tellegen, A. (1978). Common methodological problems in MMPI research. *Journal of Consulting and Clinical Psychology, 46,* 620–628.

Butcher, J. N., & Williams, C. L. (1992). *The Minnesota report: Adolescent interpretive system* [Computer software]. Minneapolis, MN: National Computer Systems.

Butcher, J. N., & Williams, C. L. (2000). *Essentials of MMPI–2 and MMPI–A interpretation* (2nd ed.). Minneapolis, MN: University of Minnesota Press.

Butcher, J. N., Williams, C. L., Graham, J. R., Archer, R. P., Tellegen, A., Ben-Porath, Y. S., et al. (1992). *MMPI–A (Minnesota Multiphasic Personality Inventory–Adolescent): Manual for administration, scoring, and interpretation.* Minneapolis, MN: University of Minnesota Press.

Caldwell, A. B. (1976, January). *MMPI profile types.* Paper presented at the 11th Annual MMPI Workshop and Symposium, sponsored by the University of Minnesota Press, Minneapolis, MN.

Capwell, D. F. (1945a). Personality patterns of adolescent girls: I. Girls who show improvement in IQ. *Journal of Applied Psychology, 29,* 212–228.

Capwell, D. F. (1945b). Personality patterns of adolescent girls: II. Delinquents and non-delinquents. *Journal of Applied Psychology, 29,* 284–297.

Cheung, F. M., & Ho, R. M. (1997). Standardization of the Chinese MMPI–A in Hong Kong: A preliminary study. *Psychological Assessment, 9,* 499–502.

Ciarlo, J. A., Edwards, D. W., Kiresuk, T. J., Newman, F. L., & Brown, T. R. (1981). *Final report: The assessment of client/patient outcome techniques for use in mental health programs* (NIMH Contract No. 278-80-0005[DB]). Denver, CO: University of Denver.

Dahlstrom, W. G., Archer, R. P., Hopkins, D. G., Jackson, E., & Dahlstrom, L. E. (1994). *Assessing the readability of the Minnesota Multiphasic Personality Inventory Instruments: The MMPI, MMPI–2, MMPI–A* (MMPI–2/MMPI–A Test Reports No. 2). Minneapolis, MN: University of Minnesota Press.

Ehrenworth, N. V., & Archer, R. P. (1985). A comparison of clinical accuracy ratings of interpretive approaches for adolescent MMPI responses. *Journal of Personality Assessment, 49,* 413–421.

Exner, J. E. (1986). *The Rorschach: A comprehensive system: Vol. 1. Basic foundations* (2nd ed.). New York: Wiley.

Finn, S. E. (1996). *Manual for using the MMPI–2 as a therapeutic intervention.* Minneapolis, MN: University of Minnesota Press.

Fontaine, J. L., Archer, R. P., Elkins, D. E., & Johansen, J. (2001). The effects of MMPI–A *T*-score elevation on classification accuracy for normal and clinical adolescent samples. *Journal of Personality Assessment, 76,* 264–281.

Forbey, J. D., & Ben-Porath, Y. S. (1998). *A critical item set for the MMPI–A* (MMPI–2/MMPI–A Test Reports No. 4). Minneapolis, MN: University of Minnesota Press.

Gallucci, N. T. (1990). On the synthesis of information from psychological tests. *Psychological Reports, 67,* 1243–1260.

Gallucci, N. T. (1997). On the identification of patterns of substance abuse with the MMPI–A. *Psychological Assessment, 9,* 224–232.

Gallucci, N. T., Kay, D. C., & Thornby, J. I. (1989). The sensitivity of 11 substance abuse scales from the MMPI to changing clinical status. *Psychology of Addictive Behaviors, 3,* 29–33.

Goldberg, L. R. (1965). Diagnosticians versus diagnostic signs: The diagnosis of psychosis versus neurosis from the MMPI. *Psychological Monographs, 79*(Whole No. 602).

Graham, J. R. (2000). *MMPI–2: Assessing personality and psychopathology* (3rd ed.). New York: Oxford University Press.

Greene, R. L. (1989). *Assessing the validity of MMPI profiles in clinical settings* (Clinical Notes on the MMPI No. 11). Minneapolis, MN: National Computer Systems.

Greene, R. L. (2000). *The MMPI–2: An interpretive manual* (2nd ed.). Boston: Allyn & Bacon.

Gumbiner, J. (1997). Comparison of scores on the MMPI–A and MMPI–2 for young adults: *Psychological Reports, 81,* 787–794.

Handel, R. W., Arnau, R., Archer, R. P., & Bolinskey, P. K. (2002). *MMPI–A PSY-5 scales: Replication and development of scale-level facets.* Manuscript in review.

Harris, R. E., & Lingoes, J. C. (1955). *Subscales for the MMPI: An end to profile interpretation.* Unpublished manuscript, University of California.

Hathaway, S. R. (1956). Scales 5 (Masculinity-Femininity), 6 (Paranoia), and 8 (Schizophrenia). In G. S. Welsh & W. G. Dahlstrom (Eds.), *Basic readings on the MMPI in psychology and medicine* (pp. 104–111). Minneapolis, MN: University of Minnesota Press.

Hathaway, S. R., & Monachesi, E. D. (1963). *Adolescent personality and behavior: MMPI patterns of normal, delinquent, dropout, and other outcomes.* Minneapolis, MN: University of Minnesota Press.

Hedlund, J. L., Won Cho, D., & Wood, J. D. (1977). Comparative validity of MMPI–168 factors in clinical scales. *Multivariate Behavioral Research, 12,* 327–329.

Henrichs, T. F. (1964). Objective configural rules for discriminating MMPI profiles in a psychiatric population. *Journal of Clinical Psychology, 20,* 157–159.

Henrichs, T. F. (1966). A note on the extension of MMPI configural rules. *Journal of Clinical Psychology, 22,* 51–52.

Herkov, M. J., Archer, R. P., & Gordon, R. A. (1991). MMPI response sets among adolescents: An evaluation of limitations of the Subtle-Obvious subscales. *Psychological Assessment: A Journal of Consulting and Clinical Psychology, 3,* 424–426.

Imhof, E. A., & Archer, R. P. (1997). Correlates of the MMPI–A Immaturity (*IMM*) scale in an adolescent psychiatric sample. *Assessment, 4,* 169–180.

Janus, M. D., deGroot, C., & Toepfer, S. M. (1998). The MMPI–A and 13-year-old inpatients: How young is too young? *Assessment, 5,* 321–332.

Janus, M. D., Tolbert, H., Calestro, K., & Toepfer, S. (1996). Clinical accuracy ratings of MMPI approaches for adolescents: Adding ten years and the MMPI–A. *Journal of Personality Assessment, 67,* 364–383.

Johnson, C., Archer, R. P., Sheaffer, C. I., & Miller, D. (1992). Relationships between the MAPI and the MMPI in the assessment of adolescent psychopathology. *Journal of Personality Assessment, 58,* 277–286.

Kopper, B. A., Osman, A., Osman, J. R., & Hoffman, J. (1998). Clinical utility of the MMPI–A content scales and Harris-Lingoes subscales in the assessment of suicidal risk factors in psychiatric adolescents. *Journal of Clinical Psychology, 54,* 191–200.

Koss, M. P., & Butcher, J. N. (1973). A comparison of psychiatric patients' self-report with other sources of clinical information. *Journal of Research and Personality, 7,* 225–236.

Krishnamurthy, R., & Archer, R. P. (1999). Empirically based interpretive approaches for the MMPI–A Structural Summary. *Journal of Personality Assessment, 73,* 245–259.

Krishnamurthy, R., Archer, R. P., & House, J. J. (1996). The MMPI–A and Rorschach: A failure to establish convergent validity. *Assessment, 3,* 179–191.

Lachar, D. (1974). *The MMPI: Clinical assessment and automated interpretation.* Los Angeles: Western Psychological Services.

Lachar, D., & Wrobel, T. A. (1979). Validating clinicians' hunches: Construction of a new MMPI critical item set. *Journal of Consulting and Clinical Psychology, 47,* 277–284.

Lewak, R. W., Marks, P. A., & Nelson, G. E. (1990). *Therapist guide to the MMPI and MMPI–2: Providing feedback and treatment.* Muncie, IN: Accelerated Development, Inc.

MacAndrew, C. (1965). The differentiation of male alcoholic outpatients from non-alcoholic psychiatric outpatients by means of the MMPI. *Quarterly Journal of Studies on Alcohol, 26,* 238–246.

Marks, P. A., & Briggs, P. F. (1972). Adolescent norm tables for the MMPI. In W. G. Dahlstrom, G. S. Walsh, & L. E. Dahlstrom (Eds.), *An MMPI handbook: Vol. I. Clinical interpretation* (rev. ed., pp. 388–399). Minneapolis, MN: University of Minnesota Press.

Marks, P. A., & Lewak, R. W. (1991). *The Marks MMPI adolescent feedback and treatment report* [Computer software]. Los Angeles: Western Psychological Services.

Marks, P. A., & Seeman, W. (1963). *The actuarial description of personality: An atlas for use with the MMPI.* Baltimore: Williams & Wilkins.

Marks, P. A., Seeman, W., & Haller, D. L. (1974). *The actuarial use of the MMPI with adolescents and adults.* New York: Oxford University Press.

McCarthy, L., & Archer, R. P. (1998). Factor structure of the MMPI–A content scales: Item-level and scale-level findings. *Journal of Personality Assessment, 71,* 84–97.

McNulty, J. N., Harkness, A. R., Ben-Porath, Y. S., & Williams, C. L. (1997). Assessing the personality psychopathology five (PSY-5) in adolescents: New MMPI–A scales. *Psychological Assessment, 9,* 250–259.

Meehl, P. E., & Dahlstrom, W. G. (1960). Objective configural rules for discriminating psychotic from neurotic MMPI profiles. *Journal of Consulting Psychology, 24,* 375–387.

Micucci, J. A. (2002). Accuracy of MMPI–A scales ACK, MAC-R, and PRO in detecting comorbid substance abuse among psychiatric inpatients. *Assessment, 9,* 111–122.

Milne, L. C., & Greenway, P. (1999). Do high scores on the adolescent-school problems and immaturity scales of the MMPI–A have implications for cognitive performance as measured by the WISC–III? *Psychology in the Schools, 36,* 199–203.

Moreland, K. L. (1983). Diagnostic validity of the MMPI and two short forms. *Journal of Personality Assessment, 47,* 492–394.

Negy, C., Leal-Puente, L., Trainor, D. J., & Carlson, R. (1997). Mexican-American adolescents' performance on the MMPI–A. Journal of Personality Assessment, 69, 205–214.

Osberg, T. M., & Poland, D. L. (2002). Comparative accuracy of the MMPI–2 and the MMPI–A in the diagnosis of psychopathology in 18-year-olds. *Psychological Assessment 14,* 164–169.

Pancoast, D. L., Archer, R. P., & Gordon, R. A. (1988). The MMPI and clinical diagnosis: A comparison of classification system outcomes with discharge diagnoses. *Journal of Personality Assessment, 52,* 81–90.

Pogge, D. L., Stokes, J. M., McGrath, R. E., Bilginer, L., & DeLuca, V. A. (2002). MMPI–A structural summary variables, prevalence of correlates in an adolescent inpatient psychiatric sample. *Assessment, 9,* 334–342.

Rogers, R., Hinds, J. D., & Sewell, K. W. (1996). Feigning psychopathology among adolescent offenders: Validation of the SIRS, MMPI–A and SIMS. *Journal of Personality Assessment, 67,* 244–257.

Scott, R. L., Butcher, J. N., Young, T. L., & Gomez, N. (2002). The Hispanic MMPI–A across five countries. *Journal of Clinical Psychology, 58,* 407–417.

Shaevel, B., & Archer, R. P. (1996). Effects of MMPI–2 and MMPI–A norms on *T*-score elevations for 18-year-olds. *Journal of Personality Assessment, 67,* 71–77.

Sherwood, N. E., Ben-Porath, Y. S., & Williams, C. L. (1997). *MMPI–A content component scales: Development, psychometric characteristics, and clinical application* (MMPI–2/MMPI–A Test Reports No. 3). Minneapolis, MN: University of Minnesota Press.

Spivack, G., Haimes, P. E., & Spotts, J. (1967). *Devereux Adolescent Behavior Rating Scale manual.* Devon, PA: The Devereux Foundation.

Stein, L. A. R., McClinton, B. K., & Graham, J. R. (1998). Long-term stability of MMPI-scales. *Journal of Personality Assessment, 70,* 103–108.

Toyer, E. A., & Weed, N. C. (1998). Concurrent validity of the MMPI–A in a counseling program for juvenile offenders. *Journal of Clinical Psychology, 54,* 395–399.

Tyler, F. T. (1951). A factorial analysis of fifteen MMPI scales. *Journal of Consulting Psychology, 15,* 451–456.

Ullmann, L. P., & Wiggins, J. S. (1962). Endorsement frequency in the number of differentiating MMPI items to be expected by chance. *Newsletter of Research in Psychology, 4,* 29–35.

Welsh, G. S. (1956). Factor dimensions *A* and *R*. In G. S. Welsh & W. G. Dahlstrom (Eds.), *Basic readings on the MMPI in psychology and medicine* (pp. 264–281). Minneapolis, MN: University of Minnesota Press.

Wiggins, J. S. (1966). Substantive dimensions of self-report in the MMPI item pool. *Psychological Monographs, 80*(22, Whole No. 630).

Wiggins, J. S. (1969). Content dimensions in the MMPI. In J. N. Butcher (Ed.), *MMPI: Research developments and clinical applications* (pp. 127–180). New York: McGraw-Hill.

Williams, C. L. (1986). MMPI profiles from adolescents: Interpretive strategies and treatment considerations. *Journal of Child and Adolescent Psychotherapy, 3*, 179–193.

Williams, C. L., Ben-Porath, Y. S., & Hevern, B. W. (1994). Item level improvements for use of the MMPI with adolescents. *Journal of Personality Assessment, 63*, 284–293.

Williams, C. L., Butcher, J. N., Ben-Porath, Y. S., & Graham, J. R. (1992). *MMPI–A content scales: Assessing psychopathology in adolescents.* Minneapolis, MN: University of Minnesota Press.

Zinn, S., McCumber, S., & Dahlstrom, W. G. (1999). Cross-validation of an extension of the MMPI–A *IMM* scale. *Assessment, 6*, 1–6.

5

Studying Outcomes in Adolescents: The Millon Adolescent Clinical Inventory (MACI) and Millon Adolescent Personality Inventory (MAPI)

Sarah E. Meagher
University of Miami

Seth D. Grossman
Institute for Advanced Studies in Personology and Psychopathology

Theodore Millon
Institute for Advanced Studies in Personology and Psychopathology

The Millon inventories have proven extremely popular with clinicians and researchers alike. Of the constellation of Millon inventories, including the Millon Clinical Multiaxial Inventory–III (MCMI–III), the Millon Behavioral Medicine Diagnostic (MBMD), and the Millon Behavioral Health Inventory (MBHI), the Millon Adolescent Personality Inventory (MAPI) and its revision, the Millon Adolescent Clinical Inventory (MACI), are the only instruments specifically designed for an adolescent population. Like the MCMI, the MAPI and MACI were constructed to be consonant with the multiaxial format of the *DSM* and are thus geared toward the assessment of both the problematic behaviors and clinical conditions of Axis I and the personality variables of Axis II. Although the main focus of this chapter is the MACI, the MAPI remains in widespread use and is presented here as well.

SCALES AND STRUCTURE OF THE MAPI AND MACI

The MAPI is a 150-item, true-false, self-report inventory consisting of eight Personality Styles scales, eight Expressed Concerns scales, and four Behavioral Correlate scales. The eight personality styles described in the MAPI mirror the styles posited by Millon's (1969) theory of personality. These styles, at maladaptive levels, correspond somewhat to the personality disorders described in the *DSM–III–R* (American Psychiatric Association, 1987). However, a decision was made to avoid the term *disorder*, defined in *DSM–III–R* as referring to "behaviors or traits that are characteristic of the person's recent (past year) and long-term functioning since early adulthood" (p. 335), as the MAPI is normed for adolescents as young as 13 years old. The eight Expressed Concerns scales focus on worries that many teens experience at one time or another, and the remaining four scales address specific behavioral issues. Previously,

TABLE 5.1
Structure and Scales of the MAPI and MACI

MAPI	*MACI*
Personality Styles	Personality Patterns
1. Introversive	1. Introversive
2. Inhibited	2a. Inhibited
	2b. Depressive
3. Cooperative	3. Submissive
4. Sociable	4. Dramatizing
5. Confident	5. Egotistic
6. Forceful	6a. Unruly
	6b. Forceful
7. Respectful	7. Conforming
8. Sensitive	8a. Oppositional
	8b. Self-Demeaning
	9. Borderline Tendency
Expressed Concerns	Expressed Concerns
A. Self-Concept	A. Identity Confusion
B. Personal Esteem	B. Self-Devaluation
C. Body Comfort	C. Body Disapproval
D. Sexual Acceptance	D. Sexual Discomfort
E. Peer Security	E. Peer Insecurity
F. Social Tolerance	F. Social Insensitivity
G. Family Rapport	G. Family Discord
H. Academic Confidence	
Behavioral Correlates	Clinical Syndromes
SS. Impulse Control	AA. Eating Dysfunctions
TT. Societal Conformity	BB. Academic Noncompliance
UU. Scholastic Achievement	CC. Alcohol Predilection
WW. Attendance Consistency	DD. Drug Proneness
	EE. Delinquent Disposition
	FF. Impulsivity Propensity
	GG. Anxious Feeling
	HH. Depression Affect
	II. Suicidal Ideation

two separate answer forms were available, the MAPI(G) for educational and guidance purposes and the MAPI(C) for clinical cases.

The MACI, with its several new clinically oriented scales, supplants the MAPI(C) for use in assessing clinical cases within the teenage population. The MAPI is now intended only for nonclinical educational and vocational appraisals and can be used with teenagers who have a sixth-grade or higher reading level. The structures of the MACI and MAPI are given in Table 5.1, and scale descriptions for the MAPI are given in Table 5.2. Additional commentary regarding specific changes in scale content is presented below.

Since the publication of the *DSM–III* in 1980, a total of 14 personality constructs have been represented in the body of Axis II or in the appendix. Sadistic and Self-Defeating were added to the appendix of *DSM–III–R*. In the *DSM–IV* (American Psychiatric Association, 1994), both of these disorders were dropped, the Depressive was added, and the Passive-Aggressive was broadened in content and renamed the Negativistic; also these latter two disorders were placed in the appendix.

The magnitude of these content changes required that the MAPI(C) be revised in order to coordinate the Millon clinical inventories more closely with the *DSM–IV*.

TABLE 5.2
MAPI Scale Descriptions

State	*Descriptors*
Personality Styles	
Introversive	Quiet and unemotional; interpersonally remote due to indifference toward others
Inhibited	Shy; socially ill at ease; lonely, yet keeps to self due to fear of rejection
Cooperative	Avoids asserting self and lets others take the lead; plays down own achievement and underestimates own abilities; kind and sentimental in relationships
Sociable	Talkative; charming; dramatic and emotionally expressive; easily bored with routine and long-term relationships
Confident	Rarely doubtful of own self-worth; seen by others as self-centered and egocentric; takes others for granted
Forceful	Tends to lead and dominate; strong willed and tough minded; blunt, unkind, and impatient with others
Respectful	Rule conscious, serious minded and efficient; lives orderly life; avoids unexpected and unpredictable situations; behaves properly
Sensitive	Unpredictable shifts of mood; negative attitude; discontented and pessimistic
Expressed Concerns	
Self-Concept	Clarity of one's identity or self-image
Personal Esteem	Level of satisfaction with oneself
Body Comfort	Level of satisfaction with body development and personal appearance
Sexual Acceptance	Attitudes regarding emerging sexuality and its associated impulses
Peer Security	Feelings of acceptance by one's peers
Social Tolerance	Degree of empathy for others, especially peers
Family Rapport	Degree of conflict and tension with family members
Academic Confidence	Extent to which one feels comfortable and/or satisfied with school Performance
Behavioral Correlates	
Impulse Control	Degree of control over problematic impulses
Societal Conformity	Inability or unwillingness to comply with social regulations
Scholastic Achievement	Influences resulting in underachievement
Attendance Consistency	Signs of either school phobia or school truancy

The resulting revision of the MAPI(C), the MACI, is a 160-item, true-false, self-report inventory that both corresponds more closely to the *DSM–IV* personality constructs and assesses those clinical issues seen more frequently among troubled adolescents. Although the distinction between incipient adolescent personality styles and adult personality disorders was retained, all MACI scales received more pathology-oriented names to reflect the inventory's clinical focus. The MACI's 12 personality scales include revisions of the original 8 from the MAPI as well as the Doleful, Forceful, Self-Demeaning, and Borderline Tendency scales. The clinical codes for these constructs parallel those of the MCMI–III and reflect the underlying generative theory on which all the Millon inventories are based.

Changes also have been made to the Expressed Concerns scales. Whereas the MAPI focused on expressed concerns within the context of a more normal adolescence, the expressed concerns of more clinically disordered youths reflect a more troublesome tone; where the MAPI measures level of Personal Esteem, the MACI assesses Self-Devaluation; Family Rapport in the MAPI is translated into Family Discord in the MACI, and so on. Similarly, the item content of these scales has been revised to allow discrimination within clinical populations. Moreover, whereas the MAPI includes four scales that address the behavioral issues of Impulse Control, Societal Conformity, Scholastic Achievement, and Attendance Consistency, the events that bring adolescents to the attention of clinicians often take the form of more maladjusted behaviors. For this reason, the MACI includes nine Clinical Indices oriented to such serious problems as eating dysfunctions, substance dependencies, mood disorders, and nonconformity behaviors. Given its increased clinical focus, approximately 70% of the MACI items are unique (i.e., not contained in the MAPI).

CONSTRUCTION OF THE MAPI AND MACI

The Role of Theory in Test Construction

Unlike most instruments widely used in psychological assessment, both the MAPI and MACI were constructed through a synthesis of theoretical and empirical perspectives, notably the biopsychosocial reinforcement (Millon, 1969, 1981) and evolutionary theories (Millon, 1990) of personality and its disorders. Although an early proponent of a relatively blind, empirical, criterion-keying approach to developing tests such as the MMPI, Meehl (1972) has since taken the view that theory should be an indispensable part of test construction:

> I now think that at all stages in personality test development, from the initial phase of item pool construction to a late-stage optimized clinical interpretive procedure for the fully developed and "validated" instrument, theory; and by this I mean all sorts of theory, including trait theory, developmental theory, learning theory, psychodynamics, and behavior genetics should play an important role. (p. 150)

The theory underlying the eight basic personality styles assessed by the MAPI can be explained using two basic dimensions to form a four-by-two matrix. One dimension describes an individual's basic coping pattern as either active or passive, depending on how the person usually behaves to obtain pleasure and minimize pain. The other dimension pertains to the primary source from which the individual gains this reinforcement, either from self or others. Individuals who receive little reinforcement from self or others are termed "Detached." Individuals whose values are based primarily on what others think and feel about them are termed "Dependent," and those who derive reinforcement through themselves are termed "Independent." Finally, some persons, termed "Ambivalent," develop a style born out of conflict between opposing dependent and independent tendencies. Crossing these theoretical dimensions results in the eight personality styles addressed by the MAPI: the passive-detached (Introversive), active-detached (Inhibited), passive-dependent (Cooperative), active-dependent (Sociable), passive-independent (Confident), active-independent (Forceful), passive-ambivalent (Respectful), and active-ambivalent (Sensitive).

In contrast, the theory on which the MACI is grounded reflects advances both in Millon's personality theory (Millon, 1990; Millon & Davis, 1996) and recent developments in the *DSM*. A supplementary dimension has been added, reflecting a reversal of reinforcement between pleasure and pain. Those termed passive-discordant were referred to as "self-defeating personalities" in the *DSM–III–R*, whereas those termed active-discordant were referred to as "sadistic personalities." Additionally, the MACI includes a scale that assesses structural pathology of personality, the Borderline Tendency scale. The Depressive personality, presented in the appendix of *DSM–IV*, is interpreted as having a passive-pain orientation; its clinical code reflects it relationship to the Avoidant personality. The former represents an acceptance of pain, whereas the later reflects more the anticipation of pain. The adolescent stylistic variants of these disorders are represented in the Doleful (2b) and Inhibited (2a) scales, respectively. Admittedly, the pervasiveness of both depression and anxiety across both Axis I and Axis II presents challenges to psychometricians who would tease apart what is long-standing and pervasive from what is transient and situational or reactive.

Stages of Development: Validity as a Central Consideration Throughout Construction

Validity is a consideration at all phases of test development, not a quality to be examined once inventory items have been finalized. In contrast to such established inventories as the MMPI–2 and MMPI–A, modern psychological inventories are constructed by balancing a variety of theoretical-substantive, internal-structural, and external-criterion parameters (Jackson, 1970; Loevinger, 1957). The paragraphs below review the construction of the MAPI, since it served as the foundation of the MACI.

The theoretical-substantive stage concerns how closely the content of the individual scale items match the guiding theory behind the instrument and the constructs its measures. For the MAPI, the initial theory-driven item pool for the personality style scales was derived from personality and abnormal psychology textbooks and a review of other psychological tests. Over a thousand items formed the initial pool, many of which were specially written for their particular constructs. After numerous studies (see Millon, Green, & Meagher, 1982, for a synopsis), the MAPI personality style scales were trimmed to just 64 items and the Expressed Concerns scales to 80 items. Six validational items were generated, for a total of 150 items.

The second stage of test construction, internal-structural validation, was driven by theoretically predicted relationships between scales, not factorial requirements. Because the underlying theory predicts a certain degree of scale overlap, internal-structural validation could not center on a factor analytic search for pure personality traits. Both the Inhibited and Introversive personality styles, for example, are related through their detached coping style. Likewise, content overlap also may occur logically between some Personality Styles scales and those in the Expressed Concerns, since some personalities are inclined toward particular concerns and issues rather than others. The goal of internal-structural validation, then, was not the elimination of items that could be logically assigned to multiple scales. Instead, internal scale consistency required that each particular item show its strongest, but not necessarily its only, correlation with its own theoretically designated scale. The assignment of items to multiple scales also allows the number of test items to be kept at a minimum.

The last stage, external-criterion validation, involved the administration of the final test form to a 2,157-member "normal" comparison group and a 430-member "problem" criterion group chosen from clinical and school counseling settings. Item responses from individuals with specific diagnosed psychopathology were then compared to the responses within the criterion group. This procedure enhances differential diagnosis and stands in contrast to the approach used to construct some other personality inventories. For example, the authors of the MMPI simply compared the responses of groups judged to belong to particular diagnostic categories with the responses of "normals." Meehl and Rosen (1955) argued persuasively against such a procedure. External validation also included clinical judgment data from the psychologists, counselors, and social workers who administered the MAPI to the 430 clinical criterion group subjects. Blind to the results of the test, these professionals were asked to rate their clients using a "clinical judgment form" that described the eight basic personality styles. The four Behavioral Correlates scales were derived by determining which items statistically differentiated criterion from comparison groups. Although the significant items were assessed later as to their content and internal consistency, empirical considerations were given primary attention with these four scales.

Construction of the MACI followed the same three-stage logic outlined above, building on the foundation created by the MAPI. The MACI now includes three modifying indices that assess the response styles of examinees. The first scale, Disclosure, appraises the degree to which patients are open and revealing of themselves. The two other scales, Desirability and Debasement, assess efforts to present oneself in a good or bad light, respectively. Because the results of these response styles affect the validity of other scales, they were used to develop certain correction factors. This idea should not be new to persons familiar with tests like the MMPI and MCMI, which use such scales for similar purposes. Additionally, the modifying scales may be, in and of themselves, of intrinsic interest to clinicians. Information regarding the way patients wish to present themselves, for example, by responding openly and frankly or by denying or concealing pathology, is often of special assistance to clinicians during early treatment planning.

Reliability

Test-retest and cross-validated internal consistency reliabilities for the MACI are presented in Table 5.3. All are sufficient to superior for clinical assessment and support the use of the MACI and MAPI in outcomes research.

SCORING AND INTERPRETATION

Third-party payers are increasingly requesting documentation in support of psychological diagnoses. Although the responsibility of mental health professionals is primarily to the welfare of their clients, psychological assessment should nevertheless serve both sides. Here, outcomes assessment is concerned with a single subject. At the beginning of treatment, the question is, What are the subject's clinical diagnoses and how do they relate to the subject's personality characteristics and level of functioning and current psychosocial milieu? Near the end of treatment, the question is, Which of the subject's problems have been addressed and what degree of progress has been made?

The Assessment Process

Step 1: Scoring. Proper use of the MACI and MAPI first requires that the instruments be properly scored. Given (a) the number of scales that make up the MAPI and the MACI, (b) their assignment to multiple scales and differential weighting, (c) the existence of separate group norms that are based on gender and age differences, (d) the various correction factors that may be invoked depending on response style, and (e) the unavoidable probability of human error at some point in the scoring process, it becomes clear that only computer scoring can reduce the probability of scoring error to negligible levels. Besides accuracy and speed, computer scoring has a number of other distinct advantages. Test forms and computer scoring are available through the

TABLE 5.3
MACI Alpha and Test-Retest Reliability Coefficients

MACI Scales	*Number of Items*	*Cross-Validation (Cronbach's Alpha)*	*Test-Retest*
Personality Patterns			
1 Introversive	44	0.82	0.63
2a Inhibited	37	0.86	0.70
2b Doleful	24	0.85	0.83
3 Submissive	48	0.73	0.88
4 Dramatizing	41	0.84	0.70
5 Egotistic	39	0.82	0.82
6a Unruly	39	0.83	0.79
6b Forceful	22	0.81	0.85
7 Conforming	39	0.86	0.91
8a Oppositional	43	0.82	0.76
8b Self-Demeaning	44	0.89	0.88
9 Borderline Tendency	21	0.86	0.92
Expressed Concerns			
A Identity Diffusion	32	0.76	0.77
B Self-Devaluation	38	0.90	0.85
C Body Disapproval	17	0.84	0.89
D Sexual Discomfort	37	0.69	0.74
E Peer Insecurity	19	0.77	0.57
F Social Insensitivity	39	0.79	0.83
G Family Discord	28	0.76	0.89
H Childhood Abuse	24	0.81	0.81
Clinical Syndromes			
AA Eating Dysfunction	20	0.85	0.78
BB Substance-Abuse Proneness	35	0.88	0.90
CC Delinquent Predisposition	34	0.76	0.80
DD Impulsive Propensity	24	0.75	0.78
EE Anxious Feelings	42	0.75	0.85
FF Depressive Affect	33	0.88	0.81
GG Suicidal Tendency	25	0.87	0.91
Modifying Indicies			
X Disclosure			0.86
Y Desirability	17	0.75	0.71
Z Debasement	16	0.85	0.84

Note. For the cross-validation, $N = 333$. For the test-retest, the interval was 3–7 days, and $N = 47$.

publisher. Completed forms may be processed for scoring and interpretation using an in-office personal computer system that provides immediate feedback or they can be mailed or scanned using telecommunications devices.

Most psychologists are familiar with the transformation of raw scores into other metrics, such as percentile ranks or *T*-scores. In contrast, in the MACI and MAPI, raw scores are transformed in what are termed "Base Rate" (BR) scores. Whereas *T*-scores implicitly assume that the prevalence of personality patterns and clinical syndromes are distributed equally and normally within the clinical population, BR scores do not. Clinical wisdom argues strongly that, within any given psychological treatment venue, certain disorders are more common than others. For example, borderline personality disorder and depression are relatively more common, whereas sadistic personality and systematic delusions are relatively rare. If approximately twice as many subjects are depressed as are schizophrenic, then the test should be constructed to mirror this reality. The BR score is a distinct shift from more conventional cutoff assignments, not only in jettisoning the tradition of identifying pathology by employing a single universal standard score cutoff for all scales, (e.g., two standard deviations above the mean) but also in establishing cutoffs on prevalence data based on representative and relevant national norms.

Step 2: Making Diagnoses. For the MAPI, prevalence estimates were provided by the clinical appraisals of mental health professionals, who rated a total of 430 subjects in terms of their basic personality style. After minor adjustments to reduce false positives, two arbitrary BR thresholds were set as signifying the presence or prominence of scale features. Scale scores of BR 75 and above identify the presence of each personality style, expressed concern, behavioral correlate, or clinical index. For the MACI, prevalence estimates were based not only on data from the normative sample but also on the author's years of experience using the MAPI.

In the MACI personality scales, scores of BR 75 and BR 85 indicate the presence of a trait (or disorder) or its prominence, respectively. The same is true for the Clinical Indices and Expressed Concerns scales. However, in cases where the term *disorder* is not applicable, as with Family Discord, for example, an elevation at BR 75 or above indicates this to be an area worthy of clinical attention. Although these cutting scores are not "absolutes," and a full contextual profile interpretation by an astute clinician is necessary for meaningful conceptualization and diagnosis, a youngster scoring between BR 75 and 84 may generally be seen as one who exhibits some of the features and problems of that particular scale, whereas one who scores at BR 85 and higher will likely display significant problematic facets of that scale's measured construct.

Step 3: Configural Interpretation. The interpretive yield of an instrument is significantly enhanced when its scales are interpreted configurally rather than one at a time. Several new resources have been published to aid clinicians in making complex configural interpretations; these resources range from basic to more sophisticated (McCann, 1997, 1999; Tringone, 1999). For the personality scales, configural interpretation is not just a matter of clinical convention. Instead, it is formally required by the nature of personality itself, the dynamic patterning of variables across all domains of the person. Just as individual scales stand in place of and assess hypothetical constructs, a personality profile should stand in place of the person. This naturally leads to the idea of "idiographic validity," the person-centered parallel of construct validity. It reflects the extent to which the clinical formulation or case conceptualization derived from the assessment in fact mirrors individual reality. Since personality is an intrinsically integrative construct, an adequate assessment of personality requires a configural synthesis of the personality scales available in any given instrument. Our view is that idiographic validity is maximized where the scales that compose the personality profile are themselves anchored to a coherent and generative personality theory. The two or three most highly elevated Axis II scales are thus taken as the basic interpretive context for case conceptualization, into which the meaning of symptom patterns in conjunction with psychosocial events and individual history are integrated. Ideally, this idiographically valid case formulation would become the foundation of treatment planning and thus the baseline against which any outcomes assessment would be made.

In contrast, there is no necessary reason why the Expressed Concerns and Clinical Indices scales must be interpreted configurally. Elevations among these scales are best interpreted in the context of the Axis II personality styles scales, the Axis IV psychosocial milieu, and current stressors. The logic of the multiaxial model holds that personality characteristics transform the meaning of clinical syndromes. For example, depression in a narcissistic patient has a different meaning and requires a different intervention than depression in a compulsive patient. In addition, valid interpretation also should take into account the individual's background, biographic history, and other auxiliary data.

Step 4: Configural Domain Synthesis. Personality styles and disorders are not unitary traits. Instead, they are higher order constructs that represent characteristics covariant across the entire matrix of the person. Although personality may be considered to be exclusively psychodynamic or exclusively biological, the authors regard such positions as narrow and restrictive. The integrative perspective encouraged here views personality as a multidetermined and multireferential construct that may be profitably studied and assessed across a variety of content areas. Diagnostic domains are best distinguished in accord with the data levels they represent—biophysical, intrapsychic, phenomenological, and behavioral—and in accord with the four historic approaches that characterize the study of psychopathology. These domains can be systematically organized in a manner similar to domains in the biological realm, that is, by categorizing them as *structural* or *functional*.

Functional domains represent "expressive modes of regulatory action," that is, behaviors, social conduct, cognitive processes, and unconscious mechanisms that manage, adjust, transform, coordinate, balance, discharge, and control the give and take of inner and outer life. The Expressive Acts domain relates to the observables seen at the "behavioral level" of data. The Interpersonal Conduct domain captures the impact of actions on others, intended or otherwise; the attitudes that underlie, prompt, and give shape to these actions; the methods by which others are engaged in satisfying needs; and the ways of coping with social tensions and conflicts. The Cognitive Style domain assesses how the patient focuses and allocates attention, encodes and processes information, organizes thoughts, makes attributions, and communicates reactions and ideas. Finally, the Regulatory Mechanisms domain captures efforts at self-protection, need gratification, and conflict resolution derived primarily from an unconscious level.

In contrast to functional domains, structural domains represent a deeply embedded and relatively enduring template of imprinted memories, attitudes, needs, fears, conflicts, and so on, which guide experience and transform the nature of ongoing life events. Psychic structures have an orienting and preemptive effect in that they alter the character of action and the impact of subsequent experiences in line with preformed inclinations and expectancies. For purposes of definition, structural domains may be conceived as substrates and action dispositions of a quasi-permanent nature. The Self-Image domain seeks to crystallize the patient's implicit sense of who he or she is, though these schemas differ greatly in clarity, accuracy, and complexity. The Object Representations domain synthesizes internalized representations of significant figures and relationships of the past. The Morphologic Organization domain conveys the overall architecture of the "psychic interior," referring to the structural strength, interior congruity, and functional efficacy of the personality system. Finally, Mood-Temperament variables are conveyed by terms such as *distraught*, *labile*, *fickle*, and *hostile* but are revealed as well by level of activity, speech quality, and physical appearance.

Domain descriptions for the DSM Avoidant personality are given in Table 5.4 for illustrative purposes. Although these have been developed for adult personalities

TABLE 5.4
Avoidant Descriptors

Behavioral Level
- (F) Expressively Fretful (e.g., conveys personal unease and disquiet, a constant timorous, hesitant, and restive state; overreacts to innocuous events and anxiously judges them to signify ridicule, criticism, and disapproval).
- (F) Interpersonally Aversive (e.g., distances from activities that involve intimate personal relationships and reports extensive history of social pan-anxiety and distrust; seeks acceptance but is unwilling to get involved unless certain to be liked, maintaining distance and privacy to avoid being shamed and humiliated).

Phenomenological Level
- (F) Cognitively Distracted (e.g., warily scans environment for potential threats and is preoccupied by intrusive and disruptive random thoughts and observations; an upwelling from within of irrelevant ideation upsets thought continuity and interferes with social communications and accurate appraisals).
- (S) Alienated Self-Image (e.g., sees self as socially inept, inadequate, and inferior, justifying thereby his or her isolation and rejection by others; feels personally unappealing, devalues self-achievements, and reports persistent sense of aloneness and emptiness).
- (S) Vexatious Objects (e.g., internalized representations are composed of readily reactivated, intense, and conflict-ridden memories of problematic early relations; limited avenues for experiencing or recalling gratification, and few mechanisms to channel needs, bind impulses, resolve conflicts, or deflect external stressors).

Intrapsychic Level
- (F) Fantasy Mechanism (e.g., depends excessively on imagination to achieve need gratification, confidence building, and conflict resolution; withdraws into reveries as a means of safely discharging frustrated affectionate as well as angry impulses).
- (S) Fragile Organization (e.g., a precarious complex of tortuous emotions depend almost exclusively on a single modality for its resolution and discharge, that of avoidance, escape, and fantasy and, hence, when faced with personal risks, new opportunities, or unanticipated stress, few morphologic structures are available to deploy and few backup positions can be reverted to, short of regressive decompensation).

Biophysical Level
- (S) Anguished Mood (e.g., describes constant and confusing undercurrent of tension, sadness, and anger; vacillates between desire for affection, fear of rebuff, embarrassment, and numbness of feeling).

and are not presented in the MACI or MAPI manuals, their characteristics may be extrapolated backward to the Inhibited scales of the MAPI and MACI. There is, after all, continuity between adolescence and adulthood. Because the personalities of adolescents are, however, presumably more malleable or less crystallized than those of adults, making the term *personality disorder* strictly inapplicable, clinicians who draw on these descriptions should adjust their interpretations to reflect lower levels of severity.

Most examinees present with multiple scale elevations. Pure prototypes are seldom encountered in clinical practice. In the vast majority of cases, individuals receive elevated scores on multiple scales.

Factor Subscales

Personality may be described on several levels of abstraction. Personality *styles* represent the covariant structure of personality *traits*. When these styles are expressed rigidly, they tend to create and perpetuate problems over and over again. Alternately, they may predispose the person to the development of symptoms and thus shade into personality disorders.

The content of personality assessment instruments can be examined using any number of empirical methods, including cluster and factor analysis. If factor analysis is chosen, a decision must be made whether to factor scales or items. If items are chosen, a further decision must be made—whether to group the items in some logical fashion. For example, should the items assigned to Axis II be factored separately from those assigned to Axis I, should only the items within a particular personality cluster be factored, or should only the items within a particular scale be factored? Further, where items are weighted depending on their centrality to the construct assessed, as in the Millon inventories, a decision must be made whether only core features should be factored (for the MACI, those weighted either three or two points) or whether the analysis should include all scales items, that is, both core and peripheral features. Different choices lead to different results.

Thus far, exploratory studies with the MACI personality scales using data from the normative sample have been conducted by factoring all the items *within each scale*. First, three-, four-, five-, six-, and seven-factor solutions were extracted for each scale. Next, the resulting item loadings were inspected to determine which solution best conformed to theoretical expectations. Finally, the internal consistencies of each subscale were calculated, and those found to be inadequate were dropped. A list of the resulting factors is presented in Table 5.5. Since factor analysis relies on the covariance of items, not the item weight, the logical distinction between more core and more peripheral features is lost. Items that are assumed to be prototypal for their constructs cannot necessarily be assumed to be prototypal for the traits extracted through factor analysis. Moreover, the relatively large number of factors relative to scales, which already share a proportion of items, means that the issue of item overlap is amplified for the subscales. Some subscales share all their items. The surviving subscales were thus named within the context of the personality style from which they were derived and not on the basis of item content alone. The advantage of this method is that it provides a loose guide to the content of the personality prototypes factored. Future factor studies will be directed toward comparing results for factors using more central items, those weighted three and two points, and factors using both more central and more peripheral items (the factors presented here are of this latter type).

The Automated Interpretive Report

In addition to their own interpretive skills, clinicians have available to them a large database of automated MACI and MAPI reports. Whereas clinicians may be able to remember some features associated with a number of the more common profile configurations, a computer provides quick access to all salient data for each possible profile. Moreover, even experienced clinicians may have difficulty interpreting novel profiles. Due to their low frequency, these relatively uncommon configurations receive little actuarial attention. Both the MACI and MAPI use the underlying theory to inform such sparse actuarial data. The resulting interpretive report is considered a professional consultation and constitutes a rich source of clinical hypotheses from which relevant descriptive paragraphs or phrases may be culled during the writing of the final interpretive report. Although every individual is unique, there are only a finite number of clinical reports and variations. Thus, clinicians are advised to personalize the reports by incorporating the unique characteristics and psychosocial situation of the subjects.

TABLE 5.5
Factor Content Scales of MACI Personality Scales

Scale	*Factor*
Introversive	Existential Aimlessness
	Anhedonic Affect
	Social Isolation
	Sexual Indifference
Inhibited	Existential Sadness
	Preferred Detachment
	Self-Conscious Restraint
	Sexual Aversion
	Rejection Feelings
Doleful	Brooding Melancholia
	Social Joylessness
	Self-Destructive Ideation
	Abandonment Fears
Submissive	Deficient Assertiveness
	Authority Respect
	Pacific Disposition
	Attachment Anxiety
	Social Correctness
	Guidance Seeking
Dramatizing	Convivial Sociability
	Attention Seeking
	Attractive Self-Image
	Optimistic Outlook
	Behavioral Disinhibition
Egotistic	Admirable Self-Image
	Social Conceit
	Confident Purposefulness
	Self-Assured Independence
	Empathic Indifference
	Superiority Feelings
Unruly	Impulsive Disobedience
	Socialized Substance Abuse
	Authority Rejection
	Unlawful Activity
	Callous Manipulation
	Sexual Absorption
Forceful	Intimidating Abrasiveness
	Precipitous Anger
	Emphatic Deficiency
Conforming	Interpersonal Restraint
	Emotional Rigidity
	Rule Adherence
	Social Conformity
	Responsible Conscientiousness
Oppositional	Self-Punitiveness
	Angry Dominance
	Resentful Discontent
	Social Inconsiderateness
	Contrary Conduct

(Continued)

TABLE 5.5
(Continued)

Scale	*Factor*
Self-Demeaning	Self-Ruination Low Self-Valuation Undeserving Self-Image Hopeless Outlook
Borderline Tendency	Empty Lonelinesss Capricious Reactivity Uncertain Self-Image Suicidal Impulsivity

TREATMENT PLANNING

The idea of using standardized instruments for treatment planning and the assessment of outcomes is controversial. According to Choca, Shanley, and Van Denburg (1992), some maintain that the most important information about a client can only be obtained through personal interview sessions, whereas others contend that testing before the onset of or during treatment obfuscates the therapeutic relationship (Dewald, 1967). In addition, some researchers attach little clinical significance to assessment or diagnoses, but others believe testing during treatment will almost always be detrimental (Langs, 1973). However, Choca et al. (1992) also cited several other sources that show that assessment is relied on and encouraged by a sizable number of clinicians (Berndt, 1983; van Reken, 1981).

In some cases, the individual's current psychic state is such that immediate intervention is warranted to protect the subject from self or others. Though these conditions are typically assessed as part of the clinical interview, the subject's status may be further inspected through the examination of so-called noteworthy responses. Here, the response to a single item suggests a condition that requires immediate clinical attention, such as suicidal or homicidal intentions. For example, Item 16 states, "I think everyone would be better off if I were dead." Alternatively, a noteworthy response may suggest conditions that should be addressed in therapy. For example, Item 137 states, "People did things to me sexually when I was too young to understand."

Most clinical cases, however, do not require immediate crisis hospitalization. In the era of managed care, therapy is brief, and the most relevant clinical goal is remediation of those problems that are currently most pressing. Although personality provides an important context for the development of Axis I symptoms, brief therapy requires that only the most troublesome issues be considered. Here, personality style scales are deemphasized, and expressed concerns and clinical indices become the proper focus of treatment efforts. Given that only the most observable and vivid problems will be treated, behavioral or cognitive-behavioral interventions can be expected to dominate. The clinical question is, How can current problems best be addressed or resolved? Whatever direction therapy eventually takes, the relatively high test-retest reliabilities of the MACI scales makes outcomes assessment a relatively simple affair. The test can simply be administered again at a later date, and the difference between beginning and final BR scores is then usable as a rough measure of therapeutic change.

Where therapy is less time limited, the focus shifts from immediate problems to the subject's characteristic way of viewing and responding to the world, which becomes treated as the major predisposing factor in the development and perpetuation of psychological symptoms. Here, the personality style scales move into the foreground. The clinical question is, What characteristics does the individual possess that cause him or her to perpetuate the same dysfunctional coping responses over and over again? Rigid and extreme personality styles are thus viewed as major factors increasing the individual's vulnerability to symptom development, be it anxiety, depression, or other Axis II syndromes. As Choca et al. (1992) stated, "In the majority of cases we see, especially after the symptomatology diminishes, the client is left to struggle with cumbersome or pathological personality traits" (p. 199). An example might be an emaciated anorexic who presents with elevated Borderline Tendency, Identity Confusion, Body Disapproval, and Eating Dysfunctions scale scores. Such a person might require immediate medical supervision supplemented with behavioral therapy. After some degree of physical stability has been attained, supportive, insight-oriented, or even family therapy might be administered, depending on the elevation and configuration of other scales.

The construction of treatment plans based on configural codes is best accomplished on the basis of the case conceptualization outlined earlier. However, knowledge of typical issues that different personalities bring to therapy in their prototypal form can be valuable when developing plans for individuals whose clinical codetypes synthesize multiple scales. For example, because an avoidant personality's mistrust of others contributes to and reinforces social withdrawal, development of a therapeutic alliance presents a special challenge. This introductory process may require an extended period of supportive enhancement of the client's self-esteem. Once the bond has been formed, the second phase of treatment may center on evoking insights regarding the client's unique etiology. Such reappraisal may help the client recognize current problems and deal with them more effectively. The following techniques may prove helpful as adjuncts: (a) medication and/or behavior modification to alleviate stresses resulting from therapy and its generalization, (b) principles of cognitive therapy to counter distorted thinking patterns, and (c) family and group therapy to improve social and communication skills.

Unlike the avoidant, the dependent personality typically poses no threat to the early development of the therapeutic bond. Such a client usually is eager to assume the familiar submissive stance within the therapeutic milieu. Thus, although the introductory stage of treatment may move quickly and smoothly, the client will be highly resistant to the therapist's later efforts to engender a healthy degree of autonomy. Directive therapies are logically contraindicated because these would simply reinforce the client's dependency needs. Nondirective dynamic and humanistic approaches usually emphasize the importance of the client and, over time, can be effective in improving self-esteem. These therapies may be too anxiety provoking for severe dependents, however. In these cases, medication may be required before the client is capable of producing the insight needed for change. Through additional group treatment, the dependent may learn new social skills and gain increased self-confidence.

In contrast to avoidant and dependent personalities, the unruly adolescent usually arrives for treatment at the insistence of family members or school administrators. Because this client has little motivation to change, prognosis generally is seen as poor. However, if the therapist can patiently withstand the client's disruptive behavior (e.g., attempts at humiliation, belittlement, bluff, arrogance), a modicum of rapport can be built in some cases. If this is achieved, the therapist can act as a model mixture of "power, reason, and fairness" (Millon, 1981, p. 214) for the teen. In addition, group therapies can help foster social and communication skills.

These examples hint at the literally infinite number of combinations of personality style, expressed concerns, and symptoms that adolescents present. The structure of the Millon inventories parallels the multiaxial model. Clinicians should be familiar with the principles of multiaxial assessment to use the instruments to their fullest potential.

ASSESSMENT OF TREATMENT OUTCOMES

The MACI fares well when evaluated against criteria for evaluating psychological instruments as outcome measures proposed by Newman and Ciarlo (1994) and Newman, Ciarlo, and Carpenter (1997) in earlier editions of this text. Whereas other inventories represent a downward extension of instruments originally constructed with adult populations, the MACI was specifically normed on adolescent subjects. Moreover, the inventory was constructed as a multiaxial instrument coordinated with both a coherent clinical theory and with the *DSM–IV* nosology. Though some adolescents will require supervision, its 160-item length and sixth-grade reading level make it basically self-administering. The inventory requires less than a half hour to complete. As with the other Millon inventories, scale scores are based on national samples, and prevalence rates are informed by clinical ratings on the normative population, external validity studies, and clinical wisdom. Correction factors are available to mitigate the influence of response biases. Assessments of the reliability and validity of the instrument were an integral part of the test construction process. Given that the inventory is still relatively new, a smaller database of publications is available than for the MCMI. However, the two inventories are based on the same clinical theory and were developed using the same underlying logic of test construction. Computer scoring is available and provides either a profile report or a more comprehensive interpretive report written in easy-to-understand language. The scale names are descriptive, and scale elevations beyond the BR cutoff scores indicate the relative prominence of the personality features or the relative severity of Expressed Concerns or Clinical Syndrome scores.

Though it is an implicit assumption among nosologists that legitimate psychological disorders should "breed true" over time, the interaction between intrinsic maturational capacities and variegated environmental influences creates diverse multiple pathways of development that make adolescent pathologies extremely difficult to study. For example, in assessments conducted approximately 5 to 10 years following hospitalization (Weiss & Burke, 1970), the majority of school phobic youths were found to be high school graduates who had performed academically at or above their expected levels. Thus, on the surface, it seemed that the therapeutic interventions had been effective. However, at the time of the later assessment, most of the subjects did not conceive of their earlier problem as being school phobia. Further, around half of the subjects were assessed as having made inadequate social adjustment.

As with any study, researchers are advised to be aware of multitrait-multimethod factors. Diagnosis and treatment planning should take into consideration not only self-reports but also reports from parents, teachers, and others associated with the youth. Outcomes assessment techniques also must advance to accommodate multiple measures from a variety of information sources. As more information is integated into the assessment, clinical baselines become successively more qualitative, less quantitative, and less amenable to empirical study simply because the individual is understood as a unique developmental entity rather than a collection of scale scores (see chap. 16, vol. 3, which discusses the MCMI).

Researchers designing outcome studies with multiaxial instruments must first define the scope of the outcome to be assessed. In a managed care setting, for example, personality change is often not addressed because therapy is intended to be palliative rather than substantive. Here, a minimal interpretation of efficacy might examine only pre- and posttreatment scores for just the Expressed Concerns and Clinical Syndromes scales to which treatment is addressed. Since the raw score distributions of most MACI and MAPI scales are not normally distributed, nonparametric statistics are recommended as a means of determining the statistical significance of change scores. Most nonparametric tests result in only modest loss of statistical power relative to parametric tests performed on larger samples.

Though pre- and posttreatment differences on the Personality Styles scales would thus appear useful only with longer term interventions where personality change becomes a primary goal, the Personality Styles scales can be incorporated into outcome studies in a variety of ways. Elevations on the Personality Styles scales could be inspected to assist subject selection—to help select primarily narcissistic subjects, for example, or to divide the sample into contrast groups with high and low levels of self-reported personality pathology on the basis of their BR scores. If a large sample is available, the raw scores of the personality scales could be factor analyzed and pre- and posttreatment scores could be compared on the resulting factors.

If the outcome assessment is intended for a single subject, MACI scores can be used to document treatment efficacy. Research done with the MCMI has shown that for some subjects the BRs of certain scales actually increase in response to therapy, namely, the Histrionic, Narcissistic, and Compulsive scales. This is likely to be the case for the MACI as well. These three constructs possess normal variants that are often highly adaptable in modern society. The self-confidence of the normal-range narcissist, for example, is seen as positive and motivating, while the sociability of the normal-range histrionic is a positive form of extroversion. For these scales, the relationship between scale score and pathology is nonlinear. Too little self-confidence is bad, too much is bad, but a certain level is valued and even envied.

Although the repeated administration of inventories is questioned by some, many clinicians find follow-up assessments to be useful. Furthermore, insurance companies, lawyers, consumer interest groups, and others are increasingly calling for documentation that supports the value of treatment. The BR thresholds built into the instrument provide reference points against which the efficacy of treatment for a single subject may be judged. Since a score of BR 75 indicates the presence of pathology for most scales, posttreatment scores that drop below BR 75 suggest pathologies that have been treated into the subclinical range. This does not mean that no further basis for treatment exists, since the scales that are often the focus of outcomes assessment are those related to Axis I–like conditions. Likewise, posttreatment scores that drop from above BR 85 to the BR 75–84 range may indicate that the severity of a particular disorder has subsided, though aspects of the disorder (whether Axis I or Axis II in nature) will likely need continued treatment.

Because the MACI is a multiaxial instrument, the focus of treatment should be understood in advance before results are communicated. For example, the best index of recovery for a patient referred for the treatment of depression is the change score in the Depressive Affect scale. The personality profile and its overall elevation and relation to the subject's symptoms may be interesting, but if the issue is the disposition of the referral issue, certain scales may not be relevant.

CONCLUSION

The MAPI and its more recent revision, the MACI, are designed to be consonant with the *DSM*'s multiaxial format, and they may be invaluable in helping to formulate a case conceptualization that fully contextualizes the clinical conditions of Axis I and the personality variables of Axis II. Derived, as all Millon instruments are, from a comprehensive theory of personality that interfaces well with the empirically based *DSM* model, these adolescent instruments provide advantages in treatment planning by allowing the clinician to focus on target issues (as may be required by some short-term models of therapy) while providing a sound basis for a comprehensive, integrated profile of personality and clinical variables. Their brevity and ease of use are complemented by their positive appraisal against established criteria for the evaluation of psychological instruments.

Since the MACI is a relatively recently published instrument, an important direction for research is the use of the MACI as an instrument in outcome studies. The reliability of the MACI scales, their basis in a coherent theory of personality and psychopathology, and their coordination with the *DSM-IV* should be attractive to researchers seeking to quantify outcomes in adolescent groups. At the same time, the availability of interpretive reports is of assistance to clinicians seeking to document baselines and progress in the therapy they provide to patients.

REFERENCES

American Psychiatric Association. (1987). *Diagnostic and statistical manual of mental Disorders* (3rd ed. rev.). Washington, DC: Author.

American Psychiatric Association. (1994). *Diagnostic and statistical manual of mental disorders* (4th ed.). Washington, DC: Author.

Berndt, D. (1983). Ethical and professional considerations in psychological assessment. *Professional Psychology: Research and Practice, 14*, 580–587.

Choca, J. P., Shanley, L. A., & Van Denburg, E. (1992). *Interpretive guide to the Millon Clinical Multiaxial Inventory*. Washington, DC: American Psychological Association.

Dewald, P. (1967). Therapeutic evaluation and potential: The psychodynamic point of view. *Comprehensive Psychiatry, 8*, 284–298.

Jackson, D. N. (1970). A sequential system for personality scale development. In C. D. Spielberger (Ed.), *Current topics in clinical and community psychology* (Vol. 2, pp. 61–92). New York: Academic Press.

Langs, R. (1973). *The technique of psychoanalytic psychotherapy* (Vol. 1). Northvale, NJ: Jason Aronson.

Loevinger, J. (1957). Objective tests as instruments of psychological theory. *Psychological Reports, 3*, 635–694.

McCann, J. T. (1997). The MACI: Composition and clinical applications. In T. Millon (Ed.), *The Millon inventories: Clinical and personality assessment* (pp. 363–388). New York: Guilford.

McCann, J. T. (1999). *Assessing adolescents with the MACI*. New York: Wiley

Meehl, P. E. (1972). Reactions, reflections, projections. In J. N. Butcher (Ed.), *Objective personality assessment* (pp. 131–189). New York: Academic Press.

Meehl, P. E., & Rosen, A. (1955). Antecedent probability and the efficiency of psychometric signs, patterns, or cutting scores. *Psychological Bulletin, 52*, 194–216.

Millon, T. (1969). *Modern psychopathology*. Philadelphia: Saunders.

Millon, T. (1981). *Disorders of personality: DSM–III, Axis II*. New York: Wiley.

Millon, T. (1990). *Toward a new personology: An evolutionary model*. New York: Wiley.

Millon, T., & Davis, R. (1996). *Disorders of personality: DSM–IV and beyond*. New York: Wiley-Interscience.

Millon, T., Green, C. J., & Meagher, R. B. (1982). *Millon Adolescent Personality Inventory manual*. Minneapolis, MN: National Computer Systems.

Newman, F. L., & Ciarlo, J. A. (1994). Criteria for selecting psychological instruments for treatment outcome assessment. In M. E. Maruish (Ed.), *The use of psychological testing for treatment planning and outcomes assessment* (pp.). Hillsdale, NJ: Lawrence Erlbaum Associates.

Newman, F. L., Ciarlo, J. A., & Carpenter, D. (1999). Guidelines for selecting psychological instruments for treatment planning and outcome assessment. In M. E. Maruish (Ed.), *The use of psychological testing for treatment planning and outcomes assessment* (2nd ed., pp. 153–170). Hillsdale, NJ: Lawrence Erlbaum Associates.

Tringone, R. (1999). Essentials of MACI assessment. In S. Strack (Ed.), *Essentials of Millon inventories assessment* (pp. 92–160). New York: Wiley.

van Reken, M. (1981). Psychological assessment and report writing. In C. E. Walker (Ed.), *Clinical practice of psychology: A guide for mental health professionals*. New York: Pergamon.

Weiss, M., & Burke, A. (1970). A 5- to 10-year follow-up of hospitalized school phobic children and adolescents. *American Journal of Orthopsychiatry, 40*, 672–676.

6

Personality Inventory for Children, Second Edition (PIC–2), Personality Inventory for Youth (PIY), and Student Behavior Survey (SBS)

David Lachar
University of Texas–Houston Health Sciences Center

This chapter introduces a family of measures used in the evaluation of school-age children: the Personality Inventory for Children Second Edition (PIC–2), the Personality Inventory for Youth (PIY), and the Student Behavior Survey (SBS). These three questionnaires have been constructed to meet the assessment needs of youth, as have measures developed by Achenbach, by Conners, and by Reynolds and Kamphaus described in other chapters of this volume. Each of these families of measures assesses multiple dimensions of problem behavior, collects observations from parents, teachers, and youth, and provides standard scores based on contemporary national samples. Lachar (1998, 2003) has offered integrated reviews of these four families of measures.

AN INTRODUCTION TO MULTIDIMENSIONAL MULTISOURCE ASSESSMENT

Multidimensional objective assessment is both efficient and accurate. Important clinical phenomena are measured using the same format and are evaluated using the same or similar standardization samples (in contrast to an assessment in which a customized selection of narrowband instruments that have different response characteristics and were standardized using different normative samples deliver results that are clinically integrated into a description of a specific child). Clinicians who use multidimensional assessment understand that the documentation of symptom or problem *absence* makes a diagnostic contribution comparable to the documentation of symptom or problem *presence*. They also recognize that a pattern of significant clinical problems is often characteristic of referred children. These problem constellations or patterns of diagnoses are designated as "comorbid" and reflect the dynamics of child referral in that the probability of such referrals is determined by the combined likelihood of referral for separate disorders (Caron & Rutter, 1991). For example, the internalizing problem dimensions of anxiety and depression are often comorbid (Brady & Kendall, 1992; King, Ollendick, & Gullone, 1991; Lonigan, Carey, & Finch, 1994). Similarly, a variety of externalizing problem dimensions have been found to be comorbid with the diagnosis of attention deficit/hyperactivity disorder (ADHD; Jensen, Martin, & Cantwell, 1997; Pliszka, 1998). Indeed, it has been stated that the measurement and treatment of these comorbid disorders are often of comparable importance to the assessment and treatment of ADHD itself (Cantwell, 1996).

Clinicians who routinely apply multidimensional assessment measures to the initial assessment also are aware that children referred for an evaluation often have problems that are different from those originally thought to be present. For example, application of a narrowly focused ADHD measure at the beginning of an evaluation of a child referred because of possible ADHD may be problematic for two reasons. The resulting descriptions from such a measure may not result in clinically elevated scale scores, leaving possible alternative explanations for observed inattention unexplored (e.g., depression, anxiety, situational maladjustment, learning disability, and acquired cognitive deficit). Alternatively, application of such a narrowly focused ADHD measure may result in one or more clinically significant scale scores but provide no evidence of the presence or absence of frequently observed comorbid conditions. It would therefore seem most logical and efficient to first apply a multidimensional measure and then subsequently focus on further differentiation of problem areas highlighted by this initial assessment effort. Such a "successive hurdles" approach recognizes the value of initial psychometric information in the design of subsequent evaluative efforts.

Multisource assessment has become the preferred model for the evaluation of child and adolescent emotional and behavioral adjustment and reflects the importance of parent and teacher observation (cf. LaGreca, Kuttler, & Stone, 2001). Unlike the evaluation of adjustment in adults, which typically relies on self-report, the evaluation of school-age children usually cannot depend solely on self-description. Indeed, the context of assessment is fundamentally different for children and adolescents, who are unlikely to refer themselves for evaluation or treatment and may not possess the academic, cognitive, or motivational competence to complete a comprehensive self-report instrument. Young children, perhaps from preschool through third grade, may be unable to describe themselves adequately through responses to questionnaire statements (cf. Flavell, Flavell, & Green, 2001). Such children are unlikely to have mastered the range of vocabulary necessary to adequately describe dimensions of adjustment; such language competence is not usually attained before the fourth or fifth grade.

Another consideration is that youth are most often referred for evaluation because they are either noncompliant with the requests of the significant adults in their lives or exhibit academic problems (often associated with inadequate reading skills). Therefore, completion of a self-report inventory of several hundred items could present quite an assessment challenge even for a high school student who is referred for an evaluation. Parents and teachers not only refer youth for assessment, they are also the primary sources of useful systematic observation. Certainly adults are the informants who can best report on the noncompliance of a child to their own requests. Parents are the only consistently available source for information on early childhood development and the child's behavior in the home. Teachers offer the most accurate observations on the age-appropriateness of the child's adjustment in the classroom and academic achievement as well as the attentional, motivational, and social phenomena unique to the classroom and to school. It is likely, however, that such observational accuracy decreases following the elementary school grades, as middle school and high school teachers have little continuous observation of students, and usually see each student only for 45 minutes a day and in the context of a class consisting of 30 other students. Youth self-description, regardless of the problems that have been documented for this source of information (Greenbaum, Dedrick, Prange, & Friedman, 1994; Jensen et al., 1996), still represents the most direct and accurate expression of personal thoughts and feelings—once the potentially distorting effects of response sets have been identified. (Note that Michael and Merrell, 1998, recently demonstrated adequate short-term temporal stability for the self-report of third- to fifth-grade students.)

The availability of two or three independent sets of child descriptions provides a compelling opportunity for comparison across informants. Achenbach, McConaughy, and Howell (1987) conducted a comprehensive literature review and found very limited concordance in general between the descriptions of parent, teacher, and youth, although relatively greater between source agreement was obtained for scales representing externalizing behaviors. A review of similar studies that evaluated the responses to parallel objective interviews of parent and child concluded that greater agreement was obtained for visible behaviors and for child-parent pairs with older children (Lachar & Gruber, 1993).

Although one reasonable approach to the interpretation of differences between parent, teacher, and youth would be to assign such differences to situation-specific variation (e.g., the child is only oppositional at home, not in the classroom), other explanations are equally plausable. Cross-informant variance may reflect the fact that scales with similar names may contain significantly different content. On the other hand, the development and application of valid strictly content-parallel measures may limit instrument validity. Assignment of only parallel scale content may restrict the diagnostic potential of each informant source by excluding the measurement of attributes that may be uniquely obtained from that source. Such attributes might be measured through a parent-completed measure of developmental delay, a teacher-completed measure of classroom behavior, or a youth-completed measure of self-concept. The PIC–2, PIY, and SBS attempt in their structure and content to provide the opportunity both to compare similar scale content across informants as well as to measure phenomena that may be uniquely obtained from only one informant.

Along with dissimilar scale content, another source of poor across-informant agreement is the substantial effect of response sets on the accuracy of one source of information found to be discrepant when compared with the observations of other informants. The child or adolescent being assessed may not adequately comply with questionnaire instructions, because of inadequate language comprehension, limited reading skills, or lack of sufficient motivation for the task. It is as likely that a youth may wish to hide a personal history of maladaptive behavior and current internal discomfort from mental health professionals, although a negative presentation of parent adjustment and home conflict may be readily provided. Youth may also be motivated in an assessment context to admit to problems and symptoms that are not present. These same motivations and conditions may also influence parent report. Indeed, there has been some concern that poor parent adjustment may compromise the validity of parent report (Achenbach, 1981). Subsequent review (Richters, 1992) and specific analysis of this issue with the Personality Inventory for Children (Lachar, Kline, & Gdowski, 1987) found no empirical support that this is an important concern. The PIC–2 and the PIY incorporate validity scales to identify the effect of response sets. These scales are designed to measure random or inadequate response to scale statements, defensive denial of existing problems, as well as admission of symptoms that are unlikely to be present or the exaggeration of actual problems.

Clinicians may interpret inconsistencies across informants in a variety of ways. At one extreme, a clinician might consider accepting any evidence of symptom presence from any informant source. At the other extreme, a clinician's focus on symptoms may exclude the interpretation of all scale dimensions not demonstrated within the clinical range by at least two or even all three informant sources. Although an optimal approach to the integrative interpretation of multi-informant questionnaires has not been established (which is not to say that the opinions of mental health professionals and parents remain unstudied; Loeber, Green, & Lahey, 1990; Phares, 1997), there is a distinct pragmatic advantage in using an assessment system with comparable parent, teacher, and youth versions. Conditions regularly occur in the conduct of psychological evaluations that make it difficult or impossible to obtain a parent, teacher, or youth report. The child may be too young, uncooperative, or language impaired. The evaluation may occur during the summer vacation, or the child may have not consistently attended one classroom or may have left school permanently. Parents may miss family appointments when their child is hospitalized, or the child may be under agency guardianship. In such instances, a set of comprehensive parent-, teacher-, and self-report measures that can be applied independently of each other provide the flexibility to facilitate psychometric assessment.

THE PERSONALITY INVENTORY FOR CHILDREN SECOND EDITION (PIC–2) AND PERSONALITY INVENTORY FOR YOUTH (PIY)

Development of the PIC–2

Over 40 years ago, two University of Minnesota psychologists began developing a new inventory approach for the evaluation of children and adolescents. They assembled a 600-item administration booklet and named it the "Personality Inventory for Children. For use with children from six through adolescence." The directions stated that each item was to be answered "True" or "False" by the child's mother in order to describe both the child and family relationships. Professors Wirt and Broen accumulated administration booklet descriptive statements following a general outline. To ensure comprehensive coverage of child behavior and adjustment, 50 statements were written for each of 11 content areas: Aggression, Anxiety, Asocial Behavior, Excitement, Family Relations, Intellectual Development, Physical Development, Reality Distortion, Social Skills, Somatic Concern, and Withdrawal. To these 550 potential scale items, 50 items were added in an effort to strengthen or clarify the meaning of certain areas of concern. Although all statements were to be completed by a parent, the statement format varied. Some statements describe historical fact ("My child has failed a grade [repeated a year] in school"), other statements report the observations of other individuals ("School teachers complain that my child cannot sit still"), and still other statements reflect direct parental report. These direct statements describe behaviors ("My child sometimes swears at me") as well as emotional states ("My child worries some"). The items as a group were found to require a sixth- to seventh-grade reading level (Harrington & Follett, 1984). Through use of many of the general procedures employed in the development of the Minnesota Multiphasic Personality Inventory, PIC scales were constructed from these potential items over a span of 20 years.

The initial 1977 published profile was a visual display of the linear *T*-scores of three validity scales, a general screening scale, and 12 measures of child ability and adjustment and family function developed through either empirical item-selection techniques or iterative content-valid procedures. In 1981 the administration booklet was revised, and the PIC–R items were sorted into four parts. Completion of part I (Items 1–131) allowed the scoring of four broadband factor-derived scales (Lachar, Gdowski, & Snyder, 1982). Completion of parts I and II (Items 1–280) generated the entire clinical profile with "shortened scales" (Lachar, 1982), and completion of parts I–III (Items 1–420) allowed the scoring of the original-length scales. The last 180 items were eventually dropped from the booklet because they did not appear on any of the standard full-length profile scales.

From the booklet's first publication, PIC scale and profile interpretation placed relatively little importance on item content (except for the construction of a critical items list). Instead, an integrated program of research established external correlatives and interpretive guidelines for individual profile scales (Lachar & Gdowski, 1979) and replicated profile patterns (Gdowski, Lachar, & Kline, 1985; Kline, Lachar, & Gdowski, 1987; LaCombe, Kline, Lachar, Butkus, & Hillman, 1991; Lachar, Kline, Green, & Gruber, 1996). A profile interpretive procedure in which similarity coefficients are calculated between the individual profile to be interpreted and the mean profiles of students receiving specific special education services has been incorporated into profile scoring and interpretation software (Kline, Lachar, Gruber, & Boersma, 1994). Special effort has also focused on demonstrating that PIC scale validity is not restricted by a child's age, gender, or ethnicity (Kline & Lachar, 1992; Kline, Lachar, & Sprague, 1985). A comprehensive review of this version of the PIC appears in the first edition of this work (Lachar & Kline, 1994). In addition, a bibliography of over 350 relevant publications is presented in the PIC–2 manual (Lachar & Gruber, 2001).

Current test revision efforts began in 1989 with the rewriting of the first 280 items of the PIC booklet in a self-report format for the construction of the Personality Inventory for Youth (PIY; Lachar & Gruber, 1993, 1995a, 1995b). Development of the PIY facilitated concurrent critical review of the structure and content of PIC–R scales and the PIC–R profile. Revision efforts have been sensitive to the need to maintain continuity with PIC interpretation principles established over the past 20 years while introducing psychometric changes that improve its efficiency. A research edition administration booklet that allowed both the scoring of the PIC–R profile and the collection of data on revised and new inventory items facilitated test revision. Over 1,000 clinical protocols have been subjected to considerable statistical analysis. As a consequence, the PIC–R (now the PIC–2) and the PIY have achieved sufficient similarity to facilitate the comparison of parent description and self-description. Their similarity includes a comparable subscale-within-clinical-scale structure. In addition, specific item revisions have improved comprehension and application, such as the removal of almost all negatively worded statements to which "True" (versus the natural response of "False") represents the unscored response (e.g., "My child has never had cramps in the legs. False"), and the substitution of "parent(s)" for the designation of either mother or father (or parent surrogates) in family descriptions. The final PIC–2 administration booklet of 275 statements generates a profile of gender-specific linear *T*-scores for 3 validity scales, 9 scales, and 21 subscales as well as a second profile of 8 shortened scales and 4 scale composites used as an abbreviated assessment and for the measurement of treatment effectiveness. The PIC–2 provides a representative normative sample of school-age children (kindergarten through 12th grade). Current efforts are focused on the development of a version of the PIC for preschool children (ages 3–5).

PIC–2 Standard Form Clinical Scales and Subscales

Each of the nine clinical scales was constructed using a uniform iterative process (Lachar & Gruber, 2001). Initial scale composition was based on previous PIC or PIY item placement or substantive item content. Item-to-scale correlation matrices generated from an initial sample of 950 clinical protocols were then inspected to establish the accuracy of the initial item placements. Each inventory statement retained on a final clinical scale demonstrated a significant and substantial correlation to the scale on which it was placed. When an item obtained a significant correlation to more than one clinical scale, it was placed, in almost all cases, on the scale to which it obtained the most substantial correlation.

Using this technique, 94% of the 264 PIC–2 statements that make up the nine adjustment scales were placed on only one scale. The 16 items that were placed on two of these final scales obtained substantial correlations to both and represented substantive content consistent with both. For example, "Others often say that my child is moody" has been placed on both the DIS2: Depression ($r = .63$) and DLQ2: Dyscontrol ($r = .61$) subscales, as "moody" may signify both dysphoria and anger. The relatively unique item composition of the nine PIC–2 clinical scales is in contrast to the previous PIC–R structure. For example, in the PIC–R, 68% of the Anxiety scale items also appeared on the Depression scale. In addition, considerable between-scale overlap occurred among the three PIC–R cognitive scales: Achievement (56%), Intellectual Screening (37%), and Development (84%).

The PIC–2 gender-specific T-score values are derived from a contemporary national sample of parent descriptions of youth 5 to 18 years of age ($n = 2{,}306$); a large sample of referred youth were analyzed to provide evidence of instrument validity ($n = 1{,}551$). As presented in Table 6.1, these scales demonstrate substantial internal consistency. PIC–2 clinical scales average 31 items in length (range = 19 to 47 items) and obtain a median coefficient alpha of .89 (range = .81 to .95). The similarity of PIC–2 to the PIC–R and PIY clinical scales was measured by percentage of item overlap as well as correlation between PIC–2 and comparable PIC/PIY scales. PIC–2 scales on average obtain 66% overlap with PIC–R scales (range = 33% to 96%) and obtain a substantial median correlation of .93 (range = .81 to .99) with the PIC–R equivalent. As would be expected, PIC–2 clinical scales obtain substantial item overlap with PIY scales similarly named (average = 79%, range = 51% to 100%). In spite of this substantial scale similarity, the difference in informants (parent to youth) resulted in only moderate concordance estimates (median correlation = .43, range = .28 to .53). As presented in Table 6.1, the strongest relationship between parent and youth description was demonstrated for subscales of Delinquency, Family Dysfunction, and Social Skill Deficits.

The items of each PIC–2 adjustment scale have been partitioned into two or three subscales. Application of principal component factor analysis with varimax rotation guided the identification of two or three relatively homogeneous item subsets for each adjustment scale. PIC–2 subscales average 13 items in length (range = 6 to 21 items), with only 3 of 21 subscales incorporating less than 10 items. Table 6.1 provides coefficient alpha values for subscales and lists a representative item for each subscale. The majority of subscales demonstrate psychometric characteristics comparable to scales on shorter published questionnaires. In all instances, the division of scales into subscales facilitates the interpretation process. For example, the actuarial interpretation of the PIC–R Delinquency scale (Lachar & Gdowski, 1979) identified T-score ranges associated with the dimensions noncompliance, poorly controlled anger, and antisocial behaviors. These dimensions are each represented by different PIC–2 DLQ subscales; their patterns of elevation represent the dominant endorsed content of this adjustment scale. (Note the comparable subscales on the PIY Delinquency scale.) Correlations between PIC–2 scale scores and clinician, teacher, and youth descriptions readily provide actuarial interpretive guidelines for these nine major adjustment dimensions. These interpretive guidelines are detailed in the PIC–2 manual:

TABLE 6.1
PIC–2 Adjustment Scales and Subscales and Selected Psychometric Performance in Youth Referred for Evaluation

Scale/Subscale (Abbr.)	*Items*	α	r_{tt}	*% PIY*	r_{PIY}	*Subscale Representative Item*
STANDARD FORMAT PROFILE						
COGNITIVE IMPAIRMENT (COG)	39	.87	.94	54		
Inadequate Abilities (COG1)	13	.77	.95		—	My child seems to understand everything that is said.
Poor Achievement (COG2)	13	.77	.91		.39	Reading has been a problem for my child.
Developmental Delay (COG3)	13	.79	.82		.39	My child could ride a tricycle by age five years.
IMPULSIVITY & DISTRACTIBILITY (ADH)	27	.92	.88	63		
Disruptive Behavior (ADH1)	21	.91	.87		.30	My child cannot keep attention on anything.
Fearlessness (ADH2)	6	.69	.86		.46	My child will do anything on a dare.
DELINQUENCY (DLQ)	47	.95	.90	85		
Antisocial Behavior (DLQ1)	13	.88	.83		.68	My child has run away from home.
Dyscontrol (DLQ2)	17	.91	.91		.46	When my child gets mad, watch out!
Noncompliance (DLQ3)	17	.92	.87		.46	My child often breaks the rules.
FAMILY DYSFUNCTION (FAM)	25	.87	.90	100		
Conflict Among Members (FAM1)	15	.83	.90		.43	There is a lot of tension in our home.
Parent Maladjustment (FAM2)	10	.77	.91		.47	One of the child's parents drinks too much alcohol.
REALITY DISTORTION (RLT)	29	.89	.92	72		
Developmental Deviation (RLT1)	14	.84	.87		—	My child needs protection from everyday dangers.
Hallucinations & Delusions (RLT2)	15	.81	.79		—	My child thinks others are plotting against him/her.
SOMATIC CONCERN (SOM)	28	.84	.91	86		
Psychosomatic Preoccupation (SOM1)	17	.80	.90		.40	My child is worried about disease.
Muscular Tension & Anxiety (SOM2)	11	.68	.88		.31	My child often has back pains.
PSYCHOLOGICAL DISCOMFORT (DIS)	39	.90	.90	82		
Fear & Worry (DIS1)	13	.72	.76		—	My child will worry a lot before starting something new.
Depression (DIS2)	18	.87	.91		.31	My child hardly ever smiles.
Sleep Disturbance/Preoccupation with Death (DIS3)	8	.76	.86		.41	My child thinks about ways to kill himself/herself.
SOCIAL WITHDRAWAL (WDL)	19	.81	.89	95		
Social Introversion (WDL1)	11	.78	.90		—	Shyness is my child's biggest problem
Isolation (WDL2)	8	.68	.88		—	My child often stays in his/her room for hours.

(Continued)

TABLE 6.1
(Continued)

Scale/Subscale (Abbr.)	*Items*	α	r_{tt}	*% PIY*	r_{PIY}	*Subscale Representative Item*
SOCIAL SKILL DEFICITS (SSK)	28	.91	.92	82		
Limited Peer Status (SSK1)	13	.84	.92		.38	My child is very popular with other children.
Conflict with Peers (SSK2)	15	.88	.87		.43	Other children make fun of my child's ideas.
BEHAVIORAL SUMMARY PROFILE						
SHORT ADJUSTMENT SCALES						
Impulsivity & Distractibility–Short (ADH-S)	12	.88	.87			
Delinquency–Short (DLQ-S)	12	.89	.85			
Family Dysfunction–Short (FAM-S)	12	.82	.86			
Reality Distortion–Short (RLT-S)	12	.82	.87			
Somatic Concern–Short (SOM-S)	12	.73	.85			
Psychological Discomfort–Short (DIS-S)	12	.81	.87			
Social Withdrawal–Short (WDL-S)	12	.76	.88			
Social Skill Deficits–Short (SSK-S)	12	.82	.89			
COMPOSITE SCALES						
Externalizing (EXT-C)	24	.94	.89			
Internalizing (INT-C)	36	.89	.89			
Social Adjustment (SOC-C)	24	.86	.89			
Total Score (TOT-C)	96	.95	.89			

Note. Scale and subscale alpha (α) values based on a referred sample $n = 1{,}551$. One-week clinical retest correlation (r_{tt}) sample $n = 38$. %PIY = percentage overlap with same-named PIY self-report dimension; r_{PIY} = correlation (when > .29) with best match PIY subscale in a sample of 588 referred youth.

Cognitive Impairment (COG). The statements that reflect limited general intellectual ability (COG1), problems in achieving in school (COG2), and a history of developmental delay or deficit (COG3) have been placed on this scale. COG2 elevation has been found to be associated with a broad range of inadequate academic habits and poor achievement in the classroom. Both teacher and clinician ratings demonstrate a strong relation between COG3 elevation and language deficits.

Impulsivity and Distractibility (ADH). The majority of these items (21 of 27) appear on the first dimension. ADH1 (Disruptive Behavior) receives substantial support from teacher ratings: Elevation on this subscale is associated with poor behavioral control and disruptive behavior in the classroom. It is also associated with impulsive, hyperactive, and restless behavior and excessive attention-seeking as reported by clinicians. The second dimension (ADH2, Fearlessness) appears to measure an aspect of bravado that may best be classified as a personality dimension.

Delinquency (DLQ). DLQ1 (Antisocial Behavior) elevation is associated with behaviors suggested by the name of the total scale. DLQ1 subscale elevation predicts admission by both clinician and youth of a variety of unacceptable behaviors: truancy, alcohol and drug misuse, theft, running away from home, deceit, and association with other youth who are similarly troubled. DLQ2 (Dyscontrol) elevation suggests the presence of disruptive behavior associated with poorly modulated anger. Teachers note fighting, and youth admit to similar problems ("I lose friends because of my temper"). Clinicians rate these children as assaultive, defiant, argumentative, irritable, destructive, and manipulative. This lack of emotional control often results in behaviors that demonstrate poor judgement. DLQ3 (Noncompliance) elevation reflects disobedience to parents and teachers, the ineffectiveness of discipline, and the tendency to blame others for problems. Youth agreement with this perception of adults is demonstrated by a variety of PIY item correlates, including "I give my parent(s) a lot of trouble."

Family Dysfunction (FAM). This scale is divided into two meaningful dimensions. FAM1 (Conflict Among Members) reflects conflict within the family ("There is a lot of tension in our home"; "My parents do not agree on how to raise me"). Clinicians note conflict between the child's guardians and concern regarding the emotional or physical abuse of the child. The second FAM dimension more directly measures parent adjustment. Self-report correlates of FAM2 (Parent Maladjustment) include "One of my parents sometimes gets drunk and mean" as well as "My parents are now divorced or living apart."

Reality Distortion (RLT). This content valid scale is considerably different from the empirically keyed PIC–R Psychosis scale, whereas substantial overlap is obtained with the PIY RLT scale (RLT1: 57%, RLT2: 80%). RLT1 (Developmental Deviation) elevation describes a level of intellectual, emotional, and social functioning usually associated with substantial developmental retardation or regression. RLT2 (Hallucinations and Delusions) describes symptoms and behaviors often associated with a psychotic adjustment.

Somatic Concern (SOM). The first dimension of SOM measures a variety of health complaints often associated with poor psychological adjustment. SOM1 (Psychosomatic Preoccupation) elevation is often associated with the self-report of similar complaints ("I feel tired most of the time," "I often have headaches," "I often have an upset stomach"). The second SOM dimension (SOM2, Muscular Tension and Anxiety) appears to measure the somatic components of internalization.

Psychological Discomfort (DIS). This relatively long scale of 39 items is best described as a measure of negative affectivity, divided, as in the PIY, into three meaningful dimensions. The first dimension (DIS1) measures fearfulness and worry and is associated with clinician description of anxiety, fear, and tearfulness as well as self-report of fear and emotional upset. The second dimension (DIS2) is a general measure of depression that obtains considerable correlation with parent, teacher, and youth description. Teachers see students with an elevated DIS2 subscale score as sad or unhappy, moody and serious, and not having fun. Clinicians note many of the classical symptoms of depression, including feelings of helplessness, hopelessness, and worthlessness. Demonstrating inadequate self-esteem, such children are overly self-critical and usually expect rejection. The third DIS subscale is similar to the PIY DIS3 dimension; it combines the report of problematic sleep and a preoccupation with death. Elevation of DIS3 correlates with clinician concern regarding suicide potential and a wide variety of self-reported symptoms, including sleep disturbance, dysphoria, and thoughts about suicide.

Social Withdrawal (WDL). This is the shortest PIC–2 adjustment scale (19 items). The two WDL dimensions parallel those of the PIY. The first WDL subscale (WDL1: Social Introversion) measures the personality dimension social introversion. Most items reflect psychological discomfort in social interactions. Clinician observation and youth self-report describe shyness and an unwillingness to talk with others. The second WDL dimension (WDL2: Isolation) is a brief subscale of eight items that describes intentional lack of contact with others.

Social Skill Deficits (SSK). This scale consists of two dimensions. Both dimensions receive considerable support from self-report correlates in the form of PIY statements. The first SSK subscale reflects limited social influence. SSK1 (Limited Peer Status) elevation relates to self-report of few friends, a lack of popularity with peers, and little social influence. Teachers note avoidance of peers and a lack of awareness of the feelings of others. SSK2 (Conflict With Peers), elevation, in contrast, measures problematic relations with peers. Self-report correlates document these conflicts, and clinicians observe poor social skills and a problematic social adjustment.

Case Study: PIC–2 Standard Form Profile Scales and Subscales

The case of "Cheryl" and the PIC–2 Standard Form profile obtained from Cheryl's mother are introduced here. (Other elements of this case appear as appropriate throughout this presentation of test characteristics.) This teenager was referred for evaluation by her parents to determine if her school performance reflected the presence of a learning disability. Comprehensive evaluation of ability and academic achievement provided no such evidence. As presented in Fig. 6.1, this PIC–2 Standard Form profile generated by the personal computer–scoring program available from the test publisher (note specific scale and subscale standard scores above 59*T* that fall within the shaded portion of the profile) demonstrated concern regarding school performance and cognitive status (COG1, COG2, RLT1) and the presence of externalizing symptoms suggesting limited behavioral control (ADH1, ADH2), noncompliance

Personality Inventory for Children, Second Edition (PIC-2)

A WPS TEST REPORT by David Lachar, Ph.D., Christian P. Gruber, Ph.D.

12031 Wilshire Blvd., Los Angeles, California 90025-1251

Version 1.110

Child Name: Cheryl		**Child ID:** Not Entered
Birthdate: 11-15-87	**Gender:** Female	**Ethnicity:** White
Age: 15	**Grade:** 9	
Respondent: Not Entered		**Relationship to Child:** Mother
Date Administered: 01/09/03	**Date Processed:** 01/09/03	**Administered By:** David Lachar

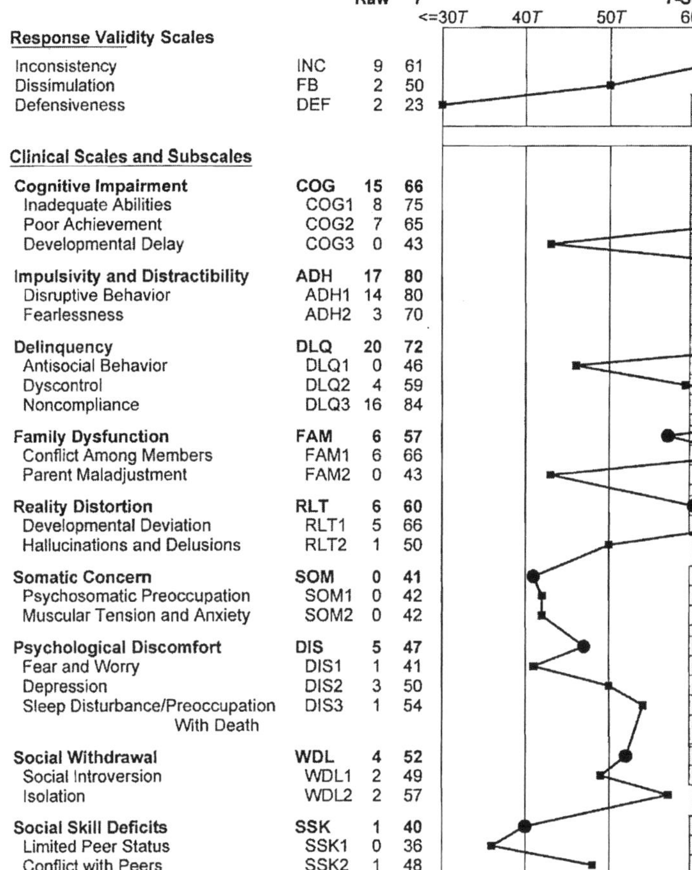

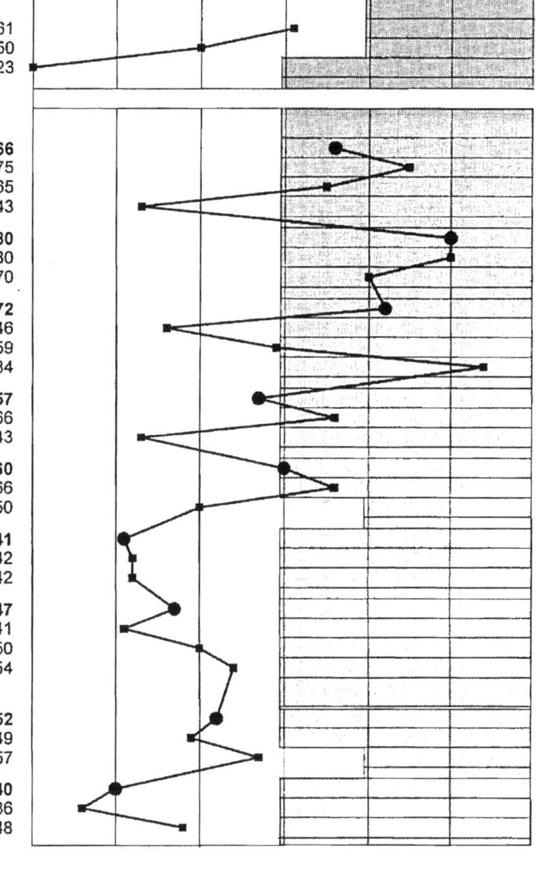

STANDARD FORM PROFILE

Scale		Raw	T
Response Validity Scales			
Inconsistency	INC	9	61
Dissimulation	FB	2	50
Defensiveness	DEF	2	23
Clinical Scales and Subscales			
Cognitive Impairment	**COG**	**15**	**66**
Inadequate Abilities	COG1	8	75
Poor Achievement	COG2	7	65
Developmental Delay	COG3	0	43
Impulsivity and Distractibility	**ADH**	**17**	**80**
Disruptive Behavior	ADH1	14	80
Fearlessness	ADH2	3	70
Delinquency	**DLQ**	**20**	**72**
Antisocial Behavior	DLQ1	0	46
Dyscontrol	DLQ2	4	59
Noncompliance	DLQ3	16	84
Family Dysfunction	**FAM**	**6**	**57**
Conflict Among Members	FAM1	6	66
Parent Maladjustment	FAM2	0	43
Reality Distortion	**RLT**	**6**	**60**
Developmental Deviation	RLT1	5	66
Hallucinations and Delusions	RLT2	1	50
Somatic Concern	**SOM**	**0**	**41**
Psychosomatic Preoccupation	SOM1	0	42
Muscular Tension and Anxiety	SOM2	0	42
Psychological Discomfort	**DIS**	**5**	**47**
Fear and Worry	DIS1	1	41
Depression	DIS2	3	50
Sleep Disturbance/Preoccupation With Death	DIS3	1	54
Social Withdrawal	**WDL**	**4**	**52**
Social Introversion	WDL1	2	49
Isolation	WDL2	2	57
Social Skill Deficits	**SSK**	**1**	**40**
Limited Peer Status	SSK1	0	36
Conflict with Peers	SSK2	1	48

NOTE: Actuarial interpretive guidelines for the scales of the PIC-2 Standard Form Profile are highlighted in chapter 3 (pages 19–53) of the 2001 PIC-2 manual.

FIG. 6.1. Personality Inventory for Children Second Edition (PIC–2) Standard Form Profile generated from maternal response for the case study of "Cheryl." The PIC–2 Standard Form Profile copyright © 2001, 2003 by Western Psychological Services. Reprinted by permission of the publisher, Western Psychological Services, 12031 Wilshire Boulevard, Los Angeles, California, 90025, U.S.A., www.wpspublish.com. Not to be reprinted in whole or in part for any additional purpose without the expressed, written permission of the publisher. All rights reserved.

(DLQ3), and conflict with significant adult family members (FAM1). The endorsed critical items (not presented here) provided additional support for the presence of a pattern of problematic behavioral adjustment that would be consistent with inadequate academic motivation and effort.

PIY Scales and Subscales

The majority of PIY items were derived from rewriting the first 280 items of the PIC–R administration booklet into a first-person format (see Table 6.2 for examples of PIY items). The PIY self-report scales and subscales were constructed in the same manner as the PIC–2 scales (Lachar & Gruber, 1993, 1995a, 1995b). The nine clinical scales were constructed with a uniform methodology, resulting in the assignment of 231 items to only one scale as well as a high degree of scale content saturation and homogeneity. In addition, each of the nine scales have been further divided into two or three nonoverlapping subscales that represent factor-guided dimensions of even greater content homogeneity. The pattern of scale and subscale elevation is a major focus of the PIY and PIC–2 interpretive process.

Gender-specific linear T-scores have been derived from a national normative sample of 2,327 regular education students in Grades 4 through 12, and a variety of analyses have been conducted using a large sample of clinically referred students ($N = 1{,}178$). PIY clinical scales average 26 items in length (range = 17 to 42 items), and the median coefficient alpha in referred protocols was .85 (range = .74 to .92). The 24 subscales average 10 items in length (range = 4 to 16 items, with 5 subscales less than 8 items in length), and the mean coefficient alpha in referred protocols was .73 (range = .44 to .84, with 8 of 24 subscales less than .70). The PIY administration and interpretation guide (Lachar & Gruber, 1995a) provides empirically derived interpretive guidelines for scales and subscales as well as 15 case studies.

Differences between the character of self-report and parent report are demonstrated when PIY scale and subscale content is compared to PIC–2 equivalents. The PIY Cognitive Impairment scale includes only half of the items of the comparable PIC–2 scale. This difference reflects the exclusion of developmental or historical items in the self-report format (children are not accurate reporters of developmental delay) as well as the reality that fewer self-report items correlated with this dimension for youth. The PIY Impulsivity and Distractibility scale also incorporated fewer scale items (17) than its PIC–2 equivalent (27). Perhaps the report of ADH disruptive behavior would be more expected from an adult informant, who likely finds such behavior distressful, than from a student, who may not find such behaviors disturbing. Such results predict that the PIC–2 COG and ADH scales will demonstrate superior diagnostic performance in comparison to these PIY scales. In contrast, the other seven PIY clinical scales achieved a significant degree of similarity in content and length with their PIC–2 scale equivalents.

Case Study: PIY Profile Scales and Subscales

Cheryl completed the PIY as part of her evaluation. As demonstrated in Fig. 6.2, the resulting scales and subscale scores that fell within the clinical range (shaded area of the profile) reflect acknowledgement of poor school performance (indeed, all COG1 items have been endorsed), and the interpretation of the remaining elevated scales and subscales is relatively straightforward: All of these values reflect problematic externalizing problem behaviors in the form of conflict at home (FAM1), noncompliance

TABLE 6.2
PIY Clinical Scales and Subscales and Selected Psychometric Performance in Youth Referred for Evaluation

Scale/Subscale (Abbr.)	*Items*	α	r_{tt}	*Subscale Representative Item*
COGNITIVE IMPAIRMENT (COG)	20	.74	.80	
Poor Achievement & Memory (COG1)	8	.65	.70	School has been easy for me.
Inadequate Abilities (COG2)	8	.67	.67	I think I am stupid or dumb.
Learning Problems (COG3)	4	.44	.76	I have been held back a year in school.
IMPULSIVITY & DISTRACTIBILITY (ADH)	17	.77	.84	
Brashness (ADH1)	4	.54	.70	I often nag and bother other people.
Distractibility & Overactivity (ADH2)	8	.61	.71	I cannot wait for things like other kids can.
Impulsivity (ADH3)	5	.54	.58	I often act without thinking.
DELINQUENCY (DLQ)	42	.92	.91	
Antisocial Behavior (DLQ1)	15	.83	.88	I sometimes skip school.
Dyscontrol (DLQ2)	16	.84	.88	I lose friends because of my temper.
Noncompliance (DLQ3)	11	.83	.80	Punishment does not change how I act.
FAMILY DYSFUNCTION (FAM)	29	.87	.83	
Parent-Child Conflict (FAM1)	9	.82	.73	My parent(s) are too strict with me.
Parent Maladjustment (FAM2)	13	.74	.76	My parents often argue.
Marital Discord (FAM3)	7	.70	.73	My parents' marriage has been solid and happy.
REALITY DISTORTION (RLT)	22	.83	.84	
Feelings of Alienation (RLT1)	11	.77	.74	I do strange or unusual things.
Hallucinations & Delusions (RLT2)	11	.71	.78	People secretly control my thoughts.
SOMATIC CONCERN (SOM)	27	.85	.76	
Psychosomatic Syndrome (SOM1)	9	.73	.63	I often get very tired.
Muscular Tension & Anxiety (SOM2)	10	.74	.72	At times I have trouble breathing.
Preoccupation with Disease (SOM3)	8	.60	.59	I often talk about sickness.
PSYCHOLOGICAL DISCOMFORT (DIS)	32	.86	.77	
Fear & Worry (DIS1)	15	.78	.75	Small problems do not bother me.
Depression (DIS2)	11	.73	.69	I am often in a good mood.
Sleep Disturbance (DIS3)	6	.70	.71	I often think about death.
SOCIAL WITHDRAWAL (WDL)	18	.80	.82	
Social Introversion (WDL1)	10	.78	.77	Talking to others makes me nervous.
Isolation (WDL2)	8	.59	.77	I almost always play alone.
SOCIAL SKILL DEFICITS (SSK)	24	.86	.79	
Limited Peer Status (SSK1)	13	.79	.76	Other kids look up to me as a leader.
Conflict with Peers (SSK2)	11	.80	.72	I wish that I were more able to make and keep friends.

Note. Scale and subscale alpha (α) values based on a clinical sample $n = 1{,}178$. One-week clinical retest correlation (r_{tt}) sample $n = 86$.

Personality Inventory for Youth (PIY)

A WPS TEST REPORT by David Lachar, Ph.D., Christian P. Gruber, Ph.D.

12031 Wilshire Blvd., Los Angeles, California 90025-1251

Version 1.110

Youth Name: Cheryl		**Youth ID:** Not Entered
Birthdate: 11-15-87	**Gender:** Female	**Ethnicity:** White
Age: 15	**Grade:** 9	
Date Administered: 01/09/03	**Date Processed:** 01/09/03	**Administered By:** David Lachar

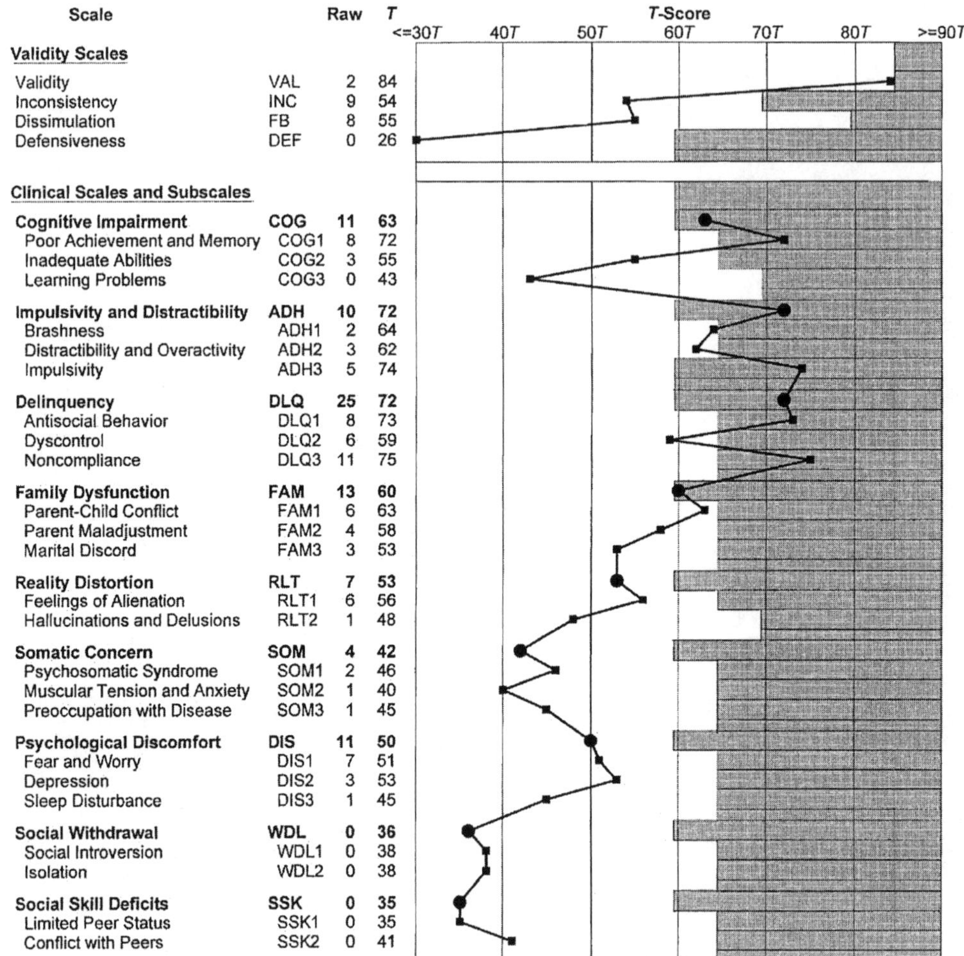

Scale		Raw	T
Validity Scales			
Validity	VAL	2	84
Inconsistency	INC	9	54
Dissimulation	FB	8	55
Defensiveness	DEF	0	26
Clinical Scales and Subscales			
Cognitive Impairment	**COG**	**11**	**63**
Poor Achievement and Memory	COG1	8	72
Inadequate Abilities	COG2	3	55
Learning Problems	COG3	0	43
Impulsivity and Distractibility	**ADH**	**10**	**72**
Brashness	ADH1	2	64
Distractibility and Overactivity	ADH2	3	62
Impulsivity	ADH3	5	74
Delinquency	**DLQ**	**25**	**72**
Antisocial Behavior	DLQ1	8	73
Dyscontrol	DLQ2	6	59
Noncompliance	DLQ3	11	75
Family Dysfunction	**FAM**	**13**	**60**
Parent-Child Conflict	FAM1	6	63
Parent Maladjustment	FAM2	4	58
Marital Discord	FAM3	3	53
Reality Distortion	**RLT**	**7**	**53**
Feelings of Alienation	RLT1	6	56
Hallucinations and Delusions	RLT2	1	48
Somatic Concern	**SOM**	**4**	**42**
Psychosomatic Syndrome	SOM1	2	46
Muscular Tension and Anxiety	SOM2	1	40
Preoccupation with Disease	SOM3	1	45
Psychological Discomfort	**DIS**	**11**	**50**
Fear and Worry	DIS1	7	51
Depression	DIS2	3	53
Sleep Disturbance	DIS3	1	45
Social Withdrawal	**WDL**	**0**	**36**
Social Introversion	WDL1	0	38
Isolation	WDL2	0	38
Social Skill Deficits	**SSK**	**0**	**35**
Limited Peer Status	SSK1	0	35
Conflict with Peers	SSK2	0	41

NOTE: Actuarial interpretive guidelines for PIY scales may be found on pages 14–21 of the 1995 PIY Administration and Interpretation Guide.

FIG. 6.2. Personality Inventory for Youth (PIY) Profile generated from youth response for the case study of "Cheryl." The PIY Profile copyright © 1994, 1997, 2003 by Western Psychological Services. Reprinted by permission of the publisher, Western Psychological Services, 12031 Wilshire Boulevard, Los Angeles, California, 90025, U.S.A., www.wpspublish.com. Not to be reprinted in whole or in part for any additional purpose without the expressed, written permission of the publisher. All rights reserved.

with the requests of adults (DLQ3), violation of rules and expectations (DLQ1), and other impulsive and poorly modulated behaviors (ADH3). Representative endorsed critical items support these diagnostic conclusions:

"It is hard for me to make good grades."
"Recently my school has sent notes home about my bad behavior."
"Punishment does not change how I act."
"Teachers complain that I cannot sit still."
"My parent(s) cause most of my problems."

PIC–2 and PIY Screening and Short Forms

The PIY and PIC–2 each incorporate a screening or a shortened assessment procedure. Thirty-two items from the first 80 items of the PIY were selected to form a screening scale (CLASS) intended to provide optimal identification of those regular education students who, when administered the full PIY, produce clinically significant results. These items also include 3 "scan items" for each clinical scale. Scan items were selected in such a manner that students who endorse at least two of each set of three items would have a high probability of scoring more than 59*T* on the corresponding clinical scale. Shortened versions of three validity scales can also be derived from these items. CLASS has demonstrated its effectiveness with nonreferred elementary school children (Wrobel & Lachar, 1998) as well as with nonreferred adolescents attending high school (Ziegenhorn, Tzelepis, Lachar, & Schubiner, 1994). In the former study, CLASS predicted elevations on PIY adjustment scales and problem descriptions from parents. In the latter study, CLASS significantly correlated with 16 of 18 potential indicators of maladjustment or behavioral risk.

The PIC–2 provides a short form designed specifically to measure change in clinical status associated with therapeutic intervention, the Behavioral Summary. Although PIC and PIC–R scales have demonstrated such sensitivity to change (see the example of treatment-related PIC–R and PIY change in Lachar & Kline, 1994), a brief form tailored specifically for this purpose was constructed by selecting items that are frequently endorsed in the context of clinical assessment and that describe clinical phenomena often the focus of short-term interventions. Using these guidelines, the 12 most favorable items from each of eight PIC–2 clinical scales were selected. (See the bottom of Table 6.1 for the psychometric characteristics of the PIC–2 Behavioral Summary measures.) Comparable items were not selected from the Cognitive Impairment scale because the majority of COG items have historical content or demonstrate a lack of appropriate associated therapeutic focus due to the global or stable nature of the descriptions on this dimension. These 96 inventory statements have been placed at the beginning of the 275-item PIC–2 administration booklet to serve as both a short form and a method of efficient reevaluation of a child following a short-term intervention. These statements are also available on a separate form with a self-scoring format. The scale scores and four scale composites may be graphed on the same profile (see Fig. 6.3) at baseline and at appropriate interim and posttreatment intervals to demonstrate both dimensions of change and dimensions of stability. The Externalization composite is the sum of the ADH and DLQ shortened scales; the Internalization composite is the sum of the RLT, SOM, and DIS shortened scales; the Social Adjustment composite is the sum of the WDL and SSK shortened scales; and all eight scales (representing the response to all 96 items) are combined into a Total Score that is placed at the end of the profile.

TABLE 6.3
Correlates of PIC–2 Short Adjustment Scales for Youth Referred for Evaluation

	r	*Rule*	*Performance*
IMPULSIVITY & DISTRACTIBILITY (ADH-S: .96[a])			
Clinician Ratings: total = 27			
Impulsive behavior	.43	> 59*T*	27%/75%
Defiant	.45	> 69*T*	24%/63%
Teacher Ratings: total = 26			
Disobeys class or school rules	.45	> 59*T*	28%/67%
Disrupts class by misbehaving	.41	> 59*T*	25%/65%
Self-Report Ratings: total = 3			
Recently my school has sent notes home about my bad behavior	.29	> 59*T*	17%/41%
Teachers complain that I can't sit still	.32	> 69*T*	28%/53%
DELINQUENCY (DLQ-S: .93)			
Clinician Ratings: total = 48			
Poorly modulated anger	.57	> 59*T*	19%/74%
Disobedient to teachers	.47	> 69*T*	22%/64%
Teacher Ratings: total = 23			
Angers other students	.32	> 59*T*	26%/69%
Complains about the requests of adults	.31	> 59*T*	28%/69%
Self-Report Ratings: total = 28			
Sometimes I lie to get out of trouble	.27	> 59*T*	48%/73%
Several times I have said that I would run away	.29	> 69*T*	37%/64%
FAMILY DYSFUNCTION (FAM-S: .93)			
Clinician Ratings: total = 3			
Conflict between parents/guardians	.35	> 59*T*	15%/43%
Emotionally abused	.31	> 69*T*	12%/32%
Teacher Ratings: total = 0			
Self-Report Ratings: total = 8			
There is a lot of tension in our home	.30	> 59*T*	31%/57%
There is a lot of swearing (cursing) at our house	.27	> 69*T*	31%/57%
REALITY DISTORTION (RLT-S: .94)			
Clinician Ratings: total = 5			
Auditory hallucinations	.30	> 79*T*	5%/21%
Inappropriate emotion (affect)	.25	> 69*T*	9%/24%
Teacher Ratings: total = 0			
Self-Report Ratings: total = 2			
I need a lot of help from others	.26	> 59*T*	18%/43%
I hear voices that no one else can hear or understand	.21	> 79*T*	21%/38%
SOMATIC CONCERN (SOM-S: .93)			
Clinician Ratings: total = 3			
Somatic response to stress	.26	> 79*T*	7%/28%
Continually tired (listless)	.19	> 79*T*	10%/28%
Teacher Ratings: total = 0			
Self-Report Ratings: total = 11			
I often get very tired	.27	> 59*T*	38%/61%
I often have headaches	.22	> 59*T*	38%/58%
PSYCHOLOGICAL DISCOMFORT (DIS-S: .92)			
Clinician Ratings: total = 23			
Depressed, sad, unhappy	.48	> 69*T*	27%/71%
Inadequate self-esteem	.42	> 69*T*	27%/61%
Teacher Ratings: total = 2			
Appears sad or unhappy	.33	> 59*T*	31%/59%
Becomes upset for little or no reason	.31	> 59*T*	28%/54%

(*Continued*)

TABLE 6.3
(Continued)

	r	*Rule*	*Performance*
Self-Report Ratings: total = 3			
I tend to feel sorry for myself	.23	> 69*T*	34%/52%
I am often afraid of little things	.23	> 79*T*	17%/43%
SOCIAL WITHDRAWAL (WDL-S: .96)			
Clinician Ratings: total = 1			
Withdrawn	.32	> 59*T*	15%/37%
Teacher Ratings: total = 0			
Self-Report Ratings: total = 1			
Shyness is my biggest problem	.25	> 69*T*	19%/49%
SOCIAL SKILL DEFICITS (SSK-S: .95)			
Clinician Ratings: total = 3			
Poor social skills	.46	> 59*T*	21%/63%
Isolated (few or no friends)	.41	> 69*T*	22%/56%
Teacher Ratings: total = 0			
Self-Report Ratings: total = 13			
Other kids make fun of my ideas	.25	> 59*T*	16%/33%
Other kids are often angry with me	.24	> 69*T*	20%/58%

Note. r = correlation between scale and external rating $p < .01$; Rule = minimum value of clinical range; Performance = endorsement rate below/above interpretive rule. Selected material from the PIC–2 copyright © 2001 by Western Psychological Services. Reprinted by permission of the publisher, Western Psychological Services, 12031 Wilshire Boulevard, Los Angeles, California, 90025, U.S.A., www.wpspublish.com. Not to be reprinted in whole or in part for any additional purpose without the expressed, written permission of the publisher. All rights reserved.

[a]Number indicates correlation between standard form and behavioral summary version of PIC–2 adjustment scale in a sample of referred students.

Insight into the empirical foundation of PIC–2 interpretation (as well as PIY and SBS interpretation) is provided by Table 6.3. (Also see the expanded detail provided in Appendix C and chap. 4 of the PIC–2 manual.) The concurrent validity of the PIC–2 shortened scales was established through the correlation of scale scores with clinician ratings, teacher descriptions, and self-report descriptions. These correlations were drawn from the data generated from a clinical project in which PIC–2, PIY, and SBS scores; clinician ratings; diagnoses; and the results of individually administered cognitive ability and academic achievement tests were collected in over 1,500 assessments. Each obtained scale descriptor was classified with only the one shortened scale with which it received the largest correlation, all correlations being significant at least at $p < .01$. Table 6.3 summarizes the number of external ratings identified in this manner from each source (clinician, teacher, and student) and provides up to two examples from each rating source for each of the eight scales. Correlations between the shortened scales and their full-length versions are also presented.

Table 6.3 documents that these 12-item scales correlate substantially with their full-length versions (r = .92 to .96) and obtain independent correlates from nonparent observers that match expressed scale content and diagnostic intent. Clinician ratings provided the greatest support for ADH-S, DLQ-S, and DIS-S, focusing on problems of disruptive and noncompliant behavior and intense and dysphoric affect that often form the basis of clinical referral. These analyses also demonstrate that ADH-S, as previously demonstrated for the PIC Hyperactivity scale (Lachar & Gdowski, 1979), assesses those behaviors most related to problems in classroom adjustment. In addition, observations obtained directly from the student being evaluated provide those internal and subjective judgments that demonstrate the clinical value of PIC–2 dimensions that do not receive robust correlates from clinicians or teachers. The PIC–2 short adjustment scales and composites are also applied in the treatment evaluation example presented in this chapter (see the following section).

Case Study: PIC–2 Behavioral Summary

Cheryl's Behavioral Summary profile is shown in Fig. 6.3. This profile clearly focuses on the presence of poor behavioral control and noncompliance (ADH-S = 80*T*, DLQ-S = 82*T*). Family issues are also indicated (FAM-S = 64*T*). The pattern of composite scale *T*-scores (EXT-C = 83*T*) provides a single summary measure of this teenager's externalizing problem behaviors and suggests that readministration of the Behavioral Summary would be a useful way to monitor response to treatment.

PIY and PIC–2 Validity Scales

Both PIY and PIC–2 profiles include three comparable validity scales. The first to appear on the profile, Inconsistency, evaluates the likelihood that responses to items are random or reflect in some manner inadequate comprehension of inventory statement content or inadequate compliance with test instructions. The Dissimulation scale identifies profiles that may result from exaggeration of current problems or a malingered pattern of atypical or infrequent symptoms. The third validity scale, Defensiveness, identifies profiles likely to demonstrate the effect of minimization or denial of current problems. The PIY also provides a fourth unique validity measure, which consists of six items written so that, in each case, one of the two possible responses would be highly improbable, such as the response false to "I sometimes talk on the telephone." These six items, although also highly infrequent in parent description, were omitted from the PIC–2, as they contributed no information beyond that provided by the other three validity scales.

PIY and PIC–2 Inconsistency (INC) scales measure semantic inconsistency (Tellegen, 1988) through the classification of responses to 35 pairs of highly correlated items drawn from all nine clinical scales (e.g., "I have many friends/I have very few friends"; "My child has a lot of talent/My child has no special talents"). For each item pair, two response combinations are consistent and two are inconsistent (both True/True and False/False or True/False and False/True). Each inconsistent pair identified in a given protocol contributes one point to the INC raw score. Application of a cutting raw score of less than 13 resulted in correct identification of 90% to 95% of clinical protocols and a score of greater than 12 correctly identified 92% to 96% of random protocols.

The PIY and PIC–2 Dissimulation scales (abbreviation FB, short for "Fake Bad") were empirically constructed through item analyses that compared clinical protocols and two sets of protocols completed by nonreferred regular education students or their mothers. The PIY or PIC–2 was first completed with directions to provide an accurate or valid description. The same student or mother then completed a second questionnaire in which the student was now described as in need of mental health counseling or psychiatric hospitalization. Selected FB items in the scored direction were very infrequent in valid normal protocols (PIY: 11%, PIC–2: 4%) and in valid clinical protocols (PIY: 18%, PIC–2: 15%), though very frequent in the "fake bad" or dissimulated condition (PIY: 83%, PIC–2: 55%). FB items reflect "erroneous stereotype" in that they reflect face valid content by naive informants but demonstrate no

Personality Inventory for Children, Second Edition (PIC-2)
A WPS TEST REPORT by David Lachar, Ph.D., Christian P. Gruber, Ph.D.

12031 Wilshire Blvd., Los Angeles, California 90025-1251
Version 1.110

Child Name: Cheryl		**Child ID:** Not Entered
Birthdate: Not Entered	**Gender:** Female	**Ethnicity:** White
Age: 15	**Grade:** 9	
Respondent: Not Entered		**Relationship to Child:** Mother
Date Administered: 01/09/03	**Date Processed:** 01/09/03	**Administered By:** David Lachar

PIC-2: BEHAVIORAL SUMMARY PROFILE (Only first 96 items were completed by respondent.)

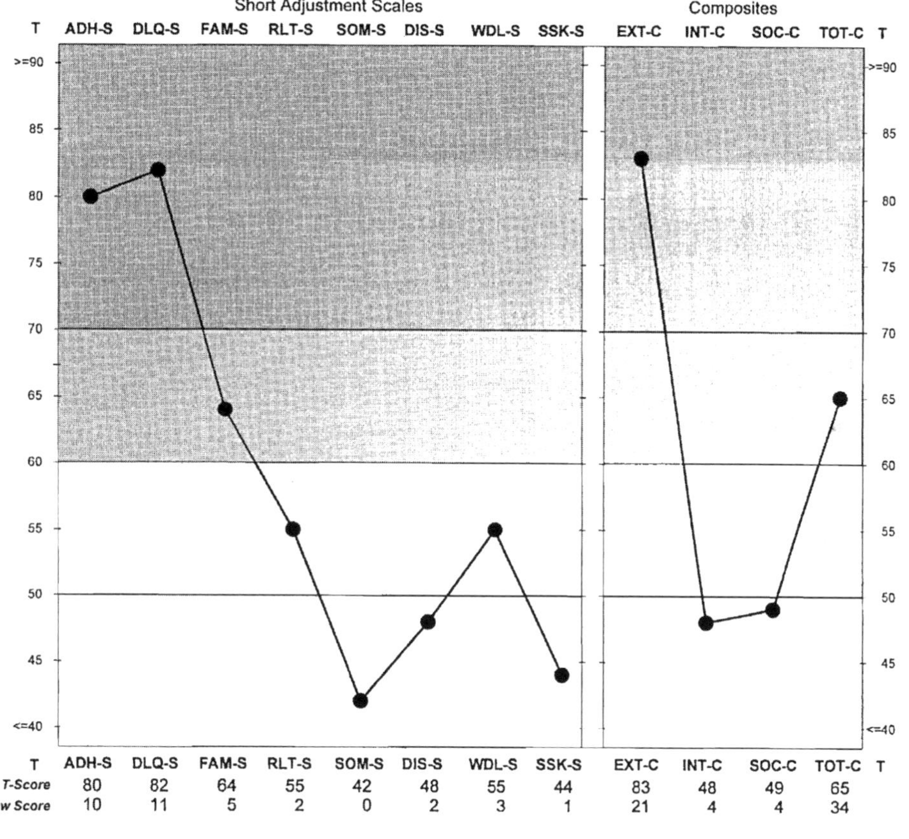

T	ADH-S	DLQ-S	FAM-S	RLT-S	SOM-S	DIS-S	WDL-S	SSK-S	EXT-C	INT-C	SOC-C	TOT-C	T
T-Score	80	82	64	55	42	48	55	44	83	48	49	65	
Raw Score	10	11	5	2	0	2	3	1	21	4	4	34	

ADH-S = Impulsivity and Distractibility - Short
DLQ-S = Delinquency-Short
FAM-S = Family Dysfunction - Short
RLT-S = Reality Distortion - Short
SOM-S = Somatic Concern - Short
DIS-S = Psychological Discomfort - Short
WDL-S = Social Withdrawal - Short
SSK-S = Social Skill Deficits-Short
EXT-C = Externalization - Composite
INT-C = Internalization - Composite
SOC-C = Social Adjustment - Composite
TOT-C = Total Score - Composite

NOTE: Actuarial interpretive guidelines for the scales of the PIC-2 Behavioral Summary Profile are highlighted in chapter 4 (pages 55–66) of the 2001 PIC-2 manual.

FIG. 6.3. Personality Inventory for Children Second Edition (PIC–2) Behavioral Summary Profile generated from maternal response for the case study of "Cheryl." The PIC–2 Behavioral Summary Profile copyright © 2001, 2003 by Western Psychological Services. Reprinted by permission of the publisher, Western Psychological Services, 12031 Wilshire Boulevard, Los Angeles, California, 90025, U.S.A., www.wpspublish.com. Not to be reprinted in whole or in part for any additional purpose without the expressed, written permission of the publisher. All rights reserved.

empirical validity (Lanyon, 1997). Examples of the 42 PIY FB items include "People are out to get me" and "I do not care about having fun." Examples of the 35 PIC–2 FB items include "My child is not as strong as most children" and "My child often talks about sickness." Application of one FB cutting score to PIY data correctly identified 99% of accurate, 98% of fake bad, and 96% of clinical protocols. Application of two potential cutting scores to similar PIC–2 protocols revealed that both correctly classified 97% to 100% of accurate regular education student descriptions. A cutting score of greater than 8 (> 69*T*) resulted in correct classification of 92% of dissimulated and 78% of clinical protocols (possible dissimulation), and a cutting score of greater than 14 (> 89*T*) resulted in correct classification of 70% of dissimulated and 95% of clinical protocols (probable dissimulation). The pattern of FB and INC scale elevation facilitates the differentiation of inadequate from inaccurate response. A deliberate exaggerated response (or, for that matter, an accurate description of a severe or atypical psychopathological adjustment) would generate an elevated FB score and an unelevated INC scale score. Protocols completed without adequate statement comprehension, in contrast, obtain raw INC and FB scores approximating 50% of each scale's length; in such a case both scales would be clinically elevated (see Figures 11 and 12 in Lachar & Gruber, 1995b).

The value of the PIC–2 FB scale is demonstrated in the following vignette. The PIC–2 was completed by the parent of a hospitalized 7-year-old boy in first grade who had a history of multiple psychiatric hospitalizations. This boy had attended a self-contained special education classroom for the emotionally impaired. His current psychiatric hospitalization was due to reported verbal and physical aggression toward family members, noncompliance, auditory and visual hallucinations, agitation, running in front of moving cars, attempting to drown himself, hair pulling, running away from home, and oppositional defiant behavior. His parents were asking for assistance in obtaining an agency placement, as they were unable to cope with his undercontrolled behavior at home. Several psychiatrists had been sufficiently impressed by the parents' reports to have treated this child with a variety of psychotropic medications (stimulants, neuroleptics, mood stabilizers, and antidepressants).

Standing in contrast to the presentation by his parents of severe emotional and behavioral psychopathology was the fact that this young boy had called children's protective services to allege physical and emotional abuse by his parents. In addition, no indication of maladjustment had been observed during his first week of hospitalization. In an attempt to resolve the discrepancy between reported history and current behavior, the treating child psychiatrist made a request for a comprehensive psychological evaluation. The boy's mother completed the PIC–2, his teacher completed the SBS, and the boy himself was administered tests of intellectual ability and academic achievement. An obtained Full Scale IQ of 122 and a SBS profile not indicative of behavioral or emotional maladjustment but rather consistent with his teacher's assessment that the boy was "a bright and cooperative student, obtaining excellent grades" were in remarkable contrast to his mother's description of a severely disturbed child. Although all nine PIC–2 adjustment scales obtained scores above 70*T* and 18 of 21 subscales were elevated into the clinical range, the pattern of validity scale elevations suggested that little credence should be given to these results (INC = 47*T*, FB = 127*T*, DEF = 27*T*). The Dissimulation raw score of 24, a value equivalent to the top third of the protocols generated by directed malingering, raised serious doubts about the validity of this PIC–2. Subsequent weeks of hospitalization documented in a variety of ways that this child had been the scapegoat in this family and had experienced considerable emotional abuse.

The third pair of PIY/PIC–2 validity scales, Defensiveness (DEF), is an expanded version of the PIC Lie scale. DEF items represent either the denial of common problems (e.g., answering "False" to "Sometimes I put off doing a chore" or "True" to "My child almost never argues") or attributions of improbable positive adjustment (e.g., answering "True" to "My child always does his/her homework on time" or "I am almost always on time and remember what I am supposed to do"). Such items represent inaccurate knowledge in the form of overendorsement (Lanyon, 1997). DEF elevations above 59*T*, even in hospitalized patients, result in profiles indicating minimization of current problems or consistent denial of the presence of most or all problems in adjustment. A secondary interpretation of an elevated PIY DEF scale is that the youth would be unlikely to be good candidate for talk therapy. Youth who respond with denial to items in an administration booklet probably will respond in a similar manner during a diagnostic interview. The INC, FB, and DEF pattern readily identifies profiles that should be interpreted cautiously. Additional support for the utility of PIY validity scales can be found in Wrobel et al. (1999). Table 6.4 presents the PIC–2 and PIY profile pairs obtained for three 12-year-old hospitalized patients.

Review of Case A's profiles identified PIC–2 and PIY validity scale *T*-score values that did not suggest that the accuracy of these profiles had been compromised in any systematic manner. It is important to observe that both profiles include clinically elevated scale scores. First, consider the similarities in scale and subscale pattern and scale and subscale clinical elevations. For example, apparent disagreement between PIY and PIC–2 COG3 (53*T* vs. 85*T*) actually represents difference in subscale content. COG3 for parent report reflects developmental issues (Developmental Delay), whereas COG3 for student report represents problems in learning (Learning Problems), a dimension much more similar to PIC–2 COG2 (Poor Achievement). Case A is a 12-year-old who is in his fifth psychiatric hospitalization and had previously attended a self-contained special education classroom for the behaviorally maladjusted. His current diagnoses were ADHD combined type, Oppositional Defiant Disorder, and Conduct Disorder. His behavior at home and in the hospital demonstrated serious behavioral dyscontrol. He had been noncompliant in taking psychotropic medication to improve his emotional and behavioral control. He had threatened to kill himself (see DIS3 scores) and had assaulted his mother, who he said did not want him at home (see PIY FAM1, Parent-Child Conflict, and FAM2, Parent Maladjustment). He attempted to escape from the hospital and required multiple time-outs and seclusions to control his rages, threats, and aggressive and inappropriate behavior (see DLQ2, Dyscontrol). Off of medication, he demonstrated an attention span of less than 15 minutes (see ADH values). He also had a history of impulsive and disruptive behavior, fighting with peers, noncompliance with adults, verbal and physical aggression, and running away from home (see elevated DLQ values for both PIY and PIC–2).

The profiles of Case B, in contrast to those of Case A, document considerable disagreement between parent and child. The only consistency in agreement was in the problem area of academic achievement (PIC–2 COG2, Poor Achievement, PIY COG3, Learning Problems). School history and psychometric assessment documented retention in grade, special class placement, and academic achievement substantially below assessed intellectual ability. Clearly the PIC–2 most accurately described this 12-year-old male who presented with multiple handicaps. The elevation of the PIY DEF scale ($T = 64$) is the most likely explanation for the fact that this PIY profile is essentially within normal limits. Indeed, this patient's medical record detailed his repeated denial and minimizing of problems during this hospitalization in an attempt

TABLE 6.4
The Influence of Respondent Defensiveness on PIC–2/PIY Profile Pairs From Three Clinical Evaluations

	Case A		*Case B*		*Case C*	
Scale/Subscale	*PIC–2*	*PIY*	*PIC–2*	*PIY*	*PIC–2*	*PIY*
Inconsistency	53	49	67	57	50	68
Dissimulation	60	72	81	48	47	72
Defensiveness	30	39	30	**64**	**65**	50
Cognitive Impairment	61	63	67	57	43	47
COG1	56	57	68	52	49	42
COG2	67	50	70	45	41	45
COG3	53	85	48	85	43	67
Impulsivity & Distractibility	79	69	81	39	44	64
ADH1	75	77	83	49	46	53
ADH2	81	62	64	37	41	62
ADH3	—	57	—	41	—	66
Delinquency	83	75	86	41	42	49
DLQ1	71	75	63	43	46	49
DLQ2	82	71	98	41	43	56
DLQ3	79	67	76	43	42	42
Family Dysfunction	60	69	58	57	67	49
FAM1	58	69	58	52	62	47
FAM2	60	74	54	57	72	49
FAM3	—	53	—	58	—	53
Reality Distortion	67	71	73	48	50	79
RLT1	69	64	83	53	55	74
RLT2	62	75	56	41	44	79
Somatic Concern	82	75	74	49	41	65
SOM1	82	66	76	38	42	59
SOM2	72	71	65	53	41	65
SOM3	—	73	—	59	—	65
Psychological Discomfort	90	59	97	63	53	68
DIS1	70	64	81	64	51	66
DIS2	88	38	92	52	49	58
DIS3	83	70	83	63	63	68
Social Withdrawal	47	83	85	41	46	59
WDL1	46	77	72	46	49	53
WDL2	50	78	88	38	42	65
Social Skill Deficits	57	43	86	56	49	57
SSK1	43	40	68	53	50	56
SSK2	74	50	97	59	48	55

to facilitate his early discharge from treatment. This child's psychiatric history was secondary to a traumatic motor vehicle accident. He felt lonely and scared; frequently cried, sobbed, and shook; avoided others; and was preoccupied with excessive worries (DIS, WDL). He externalized his problems (DLQ), had difficulties with peers and had little insight into his role in these conflicts (SSK2, Conflict with Peers). This pattern of PIY defensiveness is fairly common in inpatient settings.

Case C is quite unusual in that the PIC–2 completed by this 12-year-old girl's mother is essentially within normal limits, with the exception of FAM1 (Conflict Among Members), FAM2 (Parent Maladjustment), and DIS3 (Sleep Disturbance/Preoccupation with Death), which obtain some elevation. This PIC–2 profile would be quite difficult to interpret without the presence of validity scales, as the mother had referred her daughter for this current hospitalization. Case C presented with suicidal ideation, low self-esteem, depression, crying spells, poor appetite, and associated weight loss (DIS, WDL2, Isolation). She actively demonstrated somatic concern and somatic symptoms (SOM) in response to conflict during this hospitalization and told others that she would not talk about her problems with her mother because she was afraid that she would distress her mother, who was under psychiatric care (PIC–2 FAM2, Parent Maladjustment). The clinicians were sufficiently concerned with this patient's internalizing problems to assign discharge diagnoses of generalized anxiety disorder and depressive disorder and to continue her on antidepressant medication at discharge. Why was the mother defensive in describing her daughter's problems? It was clearly documented in the medical record that she was concerned that she would be seen as an inadequate mother because of her and her daughter's psychiatric problems and that she could thus lose custody of her daughter to another adult family member.

STUDENT BEHAVIOR SURVEY (SBS)

The development of the Student Behavior Survey (SBS; Lachar, Wingenfeld, Kline, & Gruber, 2000) consisted of several iterations in which the test authors in their review of established teacher rating scales and in the writing of new rating statements focused on content appropriate to teacher observation. SBS items are not derived from the PIY or PIC–2. Unlike measures that provide separate parent and teacher norms for the same questionnaire items (see, e.g., the Devereux Scales of Mental Disorders; Naglieri, LeBuffe, & Pfeiffer, 1994), the SBS items demonstrate a specific school focus. Review of the SBS reveals that 58 out of its 102 items specifically refer to in-class or in-school behaviors and to judgments that can only be made by school staff (Wingenfeld, Lachar, Gruber, & Kline, 1998). The SBS items are sorted into 14 scales that are placed onto a profile. The SBS assesses student academic status and work habits, social skills, parental participation in the educational process, and problems such as aggressive or atypical behavior and emotional stress. Norms that generate linear *T*-scores are gender specific and divided into two age groups, 5 to 11 years and 12 to 18 years.

The 102 SBS items and their rating options are arrayed on both sides of one sheet of paper. These items are sorted into content meaningful dimensions and are placed under 11 scale headings to enhance the clarity of item meaning rather than being presented in a random order. The SBS consists of three sections. In the first section, the teacher selects one of five ratings options (Deficient, Below Average, Average, Above Average, Superior) to describe eight areas of achievement, such as reading comprehension and mathematics, that are then summed to provide an estimate of current Academic Performance (AP). The remaining 94 items are rated on a four-point frequency scale: Never, Seldom, Sometimes, and Usually. The second section (Academic Resources) presents positively worded statements divided into three scales. The first two of these scales consist of descriptions of positive behaviors that describe the student's adaptive behaviors: Academic Habits (AH) and Social Skills (SS). The third scale, Parent Participation (PP), consists of ratings of the student's parents that are very school specific. Here the teacher is asked to judge the degree to which the parents support the student's educational program.

The third SBS section, Problems in Adjustment, provides seven scales consisting of negatively worded items: Health Concerns (HC), Emotional Distress (ED), Unusual Behavior (UB), Social Problems (SP), Verbal Aggression (VA), Physical Aggression

TABLE 6.5
SBS Scales, Representative Psychometric Performance, and Sample Items

Scale Name (Abbr.)	*Items*	α	r_{tt}	$r_{1,2}$	*Example of Scale Item*
Academic Performance (AP)	8	.89	.78	.84	Reading Comprehension
Academic Habits (AH)	13	.93	.87	.76	Completes class assignments
Social Skills (SS)	8	.89	.88	.73	Participates in class activities
Parent Participation (PP)	6	.88	.83	.68	Parent(s) encourage achievement
Health Concerns (HC)	6	.85	.79	.58	Complains of headaches
Emotional Distress (ED)	15	.91	.90	.73	Worries about little things
Unusual Behavior (UB)	7	.88	.76	.62	Says strange or bizarre things
Social Problems (SP)	12	.87	.90	.72	Teased by other students
Verbal Aggression (VA)	7	.92	.88	.79	Argues and wants the last word
Physical Aggression (PA)	5	.90	.86	.63	Destroys property when angry
Behavior Problems (BP)	15	.93	.92	.82	Disobeys class or school rules
Attention-Deficit/Hyperactivity (ADH)	16	.94	.91	.83	Waits for his/her turn
Oppositional Defiant (OPD)	16	.95	.94	.86	Mood changes without reason
Conduct Problems (CNP)	16	.94	.90	.69	Steals from others

Note. Scale alpha (α) values based on a referred sample $n = 1{,}315$. Retest correlation (r_{tt}) 5- to 11-year-old student regular education sample ($n = 52$) with average rating interval of 1.7 weeks. Interrater agreement ($r_{1,2}$) sample, fourth- and fifth-grade, team-taught, or special education students ($n = 60$).

(PA), and Behavior Problems (BP). Table 6.5 provides examples of SBS scale items, scale length, temporal stability, interrater reliability, and coefficient alphas based on protocols from students in clinical evaluation or receiving special education services in Grades K–12. Initial item and scale performance documented that 99 of 102 items statistically separated the clinical and special education protocols from the protocols of regular education students. It was demonstrated that each item had been placed on the scale with which it obtained the largest correlation. Scale scores of regular education and referred students obtained meaningful three-factor solutions (Wingenfeld et al., 1998).

Additional effort (Pisecco et al., 1999) was applied in the construction of three additional 16-item nonoverlapping scales. These scales consisted of SBS items drawn from several content dimensions that were consensually nominated as representing characteristics that would be associated with youth who obtain one of three *DSM–IV* diagnoses: Attention Deficit Hyperactivity Disorder combined type (9 items from AH, 4 items from BP, and one each from SS, UB, and SP), Oppositional Defiant Disorder (4 items each from ED and VA, 3 items each from SS and BP, and 2 items from SP), and Conduct Disorder (8 items from BP, 5 items from PA, and 3 items from VA). Item-to-scale correlations and a three-factor solution for these 48 SBS items empirically supported the placement of these scale items. The SBS Disruptive Behavior scales are named Attention-Deficit/Hyperactivity (ADH), Oppositional Defiant (OPD), and Conduct Problems (CNP).

A substantial degree of criterion validity is demonstrated when SBS scales are correlated with PIC–2 scales and subscales. Table 6.6 presents these cross-informant correlations in a sample of 520 students seen for evaluation. Inspection of each table column, with special attention to correlations greater than .49, reveals support for 11 of

TABLE 6.6
Correlations Between Teacher-Report SBS and Parent-Report PIC–2 Standard Form Scale Scores in a Clinically and Educationally Referred Sample

PIC-2	*SBS Scale*													
Scale/Subscale	*AP*	*AH*	*SS*	*PP*	*HC*	*ED*	*UB*	*SP*	*VA*	*PA*	*BP*	*ADH*	*OPD*	*CNP*
COG	**−57**	**−50**	**−40**	—	—	—	31	37	31	—	31	**46**	36	—
COG1	−36	−36	−32	—	—	—	—	32	—	—	—	33	—	—
COG2	**−55**	**−58**	**−46**	—	—	31	—	39	**40**	31	**46**	**52**	**43**	38
COG3	**−44**	—	—	—	—	—	—	—	—	—	—	—	—	—
ADH	—	**−52**	**−51**	—	—	36	—	**47**	**53**	**41**	**56**	**56**	**57**	**49**
ADH1	—	**−53**	**−51**	—	—	37	—	**47**	**50**	39	**53**	**57**	**55**	**44**
ADH2	—	−32	−32	—	—	—	—	31	**48**	38	**49**	36	**43**	**49**
DLQ	—	**−43**	**−47**	—	—	**40**	—	**45**	**60**	**54**	**64**	**45**	**60**	**64**
DLQ1	—	—	—	—	—	—	—	—	**48**	**49**	**59**	—	**41**	**64**
DLQ2	—	−36	**−44**	—	—	36	—	39	**56**	**51**	**54**	38	**54**	**56**
DLQ3	—	**−45**	**−47**	—	—	38	—	**46**	**52**	**41**	**57**	**47**	**56**	**50**
FAM	—	—	—	—	—	—	—	—	33	34	36	—	32	39
FAM1	—	—	—	—	—	30	—	—	34	33	34	—	33	37
FAM2	—	—	—	—	—	—	—	—	—	—	—	—	—	31
RLT	—	−36	−37	—	—	32	—	38	34	—	30	35	36	—
RLT1	−33	−34	−34	—	—	30	—	37	30	—	—	34	33	—
RLT2	—	−32	−34	—	—	30	—	32	34	—	32	31	34	30
SOM	—	—	—	—	—	30	—	—	—	—	—	—	—	—
SOM1	—	—	—	—	30	—	—	—	—	—	—	—	—	—
SOM2	—	—	—	—	—	—	—	—	—	—	—	—	—	—
DIS	—	−31	−38	—	—	**47**	—	38	36	31	33	30	**42**	34
DIS1	—	—	—	—	—	—	—	—	—	—	—	—	—	—
DIS2	—	−33	−39	—	—	**49**	—	**41**	39	35	39	31	**45**	38
DIS3	—	—	—	—	—	37	—	30	33	—	32	—	35	32
WDL	—	—	—	—	—	—	—	—	—	—	—	—	—	—
WDL1	—	—	—	—	—	—	—	—	—	—	—	—	—	—
WDL2	—	—	—	—	—	—	—	34	—	—	—	—	31	—
SSK	—	−34	**−41**	—	—	35	30	**46**	30	—	—	36	38	—
SSK1	—	—	−30	—	—	—	—	36	—	—	—	—	—	—
SSK2	—	−35	**−42**	—	—	34	—	**45**	37	—	34	39	**42**	30

Note. Scale/subscale abbreviations spelled out in Tables 6.1 and 6.5. Correlations less than .30 omitted. Correlations above .39 set in bold to facilitate review. $N = 520$. Selected material from the PIC–2 copyright © 2001 by Western Psychological Services. Reprinted by permission of the publisher, Western Psychological Services, 12031 Wilshire Boulevard, Los Angeles, California, 90025, U.S.A., www.wpspublish.com.

the 14 SBS scales. Teacher-rated Academic Performance correlates substantially with two of the three COG subscales—note the correlation between AP and COG2 of −.55. (Statistically significant SBS/PIC–2 correlations for AP, AH, and SS are negative because these SBS dimensions, when elevated, reflect positive attributes, whereas PIC–2 dimensions are consistently presented as problem dimensions.) Academic Habits and Social Skills obtain similar correlations to PIC–2 subscales, demonstrating that disruptive behavior and limited social adjustment at school correlate with noncompliant (DLQ3) and disruptive (ADH1) behaviors at home as well as parent report of poor school performance (COG2). Specific support was also achieved for Emotional Distress (DIS2, $r = .49$) and Social Problems (SSK2, $r = .45$; ADH1, $r = .47$; DLQ3,

$r = .46$). Parent report of poorly modulated anger (DLQ2) correlated with teacher report of both Physical Aggression and Verbal Aggression in the classroom, and ADH and other DLQ dimensions also correlated with teacher-rated Verbal Aggression. Teacher-rated Behavior Problems in students also obtained substantial correlations with undercontrolled behaviors (ADH, DLQ) as described by their parents. Health Concerns, Unusual Behavior, and Parent Participation obtained minimal if any support from this analysis. Parent and youth agreement between PIC–2 and PIY Somatic Concern performance (see Table 6.1) suggests that teachers may be less aware of these phenomena. Parent Participation is a dimension unique to the SBS, whereas Unusual Behavior may represent behaviors that are very infrequently observed in the classroom, even for students who are referred for assessment services.

Similar review of the columns headed ADH, OPD, and CNP suggests support for and subtle differences in meaning between these substantially correlated dimensions. Although correlations with PIC–2 scales ADH and DLQ are prominent in this regard, the SBS dimension ADH does not obtain significant or substantial correlation with PIC–2 subscales ADH2, DLQ1, or DLQ2, in contrast to OPD and CNP. OPD reflects not only noncompliance but anger (DLQ2) and dysphoria (DIS2) as well as poor peer relations (SSK2). Note that CNP obtained the largest correlation with the PIC–2 subscale DLQ1 (Antisocial Behavior).

Case Study: SBS Profile Scales

To complete this chapter's core case study, we now turn our attention to a teacher description of Cheryl obtained from the SBS. As demonstrated by the SBS profile presented in Fig. 6.4, although few scale *T*-scores extend into the interpretable range (shaded, > 59*T*), their interpretive meaning is consistent with the previously discussed clinically elevated PIY self-report and PIC–2 parent-report scales. The low score on AH (40*T*) reflects concern that Cheryl was not effectively engaged in classroom activities and might not be motivated to achieve. Minimal yet significant scale score elevations (61*T*) on BP and ADH suggest variable noncompliance and rule violation.

EVALUATION OF TREATMENT EFFECTIVENESS

Baseline application of the PIC–2, SBS, and PIY at intake or program admission supports treatment planning by providing an efficient, comprehensive, and expeditious focus on a youth's problems, which may then be placed within a historical or developmental as well as a family systems context. Not only is FAM valuable in this context, but independent administration of the PIC–2 to each parent allows subsequent identification of problem areas on which parents agree and those on which they do not. The provision of feedback to parents from PIC–2 profiles is quite straightforward and usually well received, as these profiles summarize parent observations.

Therapeutic effectiveness is documented through questionnaire readministration following intervention efforts. The focus and form of measure readministration should be guided by both the setting in which therapeutic intervention has occurred and the nature of the identified problem dimensions under treatment. For example, if the problem focus is inattention and disruptive behavior primarily observed in the classroom, repeated teacher ratings are most appropriate. On the other hand, if a child's individual psychotherapy focuses on current problems that have been demonstrated to be related to negative affect and a problematic self-concept, repeated assessment

Student Behavior Survey (SBS)
A WPS TEST REPORT by David Lachar, Ph.D., Christian P. Gruber, Ph.D.

Version 1.110

Student Name: Cheryl
Birthdate: 11-15-87
Age: 15
Rater: R J Patterson
Date Administered: 12/05/02

Gender: Female
Grade: 9
Role of Rater: Teacher
Date Processed: 01/09/03

Student ID: Not Entered
Ethnicity: White

Months Observing Child: 3
Administered By: David Lachar

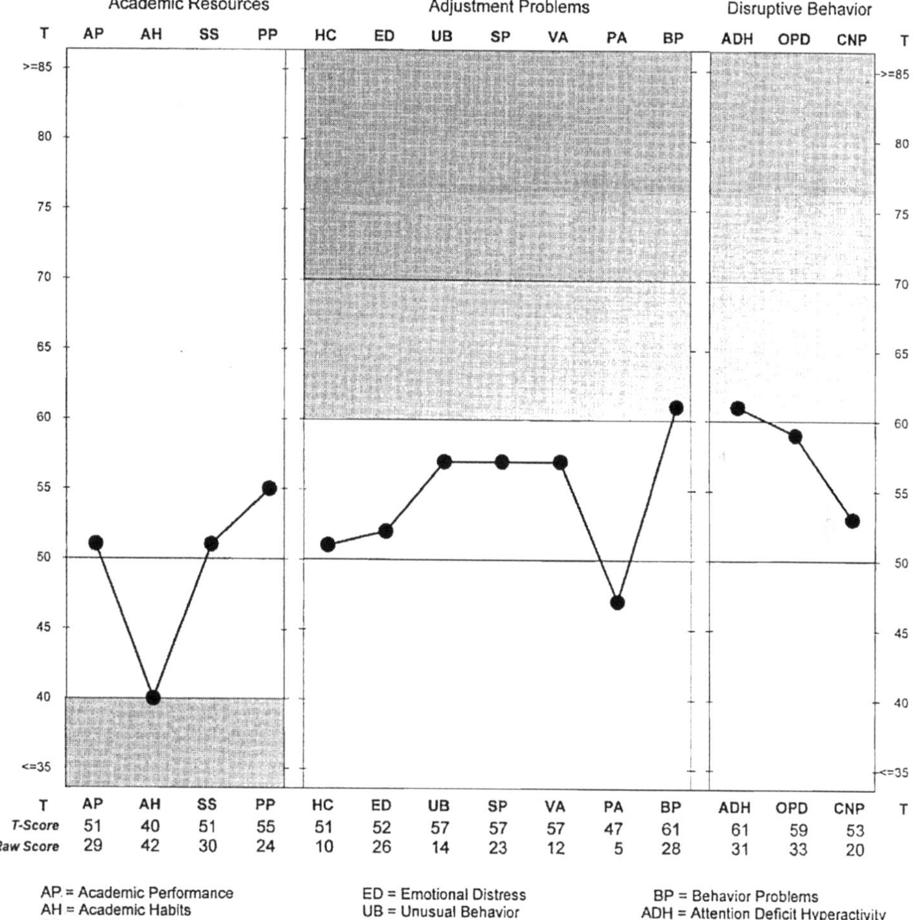

T	AP	AH	SS	PP	HC	ED	UB	SP	VA	PA	BP	ADH	OPD	CNP	T
T-Score	51	40	51	55	51	52	57	57	57	47	61	61	59	53	
Raw Score	29	42	30	24	10	26	14	23	12	5	28	31	33	20	

AP = Academic Performance
AH = Academic Habits
SS = Social Skills
PP = Parent Participation
HC = Health Concerns
ED = Emotional Distress
UB = Unusual Behavior
SP = Social Problems
VA = Verbal Aggression
PA = Physical Aggression
BP = Behavior Problems
ADH = Attention Deficit Hyperactivity
OPD = Oppositional Defiant
CNP = Conduct Problems

NOTE: Actuarial interpretive guidelines for SBS scales may be found on pages 13–17 of the 2000 SBS manual.

FIG. 6.4. Student Behavior Survey (SBS) Profile generated from teacher response for the case study of "Cheryl." The SBS Profile copyright © 2000, 2003 by Western Psychological Services. Reprinted by permission of the publisher, Western Psychological Services, 12031 Wilshire Boulevard, Los Angeles, California, 90025, U.S.A., www.wpspublish.com. Not to be reprinted in whole or in part for any additional purpose without the expressed, written permission of the publisher. All rights reserved.

using a content-appropriate self-report measure should be considered. Certainly the questionnaire or questionnaires that have documented the problems under treatment would be the most likely candidates for readministration.

Of prime consideration is the interpretation of the test differences obtained. The stability of the obtained differences may be judged against the standard error of measurement. These values are provided in each test manual and in general suggest differences in excess of 5*T* should be stable. Of greater importance in judging the clinical meaning of such differences is the benefit obtained from applying the actuarial interpretive guidelines available for these measures that define the scale scores within the normative and the clinical range as well as gradations within the clinical range. Substantive improvement is most readily documented when scores that appear in the clinical range at baseline and thereby reflect the presence of significant maladjustment fall within the normative range following an intervention. Additional attention should be given to scores that fall within the substantive clinical range at baseline and upon readministration obtain values that suggest only mild levels of maladjustment.

CASE EXAMPLE: EVALUATION AND SHORT-TERM TREATMENT OF A YOUNG CHILD

"Patrick's" mother was faced with an acute dilemma: Her son's kindergarten teacher and his elementary school had reached the end of their endurance of and capacity to deal with Patrick's behavior. Patrick could not or would not sit still, constantly talked in class, could not pay adequate attention, and frequently started fights with classmates. The assessment of Patrick began with his teacher's completing the SBS. The resulting profile and a listing of the particularly meaningful rated content are displayed in Fig. 6.5. The substantial elevation of ADH (72*T*) provides an initial diagnostic focus for this evaluation, which received additional support from AH (37*T*), BP (65*T*), and UB (63*T*) and the associated rating content presented at the bottom of Fig. 6.5.

The evaluation and initial treatment were completed in two stages. Patrick and his parents were first seen for an intake interview, at which time PIC–2s were completed by the parents. Beyond documentation of Patrick's pervasive inattention and overactivity at home and in school, this initial interview uncovered several other diagnostic issues. Patrick lived in a reconstituted family in which issues of visitation with biological noncustodial parents and the problems of new stepchildren were a source of significant stress to Patrick's biological mother. In addition, Patrick's gestational history was problematic and suggested the possibility of developmental cognitive difficulties (Patrick's delivery was substantially premature and was preceded by two months of bed rest in the hospital for his mother due to preterm labor).

The PIC–2 Behavioral Summary profiles obtained at baseline are presented in Fig. 6.6. Agreement was obtained between mother and stepfather on ADH-S and RLT-S, as well as agreement on problem status for the composite dimension EXT-C. In comparison to the profile obtained by her husband, Patrick's mother described her son as more seriously disturbed, and additional problems were suggested by elevations on DLQ-S, DIS-S, and SSK-S as well as problem status on the composite dimension INT-C. Such profile differences may reflect differences in the degree of contact the informants have had with the child, both currently and historically, although both custodial parents and the teacher reported a similar core pattern of behavior

Student Behavior Survey (SBS)

A WPS TEST REPORT by David Lachar, Ph.D., Christian P. Gruber, Ph.D.

12031 Wilshire Blvd., Los Angeles, California 90025-1251
Version 1.110

Student Name: Patrick
Birthdate: Not Entered
Age: 5
Rater: Not Entered
Date Administered: 10/22/01

Gender: Male
Grade: K
Role of Rater: Teacher
Date Processed: 01/23/03

Student ID: Not Entered
Ethnicity: White
Months Observing Child: 3
Administered By: David Lachar

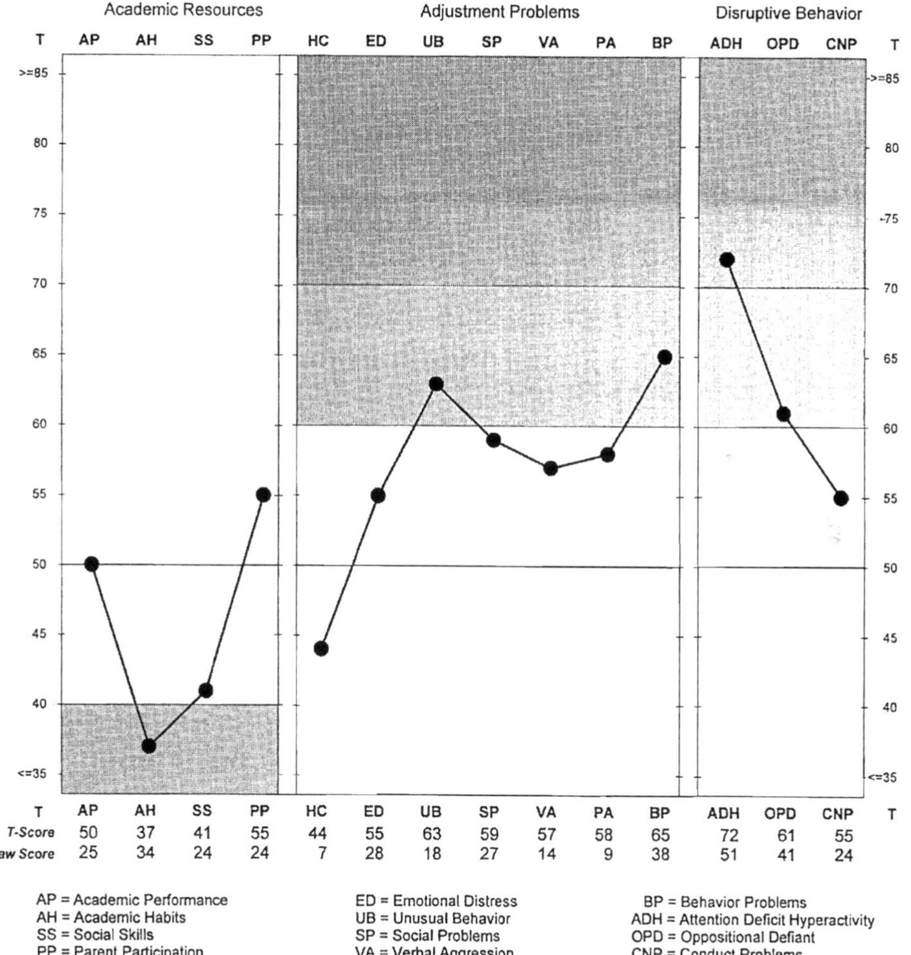

T	AP	AH	SS	PP	HC	ED	UB	SP	VA	PA	BP	ADH	OPD	CNP	T
T-Score	50	37	41	55	44	55	63	59	57	58	65	72	61	55	
Raw Score	25	34	24	24	7	28	18	27	14	9	38	51	41	24	

AP = Academic Performance
AH = Academic Habits
SS = Social Skills
PP = Parent Participation
HC = Health Concerns
ED = Emotional Distress
UB = Unusual Behavior
SP = Social Problems
VA = Verbal Aggression
PA = Physical Aggression
BP = Behavior Problems
ADH = Attention Deficit Hyperactivity
OPD = Oppositional Defiant
CNP = Conduct Problems

NOTE: Actuarial interpretive guidelines for SBS scales may be found on pages 13–17 of the 2000 SBS manual

FIG. 6.5. Baseline Student Behavior Survey (SBS) Profile (above) and Review of SBS Rating Content (below) generated from teacher response for the case study of "Patrick." The SBS Profile copyright © 2000, 2003 by Western Psychological Services. Reprinted by permission of the publisher, Western Psychological Services, 12031 Wilshire Boulevard, Los Angeles, California, 90025, U.S.A., www.wpspublish.com. Not to be reprinted in whole or in part for any additional purpose without the expressed, written permission of the publisher. All rights reserved.

WPS SBS TEST REPORT	ID: Not Entered	Page: 2

Review of SBS Rating Content

The following SBS items received ratings that may suggest problems in adjustment. Although answers to individual items should not be given too much clinical emphasis, these ratings may suggest areas for further inquiry. Only those items receiving such ratings have been printed.

Academic Habits
14. Follows the teacher's directions: Seldom
15. Maintains alert and focused attention to class presentations: Seldom
17. Persists even when activity is difficult: Seldom
18. Remembers teacher's directions: Seldom
19. Stays seated; sits still when necessary: Seldom
20. Waits for his/her turn: Seldom
21. Works independently without disturbing others: Seldom

Social Skills
25. Listens when other students speak: Seldom

Emotional Distress
45. Becomes upset by constructive criticism: Sometimes
51. Mood changes without reason: Sometimes

Unusual Behavior
59. Daydreams or seems preoccupied: Usually
62. Seems lost or disoriented: Usually
63. Talks or laughs to himself/herself: Usually

Social Problems
70. Interrupts when others are speaking: Usually
68. Engages in solitary activities: Sometimes

Verbal Aggression
76. Argues and wants the last word: Sometimes
78. Insults other students: Sometimes
80. Teases or taunts other students: Sometimes

Physical Aggression
85. Hits or pushes other students: Sometimes
86. Starts fights with other students: Sometimes

Behavior Problems
88. Associates with students who are often in trouble: Usually
91. Disrupts class by misbehaving: Usually
92. Impulsive; acts without thinking: Usually
95. Misbehaves unless closely supervised: Usually
96. Overactive; constantly on the go: Usually
102. Talks excessively: Usually
89. Blames others for his/her own problems: Sometimes
90. Disobeys class or school rules: Sometimes

FIG. 6.5. *(Continued)*

problems. Initial treatment consisted of an extended release stimulant with subsequent psychometric assessment to rule our additional emotional and cognitive issues once Patrick had been stabilized at an optimal medication dose.

Individual assessment revealed an intellectually capable youngster with a precocious reading proficiency. This assessment did not reveal emotional disturbance

Personality Inventory for Children, Second Edition (PIC-2)
A WPS TEST REPORT by David Lachar, Ph.D., Christian P. Gruber, Ph.D.

12031 Wilshire Blvd., Los Angeles, California 90025-1251
Version 1.110

Child Name: Patrick
Child ID: Not Entered
Birthdate: Not Entered
Gender: Male
Ethnicity: White
Age: 5
Grade: K
Respondent: Not Entered
Relationship to Child: Mother
Date Administered: 01/05/02
Date Processed: 01/23/03
Administered By: David Lachar

PIC-2: BEHAVIORAL SUMMARY PROFILE (Only first 96 items were completed by respondent.)

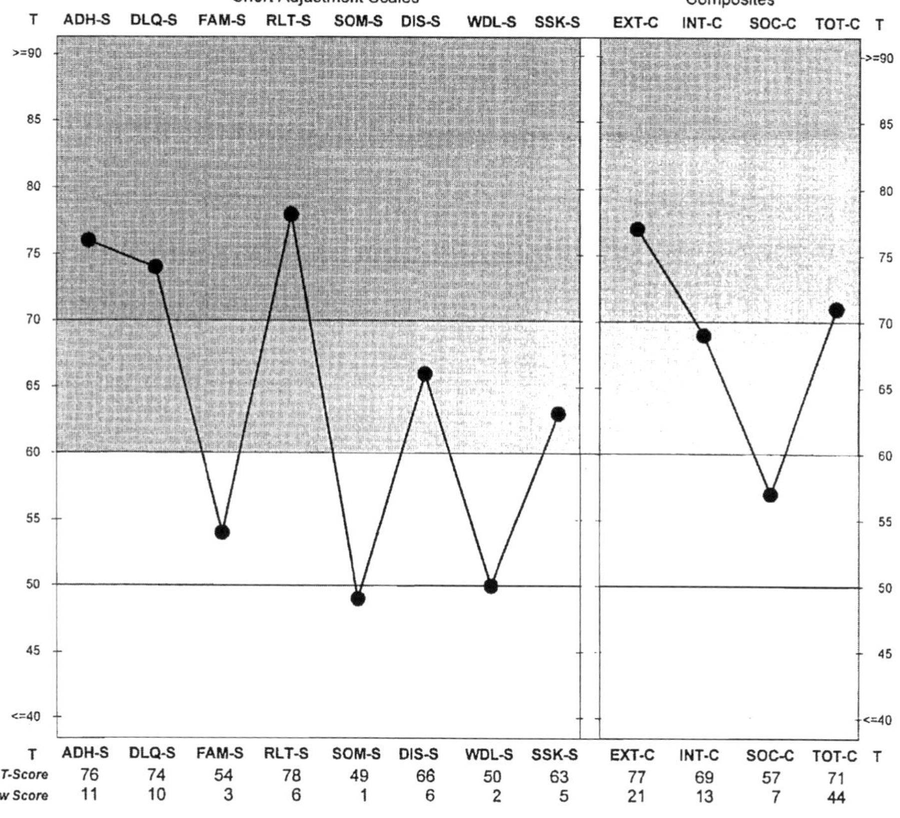

ADH-S = Impulsivity and Distractibility - Short
DLQ-S = Delinquency-Short
FAM-S = Family Dysfunction - Short
RLT-S = Reality Distortion - Short
SOM-S = Somatic Concern - Short
DIS-S = Psychological Discomfort - Short
WDL-S = Social Withdrawal - Short
SSK-S = Social Skill Deficits-Short
EXT-C = Externalization - Composite
INT-C = Internalization - Composite
SOC-C = Social Adjustment - Composite
TOT-C = Total Score - Composite

NOTE: Actuarial interpretive guidelines for the scales of the PIC-2 Behavioral Summary Profile are highlighted in chapter 4 (pages 55–66) of the 2001 PIC-2 manual.

FIG. 6.6. Baseline Personality Inventory for Children Second Edition (PIC–2) Behavioral Summary Profiles from "Patrick's" mother (above) and stepfather (below). The PIC–2 Behavioral Summary Profile copyright © 2001, 2003 by Western Psychological Services. Reprinted by permission of the publisher, Western Psychological Services, 12031 Wilshire Boulevard, Los Angeles, California, 90025, U.S.A., www.wpspublish.com. Not to be reprinted in whole or in part for any additional purpose without the expressed, written permission of the publisher. All rights reserved.

Personality Inventory for Children, Second Edition (PIC-2)
A WPS TEST REPORT by David Lachar, Ph.D., Christian P. Gruber, Ph.D.
Copyright ©2003 by Western Psychological Services
12031 Wilshire Blvd., Los Angeles, California 90025-1251
Version 1.110

Child Name: Patrick
Child ID: Not Entered
Birthdate: Not Entered
Gender: Male
Ethnicity: White
Age: 5
Grade: K
Respondent: Not Entered
Relationship to Child: Father
Date Administered: 0/05/02
Date Processed: 01/23/03
Administered By: David Lachar

PIC-2: BEHAVIORAL SUMMARY PROFILE (Only first 96 items were completed by respondent.)

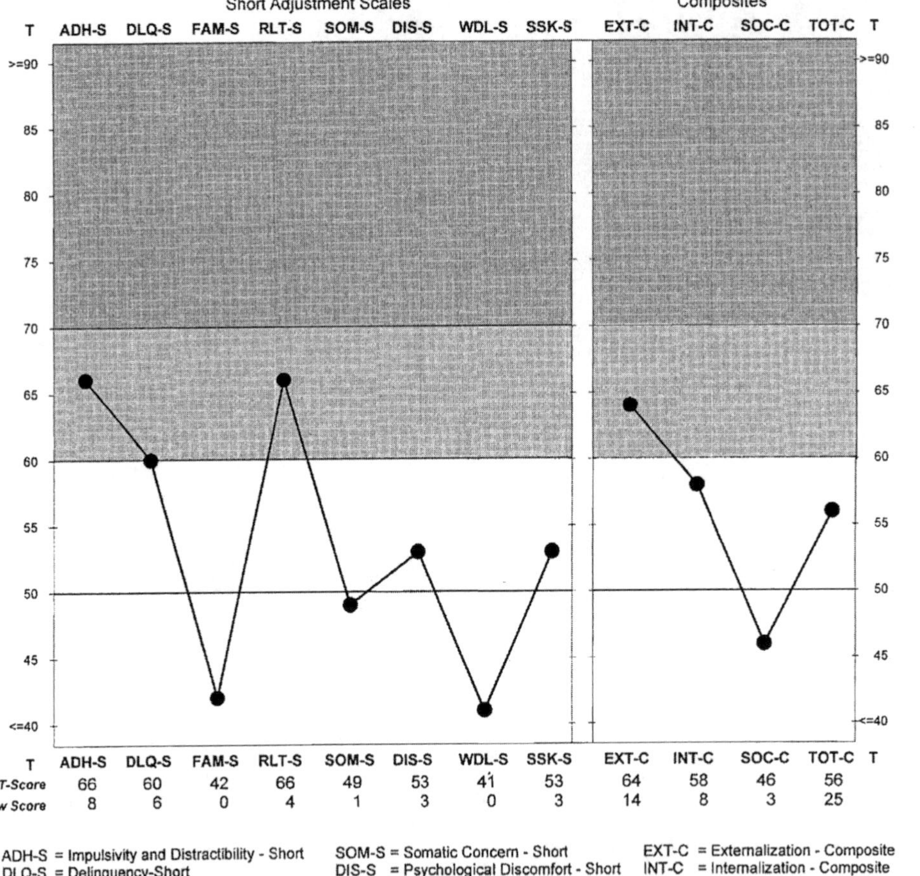

ADH-S = Impulsivity and Distractibility - Short
DLQ-S = Delinquency-Short
FAM-S = Family Dysfunction - Short
RLT-S = Reality Distortion - Short
SOM-S = Somatic Concern - Short
DIS-S = Psychological Discomfort - Short
WDL-S = Social Withdrawal - Short
SSK-S = Social Skill Deficits-Short
EXT-C = Externalization - Composite
INT-C = Internalization - Composite
SOC-C = Social Adjustment - Composite
TOT-C = Total Score - Composite

NOTE: Actuarial interpretive guidelines for the scales of the PIC-2 Behavioral Summary Profile are highlighted in chapter 4 (pages 55–66) of the 2001 PIC-2 manual.

FIG. 6.6. (*Continued*)

requiring intervention, although a recommendation was made to continue current medication and to ensure that Patrick was stimulated academically to prevent secondary academic problems caused by inadequate challenge. Patrick's SBS and his mother's PIC–2 Behavioral Summary profiles obtained following 3 months of stimulant therapy are presented in Fig. 6.7. These results demonstrate that both

Student Behavior Survey (SBS)

A WPS TEST REPORT by David Lachar, Ph.D., Christian P. Gruber, Ph.D.
Copyright ©2003 by Western Psychological Services
12031 Wilshire Blvd., Los Angeles, California 90025-1251
Version 1.110

Student Name: Patrick
Birthdate: Not Entered
Age: 6
Rater: Not Entered
Date Administered: 05/16/02

Gender: Male
Grade: K
Role of Rater: Teacher
Date Processed: 01/23/03

Student ID: Not Entered
Ethnicity: White
Months Observing Child: 10
Administered By: David Lachar

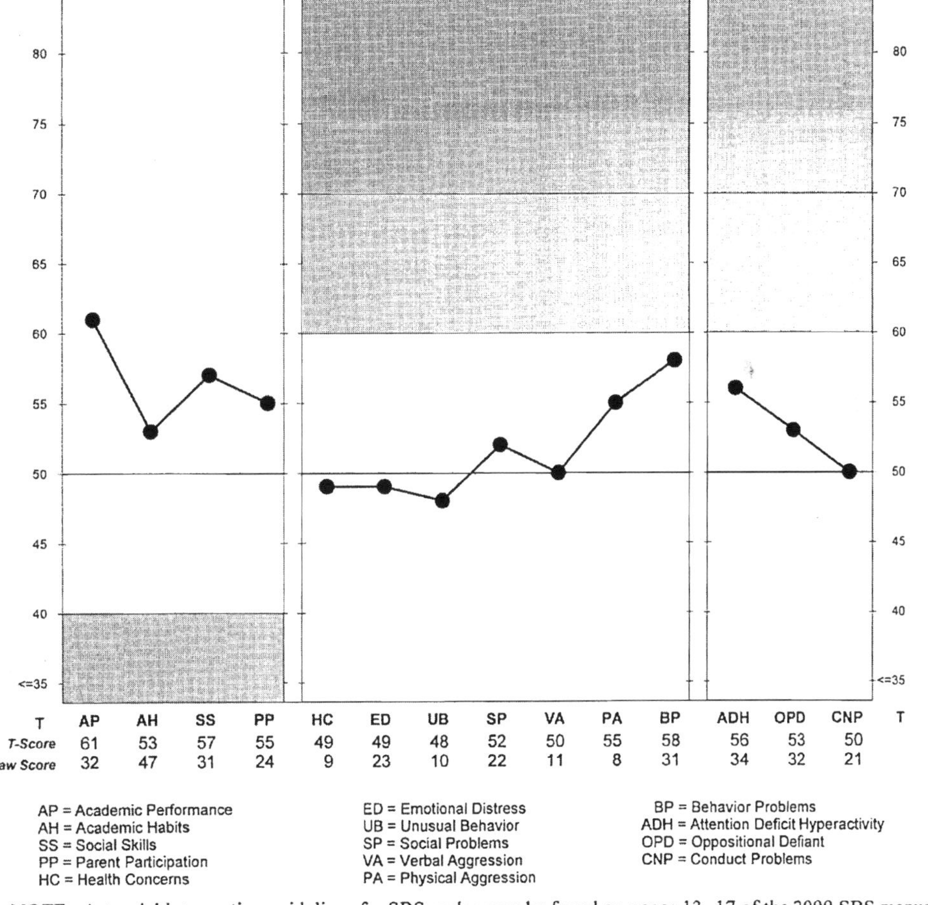

T	AP	AH	SS	PP	HC	ED	UB	SP	VA	PA	BP	ADH	OPD	CNP	T
T-Score	61	53	57	55	49	49	48	52	50	55	58	56	53	50	
Raw Score	32	47	31	24	9	23	10	22	11	8	31	34	32	21	

AP = Academic Performance
AH = Academic Habits
SS = Social Skills
PP = Parent Participation
HC = Health Concerns
ED = Emotional Distress
UB = Unusual Behavior
SP = Social Problems
VA = Verbal Aggression
PA = Physical Aggression
BP = Behavior Problems
ADH = Attention Deficit Hyperactivity
OPD = Oppositional Defiant
CNP = Conduct Problems

NOTE: Actuarial interpretive guidelines for SBS scales may be found on pages 13–17 of the 2000 SBS manual.

FIG. 6.7. Posttreatment Student Behavior Survey (SBS: above) and Personality Inventory for Children Second Edition (PIC–2) Behavioral Summary (below) Profiles for case study of "Patrick." The SBS Profile copyright © 2000, 2003 and the PIC–2 Behavioral Summary Profile copyright © 2001, 2003 by Western Psychological Services. Reprinted by permission of the publisher, Western Psychological Services, 12031 Wilshire Boulevard, Los Angeles, California, 90025, U.S.A., www.wpspublish.com. Not to be reprinted in whole or in part for any additional purpose without the expressed, written permission of the publisher. All rights reserved.

Personality Inventory for Children, Second Edition (PIC-2)

A WPS TEST REPORT by David Lachar, Ph.D., Christian P. Gruber, Ph.D.

12031 Wilshire Blvd., Los Angeles, California 90025-1251
Version 1.110

Child Name: Patrick		**Child ID:** Not Entered
Birthdate: Not Entered	**Gender:** Male	**Ethnicity:** White
Age: 6	**Grade:** K	
Respondent: Not Entered		**Relationship to Child:** Mother
Date Administered: 05/09/02	**Date Processed:** 01/23/03	**Administered By:** David Lachar

PIC-2: BEHAVIORAL SUMMARY PROFILE (Only first 96 items were completed by respondent.)

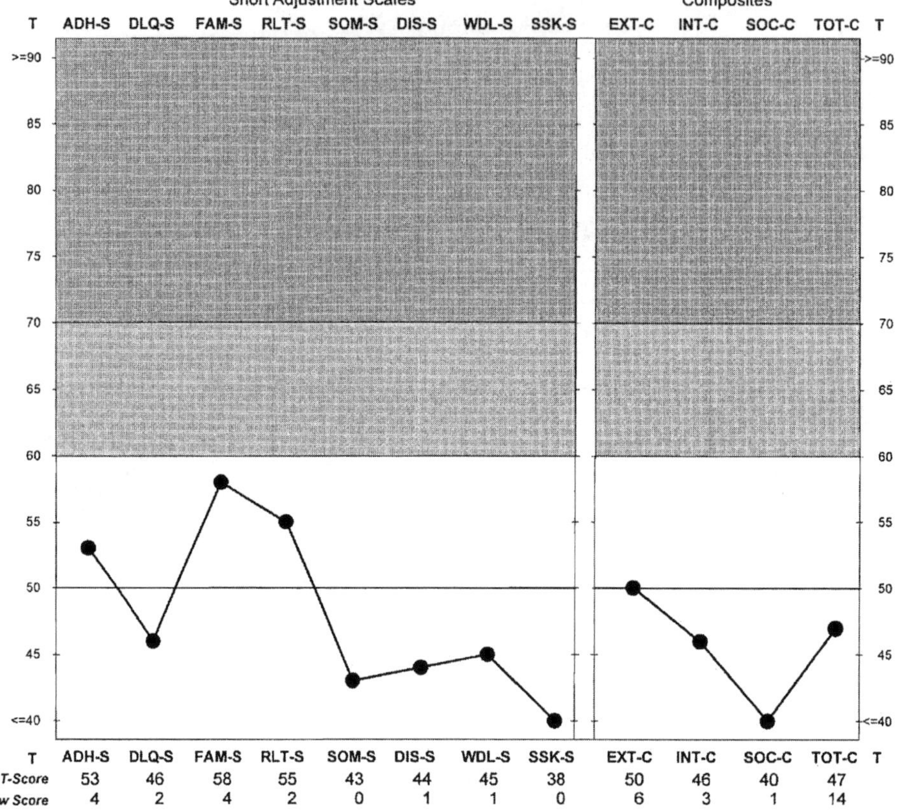

T	ADH-S	DLQ-S	FAM-S	RLT-S	SOM-S	DIS-S	WDL-S	SSK-S	EXT-C	INT-C	SOC-C	TOT-C	T
T-Score	53	46	58	55	43	44	45	38	50	46	40	47	
Raw Score	4	2	4	2	0	1	1	0	6	3	1	14	

ADH-S = Impulsivity and Distractibility - Short
DLQ-S = Delinquency-Short
FAM-S = Family Dysfunction - Short
RLT-S = Reality Distortion - Short
SOM-S = Somatic Concern - Short
DIS-S = Psychological Discomfort - Short
WDL-S = Social Withdrawal - Short
SSK-S = Social Skill Deficits-Short
EXT-C = Externalization - Composite
INT-C = Internalization - Composite
SOC-C = Social Adjustment - Composite
TOT-C = Total Score - Composite

NOTE: Actuarial interpretive guidelines for the scales of the PIC-2 Behavioral Summary Profile are highlighted in chapter 4 (pages 55–66) of the 2001 PIC-2 manual.

FIG. 6.7. (*Continued*)

questionnaires are sensitive to the behavioral changes brought about by such treatment. Particularly note the ADH shift from 72*T* at baseline to 56*T* following treatment as well as the positive increases in AP, AH, and SS. Comparable shifts in scale scores were obtained on the PIC–2 Behavioral Summary. There was an ADH-S shift from 76*T* at baseline to 53*T* following treatment and a comparable shift on EXT-C (77*T* to 50*T*) and TOT-C (71*T* to 47*T*).

COMMENTARY

The complete 2001 revision of the PIC, the addition of a multidimensional teacher-rating scale, and the collection of a national representative normative sample for each measure have gone a long way to respond to concerns that the PIC was an aging test in need of revision and update (Kamphaus & Frick, 1996; Knoff, 1989; Merrell, 1994). Critical evaluations of the SBS and PIC–2 manuals and investigation of their ability to evaluate emotional adjustment at baseline and quantify response to intervention will continue well into the new century. Indeed, traditional psychometric standards, such as reliability, are inadequate to evaluate such measures. Instead of establishing temporal stability using a test-retest paradigm for the measurement of characteristics that naturally vary over time and are often the focus of intervention, it will be necessary to establish interpretive standards for scales that are sequentially administered over time. To be applied in the evaluation of treatment effectiveness, degree of scale score change must be found to accurately track some independent estimate of treatment effectiveness (cf. Sheldrick, Kendall, & Heimberg, 2001).

The emphasis on evaluating response accuracy using validity scales and the empirical determination of interpretive guidelines continues to characterize these measures. Many psychologists unconvinced of the importance of these psychometric phenomena might not value their contributions to assessment. Although the PIC has been reduced from 420 to 275 items, into which a set of subscales and a brief 96-item form have been incorporated, some clinicians may still judge the length of these questionnaires to be problematic.

Although this chapter's author is obviously biased against the view that inventory length is intrinsically a negative attribute, it is certain that the breath and depth of a measure's content establish the potential boundaries of its utility. Even the 270 items of the PIY are easily completed in less than 45 minutes by children in the fourth grade. PIC–2, PIY, and SBS efficiency has been improved by rejecting any item not actively used in the interpretive process as well as by providing computer software for scoring and interpretation. The value of saving 10 or 15 minutes of teacher, parent, or youth effort should be balanced against what is lost in measure reliability and in the restriction of the variety of dimensions assessed.

The PIC publication history suggests the diagnostic potential of the new and revised measures, especially on the dimensions that retain the greatest similarity from original to revised formats. Continued effort will expand the diagnostic utility of these new and revised forms to achieve the demonstrated performance of the original inventory (Lachar & Kline, 1994). Such efforts have begun (see Tables 6.3 and 6.6 and the PIC–2, PIY, and SBS manuals). For example, demographically matched samples of inpatient adolescents with discharge diagnoses of either conduct disorder or major depression were correctly classified by PIY subscales in 83% of the cases (Lachar, Harper, Green, Morgan, & Wheeler, 1996). In addition, hospitalized adolescents with a diagnosis of conduct disorder obtain PIY profiles similar to adolescents incarcerated in a juvenile justice facility (Negy, Lachar, Gruber, & Garza, 2001).

CONCLUSION

This chapter reviewed the development and application of a "family" of parent-, teacher-, and self-report multidimensional inventories for use with school-age children and adolescents (Grades K–12). These objective questionnaires integrate a variety of psychometric components that improve efficiency and facilitate inventory interpretation, such as validity scales, a subscale-within-scale structure, and screening forms designed to be sensitive to treatment effects. The PIC–2, PIY, and SBS measure dimensions of internalizing and externalizing problem behaviors, social adjustment, family character, and cognitive ability. Each measure incorporates dimensions that are similar across informants as well as dimensions that are unique to a given informant source. The questionnaires can be applied independently or in combination. As this chapter demonstrated, the PIC–2, PIY, and SBS possess instrument validity and can be used in treatment planning and to document treatment effects.

REFERENCES

Achenbach, T. M. (1981). A junior MMPI? [Review of *Multidimensional description of child personality: A manual for the Personality Inventory for Children* and *Actuarial assessment of child and adolescent personality: An interpretive guide for the Personality Inventory for Children profile*]. *Journal of Personality Assessment, 45,* 332–333.

Achenbach, T. M., McConaughy, S. H., & Howell, C. T. (1987). Child/adolescent behavioral and emotional problems: Implications of cross-informant correlations for situational specificity. *Psychological Bulletin, 101,* 213–232.

Brady, E. U., & Kendall, P. C. (1992). Comorbidity of anxiety and depression in children and adolescents. *Psychological Bulletin, 111,* 244–255.

Cantwell, D. P. (1996). Attention deficit disorder: A review of the past 10 years. *Journal of the American Academy of Child and Adolescent Psychiatry, 35,* 978–987.

Caron, C., & Rutter, M. (1991). Comorbidity in child psychopathology: Concepts, issues, and research strategies. *Journal of Child Psychology and Psychiatry, 32,* 1063–1080.

Flavell, J. H., Flavell, E. R., & Green, F. L. (2001). Development of children's understanding of connections between thinking and feeling. *Psychological Science, 12,* 430–432.

Gdowski, C. L., Lachar, D., & Kline, R. B. (1985). A PIC profile typology of children and adolescents: I. An empirically-derived alternative to traditional diagnosis. *Journal of Abnormal Psychology, 94,* 346–361.

Greenbaum, P. E., Dedrick, R. F., Prange, M. E., & Friedman, R. M. (1994). Parent, teacher, and child ratings of problem behaviors of youngsters with serious emotional disturbances. *Psychological Assessment, 6,* 141–148.

Harrington, R. G., & Follett, G. M. (1984). The readability of child personality assessment instruments. *Journal of Psychoeducational Assessment, 2,* 37–48.

Jensen, P. S., Martin, D., & Cantwell, D. P. (1997). Comorbidity in ADHD: Implications for research, practice, and *DSM–IV*. *Journal of the American Academy of Child and Adolescent Psychiatry, 36,* 1065–1079.

Jensen, P. S., Watanabe, H. K., Richters, J. E., Roper, M., Hibbs, E. D., Salzberg, A. D., et al. (1996). Scales, diagnoses, and child psychopathology: II. Comparing the CBCL and the DISC against external validators. *Journal of Abnormal Child Psychology, 24,* 151–168.

Kamphaus, R. W., & Frick, P. J. (1996). *Clinical assessment of child and adolescent personality and behavior.* Boston: Allyn & Bacon.

King, N. J., Ollendick, T. H., & Gullone, E. (1991). Negative affectivity in children and adolescents: Relations between anxiety and depression. *Clinical Psychology Review, 11,* 441–459.

Kline, R. B., & Lachar, D. (1992). Evaluation of age, sex, and race bias in the Personality Inventory for Children (PIC). *Psychological Assessment, 4,* 333–339.

Kline, R. B., Lachar, D., & Gdowski, C. L. (1987). A PIC typology of children and adolescents: II. Classification rules and specific behavior correlates. *Journal of Clinical Child Psychology, 16,* 225–234.

Kline, R. B., Lachar, D., Gruber, C. P., & Boersma, D. C. (1994). Identification of special education needs with the Personality Inventory for Children (PIC): A profile-matching strategy. *Assessment, 1,* 301–313.

Kline, R. B., Lachar, D., & Sprague, D. J. (1985). The Personality Inventory for Children (PIC): An unbiased predictor of cognitive and academic status. *Journal of Pediatric Psychology, 10*, 461–477.

Knoff, H. M. (1989). Review of the Personality Inventory for Children, Revised Format. In J. C. Connolly & J. C. Kramer (Eds.), *The tenth mental measurements yearbook* (pp. 624–630). Lincoln, NE: Buros Institute of Mental Measurements.

Lachar, D. (1982). *Personality Inventory for Children (PIC) revised format manual supplement.* Los Angeles: Western Psychological Services.

Lachar, D. (1998). Observations of parents, teachers, and children: Contributions to the objective multidimensional assessment of youth. In A. S. Bellack & M. Hersen (Series Eds.) & C. R. Reynolds (Vol. Ed.), *Comprehensive clinical psychology: Vol. 4. Assessment* (pp. 371–401). New York: Pergamon.

Lachar, D. (2003). Psychological assessment in child mental health settings. In I. B. Weiner (Series Ed.) & J. R. Graham & J. A. Naglieri (Vol. Eds.) *Handbook of psychology: Vol. 10. Assessment psychology* (pp. 235–260). New York: Wiley.

Lachar, D., & Gdowski, C. L. (1979). *Actuarial assessment of child and adolescent personality: An interpretive guide for the Personality Inventory for Children profile.* Los Angeles: Western Psychological Services.

Lachar, D., Gdowski, C. L., & Snyder, D. K. (1982). Broad-band dimensions of psychopathology: Factor scales for the Personality Inventory for Children. *Journal of Consulting and Clinical Psychology, 50*, 634–642.

Lachar, D., & Gruber, C. P. (1993). Development of the Personality Inventory for Youth: A self-report companion to the Personality Inventory for Children. *Journal of Personality Assessment, 61*, 81–98.

Lachar, D., & Gruber, C. P. (1995a). *Personality Inventory for Youth (PIY) manual: Administration and interpretation guide.* Los Angeles: Western Psychological Services.

Lachar, D., & Gruber, C. P. (1995b). *Personality Inventory for Youth (PIY) manual: Technical guide.* Los Angeles: Western Psychological Services.

Lachar, D., & Gruber, C. P. (2001). *Personality Inventory for Children, Second Edition (PIC–2) Standard Form and Behavioral Summary manual.* Los Angeles: Western Psychological Services.

Lachar, D., Harper, R. A., Green, B. A., Morgan, S. T., & Wheeler, A. C. (1996, August). *The Personality Inventory for Youth: Contribution to diagnosis.* Paper presented at the 104th annual convention of the American Psychological Association, Toronto.

Lachar, D., & Kline, R. B. (1994). The Personality Inventory for Children (PIC) and the Personality Inventory for Youth (PIY). In M. Maruish (Ed.), *Use of psychological testing for treatment planning and outcomes assessment* (pp. 479–516). Hillsdale, NJ: Lawrence Erlbaum Associates.

Lachar, D., Kline, R. B., & Gdowski, C. L. (1987). Respondent psychopathology and interpretive accuracy of the Personality Inventory for Children: The evaluation of a "most reasonable" assumption. *Journal of Personality Assessment, 51*, 165–177.

Lachar, D., Kline, R. B., Green, B. A., & Gruber, C. P. (1996, August). *Contribution of self-report to PIC profile type interpretation.* Paper presented at the 104th annual convention of the American Psychological Association, Toronto.

Lachar, D., Wingenfeld, S. A., Kline, R. B., & Gruber, C. P. (2000). *Student Behavior Survey (SBS) manual.* Los Angeles: Western Psychological Services.

LaCombe, J. A., Kline, R. B., Lachar, D., Butkus, M., & Hillman, S. B. (1991). Case history correlates of a Personality Inventory for Children (PIC) profile typology. *Psychological Assessment: A Journal of Consulting and Clinical Psychology, 13*, 1–14.

LaGreca, A. M., Kuttler, A. F., & Stone, W. L. (2001). Assessing children through interviews and behavioral observations. In C. E. Walker & M. C. Roberts (Eds.), *Handbook of clinical child psychology* (3rd ed., pp. 90–110). New York: Wiley.

Lanyon, R. I. (1997). Detecting deception: Current models and directions. *Clinical Psychology: Science and Practice, 4*, 377–387.

Loeber, R., Green, S. M., & Lahey, B. B. (1990). Mental health professionals' perception of the utility of children, mothers, and teachers as informants on childhood psychopathology. *Journal of Clinical Child Psychology, 19*, 136–143.

Lonigan, C. J., Carey, M. P., & Finch, A. J., Jr. (1994). Anxiety and depression in children and adolescents: Negative affectivity and the utility of self-reports. *Journal of Consulting and Clinical Psychology, 62*, 1000–1008.

Merrell, K. W. (1994). *Assessment of behavioral, social, and emotional problems: Direct and objective methods for use with children and adolescents.* New York: Longman.

Michael, K. D., & Merrell, K. W. (1998). Reliability of children's self-reported internalizing symptoms over short to medium-length time intervals. *Journal of the American Academy of Child and Adolescent Psychiatry, 37*, 194–201.

Naglieri, J. A., LeBuffe, P. A., & Pfeiffer, S. I. (1994). *Devereux Scales of Mental Disorders manual*. San Antonio TX: The Psychological Corporation.

Negy, C., Lachar, D., Gruber, C. P., & Garza, N. D. (2001). The Personality Inventory for Youth: Validity and comparability of English and Spanish versions for regular education and juvenile justice samples. *Journal of Personality Assessment, 76*, 250–263.

Phares, V. (1997). Accuracy of informants: Do parents think that mother knows best? *Journal of Abnormal Child Psychology, 25*, 165–171.

Pisecco, S., Lachar, D., Gruber, C. P., Gallen, R. T., Kline, R. B., & Huzinec, C. (1999). Development and validation of disruptive behavior scales for the Student Behavior Survey (SBS). *Journal of Psychoeducational Assessment, 17*, 314–331.

Pliszka, S. R. (1998). Comorbidity of attention-deficit/hyperactivity disorder with psychiatric disorder: An overview. *Journal of Clinical Psychiatry, 59*(Suppl. 7), 50–58.

Richters, J. E. (1992). Depressed mothers as informants about their children: A critical review of the evidence for distortion. *Psychological Bulletin, 112*, 485–499.

Sheldrick, R. C., Kendall, P. C., & Heimberg, R. G. (2001). The clinical significance of treatments: A comparison of three treatments for conduct disordered children. *Clinical Psychology: Science and Practice, 8*, 418–430.

Tellegen, A. (1988). The analysis of consistency in personality assessment. *Journal of Personality, 56*, 621–663.

Wingenfeld, S. A., Lachar, D., Gruber, C. P., & Kline, R. B. (1998). Development of the teacher-informant Student Behavior Survey. *Journal of Psychoeducational Assessment, 16*, 226–249.

Wrobel, N. H., & Lachar, D. (1998). Validity of self- and parent-report scales in screening students for behavioral and emotional problems in elementary school. *Psychology in the Schools, 35*, 17–27.

Wrobel, T. A., Lachar, D., Wrobel, N. H., Morgan, S. T., Gruber, C. P., & Neher, J. A. (1999). Performance of the Personality Inventory for Youth validity scales. *Assessment, 6*, 367–376.

Ziegenhorn, L., Tzelepis, A., Lachar, D., & Schubiner, H. (1994, August). *Personality Inventory for Youth: Screening for high-risk adolescents*. Paper presented at the 102nd annual convention of the American Psychological Association, Los Angeles.

7

The Achenbach System of Empirically Based Assessment (ASEBA) for Ages 1.5 to 18 Years

Thomas M. Achenbach
University of Vermont

Leslie A. Rescorla
Bryn Mawr College

The Achenbach System of Empirically Based Assessment (ASEBA) comprises a family of instruments for assessing problems, competencies, and adaptive functioning for persons between the ages of 1.5 and 90 plus. In this chapter, we present ASEBA instruments for children aged 1.5 to 18. (For the sake of brevity, we use *children* to include adolescents.) In a separate chapter (chap. 4, vol. 3), we present the ASEBA for ages 18 to 90 plus.

We begin this chapter with an overview of how ASEBA instruments were developed, describing their key features and summarizing the specific ASEBA instruments for different ages and sources of data. Next, we present psychometric information, including data on norms, reliability, and validity. We then present strategies for interpreting ASEBA findings. Thereafter, we present applications of the instruments to treatment planning, monitoring, and outcomes assessment. We conclude the chapter with a case illustration demonstrating use of ASEBA instruments. More detailed data and applications are presented in the ASEBA manuals for ages 1.5 to 5 and 6 to 18 (Achenbach & Rescorla, 2000, 2001; McConaughy & Achenbach, 2001).

OVERVIEW OF THE ASEBA

The ASEBA instruments originated with efforts to identify syndromes of co-occurring problems reported for disturbed children at a time when the American Psychiatric Association's (1952) *Diagnostic and Statistical Manual of Mental Disorders (DSM–I)* provided only two diagnostic categories for child psychopathology. In the initial research, behavioral and emotional problems were scored from a large sample of child psychiatric records (Achenbach, 1966). Factor analyses revealed several patterns of problems that were not identified in *DSM-I*. These findings indicated that the *DSM-I* nosology failed to reflect patterns of co-occurring problems that were sufficiently robust to be detected by statistical analyses. Although psychiatric case histories provided relatively meager and probably unrepresentative samples of data, the findings argued for further efforts to derive "syndromes" through statistical analyses of children's problems. By *syndromes*, we mean groups of problems that tend to co-occur, with no assumptions about the causes of the problems or of their co-occurrence. This is consistent with the definition of *syndrome* as "a set of concurrent things" and with the original Greek meaning of the word *syndrome* as "the act of running together" (Gove, 1971, p. 2320).

Obtaining Data from Parents

To obtain more representative samples of data on problems that were not subject to the possible selectivity of psychiatric case records, we next developed instruments for obtaining standardized data directly from people who saw children in various settings. Because parents usually have the most comprehensive knowledge of their children's functioning, the first instrument for obtaining data from informants was designed to be completed by parents. Designated the Child Behavior Checklist (CBCL), it includes items for assessing diverse behavioral and emotional problems that most parents can easily judge. These items provide a basis for empirically identifying syndromes and also for assessing individual children. Examples of CBCL problem items are *Acts too young for his/her age; Cruel to animals;* and *Unhappy sad, or depressed.* Parents are instructed to rate each item as *0 = Not True (as far as you know); 1 = Somewhat or Sometimes True;* and 2 = *Very True or Often True,* based on the preceding 6 months. In addition to being rated 0, 1, or 2, several items request parents to provide brief descriptions of problems, such as *Strange behavior (describe).* These descriptions of problems, plus descriptions of the best things about the child, the respondent's concerns about the child, and the child's illnesses and disabilities, provide users with clinically valuable information in the respondents' own words in addition to quantitative scores.

The CBCL was tested and revised through a series of nine pilot editions completed by parents of children seen in a variety of settings from 1970 through 1976. To provide diverse clinical samples from which to derive syndromes, 2,300 parents completed CBCLs for their 4- to 16-year-old children at intake into 42 mental health services. The parents' 0-1-2 ratings of the problem items were factor analyzed to derive syndromes of co-occurring problems, as seen from the parents' perspectives. These empirically based syndromes were used to construct scales that were normed on 1,300 randomly selected nonreferred children whose parents completed the CBCL in a home interview survey.

The ASEBA approach emphasizes that competencies are as important as problems for children's adaptive development. On the CBCL, competencies are scored in terms of the quality and nature of the child's involvement in sports, other kinds of activities, organizations, jobs and chores, friendships, relations with significant others, and school. The sample that was used to norm the problem scales was also used to norm four competence scales: Activities, Social, School, and Total Competence.

The syndrome and competence scales were scored on the first edition of the Child Behavior Profile (Achenbach & Edelbrock, 1983). Later editions have been normed on nationally representative probability samples totaling 4,121 children (Achenbach, 1991; Achenbach & Rescorla, 2001). These normative samples consisted of children who had not been referred for mental health or related services during the preceding 12 months. In epidemiological terms, they are regarded as "healthy" samples.

Obtaining Data from Other Informants

Parents are vital sources of information about their children's problems and competencies. However, each parent's reports are affected by the situations in which the parent sees the child, the nature of the parent's interactions with the child, and the influence of the parent's own characteristics on what is perceived and reported. To obtain data from other perspectives, ASEBA forms were developed for completion by teachers (the Teacher's Report Form; TRF) and for completion by 11- to 18-year-olds to report their own competencies and problems (the Youth Self-Report; YSR). These forms have many items in common with the CBCL, but they are tailored to the particular informants for whom they are designed. The 2001 editions are normed on the same nationally representative sample of children as the CBCL.

The ASEBA also includes instruments for direct observations, clinical interviews, and assessment of behavior during psychological testing. The Direct Observation Form (DOF) enables observers to narratively describe and rate problems and on-task behavior in group settings, such as classrooms and group activities. The Semistructured Clinical Interview for Children and Adolescents (SCICA) provides an interview protocol, rating forms, and scoring profiles that enable clinical interviewers to apply empirically based assessment to children's self-reports and behavior during interviews (McConaughy & Achenbach, 1994, 2001). The *Test Observation Form* (TOF) enables psychological examiners to rate problems manifested by children when they are taking individual tests (McConaughy & Achenbach, 2004).

Applications of the ASEBA to Preschoolers

Although the first ASEBA instruments focused on school-age children, the past 2 decades have brought applications of ASEBA methodology to other developmental periods, including the preschool period. Like the CBCL for Ages 6 to 18 (CBCL/6–18), TRF, and YSR, the instruments for preschoolers are normed on nationally representative samples of children who had not received mental health or related services in the preceding 12 months.

The Child Behavior Checklist for Ages 1.5 to 5 (CBCL/1.5–5) is completed by parents and parent surrogates. The CBCL/1.5–5 includes open-ended questions about children's functioning as well as ratings of problems. Because language is a vital competency for young children, the CBCL/1.5–5 also includes the Language Development Survey (LDS; Rescorla, 1989; Rescorla & Achenbach, 2002). Based on parents' reports of their children's vocabulary and multi-word phrases, the LDS identifies language delays according to age and gender-specific norms for children in the 18- to 35-month age range. The Caregiver-Teacher Report Form for Ages 1.5 to 5 (C–TRF) is completed by daycare providers and preschool teachers to assess many of the same problems as the CBCL/1.5–5, plus others that are specific to daycare and preschool settings. The CBCL/1.5–5 and C–TRF yield scores on empirically based syndromes as well as a variety of other scores described later in this chapter.

Table 7.1 summarizes the ASEBA forms for ages 1.5 to 18 years.

PROFILES FOR SCORING ASEBA FORMS

ASEBA forms are scored on profiles that display scores for each item and for scales comprising sets of related items. The scale scores are displayed in relation to *T*-scores and percentiles for normative samples. Hand-scored and computer-scored versions of the profiles are available. In the following sections, we describe and illustrate the different kinds of scales.

TABLE 7.1
ASEBA Forms for Ages 1.5 to 18 Years

Name of Form	*Filled out by*
Child Behavior Checklist for Ages 1½–5 (CBCL/1½–5)	Parents, surrogates
Caregiver-Teacher Report Form for Ages 1½–5 (C–TRF)	Daycare providers, preschool teachers
Child Behavior Checklist for Ages 6–18 (CBCL/6–18)	Parents, surrogates
Teacher's Report Form for Ages 6–18 (TRF)	Teachers, school counselors
Youth Self-Report for Ages 11–18 (YSR)	Youths
Semistructured Clinical Interview for Children and Adolescents (SCICA)	Interviewers
Direct Observation Form (DOF)	Observers
Test Observation Form (TOF)	Psychological examiners

Empirically Based Syndrome Scales

Since the earliest versions of the ASEBA forms were developed in the 1960s, factor analysis has been used to derive syndromes of problems. To reflect actual patterns of co-occurring problems, the problem items of each form are factor analyzed for large samples of individuals who obtained relatively high problem scores. For the 21st-century versions of ASEBA forms, multiple factor analytic methods were applied to various samples in order to identify syndromes that are statistically robust. For instruments that are parallel to each other, such as the CBCL/1.5–5 and C–TRF for preschoolers and the CBCL/6–18, TRF, and YSR for school-age children, the factor analyses were coordinated to identify syndromes that could be scored from the parallel instruments. However, some syndromes were identified only in scores for a particular instrument. An example is the Sleep Problems syndrome that was identified in the CBCL/1.5–5 but not in the C–TRF. Furthermore, because some problems are appropriately rated by only certain types of informants, there are some small cross-informant variations in the specific problems comprising the syndromes scored from ratings by each type of informant. For example, the item *Disobedient at home* is included in the Aggressive Behavior syndrome scored from the CBCL/6–18 and YSR, but this item is not in the Aggressive Behavior syndrome scored from the TRF because teachers are not apt to know about their students' disobedience at home.

Profiles of Syndrome Scales. Figure 7.1 shows a hand-scored profile of syndrome scales scored from the CBCL/6–18 completed for 15-year-old Wayne Webster by his mother (all names of cases and other identifying details in this chapter are fictitious). By looking at the lower portion of Fig. 7.1, you can see abbreviated versions of the CBCL items that compose each syndrome. The 0, 1, or 2 rating assigned to each item by Wayne's mother is entered to the left of the item. The syndrome scores are obtained by summing the 0, 1, and 2 ratings for the items of the syndrome. For example, on the leftmost syndrome, which is Anxious/Depressed, the sum of the item ratings is 11. By looking now at the graphic display, you can see that Wayne's Anxious/Depressed score of 11 is circled in the column for ages 12–18. By looking to the left of the graphic display, you can see that Wayne's score of 11 is above the 98th percentile for 12- to 18-year-old boys. By looking to the right of the graphic display, you can see that Wayne's raw score of 11 is equivalent to a *T*-score of 72.

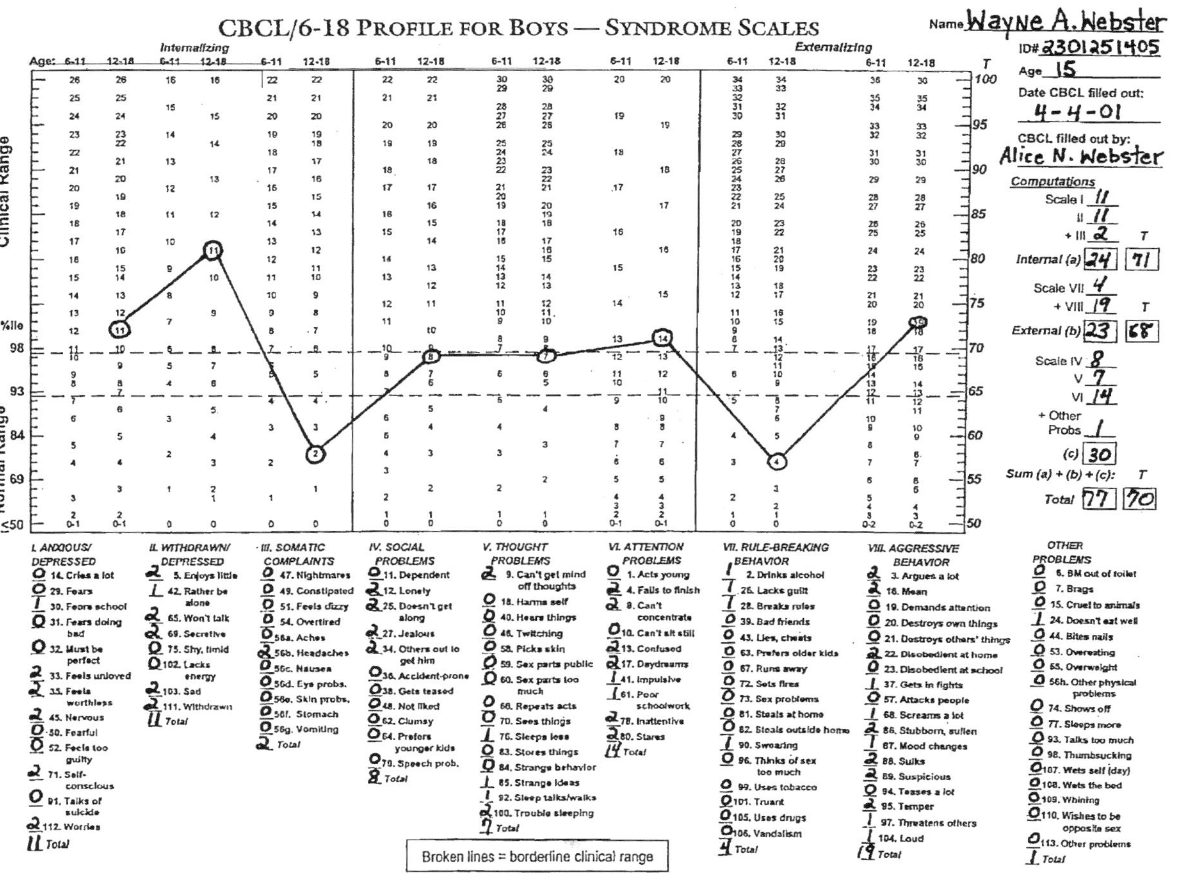

FIG. 7.1. Hand-scored Syndrome Profile from CBCL/6–18 completed for Wayne Webster by his mother (copyright Achenbach & Rescorla, 2001).

Wayne's scores were similarly calculated for the other seven syndromes: Withdrawn/Depressed, Somatic Complaints, Social Problems, Thought Problems, Attention Problems, Rule-Breaking Behavior, and Aggressive Behavior. Under the heading *Other Problems* to the right of the graphic display are items that did not load significantly on any of the empirically based syndromes but may be important in their own right. An example is *Cruel to animals.*

Borderline and Clinical Ranges. Notice now that two broken lines are printed across the profile in Fig. 7.1. Scores above the top broken line are considered to be in the clinical range because they are higher than the scores obtained by 97% of the boys in the national normative sample of nonreferred boys. A borderline clinical range is indicated between the top broken line at the 97th percentile ($T = 69$) and the bottom broken line at the 93rd percentile ($T = 65$). Scores in the borderline range are high enough to be of concern but are not so clearly deviant as those in the clinical range.

Scores below the 93rd percentile are considered to be in the normal range. Although ASEBA scale scores provide quantitative measures of problems, competencies, and adaptive functioning, the borderline and clinical ranges constitute guidelines for identifying scores that are deviant enough to indicate impairment. Statistical analyses such as odds ratios, chi squares, and receiver operating characteristic analyses (Swets & Pickett, 1982) have shown that children obtaining scores in the borderline and clinical ranges are significantly more likely to be referred for mental health services than children obtaining scores in the normal range (Achenbach & Rescorla, 2000, 2001).

As you can see in Fig. 7.1, Wayne's CBCL scores were in the clinical range on the Anxious/Depressed, Withdrawn/Depressed, Attention Problems, and Aggressive Behavior scales. Wayne's scores on the Social Problems and Thought Problems syndromes were in the borderline clinical range. His scores on the Somatic Complaints and Rule-Breaking syndromes were in the normal range, below the 93rd percentile. To take account of gender differences in the distributions of syndrome scores, norms are calculated separately for boys and girls. There is a separate hand-scored profile for girls that has separate norms for ages 6 to 11 and 12 to 18.

Internalizing and Externalizing Scores

By looking at the left side above the graphic display in Fig. 7.1, you can see the heading *Internalizing.* On the right side, you can see the heading *Externalizing.* These headings refer to two groupings of syndromes that were found through second-order factor analyses of the correlations between syndrome scores obtained by the large samples of children on whom the syndromes were derived. For the 2001 editions of the CBCL/6–18, TRF, and YSR, the factor analytic samples totaled 12,012 forms. Averaged across the second-order factor analyses for all the forms, the Anxious/Depressed, Withdrawn/Depressed, and Somatic Complaints syndromes had the highest mean loadings on one second-order factor. We designated this factor as Internalizing because it primarily reflects problems within the self. The Aggressive Behavior and Rule-Breaking syndromes had the highest mean loadings on another second-order factor, which we designated as Externalizing because it primarily reflects conflicts with other people and with social mores. Internalizing and externalizing groupings of syndromes have also been obtained in second-order factor analyses of syndromes scored from other ASEBA forms.

To indicate how individuals compare with peers in terms of the broad-band groupings of syndromes, Internalizing and Externalizing scores are computed by summing the scores of their constituent syndromes. *T*-scores for Internalizing and Externalizing can then be obtained by consulting a lookup table on the right side of the syndrome profile. Owing to space limitations, the lookup table is omitted from Fig. 7.1, but the boxes to the right of the profile in this figure indicate Wayne Webster's raw scores and *T*-scores for Internalizing and Externalizing. His *T*-score of 71 for Internalizing was above the 98th percentile, and his *T*-score of 68 for Externalizing was at the 96th percentile, according to his mother's ratings.

Total Problems Scores

The most global index of psychopathology on the ASEBA forms is the Total Problems score. This is the sum of the scores for all the problem items on the form. On hand-scored profiles, the *T*-score for an individual's Total Problems score is obtained from the lookup table to the right of the profiles. Although the lookup table is not shown in Fig. 7.1, the box labeled *Total* to the right of the graphic display shows that Wayne's Total Problems score was 77. In the box to the right of Wayne's Total Problems score, you can see that his *T*-score was 70, which is at the 98th percentile for 12- to 18-year-old boys. (The computer software for scoring ASEBA forms automatically computes all raw scores, plus gender- and age-specific *T*-scores and percentiles. The software also prints all profiles and the other results discussed in the following sections.)

DSM-Oriented Scales

The empirically based syndromes reflect patterns of co-occurring problems that were identified by factor analyzing the correlations among problems in large samples of individuals who had relatively high problem scores. This can be described as a "bottom-up" strategy because it starts with data and then derives syndromes from the data.

The psychiatric nosologies embodied in the *DSM* and in the *International Classification of Disease–10th Edition* (*ICD–10;* World Health Organization, 1992) have been developed by panels of experts who negotiated the diagnostic categories to be included. After choosing the diagnostic categories, the experts negotiated criteria for each category. This can be described as a "top-down" strategy, because it starts with concepts of diagnostic categories and then formulates criteria for determining which category an individual's problems fit.

ASEBA forms include numerous items that are empirically tested for their ability to discriminate significantly between people who are referred for mental health and related services versus demographically similar people who have not been referred for services in the preceding 12 months. The problems that compose some empirically based syndromes are similar to the symptoms that compose some *DSM–IV* and *ICD–10* diagnostic categories. Furthermore, numerous studies have found significant associations between scores on the empirically based syndrome scales and nosological diagnoses (e.g., Edelbrock & Costello, 1988; Hofstra, van der Ende, & Verhulst, 2002a; Kasius, Ferdinand, van den Berg, & Verhulst, 1997; Weinstein, Noam, Grimes, Stone, & Schwab-Stone, 1990). To facilitate crosswalks between ASEBA data and nosological categories, the 21st century ASEBA editions feature *DSM*-oriented scales for scoring ASEBA problem items in addition to the empirically based syndrome scales for scoring the problem items.

Construction of DSM-*Oriented Scales.* The *DSM*-oriented scales were constructed for each instrument by having international panels of expert psychiatrists and psychologists identify ASEBA problem items that they judged to be very consistent with particular *DSM–IV* categories (Achenbach, Dumenci, & Rescorla, 2000, 2001). Rather than matching individual ASEBA items and *DSM* symptom criteria, the experts were asked to judge ASEBA items according to their consistency with particular *DSM* diagnostic categories. Items that were identified by a substantial majority of experts as being very consistent with a *DSM* category were used to construct a scale oriented toward that category. The resulting scales were normed on the same normative samples as the empirically based syndrome scales and are displayed on analogous profiles.

Profile of DSM-Oriented Scales. Figure 7.2 shows a hand-scored version of the profile of *DSM*-oriented scales scored for Wayne Webster by his teacher. As you can see in Fig. 7.2, the *DSM*-oriented scales scored from the TRF (as well as from the CBCL/6–18 and YSR) are designated as Affective Problems, Anxiety Problems, Somatic Problems, Attention Deficit/Hyperactivity Problems, Oppositional Defiant Problems, and Conduct Problems. Note that the Attention Deficit/Hyperactivity Problems scale has subscales designated as Inattention and Hyperactivity-Impulsivity, which comprise items identified by the experts as being very consistent with the Inattentive and Hyperactive-Impulsive types of Attention Deficit/Hyperactivity Disorder (ADHD) as specified by *DSM–IV*.

Borderline and Clinical Ranges. Like the profiles for scoring the empirically based syndromes, the profiles for scoring the *DSM*-oriented scales indicate percentiles and *T*-scores based on normative samples of peers. In addition, the broken lines printed across the profiles of *DSM*-oriented scales demarcate a borderline clinical range spanning *T*-scores of 65 to 69 (the 93rd through 97th percentiles). Like the borderline clinical range on the syndrome profiles, scores below the bottom broken line are in the normal range, whereas scores above the top broken line are in the clinical range. Users can thus classify scores as normal, borderline, and clinically deviant as well as view the scores in terms of quantitative gradations.

Critical Items

Another innovation in the 21st century versions of the instruments is the identification of critical items. These items were identified by clinicians as being of particular clinical concern. Narrative reports printed by the software for scoring the ASEBA forms list scores obtained on the critical items.

Competence and Adaptive Functioning Scales

Most ASEBA forms include items for assessing developmentally appropriate competencies and adaptive functioning as well as open-ended items that request respondents to describe the best things about the individual being assessed. For the youngest preschoolers, parents' reports of their child's vocabulary and the length of their child's multiword phrases are scored. For the CBCL/6–18 and YSR, competencies are scored on scales designated as Activities, Social, School, and Total Competence. For the TRF, adaptive functioning is scored in terms of performance in academic subjects, how hard the student is working, how appropriately the student is behaving, how much the student is learning, and how happy the student is. Table 7.2 summarizes the scales that are scored from the ASEBA forms for ages 1.5 to 18.

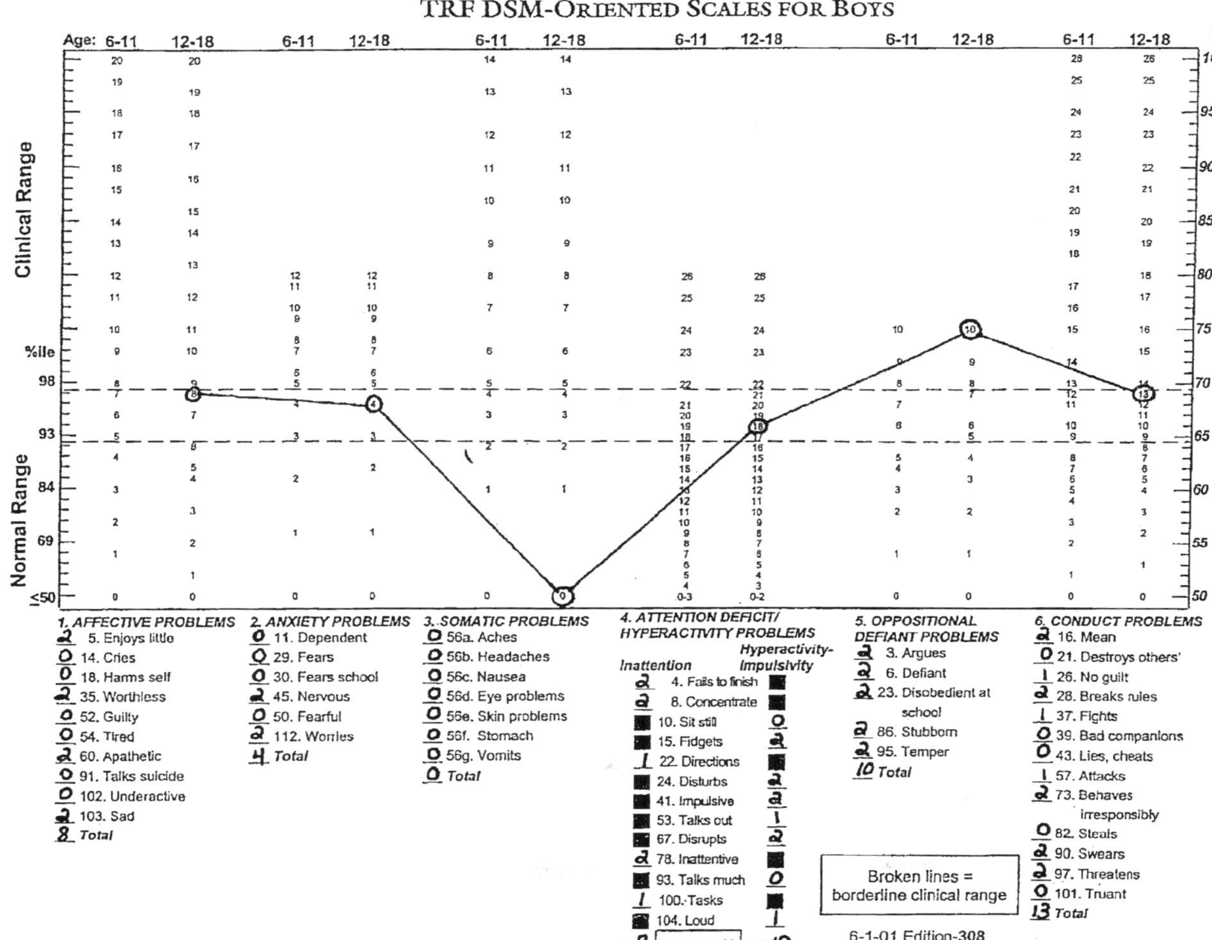

FIG. 7.2. Hand-scored *DSM*-oriented profile from TRF completed for Wayne Webster by his teacher (copyright Achenbach & Rescorla, 2001).

TABLE 7.2
Scales Scored from ASEBA Forms for Ages 1.5 to 18

Forms	*Competence & Adaptive*	*Syndromes*	*DSM-Oriented Scales*
Ages 1.5–5 CBCL, C-TRF	Language Development Survey[a] Length of Phrases Vocabulary	Emotionally Reactive Anxious/Depressed Somatic Complaints Withdrawn Sleep Problems[a] Attention Problems Aggressive Behavior	Affective Problems Anxiety Problems Pervasive Developmental Problems Attention Deficit/ Hyperactivity Problems Oppositional Defiant Problems
Ages 5–14 DOF	On-Task Behavior	Withdrawn-Inattentive Nervous-Obsessive Depressed Hyperactive Attention Demanding Aggressive	None
Ages 6–18 CBCL, TRF, YSR, SCICA	Activities[b] Social[b] School[b] Total Competence[b] Academic[c] Adaptive Functioning[c]	Anxious/Depressed Withdrawn/Depressed Somatic Complaints Social Problems[d] Thought Problems[d] Attention Problems[e] Rule-Breaking Behavior[f] Aggressive Behavior[f] Anxious[g] Language/Motor Problems[g] Self-Control Problems[g]	Affective Problems Anxiety Problems Somatic Problems Attention Deficit/ Hyperactivity Problems[e] Oppositional Defiant Problems Conduct Problems
Ages 2–18 TOF		Withdrawn/Depressed Language/Thought Problems Anxious Oppositional Attention Problems	Attention Deficit/ Hyperactivity Problems[e]

Note. Table 7.1 provides full names of forms. All forms are also scored in terms of the following groupings of problems: Internalizing, Externalizing, and Total Problems.

[a]CBCL/1.5–5 only.

[b]CBCL/6–18 and YSR only (on YSR, mean score for academic performance substitutes for the CBCL/6–18 School scale).

[c]TRF only.

[d]Not on SCICA.

[e]Attention Problems scales have subscales for Inattention and Hyperactivity-Impulsivity.

[f]These two syndromes are combined on SCICA.

[g]SCICA only.

MULTI-INFORMANT ASSESSMENT

Because children seldom seek professional help for their own behavioral and emotional problems, referrals for help typically require information from adults such as parents and teachers. Meta-analyses of many studies of various assessment instruments have yielded a mean correlation of .60 between reports of children's problems by pairs of informants who play similar roles in relation to children, including pairs of parents, pairs of teachers, and pairs of mental health workers (Achenbach, McConaughy, & Howell, 1987). The mean correlation was .28 between reports by informants who play different roles in relation to children, such as parents versus teachers versus mental health workers. Between children's self-reports and reports by adults, the mean correlation was .22. Although all these correlations were statistically significant, their modest magnitude indicates that no one informant can substitute for all others.

As described in previous sections, we have developed parallel forms for obtaining data from multiple informants for ages 1.5 to 5 and 6 to 18. Tailored to each type of informant, these forms enable users to compare quantitative item and scale scores, profile patterns, and specific comments obtained from multiple informants about the same child. To help users quickly make rigorous cross-informant comparisons, ASEBA software provides a variety of ways to systematically compare data obtained from up to eight informants for each child being assessed, as described next.

Side-by-Side Comparisons of Item Scores

To facilitate comparisons of problems reported by different informants, the ASEBA software prints a side-by-side listing of individual problem items, rated by up to eight informants, as shown in Fig. 7.3. As you can see in the box at the top of the figure, six informants completed forms for Wayne Webster, including Wayne's parents, Wayne himself, and three teachers. By looking at the leftmost columns beneath the box, you can see each informant's ratings of the items of the Anxious/Depressed syndrome. The first item beneath the Anxious/Depressed heading is *14. Cries*. On the CBCL/6–18 and TRF, the full wording of this item is *14. Cries a lot*, whereas on the YSR it is *14. I cry a lot*. By looking at the six ratings to the right of *14. Cries*, you can see that both of Wayne's parents (ratings shown in the two left columns) and all three of his teachers (three rightmost columns) rated this item 0. Under the heading *YSR*, you can see that Wayne rated this item 1, meaning that he reported *14. I cry a lot* to be *Somewhat or Sometimes True*.

By looking at each item listed in Fig. 7.3, you can identify those items that all informants reported as absent (i.e., rated 0), those items that all informants reported as present (i.e., rated 1 or 2), and those items on which the informants differed, such as *14. Cries*. By looking down the list of items for the Anxious/Depressed syndrome, you can see that Wayne was also the only one who rated item *96. Suicide* as being present (the YSR version is *I think about killing myself*). Wayne rated this item 2, whereas his parents and teachers gave ratings of 0 to the counterpart CBCL and TRF item *91. Talks about killing self*. By looking at the side-by-side items, you can quickly identify those items that were consistently reported to be present or absent and those items that revealed potentially important differences between informants' reports, such as Wayne's endorsement of items 14 and 91.

Cross-Informant Correlations

As noted earlier, meta-analyses and reviews of many studies have reported mean correlations between informants regarding children's problems (Achenbach et al., 1987). To help users judge the level of agreement between particular informants, the ASEBA software prints *Q* correlations between the 0-1-2 ratings for problem items obtained from pairs of informants for a particular individual. To obtain a *Q* correlation,

Cross-Informant Comparison - Problem Items Common to the CBCL/TRF/YSR

ID: 2301251405 Name: Wayne Webster Gender: Male Birth Date: 03/03/1986 Comparison Date: 04/13/2001

Form	Eval ID	Age	Informant Name	Relationship	Date
CBC1	001	15	Alice N. Webster	Biological Mother	04/04/2001
CBC2	002	15	Ralph F. Webster	Biological Father	04/05/2001
YSR3	003	15	Self	Self	04/08/2001
TRF4	004	15	George Jackson	Classroom Teacher {M}	04/10/2001
TRF5	005	15	Carmen Hernandez	Classroom Teacher {F}	04/11/2001
TRF6	006	15	Charles Dwyer	Classroom Teacher {M}	04/12/2001

	CBC 1	CBC 2	YSR 3	TRF 4	TRF 5	TRF 6	7	8
Anxious/Depressed								
14.Cries	0	0	1	0	0	0		
29.Fears	0	1	0	0	0	0		
30.FearSchool	1	0	0	0	0	0		
31.FearDoBad	0	0	0	0	0	0		
32.Perfect	0	0	0	0	0	1		
33.Unloved	2	2	2	0	0	0		
35.Worthless	2	2	2	2	1	0		
45.Nervous	2	2	2	2	0	0		
50.Fearful	0	0	0	0	0	0		
52.Guilty	0	0	0	0	0	0		
71.SelfConc	2	2	1	1	2	0		
91.Suicide	0	0	2	0	0	0		
112.Worries	2	2	2	2	0	0		
Withdrawn/Depressed								
5.EnjoysLittle	2	1	2	2	2	1		
42.PreferAlone	1	1	2	2	0	1		
65.Won'tTalk	2	1	2	2	1	2		
69.Secretive	2	1	2	2	1	2		
75.Shy	0	0	0	0	2	1		
102.LacksEnergy	0	1	0	0	1	0		
103.Sad	2	2	2	2	2	2		
111.Withdrawn	2	1	2	2	2	2		
Somatic Complaints								
51.Dizzy	0	1	1	0	0	0		
54.Tired	0	2	1	0	1	2		
56a.Aches	0	0	0	0	0	0		
56b.Headaches	2	0	1	0	0	0		
56c.Nausea	0	0	0	0	0	0		
56d.EyeProb	0	0	0	0	0	0		
56e.SkinProb	0	0	1	0	0	0		
56f.Stomach	0	0	0	0	0	0		
56g.Vomit	0	0	0	0	0	0		

	CBC 1	CBC 2	YSR 3	TR 4	TRF 5	TRF 6	7	8
Social Problems								
11.Dependent	0	2	2	0	1	2		
12.Lonely	2	0	2	1	0	0		
25.NotGetAlong	2	1	1	2	1	2		
27.Jealous	2	1	0	0	0	0		
34.OutToGet	2	1	2	2	1	1		
36.GetsHurt	0	2	2	0	1	0		
38.Teased	0	0	1	1	0	0		
48.NotLiked	0	1	2	2	1	2		
62.Clumsy	0	0	1	0	0	1		
64.PreferYoung	0	0	1	1	0	0		
79.SpeechProb	0	0	0	0	0	0		
Thought Problems								
9.MindOff	2	1	2	2	1	1		
18.HarmSelf	0	0	0	0	0	0		
40.HearsThings	0	0	1	0	0	0		
46.Twitch	0	0	2	0	0	0		
58.PicksSkin	0	0	0	0	0	0		
66.RepeatsActs	0	1	2	1	1	0		
70.SeesThings	0	0	0	0	0	0		
83.StoresUp	0	1	0	0	0	2		
84.StrangeBehav	0	0	1	1	0	0		
85.StrangeIdeas	1	1	2	2	0	1		
Attention Problems								
1.ActsYoung	0	2	0	0	2	2		
4.FailsToFinish	2	0	0	2	1	0		
8.Concentrate	2	2	2	2	1	1		
10.SitStill	0	2	0	0	1	1		
13.Confused	2	2	2	2	1	2		
17.Daydream	2	1	1	2	1	2		
41.Impulsive	1	2	1	2	2	2		
61.PoorSchool	1	1	1	2	0	0		
78.Inattentive	2	2	2	2	2	1		

	CBC 1	CBC 2	YSR 3	TRF 4	TRF 5	TRF 6	7	8
Rule-Breaking Behavior								
26.NoGuilt	1	2	0	1	0	0		
28.BreaksRules	1	2	0	2	1	1		
39.BadFriends	0	0	0	0	0	0		
43.LieCheat	0	0	0	0	0	0		
63.PreferOlder	0	0	0	0	0	0		
82.StealsOther	0	0	0	0	0	0		
90.Swears	1	2	1	2	0	0		
96.ThinksSex	0	0	1	0	0	0		
99.Tobacco	0	0	0	0	0	0		
101.Truant	0	0	0	0	0	0		
105.UsesDrugs	0	0	1	0	0	0		
Aggressive Behavior								
3.Argues	2	1	2	2	1	2		
16.Mean	2	1	1	2	0	0		
19.DemAtten	0	1	0	0	1	2		
20.DestroyOwn	0	0	1	1	1	1		
21.DestroyOther	0	0	0	0	0	0		
23.DisobeySchl	0	2	1	2	0	0		
37.Fights	1	2	1	1	0	0		
57.Attacks	0	0	0	1	0	0		
68.Screams	1	2	0	1	0	0		
86.Stubborn	2	2	1	2	2	2		
87.MoodChang	1	1	2	2	2	2		
89.Suspicious	2	1	2	2	0	1		
94.Teases	0	0	0	0	0	0		
95.Temper	2	2	2	2	1	1		
97.Threaten	1	2	0	2	0	0		
104.Loud	1	0	0	1	0	0		
Other Problems								
44.BiteNail	0	0	1	0	0	0		
55.Overweight	0	0	0	0	0	0		
56h.OtherPhys	0	2	0	0	0	0		

{F}=Female {M}=Male

FIG. 7.3. Cross-informant comparisons of item scores for Wayne Webster (copyright Achenbach & Rescorla, 2001).

the formula for the Pearson correlation is applied to a set of scores obtained from one rater and a set of scores obtained from another rater, e.g., the 0-1-2 ratings of items on CBCLs completed for Wayne by his mother and father. *Q* correlations can be computed between each pair of informants who rated the same individual on a common set of items. For example, Fig. 7.4 displays the *Q* correlation between ratings of Wayne by his parents, teachers, and Wayne himself on the problem items common to the CBCL/6–18, TRF, and YSR.

To provide a basis for evaluating the correlations obtained between particular informants, the printout shown in Fig. 7.4 displays each correlation (under the heading *Q Corr*) next to the 25th percentile, mean, and 75th percentile *Q* correlations found in large reference samples of similar informants. The top row of the large box displays the *Q* correlation of .51 between the 0-1-2 ratings of problem items on CBCLs completed by Wayne's mother and father. Under the heading *Cross-Informant Agreement*, this correlation is described as *Average* because it is in the interquartile range of .51 to .69 shown in the rightmost columns for *Q* correlations between the parents' ratings. As you can see from the rightmost columns, the interquartile range and mean for the *Q* correlations are lower for other combinations of informants than for pairs of parents. The correlation between each pair of informants who rated Wayne is described as *Below Average*, *Average*, or *Above Average* based on the interquartile range for correlations between those kinds of informants in the large reference samples.

Bar Graph Comparisons of Scale Scores

In addition to displaying side-by-side item ratings and correlations between pairs of informants, the ASEBA software prints bar graphs that provide side-by-side comparisons of scores for syndromes, *DSM*-oriented scales, Internalizing, Externalizing, and Total Problems obtained from each informant's ratings. As an example, Fig. 7.5 displays bar graphs showing the syndrome scores obtained from each informant who rated Wayne. By looking at the top row of bar graphs from left to right, you can see that Wayne's parents, Wayne, and one teacher scored him in the borderline or clinical range on the Anxious/Depressed syndrome, whereas two teachers scored him at the high end of the normal range. On the Withdrawn/Depressed syndrome, all raters scored Wayne in the clinical range. And on the Somatic Complaints syndrome, all raters scored him in the normal range. There was thus clear evidence for cross-situationally high levels of Withdrawn/Depressed problems, evidence for somewhat less cross-situationally consistent Anxious/Depressed problems, and little evidence for high levels of Somatic Complaints. Similar bar graphs enable you to quickly identify reports of high, medium, and low levels of problems on all the other problem scales.

NORMATIVE, PSYCHOMETRIC, AND VALIDITY DATA

Normative Data

The normative data for the cross-informant instruments for ages 1.5 to 5 and 6 to 18 were obtained in a home interview survey of a multistage national probability sample that was assessed in 1999 and 2000. At 100 sites selected to be collectively representative of the 48 contiguous states, stratified random samples of children were selected to be assessed with the relevant ASEBA forms. A parent was initially administered the

Cross-informant Comparison - CBCL/TRF/YSR Cross-Informant Correlations

ID: 2301251405 Name: Wayne Webster Gender: Male Birth Date: 03/03/1986 Comparison Date: 04/13/2001

Form	Eval ID	Age	Informant Name	Relationship	Date	Form	Eval ID	Age	Informant Name	Relationship	Date
CBC1	001	15	Alice N. Webster	Biological Mother	04/04/2001	TRF5	005	15	Carmen Hernandez	Classroom Teacher	04/11/2001
CBC2	002	15	Ralph F. Webster	Biological Father	04/05/2001	TRF6	006	15	Charles Dwyer	Classroom Teacher	04/12/2001
YSR3	003	15	Self	Self	04/08/2001						
TRF4	004	15	George Jackson	Classroom Teacher {M}	04/10/2001						

Q Correlations Between Item Scores

				Reference Group		
Forms	Informants	Cross-Informant Agreement	Q Corr	25th %ile	Mean	75th %ile
CBC1 x CBC2	Biological Mother x Biological Father	Average	.51	.51	.59	.69
CBC1 x YSR3	Biological Mother x Self	Above average	.41	.17	.29	.40
CBC1 x TRF4	Biological Mother x Classroom Teacher {M}	Above average	.54	.09	.23	.37
CBC1 x TRF5	Biological Mother x Classroom Teacher {F}	Above average	.49	.09	.23	.37
CBC1 x TRF6	Biological Mother x Classroom Teacher {M}	Above average	.42	.09	.23	.37
CBC2 x YSR3	Biological Father x Self	Above average	.56	.17	.29	.40
CBC2 x TRF4	Biological Father x Classroom Teacher {M}	Above average	.76	.09	.23	.37
CBC2 x TRF5	Biological Father x Classroom Teacher {F}	Above average	.40	.09	.23	.37
CBC2 x TRF6	Biological Father x Classroom Teacher {M}	Average	.30	.09	.23	.37
YSR3 x TRF4	Self x Classroom Teacher {M}	Above average	.60	.07	.19	.30
YSR3 x TRF5	Self x Classroom Teacher {F}	Above average	.36	.07	.19	.30
YSR3 x TRF6	Self x Classroom Teacher {M}	Above average	.35	.07	.19	.30
TRF4 x TRF5	Classroom Teacher {M} x Classroom Teacher {F}	Average	.43	.40	.51	.63
TRF4 x TRF6	Classroom Teacher {M} x Classroom Teacher {M}	Below average	.39	.40	.51	.63
TFF5 x TRF6	Classroom Teacher {F} x Classroom Teacher {M}	Above average	.67	.40	.51	.63

nc = not calculated due to insufficient data

FIG. 7.4. Cross-informant *Q* correlations for Wayne Webster (copyright Achenbach & Rescorla, 2001).

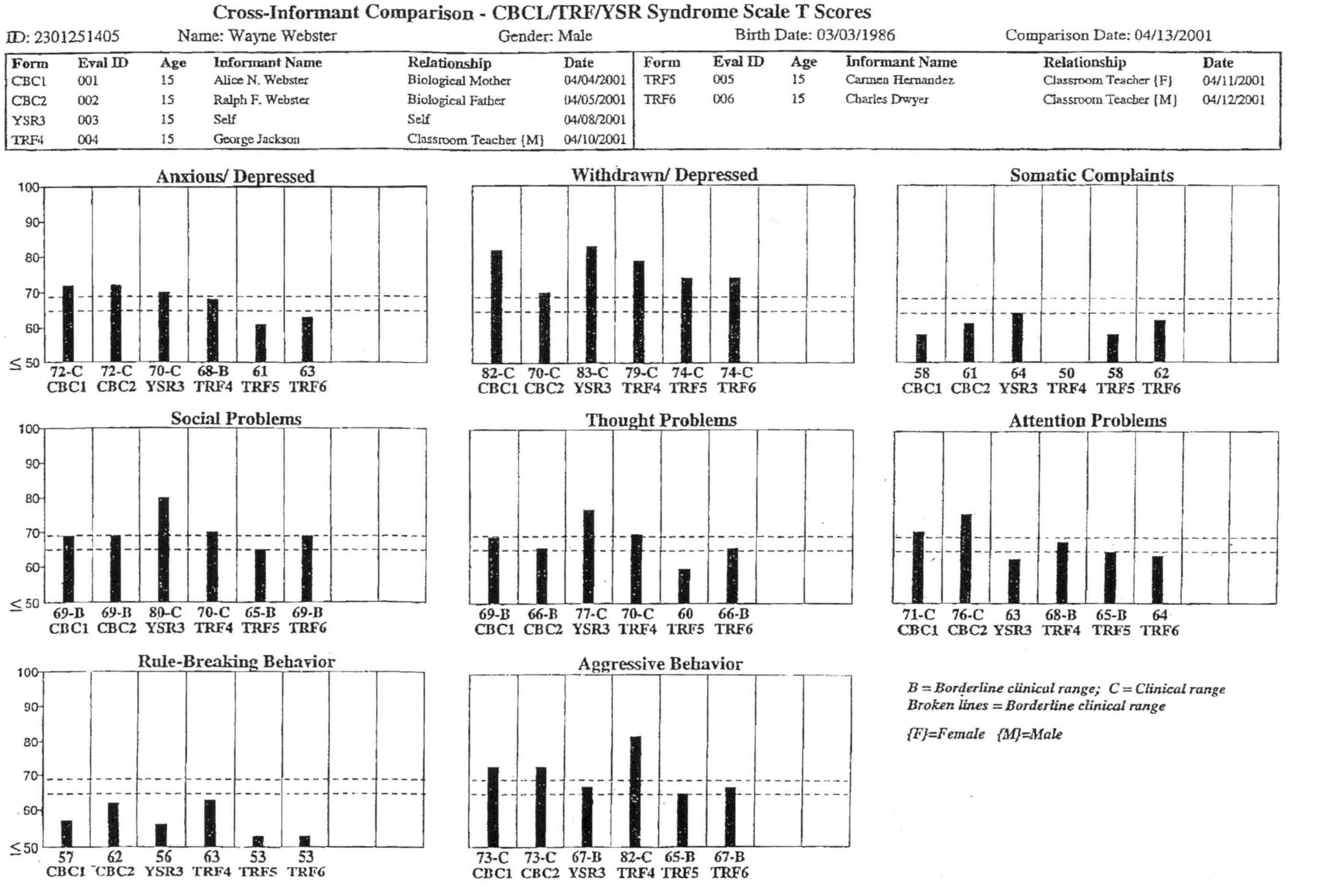

Cross-Informant Comparison - CBCL/TRF/YSR Syndrome Scale T Scores

ID: 2301251405 Name: Wayne Webster Gender: Male Birth Date: 03/03/1986 Comparison Date: 04/13/2001

Form	Eval ID	Age	Informant Name	Relationship	Date
CBC1	001	15	Alice N. Webster	Biological Mother	04/04/2001
CBC2	002	15	Ralph F. Webster	Biological Father	04/05/2001
YSR3	003	15	Self	Self	04/08/2001
TRF4	004	15	George Jackson	Classroom Teacher {M}	04/10/2001
TRF5	005	15	Carmen Hernandez	Classroom Teacher {F}	04/11/2001
TRF6	006	15	Charles Dwyer	Classroom Teacher {M}	04/12/2001

FIG. 7.5. Cross-informant comparisons of syndrome scores for Wayne Webster (copyright Achenbach & Rescorla, 2001).

CBCL/1.5–5 or CBCL/6–18. For children who attended daycare, preschool, or school and whose parents consented, the C–TRF or TRF was sent to be completed by a daycare provider or teacher. With parental consent, 11- to 18-year-olds were administered the YSR. For ages 1.5 to 5, 94.4% of the selected parents completed the CBCL/1.5–5, and for ages 6 to 18, 93.0% of the selected parents completed the CBCL/6–18. YSRs were completed by 96.5% of the 11- to 18-year-olds whose parents completed the CBCL/6–18.

For all initial interviews, the procedure was as follows: Eligible participants were first identified by interviewers who went door to door in randomly selected areas to determine the age, gender, and eligibility of residents. A stratified random sampling procedure was used to select candidates for the survey from the residents who were identified as eligible. A trained interviewer then contacted the candidate interviewees. The interviewer explained the survey and offered $10 for participating in an interview of approximately 30 minutes. A detailed informed consent form was handed to the candidate interviewee. If the candidate interviewee consented to participate, the interviewer handed him or her a copy of the relevant form (e.g., CBCL/1.5–5). The interviewer retained a second copy of the form and said, "I'll read the questions on this form and I'll write down your answers." By reading the form aloud as interviewees looked at their own copy of the form, interviewers maintained standardized administration conditions while avoiding embarrassment and errors by interviewees who could not complete forms independently. The results of this procedure have been found to be similar to the results obtained by self-administration (Achenbach, 1991).

After the ASEBA form had been completed, parent interviewees were asked whether their child had received mental health, substance abuse, or special education services in the preceding 12 months. To create nonclinical normative samples (called "healthy samples" in epidemiology), ASEBA forms for children who had received services in the preceding 12 months were excluded from the samples used to norm the profiles. Table 7.3 summarizes the national normative samples for each cross-informant instrument for ages 1.5 to 18. The manuals for the instruments provide demographic details of the normative samples (Achenbach & Rescorla, 2000, 2001).

Because it was unrealistic to seek a national probability sample for the DOF, the normative sample for the DOF consisted of children who were classmate controls for problem children observed in classrooms and group activities in 45 schools in 23 public and parochial school systems. Because the SCICA is designed for assessing children being evaluated for clinical services, the SCICA scale scores obtained by individual children are compared with scores for samples of referred children, as detailed in the manual for the SCICA (McConaughy & Achenbach, 2001). The normative sample for the TOF was drawn from the national sample that was used to norm the 5th edition of the Stanford-Binet test of intelligence (McConaughy & Achenbach, 2004).

Psychometric and Validity Data

The ASEBA manuals provide details of the high-scoring samples that were factor analyzed to derive scales. They also provide detailed data on test-retest reliability, internal consistency, cross-informant agreement, and long-term stability. Data on validity include content validity, criterion-related validity, and construct validity. Detailed analyses of discriminant validity are presented in terms of effect sizes for every problem, competence, and adaptive functioning item and scale in relation to referral status and demographic characteristics. Associations with diagnoses and other assessment instruments are also presented. Longitudinal studies have supported the predictive

TABLE 7.3
Normative and Syndrome Derivation Samples for ASEBA Instruments

Instruments	*N*	*Normative Sample Sources*	*N*	*Syndrome Derivation Sources*
CBCL/1.5–5	700	National probability sample	1,728	High-scoring children from national sample and 24 other samples
C–TRF	1,192	National probability sample; National study of early childcare; 14 other daycare and preschool programs	1,113	High-scoring children from normative sample and 18 other samples
CBCL/6–18	1,753	National probability sample	4,994	High-scoring children from national sample and 20 clinical settings
TRF	2,319	Two national probability samples	4,437	High-scoring children from National samples and 60 clinical and special education settings
YSR	1,057	National probability sample	2,581	High-scoring youths from national sample and 13 clinical settings
SCICA	686	Two mental health clinics in U.S. and Netherlands	686	Two mental health clinics in U.S. and Netherlands
DOF	287	Classroom controls for problem children in 45 public and parochial schools	212	Children referred for mental health or school psychological services in 45 public and parochial schools
TOF	3,943	Nonreferred general population sample	3,400	High-scoring children from general population sample and 4 clinical settings

Note. Table 7.1 provides full names of instruments.

validity of ASEBA scale scores for periods as long as 14 years (Hofstra, van der Ende, & Verhulst, 2001, 2002a, 2002b). Table 7.4 summarizes the psychometric data.

The *Bibliography of Published Studies Using ASEBA Instruments* (Bérubé & Achenbach, 2004) lists references for over 5,000 publications by some 8,000 authors that report use of ASEBA instruments. Many of the studies report data that support the reliability and validity of ASEBA instruments. The references are listed according to some 300 topics. Examples of the topics, with the number of references shown in parentheses, include Attention Deficit/Hyperactivity Disorder (ADHD; 450), Anxiety (155), Conduct Disorder (152), Depression (305), Drug Studies (93), Outcomes (297), Substance Abuse (108), and Suicide (58).

CROSS-CULTURAL APPLICATIONS

Because ASEBA instruments can easily obtain data directly from diverse informants without requiring specialized training or inferences, they have been widely translated for use in many cultures. At this writing, translations have been made in the 69 languages listed in Table 7.5, and over 1,000 cross-culturally relevant studies have been published from 50 countries (Bérubé & Achenbach, 2004). Among the cross-cultural studies, a number report rigorous statistical comparisons of ASEBA item and scale scores obtained in large epidemiological samples for various pairs of cultures (e.g., Lambert, Lyubansky, & Achenbach, 1998; MacDonald, Tsiantis, Achenbach, Motti-Stefanidi, & Richardson, 1995; Stanger, Fombonne, & Achenbach, 1994). In addition, rigorous statistical comparisons of CBCL scores have been made for 13,697 children across 12 cultures (Crijnen, Achenbach, & Verhulst, 1997, 1999). Comparisons of YSR scores have also been made for 7,137 eleven- to eighteen-year-olds from seven cultures

TABLE 7.4
Reliability and Validity Data

Instruments	*Reliability*[a]	*Validity*
CBCL/1.5–5	.85	1. All scales discriminate between referred and nonreferred at $p < .01$. 2. Significant correlations with Behavior Checklist (Richman, 1977), Toddler Behavior Screening Inventory (Mouton-Simien et al., 1997), Infant-Toddler Social and Emotional Assessment (Briggs-Gowan & Carter, 1998), and *DSM* criteria (Arend et al., 1996; Keenan & Wakschlag, 2000).
C-TRF	.76	1. All scales discriminate between referred and nonreferred at $p < .01$.
CBCL/6–18	.90	1. All scales discriminate between referred and nonreferred at $p < .01$. 2. Significant associations with Conners (1997a) and BASC (Reynolds & Kamphaus, 1992a) parent rating scales, plus concurrent and predictive associations with many other variables (Bérubé & Achenbach, 2004).
TRF	.88	1. All scales discriminate between referred and nonreferred at $p < .01$. 2. Significant associations with Conners (1997b) and BASC (Reynold & Kamphaus, 1992b) teacher rating scales, plus concurrent and predictive associations with many other variables (Bérubé & Achenbach, 2004).
YSR	.83	1. All scales discriminate between referred and nonreferred at $p < .01$. 2. Over periods of 3, 4, and 10 years, YSR scores predicted adult ASEBA scores, signs of disturbance, and *DSM* diagnoses (Achenbach et al., 1995, 1998; Ferdinand et al., 1995; Hofstra et al., 2001), plus they had concurrent and predictive associations with many other variables (Bérubé & Achenbach, 2004).
SCICA	.80[b]	1. All scales discriminate between referred and nonreferred at $p < .05$ in at least one age group (6–11 or 12–18). 2. Over a 3-year period, SCICA scores significantly predicted outpatient treatment, inpatient treatment, parents' wishes for help for child, school problems, and police contacts (Ferdinand et al., 2003).
DOF	Total Problems = .90[c] On-task = .84[c]	1. All scales discriminate between referred and classroom control children at $p < .001$. 2. Significant discrimination between outcomes for at-risk children receiving different interventions (McConaughy et al., 1998, 1999).
TOF	.80	1. All scales discriminate between referred and nonreferred at $p < .05$.

Note. Many other reliability and validity data are presented in the manual for each instrument and in hundreds of studies listed in the *Bibliography of Published Studies Using ASEBA Instruments* (Bérubé & Achenbach, 2004).

[a]Unless otherwise indicated, reliability is the mean of *r*s between all scale scores obtained over 8- to 16-day intervals, as reported in the instrument manuals.

[b]SCICA mean *r* is for scale scores obtained for the same children by different interviewers over a mean interval of 12 days.

[c]DOF *r*s are the means of interrater *r*s obtained in four studies (Achenbach & Rescorla, 2001, p. 172).

(Verhulst et al., 2003). Although there were some significant cross-cultural differences, the mean scores for most cultures on most scales were quite close to the "omnicultural mean," which was the overall mean for all cultures.

The availability of ASEBA forms in 69 languages and the ease of self-administration and administration by nonclinician interviewers makes the forms easy to use with people who are not proficient in English. Because the translations are laid out and scored like the English language versions, they can be scored on the English language ASEBA hand-scored profiles and can be key entered into the ASEBA software for scoring and

TABLE 7.5
Translations of ASEBA Forms

Afrikaans	French (Canadian and Parisian)	Papiamento (Curacao)
Albanian	Ga (Ghana)	Polish
American Sign Language	German	Portuguese
Amharic (Ethiopia)	Greek	Portuguese Creole
Arabic	Gujerati (India)	Romanian
Armenian	Haitian Creole	Russian
Australian Sign Language	Hebrew	Sami (Norwegian Laplanders)
Bahasia (Indonesia)	Hindi	Samoan
Bahasia (Malaysia)	Hungarian	Sepedi (South Africa)
Bengali	Icelandic	Serbo-Croatian
Bosnian	Iranian (Farsi, Persian)	Sinhala (Sri Lanka)
British Sign Language	Italian	Slovenian
Bulgarian	Japanese	Sotho (South Africa)
Cambodian	Kannada (India)	Spanish (Castilian and Latino)
Catalan (Spain)	Kiembu (Kenya)	Swahili
Chinese	Korean	Swedish
Croatian	Latvian	Tagalog (Philippines)
Czech	Lithuanian	Thai
Danish	Maltese	Tibetan
Dutch	Marathi	Turkish
Estonian	Nepalese	Ukrainian
Finnish	Norwegian	Vietnamese
Flemish	Papiamento (Aruba)	Zulu

Note. The table lists languages into which at least one ASEBA form has been translated.

cross-informant comparisons. If some informants relevant to a case prefer to complete the English language ASEBA forms while others prefer to complete translations of ASEBA forms, the data from all the forms can be included in the cross-informant comparisons.

INTERPRETIVE STRATEGY

ASEBA instruments provide psychometrically sound, standardized descriptions of problems, competencies, and adaptive functioning, as reported by different informants and compared with norms for relevant samples of peers. ASEBA instruments can be used in conjunction with virtually any other assessment procedures. However, unlike the items of many instruments, ASEBA items are designed to obtain information about particular behaviors, emotions, and aspects of functioning that are intrinsically important. In other words, the meanings of ASEBA items are intended to be clear to respondents, and the item scores are intended to measure the characteristics described by the items. Of course, all measurement is subject to error. For example, reports of people's problems, competencies, and adaptive functioning may be affected by the respondents' memory, motivation, carefulness, candor, and other factors. The aggregation of items into scales provides more reliable and valid measures of constructs than do individual items, each of which is subject to idiosyncratic error variance.

Cross-Informant Interpretations

Because there is no gold standard for assessing problems, competencies, and adaptive functioning and because correlations among informants are modest, it is desirable to have multiple informants complete ASEBA forms whenever possible. The ASEBA software makes it easy to identify problems that are reported by multiple informants versus problems that appear more variable and problems that are reported by only one informant. The respondents' written comments should be carefully considered for the light they may shed on the quantitative scores. Both the comments and the scores provide clinically useful takeoff points for interviews. For example, the practitioner can focus an interview with an adolescent on YSR items endorsed as *very true or often true*. When interviewing a parent, the practitioner might focus on written comments about what concerns the parent most about the child. Problems that are reported by multiple informants provide especially clear targets for interventions.

Discrepancies between reports by different informants are also clinically valuable because they may shed light on the children, on the informants themselves, and on the interactions between the children and informants. If potentially important problems are reported by only one or two informants, it is advisable to ask those informants to describe the problems. It is possible, for example, that some informants misconstrue or exaggerate certain behaviors or that they interact with the child in ways or in contexts that trigger certain problems. For example, if the Aggressive Behavior score is much higher in ratings by one parent than in ratings by the other parent, the practitioner can inquire about the circumstances under which each parent interacts with the child. This can help to elucidate whether differences in the conditions under which the parents see the child or differences in how the parents interact with the child may contribute to actual differences in aggressive behavior.

On the other hand, if the ASEBA software indicates that the parent who reported elevated aggressive behavior has a below-average *Q* correlation with all other informants, and if there is no evidence that the child is really more aggressive with that parent than with the other informants, this would suggest that the parent's views are idiosyncratic. Consequently, the practitioner may decide to make the parent's views of the child a focus for intervention. Multi-informant ASEBA data thus help practitioners interpret cases in terms of multiple perspectives on the functioning of children and on their interactions with other people. The ASEBA manuals provide numerous illustrations of how multi-informant ASEBA data can be interpreted in different kinds of cases seen in diverse settings.

Identifying Targets for Interventions and Outcome Evaluations

After comparing data from multiple informants and clarifying reasons for important discrepancies, the practitioner can target specific problem areas, competencies, and adaptive functioning for intervention. As described in the following sections, ASEBA data obtained at intake can provide baselines for comparison with ASEBA data obtained during the course of treatment, at termination, and at subsequent follow-ups. Comparisons between the baseline assessment and subsequent assessments can be made for individual clients and also for samples of clients who receive a particular kind of intervention for comparison with clients who receive other interventions or no intervention. Baseline and subsequent assessments can use multi-informant ASEBA data to measure changes, as seen by each informant.

USE OF ASEBA FOR TREATMENT PLANNING

Treatment should be based on the appropriate and comprehensive assessment of each child and family. ASEBA instruments are designed to assess problems and strengths in ways that are sensitive to developmental and gender differences and that utilize sources of information relevant to ages 1.5 to 5 and 6 to 18. The forms completed by parents, teachers, and youths can be used routinely for intake assessments in most settings. In addition, the SCICA can be used routinely for clinical interviews of 6- to 18-year-olds. The DOF can be used to assess children in classrooms and other group settings. Observations documented with the DOF can be especially helpful when children's school behavior is in question, when there are marked discrepancies between TRFs completed by different teachers, and when children are evaluated in residential or day treatment settings. Even for practitioners who do not work in schools or in residential or day treatment settings, it may be feasible to obtain DOF data by employing paraprofessionals, teacher aides, students, or others to make observations with the DOF. Professional training is not required to obtain reliable and valid observational data with the DOF (McConaughy, Achenbach, & Gent, 1988; McConaughy, Kay, & Fitzgerald, 1998, 1999; Reed & Edelbrock, 1983). Parents can also be assessed with the Adult Self-Report (ASR) and Adult Behavior Checklist (ABCL), as detailed by Rescorla and Achenbach in Chapter 4 of Volume 3.

By comparing the pictures of the child's problems and strengths obtained from the relevant ASEBA profiles and other assessment procedures, the practitioner can determine whether interventions may be needed. If the practitioner elects to initiate an intervention, ASEBA profiles can be shown to parents to provide a concrete basis for collaborative treatment planning. For example, if a mother and father have completed CBCLs for their child, and if they both consent, the practitioner can show them the profiles scored from their CBCLs. Working collaboratively with both parents, the practitioner can discuss the consistencies and discrepancies in what they reported about their child. Of course, a decision to show the profiles to the parents should be based on the practitioner's judgment that the parents are sufficiently sophisticated and appropriately motivated to use the information constructively. In some cases, a practitioner may also elect to show the YSR profile to a youth who has completed the YSR.

Identification of Primary and Secondary Problems

Because ASEBA instruments assess a broad range of functioning, the profiles may reveal problems and strengths that were not among the reasons for referral. For example, ASEBA profiles for children who are referred for evaluation of ADHD may reveal that their scores are more deviant on scales such as Anxious/Depressed, Social Problems, Thought Problems, or Aggressive Behavior than on the Attention Problems syndrome or the *DSM*-oriented Attention Deficit/Hyperactivity Problems scale. If the children are evaluated only for ADHD, it might be erroneously concluded that ADHD is their primary problem. Findings of greater deviance on other scales might indicate, instead, that attention problems are secondary to other problems. Furthermore, because ASEBA forms explicitly request information about a broad spectrum of strengths and problems, they may reveal areas in which functioning is especially strong or problem free.

In addition to the profiles of empirically based scales, the profiles of *DSM*-oriented scales may reveal problems that are consistent with *DSM* diagnoses other than those that were the main focus of the referral. For example, children referred for ADHD may indeed meet *DSM* criteria for ADHD, but their *DSM*-oriented profiles may also reveal clinical elevations on depressive or anxiety problems. Such elevations would prompt the practitioner to determine whether the children also meet *DSM* criteria for depressive and/or anxiety disorders. If so, these disorders could become foci for interventions along with ADHD.

It may not always be meaningful to classify problems and strengths as primary versus secondary. However, it is always essential to identify all important problems and strengths rather than assessing only those that prompted the referral. For example, widely publicized diagnostic concepts such as ADHD may sometimes deflect attention from other important problems and strengths.

Levels of Care

ASEBA scales quantitatively compare a child's problems and strengths with those of normative samples of peers. It is therefore easy to judge the degree of deviance indicated on each scale. The normal, borderline, and clinical ranges marked on the profiles provide explicit guidance for determining general levels of deviance. However, the quantitative gradations within these ranges provide more precise indices of the degree of deviance. These quantitative gradations can be helpful for determining whether relatively low or high levels of care are needed. For example, if no problem scale scores are in the clinical range, this suggests that relatively low levels of care are needed. On the other hand, scores that are at the high end of the clinical range argue for high levels of care.

The ASEBA critical items can also indicate whether relatively high levels of care are needed. Although children's *DSM* diagnoses must also be considered, categorical, yes-versus-no *DSM* diagnoses do not offer clear guidance regarding the severity of children's problems. Of course, decisions about levels of care must take account of many factors, such as past history, strengths, etiologies, available resources, and aftercare options.

Appropriate Treatment Approaches

ASEBA instruments can be used in planning most kinds of treatment. Because ASEBA items assess relatively specific kinds of behavior, thoughts, feelings, social interactions, and competencies, these can be used as targets for behavioral treatments. Because the problem items are also aggregated into syndromes and *DSM*-oriented scales, the constructs measured by these scales can be targeted for psychotherapies, cognitive behavioral therapies, and pharmacotherapies that are designed to treat disorders such as depression, anxiety, and ADHD. High scores for children and adolescents on the Rule-Breaking and Aggressive Behavior syndromes and on the *DSM*-oriented Conduct Problems scale indicate needs for highly structured treatments and settings.

ASEBA instruments facilitate consideration of different kinds of treatment from the same database. For example, if an adolescent obtains scores in the clinical range on the Anxious/Depressed, Social Problems, and Attention Problems syndromes and on the *DSM*-oriented Attention Deficit/Hyperactivity Problems scale, the practitioner might recommend stimulant drug treatment for attention problems. The practitioner might also recommend psychotherapy or cognitive behavioral therapy for the negative affectivity indicated by the Anxious/Depressed syndrome and social skills training for the problems of the Social Problems syndrome.

Over 300 publications reporting applications of ASEBA instruments to treatment are listed in the *Bibliography of Published Studies Using ASEBA* (Bérubé & Achenbach, 2004). These include studies of behavior therapy, cognitive behavioral therapy, pharmacotherapy, and psychotherapy. Table 7.6 lists examples of treatment-related topics for which published studies have reported use of ASEBA.

TABLE 7.6
Examples of Treatment-Related Topics for Which Studies Have Been Published on ASEBA Instruments

Abdominal pain (15)	Headaches (6)	Posttraumatic stress disorder (53)
Anxiety (159)	Lead toxicity (10)	Psychotherapy (20)
Asthma (60)	Learning problems (73)	Schizophrenia (31)
Attention Deficit/Hyperactivity Disorder (435)	Obesity (19)	School refusal (15)
Colitis (2)	Obsessive-compulsive behavior (24)	Seasonal affective disorder (2)
Conduct Disorder (152)	Oppositional disorder (49)	Self-concept (46)
Delinquent behavior (70)	Outcomes of problems (298)	Self-esteem (32)
Diabetes (52)	Pain (20)	Separation (14)
Divorce (66)	Parent management training (23)	Sex abuse (99)
Drug studies (94)	Parent-child relationships (289)	Sleep disturbance (26)
Eating problems (15)	Parental perceptions (214)	Stress (152)
Encopresis (11)	Parental psychopathology (133)	Suicide (56)
Enuresis (16)	Peer interaction (123)	Teacher perceptions (65)
Epilepsy (42)		Temperament (48)
Fire-setting (13)		Tourette syndrome (28)
Gender problems (25)		

Note. The *Bibliography of Published Studies Using ASEBA Instruments* (Bérubé & Achenbach, 2004) provides references to the studies relevant to each topic. The number of studies listed in the *Bibliography* for each topic is shown in parentheses.

Use of ASEBA with Other Evaluation Data

ASEBA instruments provide pictures of functioning during a particular window of time. On the instruments for ages 1.5 to 5 and on the TRF for ages 6 to 18, problems are rated on the basis of a 2-month period. On the other instruments for ages 6 to 18, problems are rated on the basis of a 6-month period. However, some competence items for ages 6 to 18 include information about longer periods, such as whether the child has ever repeated a grade. The SCICA assesses children's behavior and self-reports during a clinical interview, but the self-reports include information about functioning prior to the interview. The TOF assesses behavior during psychological testing sessions. The DOF scores observations of 10-minute samples of behavior, with three to six 10-minute samples being recommended. The ASEBA software for the DOF averages item and scale scores for up to six 10-minute observation periods for the target child and for two control children observed in the same setting as the target child.

ASEBA forms obtain demographic data from which to code socioeconomic status and ethnicity. Comprehensive assessment should also include developmental and medical histories plus information about the child's current living situation and family dynamics.

If there are questions about a child's cognitive functioning, the practitioner may opt to administer ability and achievement tests. Clinical interviews, personality tests, and projectives may also be used as desired. If ASEBA instruments are completed prior to interviews, the practitioner can use the ASEBA responses as a takeoff point for interviewing. For example, the practitioner working with an adolescent can first ask if he or she has any questions about the YSR form. This may lead to important issues to pursue. The practitioner can then ask about particular responses. As an example, the practitioner can say, "I noticed that you circled 2 for item *34. I feel that others are out to get me.* Can you tell me more about that?" Following completion of ASEBA instruments, interviews can be used to obtain details of the respondent's experience, feelings, and expectations that cannot be obtained with assessment instruments alone.

Uses and Limits of ASEBA for Treatment Planning in Managed Care and Other Settings

ASEBA instruments are very cost-effective and easy to use in managed care and most other settings. Except for the SCICA, TOF, and DOF, they are self-administered. They can all be scored by clerical staff or computers. Machine readable versions, computerized client-entry versions, and Web-based versions are available for several ASEBA instruments. For respondents who cannot complete forms independently, a receptionist or other staff member can administer the form as an interview. For respondents who are not proficient in English, translations have been made into the 69 languages listed in Table 7.4.

ASEBA forms and profiles document diverse strengths and problems. This documentation provides baseline data with which to plan interventions and compare subsequent reassessments. The practitioner can quickly look at completed forms, profiles, and cross-informant comparisons for essential information and can use them as a basis for interviews and other assessments. With appropriate permission, ASEBA forms and profiles can be sent to other practitioners who see the children. Feedback in the form of scored profiles and the narrative reports produced by the ASEBA software can be provided to other professionals and to sophisticated clients. Scale scores can also be used to provide information about individual children and groups of children.

Spanning from ages 1.5 to 18, with age- and gender-specific norms, ASEBA instruments for children can be used in school, medical, mental health, child welfare, foster care, managed care, and other service settings. Within health care organizations that have multiple services, ASEBA forms can be used in different services, such as family practice, pediatrics, internal medicine, mental health, and substance abuse services. Each service can use ASEBA instruments in its own treatment planning but can also use the instruments as a basis for referral to other services. For example, if a child seen in pediatrics or family practice is found to score in the clinical range on multiple syndromes and/or *DSM*-oriented scales, the ASEBA data can be used in a referral to the mental health service. The initial ASEBA data can thus be used by the mental health professionals as a cornerstone of their evaluation. The mental health professionals may decide whether to obtain data from other informants, such as by requesting the child's teachers to fill out TRFs.

For settings that rely heavily on *DSM* diagnoses, a possible limitation of ASEBA instruments is that they do not include all criteria for many *DSM* diagnostic categories. Although *DSM*-oriented scales are scored from ASEBA instruments, users are cautioned that high scores on these scales are not directly equivalent to *DSM* diagnoses. Instead, users should consult the *DSM* for the precise criteria for each disorder and then determine whether children meet all the criteria.

USE OF ASEBA FOR TREATMENT MONITORING

The purpose of treatment monitoring is to determine whether desired changes are occurring during the course of treatment and to detect unfavorable changes. If we assess only the target problems either initially or during the course of treatment, we might not recognize that other problems may fail to resolve or may even worsen. For example, if ADHD is identified as the target for treatment and only ADHD symptoms are monitored, treatment may be deemed successful if ADHD symptoms decline. Yet, assessment of a broad spectrum of problems may reveal that other problems, such as anxiety, depression, social problems, or aggression, were initially present or emerged or worsened during treatment.

By readministering ASEBA instruments at regular intervals appropriate for the treatment, such as every 3 months, users can track the course of all the problems and strengths assessed by them. Furthermore, by having ASEBA forms completed by informants who are not directly involved in the treatment, users can monitor the treatment free of the confounds potentially associated with involved individuals' beliefs about whether treatment is working.

If ASEBA instruments are to be readministered at intervals shorter than those stated in the standard instructions (2 months for the CBCL/1.5–5, 2 months for the TRF for ages 6 to 18, and 6 months for the CBCL/6–18 and the YSR), the rating intervals for the first administration should be similarly shortened to maintain uniform rating periods. Except for the SCICA and DOF, which obtain observations during a particular session, the other instruments should probably not be readministered at intervals of less than about 1 month. This is because the aspects of functioning that they assess take time to change. Time is also needed for the changes to stabilize and for respondents to become aware of the changes. Use of intervals shorter than the standard interval may reduce problem scores somewhat. However, if the same shortened interval is used at all administrations, this will not affect differences between scores obtained from one administration to the next.

Test-Retest Attenuation

Another reason for not readministering ASEBA or other assessment instruments over intervals of less than 1 month is *test-retest attenuation*. This is the widely found tendency for people to report fewer problems on the second administration of a test, interview, or rating form shortly after the first administration (Helzer, Spitznagel, & McEvoy, 1987; Roberts, Solovitz, Chen, & Casat, 1996; Vandiver & Sher, 1991). Although test-retest correlations are high for ASEBA instruments, as summarized in Table 7.3, there is a tendency for problem scores to decline from the first administration to a second administration a week later, which is the usual period for assessing test-retest reliability. The longer the interval between administrations, the weaker the effect of test-retest attenuation is likely to be.

Regression Toward the Mean

It should be noted that test-retest attenuation differs in the following ways from *regression toward the mean*: Whereas test-retest attenuation is the tendency for most people to report fewer problems on a second assessment shortly after an initial assessment, regression toward the mean is the tendency for people who initially obtain extremely high or extremely low scores to subsequently obtain scores that are closer to the mean of the entire sample in which they are included. In other words, test-retest attenuation is a general tendency pertaining to people's reports of problems regardless of whether they initially report exceptionally many or few problems. By contrast, regression toward the mean is a statistical phenomenon reflecting the role of chance factors in causing scores to be very deviant from the mean of their distributions. Because the individuals who initially obtain extremely deviant scores are not likely to be affected by chance factors in the same way at subsequent assessments, they will tend to obtain less extreme scores (i.e., scores closer to the mean) than they initially obtained.

Both test-retest attenuation and regression toward the mean may contribute to declines in problem scores for people who initially obtained high problem scores. Consequently, individuals should be reassessed on more than one occasion, and evaluations of particular types of services should include control groups who are assessed repeatedly in the same way as the treated groups before and after different intervention conditions, as discussed in the following section.

USE OF ASEBA FOR TREATMENT OUTCOMES ASSESSMENT

To be useful for assessing treatment outcomes, instruments should be easy to administer at intake, termination of treatment, and follow-up. They should assess problems and strengths that can potentially change during and after treatment. They should also be quantified to facilitate statistical analyses of degrees of change. To avoid contamination by participants' beliefs about the effectiveness of treatment, the instruments should be able to obtain data from sources in addition to the participants. Furthermore, the instruments should provide norms based on representative samples of peers to enable users to evaluate the degree of children's deviance both before and after treatment. Norms based on representative samples are especially important for evaluating the clinical significance of changes in terms of improvement from clinical to nonclinical levels (Achenbach, 2001; Jacobson & Truax, 1991; Sheldrick, Kendall, & Heimberg, 2001).

Research on the Effectiveness of Treatments

Instruments that have the characteristics just mentioned are useful for evaluating the effectiveness of particular kinds of treatment as well as for evaluating outcomes for individual children. To properly evaluate the effectiveness of Treatment A, it is necessary to compare Treatment A with another treatment, such as Treatment B. To determine whether Treatments A and B are better than no treatment, it is also desirable to compare them with a control condition that is as similar as possible to the treatment conditions except that children receive a placebo rather than active treatment. Although it is relatively easy to arrange placebo control conditions for pharmacotherapies, it is more difficult to do so for behavior therapies, psychotherapies, and psychosocial interventions. To provide persuasive no-treatment control conditions, it may therefore be necessary to create "Hawthorne controls" in which children receive the same amount of attention from therapists as children who receive Treatments A and B. Another option is to use waiting list control conditions whereby children who are waiting for treatment are assessed over intervals of the same lengths as children who receive Treatments A and B.

To provide valid comparisons of Treatment A, Treatment B, and a control condition, the children receiving each condition must be as similar as possible. The classic strategy for achieving similarity is to first recruit a pool of cases selected to meet criteria for the study. The selection criteria would typically include manifesting the problems for which Treatments A and B are designed. Additional selection criteria would typically include being free of problems that might interfere with or present risks for Treatments A and B, plus age, gender, and other demographic characteristics appropriate for the treatments. ASEBA instruments can be used to assess both the target problems and the exclusionary problems, because the same instruments assess diverse problems and identify deviance from norms on empirically based and *DSM*-oriented scales.

Random Assignment. After enough qualified cases are recruited and after participants have given informed consent to accept assignment to the various treatment conditions, the classic procedure is to randomly assign cases to the treatment conditions. Randomization is intended to make the samples of cases receiving each condition as similar as possible with respect to characteristics that could affect the outcomes. When large pools of cases are available, purely random assignment may be an effective way to achieve similarity between the samples receiving each condition. However, with limited pools of cases, purely random assignment may result in samples that differ in ways that are confounded with the treatment conditions. For example, if cases receiving Treatment A have less severe problems than cases receiving Treatment B or the control condition, better outcomes for Treatment A cases may be attributable to the lesser severity of their problems rather than to the superiority of Treatment A.

Randomized Blocks Designs. To avoid risks associated with purely randomized assignment, a randomized blocks design can be used to obtain samples that are similar with respect to characteristics that may affect outcomes. In a randomized blocks design, the researcher identifies "blocks" (i.e., groups) of cases that are similar with respect to important characteristics, such as profiles of problems, severity of problems, and demographic characteristics. From each block of similar cases, individual cases are randomly assigned to the different treatment conditions. If there are three conditions, such as Treatment A, Treatment B, and a control condition, each block would typically consist of three cases that are similar with respect to important characteristics.

The initial matching of cases with respect to important characteristics, followed by random assignment from blocks of similar cases, can reduce the risk of case characteristics being confounded with treatment conditions. ASEBA instruments can be especially helpful for creating blocks of cases that are matched for particular scale scores and for overall severity as measured by Total Problems scores.

Multi-Informant Data. Parallel ASEBA forms completed by multiple respondents can provide baseline data for comparison with subsequent termination and follow-up assessments using the same multiple informants. By comparing reports from multiple respondents at each assessment point, researchers can determine whether favorable or unfavorable outcomes reported by one respondent are borne out by the reports of other respondents. Although their reports cannot be considered unbiased, therapists can also complete ASEBA forms at baseline, termination, and follow-up for comparison with reports by children and other respondents.

For statistical purposes, ASEBA forms completed by each type of respondent can be analyzed separately. For example, if children receiving three treatment conditions are assessed with ASEBA self-report and other-report forms at intake, termination, and follow-up, researchers can use 3 (repeated measures at intake vs. termination vs. follow-up) $\times$ 3 (conditions A vs. B vs. control) ANOVAs to analyze the self-report and other-report data separately. Another strategy is to aggregate the self-report and other-report data by combining them in MANOVAs. Because it may not always be possible to obtain data from every informant at every assessment point, missing data can be handled by various approaches, such as maximum likelihood and Bayesian multiple imputation (Schafer & Graham, 2002). Furthermore, conclusions about interrater agreement on outcomes can be based on latent class models (Schuster & Smith, 2002).

The multiple parallel scales scored from ASEBA forms completed by each informant provide opportunities for statistically evaluating outcomes in terms of a variety of target problems such as attention problems, aggression, depression, withdrawal, and social problems. In addition, because all children can be scored on all scales, problems that were not targeted by the interventions can be statistically evaluated to determine whether they have changed as well.

Total scores for problems, competencies, and adaptive functioning can also be analyzed to provide broad measures of change after treatment. Table 7.7 summarizes features of ASEBA instruments in relation to guidelines for selection and use of measures of treatment progress and outcomes (Newman, Ciarlo, & Carpenter, 1999). Over 300 publications report treatment research employing ASEBA instruments (Bérubé & Achenbach, 2004).

Evaluating Outcomes for Individual Children

In evaluating the progress of an individual child, a key outcome question is whether the child is better in important ways after treatment than before. Because of the many idiosyncracies of each case and the common practice of mixing treatment approaches, documentation of improvement for an individual child may not indicate whether a particular treatment per se is effective. Although rigorous ABAB designs may provide convincing evidence for treatment effectiveness in some single-case studies, few practitioners are able to rigorously implement such designs in day-to-day clinical practice. Instead, practitioners need to be able to determine whether individual children are improving during treatment and whether they reach levels of functioning where additional treatment is not needed.

Because ASEBA instruments for children can be completed periodically by parents, teachers, youths, and therapists, they can be used to track the course of a child's functioning in relation to norms for the child's age, gender, and the type of informant. Thus, for example, if ASEBA forms administered several months after onset of treatment show progress toward the normal range, this would indicate that the treatment is progressing. On the other hand, if there is insufficient movement of scale scores toward the normal range, this would suggest that changes in the treatment should be considered.

ASEBA forms can be readministered periodically to help practitioners decide whether sufficient progress has been made to consider termination. If feasible, follow-up reassessments at 6-month intervals, for example, are also highly desirable. The follow-up reassessments can tell practitioners whether improvements are maintained or whether additional interventions may be needed.

In lieu of the kinds of statistical analyses that are appropriate for research on treatment, practitioners can use information provided in the appendix of each ASEBA manual to judge whether changes in scale scores exceed the error of measurement. Tables in the appendix show the standard error of measurement (*SEM*) for each ASEBA scale separately for samples of referred and nonreferred children of each age and gender as assessed by each type of informant. The manuals also provide instructions for using the *SEM* to evaluate changes in scale scores. For example, if you are assessing changes in scale scores obtained by a child referred for mental health services, identify the *SEM* listed in the manual for referred children of the child's age and gender on the scale in question. If the change in the child's scale score exceeds one *SEM*, the change exceeds the change expected by chance 68% of the time. To apply a 95% confidence interval,

TABLE 7.7
ASEBA Instruments in Relation to Guidelines for Progress-Outcome Measures

Guidelines	*Comments*
Applications	
1. Relevant to target group; independent of treatment; sensitive to treatment-related changes	Items and scales are developmentally appropriate, derived and normed on large representative samples, designed for multiple relevant informants, independent of treatment but usable for evaluation of most treatments; many studies demonstrate sensitivity to treatment-related changes.
Methods and procedures	
2. Simple, teachable methods	Self-administered by respondents having at least 5th-grade reading skills; for respondents who cannot complete forms independently, can be read aloud by nonclinicians.
3. Measures with objective referents	Quantified, factual reports cross-checked among multiple informants.
4. Multiple respondents	Parallel forms obtain data from multiple informants; ASEBA software compares and correlates data from up to 8 informants per child.
5. Process-identifying outcome measures	Periodic readministration of ASEBA forms and comparisons of changes on the different competence, adaptive, and problem scales provide markers on which to base decisions about continuing or changing treatment plans.
Psychometric features	
6. Reliable, valid, sensitive to treatment-related change, nonreactive	Table 7.4 and numerous published studies provide evidence of reliability, validity, sensitivity to treatment-related change; data from informants blind to treatment conditions are nonreactive.
Cost considerations	
7. Low costs	Forms cost 50¢ each; no per-use charge for scoring or administration by computer software; Web-Link obviates the need for supplies of forms.
Utility considerations	
8. Understanding by non-professional audiences	Meaning of items is self-evident; scale names are descriptive; profiles are easy to read.
9. Easy feedback; uncomplicated interpretation	Profiles and normed data on changes can be presented to untrained consumer groups.
10. Useful in clinical services	Can be self-administered by most clients in most services; clerical staff can score by hand or computer; clinicians can quickly glean information from profiles and can use specific responses as desired; narrative reports can be imported into word processors; item and scale scores can be imported into databases; completed forms and profiles provide documentation for case records.
11. Compatibility with clinical theories and practices	Standardized descriptive data are compatible with virtually all theories and practices; studies of ASEBA instruments report associations with many clinical constructs and measures in many practice settings.

Note. Guidelines are from Newman, Ciarlo, and Carpenter (1999), p. 155, Table 5.1.

multiply the *SEM* by 1.96. Illustrations of applications of change indices to CBCL scales and other measures are presented by Sheldrick et al. (2001) and by Achenbach (2001). Jacobson and Truax (1991) provided a statistical basis for documenting changes from pre- to posttreatment assessments in terms of the reliable change index (RCI).

For individual children as well as for research, ASEBA data can be used in conjunction with most other kinds of evaluation data. The feedback provided can include actual changes in scale scores and an indication whether scores have improved from the clinical range to the borderline or normal range. If practitioners need to consider *DSM* diagnoses in their outcome evaluations, they will need other data to determine whether children meet criteria for *DSM* diagnoses at each assessment point. ASEBA data can be used for behavioral health service report cards if ASEBA instruments are applied according to uniform protocols in the services. Such data can be especially useful for comparing services that have similar cases so that case characteristics are not confounded with the type of care.

To illustrate applications of ASEBA instruments to individual cases, the following section provides a case example (the names and other identifying data are fictitious).

Case Example: Marisa Rivera, Age 13

When Ms. Rivera took her 13-year-old daughter Marisa shopping for a new Easter outfit, she noticed scars on her forearms. Alarmed at this sight, she questioned her daughter until Marisa admitted that she had cut herself with a razor blade. Ms. Rivera had been concerned about her daughter for many months, but her husband had dismissed Marisa's behavior as typical teenage rebelliousness. However, when told about the cutting, Mr. Rivera agreed that they should take Marisa to the local community mental health center. As part of the clinic intake procedure, Marisa completed the YSR and both parents completed CBCLs as well as a developmental and family history form. Sara Bartoli, the clinician assigned to the Riveras, then interviewed Marisa and her parents.

Ms. Bartoli learned that Marisa was the oldest of Miguel and Lizabeta Rivera's four children. Mr. Rivera, a postal service supervisor, had been born in Puerto Rico and had immigrated to the United States as a young child. Ms. Rivera, whose family emigrated from Poland when she was 11 years old, worked at home taking care of their children, aged 5, 7, 11, and 13. The Riveras had met at church and had married when they were 19. According to the Riveras, there was no history of psychiatric disorder in the family. Marisa was described as a healthy child who made normal developmental progress and had been a good student until the seventh grade.

ASEBA Competence and Adaptive Functioning Scores. On the competence portion of the YSR and CBCL, Marisa and her parents listed singing and dancing among Marisa's favorite activities. They also rated her as spending more time in these activities than others of her age and as doing them better than others of her age. In the open-ended section of the YSR, where youths are asked to describe the best things about themselves, Marisa wrote "I'm a good singer and pretty good dancer." Her scores on the competence scales were all in the normal range.

With the Riveras' permission, two of Marisa's teachers completed TRFs. On the adaptive functioning portion of the TRF, the teachers rated her highly on several favorable characteristics. In the open-ended section for describing the best things about her, they mentioned that she got along well with other pupils and was musically talented. Her scores on the TRF Academic Performance and Adaptive Functioning scales were in the normal range except for ratings on the item for happiness, where the teachers rated her as somewhat less happy than typical pupils of her age.

ASEBA Syndrome Scores. Ratings from all five informants indicated a significant elevation on the Withdrawn/Depressed syndrome, with the CBCLs in the clinical range and the YSR and TRFs in the borderline range. The TRFs yielded scores in the borderline clinical range on the Attention Problems syndrome. Marisa's teachers rated the following items as "very true or often true": *4. Fails to finish things he/she starts; 8.*

Can't concentrate, can't pay attention for long; 17. Daydreams or gets lost in his/her thoughts; 61. Poor school work; and *78. Inattentive or easily distracted.*

ASEBA DSM-*Oriented Scores.* On the *DSM*-oriented scales, Mr. Rivera's ratings yielded scores in the clinical range on the Oppositional Defiant Problems scale. He rated the following items as "very true or often true": *3. Argues a lot; 22. Disobedient at home; 86. Stubborn, sullen, or irritable;* and *95. Temper tantrums or hot temper.* Ms. Rivera and Marisa rated these items as "somewhat or sometimes true." Marisa's ratings yielded a score in the borderline range on the *DSM*-oriented Affective Problems scale, with endorsements of *5. There is very little I enjoy; 14. I cry a lot; 18. I deliberately try to hurt or kill myself; 24. I don't eat as well as I should; 100. I have trouble sleeping;* and *103. I am unhappy, sad, or depressed.*

Interviews. During the initial interview, Marisa complained angrily about her father's not letting her pick her own friends and not letting her do things she wanted to do, such as going to rock concerts and parties. She also complained that her mother made her do too much house cleaning and babysitting. Mr. and Ms. Rivera acknowledged that they differed somewhat on the question of how much freedom a 13-year-old girl should have, with Ms. Rivera arguing for more independence than her husband. However, both parents agreed that Marisa was withdrawn and sullen at home, that she was rude and disrespectful to them, and that she resisted doing things that she had willingly done before, such as cleaning her room and following her mother's suggestions about clothing. When Ms. Bartoli asked Marisa about her cutting herself, she said she had been doing it for a few months. She said sometimes she got so angry and frustrated that she could not think of any other way to get rid of these feelings.

Therapy Sessions. Ms. Bartoli invited the family to return for some therapy sessions aimed at resolving these conflicts. Ms. Bartoli also asked Marisa to sign a contract promising that she would not cut herself. In subsequent sessions, Marisa and her parents discussed areas in which she could have more autonomy, such as her room, clothing, and choice of music. With Ms. Bartoli's help, the Riveras set up a behavioral plan that enabled Marisa to earn leisure time privileges in exchange for improving her schoolwork and helping at home. The Riveras wanted certain restrictions to be nonnegotiable, such as restrictions against going to unsupervised parties, staying out past 11 o'clock, and socializing with peers who used drugs and alcohol. Several therapy sessions were devoted to discussions by Mr. and Ms. Rivera of the differences between their expectations for Marisa. Ms. Bartoli encouraged them to ignore minor expressions of "attitude, " such as Marisa's rolling her eyes, not responding fully to questions, debating with them, and making scornful faces. However, she supported their view that Marisa should not be allowed to speak disrespectfully to them or defy clear directives.

Based on the ASEBA reports of Marisa's involvement in and talent for singing and dancing, Ms. Bartoli encouraged Marisa to apply to a summer dramatic arts program. She also helped the Riveras work out a plan for Marisa to earn money babysitting to pay for the program. The Riveras also agreed to Marisa's request to invite friends to practice music in their basement. As the Riveras became acquainted with Maria's friends, they began to admire their commitment to music and to appreciate Marisa's skills as a vocalist.

At a 6-month reassessment, Ms. Bartoli asked Marisa to complete the YSR, her parents to complete CBCLs, and her teachers to complete TRFs. Marisa's CBCL and YSR scores were now generally in the normal range. The TRF scores on the

Withdrawn/Depressed and Attention Problems syndromes had dropped from the borderline clinical range to the high normal range. The teachers who had rated Marisa as somewhat less happy than typical pupils now rated her as "about average." Although Marisa and her parents still had occasional differences of opinion about how she should behave, they were able to discuss their differences more effectively. Marisa succeeded in meeting her parents' goals for better school performance and cooperation at home and was thus able to obtain more social privileges.

CONCLUSION

This chapter has presented ASEBA instruments for children aged 1.5 to 18 years. These instruments apply an empirically based approach to obtaining data from parents with the CBCL/1.5–5 and CBCL/6–18; from daycare providers and preschool teachers with the C–TRF/1.5–5; from teachers with the TRF/6–18; from youths with the YSR/11–18; from clinical interviewers with the SCICA/6–18; from psychological examiners with the TOF/2–18; and from observers with the DOF/5–14. ASEBA instruments can be used for diverse clinical and research purposes in many settings, as documented by some 5,000 published studies from 50 countries, including over 300 publications that report applications to treatment. Translations of ASEBA instruments are available in 69 languages.

Profiles display item and scale scores from each ASEBA instrument in relation to norms for relevant peer groups. The scales include competencies, adaptive functioning, and empirically based syndromes derived from factor analyses of scores for thousands of children. The 21st-century editions include the following important innovations: norms based on new national probability samples; empirically based syndromes derived from new samples via new factor analytic methodology; narrative reports that include scores for critical items and that can be imported into word processors; and new *DSM*-oriented scales. The *DSM*-oriented scales consist of ASEBA items that were identified by international panels of experts as being very consistent with *DSM–IV* diagnostic categories. The ASEBA software compares item and scale scores for as many as eight informants per child. It also displays *Q* correlations that measure the degree of agreement between each pair of informants. To help users evaluate the agreement between each pair of informants, the software indicates whether agreement is below average, average, or above average in relation to *Q* correlations obtained for large reference samples of similar informants.

In interpreting ASEBA data, it is important to note that, unlike the items of many other instruments, each ASEBA item is designed to obtain information that is clinically useful in its own right in addition to contributing to scale scores. Accordingly, scores for each competence, adaptive functioning, and problem item are displayed on the ASEBA profiles along with the scale scores. Individual competence, adaptive functioning, and problem items, as well as the constructs assessed by the scales, can thus be targeted for treatment and can be reassessed for monitoring treatment and evaluating outcomes.

Interpretation of ASEBA scale scores is facilitated by norms based on distributions of competencies and problems found for children of each gender in particular age ranges as seen by different types of informants. These norms enable users to evaluate children's functioning before, during, and after treatment in relation to the functioning of their peers as reported from the perspectives of different informants. Discrepancies between reports by different informants are as clinically important as agreements, because they may reveal variations in the child's functioning and/or in the informants' views of the child, both of which can be targeted for treatment.

Because ASEBA instruments assess a broad spectrum of competencies and problems, and because they can be readministered periodically, they can reveal strengths and problems beside those that are highlighted in referral complaints. For example, ASEBA instruments may reveal that a child referred for attention problems is more deviant in other areas, such as affective problems, social problems, thought problems, or aggression. Furthermore, periodic readministration of ASEBA instruments may reveal unanticipated worsening or improvement in areas other than the problems that were thought to be primary. The multiple foci and multiple informants included in the ASEBA can provide a well-differentiated picture of each child, thereby enabling practitioners to tailor interventions to the child's various needs.

Because ASEBA instruments are self-administered and require no therapist time for administration or scoring, they can be routinely used in managed care and many other settings. They can also be readministered periodically to monitor treatment and to evaluate outcomes. Their norms and rigorous quantification facilitate measurement of clinically and statistically significant change for groups receiving different treatment conditions and for individual cases, as was illustrated with the case of Marisa Rivera.

REFERENCES

Achenbach, T. M. (1966). The classification of children's psychiatric symptoms: A factor-analytic study. *Psychological Monographs, 80(No. 615).*

Achenbach, T. M. (1991). *Manual for the Child Behavior Checklist/4–18 and 1991 Profile.* Burlington, VT: University of Vermont, Department of Psychiatry.

Achenbach, T. M. (2001). What are norms and why do we need valid ones? *Clinical Psychology: Science and Practice, 8,* 446–450.

Achenbach, T. M., Dumenci, L., & Rescorla, L. A. (2000). *Ratings of relations between DSM–IV diagnostic categories and items of the CBCL/1½–5 and C–TRF.* Burlington, VT: University of Vermont, Department of Psychiatry. Available at www.ASEBA.org

Achenbach, T. M., Dumenci, L., & Rescorla, L. A. (2001). *Ratings of relations between DSM–IV diagnostic categories and items of the CBCL/6–18, TRF, and YSR.* Burlington, VT: University of Vermont, Research Center for Children, Youth, and Families. Available at www.ASEBA.org

Achenbach, T. M., & Edelbrock, C. (1983). *Manual for the Child Behavior Checklist/4–18 and Revised Child Behavior Profile.* Burlington, VT: University of Vermont, Department of Psychiatry.

Achenbach, T. M., Howell, C. T., McConaughy, S. H., & Stanger, C. (1995). Six-year predictors of problems in a national sample: III. Transitions to young adult syndromes. *Journal of the American Academy of Child and Adolescent Psychiatry, 34,* 658–669.

Achenbach, T. M., Howell, C. T., McConaughy, S. H., & Stanger, C. (1998). Six-year predictors of problems in a national sample: IV. Young adult signs of disturbance. *Journal of the American Academy of Child and Adolescent Psychiatry, 37,* 718–727.

Achenbach, T. M., McConaughy, S. H., & Howell, C. T. (1987). Child/adolescent behavioral and emotional problems: Implications of cross-informant correlations for situational specificity. *Psychological Bulletin, 101,* 213–232.

Achenbach, T. M., & Rescorla, L. A. (2000). *Manual for the ASEBA Preschool Forms and Profiles.* Burlington, VT: University of Vermont, Department of Psychiatry.

Achenbach, T. M., & Rescorla, L. A. (2001). *Manual for the ASEBA School-Age Forms and Profiles.* Burlington, VT: University of Vermont, Research Center for Children, Youth, and Families.

American Psychiatric Association. (1952, 1994). *Diagnostic and statistical manual of mental disorders.* (4th ed.). Washington, DC: American Psychiatric Association.

Arend, R., Lavigne, J. V., Rosenbaum, D., Binns, H. J., & Christoffel, K. K. (1996). Relation between taxonomic and quantitative diagnostic systems in preschool children: Emphasis on disruptive disorders. *Journal of Clinical Child Psychology, 25,* 388–397.

Bérubé, R. L., & Achenbach, T. M. (2004). *Bibliography of published studies using the Achenbach System of Empirically Based Assessment (ASEBA): 2004 edition.* Burlington, VT: University of Vermont, Research Center for Children, Youth, and Families.

Briggs-Gowan, M. J., & Carter, A. S. (1998). Preliminary acceptability and psychometrics of the Infant-Toddler Social and Emotional Assessment (ITSEA): A new adult-report questionnaire. *Infant Mental Health Journal, 19,* 422–445.

Conners, C. K. (1997a). *Conners' Parent Rating Scale–Revised.* North Tonawanda, NY: Multi-Health Systems.

Conners, C. K. (1997b). *Conners' Teacher Rating Scale–Revised.* North Tonawanda, NY: Multi-Health Systems.

Crijnen, A. A. M., Achenbach, T. M., & Verhulst, F. C. (1997). Comparisons of problems reported by parents of children in 12 cultures: Total Problems, Externalizing, and Internalizing. *Journal of the American Academy of Child and Adolescent Psychiatry, 36,* 1269–1277.

Crijnen, A. A. M., Achenbach, T. M., & Verhulst, F. C. (1999). Comparisons of problems reported by parents of children in twelve cultures: The CBCL/4–18 syndrome constructs. *American Journal of Psychiatry, 156,* 569–574.

Edelbrock, C., & Costello, A. J. (1988). Convergence between statistically derived behavior problem syndromes and child psychiatric diagnoses. *Journal of Abnormal Child Psychology, 16,* 219–231.

Ferdinand, R. F., Hoogerheide, K. N., van der Ende, J., Visser, J. H., Koot, H. M., Kasius, M. C., et al. (2003). The role of the clinician: Three-year predictive value of parents', teachers', and clinicians' judgment of childhood psychopathology. *Journal of Child Psychology and Psychiatry, 44,* 867–876.

Ferdinand, R. F., Verhulst, F. C., & Wiznitzer, M. (1995). Continuity and change of self-reported problem behaviors from adolescence into young adulthood. *Journal of the American Academy of Child and Adolescent Psychiatry, 34,* 680–690.

Gove, P. (Ed.). (1971). *Webster's third new international dictionary of the English language.* Springfield, MA: Merriam-Webster.

Helzer, J. E., Spitznagel, E. L., & McEvoy, L. (1987). The predictive validity of lay DIS diagnoses in the general population: A comparison with physician examiners. *Archives of General Psychiatry, 44,* 1069–1077.

Hofstra, M. B.,van der Ende, J., & Verhulst, F. C. (2001). Adolescents' self-reported problems as predictors of psychopathology in adulthood: 10-year follow-up study. *British Journal of Psychiatry, 179,* 203–209.

Hofstra, M. B., van der Ende, J., & Verhulst, F. C. (2002a). Child and adolescent problems predict DSM–IV disorders in adulthood: A 14-year follow-up of a Dutch epidemiological sample. *Journal of the American Academy of Child and Adolescent Psychiatry, 41,* 182–189.

Hofstra, M. B., van der Ende, J., & Verhulst, F. C. (2002b). Pathways of self-reported problem behaviors from adolescence into adulthood. *American Journal of Psychiatry, 159,* 401–407.

Jacobson, N. S., & Truax, P. (1991). Clinical significance: A statistical approach to defining meaningful change in psychotherapy research. *Journal of Consulting and Clinical Psychology, 59,* 12–19.

Kasius, M. C., Ferdinand, R. F., van den Berg, H., & Verhulst, F. C. (1997). Associations between different diagnostic approaches for child and adolescent psychopathology. *Journal of Child Psychology and Psychiatry, 38,* 625–632.

Keenan, K., & Wakschlag, L. S. (2000). More than the terrible twos: The nature and severity of behavior problems in clinic-referred preschool children. *Journal of Abnormal Child Psychology, 28,* 33–46.

Lambert, M. C., Lyubansky, M., & Achenbach, T. M. (1998). Behavioral and emotional problems among adolescents of Jamaica and the United States: Parent, teacher, and self-reports for ages 12 to 18. *Journal of Emotional and Behavioral Disorders, 6,* 180–187.

MacDonald, V., Tsiantis, J., Achenbach, T. M., Motto-Stefanidi, F., & Richardson, S. C. (1995). Competencies and problems reported by parents of American and Greek 6- to 11-year-old children. *European Child and Adolescent Psychiatry, 4,* 1–13.

McConaughy, S. H., & Achenbach, T. M. (1994). *Manual for the Semistructured Clinical Interview for Children and Adolescents.* Burlington, VT: University of Vermont, Research Center for Children, Youth, and Families.

McConaughy, S. H., & Achenbach, T. M. (2001). *Manual for the Semistructured Clinical Interview for Children and Adolescents* (2nd ed.). Burlington, VT: University of Vermont, Research Center for Children, Youth, and Families.

McConaughy, S. H., & Achenbach, T. M. (2004). *Manual for the Test Observation Form for Ages 2 to 18.* Burlington, VT: University of Vermont, Research Center for Children, Youth, and Families.

McConaughy, S. H., Achenbach, T. M., & Gent, C. L. (1988). Multiaxial empirically based assessment: Parent, teacher, observational, cognitive, and personality correlates of Child Behavior Profiles for 6–11-year-old boys. *Journal of Abnormal Child Psychology, 16,* 485–509.

McConaughy, S. H., Kay, P. J., & Fitzgerald, M. (1998). Preventing SED through parent-teacher action: Research and social skills instruction: First-year outcomes. *Journal of Emotional and Behavioral Disorders, 6,* 81–93.

McConaughy, S. H., Kay, P. J., & Fitzgerald, M. (1999). The Achieving Behaving Caring Project for preventing ED: Two-year outcomes. *Journal of Emotional and Behavioral Disorders, 7*, 224–239.

Mouton-Simien, P., McCain, A. P., & Kelley, M. L. (1997). The development of the Toddler Behavior Screening Inventory. *Journal of Abnormal Child Psychology, 25*, 59–64.

Newman, F. L., Ciarlo, J. A., & Carpenter, D. (1999). Guidelines for selecting psychological instruments for treatment planning and outcome assessment. In M. E. Maruish (Ed.), *The use of psychological testing for treatment planning and outcomes assessment* (2nd ed., pp. 153–170). Mahway, NJ: Lawrence Erlbaum Associates.

Reed, M. L., & Edelbrock, C. (1983). Reliability and validity of the Direct Observation Form of the Child Behavior Checklist. *Journal of Abnormal Child Psychology, 11*, 521–530.

Rescorla, L. (1989). The Language Development Survey: A screening tool for delayed language in toddlers. *Journal of Speech and Hearing Disorders, 54*, 587–599.

Rescorla, L., & Achenbach, T. M. (2002). Use of the Language Development Survey (LDS) in a national probability sample of children 18 to 35 months old. *Journal of Speech, Language, and Hearing Research, 45*, 733–743.

Reynolds, C. R., & Kamphaus, R. W. (1992a). *Behavior Assessment System for Children Parent Rating Scales.* Circle Pines, MN: American Guidance Service.

Reynolds, C. R., & Kamphaus, R. W. (1992b). *Behavior Assessment System for Children Teacher Rating Scales.* Circle Pines, MN: American Guidance Service.

Richman, N. (1977). Is a behaviour checklist for preschool children useful? In P. J. Graham (Ed.), *Epidemiological approaches to child psychiatry* (pp. 125–136). London: Academic Press.

Roberts, R. E., Solovitz, B. L., Chen, Y.-W., & Casat, C. (1996). Retest stability of DSM–III–R diagnoses among adolescents using the Diagnostic Interview Schedule for Children (DISC–2.1C). *Journal of Abnormal Child Psychology, 24*, 349–362.

Schafer, J. L., & Graham, J. W. (2002). Missing data: View of the state of the art. *Psychological Methods, 7*, 147–177.

Schuster, C., & Smith, D. A. (2002). Indexing systematic rater agreement with a latent-class model. *Psychological Methods, 7*, 384–395.

Sheldrick, R.C., Kendall, P.C., & Heimberg, R. G. (2001). The clinical significance of treatments: A comparison of three treatments for conduct disordered children. *Clinical Psychology: Science and Practice, 8*, 418–430.

Stanger, C., Fombonne, E., & Achenbach, T. M. (1994). Epidemiological comparisons of American and French children: Parent reports of problems and competencies for ages 6–11. *European Child and Adolescent Psychiatry, 3*, 16–29.

Swets, J. E., & Pickett, R. M. (1982). *Evaluation of diagnostic systems: Methods from signal detection theory.* New York: Academic Press.

Vandiver, T., & Sher, K. J. (1991). Temporal stability of the Diagnostic Interview Schedule. *Psychological Assessment, 3*, 277–281.

Verhulst, F. C., Achenbach, T. M., van der Ende, J., Erol, N., Lambert, M. C., Leung, P. W. L., et al. (2003). Comparisons of problems reported by youths from seven countries. *American Journal of Psychiatry, 160*, 1479–1485.

Weinstein, S. R., Noam, G. G., Grimes, K., Stone, K., & Schwab-Stone, M. (1990). Convergence of DSM–III diagnoses and self-reported symptoms in child and adolescent inpatients. *Journal of the American Academy of Child and Adolescent Psychiatry, 29*, 627–634.

World Health Organization. (1992). *Mental disorders: Glossary and guide to their classification in accordance with the Tenth Revision of the International Classification of Diseases* (10th ed.). Geneva: Author.

8

Conners' Rating Scales–Revised

Scott H. Kollins, Jeffery N. Epstein, and C. Keith Conners
Duke University School of Medicine

The revised Conners' Rating Scales represent the culmination of 30 years of work. The original scales appeared in the mid-1960s. Empirical work on the original scales is described in an annotated bibliography and in the first edition of the present work. Whereas the original scales were developed almost entirely by the senior author of this chapter (C. K. Connors)[1] using data from children seen personally in an outpatient clinic or collected in local Baltimore public schools, the restandardization involved a number of colleagues as well as data collection from 200 sites throughout North America.[2] A technical manual and a user's manual describe the technical development, norms, reliability, validity, and user aids for acquiring and displaying data. Manuals are available for the Conners' Rating Scales (parent, teacher, and adolescent forms) and the Conners' Adult ADHD Rating Scale.

There were several reasons for undertaking a revision and restandardization of the Conners' Rating Scales in the late 1990s:

- Relatively little empirical work was available at the time the original scales were created, and in the ensuing years there had been extensive use of the scales in hundreds of studies as well as feedback regarding aspects of use.
- There had been substantial changes in the demographics of North America, with the old norms being based on relatively restricted samples in Baltimore, Pittsburgh, and Ottawa.
- Researchers often used "pirate" versions of the scales, altering them for their own purposes, so that standardized item content and format were often compromised.
- There was a need for information derived directly from adolescents by way of self-report.

[1] Parts of the original scales were in use at the Harriet Lane Home for Children at Johns Hopkins Hospital. These were created by Anita Bond from section headings of Leo Kanner's textbook of child psychiatry. The items were further modified by Leon Eisenberg, Eli Breger, and Arthur Lockman. A smaller restandardization on a census tract sample in Pittsburgh was assisted by Charles Goyette and Richard Ulrich.

[2] We are indebted for technical assistance to Gill Sitarenios, Ph.D., James D. A. Parker, Ph.D., George Huba, Ph.D., Drew Erhardt, Ph.D., Jeffery Epstein, Ph.D., and Elizabeth Sparrow, B.S. Karen Wells, Ph.D., provided invaluable insights into the construction of the adolescent self-report scales.

- A large, national survey of parents using scales by Achenbach, Conners, and Quay provided guidance regarding factor constructs and item content not previously available from restricted samples.
- New analytic methods and more sophisticated psychometric approaches were available that were not typical of earlier research with the scales.
- Most importantly, there had been a series of advances in the nosology of childhood psychiatric disorders, culminating in the fourth edition of the *Diagnostic and Statistical Manual* (*DSM–IV*; American Psychiatric Association, 1994).

The original Conners scales included short and long forms for teachers and parents as well as abbreviated (10-item) scales known as the Hyperactivity Index. Descriptors for each item included "Not at all true," "Just a little bit true," "Pretty much true," and "Very much true." The revised versions (Conners' Rating Scale–Revised [CRS–R]) add additional descriptors of frequency of occurrence: "Never, Seldom"; "Occasionally"; "Often, Quite a bit"; and "Very often, Very frequent". Short forms were constructed as exact subsets of the longer forms, and more parallel item and factor content was maintained between parent and teacher versions. Adolescent self-report and adult self-report scales were added. Additional specialty scales include *DSM–IV* subtypes and attention deficit hyperactivity disorder (ADHD) indexes. The acronyms, subscales, numbers of items, and age ranges for the CRS–R scales are shown in Table 8.1.

In this chapter we describe the development of the revised scales, present interpretive guidelines for using the various scales, and explain the use of the scales for treatment planning and outcomes assessment. We also include a case study to highlight some of the issues with scale selection, implementation, and interpretation.

OVERVIEW OF THE NEW INSTRUMENTS

The current versions of the scales have a number of features not found in the earlier versions. First, there are long and short scales, and careful attention was paid to making the shorter scales as reliable as the longer ones so that choices could be made on grounds other than the superior reliability of a longer scale. Second, factor content and item content were made as parallel as possible between the parent and teacher versions. Since the parent and teacher scales are usually collected for the same subjects, this makes it possible to plot results on the same profile sheets, enhancing the comparison of findings across settings. Third, new adolescent and adult self-report rating scales were constructed, extending the depth of coverage for the assessment of adolescents; adult norms were added for similar constructs found in childhood; and new constructs for adolescents and adults that were warranted on theoretical grounds were also added. Fourth, items closely modeled on the *DSM-IV* symptomatic criteria for ADHD and oppositional defiant disorder (ODD) were included in the revised scales. Fifth, the internalizing scales were greatly expanded. Sixth, the most often used scale, the 10-item Hyperactivity Index, was normed and factor analyzed into two subscales that retain the sensitive properties of the Hyperactivity Index.[3] Finally,

[3] This scale has often been misunderstood, as evidenced by the appellation "Hyperactivity Index." Because the scale was constructed from the highest loaded items on each of the other scales, it is really a "psychopathology index." But because it showed great efficiency in detecting hyperkinetic children and was extremely sensitive to drug treatments of hyperactive youngsters, it came to be known as a hyperactivity index.

TABLE 8.1
Overview of the Connors' Rating Scales

Scale	Acronym	No. of Items	Age Range	Administration Time (Minutes)	No. of Subscales	Subscales
Conners' Parent Rating Scale–Revised, Long Version	CPRS–R:L	80	3–17	15–20	14	Oppositional, Cognitive Problem/Inattention, Hyperactivity, Anxious-Shy, perfectionism, Social Problems, Psychosomatic, Conners Global Index: Total, Conners Global Index: Restless Impulsive, Conners Global Index: Emotional Lability, ADHD Index, DSM–IV Total, *DSM–IV* Inattentive, *DSM–IV* Hyperactive-Impulsive
Conners' Parent Rating Scale-Revised, Short Version	CPRS–R:S	27	3–17	5–10	4	Oppositional, Cognitive Problem/Inattention, Hyperactivity, ADHD Index
Conners' Teacher Rating Scale-Revised, Long Version	CTRS–R:L	59	3–17	~15	13	Oppositional, Cognitive Problem/Inattention, Hyperactivity, Anxious-Shy, perfectionism, Social Problems, Conners Global Index: Total, Conners Global Index: Restless Impulsive, Conners Global Index: Emotional Lability, ADHD Index, *DSM–IV* Total, *DSM–IV* Inattentive, *DSM–IV* Hyperactive-Impulsive
Conners' Teacher Rating Scale–Revised, Short Version	CTRS–R:S	28	3–17	5–10	4	Oppositional, Cognitive Problem/Inattention, Hyperactivity, ADHD Index
Conners-Wells' Adolescent Self-Report Scale, Long Version	CASS:L	87	12–17	15–20	10	Family Problems, Emotional Problems, Conduct Problems, Cognitive Problems/Inattention, Anger Control Problems, Hyperactivity, ADHD Index, *DSM–IV* Total, *DSM–IV* Inattentive, *DSM–IV* Hyperactive-Impulsive
Conners-Wells' Adolescent Self-Report Scale, Short Version	CASS:S	27	12–17	5–10	4	Conduct Problems, Cognitive Problems/Inattention, Hyperactive-Impulsive, ADHD Index
Conners' Global Index–Parent	CGI–P	10	3–17	~5	2	Emotional Lability, Restless-Impulsive
Conners' Global Index–Teacher	CGI–T	10	3–17	~5	2	Emotional Lability, Restless-Impulsive
Conners' ADHD/DSM–IV Scales–Parent	CADS–P	12, 18, or 26	3–17	5–10	1–4	ADHD Index, DSM–IV Total, DSM–IV Inattentive, DSM–IV Hyperactive-Impulsive

(Continued)

TABLE 8.1
(Continued)

Scale	*Acronym*	*No. of Items*	*Age Range*	*Administration Time (Minutes)*	*No. of Subscales*	*Subscales*
Conners' ADHD/DSM–IV Scales–Teacher	CADS–T	12, 18, or 27	3–17	5–10	1–4	ADHD Index, DSM–IV Total, DSM–IV Inattentive, DSM–IV Hyperactive-Impulsive
Conners' ADHD/DSM–IV Scales–Adolescent	CADS–A	12, 18, or 30	12–17	5–10	1–4	ADHD Index, DSM–IV Total, DSM–IV Inattentive, DSM–IV Hyperactive-Impulsive
Conners' Adult Rating Scale–Self-Report, Long Version	CAARS–S:L	66	18+	<30	9	Inattention/Memory Problems, Hyperactivity/Restlessness, Impulsivity/Emotional Lability, Problems With Self-Concept, Inattentive Symptoms, Hyperactive-Impulsive Symptoms, Total ADHD Symptoms, ADHD Index, Inconsistency Index
Conners' Adult Rating Scale–Self-Report, Short-Version	CAARS–S:S	26	18+	~10	6	Inattention/Memory Problems, Hyperactivity/Restlessness, Impulsivity/Emotional Lability, Problems With Self-Concept, ADDH Index, Inconsistency Index
Conners' Adult Rating Scale–Self-Report, Screening Version	CAARS–S:SV	30	18+	~10	4	Inattentive Symptoms, Hyperactive-Impulsive Symptoms, Total ADHD Symptoms
Conners' Adult Rating Scale–Observer, Long Version	CAARS–O:L	66	18+	<30	9	Inattention/Memory Problems, Hyperactivity/Restlessness, Impulsivity/Emotional Lability, Problems With Self-Concept, Inattentive Symptoms, Hyperactive-Impulsive Symptoms, Total ADHD Symptoms, ADHD Index, Inconsistency Index
Conners' Adult Rating Scale–Observer, Short Version	CAARS–O:S	26	18+	~10	6	Inattention/Memory Problems, Hyperactivity/Restlessness, Impulsivity/Emotional Lability, Problems With Self-Concept, ADDH Index, Inconsistency Index
Conners' Adult Rating Scale–Observer, Screening Version	CAARS–O:SV	30	18+	~10	4	Inattentive Symptoms, Hyperactive-Impulsive Symptoms, Total ADHD Symptoms

true ADHD indexes were developed by careful extraction of items discriminating between well-diagnosed ADHD samples and age- and gender-matched cases from the standardization sample.

Summary of Development

Normative Data Collection. Subjects for collection of all normative data were recruited by professionals at over 200 sites in North America, including 49 of 50 states and all of the provinces of Canada.[4] Forms were completed individually (not in group settings).

Item Pool. For each instrument, a large item pool was created from existing items on the earlier scales, new items based on recent diagnostic developments, and new items designed to tap constructs considered of importance to the broad range of internalizing and externalizing disorders of children, adolescents, and adults. For example, the revised parent rating scale (long version) started with an item pool of 190 items, which was ultimately reduced to 80 items. Many items were based on the clinical experience of the authors along with parent interviews, work with teachers, discussions with adolescents, and assessment of adults presenting with complaints related to attentional and self-regulation problems at an outpatient clinic.

Analytic Approach. A similar methodology was followed for each of the scales. Papers describing the development of each of the scales are available. For each scale, samples were split into a derivation sample and a confirmatory sample. The correlation matrix from the derivation sample was subject to a series of principal axis factor analyses to determine which items to retain. Items were included on the final version if the following criteria were met: (a) Items had to load significantly (>0.30) on a given factor and lower than 0.30 on the other factors (exceptions would be made for items with very high loadings on one factor and loadings only slightly above 0.30 on one or more other factors), and (b) following the rational approach to scale construction, an item was eliminated if it lacked conceptual coherence with its factor. Scree test and Eigenvalues (>1.0) were used to select the number of factors for rotation. In addition, the split-half factor comparabilities method was used to determine the most reliable factor solution. The factor structure of the final model was then tested with the cross-validation sample using confirmatory factor analysis with EQS for Windows, version 5.1. As recommended by Cole (1987) and Marsh, Balla, and McDonald (1988), multiple criteria were used to assess the goodness of fit of the factor model: the goodness-of-fit index (GFI) ; the adjusted GFI (AGFI), and the root mean-square residual (RMS). Based on the recommendations of Anderson and Gerbing (1984), Cole (1987), and Marsh et al. (1988), the following criteria were used to indicate the goodness of fit of the model to the data: GFI > 0.85, AGFI > 0.80, and RMS > 0.01. The long forms include both externalizing and internalizing scales, whereas the short scales include only scales related to the core constructs for ADHD. Thus, if assessment for only these core ADHD scales is desired, then the short forms will suffice. However, as noted later, we recommend the long forms for an initial assessment of most children.

---

[4] A complete list of site coordinators may be found in the technical manual.

Types of Available Norms

Normative data are fully described in the technical manuals. Data are provided for ages 3–17, separately for each gender, as *T*-scores, percentile ranks, and mean/standard deviations. The normative sample for the child scales included 2,482 children, of whom 83% were Caucasian, 4.8% African American, 3.5% Hispanic, 2.2% Asian, 1.1% Native American, and 4.9% "Other." The adolescent self-report scale included 3,394 adolescents between the ages of 12 and 17. Of these, 62% were Caucasian, 29.9% African American, 2.3% Hispanic, 1.6% Asian, 1.3% Native American, and 3.1% Other. Age, sex, and ethnicity effects on each of the scales are fully described in the manual (pp. 102–110). The new adult scale standardization sample included 839 normal adults between the ages of 18 and 81 years of age, approximately divided equally between males and females.

BASIC VALIDITY AND RELIABILITY INFORMATION

Reliability. Overall, for all forms, the coefficients of internal consistency (Cronbach's alpha) are highly satisfactory across the normative groups. For the CPRS-R:L, the total reliability coefficients ranged from .728 to .942. For the CPRS–R:S, the coefficients ranged from .857 to .938; for the CTRS–R:L they ranged from .773 to .958; for the CTRS–R:S, they ranged from .882 to .952; for the adolescent self-report scale (CASS:L), they ranged from .754 to .917; and for the CASS:S, they ranged from .752 to .852. Test-retest reliability was estimated from samples tested 6–8 weeks apart. Median reliabilities ranged from .70 to .87. The reliability of the Conners Adult ADHD Rating Scales has also been estimated using coefficient alphas to assess internal reliability and Pearson product moment correlations to examine test-retest reliability. Coefficient alphas for the four CAARS factor scales ranged from .86 to .92; and test-retest correlations ranged from.80 to .91.

Factorial Validity. The factor structure for each of the scales was evaluated (a) by examining intercorrelations between the subscales to see if the intercorrelations met theoretical expectations, separately for males and females, and (b) by applying a statistical procedure to test the replicability of the subscale structure. To test for gender differences in the pattern of intercorrelations, the equality of the correlation matrices was examined, as recommended by Tanaka and Huba (1984). In all cases, the patterns of intercorrelations for the two sexes were virtually identical. As noted earlier, the factor comparabilities method and confirmatory factor analysis were employed to examine the replicability of the scales. In all cases, the scales met rigorous criteria for comparability. The CAARS scales went through comparable factor analytic confirmation procedures. Similar factor structures were confirmed for males and females.

Convergent and Divergent Validity. Given the overlap between items in the short and long forms, it would be expected that the correlations between the long and short forms would be high. The correlations were very near 1.0 in all cases (range = 0.96 to 0.99). The correlations between the parent and teacher scales for the ADHD Index were 0.49. But, as expected, the correlations among the other scales were somewhat lower between parents and teachers (.12 to .55). These low correlations are consistent with the findings of other studies on parent-teacher agreement about ADHD symptom ratings, but the positive predictive power of teacher ratings was high, as evidenced by the correlation among informants on the ADHD Index (Biederman, Keenan, & Faraone, 1990). In all cases across informants, the ADHD Index showed the highest correlations, generally averaging about .50. This suggests that, for the core features of ADHD, parents, teachers, and adolescents are in reasonable agreement about the degree of the key symptoms. Because the new scales included the 18 *DSM–IV* diagnostic items for ADHD, it was possible to calculate prevalence rates. When presence of a symptom is defined as a score of 3 on the 0–3 scale, the prevalence rates for ADHD are 3.84 for teacher ratings and 2.30 for parent ratings, consistent with the prevalence figures reported in the *DSM–IV* (3% to 5%). It should be noted in this regard that if one uses the *DSM–IV* criterion of "Often" for each symptom (the equivalent of a 2 on our scales), the prevalence figures would have been substantially larger.

For the specialty index scales, samples of comprehensively studied ADHD patients were age and gender matched to samples from the normative database, and discriminant function analyses were conducted to identify the subset of items from the long form that provided the best discrimination. As recommended by Kessel and Zimmerman (1993), a variety of diagnostic efficiency statistics were calculated: sensitivity, specificity, positive predictive power, negative predictive power, false-positive rate, false-negative rate, kappa, and overall classification rate. Sensitivity ranged between 91% and 100%, specificity ranged between 77% and 98%, and overall classification rates ranged between 84% and 96%. An important finding was that teacher ratings produce considerably higher false-positive rates (17% to 18%) than parent ratings (2% to 8%). These data are presented in Table 8.2.

For the CAARS scales, correlations between the CAARS scales and the Wender Utah Rating Scale (WURS; Ward, Wender, & Reimherr, 1993) were examined. The WURS is a 61-item retrospective self-report scale that requires adults to retrospectively recall their own childhood ADHD symptomatology. Pearson product moment correlations ($N = 101$) revealed significant correlations between the WURS total score and all four of the CAARS factors: Inattention Problems ($r = .37$, $p < .001$), Hyperactivity-Restlessness ($r = .48$, $< .001$), Impulsivity/Emotional Lability ($r = .67$, $p < .001$), and Problems with Self-Concept ($r = .37$, $p < .001$).

Two groups of adults were used in the criterion validity study. The first group consisted of 39 adults (23 males and 16 females) who met *DSM–IV* criteria for ADHD.

TABLE 8.2
Diagnostic Utility of Empirically Derived ADHD Index for Teacher, Parent, and Adolescent Self-Report Ratings

	Teacher Rating Scale		*Parent Rating Scale*		*Adolescent Self-Rport*	
	Original	*Replication*	*Original*	*Replication*	*Original*	*Replication*
Sensitivity	98.2	97.1	92.3	100	90.7	90.7
Specificity	82.5	81.6	98.1	92.5	88.4	76.7
Positive predictive power	84.8	84.0	98.0	93.0	88.6	79.6
Negative predictive power	97.9	96.6	92.7	100	90.5	89.2
False-positive rate	17.5	18.4	1.9	7.5	11.6	23.3
False-negative rate	1.8	2.90	7.7	0.0	9.3	9.3
Kappa	.807	.786	.904	.925	.791	.674
Overall classification	90.4	89.3	95.2	96.3	89.5	83.7
N	114	206	104	80	86	86

The second group (nonclinical) consisted of 39 normal adults who were randomly selected and matched with the ADHD sample on the basis of age and sex. The ADHD group scored significantly higher (using *t*-tests) than the nonclinical group on all four scale factors. In addition, a variety of diagnostic efficiency statistics were calculated for the CAARS: the sensitivity was 82%, the specificity was 87%, the positive predictive power was 87%, the negative predictive power was 83%, the false-positive rate was 13%; the false-negative rate was 18%, kappa was 0.692, and the overall correct classification rate was 85%.

Basic Interpretive Strategy

As with many similar instruments, an understanding of *T*-scores and their relationship to percentiles is necessary for interpretation. *T*-scores allow direct comparison of relative standing on each factor dimension without regard to the factorial composition or number of items involved. The revised rating scales are sensitive to developmental trends and sex differences, so *T*-scores are also important in comparing relative performance at different ages or between genders. These conversions can be misleading, however. Consider a child who recently turned 12 and who obtained a *T*-score of 70. This score would be interpreted as "moderately atypical" in terms of the conventions used in the manual for 12- to 14-year-olds. If the same raw score is applied to the 9–11 age range, the score would be interpreted as "mildly atypical." Thus caution is urged when repeated measures span age ranges.

In terms of interpretations for ethnic subgroups, when age and gender are taken into account, there is practically no variance attributable to ethnicity. This finding is similar to the findings of other large-scale studies: Ethnicity vanishes as an effect when the sample is large enough and age, sex, and social class effects are controlled. However, in the case of the adolescent self-report scale, there are sufficiently large numbers of African Americans across age and gender to allow the provision of separate norms.

We have suggested the following 8-step interpretation sequence.

Examine Threats to the Validity of the Scale. Threats should be examined, including random responding due to poor motivation, rushed responding due to time limits, reading difficulties, or misunderstanding of how the instrument is to be used. Consider different forms of response bias, such as overreporting to obtain a diagnosis or underreporting due to fear of labeling. Self-reports by adolescents may underreport as an oppositional strategy or social desirability response. It should be noted that the normative data were collected under conditions of anonymity, so clinic patients may appear less impaired than the normative sample if they minimize their behavior difficulties for reasons of social desirability. Note logical inconsistencies, such as endorsing the item "fidgeting" while denying the item "Fidgets with hands or feet or squirms in seat." Try to determine the reason for inconsistencies across raters (e.g., between mother and father or between parent and teacher). Sometimes such differences reflect true differences in the subjective perceptions of the raters, but other times they are clues to invalid responses created by differing standards. For example, one parent rater might be using him- or herself during childhood as the standard of comparison whereas the other is using same-age children in the neighborhood as the referent against which to judge the severity or intensity of a behavior.

Analyze the Index Scores. For each scale, the ADHD Index is the best initial indicator of whether a child is likely to have an attentional or hyperactive-impulsive problem.

The Global Index (called the Hyperactivity Index in the previous version of the scales) also may be elevated, with or without an elevated ADHD Index. This situation suggests the presence of internalizing problems along with a significant restless-impulsive component. A recent factor analysis of this scale indicates that both restlessness and emotional lability contribute to the Global Index.

Examine the Overall Profile and Subscale Patterns. Several basic patterns are of interest: *The typical or normal profile* has scores within a few points of 50 (the average for the standardization sample). The *mildly elevated profile* shows one or more scales hovering close to 60, that is, one standard deviation above the mean. Though such scores may cause suspicion of a problem, they need careful further investigation. The *Elevated Profile, Type G* is a profile in which three or more *independent* subscales are elevated above 60 or 65. "Independent" refers to scales that are conceptually different; for example, the three internalizing scales (Anxious-Shy, Perfectionistic, Psychosomatic) are conceptually different from the three externalizing scales (Hyperactivity, Conduct, and ADHD Index). The *Elevated Profile, Type P* exhibits a more focused elevation of scales, as when the Hyperactivity and Cognitive/Inattention scales are elevated. This type of profile typically points to particular problem areas such as ADHD. Certain patterns are consistent with "pure ADHD," such as elevated Hyperactivity, Inattention, and ADHD Index in the absence of other elevations. Others suggest common comorbidities, as when these three scales are elevated in the presence of oppositional problems. Comorbid learning disorders are indicated by elevations of the ADHD Index along with high elevations on the Cognitive/Inattention dimension. One should note that this latter dimension includes academic subjects that are not found in the *DSM–IV* categorical approach, where learning problems have been relegated to other Axis I disorders (e.g., developmental writing or reading disorders). The fact that there is empirical clustering of academic and inattention items is noteworthy and reflects the common perception that problems of inattention are closely linked to academic failure.

Analyze Subscale Scores. This is the most common approach to interpretation of the Conners scales. Each factor can be interpreted according to the predominant conceptual unity implied by the item content. Special parent and teacher feedback forms are available for ease of communicating the meaning of the factors to referring teachers or to the parents.

Analyze the DSM–IV *Symptom Subscales.* The interpretive position adopted in the manual for the Conners scales is a conservative one. It is recommended that only those items scored as 3 (i.e., "Very much true," "Very often," "Very frequent") count toward a categorical *DSM–IV* diagnosis. This will sometimes lead to a discrepancy between the *DSM-IV* item count and the dimensional, *T*-score, normatively based approach. *DSM-IV* itself words items beginning with "Often" but gives no criteria as to what counts as often. If we were to literally use this definition, we would count items with a score of 2 ("Pretty much true," "Often," "Quite a bit") toward the criterion symptom count. How one approaches this problem depends on whether one is more concerned about over- or underdiagnosis when using the categorical approach. Our preference is to rely on the dimensional, *T*-score approach, counting the presence of Hyperactivity-Impulsivity and Inattention only when the scores reach a *T*-score level of 65 or greater (i.e., one and a half standard deviations above the mean). But in a managed care environment, where more literal (and liberal) interpretation might be required to obtain services, it is possible for one to prefer the "often..." approach, counting items toward the *DSM-IV* criterion that are 2 or greater.

Examine Individual Item Responses. Interpretations at the item level are best considered hypotheses for further exploration. For example, a teacher rating may not show an elevated factor score for Cognitive Problems/Inattention, but perusal of the items might show that she gave a 3 on the item "Seems tired or slowed down all the time." This might suggest further inquiry regarding some physical impairment such as a hormonal imbalance, a vitamin deficiency, or lack of sleep. One should remember that many treatable problems do not rise to the level of a disorder or syndromal level of impairment but are nevertheless important. Although statistically coherent, the factors can be considered to contain subfactors of interest. For example, the reading, spelling, and handwriting items on the Cognitive/Inattention factor might suggest an academic or learning problem; elevations on items that concern forgetting things already learned and frequently misplacing items might suggest specific memory problems. Though hazardous as conclusions, such findings provide rich material for investigative hypotheses.

Integrate Results with All Other Available Information. The real art of clinical practice consists in reconciling data from many different sources, including the rating scales, family psychiatric and medical histories, family interactions, child developmental history, educational information, intrapsychic functioning such as self-efficacy and self-esteem, early temperament, language and motor development, and so on. Rating scales are good guides to narrowing the focus of an inquiry but by themselves are insufficient to tell a comprehensive and accurate story regarding individual patients. Used in conjunction with other relevant historical, medical, and current function data, they can act as important adjuncts to the descriptive and diagnostic enterprise as well as guides for treatment and instruments for treatment monitoring.

Using All Sources of Information, Determine the Appropriate Intervention or Remediation Strategy. This treatment planning is the final part of any comprehensive assessment/interpretation. After information is collected from multiple sources, however, there are several questions that need to be considered. First, what is appropriate and ethical in terms of feedback? For example, should a teacher be made aware of extreme ratings of anxiety by the parent? Second, who should have access to the information? For example, should an after-school daycare worker be allowed to learn the results of the evaluation? Third and finally, who should participate in the treatment-planning deliberations? To what extent does someone's involvement with the patient's life warrant participation in the treatment-planning process. Of course, the answers to these questions will vary depending on each individual case, but they invariably need to be addressed to allow for proper treatment planning.

TREATMENT PLANNING

General Treatment-Planning Issues

The revised versions of the CRS–R were developed after 30 years of clinical practice and experience with the earlier versions. Of course, many researchers have utilized the scales in a variety of research contexts as well. But the individual, person-to-person application of the scales has usually been done in the context of a full clinical evaluation whose central focus is the development of a treatment plan for the clients.

With parents, the scales provide a convenient and direct method of summarizing the behavior pattern of the child. Typically, this involves providing parents with either a typed summary (obtained from the output of the computer version) or a special feedback form on which the *T*-scores have been entered. One begins by perusal of individual items, particularly those rated as 3 ("Very much true"), to highlight the most salient individual behaviors. Then the meaning of the factor clusters to which the items belong is discussed, using the plotted profile to focus on the overall pattern of findings. This information is then integrated with the entire "story" of the child's life, including the family context, developmental trends, cognitive and academic strengths and weaknesses, and social interaction style.

The essential aim of this stage of feedback to the parents is to provide a meaningful and coherent account of the child's current state and how he or she got to that point. Often this will require a summary of the family psychiatric history as it bears on the current problems (e.g., pointing out family genetic trends that help explain the findings). Or it might require interpreting the problem in the context of significant birth or developmental risks uncovered by early birth and developmental information. The parent rating scale profiles constitute a concrete and visible document to which the complex life story can be anchored. This process is enhanced by using a systematic recording form filled out by parents or adults.

Identification of Primary and Secondary Problems

The primary problems for treatment planning are generally suggested by those factors that are most significantly elevated (e.g., 1 to 2 standard deviations above the normative mean). Secondary problems are often individual behaviors that are prominent even though the factors from which they come are not significantly above the normative mean. For example, a child might not have an elevated Cognitive/Inattention factor score but have ratings of 3 on reading, spelling, or handwriting items. These could in fact become *primary* treatment targets, requiring vigorous intervention at the school level before other factors are addressed. The timing of the introduction of treatments is determined by a number of factors, such as which behaviors are causing the most immediate distress or functional impairment. This information can only be obtained as part of the overall assessment.

Selecting the Appropriate Treatment Approach

Each of the factors carries with it certain implications regarding treatment based on a large body of clinical research evidence and experience. For example, oppositional or aggressive conduct suggests the need for parent training and behavioral interventions at home, and comparable behaviors at school might imply the need for similar programs there. Also, the fact that a diagnosis based on parent report is a high predictor of diagnosis based on teacher report should not deter a clinician from acquiring information from both settings, as treatment in both settings may well be required. *DSM-IV* actually requires cross-situational presence of symptoms for a diagnosis of ADHD. On the other hand, clinicians should remember to point out to parents that aggressive or oppositional problems are also responsive to stimulants. An elevated hyperactivity score will clearly raise the issue of the need for medication, whereas high anxiety, perfectionism, or psychosomatic anxiety elevations suggest caution in the use of stimulants while pointing to the possible need for antistress techniques such as progressive relaxation, cognitive behavioral therapies, or antianxiety or mood-stabilizing medications.

Many ADHD children have significant cognitive and academic problems, as indicated by elevated scores on the Cognitive Problems/Inattention scale. A variety of classroom management and academic interventions will then be appropriate. For example, the use of a home-based reward system, such as a daily report card, might be suitable intervention for classroom disruptive, interfering, or other off-task behavior. Elevations on this factor might also suggest the need for further intellectual and academic assessment if these are not already available.

Many parents will justifiably be concerned about recommendations regarding medication for ADHD and related behavior problems. By using the rating profile to indicate that "this is the type of pattern that research and clinical experience shows to be responsive to medication," the parents may be reassured. Of course, a thorough understanding of the research literature on medications is important in order to avoid embarrassing "show me" responses by the parents. It is often wise for nonspecialists to share the findings with a pediatrician or psychiatrist and leave the discussion of medication to that professional.

Treatment planning in the school is often facilitated by using the scales as a focus for describing the overall pattern of the child's behavior. Convenient feedback forms for the teacher provide the essential descriptive information that can be useful in a teacher or school team treatment-planning conference. For teacher and parents, the scales help prevent a focus on only one area of behavior to the exclusion of other and possibly equally important treatment targets. For example, a child may require counseling or therapy directed at inappropriate goal-setting when excessive perfectionism causes a high level of frustration in achievement-related areas.

With adolescents and adults, self-report rating scales provide an important focus for direct feedback regarding the nature of their problems. Of particular importance is the identification of specific cognitive deficits that are responsible for academic and vocational impairment. Treatment of these specific deficits constitutes an important element in the management of adolescent and adult ADHD.

With adolescents, complaints regarding anger management suggest specific cognitive anger-management interventions. Also, among both children and adolescents with ADHD, family processes can be prominently implicated in the disorder, frequently requiring family interventions.

Potential Use for Planning in Managed Care Settings

The Conners' Rating Scales are particularly appropriate for use in a managed care environment. The scales provide a standard, economical, and well-validated descriptive framework for determining when treatment is needed. They also provide a sensitive and well-established method for monitoring treatment response and determining when the target behaviors are within normal limits. The scales are ideally suited as documentation for managed care case workers, provided that certain guidelines are followed. If the scales are going to be useful and interpretable over time, practitioners should identify the target behaviors of interest. In addition to highly elevated factors, individual target behaviors should be identified by asking parents, teachers, or clients to circle three to five items that are the most important.

Limitations and Potential Problems in the Use of the CRS–R for Treatment Planning

Certain limitations in the use of rating scales for treatment planning are apparent. For example, an adolescents may refuse to reveal ongoing problems and instead deny the presence of symptoms. This problem is especially likely to arise when the adolescent is an unwilling participant in the evaluation process. It may be necessary to develop a trusting relationship in which the adolescent feels comfortable in revealing problems. In any case, it is often advisable to structure the administration of the self-report scales by indicating that, if the adolescent chooses, the results will not be shared directly with his or her parents. Instead, the adolescent can be reassured that admission of specific problems (e.g., covert substance use or criticisms of the family process) will only be shared in a general way to help find appropriate treatments or problem-solving strategies. A review of how the scale is to be used will often calm the fears of adolescents that they will get themselves into more hot water by being honest about their current behavior.

Many adult patients have poor insight into their own behavior and often underestimate the impact of their behavior on family members. For this reason, a separate form filled out by a significant other is often a useful supplement for treatment planning and monitoring. For example, whenever possible, the spouse of an adult ADHD client should be asked to provide an independent assessment and agree to be repeatedly administered measures during the course of treatment. This is particularly desirable in clinical trials research where treatment sensitivity to medications is an important issue. In many cases, an adult with ADHD will believe that there has been little change from a stimulant drug whereas the spouse will have noticed many areas of improvement.

The main limitations on use of rating scales in planning treatments come from the classic "garbage-in, garbage-out" problem. When the responses are invalid because of positive or negative halo effects, logical inconsistencies, inappropriate referents for what is normative, and various other limitations, rating-instrument then treatment planning is hazardous. Usually these problems can be dealt with by following the eight-step interpretive approach described here.

USE OF THE REVISED CONNERS SCALES IN TREATMENT OUTCOMES ASSESSMENT

General Issues in Assessing Treatment Outcomes With Rating Scales

As described in the second edition of this volume (Maruish, 1999), the validity of outcomes assessment with the Conners scales is highly dependent on task setting and task complexity. Research indicates that these global ratings tend to be most valid when applied to structured activities (Oettinger, Majovski, & Gauch, 1978) and tasks that are somewhat demanding in terms of difficulty and complexity (Steinkamp, 1980). Thus, in planning an outcome study, it is important to encourage teachers and parents to make their ratings based on performance in structured academic subjects such as arithmetic or language arts, not free play or recess. Similarly, observations at home might best be considered in homework situations or when the child is responding to task demands or chores, not while watching television or playing Nintendo-like games. Situations involving structured problem-solving (Cohen, Sullivan, Minde, Novak, &

Keens, 1983) or response delay or transitions between tasks (Zentall, et al., 1983) are likely to be more sensitive to the Global Index or ADHD Index measures. Ratings for externalizing problems such as hyperactivity are likely to be more valid when made in contexts with high levels of activity cues in the environment (Copeland & Weissbrod, 1978).

Many research studies use pre- and postmeasures in an experimental and control group design. It is important to recall that research with earlier versions of the scales show short-term drops in symptoms after a single readministration (Milich, Roberts, Loney, & Caputo, 1980) and indicates that long-term administration may result in gradual increases over time (Diamond & Deane, 1990). Single case studies without controls are therefore suspect. It is highly recommended that at least two administrations of the scales be obtained at baseline to avoid artifactual decreases unrelated to treatment and to establish a benchmark for comparing subsequent change. A form for recording repeated observations is available, and it also allows tracking of responses by multiple observers over time. Though it is important to try to record teachers' observations for children receiving drug treatment, during summer and holidays the reports by parents may be crucial. But parents should be made aware that the dosing schedule might mean they see the child when most of the treatment effects have worn off (e.g., at the end of the day). The question of which scales to use in outcome research depends on several factors. If the research is highly focused on a narrow condition, such as ADHD, then it seems reasonable to use only those factors that pertain to the condition or to use the short ADHD Index or Global Index. The robustness of past versions of the Global Index in treatment studies, the ease of administration, and the lack of subject burden all recommend the new indexes as dependent measures in treatment outcome research. Similarly, if anxiety is the target behavior, the anxiety scale could be extracted as a dependent measure. However, based on our clinical experience, it is unusual to have a single condition presenting in the absence of comorbid characteristics. For instance, ADHD is often associated with oppositional-defiant behaviors or conduct disorder. Only if frequently repeated measures are called for would we recommend using a brief 12-item scale such as the ADHD Index or the 10-item Global Index by themselves. If only a few repeated measures are required, it is reasonable to use the short forms. We typically use the long forms at the very beginning (e.g., screening or baseline) and for the last posttreatment assessment. Since the short scales and indexes are exact subsets of the longer scales, they can always be extracted from the longer versions for comparison with briefer interim measures.

In the chapter on these scales in the second edition of this work (Maruish, 1999), it was noted that the revisions of *DSM–IV* are likely to have a significant impact on outcome research. It was for this reason that all of the *DSM* items for ADHD were included in the standardization of the revised parent and teacher scales. It is now possible to use the *DSM* scales as outcome measures when it would be judicious to do so. In an ADHD drug trial, Food and Drug Administration (FDA) guidelines might require documentation regarding the disease entity being targeted by the new drug. The symptom criteria for ADHD in *DSM–IV* use the descriptor "often" to indicate the frequency required for each symptom to meet criteria. Our experience suggests that this would lead to an overdiagnosis of the condition compared with normative data and that it may be less sensitive to treatment response than the data obtained in comparison with norms. However, where the relatively undifferentiated *DSM* criteria are needed, then symptom scores based on ratings of 2 or greater are certainly possible and appropriate.

Typically one will examine the *T*-scores and focus on treatment changes of half a standard deviation or more (*T*-score changes of five or more scale points). However, it is important to remember that the factor scales represent a structure derived from large numbers of cases, and individuals may have only a few target symptoms relevant to themselves within a particular factor. Clinically, therefore, it is always useful in assessing change to have parents or teachers circle three to five items that they think represent the most crucial problem areas. Then, regardless of changes in factor scores, it is possible to examine particular target symptoms or behaviors for evidence of treatment effect. Obviously, in clinical situations involving a single client, it is necessary to be mindful of the possibility of interpreting random fluctuations as real change, but this is precisely the reason for not relying on a single outcome measure. One factor might show significant change whereas a particular target symptom of interest to the parent or teacher might not change. It is therefore important to maintain an "ipsative" mindset as well as a normative one in evaluating change in the clinical setting with rating scales. In a research context, the target-symptom approach may be important because the symptoms most troubling or most elevated are likely to show the most treatment gain. Thus, target symptom scores may be more sensitive to treatment than general factor score elevations.

In general, endorsements of "Pretty much" or "Very much" represent clinically significant levels of behavior or symptomatology. But some raters use a constricted scale, so that a change from "Not at all" to "Just a Little" represents a major shift in the judgment of symptom intensity. It is therefore important in a clinical context to note the overall pattern of parent or teacher item endorsements and judge the impact of treatment accordingly. For the most part, however, we have interpreted clinically significant change as constituting a change from "Very much" or "Pretty much" to "Not at all" or "Just a little." Based on this reasoning, average scale changes (where each item is scored 0, 1, 2, or 3) of 2 raw score points are considered clinically meaningful.

Other collateral information of importance is Who, Where, and When: Who made the ratings, in what setting, and when were they done in relation to the treatment? Obviously this information is most pertinent to time-sensitive and context-sensitive treatments such as pharmacologic agent regimens, but experience shows that changes in raters from pre to posttreatment as well as variations in the time and place of data collection affect the amount of noise in the rating data. A change in rater from one parent to the other, one classroom or teacher to another, or a change to a different time of day will add an unpredictable element to the assessment of the outcomes and most likely will diminish the sensitivity of ratings.

Limitations in the Use of Rating Scales for Assessing Treatment Outcomes

Some cautions are needed regarding the use of the new adolescent and adult self-rating scales in treatment outcome research. By their very nature, these scales allow the patient or research subject to estimate the level of their own symptomatology. What these patients may reveal can be greatly affected by the demand characteristics of the treatment situation as well as their own attitudes regarding the treatment. Adolescents, for example, may deliberately minimize their symptoms or the extent to which the treatment affects them as part of their general oppositionality to adult authority. It is therefore important to clarify this issue up front in order to avoid a common error with global scales that arises when the internal referent for severity and change is different than expected by the investigator or clinician. Adults may wish to receive a drug and therefore exaggerate the severity of their symptoms or the amount of change the drug evoked. Since the scales were standardized under anonymous conditions, some attempt to replicate this context of assessment should be made with the adolescent and adult (e.g., by ensuring anonymity in published results, privacy with respect to parental or spousal access, etc.).

By the very nature of their problems, it is to be expected that adolescents and adults with ADHD will have poorly organized recall of information that is not recent. For this reason, in treatment outcome studies where self-report is used as an outcome or study entry criterion, we typically obtain several measures using a daily diary format. In this approach, the time frame for the presence and severity of the symptoms is one day rather than the typical weekly or monthly time frame.

CASE STUDY: MONITORING TREATMENT EFFECTIVENESS[5]

K.H. is a 10-year-old male who was referred to a university clinic by his mother after his fifth-grade teacher reported increasing behavior problems in the academic setting. Specifically, since the beginning of the school year, K.H. had been increasingly disruptive in class, was noted to talk out of turn frequently, made noises, and was referred to as "immature." Although his grades had generally been good, this year and in years past, K.H.'s teachers reported that he had not been working up to his potential. K.H.'s mother reported that at home he has always been difficult to manage, he has never sat through a full meal with his family, and either is "going full speed" or is asleep. K.H.'s mother was interested in an evaluation to determine the presence of ADHD and to obtain specific recommendations for improving K.H.'s behavior at home and in school.

K.H. was given a full clinical evaluation. Both teacher and parent ratings on the long forms of the CRSs were consistent and showed *T*-score elevations of 74 and 87 for parent and teacher, respectively, on the Hyperactive subscale. *T*-scores for the Cognitive Problems/Inattention subscale were 67 and 72 for parent and teacher, respectively, and *T*-scores for the ADHD Index were 71 and 80 for parent and teacher, respectively. These rating scale scores, combined with a careful clinical interview, supported a diagnosis of ADHD, Hyperactive-Impulsive subtype. Several treatment strategies were recommended, including a home-based contingency plan for school and parent behavior management classes. After trying and considering these interventions without significant changes in K.H.'s behavior, a recommendation was made for a trial of stimulant medication. The decisions involved in introducing and monitoring medication are complex . But in situations where medications are being recommended, as in K.H.'s case, several steps are in order.

Identify the Target Behavior and Subscales/Items for Monitoring Change. The first step in the process is to select a subscale or subscales for monitoring change. Because multiple readministration of scales is required, K.H.'s clinician decided to use the CADS–P and CADS–T because they are short, provide data on attention problems, and provide information that can be linked directly to diagnostic symptoms. The CADS scales include the ADHD Index and the *DSM–IV* symptoms subscales for both ADHD subtypes.

[5] This section is excerpted from the technical manual with permission from the publisher.

Choose and Follow a Specific Protocol. In this case, the child's classroom behavior was of particular concern, so increased emphasis was placed on the teacher's responses. Additionally, the teacher was not told when the medication was begun to minimize the possibility of bias. Scores from the ADHD Index and the *DSM–IV* subscales from the initial administration of the CTRS–R:L were used as baseline measures. It was decided to start methylphenidate at 5 mg twice daily and to increase the dosage once every two weeks. Since academic performance was of interest, brief samples of handwriting and math were obtained to use for curriculum-based measurement.

Examine Results on the Subscale Level and Evaluate Medication/Dosage Effectiveness. Figure 8.1 summarizes the scores on two relevant subscales across the trial period of medication. It shows the scores on seven administrations (one premedication result and six postmedication results). Normally, it would be desirable to have at least two baseline measures. Although there was some improvement with 5 mg, the change was less than half a standard deviation and cannot be taken as a meaningful effect. The increase to 10 mg produced a drop of almost 2 standard deviations. The level of improvement was roughly from the 98th percentile for elevated symptoms to the 66th percentile, or near normal performance. Notably, a further increase of dosage failed to show any further decrease in symptoms, so K. H. was maintained on a regimen of 10 mg twice daily. Note that it would have been possible to also use self-ratings if the patient had been an adolescent. Usually, it would also be desirable to include ratings by parents so that improvement can be compared across settings.

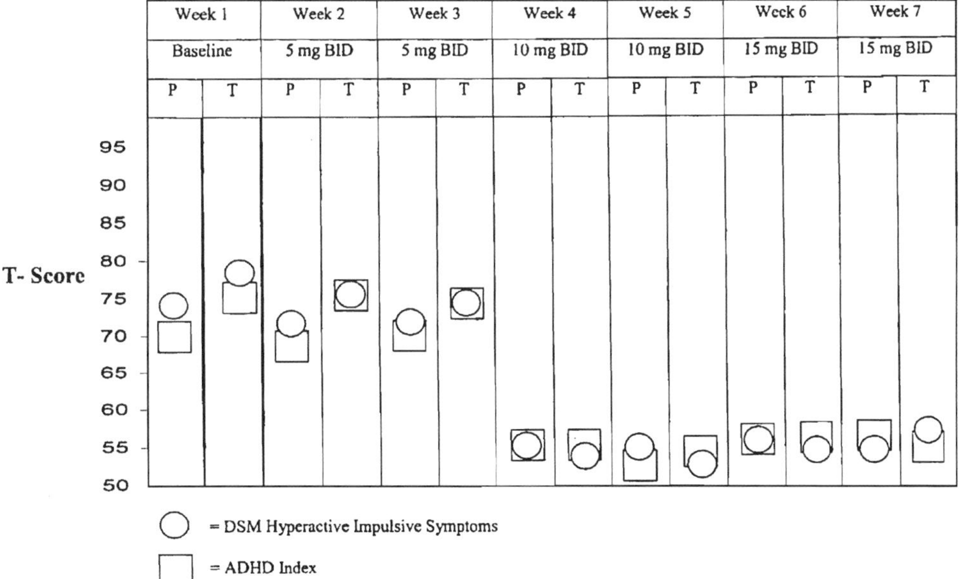

FIG. 8.1. Weekly CADS–P and CADS–T scores for two subscales identified as targets for evaluating a stimulant medication intervention. P corresponds to the parent report and T corresponds to the weekly teacher report. The circles indicate scores for the *DSM–IV* Hyperactive Impulsive Symptoms, and the squares refer to scores for the ADHD Index. BID = twice daily.

CONCLUSION

ADHD is a developmental disorder that covers the entire lifespan. However, its presentation is different for each sex, and the manifestation of symptoms differs at different developmental stages. There is usually a set of other symptoms that either reflect comorbid disorders or the cumulative developmental consequences of the primary disorder of behavior, cognition, or learning. Current categorical methods of diagnosis do not provide a sound empirical basis for assessment and treatment monitoring because they provide no empirical standards for levels of impairment. Nor do they account for the changing threshold for diagnosis that should be required in older patients. As normal development occurs, the frequency and intensity of behaviors change so that what previously may have been abnormal is no longer appropriate as a referent.

The Conners' Rating Scales–Revised provide a national normative database and rigorously developed psychometric standards for scales that are now applicable across the lifespan. No diagnostic category can be fully assessed in isolation from potential alternative diagnoses. Therefore, in addition to scales primarily focused on issues related to ADHD, scales for other important behaviors relating to conduct, oppositionality, anxiety, somatization, self-esteem, mood, and family function have been carefully developed. The scales now include the *DSM–IV* categorical symptom list, and it is possible to use them simply as symptom counts as in the *DSM–IV* field trials. However, the scalar and normative features also allow one to bring to bear the powerful dimensional measurement concept, which views each individual as the intersect of several underlying dimensions or influences. In combination with the categorical approach, dimensional measures provide a crosscheck that places diagnoses within a normative and developmental framework.

The rating scales are particularly well suited for treatment monitoring by virtue of having brief but highly reliable subscales such as the ADHD Index. These scales represent the optimum set of items for discriminating well-diagnosed ADHD from non-ADHD and have been carefully replicated on independent samples. Their use in drug studies may be of particular value, as the earlier versions (the so-called Hyperactivity Index), besides being brief, have proven to be drug sensitive and well liked by teachers, parents, and professionals.

REFERENCES

American Psychiatric Association. (1994). *Diagnostic and statistical manual of mental disorders* (4th ed.). Washington, DC: Author.

Anderson, J. C., & Gerbing, D. W. (1984). The effect of sampling error on convergence, improper solutions, and goodness-of-fit indices for maximum likelihood confirmatory factor analysis. *Psychometrika, 49,* 155–173.

Biederman, J., Keenan, K., & Faraone, S. V. (1990). Parent-based diagnosis of attention deficit disorder predicts a diagnosis based on teacher report. *Journal of the American Academy of Child and Adolescent Psychiatry, 29,* 698–701.

Cohen, N. J., Sullivan, J., Minde, K., Novak, C., & Keens, S. (1983). Mother-child interaction in hyperactive and normal kindergarten-aged children and the effect of treatment. *Child Psychiatry and Human Development, 13,* 213–224.

Cole, D. A. (1987). Utility of confirmatory factor analysis in test validation research. *Journal of Consulting and Clinical Psychology, 55,* 584–594.

Copeland, A. P., & Weissbrod, C. S. (1978). Behavioral correlates of the hyperactivity factor of the Conners Teacher Questionnaire. *Journal of Abnormal Child Psychology, 6,* 339–343.

Diamond, J. M., & Deane, F. P. (1990). Conners Teachers' Questionnaire: Effects and implications of frequent administration. *Journal of Clinical Child Psychology, 19,* 202–204.

Kessel, J. B., & Zimmerman, M. (1993). Reporting errors in studies of the diagnostic performance of self-administered questionnaires: Extent of the problem, recommendations for standardized presentation of results, and implications for the peer review process. *Psychological Assessment, 5,* 395–399.

Marsh, H. W., Balla, J. R., McDonald, R. P. (1988). Goodness-of-fit indexes in confirmatory factor analysis: The effect of sample size. *Psychological Bulletin, 103,* 391–410.

Maruish, M. E. (Ed.). (1999). The use of psychological testing for treatment planning and outcomes assessment (2nd ed.). Hillsdale, NJ: Lawrence Erlbaum Associates.

Milich, R., Roberts, M. A., Loney, J., & Caputo, J. (1980). Differentiating practice effects and statistical regression on the Conners Hyperkinesis Index. *Journal of Abnormal Child Psychology, 8,* 549–552.

Oettinger, L., Majovski, L. V., & Gauch, R. R. (1978). Coding A and Coding B on the WISC are not equivalent tasks. *Perceptual and Motor Skills, 47,* 987–991.

Reynolds, C. R., & Richmond, B. O. (1978). Factor structure and construct validity of "What I Think and Feel": The Revised Children's Manifest Anxiety Scale. *Journal of Personality Assessment, 43,* 281–283.

Steinkamp, M. W. (1980). Relationship between environmental distractions and task performance of hyperactive and normal children. *Journal of Learning Disabilities, 13,* 209–214.

Tanaka, J. S., & Huba, G. J. (1984). Confirmatory hierarchical factor analyses of psychological distress measures. *Journal of Personality and Social Psychology, 46,* 621–635.

Ward, M. F., Wender, P. H., & Reimherr, F. W. (1993). The Wender Utah Rating Scale: An aid in the retrospective diagnosis of childhood attention deficit hyperactivity disorder. *American Journal of Psychiatry, 150,* 885–890.

Zentall, S. S., Gohs, D. E., & Culatta, B. (1983). Language and activity of hyperactive and comparison children during listening tasks. *Exceptional Children, 50,* 255–266.

9

Youth Outcome Questionnaire (Y–OQ)

Gary M. Burlingame, M. Gawain Wells, Michael J. Lambert,
and Jonathan C. Cox
Brigham Young University

As we have observed elsewhere (Burlingame, Mosier, et al., 2001), three rather disparate influences meet and perhaps even appear to collide when psychotherapy outcome is assessed: the demands of rigorous research, the concerns of clinicians in practice, and the call for accountability from customers and third-party payers. This chapter introduces and updates our earlier chapter on the Youth Outcome Questionnaire (Y–OQ; Wells, Burlingame, & Lambert, 1999), which emerged from the mutual effort of individuals from the four sectors just alluded to: a university-based research team, administrators from a large managed health organization, parents and child patients, and clinicians in practice. Though many of the major assessment instruments for children and adolescents were designed for diagnosis of psychopathology, employing a test specifically for the evaluation of psychotherapy outcome has been of more recent interest. The Y–OQ is a parent-report measure constructed specifically to track treatment progress and is a continuation and extension of an adult outcomes instrument, the Outcome Questionnaire (OQ–45; see chap. 6, vol. 3). We begin with a brief review of the current "intersect" between the stakeholders and construction of the instrument before considering its characteristics and its utility.

INTERSECTION OF RESEARCH, CLINICAL WORK, AND MANAGED HEALTH CARE

Research

Reviews of psychotherapy research describe significant gains in demonstrating the effectiveness of psychotherapy (Lambert & Ogles, 2003). However, the parallel research on the treatment of emotional and behavior difficulties of children and adolescents is smaller and less developed (Kazdin, 1988, 1991, 1993; Kazdin, Bass, Ayers, & Rodgers, 1990; Shirk & Russell, 1992; Weisz, Weiss, Alicke, & Klotz, 1987; Weisz, Weiss, & Donenberg, 1992). J. S. Allen, Tarnowski, Simonian, Elliot, and Drabman (1991) examined more than 15,000 studies and found that only 6% of them related to children. Early estimates (Tramonta, 1980) described the adolescent outcomes literature as lagging 15 years behind the adult literature. Fortunately, more recent commentaries suggest significant progress (Kazdin, 1991, 1993; Kendall & Morris 1991). For instance, conclusions from several meta-analytic reviews (Barrnett, Docherty, & Frommelt, 1991; Casey & Berman, 1985; Hoag & Burlingame, 1997; Kazdin, 1990; Kovacs & Paulaskas, 1986; Weisz et al., 1987) indicate that (a) psychotherapy for children and adolescents is effective (Kazdin, 1993), with the average treated child showing improvement (effect size = .71) that exceeds 76% of children in a comparable untreated sample (Hoag & Burlingame, 1997); (b) individual therapy with children is approximately as effective as that with adults (Brown, 1987); and (c) comparisons of alternative treatment techniques appear to favor behavioral approaches thus far, although methodological confounds may also explain these results (Kazdin, 1993).

The last decade has seen significant research advances in child psychotherapy research. Kazdin (2004) reported that studies of the effectiveness of therapy for children and adolescents now exceed 1,500 and include over 500 methods for treating youth. Unfortunately, most of these methods have never been subjected to empirical research and evaluation. Kazdin (1995) noted that therapy research as a whole is restricted and narrow as presently conceived and called for much more varied and careful methodological research to explicate a variety of issues. One problem mentioned by Kazdin (2004) is the dichotomy between the lower severity of distress in youths recruited for studies compared with those found in clinical practice. This methodological problem limits the generalizability of current research and may actually underestimate the amount of improvement realized in clinical practice, as greater gains are associated with more severely disturbed patients on the Y–OQ (Brown, Burlingame, Lambert, Jones, & Vaccaro, 2001). Kazdin (1995) further noted that there is no standard outcomes assessment practice, which prevents the combination of findings that would build a common knowledge base. Standardized measures, he suggested, would serve to profile children and adolescents in a consistent way to enable researchers to integrate studies about specific types of problems.

Durlak, Wells, Cotten, and Johnson (1995) found reason for more optimism than Kazdin in a study of 516 clinical interventions with children under the age of 13. Their data suggest that the methodologies employed have improved significantly, including a majority of investigations with adequate controls, random assignment to treatment groups, multiple outcome measurements, and assessment of generalization of treatment effects. On the other hand, Durlak et al. noted a number of important neglected variables in child psychotherapy research, among them the need for normed outcome measures that would permit assessment of the clinical significance (as opposed to the statistical significance) of treatment effects. They concluded, "There is, however, certainly room for improvement. In general, child psychotherapy research would be strengthened by greater use of normed outcome measures, assessing the general as well as the specific impact of treatment, using attention-placebo controls, and collecting follow-up data" (p. 143).

Clinicians

Theoretically, the fundamental consumers of psychotherapy research are the therapist practitioners who read the literature to keep abreast of new developments. However, practitioners are often reluctant and suspicious participators in the research process, for two reasons. First, for many, a careful reading of psychotherapy research suggests that it is such a dissimilar enterprise as to be irrelevant. Kazdin (1991) noted, "Research and clinical practice differ in who is treated, how they are treated, with what treatment approaches, how long they are treated, and range of persons involved in the child's treatment. There is genuine risk that the generalizability of research findings to clinical practice is quite strained. A critical research issue for the field is the deep chasm between research and practice on child treatments" (p. 795). Accordingly, it is not surprising that some clinicians dismiss psychotherapy research as irrelevant to their practice needs.

A second and perhaps more fundamental reason for the "chasm" between researchers and clinicians is that, whereas research findings may be irrelevant to the clinicians, they are not irrelevant to third-party payers. Many therapists feel that they face the prospect of losing their jobs or positions on provider panels if they do not produce apparent substantial improvement in brief periods of time with more severe clients and more chaotic families than the researchers have ever attempted to treat (Brown et al., 2001).

The Durlak et al. (1995) review directly addresses this latter point. They examined several practitioner concerns, including (a) that there have been few studies of nonbehavioral treatments, (b) that child research has seldom been conducted on subjects from minority populations, (c) that long-term treatments have not been studied, and (d) that few treatments have been investigated. They found that approximately 40% of the recent studies evaluated nonbehavioral interventions, 18% studied minority children, and 20% evaluated treatments of 20 sessions or longer, and they also found that 19 categories were required to describe the types of treatment entailed. Thus, Durlak et al. opined that the quality of child psychotherapy research is clearly germane to clinical practice.

Health Care Corporations

Though the costs of providing mental health treatment to children and adolescents is difficult to estimate, the evidence from several sources justify the concern in the health care marketplace for cost-containment and accountability in quality care (e.g., Burlingame, Lambert, Reisinger, Neff, & Mosier, 1995). The total cost of health care in the United States in 1996 was estimated to be $943 billion (Department of Health and Human Services, 1999). In the same year, health care costs for the treatment of psychiatric disorders in the United States accounted for 10.5% of total health costs (Department of Health and Human Services, 1999). Though mental health costs grew at an alarming rate of 30% to 40% during the early 1980s (Cummings, 1987), the rate of growth appears to have decreased substantially. Specifically, the U.S. Department of Health and Human Services (1999) reported that "between 1986 and 1996, mental health expenditures grew at an average annual growth rate of more than 7 percent," which was equivalent to the growth seen in total health care costs during the 1990s.

The health care industry's response to such spiraling costs has led to managed health care systems and the so-called era of accountability. Thus, in spite of the suspicions of practitioners, third-party payers make it essential for health care providers to be able to document therapeutic progress. Consequently, psychotherapy outcomes research has been pushed into the center arena as a means of tracking the quality of mental health treatment. Moreover, the adoption of the CQI (continuous quality improvement) model in 1992 by the Joint Commission on the Accreditation of Healthcare Organizations (JCAHO) requires ongoing monitoring of patient care in addition to traditional outcomes assessment. In this setting, standardized outcomes assessment becomes vital, as described by Burlingame et al. (1995): "Continuous monitoring of outcome ideally requires standardized data to profile reliable and valid patterns of improvement across time, providers, programs, and patient groups rather than data generated solely from professional judgment that tends to be more variable and unstable" (p. 227).

This chapter describes the development and uses of the Y–OQ (Burlingame, Wells, & Lambert, 1996), a 64-item parent-report measure constructed specifically to track treatment progress. Parents or others with reasonably extensive interaction with the client complete the questionnaire at intake to establish a severity baseline and then complete it at regular intervals to follow their perception of the child's psychological state. As described later, psychometric calculations from the normative database permit determination of the client's behavioral similarity at each measurement interval to inpatient, residential, in-home, and outpatient populations as well as a large untreated community sample. Utilizing cutoff scores and a reliable change index, clinicians and/or administrators can determine if and when the client's behavior has entered the "normal" range of behavior. Though the Y–OQ publication is still recent and much research remains to be done, its use has spread at a surprising rate.

OVERVIEW OF THE INSTRUMENT

Summary of Development

Originally conceived as the child and adolescent equivalent of the OQ–45.2 (Lambert, Hansen, et al., 1996), the Y–OQ, like its predecessor, was constructed to be brief, sensitive to change over short periods of time, and available at a nominal cost while maintaining high psychometric standards of reliability and validity. Inasmuch as psychotherapy outcome research for children and adolescents has been considered as less "mature" than the research on adult outcomes (Kazdin, 1995), a comprehensive instrument construction process, encompassing a literature search, focus groups, and chart reviews, was undertaken to identify the most salient content domains to include in the instrument. Thus, input was sought from all stakeholders in outcomes assessment.

Initial Literature Review. A comprehensive review of the literature was performed, including both narrative and meta-analytic reviews of the general psychotherapy treatment literature for children and adolescents. The search utilized PsycLit, recent relevant publications, and reference sections of previous reviews of child and adolescent psychotherapy to identify studies related to outcomes in psychotherapy. Topics searched included treatment acceptance, factors contributing to dropout, satisfaction with treatment, expectations for psychotherapy, the development of other outcome measures, evaluating outcomes with children as well as adults, and assessing clinically significant change. The primary purpose of such an exhaustive literature review was to search for content domains that had empirical support for being sensitive to change in clinical work with children and adolescents from a wide variety of orientations and for a wide variety of disorders. Similarly, from recent meta-analytic reviews, content domains were considered in which a 0.5 effect size was obtained in particular content areas (e.g., Baer & Nietzel, 1991; Casey & Berman, 1985; Grossman & Hughes, 1992; Prout & DeMartino, 1986; Roberts & Camasso, 1991; R. L. Russel, Greenwald, & Shirk, 1991; Shirk & Russell, 1992; Weisz et al., 1987). We reasoned that areas of child functioning that had a demonstrated research record of being amenable to change as a consequence of treatment would be particularly suitable for inclusion in the outcome measure.

Focus Groups. Next, focus groups made up of consumers (i.e., former clients and their parents) as well as inpatient and outpatient providers (i.e., psychologists, psychiatrists, and other support staff) were used to query participants about their perceptions of patient change. We felt that the incorporation of this qualitative method ensured a rich source of information from those most intimately involved with the mental health change process in children and adolescents. Both consumers and providers were drawn from a large western health care corporation (Intermountain Health Care, Inc.). Professional focus group leaders led 10 separate groups of 5–10 participants to identify characteristics of change thought to be the direct results of treatment. Of particular importance were the following questions: In what ways does treatment affect children and their families, and when change was taking place, what was changing? Audiotapes of the focus groups were transcribed and became part of the material reviewed for selection of item content and subscale development.

Hospital Records. Hospital records were examined to assess characteristic behavior change goals being addressed in treatment planning for both inpatient and outpatient clients. A manifest content analytic process was used to delineate the most frequently occurring change themes noted by providers in these two settings. A list of these themes was then compared to domains generated by both the literature review and the focus groups. In some cases, item content for the Y–OQ directly reflects change described in patient records.

The results from literature reviews, focus groups, and hospital charts constituted the sources from which the final common content domains were developed. Six general domains were identified that were sufficiently distinct to require the generation of a subscale. For example, inpatient therapist focus groups argued that the purposes and goals for inpatient treatment in the current health care market were stabilization and referral, goals very different from outpatient treatments. The Critical Items subscale (described later) was the content domain intended to capture behaviors that would be particularly representative of and amenable to change during inpatient hospitalizations.

Fifteen to 20 items from each of the domains were created and compared to existing items from other instruments. A final review to winnow out items that duplicated content in other subscales or described diagnostic symptoms unlikely to be amenable to change (e.g., historical facts) resulted in the current format of the instrument.

Normative data have been gathered from children in four different settings: residential treatment, inpatient, outpatient, and community (Gillman, 1998; Burlingame, Mosier, et al., 2001; Burlingame, Wells, et al., 2001). Children for whom normative data were obtained range in age from 4 to 17. Most parents require from 5 to 7 minutes to complete the measure, although particularly careful parents may take as long as 20 minutes. Each item is rated on a five-point Likert scale (0–4). Seven of the items are written in a reverse direction, identifying healthy behaviors that may be seen to increase during treatment. Thus, sensitivity to change in the measure may be seen in the increase of socially approved behaviors as well as in the decrease of disruptive symptoms. Methodologically, the inclusion of positive items increases the range of measurement to avoid an artificially low floor. These items are scored differently to reflect the continuum between the absence of healthy behaviors and their emergence (e.g., "My child handles frustration or boredom appropriately").

Description of Subscales

Six subscales were found to be optimal in capturing the domains of change identified by the aforementioned sources.

Intrapersonal Distress (ID). This subscale, consisting of 18 items, assesses the amount of emotional distress in the child (or adolescent). Anxiety, depression, fearfulness, hopelessness, and self-harm are aspects measured by the ID subscale. Since depression and anxiety are frequently correlated in assessment instruments and patients who come for treatment (Burlingame et al., 1995), no attempt was made at differentiating these symptoms. High scores indicate an elevated sense of distress in the child.

Somatic (S). This subscale, consisting of 8 items, assesses change in somatic distress that the child may be experiencing. Items address symptoms that are typical presentations, including headaches, dizziness, stomachaches, nausea, bowel difficulties, and pain or weakness in joints. High scores indicate that the child's caregiver is aware of a large number of somatic symptoms, and low scores indicate either absence or a lack of awareness of such symptoms.

Interpersonal Relations (IR). This subscale, consisting of 10 items, assesses issues and actions relevant to the child's relationship with his or her parents, other adults, and peers. Parents or caretakers evaluate the patient's attitude toward others and his or her communication and interaction with friends, cooperativeness, aggressiveness, arguing, and defiance. High scores indicate that the caregiver is reporting significant interpersonal difficulty, and low scores reflect a cooperative, pleasant interpersonal demeanor.

Social Problems (SP). This subscale, consisting of 8 items, assesses problematic social behaviors, particularly delinquent or aggressive behaviors that precipitate bringing a child into treatment for conduct difficulties. Though aggressiveness is also assessed with the IR scale, the aggressive content tapped by this subscale is of a more severe nature, typically involving the breaking of social mores. Items include truancy, sexual problems, running away from home, destruction of property, and substance abuse.

Behavioral Dysfunction (BD). This subscale, consisting of 11 items, evaluates the child's ability to organize tasks, complete assignments, concentrate, and handle frustration, including times of inattention, hyperactivity, and impulsivity. Many of the items in this scale tap features of specific disorders such as attention deficit hyperactivity disorder. However, the intent of the scale is to identify difficulties and their severity and then to observe the emergence of behavior change, not to attempt to facilitate a diagnostic decision.

Critical Items (CI). This subscale, consisting of 9 items, describes features of children and adolescents often found in inpatient services, where short-term stabilization is the primary change sought. It assesses the presence of paranoid ideation, obsessive-compulsive behaviors, hallucinations, delusions, suicidal feelings, mania, and eating disorder issues. High scores are indicative of those who may need immediate intervention beyond standard outpatient treatment (inpatient, day treatment, or residential care). Moreover, a high score on any individual item warrants serious attention and follow-up assessment by the provider, and significant change should be observed before moving the child to less protected environments.

Scoring

Scoring the Y–OQ is a straightforward procedure involving simple addition of item values. For example, if Item 1 is endorsed at a 3, the weight given Item 1 for the subscale and total Y–OQ score is 3. Subscale scores are calculated by adding items that are assigned to each. Three subscales (ID, IR, and BD) each contain two healthy behavior items, with an additional healthy behavior item found in the SP subscale. The seven healthy behavior items are scored from a −2 to +2 to adjust for the presence or absence of positive behaviors in the child.

The total score is simply a summation of item weights from all six scales. It reflects total distress in a child's life and can range from −16 to +240. A child rated as having no pathological symptoms and the highest level of all positive behaviors would receive a total Y–OQ score of −16 whereas a child rated as having the highest level of all symptoms would receive a total score of 240. Like the OQ–45 total (Lambert, Thompson, Nebeker, & Andrews, 1996), this value tends to be the best index to track global change and has the highest reliability and validity. A computerized scoring program and a graphic presentation of patient scores across time are available.

Types of Available Norms

Normative data were drawn from several samples across the Rocky Mountain region, primarily in Utah and Idaho. Previous studies of geographic or regional norms on the OQ–45 found no differences; similarly, our data collection from sites extending across 12 eastern, southern, and western states suggest no reason for geographic norms. A large community normal sample was collected by randomly telephoning residents in a western community of 250,000. After identifying themselves and the research project, the telephone solicitors asked if the household had children in the age range 4–17. If there were children in the age range who were not currently receiving mental health treatment (either medication or therapy), the parent was invited to complete a Y–OQ on only one child or adolescent in the household. The questionnaire, along with a self-addressed stamped envelope, a brief summary of the project, and a consent form were mailed to parents who agreed to participate in the project. Approximately 50% of those who agreed to participate returned completed, usable questionnaires.

In addition, two separate inpatient and outpatient samples totaling approximately 500 children and adolescents were collected using a cluster sampling procedure through the intake offices of a large multistate western health care corporation. All parents of children and adolescents who presented for treatment at outpatient and inpatient facilities located in Utah and Idaho owned by the corporation completed the Y–OQ as part of their initial screening. By collecting data at intake from all new patients, initial level of disturbance was captured on each child. Furthermore, two community mental health centers (CMHC) also contributed to the outpatient data. These CMHCs are operated by state-funded public mental health systems in the western United States (one services a city of approximately 1 million, and the other covers a diverse western county). These two samples contributed approximately 600 protocols to the normative sample. Another part of the outpatient clinical sample came from a western state's youth protection and reform system. This state system typically requires psychosocial interventions as well as detention or probation. A total of 719 adolescents (64% male, 36% female) from this state system contributed to the norms.

TABLE 9.1
Normative Group Data for the Y–OQ Total Score

Sample	N	M	SE
Residential	242	115.4	2.13
Inpatient	435	110.4	1.70
Outpatient	2297	68.4	.82
Community	1091	21.4	.80

Collectively across the three samples (community normal, outpatient, and inpatient), males slightly outnumbered females (approximately 60% to 40%). Of the total normative sample, 29% were children of the community normal group, 60% were outpatients, and 11% were inpatients. Means and standard errors for the normative sample groups are presented in Table 9.1. Analyses found large differences on the total Y–OQ scores between the three samples, $F(2,3822) = 1137.3$, $p < .000$. As can be seen, community sample total means were substantially below those taken from the two clinical settings. Reliable differences also occurred between the two patient populations, with inpatients demonstrating more overall symptoms than outpatients and residential patients posting the highest distress scores.

Analysis of the domain or subscale scores presented in Table 9.2 supports similarly strong significant differences between the community normal sample and the two clinical samples on nearly every subscale. Using a Bonferroni correction at an alpha of .05, all subscales reliably distinguished between all three groups.

Table 9.3 presents data from three HMOs with diverse geographic locations and demographic characteristics, illustrating the comparability of the Y–OQ across settings. No significant differences exist between sites on total or subscale means.

Recently, Gillman (1998) conducted a study testing the need for separate norms for residential treatment. Using a sample ($N = 242$) of adolescents at a residential treatment facility, he found that the mean score for his residential patients was significantly higher, $F(3,3096) = 879.85$, $p < .001$, than the means for all previous normative groups, including the inpatient sample. Gillman found that all subscale scores were significantly different from the subscale scores of the community and outpatient samples. Additionally, four of the six subscale scores for the residential sample were significantly different from those of the inpatient sample, with the ID and CI subscales failing to reach significance. These findings suggest the need to develop residential norms to accompany the other treatment settings already included in the Y–OQ

TABLE 9.2
Normative Group Raw Score Data for the Y–OQ Domains

	Residential (N = 242)		*Inpatient* (N = 435)		*Outpatient* (N = 2, 297)		*Community* (N = 1, 091)	
Domain	M	SE	M	SE	M	SE	M	SE
Intrapersonal Distress	34.1	0.72	34.6	0.58	22.2	0.27	8.1	0.80
Somatic	8.1	0.33	8.6	0.26	5.9	0.10	3.1	0.10
Interpersonal Relations	18.5	0.40	16.5	0.36	9.4	0.16	0.3	0.15
Social Problems	16.6	0.41	14.3	0.33	6.7	0.12	0.6	0.09
Behavioral Dysfunction	26.6	0.50	24.8	0.41	17.3	0.21	6.5	0.23
Critical Items	11.7	0.39	11.6	0.28	6.9	0.11	2.7	0.09

TABLE 9.3
Total and Subscale Y–OQ Raw Scores for Outpatients from Three HMOs

Source	*Total Y–OQ*	*Subscales*					
		BD	CI	ID	IR	S	SP
Company A							
M	71.2	18.1	7.5	24.1	9.2	6.2	5.5
N	171.0	189.0	190.0	179.0	187.0	189.0	187.0
SD	36.3	9.2	5.1	12.3	7.5	4.9	5.3
Company B							
M	84.9	20.2	8.5	26.2	12.8	6.6	9.0
N	226.0	328.0	339.0	297.0	340.0	340.0	330.0
SD	37.9	8.9	5.4	12.4	7.4	5.2	5.9
Company C							
M	66.6	19.3	6.4	22.1	8.4	5.5	4.9
N	255.0	255.0	255.0	255.0	255.0	255.0	255.0
SD	32.7	9.1	4.3	11.8	7.0	4.4	4.2
Total							
M	74.1	19.5	7.6	24.3	10.5	6.1	6.8
N	652.0	772.0	784.0	731.0	782.0	784.0	772.0
SD	36.4	9.1	5.1	12.3	7.6	4.9	5.6

Note. Company A is a large multistate HMO based on the Eastern seaboard. It includes a hospital but is primarily an outpatient facility. Company B is a large community mental health center in the western United States serving a catchment area of 750,000 people. It serves primarily Medicare and Medicaid patients. Company C is a large multistate HMO serving patients throughout the United States. The current sample primarily comes from East and West Coast offices and the southern states.

scoring and administration manual (Burlingame, Mosier, et al., 2001; Burlingame, Wells, et al., 2001). Although replication is essential, we provide Gillman's norms in Table 9.1 for the interested reader.

Gender. Analysis of Y–OQ total scores found no differences between males and females in any of the three normative samples, nor were any significant interactions observed. See Table 9.4 for means and standard errors for each sample.

As depicted in Table 9.5, gender differences were observed on two Y–OQ subscales, Behavior Dysfunction (males score higher across all samples), $F(1, 1128) = 16.23$, $p < .01$, and Somatic (females score higher than their male counterparts across all samples),

TABLE 9.4
Comparison of Total Scores on the Y–OQ by Gender and Setting

Sample	N	M	SE
Inpatient			
Male	108	97.9	3.87
Female	65	104.0	5.07
Outpatient			
Male	208	79.4	2.43
Female	132	77.2	3.37
Community			
Male	361	24.5	1.41
Female	320	22.0	1.48

Note. Gender differences are not statistically significant.

TABLE 9.5
Comparison of Gender Scores on the Y–OQ Domains

	Inpatient (N = 108/65)		*Outpatient* (N = 208/132)		*Community* (N = 361/320)	
Domain	M	SE	M	SE	M	SE
Intrapersonal Distress						
Male	33.1	1.42	25.9	0.86	8.60	0.51
Female	36.6	1.76	27.1	1.21	9.30	0.56
Somatic						
Male	8.6	0.55	7.3	0.39	2.90	0.16
Female	10.4	0.68	8.5	0.50	3.60	0.20
Interpersonal Relations						
Male	12.8	0.78	10.5	0.54	0.95	0.28
Female	13.4	1.04	10.2	0.69	0.16	0.27
Social Problems						
Male	9.8	0.61	6.6	0.41	1.10	0.18
Female	10.9	0.92	5.6	0.52	0.20	0.15
Behavioral Dysfunction						
Male	22.1	0.94	21.3	0.59	7.90	0.41
Female	21.0	1.29	18.1	0.85	5.70	0.38
Critical Items						
Male	11.4	0.63	7.7	0.34	3.00	0.15
Female	11.7	0.76	7.5	0.46	3.00	0.17

$F(1, 1128) = 16.46$, $p < .01$. Inasmuch as the Behavior Dysfunction scale taps behavior frequently associated with attention deficit disorder, this finding might be expected, given that 3 to 6 times more males than females are diagnosed with ADHD (Whalen, Henker, Hinshaw, & Granger, 1989). Similarly, Werry, Reeves, and Elkind's (1987) review found that females predominate in the incidence of somatization disorders.

Age. Data from the community normal sample were examined by four age groups that correspond somewhat to those used in other diagnostic instruments (e.g., Connors Parent Rating Scale, Achenbach Child Behavior Checklist). Analysis by age found no reliable differences between age groups on the Y–OQ total, $F(3, 555) = 2.14$, $p > .05$, although slightly higher mean elevations (4- to 7-point spread) were noted for the adolescent age groups (12–14 and 15–17) than for preschool and latency age children (see Table 9.6).

Subscale means from the community sample highlight a few significant differences that may be developmental in nature (see Table 9.7). The greatest age difference was

TABLE 9.6
Y–OQ Total Score by Age in Community Normal Sample

		Total Score	
Age Range	N	M	SE
6–8 years	170	20.4	1.73
9–11 years	155	22.8	2.15
12–14 years	123	27.2	2.80
15–17 years	111	27.0	2.89

TABLE 9.7
Y–OQ Subscale Scores by Age in a Sample of Community Normals

	6–8 Years (N = 170)		*9–11 Years* (N = 155)		*12–14 Years* (N = 123)		*15–17 Years* (N = 111)	
Subscale	M	SE	M	SE	M	SE	M	SE
Intrapersonal Distress	7.60	0.61	9.3	0.79	10.8	1.07	10.7	1.09
Somatic	2.80	0.22	3.7	0.30	3.5	0.31	3.8	0.37
Interpersonal Relations	0.05	0.33	−0.2	0.41	1.6	0.54	1.7	0.54
Social Problems	0.50	0.20	0.3	0.23	0.7	0.30	1.4	0.40
Behavioral Dysfunction	6.60	0.53	6.8	0.60	7.2	0.70	6.3	0.69
Critical Items	2.80	0.19	2.9	0.23	3.5	0.32	3.1	0.28

on the Intrapersonal Relations subscale, where the two older groups showed reliably higher distress scores than the 9- to 11-year-olds, $F(3, 555) = 5.09$, $p < .05$. Scores on the Intrapersonal Distress scale are also higher for the 15- to 17-year-olds than for the youngest group, the 6- to 8-year-olds. Finally, the Social Problems scale is also higher for the 15- to 17-year-olds than for the 9- to 11-year-olds, $F(3, 305) = 2.66$, $p < .05$. The Social Problems subscale contains items that assess behaviors that are irrelevant to younger children (e.g., "Uses alcohol or drugs"). Thus, the therapist interpreting individual protocols should be aware that high scores on the Social Problems subscale for young children signal potentially more serious difficulties than for adolescents. Analyses by age in clinical groups found virtually identical profiles, with the exception that the 15- to 17-year-old group reported higher total distress than did the two youngest groups. The 6- to 8-year-old group had the lowest Social Problems subscale. Taken as a whole, the group differences in particular subscales appear to represent issues relevant to the particular developmental stage of the child.

Clinical Cutoff Score. Utilizing the formula from Jacobson and Truax (1991) and the rationale for multiple cutoffs proposed by Tingey, Lambert, Burlingame, and Hansen (1996), a cutoff score has been calculated between the community sample and the two clinical samples (inpatient and outpatient combined). The cutoff score for the Y–OQ total score is 46; in other words, total severity scores that fall *below* that figure suggest that the patient is demonstrating behaviors no more extreme than that of the untreated normal population. Cutoff scores for the subscales are as follows: Intrapersonal Distress, 16; Somatic, 5; Interpersonal Relations, 4; Social Problems, 3; Behavioral Dysfunction, 12; Critical Items, 5. The accuracy of the present cutoff scores is described in the section "Sensitivity and Specificity."

Reliable Change Index. A reliable change index (RCI) is used to determine if the change exhibited by an individual in treatment is greater than chance variation (i.e., measurement error). It is one of the two hurdles necessary for estimating clinically significant change (Jacobson & Truax, 1991). In order for an individual's score to represent a *clinically* significant change, it must cross a cutoff score *and* have a magnitude equal to or greater than the RCI. The RCI value that has been computed using reliability estimates from the community samples is 13, meaning that the change in an individual's score must equal at least 13 points on the Y–OQ to be considered clinically significant. The RCIs for each of the subscales are as follows: Intrapersonal Distress, 8; Somatic, 5; Interpersonal Relations, 4; Social Problems, 5; Behavior Dysfunction, 8; and Critical Items, 5. Inasmuch as the RCI value represents a large and diverse normative sample, it will be serviceable for most general purposes. If specialized or more specific RCI values are desired, appropriate norms can be gathered for the computation of new RCI values according to the Jacobson and Truax formula.

Other Normative Groups. Thus far, the Y–OQ has been translated into Spanish, French, German, Hmong, and Laotian. Data gathering is underway for African American families and Hawaiian Island and Polynesian families. Analyses of Lao-speaking families (Mills et al., 1997) found the mean Y–OQ total scores to be significantly higher (46.58) than the means of the community normal sample (22.40) but less elevated than the outpatient treatment sample (77.41). It is possible, of course, that the findings are spurious, as Southeast Asians have been reported to have less favorable attitudes toward psychology and psychologists, and the attitudes of the respondents may have affected their scores (Dinh, Sarason, & Sarason, 1994). Moreover, verbal reports from those assisting in the project found that some parents were confused about the structure of a Likert scale format even after having it explained to them in Laotian. If the findings accurately reflect differences, however, it would appear that Laotian parents are experiencing somewhat more agitation or perturbation with their children than parents of the English-speaking normative community sample. Dinh et al. (1994), for example, found that Vietnamese students consistently reported more problems in their relationships with their parents than did American-born Asian students.

Basic Reliability and Validity Information

Reliability. Internal consistency reliability estimates of the Y–OQ used Cronbach's alpha (Cronbach, 1970) and were based on a nonclinical sample drawn from a large elementary school ($N = 423$), the original community normative sample of 681 participants, and the two clinical normative samples, outpatient ($n = 342$) and inpatient ($n = 174$), which together equal 516. The Y–OQ total score had a remarkably high and similar internal consistency estimate of .94 across the four samples (Burlingame, Mosier, et al., 2001). This finding has been validated through subsequent independent research (Gironda, 2000). Estimates for separate subscale consistency ranged from .51 to .90. Of the six subscales, the Critical Item and Somatic subscales had the lowest internal consistency estimates, suggesting greater item heterogeneity (see Table 9.8). These findings make intuitive sense in that these scales cover very broad content areas (e.g., diverse somatic complaints and equally diverse behaviors suggesting a need for inpatient treatment). Overall, the high reliability estimate for the Y–OQ total score suggests a strong single factor underlying the six subscales of the instrument. The presence of

TABLE 9.8
Internal Consistency Values for the Y–OQ Total and Domain Scores

Subscale	*Student* (N = 427)	*Community* (N = 681)	*Inpatient* (N = 174)	*Outpatient* (N = 342)
Intrapersonal Distress	.84	.90	.87	.88
Somatic	.72	.68	.66	.70
Interpersonal Relations	.69	.79	.79	.81
Social Problems	.51	.71	.74	.76
Behavioral Dysfunction	.85	.86	.85	.85
Critical Items	.61	.63	.64	.70
Total Score	.93	.95	.94	.94

TABLE 9.9
Reliability Estimates for the Y–OQ Using Normal Sample

Time Elapsed Between Administrations	*Subscales*						*Total*
	ID	S	IR	SP	BD	CI	
Two weeks ($n = 56$)	.82	.70	.75	.78	.82	.56	.84
Four weeks ($n = 93$)	.79	.67	.57	.71	.78	.65	.81
Total ($N = 149$)	.78	.69	.66	.75	.79	.61	.83

Note. Scores are significant at $p < .001$.

a strong single factor was also found on the OQ–45.2 (Lambert, Hansen, et al., 1996), which is particularly useful, as the most frequently used score is the total score.

Atkin et al. (1997) calculated test-retest reliability correlation coefficients from two separate community subsamples drawn from local elementary schools; the retests were completed at 2 weeks and 4 weeks. As Table 9.9 illustrates, a strong relationship is seen between the first administration of the Y–OQ and the administrations at 2 weeks ($r = .84$, $n = 56$) and 4 weeks ($r = .81$, $n = 93$), producing an average test-retest reliability coefficient of .83. Similarly, all subscale test-retest correlations were significant at $p < .001$, with a range from .56 to .82. Thus, the total instrument as well as its separate subscales appear to have good to excellent test-retest reliability (Burlingame, Mosier, et al., 2001). Of note is that the lowest values were associated with the CI scale, possibly because of the low endorsement of these items (i.e., restricted range) as well as the small number of items.

Taken together, these findings indicate that the Y–OQ has excellent reliability. And although Durham et al. (2002) found a retest artifact with different administration schedules for the Y–OQ, the impact of this confound is diminished when the change associated with retest is compared to the Reliable Change Index (RCI) calculated for the measure (see the "Frequency of Administration" section for more details).

Validity. A concurrent validity study (Atkin, 2000) compared the relationship between the Y–OQ total and subscale scores to parallel subscales from the Child Behavior Checklist (CBCL; Achenbach, 1991) and the Connors Parent Rating Scale–93 (CPRS; Connors, 1989). The parents of a sample of 423 children completed the three instruments. Data analyses found a highly significant correlation ($p < .001$) of .78 between the Y–OQ total score and the CBCL total score, suggesting high convergent validity between the two tests (see Table 9.10). Moreover, each Y–OQ subscale correlated most highly with the analogous subscale of the CBCL. Inasmuch as a total score is not computed for the CPRS, no total comparisons could be made. However, again, each Y–OQ subscale correlated most highly with the corresponding subscale from the CPRS, with one (nonsignificant) exception: there was a slightly higher correlation between the Y–OQ Behavior Dysfunction subscale and the CPRS Conduct Disorder subscale ($r = .61$) than between the Behavior Dysfunction subscale and the CPRS Hyperactive-Immature subscale ($r = .59$). Although not as distinctive as one might like, given the substantial comorbidity between attention deficit disorder and conduct disorder in the literature, this finding is not surprising. Moreover, small and nonsignificant coefficients can be noted between dissimilar subscales, suggesting adequate divergent validity.

In addition to the community sample comparison performed by Atkin (2000), Burlingame, Mosier, et al. (2001) compared Y–OQ subscale and total scores to subscale

TABLE 9.10
Validity Estimates Between Y–OQ Subscale Scores and the CBCL and CPRS–93

	ID	S	IR	SP	BD	*Total*
CBCL (normal sample, $N = 423$)						
Anxious/Depressed	.70	.41*	.42*	.19*	.42*	.60
Withdrawn	.64	.38*	.39*	.25*	.39*	.56
Somatic Complaints	.44*	.61	.24*	.20*	.32*	.44
Aggressive Behavior	.55*	.36*	.63	.49*	.62	.67
Delinquent Behavior	.48*	.37*	.49*	.58	.53*	.60
Attention Problems	.48*	.36*	.41*	.32*	.64	.58
Total Problems	.73	.57	.61	.42	.69	.78
CPRS–93 (normal sample, $N = 423$)						
Anxious-Shy	.67	.48*	.44*	.25*	.46*	.62
Psychosomatic	.38*	.62	.22*	.15*	.32*	.41
Conduct Disorder	.60*	.39*	.60	.44	.61*	.68
Antisocial	.35*	.25*	.42*	.48	.41*	.41
Hyperactive-Immature	.52*	.40*	.48*	.38*	.67	.64
Restless-Disorganized	.60*	.46*	.48*	.31*	.59*	.64
CBCL (clinical sample, $N = 61$)						
Anxious/Depressed	.78	.48	.45*	.27[a]*	.38	.67
Withdrawn	.55*	.35*	.37*	.25[a]*	.16[a]*	.45
Somatic Complaints	.33[a]*	.63	.21[a]*	.20[a]*	.19[a]*	.38
Aggressive Behavior	.42*	.26[a]*	.71	.62	.67	.65
Delinquent Problems	.41*	.25[a]*	.57	.60	.37	.55
Attention Problems	.43*	.25[a]*	.35*	.32*	.57	.50
Total	.69	.50	.65	.56	.61	.78

Note. Underlined values correspond to hypothesized criterion index. All values are significant at $p < .001$ unless otherwise noted.

*Indicates significant value ($p < .01$) on t-test comparison of differences between hypothesized criterion and divergent subscales in the same column.

[a]Correlation coefficient is not significantly different than $r = .00$ at $p < .01$ in concurrent validity comparison.

and Total Problems scores of the CBCL in a clinical sample ($N = 61$). They found the pattern of correlations between Y–OQ and CBCL scores in their clinical sample to be quite similar to that found by Atkin. These correlations are found in Table 9.10. Overall, the findings from these two samples suggest that the relationships between the Y–OQ and established criteria are very promising. Additionally, Gironda (2000) used the Y–OQ as the reference criterion in a validity study of the Ohio Scales. In this study, he found the Y–OQ total score to have concurrent validity with the Ohio Scales both at pre- and posttest (.70/.76, $p < .05$), lending further strength to the criterion validity of the Y–OQ.

Support for the construct validity of the Y–OQ was also sought by comparing inpatient and outpatient scores on the Y–OQ with those of the community samples. Assuming that scores would be ordered from most pathological to least pathological, Burlingame, Mosier, et al. (2001) demonstrated the inpatient sample to be most disturbed, followed by the private outpatient, the community mental health outpatient, and the community sample. These samples were found to be reliably different, $F(3, 4080) = 680.9$, $p < .001$, as predicted. However, post hoc comparison found no significant difference between the average symptoms reported by the community mental health and private sector outpatients. Table 9.11 demonstrates the clear differences between clinical and nonclinical groups; children in the community sample were, on average, the most healthy, and inpatient children, on average, were most

TABLE 9.11
Comparison of Level of Psychopathology as Measured by the Total Y–OQ Score Across Patient and Nonpatient Samples

Comparison Group	N	M	SE
Community normal	683	23.9	6.77
Community mental health outpatient	2881	76.6	9.21
Private care outpatient	342	76.3	8.89
Inpatient	174	110.8	8.74

Note: $F(3, 4080) = 680.9$, significant at $p < .001$.

severely disturbed. A fourth normative group, adolescents in residential treatment settings, was the focus of two different studies. In the first study, Gillman (1998) found that a sample of youths at a residential treatment center had significantly higher scores on the Y–OQ, $F(3, 3096) = 879.85$, $p < .001$, than all other previous normative groups. Additionally, Mosier et al. (2001) conducted a study in which the Y–OQ was used to evaluate a new in-home treatment program meant to replace inpatient treatment for children and adolescents. They found that the mean Y–OQ score of initial severity for this sample was significantly higher, $t(276) = 1.99$, $p < .05$, than for the Y–OQ inpatient normative sample. This finding indicates that residential treatment youths constitute a distinct treatment group in terms of severity and pattern of Y–OQ scores.

Additional support for the construct validity of the Y–OQ can be found in two different studies. Neeleman (2001), through exploratory factor analysis, found that two higher order factors underlay the items of the Y–OQ. Preliminary internalizing and externalizing subscales based on these two factors have been created. Table 9.12 contains Y–OQ item composition and normative data for these two factors. These normative data are broken down by setting. It is important to note that these preliminary subscales should only be used for further study. At this time, clinical decisions should not be based on internalizing and externalizing scores from the Y–OQ. Based on the composition of their items, Neeleman conceptualized these factors as externalizing and internalizing behaviors. These two factors are congruent with the factor structures of other measures in the youth and adolescent literature, lending support to the construct validity of the Y–OQ. Lastly, Berrett (1999), using hierarchical linear modeling, found that the Y–OQ is sensitive to change. One of the major requirements for outcome measures is that they be sensitive to change. Thus, Berrett's findings contribute to the accumulation of support for the construct validity of the Y–OQ.

Sensitivity and Specificity. Sensitivity is the proportion of the "true positives" (i.e., members of the clinical groups who are correctly identified). Burlingame, Mosier, et al. (2001) found the sensitivity of the Y–OQ to be .82. In other words, approximately 82%

TABLE 9.12
Y–OQ Externalizing and Internalizing Factors

	Externalizing		*Internalizing*	
Setting	M	SD	M	SD
Community ($N = 1093$)	7.01	11.57	6.63	6.29
Day Treatment ($N = 194$)	29.72	17.00	18.71	9.10
Residential ($N = 245$)	48.61	12.83	21.06	8.54
Outpatient ($N = 2,190$)	28.94	15.12	17.07	8.89

of the true members of the clinical groups were properly classified as clinical and 18% were misclassified (put in the normal group) using a cutoff score of 46. Specificity is the proportion of the "true negatives" (i.e., members of the community normal group who are correctly identified). Burlingame, Mosier, et al. found the specificity of the Y–OQ to be .89; that is, 89% of the members of the normal group were correctly placed using a cutoff score of 46. As for other operating characteristics, the positive predictive power (PPP) equaled .77 and the negative predictive power (NPP) equaled .81. The sensitivity, specificity, and PPP values were reaffirmed in a study by Atkin (2000). Atkin performed a receiver operating characteristic (ROC) analysis to determine the sensitivity (true positives) and the specificity (false positives) produced by the Y–OQ. A ROC analysis plots a curve indicating the sensitivity of the measure in question. The area under the curve (AUC) demonstrates the measure's predictive ability. Atkin found that, with AUC values up to .94, the Y–OQ could accurately discriminate between normal and clinical samples. Furthermore, using a population of children and adolescents presenting at their primary care physicians' offices, A. C. Tzoumas (2001) demonstrated that the Y–OQ total score correctly classified 85% of his sample into the correct treatment categories. The sensitivity and specificity values are similar to those obtained by the OQ–45.2 (Lambert, Hansen, et al., 1996) and provide an index of the accuracy of the Y–OQ as a screening tool.

It is important to note that, though the sensitivity, specificity, and other operating characteristics are clearly useful at the levels obtained, some consideration of the measurement process itself may indicate why they are not even higher. By definition, we have considered the children from the community sample as normal and the children from the patient samples as abnormal. Yet, parents have individually defined thresholds of sufficient concern for seeking treatment for their children; therefore, some children who in the opinion of most professionals should be receiving treatment, are not receiving help (false negatives) because their parents have not chosen to refer them. Other parents may refer their children for much less serious difficulties, even prophylactic reasons such as divorce adjustment (false positives).

Basic Interpretive Strategy

The Y–OQ is designed to serve two general purposes: to evaluate the outcomes of mental health treatment through repeated administrations and to act as a screening instrument (i.e., to establish the need for treatment or alert mental health professionals to the need for more careful evaluation).

In the first edition of this book, Derogatis and DellaPietra (1994) commented on the use of screening measures in psychiatry:

> The screening process represents a relatively unrefined sieve that is designed to segregate the cohort under assessment into "positives," who presumptively have the condition, and "negatives," who are ostensibly free of the disorder. Screening is not a diagnostic procedure per se. Rather, it represents a preliminary filtering operation that identifies those individuals with the highest probability of having the disorder in question for subsequent specific evaluation. Individuals found negative by the screening process typically are not evaluated further. (p. 23)

Thus, when parents complete the Y–OQ at intake, the scores may be utilized at three different levels to determine the need for treatment. The first and most conservative procedure is to examine the Y–OQ total severity elevation. The Cronbach's alpha coefficients clearly suggest that the test is best understood as having one main underlying factor common to all the subscales. Comparing the individual case to the current normative groups, the clinician can immediately determine if the child's scores suggest that he or she is in need of treatment and what level of treatment is most likely to be warranted—outpatient treatment or treatment in a more restrictive environment.

Recent research has shown that the Y–OQ total score can be used to place patients into appropriate treatment settings (Atkin, 2000; Burlingame, Mosier, et al., 2001; Gillman, 1998; A. C. Tzoumas, 2001). Moreover, a recent modification of the Y–OQ (the Y–OQ PCM) shows promise as a screening tool for primary care settings. However, it must again be emphasized that the Y–OQ should be used as a screening measure, not as a diagnostic tool. In the words of one psychiatrist who uses the Y–OQ with his clientele, "It's like being able to take a child's mental health temperature. It is not a diagnostic blood test. It just tells you something is wrong and a little about how wrong and where to look" (R. Ferre, personal communication, 1997).

The second and third levels of interpretation speak to the issues of "how wrong and where to look." The clinician studying the Y–OQ printout can next examine the subscale elevations, particularly the Critical Items (CI) subscale. The questions in this subscale are written specifically to speak to the issue of whether increased protective actions, such as inpatient hospitalization, are necessary (e.g., "Sees, hears, or believes things that are not real," "Has times of unusual happiness or excessive energy," etc.). At the third level, further evaluation of both subscale elevations as well as individual items assist the clinician in generating hypotheses about the most effective treatment protocol. Again, for example, frequent endorsement of Critical Items such as "Believes that others can hear her/his thoughts, or that s/he can hear the thoughts of others" signals the need for psychiatric evaluation for medication as opposed to planning for parent training.

The Y–OQ is designed to be brief enough to allow for repeated administrations to parents. The scores can be plotted on a Y–OQ tracking sheet to monitor the parent's report of perceived changes over the course of treatment. When the total score drops below the community normal cutoff score of 46, the clinician knows that the parent sees the child as behaving "within normal limits" and can adjust treatment accordingly (e.g., work to consolidate gains, prepare for termination, etc.). Erratic scores may suggest to the clinician the need for careful evaluation of the treatment protocol, the introduction of second-level treatment, the influence of risk factors that militate against rapid treatment response, and so on. Brown et al. (2001) demonstrated that clinicans can apply regression analysis to the patient's intake Y–OQ score and a change score from repeated administrations to identify those patients most at risk for premature termination. These patients can then receive more intensive treatment to improve their chances of a positive outcome. Greater consideration is given to these issues in later sections.

USE OF THE INSTRUMENT FOR TREATMENT PLANNING

General Treatment-Planning Issues

Given that published literature on the Y–OQ has not addressed many issues related to treatment planning, the following should be seen as possibilities for clinical practice. It is equally clear, however, that the same statement could be applied to the entire topic of treatment planning in child and adolescent psychotherapy. Though significant

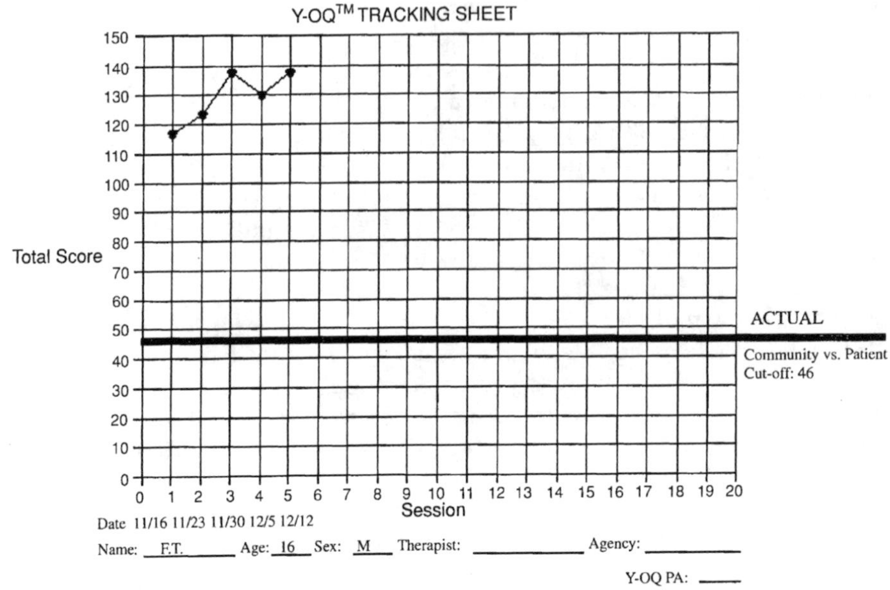

FIG. 9.1. Case example of F.T., aged 16, diagnosed with attention deficit hyperactivity disorder and oppositional defiant disorder.

advances have been made, Kazdin (1995) asserted that, in child and adolescent treatment, "research is at an early stage in relation to the range of clinical dysfunctions that has been systematically studied and the types of research questions that are addressed" (p. 125). Fonagy (1996) similarly noted that, at this point, research should direct efforts toward studies of "ecological" relevance, with somewhat less emphasis on those designed for maximal internal validity.

Given this caveat, the Y–OQ may be employed as a means of tracking a parent's perceptions of a child's change. Consider the following example of an actual treatment failure. The tracking sheet for F.T., a 16-year-old male being treated for oppositional defiant disorder and attention deficit hyperactivity disorder, is shown in Fig. 9.1. It demonstrates reliable negative change over the first five sessions; that is, the repeated Y–OQ administrations document deterioration, at least to this point in treatment. The graph also illustrates the clinical expectation that children with such co-morbid conditions are very difficult to treat successfully in their mid to late adolescence. Though there is not sufficient information to ascertain if what the graph shows is the frequent upward swing before the drop in an extinction curve, the data do clearly demonstrate the need for careful treatment monitoring and possibly the need for a different level of treatment. Regrettably, F.T.'s case was transferred to a different treatment facility, precluding a definitive conclusion.

Similarly, the watchful clinician or treatment team may, by repeated administrations of the Y–OQ, observe the effects of additional interventions or environmental impacts, such as psychotropic medications or the filing for divorce of parents. Figure 9.2 illustrates the continuing problem of medication compliance. D.M., a 14-year-old female was diagnosed with bipolar disorder. At intake, her Y–OQ total score was well within the range of the inpatient treatment population. Time 2 administration demonstrates the stabilization effect of inpatient treatment and initiation of lithium treatment. The Time 3 Y–OQ was given 2 months later, upon her readmission to the

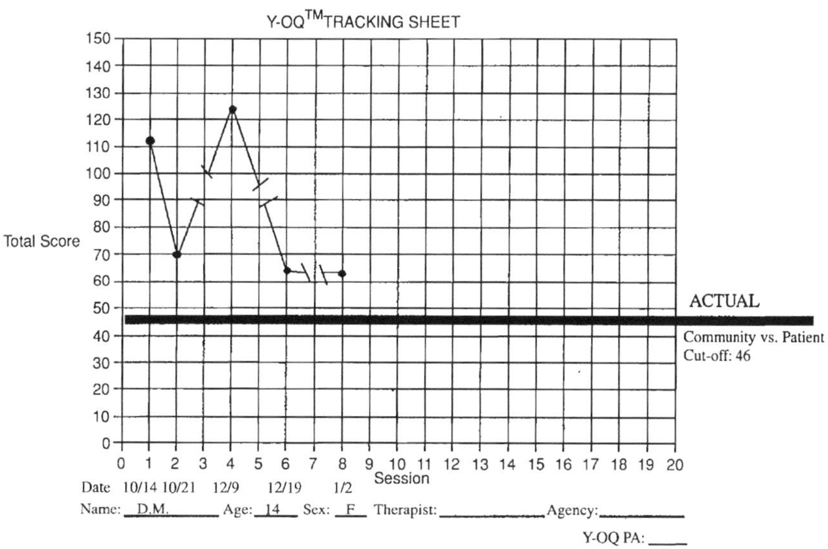

FIG. 9.2. Case example of D.M., a 14-year-old female diagnosed with bipolar disorder.

inpatient unit. D.M. had stopped attending her therapy group and had stopped taking her medication. Y–OQs administered at Times 4 and 5 were completed by the parent at 2-week intervals following D.M.'s resumption of medication and psychotherapy. According to her mother's perception, D.M. has maintained her therapeutic gains.

Clinically, Y–OQ administrations provide something akin to a structured anecdotal report from a parent (M. Latkowski, personal communication, October 1997) and decreases the time the clinician must take to query the parent about the child's progress. The first administration provides a baseline level from which treatment effects can be monitored. When scores fluctuate in unpredictable directions, the therapist can often learn about other external stressors that would not otherwise be discovered but may need to be addressed therapeutically. Latkowski has also found that clinicians who carefully review the Y–OQ tracking sheet are shifting slightly toward therapeutic impact questions as opposed to diagnostic questions. In other words, he has noticed that, because the parents are providing the clinicians with the treatment targets, the clinicians spend less time in evaluation and move more directly to the question, "What needs to be done to address this difficulty?"

Child psychiatrists in the managed health care corporation who assisted in the development of the Y–OQ have employed it as a "need-for-treatment monitoring device" (R. Ferre, personal communication, March 1997). Once a stable, therapeutic dose of medication has been reached, a portion of the practice of child psychiatry is devoted to quarterly checkups for medication evaluation. These physicians have clinic secretaries regularly mail out Y–OQ protocols. When they are received, they are scored and the results are entered on the Y–OQ tracking sheet. The practice of mailing Y–OQs to patients' caretakers does not represent an ecological validity problem since the community normative samples were obtained through the same method. Admittedly, most clinical normative samples for the Y–OQ were obtained in the waiting room. It is not known if there are any differences in clinical level scores obtained on the measure when it is mailed compared with waiting rooms. This is an important area for further research. In the capitated health care system, the physician's timely review of tracking sheets alerts him or her to the continuing efficacy of treatment or the need for a new evaluation, intensive focus on patient retention, resumption of more intensive treatment, or further treatment modifications (Brown et al., 2001).

Application to Treatment-Planning Issues

Identification of Primary and Secondary Problems. As described above, the Y–OQ was not devised as a diagnostic instrument as such. Existing standardized diagnostic instruments such as the CBCL (Achenbach, 1991) and the Personality Inventory for Children (PIC; Lachar, 1982) are more appropriate for that purpose. Conceptually, however, the clinician may examine subscale patterns of the instrument to glean overall presenting problems as perceived by parents. So-called broadband difficulties with externalizing or internalizing behavior or potential psychotic spectrum difficulties will become apparent. Individual item responses may key further questioning or evaluation in such arenas as eating disorders (e.g., "Has lost significant amounts of weight without medical reason") or somatization (e.g., "Complains of stomach pain or feeling sick more than other children of the same age"). Some clinicians have used extreme item or subscale scores as treatment targets; however, the nature of the symptom(s) expressed and the child's parents' concern may not match the measure. A problem diagnosed as primary may not be the most important problem to be treated. It is possible, for instance, that the long-term success of the ADHD child depends more on improvements in social skill than study and homework skills, the more usual focus of concern. In other words, the 14-year-old girl who lives with the recognition that she has never been invited to a party may be ultimately more at risk than if she has never received better than a C in math or history.

Appropriate Level of Care. As described above, total score elevations on the Y–OQ differ significantly between inpatient and outpatient clinical samples. Thus, in a rough clinical sense the clinician employing the Y–OQ can say that a total score of 110, for instance, is most comparable to the total scores of children being treated on an inpatient basis. Similarly, high scores on the Critical Items subscale reveal the need for treatment in a more protected or restricted environment, such as inpatient or residential treatment. However, studies by Gillman (1998) and Mosier (2001) provide a cautionary note. Both demonstrated that the Y–OQ subscale scores of youths in residential treatment or in-home settings differed significantly from community and outpatient norms and that these youths had significantly elevated subscale scores when compared with inpatient samples.

Potential Use or Limits of Treatment Planning in a Managed Care Setting. Many managed care organizations are doing more with outcomes assessment than ever before. A recent study (Brown et al., 2001) illustrates the practical CQI application of the Y–OQ and its related measures in a large managed care setting. PacifiCare Behavioral Health, Inc. (PBH) requires each of its providers to regularly administer the Youth Outcome Questionnaire 30 (Y–OQ 30), a shorter form of the Y–OQ, to a parent of each patient (see the "Related Instrument" section for a description of the Y–OQ 30). The Y–OQ is completed at regular intervals to track therapeutic progress. In the office, the measure is faxed to a central PBH location, where it is scored and entered into PBH's database. PBH then includes the patient's therapist in a feedback loop, informing him or her of the client's progress. The results can then be entered into the client's chart.

The therapist employs the measure as (a) an intake measure of initial severity of symptoms and an index of risk factors that moderate expectations for rapid improvement, (b) a device for tracking therapeutic change, (c) a warning system to alert the therapist of the danger of premature termination and the need for more intensive intervention, and (d) a potential summary source for demonstration of effectiveness of therapeutic interventions.

This same process can be effective for clinicians whose practice is independent of third-party payers. One therapist created a data set of Y–OQ scores for the patients in his private practice (Asay, Lambert, Gregersen, & Goates, 2002). Examining the individual recovery curves plotted from repeated administrations of the Y–OQ for each child and adolescent ($N = 40$), he was able to track the effectiveness of treatment. The data indicated that 75% of his sample met requirements for reliable change after 12 sessions. Asay et al. asserted that a clinician could create a database of his or her patients' scores and compare individual improvement to the clinician's average client recovery as well as to national norms, thus assessing client change and therapeutic effectiveness.

Brown et al. (2001) further demonstrated the corporate application of the Y–OQ to treatment-planning programs. As mentioned above, each completed measure was electronically received at the PBH central corporate office and entered into a data bank. Brown et al. employed regression models based on intake score and a change score at a given session to identify patients who were at risk for premature termination and patients who were progressing more rapidly than anticipated. By alerting therapists to the unusual progress of some patients, PBH created a dialogue wherein the treatment of patients was adjusted according to need. Brown et al. asserted that, by limiting the sessions of those who have improved and increasing the sessions of at-risk clients, PBH improved their cost-benefit ratio and client needs were met.

In addition to establishing decision algorithms to empirically determine appropriate session limits, corporations can use analyses of Y–OQ and Y–OQ 30 scores for (a) reporting therapeutic effectiveness to subscriber companies and profiling individual providers and (b) investigating research issues such as the efficacy of innovative approaches to treatment. The Y–OQ has been shown to be effective in this area. Hoag et al. (1998) employed the Y–OQ to measure the effectiveness of an experimental treatment program for delinquent and ungovernable youths. In their study, 87% of the experimental group, compared with 56% of the controls, demonstrated recovery (scores below the community normal cutoff of 46) or improvement (scores lower than the pretest scores by 13 or more points). They demonstrated that the Youth Reclamation Incorporated intensive treatment protocol produced more clinically significant change and was more cost-effective than the standard court-ordered residential treatment for ungovernable youths. Similarly, Mosier et al. (2001) used the Y–OQ as a measure to evaluate the effectiveness of an in-home service program designed to be an alternative to inpatient treatment for severely disturbed children and adolescents. K. C. Russell (2002) demonstrated the effectiveness of outdoor behavioral health care programs by using the Y–OQ in a pre/post design to measure outcome. Robinson (2000) employed the Y–OQ to gauge the clinical effectiveness of a partial-day treatment program for children with severe emotional disturbances. Each study demonstrated the appropriateness of using the Y–OQ to evaluate the usefulness of clinical programs.

In a similar vein, a hypothetical therapist may summarize her psychotherapy services for managed care Company X in the year 1997, illustrated in Table 9.13. The therapist details the outcomes of patients referred from the managed care company,

TABLE 9.13
Hypothetical Summary Prepared by Psychologist for Demonstration of Effectiveness as Psychotherapist: Summary of Services for Managed Care Company X, 1996

Severity Level	*No. of Patients Seen*	*Mean Initial Severity (Y–OQ)*	*Mean Treatment Duration*	*Mean Termination Level (Y–OQ)*
High	12	109	33	90
Medium	44	91	20	68[a]
Low	21	68	9	47[a]

Note. The median time lapse between initial contact and date of first appointment is 5 days. The percentage of high risk factor patients is 13%.
[a]Score within the normal population.

with appropriate case-mixing information drawn from initial severity ratings of the Y–OQ. We envision this type of summary to be useful as a report to Company X and as a tool for applying for admission to other panels.

USE OF THE INSTRUMENT FOR TREATMENT MONITORING

Purpose of Treatment Monitoring

This chapter began by considering the interface between three audiences: researchers, clinicians, and health care administrators. In the development of the measure, we added an obvious additional stakeholder, the client—or in the case of the Y–OQ, the parents of the child being treated. Treatment monitoring has obvious albeit different roles to play for the various stakeholders. Much has been said already about the relatively immature state of the art in child and adolescent psychotherapy outcomes research. For the researcher and ultimately the clinician, treatment monitoring provides ecological relevance and an answer in standardized format to the question, How is the patient doing at this stage of treatment? For Fonagy (1996), monitoring is essential to bridge the gap between academic research and everyday clinical practice:

> Monitoring the process of a service goes hand in hand with routine monitoring of outcomes of clinical practice. . . .Where outcomes are poorer than anticipated on the basis of research findings, and the discrepancy is not accounted for by the deviations from laid down standards of performance, the monitoring process has provided further research questions about the essential components of treatment or patient characteristics which place limits on treatment effectiveness. In an ideal world further theoretical and clinical development follow, leading to research which in turn addresses the shortcomings of the treatment protocol. (p. 39)

Administrators of health care organizations find treatment monitoring equally essential to build a knowledge base for determining which patients benefit from particular services and what the duration and intensity of treatment should be. Research such as that conducted by Hoag et al. (1998), Mosier et al. (2001), Robinson (2000), K. C. Russell (2002), and Brown et al. (2001) demonstrating the effectiveness of the Y–OQ in assessing the usefulness of clinical programs, as well as studies demonstrating the ability of the Y–OQ to correctly place patients in appropriate treatment settings (Gillman, 1998; A. C. Tzoumas, 2001), lay the groundwork for applying the

Y–OQ in treatment-monitoring efforts. Echoing Fonagy's vision of treatment monitoring, Burlingame et al. (1995) urge that administrators see treatment monitoring as an informational process by which the organization as well as providers can refine the treatment process and therefore its "products."

Families, too, are benefited by treatment monitoring. They, too, are asking, "How is my child doing?" In the absence of more regularized information, they are unable to track for themselves gradual but substantial changes that may have occurred and must rely on their impressions of the recent past. Clinicians reported increased consumer satisfaction in a child psychiatry practice when they routinely shared the Y–OQ tracking charts with the parents of patients.

How to Use the Instrument for Treatment Monitoring

Practitioners who have integrated the Y–OQ into their practices request parents to complete the questionnaire at each session. They reportedly interpret the printout at three levels. First, the overall severity score and/or the responses to Critical Items indicate the parents' sense of crisis or agitation with their child. Even in the midst of ongoing treatment, the occurrence of three data points that suggest increasing behavioral problems prompts a search by the clinician and the parents to determine the source of negative change. Second, initial examination of subscales frequently indicates the general therapeutic thrust required (e.g., higher levels of externalizing behaviors require a different therapeutic protocol than higher levels of internalizing behaviors). And third, when the child has made significant progress, the clinician is alerted to consider less restrictive treatment alternatives for the child.

The following example, illustrated in Fig. 9.3, may serve to demonstrate the utility of treatment monitoring, although therapy continued beyond the last available data point. T.S., a 9-year-old male with mild attention deficit difficulties, was being treated

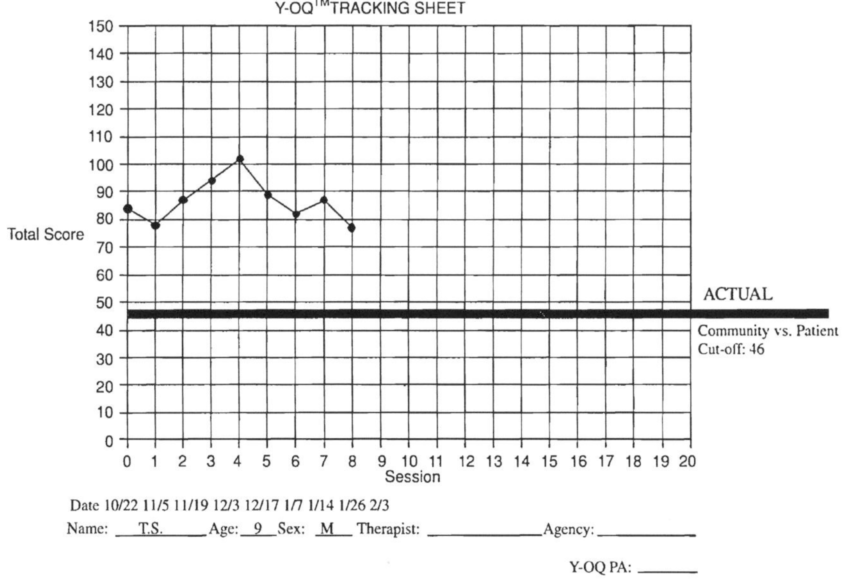

FIG. 9.3. Case example of T.S., a 9-year-old male with mild attention deficit disorder and adjustment reaction to divorce.

for an adjustment reaction to his parents' divorce. As can be seen in the figure, T.S. was experiencing moderate distress at intake, the point at which we usually attempt to collect the initial Y–OQ protocol. Perusal of subscales, as well as his mother's report, revealed considerable intrapersonal distress; moderate conflict with his mother, who, already feeling overwhelmed by the changing family circumstances, was unnerved by his acting-out behaviors; and mild difficulties with behaviors associated with attention-related problems. In other words, T.S. presented the picture of a boy experiencing a welter of confused feelings about his parents' divorce, including depression, anxiety, anger, and increased distractability.

The Y–OQ tracking sheet covers a 3-month period of outpatient supportive treatment to mother and child. Though the chart illustrates essentially a continuing course of difficulty without significant improvement, it is noteworthy that the session-by-session Y–OQs capture the agitation and pain of Christmas holidays for this boy, followed by a return to his earlier level of difficulty. His mother, when shown the tracking sheet, admitted that she was not surprised given the turmoil everyone in the family was experiencing. She stated, however, that her expectation was that her son would have been much worse without the support of the child's therapist. She saw the tracking sheet as evidence that the entire family was still in the middle of some distressing adjustments. Nevertheless, the clinician, recognizing the lack of change, may have considered a second-level form of treatment, such as a divorce adjustment group for the mother and children.

Frequency of Administration

Recent research on psychotherapy outcomes has found value in and scientific justification for increasing the number of administrations of outcome measures (Bryk & Raudenbush, 1988; Willet, 1989). Willet contended that increasing the number of administrations ("waves") increases the reliability of growth rate data, although repeated administrations may result in retest effects whereby raters respond with increasing carelessness (mechanical responding) or with social desirability motives.

In a direct examination of these issues using a randomized block design, Durham et al. (2002) studied 172 subjects who completed the Y–OQ in one of four experimental conditions (weekly, biweekly, monthly, pre/post) over an 8-week period. For each of the experimental conditions, the slopes of the growth curves were plotted and found to show reliable decline: weekly = −1.49, $t(32) = -4.5$, $p < .05$; biweekly = −1.16, $t(25) = -3.95$, $p < .05$; monthly = −.88, $t(31) = -2.67$, $p < .05$; pre/post = −.62, $t(80) = -3.04$, $p < .05$. These findings indicate that there may be a retest artifact with the Y–OQ. Furthermore, the growth curve slopes of the pre/post condition differed significantly from those of the weekly condition, $t(212) = -2.24$, $p < .05$, and the biweekly condition, $t(212) = -2.16$, $p < .05$, indicating that the magnitude of the retest artifact increases with the administration schedule. Interestingly, the authors reported no evidence that social desirability and mechanical responding affected total Y–OQ scores, and they noted that the average retest effect approximated half the value of the RCI. Although statistically significant, the retest artifact value is not clinically significant, but it needs to be considered as the number of repeat administrations increases. Repeat administrations of the Y–OQ provide the most sensitive tracking process but may also be affected by retest artifacts. It is recommended that the Y–OQ be administered on a weekly or biweekly schedule, according to the discretion of the clinician, with recognition of the influence of the retest artifact on patients' scores.

USE OF THE Y–OQ FOR TREATMENT OUTCOMES ASSESSMENT

As noted earlier, the Y–OQ was developed specifically for the purpose of tracking outcomes. We discuss here some of its advantages and limitations for this purpose. It is important to note that the Y–OQ in its present form is limited to addressing outcomes from the point of view of the patient's primary caretaker. Unlike adults, children are not considered reliable informants of their behavioral and mental states. Adolescents who are coerced into treatment are notoriously poor informants. It would be desirable if there were a form of the test that could be administered to the child, mental health specialists, teachers, or other relevant sources besides the parents. As mentioned earlier, such Y–OQ forms have been developed or are currently under development. For example, the Y–OQ 30 is a shortened version of the Y–OQ developed by Burlingame, Jasper, et al. (2001) to provide a method to quickly assess the symptomatic status of an adolescent from his or her own perspective. This sampling of the client's own experience is a rich potential data source for clinicians. For instance, adolescent-reported change on the Y–OQ 30 covaries highly with parent-reported change on the same instrument even though the absolute values of symptom distress differ.

Naturally, using only the original parent-completed Y–OQ limits the generalizability and usefulness of outcome data, as these data come from a single source (i.e., the parent or guardian). Additional factors affect the value of outcome data resulting from ratings by significant other. For example, if outcome data are collected on a weekly basis, different informants (e.g., mother, father, an older sibling, etc.) may bring the child to weekly sessions. In this instance, there may be large differences between informants because of the amount of information they possess or their response bias toward the child; consequently, the outcome data collected may not be meaningfully interpreted. Future research could focus on differences in scores caused by completion of the measure by different caretakers. This source of variance has not, as of yet, been systematically studied. Similar problems exist within inpatient treatment centers where parents may not have enough contact to adequately rate the child. Additionally, no one particular inpatient staff member may have spent enough time with the child to accurately rate the full range of behaviors covered by the Y–OQ. Thus, the development of other versions of the Y–OQ, such as the Y–OQ 30 self-report form, significantly increases the availability of data obtained from different sources concerning the efficacy of treatment and hence directly addresses the problems associated with outcome research with youths.

The knowledgeable reader will recognize these problems as inherent in the collection of data from significant others and therefore not unique to the Y–OQ. Nevertheless, it is important to note that these and related shortcomings will affect conclusions about the effectiveness of treatment interventions as measured by the Y–OQ.

Evaluation of the Y–OQ against NIMH Criteria for Outcome Measures

Newman, Ciarlo, and Carpenter (1999) suggested 11 criteria by which measures of outcome can be judged. These criteria were based on the recommendations of a panel of experts convened by the National Institute of Mental Health. The following summarizes each criterion and provides our evaluation of the Y–OQ's compliance with these criteria.

1. *Relevant to Target Group and Independent of Treatment Provided.* The Y–OQ is relevant for children aged 4 to 17 who have a primary caregiver able to read at the

sixth-grade level. It is most appropriate for tracking outcomes in outpatients. It can be applied in inpatient and residential settings, although with greater difficulty owing to the caregiver's infrequent contact with the child. Its content is related to day-to-day functioning and is not based on any particular treatment theory or modality. It has proven to be as appropriate for monitoring patients undergoing psychoactive pharmaceutical interventions as well as those undergoing psychological interventions, no matter what the theory of change.

2. *Simple, Teachable Methods.* The Y–OQ was specifically designed for ease of administration. It is intended to be administered by a wide range of service professionals ranging from clinic receptionists to clinicians themselves. Administrative instructions are straightforward. Scoring may be accomplished in a number of ways depending on the version of the instrument being used. The most straightforward version provides the Likert point values on the form itself, allowing it to be scored by simply transferring the point value to the appropriate subscale column (also clearly indicated) and then adding up the columns. A commercially released software package also allows for actual Y–OQ administration on the computer, with automatic scoring and storage of the data in a cumulative database for each client as well as tabled treatment summaries by treatment providers.

3. *Use of Measures With Objective Referents.* The items on the Y–OQ are based on objective constructs indicative of issues of importance to families, third-party payers, mental health professionals, and government agencies. However, the very nature of an observer-based measure derived from the judgments of parents and their subjective understanding of their child's current condition limits the usefulness of the data collected. The Y–OQ is not exempt from this limitation. In fact, it requires not only personal conceptualization of current psychological functioning but also a rating of intensity. It does not call for counting behavior, reporting school grades, or recording actual behavior as they occur. Typical items involve rating child behaviors on a scale from "Never" to "Almost always" (e.g., "Steals or lies," "Is fidgety," "Is restless," and "Is hyperactive").

4. *Use of Multiple Respondents.* The Y–OQ currently does not make use of multiple respondents. It is limited to the responses of a caretaker who has daily interaction with the patient. Forms are being developed for completion by older patients and other informants, such as inpatient clinicians and nurses. Furthermore, the development of the Y–OQ 30 (Burlingame, Jasper, et al., 2001) also directly addresses this requirement.

5. *More Process-Identifying Outcome Measures.* Again, the Y–OQ focuses on a subjective understanding of current psychological functioning. It is not intended to identify the process, course, or likely outcome of a pathological condition. Were the Y–OQ designed to measure such constructs, it would likely lose many of its most desirable attributes: ease of administration, short administration time, and straightforward scoring and interpretation. It is likely that repeated administrations of the Y–OQ combined with other meaningful diagnostic data and professional interpretation can provide valuable information leading to process identification.

6. *Psychometric Strengths: Reliable, Valid, Sensitive to Treatment-Related Change, and Nonreactive.* As reported in the reliability, validity, and sensitivity sections of this chapter, the Y–OQ is a psychometrically sound instrument exhibiting high validity,

consistent reliability, the ability to measure client change across sessions, and the ability to discriminate between normal, outpatient, and inpatient populations. It is not known whether the Y–OQ is reactive to extraneous factors.

7. Low Costs. One of the requirements of the Y–OQ design protocol was that the instrument be very cost-effective. Use of the Y–OQ requires a nominal licensing fee, which allows the licensee the lifetime right to reproduce and administer this instrument as well as the OQ–45.2. Cost per administration thus becomes limited to reproduction and administration costs.

8. Understanding by Nonprofessional Audiences. The Y–OQ was intended for general use in a wide range of settings and was thus designed to be easily understood, both conceptually and practically, by laypersons and professionals alike. Not only has this developmental tactic made the Y–OQ easy to administer, but the results of Y–OQ administrations can be easily understood by older patients and parents as well as other nonprofessional observers when clinicians choose to share the findings. Most people appear to understand its utility as analogous to that of a thermometer used to take a patient's temperature for analysis of current physical functioning. A lower score indicates better functioning and less pathology, and a high score represents some level of psychological distress.

9. Easy Feedback and Uncomplicated Interpretation. Development of computer scoring as well as hand-scored Y–OQ forms has yielded a straightforward instrument that is typically easy to interpret. Interpretation can begin with comparing the total score of one administration against the norms, establishing the level of distress currently being experienced, and determining whether this would be considered normal or abnormal. Interpretation of a single protocol can become more complicated if the individual subscale domains are looked at as well as the responses to individual items. However, even this level of interpretation is not very complex. The Y–OQ is also capable of presenting a slightly more complex interpretive picture when repeated measures are used to track individual client progress across sessions. Interpretation can also be expanded to include evaluation of score profiles for a specific treatment provider, therapeutic intervention, or patient population. Feedback follows a similar course, from a simple explanation of the total score to complex statistical analysis and explanation of trends, patterns, and cycles.

10. Useful in Clinical Services. The Y–OQ has proven to be very useful in a number of clinical settings. It can help establish levels of needed treatment, justify or nullify an extended number of sessions, track patient progress across time, and monitor treatment effectiveness. Simplicity of use, low cost, and straightforward interpretation are additional features that make the Y–OQ a very useful tool in a clinical setting.

11. Compatibility With Clinical Theories and Practices. The Y–OQ was intentionally developed to be atheoretical with regard to extant psychological theories. This was done with the hope that it would allow the Y–OQ to be a powerful and meaningful instrument for any clinician to use regardless of clientele, theoretical perspective, or therapeutic style. The current research (Brown et al., 2001) with the Y–OQ has shown that it can be used effectively in a diverse range of settings, providing meaningful if not different information in each instance. One recent study employed the Y–OQ to track the treatment effectiveness of a psychodymanically oriented therapist (Asay et al., 2002). Obviously, different theories and practical applications are going to require varied implementation strategies; however, to date, the Y–OQ appears to be flexible enough to meet these needs and demands.

Research Findings Relevant to Use of the Y–OQ as an Outcome Measure

Since the Y–OQ was not designed to be a diagnostic instrument but rather an assessment tool for tracking patient progress and treatment outcomes, its utility rests on its ability to be sensitive to change during and following participation in therapy or treatment. A logical criterion against which to compare the Y–OQ's sensitivity to change is its performance on subsequent administrations. The Y–OQ has proven to be a very stable measure, which suggests that over brief periods of time (e.g., 2- and 4-week intervals), Y–OQ scores should remain relatively constant. Therefore, observed changes in Y–OQ scores over relatively brief time periods that exceed the magnitude expected by known instability coefficients (test-retest estimates) are suggestive of meaningful changes in the pattern and level of a subject's symptomatology. Thus, to a great extent the Y–OQ's construct validity depends on its ability to detect change following interventions such as psychotherapy. Accordingly, it is expected that the scores of patients receiving psychological or psychopharmacological interventions would become lower over time. Unfortunately, there are several methods to operationalize "sensitivity to meaningful change." The simplest is to calculate a pre- to posttreatment difference score. The reliability of this difference score, calculated according to the method described by Allen and Yen (1979), provides a frame of reference for comparing difference scores. This method essentially estimates the inflation in difference scores due to shared variance in pretreatment and posttreatment observations (i.e., correlation between the two scores).

A second method of measuring sensitivity to change is by using methods proposed by Jacobson and Truax (1991). This involves applying two statistical indices to the pre- to posttreatment change to classify clients as "recovered" or "significantly changed." The first index is based on the principle that, following clinical intervention, a client's posttest score should be in the normal population range of functioning rather than in the dysfunctional population range. The cutoff score of 46, described earlier, establishes the threshold between the functional and dysfunctional populations. The second statistical index, the Reliable Change Index (RCI), controls for variation in pre- to posttest scores that can be attributed to measurement error inherent in the test (known test-retest variability). When both of these criteria are met, a client is considered to have demonstrated clinically significant change. Specifically, if the pre- to posttest difference score exceeds the RCI value (13) *and* the posttest score has crossed the threshold between a dysfunctional and functional population, then the client is classified as having demonstrated clinically significant change.

Speer (1992) describes a third method of classifying client change. This approach, known as the Edwards-Nunnally method, involves centering confidence intervals of 2 standard errors of measurement on the client's unbiased estimated or true initial score. If the client's posttest score then falls outside the confidence interval, it is considered significantly different from the pretest score at $p < .05$. The Edwards-Nunnally method is somewhat more conservative than the RCI method because it adjusts for regression to the mean by using the estimated true score. The formulas used in calculating these methods are listed in Table 9.14.

Mosier, Burlingame, Nebeker, and Wells (1997) gathered data from an outpatient sample ($N = 185$) on the Y–OQ to directly compare these three methods for detecting

TABLE 9.14
Formulas Used in Measuring Sensitivity to Change

Method	*Formula*
Allen and Yen	$r_{DD'} = \frac{1}{2}(r_{xx} + r_{yy}) - r_{yx}/1 - r_{yx}$
Jacobson and Truax	$\text{RCI} = x_A - x_L/S_{\text{diff}}$
Edwards-Nunnally	$x_L >$ or $< [r_{xx}(X_A - M) + M]Å\ 2\ SD(1 - r_{xx})^{1/2}$

Note. In the Allen and Yen formula, r_{xx} = internal reliability estimate of Time 1 Y–OQ total scores; r_{yy} = internal reliability estimate of Time 2 Y–OQ total scores; r_{yx} = the correlation between Time 2 Y–OQ total score and Time 1 Y–OQ total score. In the Jacobson and Truax formula, x_L = individual's raw last assessment score; x_A = individual's raw assessment score; S_{diff} = standard error of the differences between x_A and x_L. In the Edwards–Nunally formula, M = population mean of total Y–OQ scores; SD = population standard deviation of Y–OQ total scores; r_{xx} = test-retest reliability of the Y–OQ.

and interpreting change. The sample included 103 males and 83 females ranging in age from 4 to 18 years ($M = 12.24$, $SD = 3.40$). The majority ($n = 124$) were seen in an outpatient setting; however, the sample also included children and adolescents receiving day or residential treatment. Pre- to posttest difference scores were normally distributed, ranging from −151 to 82. The average participant change score was 16.6 ($SD = 37.8$), indicating overall improvement that met the RCI criteria.

The reliability of Mosier et al.'s (1997) pre- to posttest difference scores, when estimated via the method suggested by Allen and Yen (1979), yielded an estimate of .78. This value is within the conventional range of acceptability and leads to greater confidence in drawing comparative conclusions of the difference scores. Though high difference score reliability is expected (given the aforementioned reliability of the Y–OQ), it cannot be guaranteed. Thus, the importance of generating empirical estimates of such cannot be underestimated.

Although all methods support the Y–OQ with regard to sensitivity to change in the Mosier et al. (1997) sample, each produces a different profile of overall patient change. The Edwards-Nunnally method determined that, of the 185 patients, 85 were improved, 22 were unchanged, and 78 had deteriorated. Using the Reliable Change Index, 91 patients were classified as significantly improved, 59 as unchanged, and 35 as deteriorated. The actual frequency totals and the percentage of hits and misses are presented in Table 9.15. Although there is a high rate of agreement between the two methods on which children are improving (93%), more discrepancy exists for those patients classified as either remaining the same (45%) or deteriorating (45%).

The Edwards-Nunnally method classified 46% of Mosier et al.'s (1997) patients as improved, and the RCI method classified 49% as improved. These findings fit literature-based expectations: the majority of children typically exhibit improvement but a portion consisting of presumably more difficult or recalcitrant cases remain the same or deteriorate. The Edwards-Nunnally method classifies more subjects as deterioraters (i.e., worse off than at admission or initial administration) and fewer subjects as unchanged children than the RCI method. However, this is largely owing to the asymmetrical confidence interval that is generated via the Edwards-Nunnally method and should not be interpreted to mean that it is necessarily superior to the RCI method. Moreover, the differences in clarification rates found in this study replicate those reported by Speer (1992).

TABLE 9.15
Cross-Tabulation of the Edwards-Nunally and Reliable Change Index Classification Methods

	Reliable Change Index			
Edwards-Nunnally	*Improved*	*Unchanged*	*Deteriorated*	*Total*
Improved	(87%) 79 (93%)	(10%) 6 (7%)	—	85
Unchanged	(13%) 12 (55%)	(17%) 10 (45%)	—	22
Deteriorated	—	(73%) 43 (55%)	(100%) 35 (45%)	78
Total	91	59	35	185

Note. Percentages for Edwards-Nunally values are on the left side and are read from top to bottom. Percentage values of classification for the RCI method are to the right of the actual frequency count and are read horizontally.

Sensitivity to change is the raison d'etre for a treatment outcome instrument. In the ideal circumstance, any recorded change of scores would represent actual change in behavior. In the clinical world, however, measurement error, regression to the mean, and other possible confounding variables require statistical techniques to determine how much change in recorded scores is necessary to validly assume that meaningful behavioral change has occurred. Overall, the findings of the Mosier et al. (1997) study suggest that change is occurring in the expected direction, and they support the Y–OQ as a measure that is sensitive to the changes occurring in the pattern and level of subjects' symptomatology when measured over the course of treatment. Four other Y–OQ studies also speak to this question: a study comparing the change demonstrated by Y–OQ scores in a clinical and a community normal sample (Burlingame, Mosier, et al., 2001), an inpatient treatment study designed primarily to test the effectiveness of the current "stabilization" goals of managed health care (Wells et al., 1997), a psychoeducational treatment study of adjudicated youth (McCollam, Burlingame, Vanderwal, Hardinger, & Wells, 1997), and a regression analysis of the growth curves of an archival sample of 729 subjects (Berrett, 1999).

Burlingame, Mosier, et al. (2001) found significant differences, $t(927) = 3.44$, $p < .001$, between the amounts of change demonstrated by Y–OQ scores in a clinical sample ($n = 849$) and community normal sample ($n = 81$). Using the RCI value of 13 and a cutoff score of 46, 147 (17%) clinical subjects were designated as recovered, 308 (37%) as improved, 260 (31%) as unchanged, and 125 (15%) as deteriorated. Burlingame, Mosier, et al. discovered that the average amount of change between pre- and posttest Y–OQ scores across the clinical sample was 17.7 points ($SD = 34.8$), which is greater than the 13 point RCI. In comparison, the community normal sample showed an average pre- to posttest difference in Y–OQ total scores over the same period of 4.34 points ($SD = 2.48$). This demonstrates the sensitivity to clinical change of the Y–OQ and further supports its use as an outcome measure.

Wells et al. (1997) focused on evaluating behavior change via RCI standards in an inpatient population of 36 children and adolescents. They found that 61% of the sample achieved clinically significant change (difference scores exceeding the RCI of 13 plus Time 2 scores falling within the normative cutoff score), 28% achieved change that was less than the RCI (defined as no change), and 11% experienced reliable deterioration (i.e., more severe symptomatology at Time 2 than at Time 1). Note that Weisz, Weiss, Han, Granger, & Morton's (1995) meta-analysis reported a similar pattern of effectiveness for child mental health interventions.

McCollam et al. (1997) evaluated sensitivity to change in a psychoeducational group program for court-adjudicated youth. Parents of 95 adolescents completed Y–OQs at intake and at the final treatment session. Matched-pair *t*-test comparisons of pre- and posttest scores found no significant differences. However, RCI indexes of change found that approximately 25% of the sample reached the criterion for reliable improvement and an additional 25% reached the criterion for reliable deterioration. Thus, the net "no-change" finding on the *t*-test comparisons can be explained by the change exhibited by the improvers being cancelled out by the change exhibited by an equivalent number of deterioraters.

Finally, Berrett (1999) employed hierarchical linear modeling to examine the item sensitivity to change of the Y–OQ. Using an archival sample of 729 subjects (110 nonclinical, 619 clinical), Berrett demonstrated that 75% of items on the Y–OQ were sensitive to change in at least one clinical subsample and that each of the subscales contained items that were sensitive to change. These findings directly demonstrate that the Y–OQ fulfills its designated purpose and is appropriate for use as an outcome measure.

Use of Findings From the Y–OQ With Other Evaluation Data

To date, the Y–OQ has rarely been used simultaneously with other measures of treatment outcome. Thus it is difficult to compare outcomes across measures for the purpose of identifying measures that produce larger or smaller effect sizes. One study performed by Gironda (2000) used the Y–OQ as the reference criterion against which a newer outcome measure, the Ohio Scales (OS), was validated. Concurrent validity for the Y–OQ and the OS was calculated to be .76 ($p < .05$). Similarly high correlations have been found between the Y–OQ and other outcome measures such as the CBCL and CPRS (Burlingame, Mosier, et al., 2001; Atkin, 2000). What remains for future research is the comparison of differential sensitivity to change among these outcome measures (i.e., whether some measures are more capable of detecting change in particular populations than other measures).

Provision of Feedback Regarding Outcomes Assessment Findings

Feedback based on the results of Y–OQ administrations may be used in a wide range of applications. Frequently, parents will ask what purpose the measure serves and inquire as to their personal results. The course of action to be followed here is typically left for the clinician to determine. This may include a full disclosure of the results. Such an inquiry is essentially the equivalent of a patient's parents asking, "How is my son doing? Is he getting better?" and should be handled on a case-by-case basis. Charting the progress of a specific client may also be quite informative to a clinician and can even provide validating feedback as to therapeutic setbacks, stagnation, or rate and pattern of progress (Asay et al., 2002; Brown et al., 2001).

For a clinician or a third-party payer, the most meaningful feedback is typically provided by aggregating clients and sessions. Once Y–OQ results have been accumulated across multiple clients and sessions, the data may provide critical feedback on the progress of patients, typical patterns of improvement for the patients of different clinicians, and the effectiveness of treatments found in various hospitals and regions. One avenue for accessing this information is through the use of the computerized administration and scoring program. Clients can take the Y–OQ on the computer terminal itself; the program will then provide tabled results describing clinician or clinic efficacy in terms of percentage of clients improved and/or recovered across the number of sessions used.

	Mean Pre-Therapy Score	*Mean Post-Therapy Score*	*Mean # of Sessions or Days*	*% Improved*	*% No Change*	*% Deteriorated*
Clinic A	76.20	63.20	6.1	40	50	10
Clinic B	89.10	72.10	4.7	25	55	20
Clinic C	77.30	65.10	5.1	45	45	10
Clinic D	91.50	70.20	4.5	20	60	20

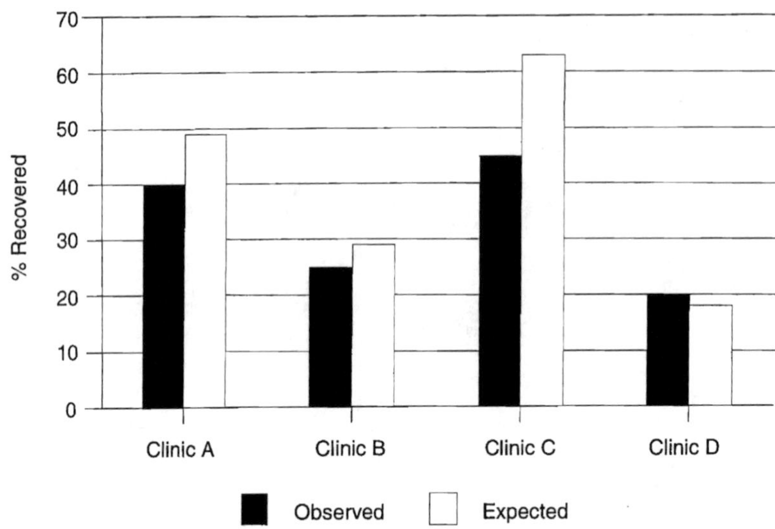

FIG. 9.4. Y–OQ-OATS printout comparison across treatment settings.

A sample clinician record is presented in Fig. 9.4. It contains the output graph comparing the work of four different clinics connected with a large metropolitan children's hospital. This routine report allows clinicians and program directors to see a summary of patient outcomes. A glance at the report shows the percentage of patients who have made clinically significant improvement at the time of the report as well as those who suffered reliable deterioration. Additionally, the report allows clinicians to evaluate (to some degree) the severity of their caseload relative to those of other clinicians. For example, there are obvious average differences between Clinic A's and Clinic B's clients at intake as well as interesting differences between the amount of change they show at intake and last testing.

Brown et al. (2001) asserted that outcomes are difficult to compare and interpret without a valid statistical method of accounting for variations in severity and difficulty of cases. When comparisons across hospitals, clinics, programs, or providers are made, they must be initially case mix–adjusted to produce equivalent findings. Case-mix adjustment is accomplished through a variety of methods on any number of relevant variables (e.g., initial severity scores, patient diagnosis, chronicity of disorders), with the goal of allowing a balanced or matched comparison to be made based on the patient disorders or severity of illness. Brown et al. (2001) demonstrated that using a patient's initial score on the Youth Life Status Questionnaire (Y–LSQ), the predecessor to the Y–OQ 30 (see the "Related Instruments" section), is one effective method of case-mix adjustment. In their study, this method was employed by a large health maintenance organization to compare treatment outcomes and provide therapists with feedback regarding patient progress and outcomes.

Limitations in the Use of the Y–OQ for Outcomes Assessment

Perhaps the biggest limitation of the Y–OQ remains in the area of implementation. As with all outcome measures, the most difficult challenge with the Y–OQ is to systematically collect data from informants across clinical sessions in order to interpret the overall pattern of change. It may be that the problem of missing data will be somewhat resolved, as more and more HMOs require such data from their health care provider panels. As mentioned, Brown et al. (2001) demonstrated the use and efficacy of one such corporate application in a large western behavioral health care corporation. Their study reflects initial efforts to implement treatment planning using outcomes assessment. Furthermore, confirming the usefulness of the program, Brown et al. reported that PBH plans to apply the program systemwide in the near future.

Psychometric limitations include evidence of a retest artifact (Durham et al., 2002) and the absence of factor analyses to support the rationally derived subscales (Hughes, Lambert, Burlingame, & Wells, 2000). These limitations are balanced by strong evidence of the test's reliability and validity as well as the test's demonstrated sensitivity to change.

Potential Use of the Y–OQ as a Data Source for Mental Health Service Report Cards

As noted, as the costs of mental health care rise, third-party providers are more frequently requiring health care providers to document therapeutic progress. This requirement for "accountability" leaves clinicians in fear of losing their livelihood if their patients do not exhibit documentable improvement. Further concerns revolve around comparisons that are not case mix adjusted to factor the severity of client pathology into health care administrators' expectations for therapeutic progress (Wells, Burlingame, Lambert, Hoag, & Hope, 1996).

We believe there is reason for optimism. Our outcome research, which is based on HMOs covering tens of millions of lives, has begun to paint a realistic picture of treatment outcomes (Brown et al., 2001). This portrait appears to be in line with the actual experiences of providers rather than the assumed limits and restraints of health care management and provider systems. Nonetheless, the age of accountability no longer gives clinicians the same degree of freedom they once enjoyed (Burlingame et al., 1995). We contend that the marriage of outcome research and managed health care has not resulted in the grim demise of the health care system that has been predicted.

Y–OQ–Related Instruments

An early attempt was made at developing a companion to the Y–OQ that would assess risk factors associated with poor treatment. The Y–OQ Prognostic Assessment (Y–OQ PA) initially demonstrated the ability to predict whether a client was at risk for low levels of improvement or even deterioration. An initial pilot study of the Y–OQ PA reported excellent test-retest reliability and moderate internal reliability of scores on the measure using a sample of 185 youths in treatment (Mosier, 1998). A subsequent study by Gillman (1998) also provided initial support. More specifically, this study demonstrated that the Y–OQ PA, along with the Y–OQ total score, could correctly classify up to 67% of clients with respect to treatment setting (outpatient, inpatient, and residential). However, the Y–OQ total score was the most powerful of the two. Subsequent research (Mosier, 2001) demonstrated that the Y–OQ PA did not account for statistically or clinically meaningful patient classification. Furthermore, there was no significant interaction with this instrument and Y–OQ scores over time, refuting the earlier predictive validity of the measure.

Another modification of the Y–OQ has shown more success. A. C. Tzoumas (2001) hypothesized that the Y–OQ's high positive predictive power might assist pediatricians in identifying children in need of mental health treatment. With this goal in mind, Tzoumas demonstrated that the Y–OQ total score correlated with high utilization of primary care. He also identified 12 items on the original Y–OQ that discriminated between community and clinical samples. These 12 items form the Y–OQ Primary Care Medicine Screening Instrument (Y–OQ PCM), a quick, psychometrically sound screening tool for use in physicians' offices. In subsequent research, J. L. Tzoumas (2001) demonstrated that the Y–OQ PCM had adequate internal consistency (.87). The new measure showed good sensitivity (.77 to .99) and adequate specificity (.62 to .77), with values varying by clinical setting. These initial statistics show that the Y-OQ PCM exhibits promising psychometric properties and indicate it may be useful for the quick assessment of mental health treatment needs in a primary care setting. The Y–OQ PCM has not demonstrated sensitivity to change and is not applicable as a short measure of treatment progress and outcome.

A frequent request from clinicians was for a shorter form of the Y–OQ that could quickly and accurately gauge the current distress of a child or adolescent. Based on this feedback, Berrett (1999) identified items on the Y–OQ that were differentially sensitive to change. This study laid the foundation for the 30-item instrument (Y–OQ 30) initially developed under the proprietary label Youth Life Status Questionnaire (Y–LSQ; Burlingame, Jasper, et al., 2001; Brown et al., 2001). The Y–OQ 30 provides a single total score and none of the original Y–OQ subscales. The earlier parent and adolescent self-report forms were collapsed into a single omnibus instrument, eliminating the need for two forms. Moreover, the initial psychometric properties of this omnibus form when used by parents of adolescents are promising. Internal consistency estimates based on parent report and self-report (.96 and .93, respectively) approximate the internal consistency found on the longer version. Moreover, sensitivity and specificity for both parent report (.80 and .75, respectively) and adolescent self-report (.70 and .63, respectively) are good. Initial research suggests the measure is able to capture patient change in a manner comparable to that of the parent instrument, the Y–OQ.

In summary, recent efforts to modify the original Y–OQ have produced mixed results. As with many attempts to capture risk (Bickman et al., 1995), the Y–OQ PA appears to have little predictive power. Other instruments (the Y–OQ PCM, Y–OQ 30, and Y–OQ SR) show more promise. Future research will be the ultimate judge of the long-term utility of these modifications and extensions to the Y–OQ.

CASE STUDIES

The cases presented here are actual treatment cases from a large inpatient and outpatient treatment facility. As with many cases from hospital charts, more details about significant treatment and environmental events, not to mention more frequent

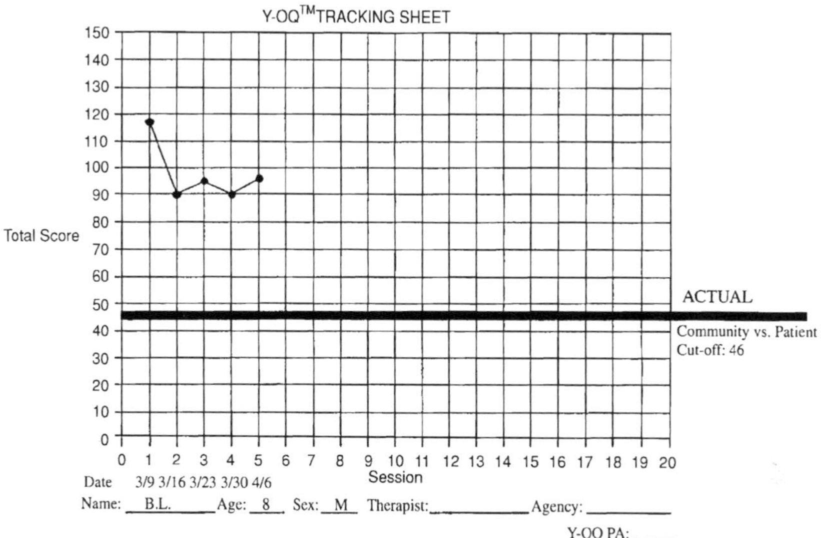

FIG. 9.5. Case example of B.L., an 8-year-old male treated for intense aggressive behaviors.

administrations of the Y–OQ, would be most helpful. Nevertheless, these cases illustrate how the Y–OQ is used in actual practice.

Figure 9.5 presents the tracking sheet for B.L., an 8-year-old boy being treated for intense aggressive behaviors. He had received a diagnosis of attention deficit hyperactivity disorder and oppositional defiant disorder. B.L.'s level of initial severity placed him in the range most often seen with children being treated by an inpatient service; however, he was treated on an outpatient basis, and his parents received corollary intervention in the form of parent training. Though the imposition of a behavior modification program had a positive effect on his total symptomatic profile (Y–OQ total), as evidenced by improvement extending beyond the RCI index, his acting out was still extreme enough to be particularly problematic when his parents moved rather suddenly from the community to seek other employment. Examination of his chart notes suggests that a careful diagnostic workup might have found B.L. to fit the criteria for early onset conduct disorder (Hinshaw, Lahey, & Hart, 1993).

Figure 9.6 highlights the rapid and very beneficial response to antidepressant medication and psychotherapy experienced by I.H., a 10-year-old female subject to major depression and suicidal feelings. Y–OQs were completed by the mother at intake, at 1 month into treatment, and at termination, after 3 months of treatment. The chart clearly and succinctly illustrates the progress of the child. Note that clinicians have found the availability of the tracking sheets helps to decrease the length of progress and termination reports.

CONCLUSION

Like its predecessor, the OQ–45, the Y–OQ is designed to be a brief, psychometrically standardized instrument for tracking the progress of child and adolescent patients receiving mental health treatment. Parents or other caretakers with reasonable acquaintance with the patient's behavior complete the questionnaire at intake and then at intervals throughout treatment. Scores from six content domains are summed to

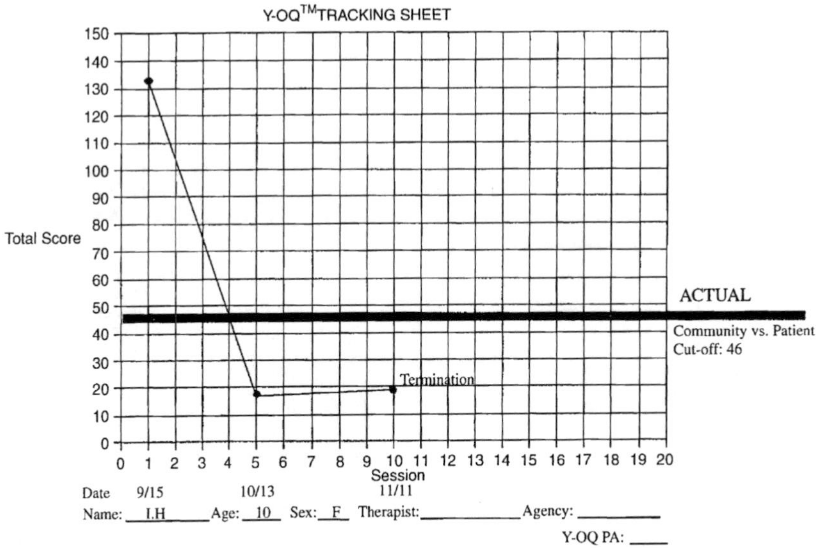

FIG. 9.6. Case example of I.H., a 10-year-old female diagnosed with major depression.

provide an overall severity score, which may roughly indicate the appropriate level of treatment. Repeated administrations of the measure permit evaluation of the patient's changes in behavior as perceived by the parent or caretaker respondent. Established cutoff scores and RCI values signal significant symptomatic change and indicate when the patient's behavior has become similar in elevation to the untreated community normal group.

Though much research remains to be done, the evidence gathered thus far suggests that the Y–OQ holds considerable promise. It requires little time to complete, is easy to administer, and is available at nominal cost. It has been translated into Spanish, French, German, Hmong, and Laotian, and ethnic group comparisons are underway. It has demonstrated acceptable to excellent reliability and validity, has been shown to be sensitive to change, and has been found to be useful both by clinicians and health care administrators.

Currently, data analyses suggest that, as with the OQ–45, interpretation of the total score rather than the subscale scores is the most justifiable tracking procedure. However, subscales and individual item responses may be used for hypothesis generation, like any other objective measure. Recent refinements include confirmatory factor analyses, establishment of norms for more specific treatment populations (patients undergoing residential treatment), parallel self-report versions for adolescents, and a primary care physician screening version. Each of these developments has expanded the applicability of the Y–OQ as a useful tool in clinical, research, and administrative settings.

REFERENCES

Achenbach, T. M. (1991). *Manual for the Child Behavior Checklist/4–18 and 1991 profile.* Burlington, VT: University of Vermont, Department of Psychiatry.

Allen, J. S., Jr., Tarnowski, K. J., Simonian, S. J., Elliot, D., & Drabman, R. S. (1991). The generalization gap revisited: Assessment of generalized treatment effects in child and adolescent behavior therapy. *Behavior Therapy, 22,* 393–405.

Allen, M. J., & Yen, W. M. (1979). *Introduction to measurement theory.* Monterey, CA: Brooks/Cole.

Asay, T. P., Lambert, M. J., Gregersen, A. T., & Goates, M. K. (2002). Using patient-focused research in evaluating treatment outcome in private practice. *Journal of Clinical Psychology, 58,* 1213–1225.

Atkin, G. Q. (2000). Concurrent-criterion validity of the Youth Outcome Questionnaire. (Doctoral dissertation, Brigham Young University, 2000). *Dissertation Abstracts International, 61,* 582.

Atkin, G. Q., Whoolery, M. L., Peterson, G., Burlingame, G. M., Wells, M. G., & Nebeker, R. S. (1997, April). *Reliability and validity of the Youth Outcome Questionnaire.* Paper presented at annual meeting of the Western Psychological Association, Seattle, WA.

Baer, R. A., & Nietzel, M. T. (1991). Cognitive and behavioral treatment of impulsivity in children: A meta-analytic review of the outcome literature. *Journal of Clinical Child Psychology, 20,* 400–412.

Barrnett, R. J., Docherty, J. P., & Frommelt, G. M. (1991). A review of psychotherapy research since 1963. *Journal of the American Academy of Child and Adolescent Psychiatry, 30,* 1–14.

Berrett, K. M. S. (1999). Youth Outcome Questionnaire: Item sensitivity to change. (Doctoral dissertation, Brigham Young University, 1999/2000). *Dissertation Abstracts International, 60,* 4876.

Bickman, L., Guthrie, P. R., Foster, E. M., Lambert, E. W., Summerfelt, W. T., Breda, C. S., et al. (1995). *Evaluating managed mental health services: The Fort Bragg experiment.* New York: Plenum.

Brown, J. (1987). A review of meta-analyses conducted on psychotherapy outcome research. *Clinical Psychology Review, 7,* 1–23.

Brown, G. S., Burlingame, G. M., Lambert, M. J., Jones, E., & Vaccaro, J. (2001). Pushing the quality envelope: A new outcomes management system. *Psychiatric Services, 52,* 925–934.

Bryk, A. S., & Raudenbush, S. W. (1988). Toward a more appropriate conceptualization of research on school effects: A three level hierarchical linear model. *American Journal of Education, 21,* 65–108.

Burlingame, G. M., Jasper, B. W., Peterson, G., Wells, M. G., Lambert, M. J., Reisinger, C. W., et al. (2001). *Youth-Life Status Questionnaire.* Wilmington, DE.: American Professional Credentialing Services.

Burlingame, G. M., Lambert, M. J., Reisinger, C. W., Neff, W. L., & Mosier, J. I. (1995). Pragmatics of tracking mental health outcomes in a managed care setting. *Journal of Mental Health Administration, 22,* 226–236.

Burlingame, G. M., Mosier, J. I., Wells, M. G., Atkin, Q. G., Lambert, M. J., Whoolery, M., et al. (2001). Tracking the influence of mental health treatment: The development of the Youth Outcome Questionnaire. *Clinical Psychology and Psychotherapy, 8,* 361–379.

Burlingame, G. M., Wells, M. G., Hoag, M. J., Hope, C. A., Nebeker, R. S., Konkel, K., et al. (2001). *Youth Outcome Questionnaire.* Wilmington, DE: American Professional Credentialing Services.

Burlingame, G. M., Wells, M. G., & Lambert, M. J. (1996). *Youth Outcome Questionnaire.* Stevenson, MD: American Professional Credentialing Services.

Casey, R. J., & Berman, J. S. (1985). The outcome of psychotherapy with children. *Psychological Bulletin, 98,* 388–400.

Connors, C. K. (1989). *Manual for Conners Rating Scales.* North Tonawanda, NY: Multi-Health Systems.

Cronbach, L. J. (1970). *Essentials of psychological testing* (3rd ed.) New York: Harper & Row.

Cummings, N. A. (1987). The future of psychotherapy: One psychologist's perspective. *American Journal of Psychotherapy, 41,* 349–360.

Derogatis, L. R., & DellaPietra, L. (1994). Psychological tests in screening for psychiatric disorder. In M. E. Maruish (Ed.), *The use of psychological testing for treatment planning and outcomes assessment* (pp. 22–54). Hillsdale, NJ: Lawrence Erlbaum Associates.

Dinh, K., Sarason, B., & Sarason, L. (1994). Parent-child relationships in Vietnamese immigrant families. *Journal of Family Psychology, 8,* 471–488.

Durham, C. J., McGrath, L. D., Burlingame, G. M., Schaalje, G. B., Lambert, M. J., & Davies, D. R. (2002). The effects of repeated administrations of self-report and parent-report scales. *Journal of Psychoeducational Assessment, 20,* 240–257.

Durlak, J. A., Wells, A. M., Cotten, J. K., & Johnson, S. (1995). Analysis of selected methodological issues in child psychotherapy research. *Journal of Clinical Child Psychology, 24,* 141–148.

Fonagy, P. (1996, October). *Evaluating the effectiveness of interventions in child psychiatry: The state of the art.* Invited address at the Kansas Conference on Clinical Child Psychology, Lawrence, KA.

Gillman, K. D. (1998). Symptom status and risk factors of adolescents in residential treatment: Developing norms for the Youth Outcome Questionnaire (Y–OQ) and determining the utility of the Y–OQ and the Y–OQ Prognostic Assessment (Y–OQ PA) in predicting treatment setting (Doctoral dissertation, Brigham Young University, 1998). *Dissertation Abstracts International, 59,* 416.

Gironda, M. A. (2000). A validity study of the Youth-Outcome Questionnaire and the Ohio Scales (Doctoral dissertation, Pace University, 2000). *Dissertation Abstracts International, 61,* 2813.

Grossman, P. B., & Hughes, J. N. (1992). Self-control interventions with internalizing disorders: A review and analysis. *School Psychology Review, 21,* 229–245.

Hinshaw, S. P., Lahey, B. B., & Hart, E. L. (1993). Issues of taxonomy and comorbidity in the development of conduct disorder. *Development and Psychopathology, 5,* 31–49.

Hoag, M. J., & Burlingame, G. M. (1997). Evaluating the effectiveness of child and adolescent group treatment: A meta-analytic review. *Journal of Clinical Child Psychology, 26,* 234–246.

Hoag, M. J., Lambert, M. J., Jenkins, P. H., Hyde, R. F., Lindsey, S. B., & Harvey, Q. (1998, October). An intensive family-centered early warning intervention pilot project program for juvenile delinquents and ungovernable youth: An outcome analysis of the Youth Reclamation Program. Paper presented at the annual meeting of the Kansas Conference on Clinical Child Psychology, Lawrence, KS.

Hughes, L. N., Lambert, M. J., Burlingame, G. M., & Wells, M. G. (2000, April). Factor analysis of the Youth Outcome Questionnaire: Further evidence of construct validity. In G. M. Burlingame (Chair), *Innovations in tracking outcome: The Youth Outcome Questionnaire—construct validity, outcome predictions, psycho-social screening, and in-home treatment evaluation.* Symposium conducted at the 80th annual convention of the Western Psychological Association, Portland, OR.

Jacobson, N. S., & Truax, P. (1991). Clinical significance: A statistical approach to defining meaningful change in psychotherapy research. *Journal of Consulting and Clinical Psychology, 59,* 12–19.

Kazdin, A. E. (1988). *Child psychotherapy: Developing and identifying effective treatments.* Elmsford, NY: Pergamon.

Kazdin, A. E. (1990). Premature termination from treatment among children referred for antisocial behavior. *Journal of Child Psychology and Psychiatry, 31,* 415–425.

Kazdin, A. E. (1991). Treatment research: The investigation and evaluation of psychotherapy. In M. Hersen, A. E. Kazdin, & A. S. Bellack (Eds.), *The clinical psychology handbook* (2nd ed., pp. 293–312). New York: Pergamon.

Kazdin, A. E. (1993). Psychotherapy for children and adolescent psychotherapy research: Limited sampling of dysfunctions, treatments, and client characteristics. *Journal of Consulting and Clinical Psychology, 58,* 729–740.

Kazdin, A. E. (1995). Scope of child and adolescent psychotherapy research: Limited sampling of dysfunctions, treatments, and client characteristics. *Journal of Clinical Child Psychology, 24,* 125–140.

Kazdin, A. E. (2004). Psychotherapy for children and adolescents. In M. J. Lambert (Ed.), *Bergin and Garfield's handbook of psychotherapy and behavior change* (5th ed., pp. 543–589). New York: Wiley.

Kazdin, A. E., Bass, D., Ayers, W. A., & Rodgers, A. (1990). Empirical and clinical focus of child and adolescent psychotherapy research. *Journal of Consulting and Clinical Psychology, 58,* 729–740.

Kendall, P. C., & Morris, R. J. (1991). Child therapy: Issues and recommendations. *Journal of Consulting and Clinical Psychology, 59,* 777–784.

Kovacs, M., & Paulaskas, S. (1986). The traditional psychotherapies. In H. D. Qual & J. S. Werry (Eds.), *Psychopathological disorders of childhood* (3rd ed., pp. 496–522). New York: Wiley.

Lachar, D. (1982). *Personality Inventory for Children (PIC) revised format manual supplement.* Los Angeles: Western Psychological Services.

Lambert, M. J., Hansen, N. B., Umphress, V., Lunnen, K., Okiishi, J., & Burlingame, G. M., et al. (1996). *Outcome Questionnaire 45.2.* Wilmington, DE: American Professional Credentialing Services.

Lambert, M. J., & Ogles, B. M. (2004). The efficacy and effectiveness of psychotherapy. In M. J. Lambert (Ed.), *Bergin and Garfield's handbook of psychotherapy and behavior change* (5th ed., pp. 139–193). New York: Wiley.

Lambert, M. J., Thompson, K. C., Nebeker, R. S., & Andrews, A. (June, 1996). *The re-test artifact and its implications for establishing dose-effect estimates of patient change following psychotherapy.* Paper presented at the annual meeting of the Society for Psychotherapy Research, Amelia Island, FL.

McCollam, P. M., Burlingame, G. M., Vanderwal, G., Hardinger, C., & Wells, M. G., (1997, April). *The Youth Outcome Questionnaire: Characteristics of a juvenile delinquent population.* Paper presented at the annual meeting of the Western Psychological Association, Seattle, WA.

Mills, J. R., Manivanh, T., Burlingame, G. M., Wells, M. G., Peterson, G., & Nuttall, M. (1997, April). *Developing the Youth Outcome Questionnaire (Y–OQ) for Lao refugeee children and adolescents.* Paper presented at the annual meeting of the Western Psychological Association, Seattle, WA.

Mosier, J. (1998). *The predictive validity of the Youth Outcome Questionnaire: Prognostic assessment.* Unpublished master's thesis, University of Utah, Salt Lake City.

Mosier, J. (2001). Predicting treatment outcome using psychosocial characteristics: A re-examination of the Youth Outcome Questionnaire Prognostic Assessment (Doctoral dissertation, Brigham Young University, 2001). *Dissertation Abstracts International, 62,* 2070.

Mosier, J. I., Burlingame, G. M., Nebeker, R. S., & Wells, M. G. (1997, April). *Correlates of change in treatment in a clinical sample of children and adolescents.* Paper presented at the annual meeting of the Western Psychological Association, Seattle, WA.

Mosier, J., Burlingame, M. G., Wells, M. G., Ferre, R., Lakowski, M., Johansen, J., et al. (2001). In-home, family-centered psychiatric treatment for high-risk children and youth. *Children's Services: Social Policy, Research, and Practice, 4,* 51–68.

Neeleman, L. (2001). Factor analysis of the Youth-Outcome Questionnaire: Further evidence of construct validity (Doctoral dissertation, Brigham Young University, 2001). *Dissertation Abstracts International, 62,* 2110.

Newman, F. L., Ciarlo, J. A., & Carpenter, D. (1999). Guidelines for selecting psychological instruments for treatment planning and outcome assessment. In M. E. Maruish (Ed.), *The use of psychological testing for treatment planning and outcomes assessment* (2nd ed., pp. 153–170). Mahwah, NJ: Lawrence Erlbaum Associates.

Prout, H. T., & DeMartino, R. A. (1986). A meta-analysis of school based studies of psychotherapy. *Journal of School Psychology, 24,* 285–292.

Roberts, A. R., & Camasso, M. J. (1991). The effects of juvenile offender treatment programs on recividism: A meta-analysis of 46 studies. *Notre Dame Journal of Law, Ethics, and Public Policy, 5,* 421–441.

Robinson, K. E. (2000). Outcomes of a partial-day treatment program for referred children. *Child and Youth Care Forum, 29,* 127–137.

Russell, K. C. (2002). Outdoor treatment for adolescents with problem behaviors: An outcomes study. *Behavioral Health Management, 22,* 14–18.

Russell, R. L., Greenwald, S., & Shirk, S. R. (1991). Language change in child psychotherapy: A meta-analytic review. *Journal of Consulting and Clinical Psychology, 51,* 42–53.

Shirk, S. R., & Russell, R. L. (1992). A reevaluation of estimated of child therapy effectiveness. *Journal of American Academy of Child and Adolescent Psychiatry, 31,* 703–709.

Speer, D. C. (1992). Clinically significant change: Jacobson and Truax (1991) revisited. *Journal of Consulting and Clinical Psychology, 60,* 402–408.

Tingey, R., Lambert, M., Burlingame, G., & Hansen, N. (1996). Assessing clinical significance: Proposed extensions to method. *Psychotherapy Research, 6,* 109–123.

Tramonta, M. G. (1980). Critical review of research on psychotherapy outcome with adolescents: 1967–1977. *Psychological Bulletin, 88,* 429–450.

Tzoumas, A. C. (2001). The Youth-Outcome Questionnaire–Primary Care Medicine screening instrument (Doctoral dissertation, Brigham Young University, 2001/2002). *Dissertation Abstracts International, 62,* 3817.

Tzoumas, J. L. (2001). *Validation study of the Youth Outcome Questionnaire–Primary Care Medicine (YOQ–PCM) screening instrument.* Unpublished doctoral dissertation, Brigham Young University, Provo, UT.

U.S. Department of Health and Human Services. (1999). *Mental health: A report of the Surgeon General.* Retrieved December 28, 2002 from http://www.surgeongeneral.gov/Library/MentalHealth/home.html

Weisz, J. R., Weiss, B., Alicke, M. D., & Klotz, M. L. (1987). Effectiveness of psychotherapy with children and adolescents: A meta-analysis for clinicians. *Journal of Consulting and Clinical Psychology, 55,* 542–549.

Weisz, J. R., Weiss, B., & Donenberg, G. R. (1992). The lab versus the clinic: Effects of child and adolescent psychotherapy. *American Psychologist, 47,* 1578–1585.

Weisz, J. R., Weiss, B., Han, S. S., Granger, D. A., & Morton, T. (1995). Effects of psychotherapy with children and adolescents revisited: A meta-analysis of treatment outcome studies. *Psychological Bulletin, 117,* 450–468.

Wells, M. G., Burlingame, G. M., & Lambert, M. J. (1999). Youth Outcome Questionnaire. In M. E. Maruish (Ed.), *The use of psychological testing for treatment planning and outcome assessment* (2nd ed., pp. 497–453). Mahwah, NJ: Lawrence Erlbaum Associates.

Wells, M. G., Burlingame, G. M., Lambert, M. J., Hoag, M., & Hope, C. (1996). Conceptualization and measurement of patient change during psychotherapy: Development of the Youth and Adult Outcome Questionnaires. *Psychotherapy: Theory, Research, and Practice, 33,* 275–283.

Wells, M. G., Mohlman, J., Trecarico, S., Gandhi, P., Turner, L., Stark, C., et al. (1997, April). *Measuring therapeutic change among child and adolescent inpatients using the Youth Outcome Questionnaire.* Paper presented at the annual meeting of the Western Psychological Association, Seattle, WA.

Werry, J. S., Reeves, J. C., & Elkind, G. S. (1987). Attention deficit, conduct, oppositional, and anxiety disorders in children: 1. A review of research on differentiating characteristics. Journal of The American Academy of child and Adolescent Psychiatry, 26, 133–143.

Whalen, C. K., Henker, B., Hinshaw, S. P., & Granger, D. A. (1989). Externalizing behavior disorders, situational generality, and the type A behavior pattern. *Child Development, 60,* 1453–1462.

Willet, J. B. (1989). Some results on reliability for the longitudinal measurement of change: Implications for the design of studies of individual growth. *Educational and Psychological Measurement, 49,* 587–602.

10

The Ohio Scales

Benjamin M. Ogles, Kathy Dowell, Derek Hatfield,
Gregorio Melendez, and David L. Carlston
Ohio University

As the service system for children and adolescents with emotional and behavioral disorders has evolved, increasing emphasis has been placed on developing ongoing evaluation procedures to determine the effectiveness of community-based interventions. As a result, the Southern Consortium for Children (SCC), an administrative agency dedicated to improving mental health services for children in a 10-county area of southeastern Ohio, embarked on a search for outcome assessment instruments that could be used to evaluate local mental health systems and services. After an extensive search for practical measures, the SCC decided to work with local university partners to develop a clinical outcome measure that would be practical yet scientifically sound. The Ohio Youth Problems, Functioning, and Satisfaction Scales (Ohio Scales) evolved out of this collaboration and has now been adopted statewide in Ohio for the assessment of outcome for children receiving publicly funded mental health services (Ohio Department of Mental Health, 2000; Vital Signs, 1998). In this chapter, the conceptualization, development, validation, and potential uses of the Ohio Scales are described.

CONCEPTUALIZATION

Although a variety of instruments were available for assessing outcome at the initiation of this project, the Ohio Scales were developed to address the need for more pragmatic methods of gathering data. Initially, four areas of concern were considered relevant to the assessment of clinical outcomes: (1) the problems associated with rural service provision, (2) the perspective of various stakeholders, (3) research-based methods of outcome measurement, and (4) theoretical and conceptual models of outcome assessment. Perspectives regarding these issues were used to develop a set of desirable characteristics for a clinical outcome measure that then guided the development of the Ohio Scales.

Problems in a Rural Setting

Although the Ohio Scales are now being used in a variety of settings and locations, the initial development was based on needs specific to rural, southeastern Ohio. The rural location presented some unique problems for both the provision of services, the establishment of evaluation programs, and the development of an appropriate instrument. The designated service area of the initial project was composed of 10 Ohio counties located in the scenic foothills of the Appalachian Mountains and in the heart of Ohio's 29 designated Appalachian counties. The terrain is rough and hilly and marked with poor roads and no public transportation system. A sparse population, economic underdevelopment and a low tax base characterize the region. Nearly 25% of the individuals within the 10-county area have incomes that fall below the federal poverty guidelines. The rural nature of the counties also limits financial resources and results in large distances between agencies. Similarly, there is limited availability of many medical and mental health services resulting in placements that may isolate the child from the family. These difficulties influence both the provision of services and the assessment of outcome. Evaluating the effectiveness of services in these rural, poverty-stricken areas is difficult to implement and of necessity demanded practical, brief, inexpensive methods of outcome assessment that have intuitive value for the consumer. Otherwise, little useful data from consumers would be collected.

Practical challenges that hamper the implementation of outcome evaluation plans in applied settings are certainly not unique to rural areas. In fact, when serving at-risk populations many of the issues (e.g., poverty, transportation, availability of services) are identical irrespective of geographic location. Especially in service agencies where clinical skills and client advocacy are predominant, the resources and expertise for selecting measures and developing strategies for collecting data may not be available.

One example of such a practical constraint may illustrate the point. Some community mental health providers find that the formats of research-based measurement tools are impractical (Mordock, 2000; Rosenblatt, 1998; Weber, 1998). Research-based tools may be lengthy, difficult to score and interpret, or costly. As a result, some organizations throw together a few items that assess satisfaction and make their own "outcome" measure. In so doing, they neglect the need for psychometric rigor. These agencies acknowledge the importance of assessing outcome yet desire methods of evaluating services using cost-efficient, practical measures. Especially if one is searching for a multicontent, multisource measure in a practical format that can be used repeatedly over time, the possibilities are few. In fact, Rosenblatt (1998) stated, "There simply is no perfect outcome measure for the delivery of behavioral health services to children. It is extraordinarily difficult, given the current state of measurement development, to strike a balance between practicality and rigor" (p. 42).

It is interesting that these problems were also evident in the 1970s. For example, Ihilevich and Gleser (1982) summarized their work on the Progress Evaluation Scales after discussing the problems that agencies encountered when attempting to evaluate mental health services. Among the difficulties mentioned in their book, they suggested that "standardized instruments for measuring outcome that are reliable, valid, and relevant for clinical and programmatic decision making yet are sufficiently broad to be applicable to the great variety of programs and clients served by mental-health professionals in the community are largely unavailable" (Ihilevich & Gleser, 1982, pp. 1–2). As a result, agency administrators and service providers must balance the need for accountability with the practical demands of collecting data. When developing the Ohio Scales, issues that could have precluded adequate application in areas with limited resources were carefully considered. To that end, when facing any choice point, the practical issues were emphasized.

The Input of Stakeholders

Key members of the public who are potentially most affected by services are referred to as stakeholders (Gold, 1983). Several potential stakeholders have a vested interest in mental health outcomes of which three have been emphasized: society (those not involved in treatment but who have a vested interest in the outcome and costs of services), the consumer, and the mental health professional (Strupp & Hadley, 1977). Based on the viewpoint of the interested party, different criteria may be emphasized or selected to measure successful treatment. Certainly, one's perspective plays a role in determining what one values as successful intervention. As a result, we attempted to gain input from a variety of stakeholders to assess success from several perspectives.

More specifically, a Social Validation Survey of the various stakeholders was conducted (Gillespie, 1993). This survey was administered to gather input from stakeholders regarding what they found important and to what degree they were satisfied with certain aspects of services and potential outcomes. This approach originated in the behavioral and social validation research, which first made the case for subjective measurement of behavioral interventions (Kazdin, 1977; Schriner & Fawcett, 1988; Wolf, 1978). The Social Validation Survey instrument used in this project was developed in Pennsylvania by VanDenBerg, Beck, and Pierce (1992) and was originally based on the work of Wolf (1978). The instrument was obtained, and the survey was conducted, with slight changes based on an item analysis of the original data (Gillespie, 1993). The revised survey was then administered in southeastern Ohio. Stakeholders were asked a series of questions regarding the importance and satisfaction levels associated with various service issues.

One hundred and ninety-two stakeholders of child and family services were selected for participation in the survey. In all, 95 responses were received from a variety of stakeholders (e.g., children, parents, judges, mental health professionals, social service professionals, influential community members). The overall goal was to identify issues that stakeholders deemed most important to include these issues in the final measure.

Use of a Theoretical and Conceptual Scheme

Because of the divergent processes that occur during mental health intervention, a variety of measurement methods have been used as a way of capturing the complexity of human functioning and change. When multiple assessment methods are used, the importance of different sources or content areas of outcome becomes an issue. A conceptual scheme (see Lambert, Ogles, & Masters, 1992) was used in this project to help prioritize among central elements of outcome measurement.

The conceptual scheme included four theoretical dimensions on which outcome instruments vary: (a) the content area addressed by the instrument, (b) the source of outcome ratings sampled by the instrument, (c) the outcome instrument's method or technology of data collection, and (d) the time orientation or stability of the instrument. For the Ohio Scales, we used the scheme as the basic underlying model for conceptualizing the important sources, contents, and methods for collecting outcome data.

Research Input

To include the perspective of empirical research, studies investigating the effectiveness of mental health services for children and youth were also examined. This review focused on the instruments used to evaluate outcome and identified areas of outcome thought important to assess. Although the focus of this project did not include all areas of assessment, reviewing several well-designed studies helped to ascertain the most important domains of assessment to include in an initial outcome instrument. We identified and examined several studies investigating the effectiveness of mental health services for children and youth (e.g., Bickman et al., 1995; Duchnowski, Johnson, Hall, Kutash, & Friedman, 1993; Evans, Dollard, Huz, & Rahn, 1990; Kutash, Duchnowski, Johnson, & Rugs, 1993; Stroul & Friedman, 1986). For example, Duchnowski et al. (1993) describe their multisource, multimethod data collection strategy, which included assessment instruments from five domains: (1) demographic data, (2) a history of services received, (3) family characteristics and functioning, (4) emotional and behavioral problems and competence, and (5) academic achievement (including IQ). A variety of well-established instruments were selected to assess various aspects of these domains to "obtain an ecological overview of the youth and their families" (p. 18; Duchnowski et al., 1993). Although the focus of this project did not include all areas of assessment, reviewing several well-designed studies helped to ascertain the most important domains of assessment to include in an initial outcome instrument.

The assessment of outcome within children's behavioral health services is also complicated by the need to include multiple sources of outcome. Children's outcome assessment often includes the perspective of multiple sources (e.g., parents, youth, agency worker, and teacher; Cross, McDonald, & Lyons, 1997). Especially when examining the effectiveness of services for youth with serious emotional disturbances, the involvement of multiple child-serving systems necessitates the gathering of outcome from multiple points of view (Burchard & Shaefer, 1992).

Summary of Conceptualization

Based on our consideration of assessment in resource-deprived settings, input from stakeholders, review of current studies and instruments, and using a conceptual scheme of outcome assessment, a list of desirable characteristics for the assessment of clinical outcomes was developed:

1. Measurement instruments need to be pragmatic in terms of time, expense, and clinical utility. The practical constraints of service provision must be considered when developing useful outcome instruments (Rosenberg, 1979).
2. Current mental health care practices require increased involvement of paraprofessionals in assessment. This necessitates measures that require minimal professional training for interpretation. Similarly, instruments are needed that provide immediate and understandable results for parents and children receiving services.
3. Effective outcome assessment devices for youth should include input from multiple sources (Lambert, Christensen, & DeJulio, 1983; Ogles, Lambert, & Masters, 1996; VanDenBerg et al. 1992). Information from the youth as well as their parents and service provider can create a more comprehensive clinical picture. In addition, the different sources of input provide an index of the authenticity of the youth's self-report information. Multiple sources are also important, given the growing emphasis on consumer satisfaction with treatment and involvement of parents and children in the treatment planning process (Barth, 1986; Friesen, Koren, & Koroloff, 1992).
4. Multiple content areas of outcome should be considered. Potential content areas included: overall well-being or hopefulness, severity of problems, life functioning,

satisfaction with services, family functioning, restrictiveness of living setting, school performance, and others. Including multiple content areas allows for the development of individual profiles necessary for individualized treatment planning. In addition, the assessment of multiple content areas helps to identify areas of change for youth who have multiple and severe problems. The assessment of client and family strengths is an area that may be especially useful (Burchard & Clarke, 1990; Cochran, 1987; Dunst, Trivette, & Deal, 1988; Friesen & Koroloff, 1990; Poertner & Ronnau, 1992). Unfortunately, many existing measures focus on the child's psychopathology but exclude their strengths. With many new programs that focus on developing individualized plans of intervention, or "wraparound" services, the child's strengths within his or her social context should be considered (Burchard & Clarke, 1990; Cochran, 1987; Dunst, Trivette, & Deal, 1988; Friesen & Koroloff, 1990).

5. Any outcome measures should be psychometrically sound. Although an emphasis on pragmatics is necessary, this emphasis should be counterbalanced by the need to develop instruments with demonstrated psychometric properties, including reliability, validity, and sensitivity to change (Kutash, Duchnowski, Johnson, & Rugs, 1993).

Based on this list of desirable characteristics for outcome assessment instruments, we began the process of developing practical (brief, inexpensive, understandable, easy to administer and score) measures of clinical outcome that could cover multiple content areas and provide input from multiple sources while attempting to maintain a level of psychometric integrity. Our final goal was a practical set of outcome instruments that would be useful for agencies and practitioners without the problems that accompany some research-based instruments (e.g., lengthy, difficult scoring, difficult to interpret, costly, time-consuming).

DEVELOPMENT OF THE INSTRUMENT

There are three parallel forms of the Ohio Scales completed by the youth's parent or primary caregiver (P-form), the youth (Y-form), and the youth's agency worker (W-form). This allows assessment of the client's current strengths and weaknesses from multiple perspectives. The youth form is designed for youth aged 12 to 18. The parent and agency worker versions are designed for youth aged 5 to 18.

Four content areas were selected for the final scale—problem severity, functioning, satisfaction, and hopefulness. Problem severity and functioning were included because of their frequent inclusion as important dimensions of outcome in studies of mental health interventions with children (e.g., Duchnowski et al., 1993) and frequent use in applied settings (Koch, Lewis, & McCall, 1998; Maruish, 1999). In addition, the problem severity (or symptom), hopefulness, and functioning domains were also selected because of their consistency with the phase model of therapy outcome proposed by Howard, Lueger, Maling, and Martinovich (1993). The phase model suggests that participants in treatment experience change in a succession of phases—remoralization, remediation, and rehabilitation. In short, the model proposes that consumers first gain hope (remoralization) in the early stages of treatment. This renewed hope is followed by an improvement in symptoms (remediation) with continued treatment. Finally, as treatment continues and symptoms continue to abate, the individual experiences improvement in life functioning (rehabilitation). Although the model was generated based on studies of outpatient psychotherapy with adults, the notion that families and youth may also improve in phases is appealing and must be investigated empirically.

The Problem Severity Scale was initially comprised of 44 items covering common problems reported by youth who receive behavioral health services. Later, in response to feedback from focus groups composed of consumers and service providers involved in the initial studies of the Ohio Scales, the Problem Severity Scale was shortened to 20 items. Items were selected based on a factor analysis of the original data set along with examination of the ability of the items to discriminate between clinical and community samples (Melendez, 2000). Correlations between the total scores for the long and short forms of the Problem Severity Scale fell in the range of .95 to .97, indicating that the two measures tap similar constructs. From this point, all discussion regarding the Problem Severity Scale will focus on the short version. Each item on the Problem Severity Scale is rated for severity/frequency (0 "Not at all" to 5 "All the time") on a 6-point scale. A total score is calculated by summing the ratings for all items and can range from 0 to 100. Problem severity is included on all three forms of the scale (youth, parent, and agency worker). The individual completing the form rates the youth (or self) for the past 30 days. Total scores are then calculated. There are no reverse scored items, and to date there are no subscale scores.

The Functioning Scale is comprised of 20 items designed to rate the youth's level of functioning in a variety of areas of daily activity (e.g., interpersonal relationships, recreation, self-direction, and motivation). Each item is rated on a 5-point scale (0 "Extreme troubles" to 4 "Doing very well"). The Functioning Scale provides a broader range of ratings, including "OK" and "Doing very well." This provides an opportunity for raters to identify areas of functional strength. The youth is rated on their "current functioning," and a total functioning score is calculated by summing the ratings for all 20 items and range from 0 to 80. There are no reverse-scored items and no subscales. Higher scores are indicative of better functioning. The Functioning Scale is included on all three forms of the scale (youth, parent, and agency worker).

Four additional items on the parent and youth forms tap levels of hopefulness and well-being either about parenting or self, or future, respectively. Agency workers do not rate this scale. Each of the items is rated on a 6-point scale. The total hopefulness score is calculated by summing the four items and can range from 4 to 24. Lower scores denote more hope.

Satisfaction with services was selected as the final content area, because it is frequently assessed in applied settings (Pratt & Moreland, 1996). We also felt agencies may be more inclined to assess outcome if they could replace their existing satisfaction measurement procedures with a brief instrument that assessed both satisfaction and other content areas. Four items assess satisfaction with and inclusion in behavioral health services on a 6-point scale (1 "Extremely satisfied" to 6 "Extremely dissatisfied"). The total satisfaction score is calculated by summing the four items and ranges from 4 to 24. Lower scores denote greater satisfaction. Satisfaction is only assessed from the youth and parent perspectives and is not included on the agency worker version of the scales.

The instrument is two pages long, placed on the front and back of a single sheet. The questions for problem severity and functioning are identical on the three parallel forms (youth, parent, agency worker). The satisfaction and hopefulness scales are slightly different depending on perspective (of parent or youth). On the front side of all three forms is the Problem Severity Scale, along with several demographic questions. The remaining scales are on the back of the page. Although other potential sources of outcome may be relevant (e.g., teachers), three sources were selected, because they represent the primary sources of outcome for mental health interventions with youth. Youth and parents rate all four scales (Problem Severity, Functioning, Satisfaction, and Hopefulness). Agency workers rate problem severity and functioning.

Because the Ohio Scales include multiple content areas, it is easily compartmentalized. In other words, an agency or clinician could choose to use just a selected content area rated by all three sources or one source using all content areas for their outcome measure. For example, one could choose to use only the youth self-report of problem severity combined with other measures for parent (e.g., Child Behavior Checklist) and therapist data collection (e.g., Child and Adolescent Functional Assessment Scale). The Ohio Scales includes multiple sources and contents to help avoid the need for different measures, yet the compartmentalization allows flexibility for the user. The Ohio Scales are also available in several languages, including Spanish (Mexican and Puerto Rican), Russian, Korean, Japanese, and Chinese. To date, the psychometric properties of these versions have not been verified. Various technologies for administration have also been developed, including scannable forms, telephone or Web-based entry, and point-of-view entry. These administration methods are available from vendors of the technology that are referenced on the Ohio Department of Mental Health Web site (http://www.mh.state.oh.us/initiatives/outcomes/outcomes.html).

PSYCHOMETRIC PROPERTIES

The psychometric evaluation of the original and short form of the Ohio Scales is summarized in the technical manual (Ogles, Melendez, Davis, & Lunnen, 1999) and in published format (Ogles, Melendez, Davis, & Lunnen, 2001), and is briefly summarized here. Additional data sets have been gathered since the technical manual was assembled. Some of this evidence is presented here. Evidence for reliability, validity, and sensitivity to change is presented.

Reliability

Internal Consistency. Internal consistency data has been evaluated for both clinical and community samples for all three perspectives (youth, parent, and agency worker). In addition, the initial evaluation of the Ohio Scales included an item analysis to evaluate the degree to which items within each scale correlated with the total score. Adjusted item-total correlations for all items within scales fell above .40, with two exceptions. Items with lower item–total correlations had low base rates of endorsement and were retained for their informative value. Alpha coefficients for the three scales by rater and averaged across samples are presented in Table 10.1.

TABLE 10.1
Average Internal Consistency Estimates (Cronbach's Alpha) for Each Scale by Rater

Scale	*Parent*	*Youth*	*Agency Worker*
Problem Severity	.91	.93	.86
Functioning	.93	.86	.95
Hopefulness	.77	.78	—
Satisfaction	.76	.77	—

TABLE 10.2
Average Two-Week Test–Retest Reliability Estimates for the Parent- and Youth-Rated Instruments

Scale	*Parent*	*Youth*
Problem Severity	.88	.72
Functioning	.77	.63
Hopefulness	.79	.74
Satisfaction	.67	.67

TABLE 10.3
Interrater Reliability Estimates Averaged for Graduate Students, Undergraduate Students, and Case Managers on Four Measures of Functioning Using Clinical Vignettes

Measure	*Standardized Vignettes*	*Random Clinical Forms*
CGAS	.77	.33
CAFAS	.90	.66
Ohio Scales	.88	.22
Vanderbilt	.86	.59

Note. CGAS = Children's Global Assessment Scale.

Test–Retest Reliability. Test–retest reliability (after two weeks) was evaluated for the parent and youth versions of the Ohio Scales. Test–retest reliability estimates for both parent and youth samples on four scales are presented in Table 10.2. As can be seen, the test–retest reliability was adequate though not exceptional for the satisfaction and functioning scales. Small *n*'s may have reduced the reliability coefficients for the youth sample.

Interrater Reliability. The interrater reliability was investigated for the agency worker version of the Functioning Scale using four undergraduate students, four graduate students, and four case managers who rated 20 cases as described on paper (10 sets of unmodified clinical intake paperwork and 10 standardized vignettes; Hodges & Wong, 1996). The raters used four measures of functioning, including the Ohio Scales Functioning Scale, the Child and Adolescent Functional Assessment Scale (CAFAS), the Vanderbilt Functioning Index, and the Children's Global Assessment Scale. More details regarding the study are available elsewhere (Ogles, Davis, & Lunnen, 1998).

To examine the interrater reliability, interrater correlations were calculated for each pair of undergraduates, graduates, and case managers, respectively. Correlations were then averaged (across measures and methods) to examine the influence of rater level of training on interrater reliability. Table 10.3 presents average correlations for each measure for the 10 standardized vignettes and the 10 randomly selected and unaltered clinical records. The vignettes were produced by Hodges and Wong (1996) for training on the CAFAS. The clinical forms were basic first contact data for 10 different children who were seen by several different clinicians at a community mental health center. The material used for rating included a brief set of intake paperwork completed by the clinician.

Overall, the level of training did not influence interrater reliability. However, the standardized format of the vignettes substantially improved reliability. When raters examined and rated the unmodified clinical paperwork, reliability was significantly attenuated (see Table 10.3). The clinical forms varied widely in their degree of completeness, accuracy, and adequacy. As a result, raters had a difficult time knowing how to rate all 20 functioning items of the Ohio Scales based on the incomplete information. This suggests that a standardized, comprehensive method of data collection and presentation may be needed in applied settings to obtain reliable ratings. For example, Hodges and Wong (1996) developed a standardized telephone interview for collecting and organizing information to be used when making CAFAS ratings. This or another similar structured format for gathering information may improve interrater agreement through minimizing differences in available information.

Validity

Several analytic strategies were used to examine the validity of the scales. Measures were correlated with other measures of symptoms, functioning, and satisfaction, respectively. Ratings of clinical samples were compared with community samples to establish the ability of the measures to discriminate between samples. Factor analysis was also used to examine the construct validity.

The parent-rated Problem Severity Scale was correlated with the Connor's Parent Rating Scale ($r = .89, p < .05$) and the Child Behavior Checklist ($r = .85, p < .05$). Parent-rated functioning was correlated with the Child Behavior Checklist ($r = .77$, $p < .001$) and the Vanderbilt Functioning Index ($r = .54, p < .001$). The youth-rated Problem Severity and Functioning Scales were correlated with ratings on the youth self-report ($r = .82, p < .05$) and ($r = .46, p < .05$), respectively. The agency worker Functioning Scale ratings were correlated with the Progress Evaluation Scales (Ihilevich & Gleser, 1982) and the Child and Adolescent Functional Assessment Scale ($r = .58, p < .001$) and ($r = -.61, p < .001$), respectively. The parent- and youth-rated Satisfaction Scales were correlated with the Client Satisfaction Scale (CSQ–8) ($r = -.68, p < .05$) and ($r = -.52, p < .05$), respectively (correlations are negative, because the scales are scored in reverse directions). The Hopefulness scale has not been evaluated for concurrent validity.

Additional evidence for validity is obtained through comparing the community and clinical samples. As can be seen in Table 10.4, community and clinical samples are significantly different (Ogles et al., 1999). Additional analyses within the community

TABLE 10.4
Means and Standard Deviation on the Ohio Scales for Community and Clinical Samples.*

Population: Form	*N*	*Problems M (SD)*	*Functioning M (SD)*	*Hope M (SD)*
Community				
Youth	166	18.18 (15.04)	61.07 (12.99)	9.61 (3.78)
Parent	329	10.29 (9.88)	63.95 (12.67)	8.31 (3.52)
Agency worker	40	17.58 (9.62)	67.03 (9.01)	NA
Clinical				
Youth	76	36.31 (20.96)	55.09 (13.42)	10.57 (4.35)
Parent	137	39.35 (17.71)	41.65 (16.03)	13.81 (5.26)
Agency worker	134	41.04 (14.40)	33.94 (12.91)	NA

*These numbers are the combined data for multiple samples described in the technical manual.

sample were also conducted and are described in the technical manual for the Ohio Scales, which indicate that youth who have participated in various services (e.g., mental health services, classes for students with behavioral difficulties) have higher scores on the Problem Severity and Functioning Scales as rated by both youth and parents (Ogles, Melendez, Davis, & Lunnen, 1998). In addition, the construct validity of the Ohio Scales has been examined through factor analysis both in the technical manual and with an independent sample (Baize, 2001).

In the technical manual, factor analyses were conducted using the original parent-rated Problem Severity, Functioning, and Hopefulness Scales. The analysis of the Problem Severity Scale resulted in a three-factor solution with and Externalizing, Internalizing and Delinquency factors. With the Ohio Scales short form, Baize (2001) found the same three factors—Externalizing (Items 1–6 and 10–11), Internalizing (Items 12–20), and Delinquency (Items 7–9). Baize (2000) also found, however, that this factor structure was consistent for parent, youth, and agency worker ratings. The factor analysis of the Functioning Scale in the technical manual identifies two factors—a central factor of functioning with all of the items except the two of the three items on the second factor (Items 3, 13, 17) which included items that are more relevant to adolescents. Baize (2000) found a quite different factor structure in an analysis of parent, youth, and agency worker ratings on the Functioning Scale and concluded, "In general, the factor analysis does not provide a suitable basis for constructing reliable scales and a cautious researcher or user should consider using the full set of items as a single scale, as designed" (p. 8).

Agreements of ratings were also examined within the first wave of the Ohio Department of Mental Health Consumer Outcomes System (Ohio Department of Mental Health, 2003). Youth, parent and agency worker ratings were correlated with one another using both the Problem Severity and Functioning Scales to examine the degree of concordance in scores. For problem severity, parents and youth ($r = .46, p < .001$), parents and agency worker ($r = .62, p < .001$), and youth and agency worker ($r = .52, p < .001$) were significantly correlated. Similarly, functioning scores for parents and youth ($r = .37, p < .001$), parents and agency worker ($r = .59, p < .001$), and youth and agency worker ($r = .39, p < .001$) were smaller yet significantly correlated. It is important that these correlations might be considered in the context of other instruments and studies. For example, Achenbach, McConaughty, and Howell (1987) examined cross-informant consistently using meta-analytic procedures. They found modest agreement at best ($r = .25$) between parent and youth when averaging across a small number of studies.

Sensitivity to Change

The sensitivity of the Problem Severity and Functioning Scales has been examined in several samples. In the initial Ohio Scales validation study, case managers rated youth problems and functioning twice, with a 4-month interval between ratings. Ratings were also collected for the seven-item, Progress Evaluation Scales (Ihilevich & Gleser, 1982). All youth were participating in behavioral health services. Changes in scores on the Problem Severity and Functioning Scales were then correlated with changes in scores on the Progress Evaluation Scales. Change scores on both the Problem Severity ($r = .54, p < .05$) and Functioning Scales ($r = .56, p < .05$) were significantly correlated with change scores on the Progress Evaluation Scales. This suggests that changes on an instrument that has been used to assess outcome co-occur with changes on the Ohio Scales.

TABLE 10.5
Means and Standard Deviation, and Significance Test for Three Sources of Information in Content Areas From Intake to 3-Month Assessment

Rater *Scale*	*Intake* *Mean (SD)*	*3 months* *Mean (SD)*	*T*	*Significance*
Parent ($n = 25$)				
Problem Severity	69.4 (32.8)	50.0 (32.0)	3.64	.001
Functioning	41.6 (15.8)	45.0 (14.2)	−1.24	.225
Hopefulness	12.8 (4.84)	11.9 (4.17)	.854	.401
Agency Worker ($n = 26$)				
Problem Severity	57.5 (24.1)	41.6 (18.0)	3.06	.005
Functioning	39.3 (12.8)	40.3 (11.9)	−.634	.532
Youth ($n = 7$)				
Problem Severity	60.3 (30.8)	36.7 (23.2)	2.35	.057
Functioning	50.6 (14.7)	47.0 (13.7)	.624	.556
Well-being	11.4 (3.30)	10.0 (2.58)	1.59	.162

In addition, sensitivity to change was examined through tracking changes occurring as the result of treatment in two samples. In the first sample, children ($n = 53$) who were enrolled in community support services at four offices within two agencies were enrolled in a longitudinal study. Families that agreed to participate were asked to complete the Ohio Scales at intake and every 3 months thereafter while they were receiving services up to a 1-year follow-up. Parents completed all four content areas of the Ohio Scales, agency workers rated the youth using the Problem Severity and Functioning Scales, and youth who were 12 or older completed the four content areas of the youth self-report version of the Ohio Scales.

Although the number of dropouts was high, we conducted analyses to examine change in problem severity, hopefulness, and functioning during the first 3 months. Means, standard deviations, and significance tests for the measures are presented in Table 10.5. As can be seen, the parents, case managers, and youth all reported significant changes in problem severity. No changes were noted, however, in functioning or hopefulness/well-being. In a second sample of youth who were receiving wraparound services, similar changes were observed over the first 3 months of treatment (Hatfield et al., 2002). Finally, examination of youth self-report change while enrolled in outpatient therapy, using the Functioning Scale, was examined for a large group of adolescents ($n = 757$) and resulted in evidence for steady yet small changes over the duration of treatment (Ogles et al., 1998)

Qualitative Ratings of Measure Pragmatics

In addition to examining the reliability, validity, and sensitivity to change, we gathered qualitative ratings of the short form to assess parent and case manager views of the instrument. Twenty-seven case managers at a mental health agency located in a large urban area were presented with the short form of the Ohio Scales and asked to make qualitative judgments (Melendez, 2000). Each case manager rated five current clients using the newly shortened agency worker version of the scale. In addition, they were asked to collect five parent and youth ratings using the Ohio Scales–Short Form. The average time taken to fill out the short form (included the problem severity and functioning scales) was just over 9 minutes, whereas the modal response was 6 minutes. Participants were then asked to make qualitative comments about the scale

TABLE 10.6
Comparison of Case Manager Ratings of Minority and Majority Youth

Scale	*Group*	*Mean*	*SD*
Problem Severity	Majority	40.88*	12.52
	Minority	41.16	15.91
Functioning	Majority	33.80	12.84
	Minority	34.05	13.05

*$n = 135$; no significant differences between means evident.

in relationship to other measures. In comparison to instruments that they used in the past, participants reported that the Ohio Scales–Short Form was easier to use and understand, quicker, more efficient, and useful. Three of the 27 participants reported that the short form was not as detailed as other measures, but two of these preferred the quickness and ease of use over detail. One respondent criticized the lack of items that focused on "mental health concerns," such as thought problems. The majority of users endorsed the short form as an instrument for assessing progress, outcomes, and functioning in a practical, concise, and clear manner. Similarly, a small sample of parents from an urban setting ($n = 22$) made qualitative ratings of the short form after completing ratings of their children. The items offended none of the 22 parents. Most of the parents (21 out of 22) understood the questions, and the majority felt comfortable responding to them (82%).

The California Department of Mental Health (2001) conducted a pilot study using the Ohio Scales to investigate the possibility of changing the measures that were used as part of their performance outcome measurement system. They asked a group of mental health system administrators and clinicians to rate the Ohio Scales in comparison to the existing measures of outcome. The sample of 107 rated the Ohio Scales as practical, easy to understand, culturally unbiased, strengths based, easily integrated with data management and clinical work, and preferable to the existing measures.

Rating Differences in a Diverse Sample

Because the original validation of the Ohio Scales used samples from southeastern Ohio, little information regarding diverse groups was available. As a result, a set of data were collected from a metropolitan site (Cleveland) to investigate the possibility of any systematic differences in scores based on race (Melendez, 2000). In this sample, 27 case managers rated five clients each. Total scores for problem severity and functioning for minority (predominantly African American) and majority youth were compared to see if differences existed. No significant differences existed between the case manager ratings of majority ($n = 62$) and minority ($n = 73$) youth. Similarly, data collection from youth and parents from the urban location revealed no differences between majority and minority group ratings by parents or youth report (see Tables 10.6 and 10.7). Finally, there were no differences in hopefulness or satisfaction with services between majority and minority group ratings by parents and youth report.

Summary

Based on the current evidence, the Ohio Scales appear to be well on the way toward meeting the original set of goals. That is, a brief, practical set of measures representing youth, parent, and agency worker views of multiple content areas were created that

TABLE 10.7
Comparison of Parent Ratings of Minority and Majority Youth

Scale	*Group*	*Mean*	*SD*
Problem severity	Majority	38.42*	19.97
	Minority	41.67	17.21
Functioning	Majority	42.07	14.08
	Minority	38.17	18.85

*$n = 38$; no significant differences between means evident.

are reliable, valid, and sensitive to change. Practically speaking, the work on the Ohio Scales is an effort to establish the psychometric properties of 10 separate scales (youth-rated functioning, problem severity, hopefulness, and satisfaction; parent-rated functioning, problem severity, hopefulness, and satisfaction; and agency worker–rated functioning and problem severity). As a result, many studies will be needed to verify that the instruments are practical as well as valid for the many potential uses. To date, the evidence for the problem severity scale is most firmly in place, with solid evidence of reliability, validity and sensitivity to change for all three sources. Data regarding the validity of the Functioning Scale is also significant, with good evidence of reliability and validity. Questions about the sensitivity of the Functioning Scales to change must be investigated further. In addition, the youth-rated Functioning Scale could also benefit from further validation. The Satisfaction Scale is reliable and correlated with another measure of satisfaction. Further data would be useful to firmly establish the psychometric properties of the four-item Satisfaction Scale. Finally, the four-item Hopefulness Scale requires significant further study. In short, the establishment of psychometric properties for the various sources and contents of the Ohio Scales is just beginning and must continue so that it may provide a firm foundation of support for their use.

USING THE OHIO SCALES FOR TREATMENT PLANNING

Like many measures (such as those presented in this book), the Ohio Scales can be readily used in treatment. The Ohio Scales were designed to be pragmatic to specifically facilitate repeated administration as part of an outcome assessment plan for the individual client. However, the Ohio Scales may also be used for treatment planning, evaluation, research, and other purposes.

The methods for using the Ohio Scales in treatment planning are not necessarily unique. Indeed, many instruments may be used in a similar fashion to inform the treatment plan. The methods described below are discussed in greater detail in several publications that provide methods for using any of a variety of outcome measures for treatment planning and outcome assessment (Maruish, 1999, 2002; Ogles, Lambert, & Fields, 2002; Ogles et al., 1996; Ogles & Owens, in press).

In many clinical settings, the development of a treatment plan is governed by state regulations, insurance requirements, or both, for payment. These regulations and requirements often necessitate the formulation of a standard format treatment plan within a specified period of time (e.g., within 30 days of the first contact). Administration of the Ohio Scales prior to the first clinical contact can help inform the initial assessment and treatment plan by helping the clinician to assess critical issues, narrow in on target problems, identify client areas of strength, and establish unique goals for treatment.

Given the brevity, yet wide range of assessment areas of the Ohio Scales, agency workers may administer and score the measure just prior to the initial intake interview. The completed forms can be used by the clinician to direct the interview and to inform the treatment planning. In addition, the clinician may use the results to provide both the parents and youth immediate and understandable feedback regarding the youth's current problems, as well as strengths and weaknesses in functioning.

Critical Issues

The most immediate use of the information on the completed Ohio Scales is to note responses to critical items. Prior to the initial clinical contact, the clinician can look at the youth and parent responses on items that may indicate the need for immediate intervention. Endorsement of items (by either the youth or parent rating of the youth) such as "hurting self (cutting or scratching self, taking pills)," "talking or thinking about death," or "using drugs or alcohol" will require prompt clinical attention and a more focused line of verbal assessment in the interview. For example, the youth may need further assessment for serious suicidal or homicidal risk or for disturbed thought processes.

Of course, questions concerning these issues are often routinely asked in an initial clinical interview. The addition of a standardized rating by the youth and parent, however, documents the level of client concern, establishes a baseline for later comparison (outcome), and standardizes a portion of the initial assessment.

Target Problems

A quick scan of the Problem Severity Scale on the front page of the Ohio Scales will allow the clinician to quickly identify problems that are reported as occurring most frequently, as well as identify significant differences or agreement between the parent and the youth self-report forms. Noting the problems before the interview may guide the line of questioning in the verbal assessment. The central problems noted on the forms may also be included as primary and secondary problems in the treatment plan, because they are likely to be the most relevant to the treatment. The targeted problems may include a cluster of items (e.g., depression-related items) or a single item (e.g., arguing). Additional symptom measures may be administered at this point if there is a need for more detailed and specific assessment (e.g., measures specific to disorders such as obsessive compulsive disorder, encopresis, depression, or attention deficit hyperactivity disorder). A brief look at the first 11 items on the Problem Severity Scale in comparison to the last 9 items also provides a quick and gross snapshot of whether the problem is more in line with an externalizing (first 11 items) or an internalizing (last 9 items) set of problems.

The multiple forms also permits input from multiple sources. Given the growing emphasis on consumer involvement, gathering parent and child ratings is an important part of seeking their input to the treatment planning process (Friesen, Koren, & Koroloff, 1992; Lambert, Christensen, & DeJulio, 1983). Because the items on the Problem Severity Scale and the Functioning Scale are worded identically across different raters, the clinician can easily compare specific items and incorporate information from both sources into the treatment plan. Thus, input from multiple sources would likely lead to a treatment plan in which both the parent and youth contributes to the therapeutic goals.

In addition, the clinician should note differences in ratings of severity between youth and parents. Discrepancies in ratings may provide information regarding the nature of the problems (e.g., internalizing versus externalizing) or preferred treatment approach. For example, if parents are reporting more frequent problems than the youth, clinicians may tailor the treatment plan to include the parents as key participants in treatment.

Level of Severity

In addition to using the individual item responses when developing treatment plans, total scale scores may also be useful to establish a standardized measure of symptom severity and subsequent improvement. There are several ways in which this may be done. First, the youth's total scale score may serve as a baseline measurement used to set specific goals. For example, one potential treatment goal may be for the youth self-report score, the parent-report score, or both on the problem severity scale to decrease by 10 points. Another way in which total scores may be used in treatment planning is by comparing the youth's self-report or parent-report scores to average scores in the comparison sample. This gives the clinician an overall indication of the severity of the youth's score by comparing it to a sample of youth who are not receiving services. For example, a parent who rated his or her child using the Problem Severity Scale and obtained a total scale score of 45 could note that the score was above the average (39.35) for parents of children receiving clinical services, and well above the average (10.29) of parent ratings of youth in the community who were not receiving behavioral health services. Means and standard deviations for a community sample and a clinical sample are presented in Table 10.4.

In addition, a figure can be developed that allows clinicians to record the youth's total scale score (see the example included with the case study later in this chapter). The horizontal lines of the chart indicate potential cutoff scores to identify youth with significant problems when compared to a nonclinical community sample. Finally, ranges of scores that identify current level of severity can be used to assess the current level of severity in problems or functioning.

For the Problem Severity Scale, the bottom line indicates the average parent rating within a community sample. (Youth who reported having received mental health services, had been arrested, or were assigned to a special class because of behavioral problems were excluded when calculating the average.) The middle line represents one standard deviation above this mean (total score = 20), and the top line represents two standard deviations above this mean (total score = 30). Youth whose parents rate them as having more severe or frequent problems than the top line are considered to have more clinically severe problem behaviors.

Similarly for the Functioning Scale: The top line of the chart indicates the average parent rating of functioning in a community sample, which used the same exclusion criteria previously mentioned. However, the next line moving down represents one standard deviation below the community sample mean (total score = 52), and the third line represents two standard deviations below this mean (total score = 40). Youth whose parents rate them as functioning more poorly than either the first or second cutoff are considered to have clinically meaningful impairment in functioning.

Data are also available for comparing agency worker ratings to a sample of children who are not receiving services (see Table 10.4). Four case managers were asked to think of 10 youth each who were not receiving services and to rate the youth. The ratings were conducted independent of any interview or other data gathering by the caseworkers. Nevertheless, these data provided a start for a community sample of agency worker ratings. Unfortunately, many rater-based assessment measures do not include normative data. For example, the Hamilton Rating Scale for Depression, a measure frequently used in empirical studies, does not currently include a nonclinical normative sample (Grundy, Lambert, & Grundy, 1996; Grundy, Lunnen, Lambert, Ashton, & Tovey, 1994). Consequently, these data were collected for the Ohio Scales to initiate the process of developing a rater-based nonclinical normative sample that could be compared to clinical samples. Clearly, additional data is necessary to establish a more dependable data set for comparison.

Identifying Strengths

After identifying critical items, scanning the Problem Severity Scale for commonly occurring items, noting discrepancies between parent and youth ratings, and examining the severity of total scores, specific responses to the functioning scale on the back page of the Ohio Scales should be evaluated. Functioning items that are rated highly, such as a "3—ok functioning" or "4—Doing very well," may be noted as specific attributes or activities that can be included in the treatment plan as the youth's personal strengths. These strengths can then be incorporated into the treatment plan. The clinician may also note any specific functioning questions that may be quickly responsive to treatment and therefore potentially helpful later in treatment when working on target problems. For example, improved participation in appropriate recreational activities or hobbies may lead to additional improvements in self-esteem or interpersonal relationships with peers or family.

One essential component for family involvement in children's mental health services is the parent's optimism and hopefulness about being able to parent and care for their child, as well as the likelihood of the child improving with treatment. When families seek services, they are often emotionally overwhelmed by the challenges of raising a child with serious emotional and behavioral problems. Similarly, the youth may lack hope about the future. The Ohio Scales Hopefulness Scale provides a method to briefly assess the parents' and youth's outlook on the future. Clinician's may incorporate parent or youth report of the presence of hopefulness as a strength to be used in treatment, or lack of hopefulness as a target for treatment.

Summary

Although the Ohio Scales were primarily developed for outcome assessment, they may also be used to identify critical issues, target problems, level of severity or impairment, and functional strengths at the initiation of treatment. In addition, the identical items on each form make it possible to easily compare ratings by the three sources (parent, youth, agency worker). These bits of information can be integrated into the treatment plan and goals with little effort. In the most structured form, a protocol could be developed that integrates the measurement results into a standard initial assessment form and process. In a more flexible format, the scales may be used at the clinician's discretion to supplement their routine verbal intake process. Of course the inclusion of a measure adds to a verbal clinical intake by providing standardized information in comparison to community-and agency-specific samples. In addition, once the scales are administered at intake, they provide a natural baseline for later comparison to assess outcome.

USING THE OHIO SCALES FOR OUTCOME ASSESSMENT

The Ohio Scales is an instrument that can be successfully utilized to measure, monitor, or manage outcome of mental health services for youth. In addition, the Ohio Scales could be used to in an aggregate fashion for evaluation or research regarding the effectiveness of mental health interventions for youth.

Measuring Outcome

In its most elementary form, the assessment of outcome occurs independently of the clinical process. For example, in the typical evaluation of mental health services, data are gathered regarding client outcomes without necessarily providing immediate or ongoing information to the clinician or client. The data are used to inform treatment much later—once the data are gathered, aggregated and summarized in a report or published article format. Once summarized, the data can be used to inform the treatment for later clients. The data are not typically immediately available, however, to modify treatment for the current client. In this method, the main purpose of gathering the data is for later aggregation.

A variety of instruments have been developed over the years to measure outcome in this way (see Ogles et al., 1996; Ogles et al., 2002; Maruish, 1999; and measures in this volume). Fewer outcome measures are available for use with children and adolescents, yet enough are available that an agency or clinician must have some basis for deciding among various measures to use. To help guide the process for developing or selecting outcome measures, several authors have developed categorical or conceptual models of outcome measurement. For example, Cross, McDonald, and Lyons (1997) divided child mental health measures into eight categories: symptoms, behavioral problems, life functioning, family environment and behavior, self-esteem, measures for young children, client satisfaction, and other quality of care. They go on to describe six principles that might guide selection of measures, depending on the needs of the organization, and provide information regarding several existing measures. Lambert et al. (1992), described a broad conceptual model for categorizing outcome measures. They discussed four characteristics of measures, including the content, the source, the methodology or technology of data collection, and the time frame of each instrument. They also presented a method for examining and selecting measures using the conceptual model. McGlynn (1996) identified six primary outcome domains: clinical status, functional status, quality of life, adverse events, satisfaction with care, and expenditures. Finally, Rosenblatt and Attkisson (1993) outlined a conceptual framework for outcomes related to services for individuals with severe mental disorders. The three-dimensional model includes the domain of outcome assessment, the respondent, and the social context of the assessment. The domain of outcome assessment can include one of four areas of treatment outcome: clinical status, functional status, life satisfaction and fulfillment, and safety and health.

In perhaps the most comprehensive effort to date, Ciarlo, Brown, Edwards, Kiresuk, and Newman (1986) summarized a set of guidelines for the development, selection, or use of outcome measures. These guidelines were developed by a panel of experts who were assembled via funding from the National Institute of Mental Health (see Newman, Ciarlo, & Carpenter, 1999; and Newman, Rugh, & Ciarlo, Vol. 1, chap. 6). The guidelines present a mix of instrument characteristics, including five categories: application of the measures (e.g., relevance to the target group), methods and procedures (e.g., simple methods), psychometric features (e.g., reliability), cost, and utility

TABLE 10.8
Ohio Scales' Characteristics Matched With the Newman, Ciarlo, and Carpenter (1999) Guidelines for Selecting an Outcome Assessment Instrument

	Guideline	*Ohio Scales Characteristics*
1	Relevance to target group	Broad measure of severity and functioning that is applicable to a wide range of children receiving services. Weakness—may need more specific outcome for some target groups (e.g., children with enuresis, encopresis, eating disorders, etc.)
2	Simple, teachable	Short, easy to score (just sum the numbers); no reverse-scored items; no transformation of scores, no subscales to date
3	Objective referents	Items rated for frequency/severity, community comparison groups available
4	Multiple respondents	Parent, child, agency worker
5	Process of identifying	Only through potential changes through stages that relate to the content areas of the scales
6	Psychometric strengths	Evidence for reliability, validity, and sensitivity to change described in this chapter
7	Cost	Modest one-time fee for unlimited use ($0–$500 depending on the organization)
8	Understanding by nonprofessionals	Easily understood by nonprofessionals; parents and community support workers involved in the instrument development
9	Easy feedback	Quick administration and scoring facilitate prompt feedback that is easily provided
10	Useful in services	Brevity, understandability, simplicity of use, and low cost all facilitate utility
11	Compatibility with theories	Compatible with assessing the outcome of mental health services in a broad way, also potential to assess a phase theory of change

considerations (useful, easy feedback). The guidelines are used to examine the various features of a variety of outcome instruments and to guide selection of an instrument for use in an agency, practice, or evaluation or research project.

The Ohio Scales are matched with the Ciarlo et al. (1986) guidelines in Table 10.8. As can be seen, the Ohio Scales match especially well with the guidelines that target practical relevance in terms of administration, cost, and application. Many instruments have been used to evaluate outcome over the years, and the Ohio Scales are also available to measure outcome. The practical nature of the Ohio Scales, however, allows them to be quickly scored and examined during the clinical hour. This possibility makes it possible to use the Ohio Scales to inform the treatment of the current client rather than solely as a means of evaluating outcome after treatment in an aggregate fashion. This ongoing monitoring of client progress is the primary reason for the Ohio Scales development.

Monitoring Outcome

Continuous treatment monitoring is a tool that has the potential to greatly aid clinicians in their practice. One of the most important ways in which treatment monitoring can be beneficial occurs when practitioners receive feedback concerning the current level of the client's problem severity or functioning and the progress that has been obtained since treatment started. This method of use goes beyond the gathering of data for later aggregation to the immediate use of the data to monitor treatment progress. When practitioners receive feedback obtained from outcome measures, such as the Ohio Scales, they can use the data to inform treatment decisions, such as the need to modify, supplement, or end treatment.

The Ohio Scales can be used as the central outcome measure in a treatment monitoring system. The easy administration and good reliability of the Ohio Scales allows the instrument to be used as frequently as the clinician would like. Over time, it is then possible to track any clinical change in an objective manner, free from the difficulties of relying on memory. There are several ways in which the Ohio Scales can be used to produce valuable outcome monitoring information, which is described next.

Change in Total Scores. Viewing scale total scores, it is possible to see the client's overall amount of improvement. Using the Reliable Change Index, developed by Jacobson and Truax (1991), a change of ten points on the problem severity scale or eight points on the Functioning Scale would be indicative of reliable improvement (or deterioration if scores worsen). In addition, total scale scores can be compared to similar community samples. For example, the clinician can examine scale total scores at intake and after 3 months to see if there were changes in overall problem severity or functioning. Using the figure presented earlier, the clinician can track change over time from the perspective of the youth, parent, and agency worker using the same graph. Total problem severity and functioning scores for all three sources (child, parent, and agency worker) can be charted on the two figures. The lines on the figure, however, represent the means and cutoff scores for parent ratings in the comparison sample.

Once the current scores are plotted on the graph, change at the current time can be compared with the initiation of treatment, across sources of the ratings (youth, parent, and agency worker), and with community norms. Thus, relative change (change since intake), concordance of change (degree to which all three sources see and agree about the change), and clinical meaningfulness of the change (degree to which the change moves the child into the range of scores for the community) can all be examined.

If a particular youth is not improving as expected, then the clinician can make a closer examination of the appropriateness of the current treatment plan and alter it accordingly. Similarly, the clinician might choose to seek out peer consultation on the case. Clients who get worse in therapy are much more likely to prematurely drop out of treatment. With the aid of information provided by the Ohio Scales, clinicians can potentially be warned of lack of progress and take steps to both prevent dropout and alter the progress of treatment.

Change in Items. In addition to tracking change in overall problem severity scores, it can also be beneficial to track changes on individual items of the Ohio Scales. For example, it may be useful in some cases to selectively track specific problem areas that were identified for clinical work. In this case, the client completes the all of the scales, but responses to relevant questions (items), in addition to changes in the total scores, are tracked. This allows greater individualization of the treatment goals and outcome, because each child will have a unique set of target problems that are identified by selected items. Tracking change with the total score facilitates standardization, aggregation, and comparison with community norms. Tracking change on selected treatment targets and the items that represent them facilitates individualization and idiographic treatment planning and outcome assessment.

One way that this can be beneficial to clinicians is through the development of dose–effect curves (Howard, Kopta, Krause, & Orlinsky, 1986). The dose–effect relationship predicts how well a client is expected to improve after a certain number of sessions. This is called patient profiling, and the benefits of this approach can be very important to the practicing clinician. By using patient profiling to predict improvement across treatment on the basis of intake clinical characteristics, clinicians can also begin to predict, with reasonable accuracy, which clients will follow the predicted dose–effect curve and which will not. Therefore, based on the specific client characteristics, clinicians can know which dose–effect curve a particular client can be expected to follow and thereby how much change should be expected with that individual. If the client is not improving as expected, then the therapist can be alerted to this and either begin a further assessment to investigate the reasons or alter the treatment if deemed necessary. Lambert et al. (2001) found that clinicians who are alerted (through a treatment monitoring system) to clients who are getting worse are better able to help those clients make clinically significant improvement.

In using a system similar to the one described, practitioners can use a treatment monitoring strategy to help guide them in their decision-making processes. Lambert et al. (1998) suggested that using such a system aids in decision making in various ways. If the therapist's treatment monitoring strategy shows that a patient has returned to normal functioning, termination, or a spacing of sessions, might be considered. A lack of progress might result in consultation and revision of the treatment plan. Progress, but failure to achieve critical results, might indicate the need for continued treatment. The scores from the Ohio Scales would, of course, not be the only factor in treatment plan decisions, but could provide a valuable source of information that the therapist might consider in making those treatment plan decisions.

Change in Hopefulness. One key ingredient for family involvement in behavioral health services is the parents' hopefulness about being able to parent and care for their child. When families seek services, they are often physically tired and emotionally discouraged by the challenges of raising a child with serious emotional and behavioral problems. Similarly, the youth may lack hope about the future. Because of this, the Ohio Scales incorporates a four-item scale to track hopefulness over time. Clinician's may find useful information about the parents' or youth's level of hopefulness over time by tracking changes in the hopefulness total scale score. The clinician may also examine the satisfaction scale to see if the client is satisfied with behavioral health services.

Compare Change in Scales. In constructing case conceptualizations, the clinician may also find it useful to use scale totals (or even specific item responses) to better understand theoretically how a client is improving. Specifically, the clinician may look at the improvement over time in the Problem Severity Scale versus the Functioning Scale. Does it seem with a particular youth that problems have been disrupting functioning and an improvement in the Problem Severity Scale precedes an improvement in the Functioning Scale? Or, does it seem with a particular case that functioning improvement provides help with problems? The Ohio Scales can provide specific information on an individual's changes to help address issues such as these. Incidentally, the researcher may also be interested in the pattern of change in various content scores. As mentioned earlier, Howard et al. (1993) proposed a phase model of change for adult clients in outpatient treatment. A phase model of change may also be relevant for youth. With data from multiple contents, patterns or processes of change may be examined to identify the potential paths of progress for youth.

Summary. The Ohio Scales can be used to track change at the individualized level through examination of central targets (items) or in a more standardized fashion (by using total scores). In addition, the multiple sources and contents allow for rich clinical comparisons to inform both treatment planning and treatment monitoring.

Managing Outcome

Outcome data from the Ohio Scales may also be used to manage outcome. When measuring outcome, the data are gathered but are not used for the current client. When monitoring outcome, the data are used by the clinician to inform treatment by tracking client progress. For the management of outcome, the data are used by an administrator, supervisor, or other third party to help manage the case. A practical example of this is using Ohio Scales data to assist with clinical supervision.

Informing Supervision. When therapists chart client progress for each of the clients in their caseload, the data can also inform the supervisory process. Supervisors can review the outcome data for each therapist's caseload to help prioritize clients for review in supervision. For example, examination of the outcome data for a particular therapist or case manager may result in the identification of a particular youth who is not responding to treatment as expected. This case can then be scheduled for further review and discussion by the therapist and case manager, the treatment team, the family, or all three. Similarly, a client who is progressing as expected may be reviewed to consider the remaining steps necessary to finish treatment and maintain treatment gains. Going beyond the monitoring of the individual case, patterns of success or difficulties may be identified by the supervisor through an examination of the clinician's caseload. Steps can then be taken to provide additional training or tailor the caseload to the clinician's strengths.

Administrative Issues. Aggregate outcome data may also be used by administrators to manage treatment in a variety of ways. Funders of treatment may track the progress of treatment for clients who are receiving services. Data can then be used to manage the case by informing decisions about continued funding, supplementing treatment, or ending treatment. Although managed care has developed a poor reputation because of its emphasis on decision making guided solely by financial concerns, the potential to manage cases with a focus on quality is an equally plausible option. For example, a youth with a psychotic disorder who appears to be deteriorating in outpatient treatment (based on increasing problem severity scores) may be provided with additional support services, a review of medication issues, or a brief stay in a respite facility in an effort to stabilize the situation without the need for hospitalization. Management of a case is likely to occur anyway, but may benefit by being informed by outcome data.

Research and Evaluation

In addition to using outcome data to monitor or manage the current case, data may be aggregated for research or evaluation purposes. The evaluation may take the form of specific investigator-formed hypotheses regarding the effectiveness of programs or through the applied questions of the administrator. For example, when practitioners keep track of the outcomes of the clients they serve, they can also compile the results into one database to examine their own effectiveness with their clients. They could possibly begin to determine if there are groups of clients with which they are more or less effective. For example, there may be individuals with certain diagnoses that their personal therapeutic interventions are most effective with. They can also look at their personal effectiveness in combination with a wide array of demographic variables, such as age, gender, ethnicity, socioeconomic status, or anything else that the clinician might desire to examine. For example, after viewing outcome data for all clients that a particular clinician has seen in the past year, he or she might realize that outcomes have been somewhat higher for older females, and with people diagnosed with severe depression more than with people who have anxiety disorders.

Aggregate Change. Combined databases also provide useful information to administrators, as well as clinicians. Administrators may aggregate or average the improvement numbers for all clients or groups of clients to obtain information regarding specific programs. These numbers may be very useful in reporting to regulatory bodies or in attempting to gain agency funding. For example, data may be examined for all clients who were referred from the juvenile court or child welfare agency. Similarly, data could be examined for all youth in a particular program (e.g., an eating disorders group) or of a certain demographic (e.g., youths under 12, girls, Spanish speakers). It should be noted that average change scores reported in this fashion do not include information regarding the causes of change. Unless control groups or some other form of control has been used in an experimental fashion, client improvement could be because of factors other than treatment. As a result, administrators should be careful how they make attributions about evaluation data collected from a single group tracked over time.

A more controversial use of the data would be to examine and compare the effectiveness of clinicians within an agency (Ogles et al., 2002). Data regarding all the clients from a given agency may also provide information that is useful in examining and comparing each clinician's effectiveness with his or her caseload. In addition to overall effectiveness with all clients, specific strengths or challenges may also be identified for the individual clinician. For example, certain therapists may excel with youth who have externalizing disorders, whereas others may match better with older adolescents with internalizing disorders. With sufficient numbers, patterns of effectiveness may be identified.

Satisfaction With Service. In addition, the satisfaction scales may be aggregated to give an overall picture of client satisfaction with services. Reports of high client satisfaction with services can be helpful in communicating overall agency effectiveness. Conversely, if client satisfaction ratings were less favorable, this would provide important feedback to the administrator regarding specific programs. Again, the data may be aggregated for certain subgroups by referral source, demographic characteristics, or treatment program.

Case Example of Monitoring Change

Ann Smith is a community support worker in a community mental health center. She works primarily with families receiving intensive outpatient treatment. She often works with families in which the child is returning to the home after a stay in the hospital or residential treatment or when the child is at risk for such a placement. Her agency selected the Ohio Scales to assess all services delivered to children and adolescents. In addition, the clinical workers, including Ann, use the data from the scales to inform the treatment plan and treatment progress reports.

Each client that enters treatment is asked by the receptionist to complete the Ohio Scales prior to their visit with an intake worker. If the identified child client is 12 or older, then the child completes the youth form of the Ohio Scales, and a parent or parent surrogate completes the parent form. For children under 12, only the parent completes the forms. The forms are completed and then scored by the receptionist. They are entered into a database, and brief reports are produced using the data. The reports are given to the clinician prior to the intake interview. Following the interview and collection of additional information, the clinician rates the youth using the agency worker form of the Ohio Scales.

The clinician completes a treatment plan after interviewing the family, reviewing the paperwork, and examining the Ohio Scales reports. Roberta Jones is a 17-year-old youth who was returning to her home after a brief stay in the hospital related to suicidal thoughts and expressions of intent to harm herself. R. J. lives with her mother, Florence, and one younger half sister. Her father lives in another state and has infrequent visits with R. J. (about once per year).

When Ann was first referred the case, she reviewed the Ohio Scales reports, which indicated that R. J. had some lingering suicidal ideation. Examination of the four critical items—thoughts of death, self-harm, drug and alcohol use, and breaking the law—indicated that both R. J. and her mother, Florence, reported that R. J. had some thoughts of death (rated a 4—"Most of the time" by R. J. and a 1—"Once or twice" by Florence) and self-harm (rated 4—"Most of the time" by R. J. and 1—"Once or twice" by Florence). The other critical items were rated 0—"Not at all" by both Florence and R. J. As a result, Ann conducted a more thorough assessment of risk for self-harm in the interview and developed a safety plan with R. J. and Florence in the first clinical contact.

R. J.'s total problem severity score of 39 falls in the moderate range, compared to the community sample. Similarly, Florence's ratings of R. J.'s problem behaviors produced a score of 31, which falls in the moderate range. Noticeably, Florence's ratings of the more internalizing items (e.g., depression, anxiety, thoughts of death) were similar to R. J.'s ratings, with the exception of the two items concerning thoughts of death and hurting self. After reviewing the reports and conducting the intake, Ann rated R. J. as a 37 (moderate range).

When examining the items to find potential targets for treatment, Ann noticed first that the last nine items (internalizing items) are the main source of concern for both R. J. and Florence (see Figs. 10.1 and 10.2). In addition, she noticed that R. J. rated a cluster of five items as 4 "Most of the time" or 5 "All of the time"—self-harm, thoughts of death, feeling worthless or useless, feeling sad or depressed, and feeling lonely and having no friends. In addition, she rated the two anxiety items, feeling anxious or fearful and worrying that something bad is going to happen—as 3—"Often." Florence identified a similar group of items as the most troublesome, but also added nightmares as a potential issue to address. Ann also noted that Florence and R. J. rated several items as high on the Functioning Scale (lower scores are more impairment on this scale), including: self-care (e.g., hygiene), relationships with peers, hobbies, recreational activities, and accepting responsibility for actions. These items may be indicative of strengths that might be used to support change in treatment.

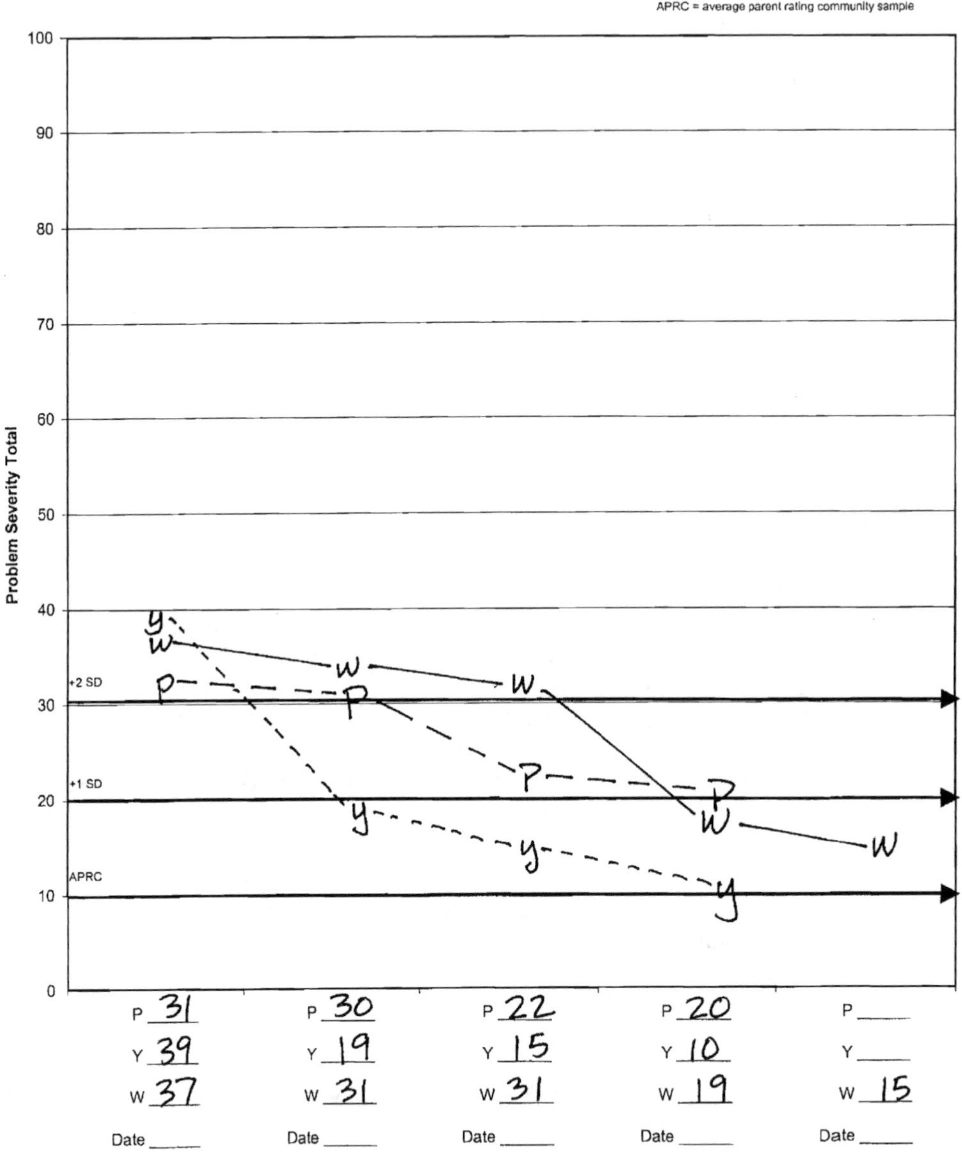

FIG. 10.1. R. J.'s Parent Ratings

Based on this data, Ann meets with R. J. and Florence in their home for the second clinical contact. At this session, they agree to begin treatment with intermittent family contacts at home and individual sessions with R. J. at the clinic. In addition, R. J. is referred to the psychiatrist to continue the medications that were prescribed during the hospital stay.

In this agency, outcome data are gathered every month to track the progress of the case and when finishing the case. In this particular case, five data points were

Ohio Youth Problem, Functioning, and Satisfaction Scales

Parent Rating – Short Form **P**

Child's Name: Roberta Date: ______ Child's Grade: 11 ID#: ______ (Completed by Agency)

Child's Date of Birth: 3/6/86 Child's Sex: ☐ Male ☒ Female Child's Race: ______

Form Completed By: ☒ Mother ☐ Father ☐ Step-mother ☐ Step-father ☐ Other: ______

Instructions: Please rate the degree to which your child has experienced the following problems in the past 30 days.	Not at All	Once or Twice	Several Times	Often	Most of the Time	All of the Time
1. Arguing with others	0	(1)	2	3	4	5
2. Getting into fights	(0)	1	2	3	4	5
3. Yelling, swearing, or screaming at others	0	(1)	2	3	4	5
4. Fits of anger	(0)	1	2	3	4	5
5. Refusing to do things teachers or parents ask	0	(1)	2	3	4	5
6. Causing trouble for no reason	(0)	1	2	3	4	5
7. Using drugs or alcohol	(0)	1	2	3	4	5
8. Breaking rules or breaking the law (out past curfew, stealing)	(0)	1	2	3	4	5
9. Skipping school or classes	(0)	1	2	3	4	5
10. Lying	0	(1)	2	3	4	5
11. Can't seem to sit still, having too much energy	(0)	1	2	3	4	5
12. Hurting self (cutting or scratching self, taking pills)	0	(1)	2	3	4	5
13. Talking or thinking about death	0	(1)	2	3	4	5
14. Feeling worthless or useless	0	1	2	3	(4)	5
15. Feeling lonely and having no friends	0	1	2	3	4	(5)
16. Feeling anxious or fearful	0	1	2	3	(4)	5
17. Worrying that something bad is going to happen	0	1	2	3	4	(5)
18. Feeling sad or depressed	0	1	2	3	(4)	5
19. Nightmares	0	1	2	(3)	4	5
20. Eating problems	(0)	1	2	3	4	5
		6		3	12	10

(Add ratings together) Total 31

Copyright © Benjamin M. Ogles & Southern Consortium for Children September 1999 (Parent-1)

Instructions: Please circle your response to each question.

1. Overall, how satisfied are you with your relationship with your child right now?
   1. Extremely satisfied
   2. (2) Moderately satisfied
   3. Somewhat satisfied
   4. Somewhat dissatisfied
   5. Moderately dissatisfied
   6. Extremely dissatisfied
2. How capable of dealing with your child's problems do you feel right now?
   1. Extremely capable
   2. (2) Moderately capable
   3. Somewhat capable
   4. Somewhat incapable
   5. Moderately incapable
   6. Extremely incapable
3. How much stress or pressure is in your life right now?
   1. Very little
   2. Some
   3. Quite a bit
   4. (4) A moderate amount
   5. A great deal
   6. Unbearable amounts
4. How optimistic are you about your child's future right now?
   1. The future looks very bright
   2. The future looks somewhat bright
   3. (3) The future looks OK
   4. The future looks both good and bad
   5. The future looks bad
   6. The future looks very bad

Total: 11

Instructions: Please circle your response to each question.

1. How satisfied are you with the mental health services your child has received so far?
   1. Extremely satisfied
   2. (2) Moderately satisfied
   3. Somewhat satisfied
   4. Somewhat dissatisfied
   5. Moderately dissatisfied
   6. Extremely dissatisfied
2. To what degree have you been included in the treatment planning process for your child?
   1. A great deal
   2. (2) Moderately
   3. Quite a bit
   4. Somewhat
   5. A little
   6. Not at all
3. Mental health workers involved in my case listen to and value my ideas about treatment planning for my child.
   1. A great deal
   2. Moderately
   3. (3) Quite a bit
   4. Somewhat
   5. A little
   6. Not at all
4. To what extent does your child's treatment plan include your ideas about your child's treatment needs?
   1. A great deal
   2. (2) Moderately
   3. Quite a bit
   4. Somewhat
   5. A little
   6. Not at all

Total: 9

Instructions: Please rate the degree to which your child's problems affect his or her current ability in everyday activities. Consider your child's current level of functioning.	Extreme Troubles	Quite a Few Troubles	Some Troubles	OK	Doing Very Well
1. Getting along with friends	0	1	2	(3)	4
2. Getting along with family	0	(1)	2	3	4
3. Dating or developing relationships with boyfriends or girlfriends	0	1	(2)	3	4
4. Getting along with adults outside the family (teachers, principal)	0	1	(2)	3	4
5. Keeping neat and clean, looking good	0	(1)	2	3	4
6. Caring for health needs and keeping good health habits (taking medicines or brushing teeth)	0	1	(2)	3	4
7. Controlling emotions and staying out of trouble	0	1	(2)	3	4
8. Being motivated and finishing projects	0	1	2	(3)	4
9. Participating in hobbies (baseball cards, coins, stamps, art)	0	1	2	(3)	4
10. Participating in recreational activities (sports, swimming, bike riding)	0	1	(2)	3	4
11. Completing household chores (cleaning room, other chores)	0	1	(2)	3	4
12. Attending school and getting passing grades in school	0	1	(2)	3	4
13. Learning skills that will be useful for future jobs	0	(1)	2	3	4
14. Feeling good about self	0	(1)	2	3	4
15. Thinking clearly and making good decisions	0	1	(2)	3	4
16. Concentrating, paying attention, and completing tasks	0	1	2	(3)	4
17. Earning money and learning how to use money wisely	0	1	(2)	3	4
18. Doing things without supervision or restrictions	0	1	2	(3)	4
19. Accepting responsibility for actions	0	1	2	(3)	4
20. Ability to express feelings	0	1	(2)	3	4
		4	20	18	

(Add ratings together) Total 42

Copyright © Benjamin M. Ogles & Southern Consortium for Children September 1999 (Parent-2)

FIG. 10.2. R. J.'s Youth Ratings

Ohio Youth Problem, Functioning, and Satisfaction Scales **Y**

Youth Rating – Short Form (Ages 12-18)

Name: Roberta Date: ______ Grade: 11 ID#: ______ (Completed by Agency)

Date of Birth: 3/6/86 Sex: ☐ Male ☒ Female Race: ______

Instructions: Please rate the degree to which you have experienced the following problems in the past 30 days.	Not at All	Once or Twice	Several Times	Often	Most of the Time	All of the Time
1. Arguing with others	0	1	(2)	3	4	5
2. Getting into fights	(0)	1	2	3	4	5
3. Yelling, swearing, or screaming at others	0	(1)	2	3	4	5
4. Fits of anger	0	1	(2)	3	4	5
5. Refusing to do things teachers or parents ask	0	(1)	2	3	4	5
6. Causing trouble for no reason	0	(1)	2	3	4	5
7. Using drugs or alcohol	(0)	1	2	3	4	5
8. Breaking rules or breaking the law (out past curfew, stealing)	(0)	1	2	3	4	5
9. Skipping school or classes	0	(1)	2	3	4	5
10. Lying	(0)	1	2	3	4	5
11. Can't seem to sit still, having too much energy	(0)	1	2	3	4	5
12. Hurting self (cutting or scratching self, taking pills)	0	1	2	3	(4)	5
13. Talking or thinking about death	0	1	2	3	(4)	5
14. Feeling worthless or useless	0	1	2	3	4	(5)
15. Feeling lonely and having no friends	0	1	2	3	(4)	5
16. Feeling anxious or fearful	0	1	2	(3)	4	5
17. Worrying that something bad is going to happen	0	1	2	(3)	4	5
18. Feeling sad or depressed	0	1	2	3	4	(5)
19. Nightmares	0	1	(2)	3	4	5
20. Eating problems	0	(1)	2	3	4	5
		5	6	6	12	10

(Add ratings together) Total 39

 September 1999 (Youth-1)

Instructions: Please circle your response to each question.

1. Overall, how satisfied are you with your life right now?
   1. Extremely satisfied
   2. Moderately satisfied
   3. Somewhat satisfied
   (4) Somewhat dissatisfied
   5. Moderately dissatisfied
   6. Extremely dissatisfied
2. How energetic and healthy do you feel right now?
   1. Extremely healthy
   2. Moderately healthy
   3. Somewhat healthy
   (4) Somewhat unhealthy
   5. Moderately unhealthy
   6. Extremely unhealthy
3. How much stress or pressure is in your life right now?
   1. Very little stress
   2. Some stress
   3. Quite a bit of stress
   (4) A moderate amount of stress
   5. A great deal of stress
   6. Unbearable amounts of stress
4. How optimistic are you about the future?
   1. The future looks very bright
   2. The future looks somewhat bright
   3. The future looks OK
   4. The future looks both good and bad
   (5) The future looks bad
   6. The future looks very bad

Total: 17

Instructions: Please circle your response to each question.

1. How satisfied are you with the mental health services you have received so far?
   1. Extremely satisfied
   2. Moderately satisfied
   3. Somewhat satisfied
   (4) Somewhat dissatisfied
   5. Moderately dissatisfied
   6. Extremely dissatisfied
2. How much are you included in deciding your treatment?
   1. A great deal
   2. Moderately
   (3) Quite a bit
   4. Somewhat
   5. A little
   6. Not at all
3. Mental health workers involved in my case listen to me and know what I want.
   1. A great deal
   (2) Moderately
   3. Quite a bit
   4. Somewhat
   5. A little
   6. Not at all
4. I have a lot of say about what happens in my treatment.
   1. A great deal
   (2) Moderately
   3. Quite a bit
   4. Somewhat
   5. A little
   6. Not at all

Total: 11

Instructions: Below are some ways your problems might get in the way of your ability to do everyday activities. Read each item and circle the number that best describes your current situation.	Extreme Troubles	Quite a Few Troubles	Some Troubles	OK	Doing Very Well
1. Getting along with friends	0	1	2	3	(4)
2. Getting along with family	0	1	(2)	3	4
3. Dating or developing relationships with boyfriends or girlfriends	0	1	2	(3)	4
4. Getting along with adults outside the family (teachers, principal)	0	1	2	(3)	4
5. Keeping neat and clean, looking good	0	1	2	3	(4)
6. Caring for health needs and keeping good health habits (taking medicines or brushing teeth)	0	1	2	(3)	4
7. Controlling emotions and staying out of trouble	0	1	(2)	3	4
8. Being motivated and finishing projects	0	1	2	(3)	4
9. Participating in hobbies (baseball cards, coins, stamps, art)	0	1	2	(3)	4
10. Participating in recreational activities (sports, swimming, bike riding)	0	1	2	(3)	4
11. Completing household chores (cleaning room, other chores)	0	1	(2)	3	4
12. Attending school and getting passing grades in school	0	1	(2)	3	4
13. Learning skills that will be useful for future jobs	0	1	(2)	3	4
14. Feeling good about self	0	1	(2)	3	4
15. Thinking clearly and making good decisions	0	1	2	(3)	4
16. Concentrating, paying attention, and completing tasks	0	1	2	(3)	4
17. Earning money and learning how to use money wisely	0	1	2	(3)	4
18. Doing things without supervision or restrictions	0	1	2	(3)	4
19. Accepting responsibility for actions	0	1	2	(3)	4
20. Ability to express feelings	0	1	(2)	3	4
			14	33	8

(Add ratings together) Total 55

 September 1999 (Youth-2)

FIG. 10.3. Tracking Graph for R. J.

gathered—intake, 1 month, 2 months, 3 months, and 4 months following initiation of treatment. The tracking graph is displayed in Fig. 10.3. As can be seen, only the agency worker rating is available at 4 months, because R. J. and Florence dropped out of treatment and did not complete the final outcome assessment ratings.

As can be seen, R. J. made some apparent progress from all three perspectives while enrolled in treatment. In addition, an examination of the central items revealed movement from ratings of 4 and 5 to ratings of 0, 1, or 2.

CONCLUSION

In this chapter, we presented the conceptualization and development of the Ohio Scales—brief measures of outcome that were developed with specific emphasis on practical everyday use. Although we wanted to maintain a focus on the psychometric properties and theoretical underpinnings that are common to most research-based measures, we were particularly mindful of pragmatic issues. Our hope was to develop a set of multisource, multicontent measures that might actually be used in practice by clinicians who are not as well acquainted with the day-to-day requirements of research or evaluation. Consistent with this focus, we described the development of practical measures, including the substantiation of both their psychometric properties and their utility. Although validation efforts must continue, early evidence suggests that the Ohio Scales may provide a useful method for tracking change that occurs during treatment for youth receiving mental health services. It is important that we provided potential uses of the Ohio Scales for both treatment planning and outcome assessment. We hope that our efforts will encourage those who are involved in the routine delivery of mental health services to consider evaluating their services through the use of the Ohio Scales or other practical measures. Our clients deserve services that have evidence to support their effectiveness and methods for tracking their progress and outcome. As clinicians and agencies integrate routine assessment into their clinical protocols, both clients and clinicians will benefit.

ACKNOWLEDGMENTS

Much of the research summarized in this chapter was supported by the Office of Program Evaluation and Research, the Ohio Department of Mental Health, Grant No. 96-1105. Early work on the Ohio Scales was also supported by the Southern Consortium for Children.

REFERENCES

Achenbach, T. M., McConaughty, S. H., & Howell, C. T. (1987). Child/adolescent behavioral and emotional problems: Implications of cross-informant correlations for situational specificity. *Psychological Bulletin, 101*, 213–232.

Baize, H. (Oct., 2001). *Implications of the Ohio Scales factor structure for scale utility and scoring*. The fourth Annual California Children's System of Care Model Evaluation Conference, San Francisco.

Barth, R. P. (1986). *Social and cognitive treatment of children and adolescents*. San Francisco: Jossey-Bass.

Bickman, L., Guthrie, P. R., Foster, E. M., Lambert, W., Summerfelt, W. T., Breda, C. S., & Heflinger, C. A. (1995). *Evaluating managed mental health services: The Fort Bragg experiment*. New York: Plenum.

Burchard, J. D., & Clarke, R. T. (1990). The role of individualized care in a service delivery system for children and adolescents with severely maladjusted behavior. *The Journal of Mental Health Administration, 17*, 48–60.

Burchard, J. D., & Schaefer, M. (1992). Improving accountability in a service delivery system in children's mental health. *Clinical Psychology Review, 12*, 867–882.

California Department of Mental Health. (2001, October). *Post-Pilot Survey Results*. Retrieved September 1, 2003 from http://www.dmh.cahwnet.gov/rpod/PDF/Post-Pilot-Survey-Results_10-01.pdf

Ciarlo, J. A., Brown, T. R., Edwards, D. W., Kiresuk, T. J., & Newman, F. L. (1986). *Assessing mental health treatment outcome measurement techniques* (U.S. Department of Health and Human Services Pub. No. ADM 86-1301). Washington, DC: U.S. Government Printing Office.

Cochran, M. (1987). Empowering families: An alternative to the deficit model. In K. Hurrelmann, F. Hurrelmann, & F. Lostel (Eds.), *Social intervention: Potential and constraints* (pp. 105–119). Berlin: DeGruyter.

Cross, T. P., McDonald, E., & Lyons, H. (1997). *Evaluating the outcome of children's mental health services: A guide for the use of available child and family outcome measures (2nd* ed.*)*. Boston: Judge Baker Children's Center.

Duchnowski, A. J., Johnson, M. K., Hall, K. S., Kutash, K., & Friedman, R. M. (1993). The alternatives to residential treatment study: Initial findings. *Journal of Emotional and Behavioral Disorders, 1*(1), 17–26.

Dunst, C. J., Trivette, C. M., & Deal, A. G. (1988). *Enabling and empowering families: Principles and guidelines for practice*. Cambridge, MA: Brookline Books.

Evans, M. E., Dollard, N., Huz, S., & Rahn, D. S. (1990). *Outcomes of Children and Youth Intensive Case Management in New York State*. Paper presented at the Annual American Public Health Association Meetings, Atlanta, GA.

Friesen, B. J., Koren, P. E., & Koroloff, N. M. (1992). How parents view professional behaviors: A cross-professional analysis. *Journal of Child and Family Studies, 1*, 209–231.

Friesen, B. J., & Koroloff, N. M. (1990). Family-centered services: Implications for mental health administration and research. *The Journal of Mental Health Administration, 17*, 13–25.

Gillespie, D. K. (1993). *Enhancing the methodology of social validation: The application of psychometric measures to the Pennsylvania project social validation instrument*. Unpublished masters's thesis, Ohio University.

Gold, N. (1983). Stakeholders and program evaluation: Characteristics and reflections. In Bryk (Ed.), *Stakeholder-based evaluation* (pp. 63–72). San Francisco: Jossey-Bass.

Grundy, C. T., Lambert, M. J., & Grundy, E. M. (1996). Assessing clinical significance: Application to the Hamilton Rating Scale for Depression. *Journal of Mental Health, 5*, 25–33.

Grundy, C. T., Lunnen, K. M., Lambert, M. J., Ashton, J. E., & Tovey, D. (1994). Hamilton Rating Scale for Depression: One scale or many? *Clinical Psychology—Science & Practice, 1*, 197–205.

Hatfield, D., Ogles, B. M., Carlston, D., Dowell, K. A., Melendez, G., & Fields, S. A. (2002, March). *The role of continuous feedback in the wraparound approach*. Paper presented at the Research and Training Center for Children's Mental Health's 15th Annual Research Conference, Tampa, FL.

Hodges, K., & Wong, M. M. (1996). Psychometric characteristics of a multidimensional measure to assess impairment: The Child and Adolescent Functional Assessment Scale. *Journal of Child and Family Studies, 5*, 445–467.

Howard, K. I., Kopta, S. M., Krause, M. S., & Orlinsky, D. E. (1986). The dose–effect relationship in psychotherapy. *American Psychologist, 41*, 159–164.

Howard, K. I., Lueger, R. I., Maling, M. S., & Martinovich, Z. (1993). A phase model of psychotherapy outcome: Causal mediation of change. *Journal of Consulting and Clinical Psychology, 61*, 678–685.

Ihilevich, D., & Gleser, G. C. (1982). *Evaluating mental health programs: The Progress Evaluation Scales*. Lexington, MA: D.C. Heath.

Jacobson, N. S., & Truax, P. (1991). Clinical significance: A statistical approach to defining meaningful change in psychotherapy research. *Journal of Consulting and Clinical Psychology, 59*, 12–19.

Kazdin, A. E. (1977). Assessing the clinical or applied importance of behavior change through social validation. *Behavior Modification, 1*, 427–452.

Koch, J. R., Lewis, A., & McCall, D. (1998). A multistakeholder-driven model for developing an outcome menagement system. *Journal of Behavioral Health Services and Research, 25*, 151–162.

Kutash, K., Duchnowski, A., Johnson, M., & Rugs, D. (1993). Multi-stage evaluation for a community mental health system for children. *Administration and Policy in Mental Health, 20*, 311–322.

Lambert, M. J., Christensen, E. R., & DeJulio, S. S. (1983). *The Assessment of Psychotherapy Outcome*. New York: Wiley.

Lambert, M. J., Ogles, B. M., & Masters, K. S. (1992). Choosing outcome assessment devices: An organizational and conceptual scheme. *Journal of Counseling and Development, 70*, 538–539.

Lambert, M. J., Okiishi, J. C., Finch, A. E., & Johnson, L. D. (1998). Outcome assessment: From conceptualization to implementation. *Professional Psychology:Research & Practice, 29*, 63–70.

Lambert, M. J., Whipple, J. L., Smart, D. W., Vermeersch, D. A., Nielsen, S. L., & Hawkins, E. J. (2001). The effects of providing therapists with feedback on patient progress during psychotherapy: Are outcomes enhanced? *Psychotherapy Research, 11*, 49–68.

Maruish, M. E. (Ed.). (1999). *The use of psychological testing for treatment planning and outcomes assessment* (2nd ed.). Mahwah, NJ: Lawrence Erlbaum Associates.

Maruish, M. E. (2002). *Essentials of treatment planning*. New York: Wiley.

McGlynn, E. A. (1996). Domains of study and methodological challenges. In L. I. Sederer & B. Dickey (Eds.), *Outcomes assessment in clinical practice*. Baltimore: Williams & Wilkins.

Melendez, G. (2000). *The Brief Ohio Scales: Development and validation of a brief child outcome measure*. Unpublished master's thesis, Ohio University.

Mordock, J. B. (2000). Outcome assessment: Suggestions for agency practice. *Child Welfare, 79*, 689–710.

Newman, F. L., Ciarlo, J. A., & Carpenter, D. (1999). Guidelines for selecting psychological insturments for treatment planning and outcome assessment. In M. E. Maruish (Ed.), *The use of psychological testing for treatment planning and outcomes assessment* (2nd ed.), (pp. 153–170). Mahwah, NJ: Lawrence Erlbaum Associates.

Ogles, B. M., Davis, D C., & Lunnen, K. M. (1998, March). *The interrater reliability of four measures of functioning*. Paper presented at the Research and Training Center for Children's Mental Health's 11th Annual Research Conference, Tampa, FL.

Ogles, B. M., Lambert, M. J., & Fields, S. (2002). *Essentials of outcome assessment*. New York: Wiley.

Ogles, B. M., Lambert, M. J., & Masters, K. S. (1996). *Assessing outcome in clinical practice*. Boston: Allyn & Bacon.

Ogles, B. M., Melendez, G., Davis, D. C., & Lunnen, K. M. (1998). *The Ohio Youth Problem, Functioning, and Satisfaction Scales: Technical manual*. Columbus, OH: Ohio Department of Mental Health.

Ogles, B. M., Melendez, G., Davis, D. C., & Lunnen, K. M. (1999). *The Ohio Youth Problem, Functioning, and Satisfaction Scales (short form): Users manual*. Columbus, OH: Ohio Department of Mental Health.

Ogles, B. M., Melendez, G., Davis, D. C., & Lunnen, K. M. (2001). The Ohio Scales: Practical outcome assessment. *Journal of Child and Family Studies, 10*, 199–212.

Ogles, B. M., & Owens, J. S. (in press). Outcome assessment for evaluating and monitoring school-based mental health programs. In K. E. Robinson (Ed.), *Advances in school-based mental health: Best practices and program models*. Kingston, NJ: Civic Research Institute.

Ohio Department of Mental Health (2000). *Ohio mental health consumer outcomes initiative*. Retrieved Sept. 1, 2003 from http://www.mh.state.oh.us/initiatives/outcomes/outcomes.html

Ohio Department of Mental Health. (2003). *Ohio mental health consumer outcomes system: Initial statewide report*. Columbus, OH: Author.

Poertner, J., & Ronnau, J. (1992). A strengths approach to children with emotional disabilities. In D. Saleebey (Ed.), *The strengths perspective in social work practice* (pp. 111–121). New York: Longman.

Pratt, S. I., & Moreland, K. L. (1996). Introduction to treatment outcome: Historical perspectives and current issues. In S. I. Pfeiffer (Ed.), *Outcome assessment in residential treatment* (pp. 1–28). New York: Haworth.

Rosenberg, M. (1979). *Conceiving the self*. New York: Basic Books.

Rosenblatt, A. (1998, August). A primer on outcome measures for children's services. *Behavioral Healthcare Tomorrow*, 41–43.

Rosenblatt, A., & Attkisson, C. C. (1993). Assessing outcomes for sufferers of severe mental disorder: A conceptual framework and review. *Evaluation and Program Planning, 16*, 347–363.

Schriner, K. F., & Fawcett, S. B. (1988). Development and validation of a community concerns report method. *Journal of Community Psychology, 16*, 306–316.

Sederer, L. I., & Dickey, B. (Eds.). (1996). *Outcomes assessment in clinical practice*. Baltimore: Williams & Wilkins.

Stroul, B. A., & Friedman, R. M. (1986). *A system of care for severely emotionally disturbed children and youth* (Rev. ed.). Washington, DC: Georgetown University Child Development Center.

Strupp, H. H., & Hadley, S. W. (1977). A tripartite model of mental health and therapeutic outcome: With special reference to negative effects in psychotherapy. *American Psychologist, 32*, 187–196.

VanDenBerg, J., Beck, S., & Pierce, J. (1992). *The Pennsylvania outcome project for children's services*. Paper presented at the fifth annual research meeting of the Research and Training Center for Children's Mental Health, Tampa, FL.

Vital Signs. (1998). Final report of the Ohio Mental Health Outcomes Task Force. Columbus, OH: Ohio Department of Mental Health.

Weber, D. O. (1998). A field in its infancy: Measuring outcomes for children and adolescents. In K. J. Midgail (Ed.), *The behavioral outcomes & guidelines sourcebook*. Washington, DC: Faulkner and Gray's Healthcare Information Center.

Wolf, M. M. (1978). Social validity: The case for subjective measurement or how applied behavior analysis is finding its heart. *Journal of Applied Behavior Analysis, 11*, 203–214.

11

Use of the Devereux Scales of Mental Disorders for Diagnosis, Treatment Planning, and Outcome Assessment

Jack A. Naglieri
George Mason University

Steven I. Pfeiffer
Duke University

The purpose of this chapter is to describe the use and interpretation of the Devereux Scale of Mental Disorders (DSMD; Naglieri, LeBuffe, & Pfeiffer, 1994). The scale is described in detail, as is its development, standardization, and norming procedures. The interpretation method described in the DSMD manual is presented. In addition, the computer scoring and interpretation program is used to illustrate how the DSMD can be used. Special attention is given to the issue of treatment planning and evaluation of treatment effectiveness.

OVERVIEW OF THE INSTRUMENT

The DSMD is a behavior rating scale that can be used to assess maladjustment in children and adolescents from age 5 to 18. The instrument is designed to identify psychopathological and behavioral problems in children and adolescents by evaluating overt behaviors exhibited by the individual. The DSMD provides this information from the report of the parent, teacher, or professional. Ratings from each of a child's parents, as well as from teachers or other professionals who have had the opportunity to observe the child, can provide a rich source of information about the variability or consistency of behavior across several settings and under different environmental conditions. The behavior rating scale is easy to administer and score either by hand or by using the computer scoring system. The DSMD is especially useful for the direct assessment of changes in behavior over time as a function of psychological, psychiatric, or behavioral treatment, as described by Pfeiffer (1989), because of several unique psychometric features included during development of the instrument.

The DSMD is comprised of 111 (age 5–12) or 110 (age 13–18) items included on a two-page record form. Each item begins with the stem "During the past 4 weeks, how often did the child . . ." or "During the past 4 weeks, how often did the adolescent . . ." for the two versions of the scale. Teachers and parents rate the child using the same form. The ratings "Never," "Rarely," "Occasionally," "Frequently," and "Very Frequently" are assigned scores of 0 through 5, respectively, on the second page of the record form.

The rater's marks are automatically transferred from the page they see to the second page that contains the scoring system.

Scoring the DSMD is easily completed and accomplished with the assistance of a well-organized and visually informative record form. For example, arrows are used to tell the user of the flow of the scoring system and text is included that instructs the practitioner which norms tables to use. Scoring involves the following four steps:

1. Item scores are summed to yield raw scores for each of six scales.
2. Each scale's raw score is converted to a *T*-score using a conversion table.
3. The six scales are combined into three pairs to yield a sum of *T*-scores used to obtain a *T*-score for Externalizing, Internalizing, and Critical Pathology Composite scales.
4. The sum of the six scale *T*-scores is used to obtain a *T*-score for the Total scale.

The DSMD yields an overall score and scores for several factorially derived scales (see the Validity section later) that reflect major categories of psychopathological symptoms. The rating scale yields standard scores for the three broad scales of Externalizing, Internalizing, and Critical Pathology. Within each of these three scales are two separate scales: Conduct, Attention (for age 5–12 only), Delinquency (for age 13–18 only), Anxiety, Depression, Autism, and Acute Problems. Additionally, the DSMD provides an approach for the evaluation of specific item scores outside of the normal range and can be used to guide diagnosis and treatment planning. The DSMD can therefore aid professionals in identifying psychological or emotional difficulties, in specifying the type of psychopathology, and in formulating a treatment plan.

Summary of Development

The DSMD is a revision of the Devereux Child Behavior Rating Scale (Spivack & Spotts, 1966) and Devereux Adolescent Behavior Rating Scale (Spivack, Spotts, & Haimes, 1967), which were among the first behavior rating scales developed. These scales were developed as measures of behaviors that provide information about how "the child relates to his world of things and people" (Spivack & Levine, 1964, p. 702). The identification of the original behaviors included in the scales was based on extensive field research that proved to be an effective and efficient method of detecting behavioral problems associated with psychopathology in children and adolescents.

Item construction for the DSMD was based on three sources. The original items included in the previous behavior scales were examined. These items were categorized according to the *DSM–III–R* (American Psychiatric Association, 1987) and the *DSM–IV Options Book: Work in Progress* (American Psychiatric Association, 1991). Additional items were written where needed. Other relevant literature (e.g., Garfinkel, Carlson, & Weller, 1990; Hooper, Hynd, & Mattison, 1992; Lewis & Miller, 1990) was considered, as was the need to modify items that included outdated language (e.g., terms no longer in use, sexist language). The results of these efforts served as the starting point in the construction of the DSMD.

One important value of using the *DSM* as a structure for item identification was to formalize the assessment of a large set of behaviors associated with psychopathology that are representative of the major categories. The advantage of using the *DSM* as a base is that it provides a rich source of options to include and then evaluate from a psychometric perspective. Second, this approach provides the kinds of information that can aid professionals in the selection of an appropriate therapeutic intervention. Although diagnosis does not necessarily determine the exact type of therapy, it may narrow the field of choices considerably and, therefore, add to the efficiency, quality, and effectiveness of treatment. Accurate diagnosis can be especially important when selecting, for example, behavioral, cognitive, and psychopharmacological therapies that can have differential effectiveness. This was noted by Dougherty, Saxe, Cross, and Silverman (1987), who concluded that

> behavioral treatment is clearly effective for phobias and enuresis, and cognitive behavioral therapy is effective for a range of disorders involving self-control (except aggressive behavior). Group therapy has been found to be effective with delinquent adolescents, and family therapy appears to be effective for children with conduct disorders and psychophysiological disorders. Psychopharmacological treatment, while not curative, has been found to have limited effectiveness with children with ADD-H, depression, or enuresis, and also in managing the behavior of children who are severely disturbed. (p. 114)

These conclusions emphasize the need for accurate differential diagnosis, which should influence the selection of the most appropriate therapeutic intervention and eventual outcomes. Using a child's scores on the various scales of the DSMD in conjunction with information from item-level analysis, along with a psychosocial history and other findings, the professional can determine the existence of psychological or emotional difficulties, specify the type of psychopathology according to the *DSM–IV*, and develop an effective treatment plan.

The reading level of the items and rater directions were also carefully written so that the overall readability level of the text would be as low as possible. All text was evaluated according to the Living Word Vocabulary (Dale & O'Rourke, 1981), which provides a percentage score on more than 44,000 words and terms familiar to students in grades 4, 6, 8, 10, 12, 13, and 16. Words that were too difficult were eliminated. Direct and simple instructions were written with readability of the average newspaper (about sixth-grade level).

The item development phase also included a review of the items for possible cultural, racial, and gender bias. Experts in the field qualitatively examined every item for racial, ethnic, and gender bias. Statistical analyses were also conducted that would indicate the extent to which the items showed mean score differences. Based on both the review of content and statistical evidence of mean score differences, a small number of items (approximately five) were deleted from the DSMD.

Development of DSMD Scales

Items were organized into statistically and logically derived scales. Statistically derived scales were identified with the aid of item factor analyses. Item factor analyses guided the assignment of items onto six factorially defined scales. The factor-based scales were consistent with generally accepted conceptualizations of developmental psychopathology. There were three superordinate categories within which three pairs of scales could be subsumed. For age 5 through 12, both Conduct and Attention factors could be viewed as Externalizing problems; Anxiety and Depression both suggested an Internalizing dimension; and the Autism and Acute Problems factors together formed a Critical Pathology category. Similarly, for age 13 through 18, the Conduct and Delinquency factors represented Externalizing problems; Depression

Ages 5-12	TOTAL SCALE	Ages 13-18
Conduct & Attention	**Externalizing**	Conduct & Delinquency
Anxiety & Depression	**Internalizing**	Anxiety & Depression
Autism & Acute Problems	**Critical Pathology**	Autism & Acute Problems

FIG. 11.1. Organization of the DSMD scales and composites.

and Anxiety constituted an Internalizing dimension; and the Autism and Acute Problems factors a Critical Pathology group. This categorization of the factor-based scales formed the basis of the organization of the DSMD into Externalizing, Internalizing, and Critical Pathology composites shown in Fig. 11.1. (See the Validity section for more information about the factor analytic results.)

Standardization

The DSMD was carefully standardized so that the sample would be representative of the U.S. population. The data collection process included both regular education (for generation of norms) and special education and clinical (for standardization and validity studies) samples of children and adolescents from age 5 to 18. Data were collected from spring through summer 1991 from public school districts, private special education settings, and clinical treatment programs from across the United States. Students who attended regular education classes at least part time were included in the normative sample, as were those enrolled in part-time special education classes and identified as having learning disabilities, speech or language impairments, or other disabilities. Children and adolescents who were receiving either part- or full-time special education services for the seriously emotionally disturbed or the mentally retarded were not included in the normal standardization sample, but those identified as seriously emotionally disturbed were included in the validity studies. Parents and/or teachers rated each of the students.

The DSMD standardization sample is comprised of 3,153 children and adolescents from age 5 to 18. The sample was stratified according to age, gender, geographic region, race, ethnicity, socioeconomic status, community size, and educational placement. There were, on average, 225 children across the fourteen 1-year age groups included. Data were collected from sites in 17 states in the four geographic regions: northeast, midwest, south, and west. The sample closely matches the United States on the basis of five major race categories: White, African American, Asian/Pacific Islander, Native American, and other. The proportions of children and youth of Hispanic origin included in the standardization sample are also very similar to that of the U.S. population.

Norming Procedures

Following collection on the standardization sample, a series of procedures was conducted to ensure the quality of the norms. First, the Total scale raw scores (i.e., the sums of all item raw scores) were examined for age, rater, and gender differences. Results of the analyses of these data indicated that the scores across each of the 14 ages differed by gender and rater but showed no meaningful age progression within the 5 to 12 or 13 to 18 age groups—thus standard scores by age were not needed. Analyses of the differences in total raw scores by gender were small to moderate but statistically significant (Naglieri, LeBuffe, & Pfeiffer, 1994). For those in the 5 to 12 and 13 to 18 year age groups, the total scale mean raw score was significantly greater for males than for females. These results suggested that separate norms by gender were appropriate. Similarly, analysis of differences by rater (teachers or school staff vs. parents or other appropriate caregiver) varied and therefore separate norms by rater were needed to account for the differences. The final norms for the DSMD are by rater by gender.

Normality of the Total Scale Raw Score Distributions

The distributions of scores by rater, gender, and age all approached a normal distribution but were positively skewed (Naglieri et al., 1994). In each case, the range of scores extended approximately one standard deviation below the mean and about three standard deviations above the mean. Typically, the Total scale raw score mean and median values differed by approximately 8 to 10 raw score points. Given that the distributions were skewed, normalization was considered but rejected. If a nonnormal raw score distribution represents the distribution of scores that would have been obtained if the entire population were tested, then a linear standard score approach that retains the shape of the original distribution should be used (Crocker & Algina, 1986). Moreover, because it was assumed that emotional functioning, as measured by the DSMD, is not normally distributed (because behaviors associated with developmental psychopathology are not typical in the general population), and current standardization results support this view (normal distributions were not obtained), normalization was further contraindicated. Normalization of the raw scores, therefore, was not conducted because the nonnormal shape of the raw score distribution is believed to accurately reflect the distribution of behaviors associated with severe emotional disturbance in the population (Crocker & Algina, 1986).

Derivation of Standard Scores

Standard scores for the DSMD were computed separately for the six scales, the Externalizing, Internalizing, and Critical Pathology composites, and the Total scale (Naglieri et al., 1994). *T*-scores for each scale and composite and for the Total scale, set at a mean of 50 and a standard deviation of 10, were developed. The *T*-scores for the DSMD Externalizing, Internalizing, and Critical Pathology composites and Total scale, were calculated on the basis of the sum of the *T*-scores. For each composite, the *T*-score was based on the sum of the *T*-scores on the contributing scales (e.g., the Externalizing *T*-score was based on the sum of the *T*-scores on the Conduct and Attention scales). The Total scale *T*-score was calculated on the basis of the sum of the *T*-scores on the six scales. This method weights each scale equally in the derivation of composite and Total scale scores.

Percentile Rank

The DSMD percentile scores are based on the actual distributions of scores obtained from the standardization sample (Naglieri et al., 1994). These scores are not the same as those that would be obtained if the distributions of raw scores were normal. Tables for converting standard IQ scores to percentiles have been reported by many authors who used a normalization procedure (e.g., Wechsler, 1991). The conversion

TABLE 11.1
Median DSMD Internal Consistency Reliability Coefficients Across Rater and Gender

Scale	*5–12 years*	*13–18 years*
Externalizing	.97	.94
Conduct	.96	.97
Attention	.84	—
Delinquency	—	.75
Internalizing	.94	.96
Anxiety	.88	.84
Depression	.89	.93
Critical Pathology	.90	.93
Autism	.90	.88
Acute Problems	.78	.90
Total Scale	.98	.98

of IQ scores to percentiles in these cases is based on the normal curve. Because DSMD *T*-scores are based on the actual distribution of Total scale raw scores obtained during standardization and these scores are positively skewed, *T*-score to percentile rank conversions based on the normal curve technically do not apply to the DSMD, although the differences between the two are not large (Naglieri et al., 1994).

Reliability

Internal Consistency Reliability. Internal consistency reliability of the DSMD was determined using Cronbach's alpha for each of the 10 scales (Naglieri et al., 1994). The median reliability coefficients (across rater and gender) provided in Table 11.1 show that the scale has excellent internal consistency reliability. These data are especially important because they are used to obtain the standard errors of measurement, which in turn are used to guide interpretation of the scales. For example, to determine the significance of the difference between scores obtained by different raters, comparisons of scores for an individual child, and the comparison of scores over the course of treatment, standard errors of measurement are used to obtain the values needed for significance. Each of these issues is discussed more fully in the Interpretation section of this chapter.

Test–Retest Reliability. Test–retest reliability was examined from data obtained from the same rater for the same individual on two occasions. The magnitude of the obtained value informs about the degree to which random changes influence the scores (Anastasi, 1988). Two test–retest reliability studies were conducted for the DSMD: one with a clinical sample, the other with a regular education sample. Participants in the clinical study ($n = 48$) attended psychiatric day or residential treatment programs at Devereux facilities and represented a wide range of severe psychiatric disorders. Two ratings by the same rater were obtained for each participant over a 24-hour interval. Teachers provided paired ratings for 30 participants who were mostly males (67%) and White (83%), who ranged in age from 10 to 17 years ($M = 14.5$). The median scale test–retest reliability coefficient was .81. At the composite level, the reliabilities were .89 for Externalizing, .85 for Internalizing, .91 for Critical Pathology, and .90 for the Total scale. Similar results were obtained for a regular education sample from public schools (Naglieri et al., 1994).

Interrater Reliability. Interrater reliability for the DSMD was also examined for a sample of 45 children evaluated by their teachers and teacher's aides. The sample resided in the inpatient unit of a children's psychiatric hospital in the mid-Atlantic area. The paired teachers and teacher's aides completed ratings for the same child within a 1-week period. The results of this study indicate that the DSMD has good interrater reliability with a clinical population. The interrater reliability coefficients were .66 (Conduct), .55 (Attention), .48 (Anxiety), .52 (Depression), .46 (Autism), .44 (Acute Problems), .61 (Externalizing), .44 (Internalizing), .45 (Critical Pathology), and .52 (Total scale). All of the coefficients are significant ($p < .01$; Naglieri et al., 1994). The median coefficient for the six scales is .50, and for the three composites, .45. Coefficients of this magnitude are typical of those found in interrater studies with behavior rating scales. For example, in their review of 119 articles reporting interrater reliability findings with behavior rating scales, Achenbach, McConaughy, and Howell (1987) found a mean correlation coefficient of .60 with similar informants (e.g., teachers and teacher's aides).

Validity

The validity of the DSMD was examined through an extensive program designed to evaluate several types of validity evidence. Content-related validity was assessed to examine the extent to which the items included in the test represent the domain(s) being assessed. Construct-related validity was studied to determine the extent to which the DSMD measures the relevant theoretical constructs or traits. Especially important was criterion-related validation that involved the examination of how the test is related to an individual's performance within a particular domain. These dimensions of validity are summarized in the following sections. For more details, interested readers should consult chapter 4 of the DSMD manual (Naglieri et al., 1994).

Construct Validity. The DSMD items were subjected to a series of factor analyses so that the number of factors that best describes the underlying relations among the items could be identified. Analyses were conducted for the 5 to 12 and 13 to 18 age groups separately. Each correlation matrix was subjected to principal component analyses to obtain an indication of the size of the eigenvalues and guidance on the number of factors to consider. Next, principal factor analyses was used with multiple R^2 in the diagonal and varimax rotations.

Factor Analysis. The results of the factor analyses for the 5 to 12 age group indicated a large first factor (eigenvalue of 34.6) and eight additional factors with eigenvalues greater than 1.0 (Naglieri et al., 1994). Following this first step, factor analyses of four- through nine-factor solutions were obtained. First a nine-factor solution was selected, then eight, followed by seven, and so on until a factor solution that produced the clearest groups of items was found. The solutions with more than six factors had no items with their highest loadings on the sixth, seventh, eighth, or ninth factors. Over-factoring suggested that the six-factor solution was the best solution. This solution also contained the closest approximation of simple structure with the most number of factors that were interpretable. With this solution, nearly all the items loaded decisively on a factor, and seldom did an item's loading on any other factor approach its highest loading.

The results of the factor analyses for the 13 to 18 age group were remarkably similar to those obtained for the younger sample. Initial results indicated there was a large first factor (eigenvalue of 33.6) and eight additional factors with eigenvalues greater than 1.0 (Naglieri et al., 1994). Solutions with more than six factors had no items with their highest loadings on the sixth, seventh, eighth, or ninth factors. Also with the six-factor solution, the items had high loadings on one factor and low loadings on the other factors. Therefore, the six-factor solution appeared to be the best solution. In addition, the six-factor solution was easily interpretable from a conceptual framework based on the present understanding of developmental psychopathology.

Confirmatory Factor Analysis. The DSMD organization of six scales into three composites was evaluated with confirmatory factor analyses. LISREL-7 structural equation modeling program (Joreskog & Sorbom, 1989) was employed to contrast models of one, two, and three composite factors with a null-factor model (Naglieri et al., 1992). The organization of the six DSMD scales were examined for the 5- to 12-year-olds and 13- to 18-year-olds in the standardization sample and several indices of model-data fit were computed (Marsh, Balla, & McDonald, 1988). These included LISREL goodness-of-fit index (GFI), the goodness-of-fit index adjusted for degrees of freedom (AGFI), the root mean squared residual (RMSR) index, and the Bentler (1990) comparative fit index (CFI).

The results of the fit statistics appear comparable and within acceptable ranges for all three models. Logical and theoretical decisions, as well as the statistical quality of the fit, drove the selection of a three-factor composite model. For children age 5 to 12, the three-factor model yielded a superior GFI (.989), AGFI (.963), and CFI (.993) relative to the alternative models. For adolescents from age 13 to 18, the three-factor solution yielded a higher GFI (.931) and CFI (.935), but a somewhat reduced AGFI (.758) relative to the alternative models. These results provide strong support for the organization of the six scales into three composites. Together with expectations based on current understanding of mental disorders, both statistical and theoretical support for organization of the DSMD was found (Naglieri et al., 1994).

Criterion-Related Validity

Diagnostic Criterion Groups for Clinical Samples. The sensitivity of the DSMD's six scales and three composites to differences between samples provides important criterion-related evidence related to the diagnostic utility of the scales. The degree to which DSMD scores assist in this process provides a measure of criterion-related validity (Anastasi, 1988) and is especially important in validating the DSMD. Naglieri et al. (1994) provided considerable information about several investigations that compared the mean scale, composite, and Total scale scores for groups of patients with specific psychiatric diagnoses. The six groups included diagnoses of conduct, attention deficit hyperactivity, anxiety, depressive, autistic, and psychotic disorders. These diagnoses are among the most prevalent child and adolescent disorders. The subjects in the diagnostic groups criterion validity studies were carefully selected from a large pool of clinical samples. Participants were included if they had only one *DSM–III–R* psychiatric diagnosis from one of the six groups already noted. Over 750 cases were reviewed to obtain the 128 cases. Each child or adolescent was rated by a teacher or parent and the results are graphically presented in Fig. 11.2 and discussed here.

The results for the *conduct disorder* sample are clear. The Externalizing composite mean score of 75 is more than one standard deviation greater than the next highest composite mean score (Critical Pathology, 62). The profile of scale mean scores is characterized by elevations on the Conduct scale ($M = 71$) and the Delinquency scale

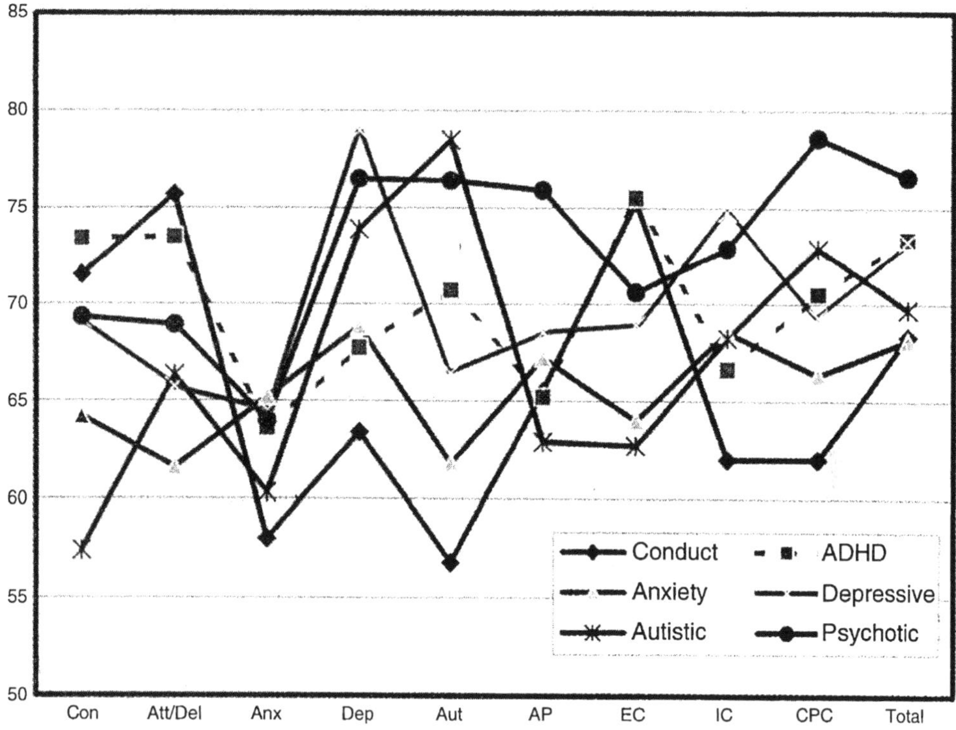

FIG. 11.2. Mean scale, composite, and total scores for six diagnostic groups.

($M = 75$), as would be expected in adolescents with conduct disorders. The third highest scale mean score, 65 on the Acute Problems scale, is the result of items on that scale associated with severe conduct disorders (e.g., "set or threaten to set a fire, hurt or torture animals, run away from home").

The children in the *attention deficit hyperactivity disorder (ADHD)* sample earned a Total scale mean in the Very Elevated range (73). The highest composite mean score (75) is on the Externalizing composite and consistent with an ADHD diagnosis. The highest mean scores (73 and 73) were found on the Conduct and Attention scales, respectively. The relatively high score on the Autism scale is attributable to a small number of items on that scale related to ADHD (e.g., "show a lack of fear of getting hurt in dangerous activities," "become easily overexcited").

The *anxiety disorders* group included diagnoses of posttraumatic stress disorder, separation anxiety disorder, obsessive-compulsive, and overanxious disorders and was considered a more heterogeneous group. The Total scale mean for this group is 68, which is in the Elevated range. The sample earned their highest mean score (68) on the Internalizing composite—which is not unexpected. The sample earned high scores on the Depression scale (68), Acute Problems (67) and Anxiety (65) scales. The profile for the anxiety disorders sample is not characterized by distinct scale elevations as is apparent for the other groups, which likely reflects the more heterogeneous nature of this sample.

The *depressive disorders* group was a relatively homogeneous sample with each participant having a single diagnosis of major depression. The Total scale mean score for this group is in the Very Elevated range (73). The Internalizing composite mean score of 74 is also in the Very Elevated range. The profile of scores shows a pattern with a distinct elevation on the Depression scale (79), which is clearly consistent with this group's diagnoses.

The results for individuals with *autism* shows that the group had a high Total scale mean (70), which is in the Elevated range. The Critical Pathology composite, which incorporates the Autism scale, has the highest mean score (73). The profile of the six scale scores shows distinct elevations on the Autism scale (79) and the Depression scale (74). The high score on the Depression scale is logical because this scale includes items related to social withdrawal and isolation, which are key clinical features of autism.

The results for individuals with *psychotic disorders* included persons with undifferentiated schizophrenia, psychotic disorder not otherwise specified, paranoid schizophrenia, and brief reactive psychosis. The group's Total scale mean (77) is in the Very Elevated range and is the highest for all the diagnostic criterion samples. The Critical Pathology composite mean score of 79 is also in the Very Elevated range. The profile of mean scores, including elevations on the Depression (77), Autism (76), and Acute Problems (76) scales, reflects the variety of symptoms associated with the different phases in the clinical course of schizophrenia.

Summary of Clinical Group Studies. The Total scale mean scores of the six diagnostic groups are all elevated, which indicates that the groups are comparable in their total level of pathology. For each of the six samples there were appropriate elevations in the composite scales. For example, Externalizing was elevated for the conduct disorder and attention deficit hyperactivity disorder samples, Internalizing was elevated for the anxiety disorders and depressive disorders samples, and Critical Pathology was elevated for the autistic and psychotic disorders samples. The profiles are pronounced for the five diagnostic groups that were characterized by relatively homogeneous diagnoses (conduct disorder, attention deficit hyperactivity disorder, depressive disorders, autistic disorder, and psychotic disorders). For the anxiety disorders sample, the complexity of the profile is consistent with the presence of diverse diagnoses. In conclusion, "these data provide strong evidence that the DSMD is sensitive to differing psychiatric diagnoses and that the DSMD can contribute to psychological and psychiatric assessment, diagnosis, and treatment planning" (Naglieri et al., 1994, p. 79).

Diagnostic Criterion Groups for Special Education Samples

In addition to studying several samples of individuals in clinical settings, Naglieri et al. (1994) also provided results of research with children in special education settings. The results of these studies are provided here and summarized in Table 11.2 by study and age of the sample. The table provides two important statistics. First, in all instances, the experimental and control samples were matched on the basis of age, sex, race, and geographic region. In every study, mean scores were compared between the samples and the percentage of correct classification and the *d*-ratio between the experimental and control samples was computed. The percentage of correct classification was determined using a cutoff score of 60 on the DSMD Total scale. The efficiency of differentiation between hospitalized individuals and those in the control sample was evaluated by chi-square analysis. That is, all the subjects in the experimental and control groups who had a Total scale *T*-score of 60 or more (i.e., 1 or more SDs above the mean) and those with a *T*-score less than 60 were identified as having significant emotional problems or not, respectively. These results were compared with their actual group membership (experimental vs. control). This provided a measure of the

TABLE 11.2
DSMD Total Scale Classifications Accuracy for Several Samples of Children Identified as SED and Regular Education by Age Group

	Ages 5–12			Ages 13–18		
Study	*Percent*	d-*ratio*	n	*Percent*	d-*ratio*	n
SED National Special Ed	72.2	1.0	223	65.5	1.4	142
SED Local Special Ed	78.1	1.3	64	69.0	1.2	84
SED/LD	—	—	—	87.5	1.2	88
SED in Psychiatric	69.6	1.5	112	89.7	2.5	58
SED in Residential	81.1	1.7	106	77.8	1.9	180
SED in Clinical Treatment	77.5	1.8	209	72.7	1.6	132
Average	75.7	1.5		77.0	1.6	
Total *n* of cases			714			684

Note. From DSMD manual, p. 99. Copyright © 1992, The Devereux Foundation. Adapted with permission.

percentage of the total sample correctly identified by the DSMD Total scale score. Additional statistical results, such as multivariate analysis of variance (MANOVA), chi-square analyses, and so on are provided in the DSMD manual (Naglieri et al., 1994). Each study is described next.

SED in National Special Education Settings. Seriously emotionally disturbed (SED) students who were receiving public special education services were contrasted to a matched regular education national sample. Both part- and full-time students identified by the local school systems as having a serious emotional disturbance and placed in special educational settings were included in this investigation. The regular education control sample for this investigation was selected from the standardization sample matched on the basis of age, race, ethnicity, and gender.

SED in a Local Special Education Setting. Seriously emotionally disturbed students who were receiving public special education services were compared with a matched regular education control sample. Both groups were from greater Philadelphia area. The control sample of regular education students was matched to the SED sample on the basis of age, race, ethnicity, and gender.

SED LD in Private Special Education. Dually Diagnosed Learning Disabled (LD) and Emotionally Disturbed students in private educational settings were compared with a normal control sample. The samples were similar on the basis of age, race, ethnic origin, and gender. The students with learning and emotional problems attended a private school, where they received specialized educational intervention as well as group and individual counseling. Students with learning and emotional problems were included in this sample if school records contained evidence of both educational and psychological problems. Criteria for selection included psychological treatment in school or community-based settings or a history of behavioral problems.

SED—Psychiatric. Severely emotionally disturbed students in psychiatric hospitals were compared with a normal control group selected from the standardization sample on the basis of age, race, ethnicity, and gender. Two groups of children from age 5 to 12 and adolescents from age 13 to 18 were included in this study, each group included an experimental (SED) and control sample.

SED—Residential. Severely emotionally disturbed children and adolescents in residential treatment were compared with a matched normal control sample. The experimental group included individuals in long-term psychiatric treatment for severe psychological problems. The clinical sample was matched with a control group selected from the standardization sample on the basis of age, race, region (all from the northeast region), ethnicity, and gender. Both 5 to 12 and 13 to 18 year age groups were included.

SED—in Clinical Treatment. Clinically diagnosed individuals receiving special education services were compared with a normal control sample that participated in this study. The clinical sample was composed of Devereux Foundation clients served in residential and day special education and psychiatric treatment programs in Arizona, Florida, Massachusetts, New Jersey, and Texas. They exhibited a wide range of psychopathological disorders. The comparison group was drawn from public facilities in Pennsylvania and Kentucky. Any individual who was receiving counseling, psychotherapy, or special education services was excluded from the normal comparison group.

A summary of these results is provided in Table 11.2. Included are the Total scale classification accuracy rates by age level for each of the six studies. The results clearly indicate that the DSMD did an excellent job of separating children with various degrees of mental disorders from normal control samples. For age 5 to 12, the accuracy rates varied from 69.6% (Validity Study 4) to 81.1% (Study 5). For ages 13 to 18, the lowest accuracy rate was 65.5% (Study 1), and the highest, 89.7% (Study 4). The average total classification rates are 75.7% and 77.0% for the 5 to 12 and 13 to 18 age levels, respectively (Naglieri et al., 1994).

The overall *d*-ratio values at the two age levels were also very large. These *d*-ratios indicate the extent to which the group mean scores for children and adolescents with serious emotional problems differ from those for individuals who do not have emotional problems. These results provide considerable support for the criterion validity of the Devereux Scales of Mental Disorders as a measure that can separate those who have emotional disorders from those who do not (for more details, see Naglieri et al., 1994).

INTERPRETATION OF THE DSMD

Interpretation of the DSMD involves a carefully prescribed sequence of examination that moves from most general (composite scales) to most specific (item level). Although attention is paid to the three basic elements of the scale—Externalizing, Internalizing, and Critical Pathology—scales within these three composites are carefully examined. Finally, analysis of the individual item scores is used to facilitate treatment planning. Follow-up analysis includes comparisons of pre- and posttest scores on the three composites and six scales.

Definition of Composite Scales

Externalizing behaviors involve problems that relate to a person's conflicts with others in the environment. A child or adolescent with a high score on the Externalizing composite will likely be seen as aggressive, disobedient, annoying, disruptive, undercontrolled, restless, or inattentive. This includes Conduct (disruptive and hostile acts in which the basic rights of others are violated and age-appropriate norms are disregarded), Attention (difficulty with concentration and distractibility), and Delinquency (those behaviors considered to be out of accord with societal standards or the law) problems.

Internalizing problems involve excessive worrying, social withdrawal, anxiety, and overcontrol or inhibition associated with the individual's state of well-being. Included are behaviors reflecting Anxiety (excessive worry, fears, tension, low self-concept, and somatic complaints) and signs of Depression (withdrawal from social contacts, depressed mood, and decreased interest or pleasure in activities).

Critical Pathology behaviors represent severe mental, behavioral, or emotional disturbances. This includes behaviors that are often symptomatic of an individual who may be out of contact with reality resulting in disruption of daily functioning. The behaviors in the Critical Pathology composite scale are not seen in normal individuals and are problematic if they occur at all. This includes behaviors that indicate impaired social interaction and communication, such as disorganized and echolalic speech, inappropriate social interactions, and odd motoric responses (Autism scale). The hallucinatory and bizarre behaviors described in the Acute Problems scale are typical of individuals with severe psychological disturbances that can be described as psychotic. Descriptions of the DSMD Total scale and its composites and scales are summarized in Fig. 11.3.

DSMD Scores

The DSMD Total scale, three composites, and six scales all have a mean of 50 and a standard deviation of 10. The Total scale *T*-score is the most reliable way of describing a child's or adolescent's performance across the areas measured by the six scales of the DSMD. The scores on the composites (Externalizing, Internalizing, and Critical Pathology) and scales (Conduct, Attention, Anxiety, Depression, Autism, and Acute Problems for ages 5–12 and Conduct, Delinquency, Anxiety, Depression, Autism, and Acute Problems for ages 13–18) describe the individual's performance at more specific levels, and therefore, are most informative. These scores are further described using percentile and categorical ratings. Naglieri et al. (1994) suggested that a cutoff score of 60 (1 *SD* above the mean) could be used for determining when a person's scores on the DSMD depart substantially from the average for the standardization sample and therefore are indicative of significant problems reported by the rater.

Summary of Interpretive Steps for the DSMD

The following steps should be followed when interpreting the DSMD. These steps are listed first, then described in some detail. The steps presented graphically in flow charts in Figs. 11.4 and 11.5 (see Naglieri et al., 1994, for more information), are as follows:

1. Examine the Total Test, and Externalizing, Internalizing, and Critical Pathology scales to determine if any fall above a *T*-score of 59.
2. Compare the Externalizing, Internalizing, and Critical Pathology scales to determine if any one of these is significantly higher than the child's or adolescent's mean.
3. Compare the Conduct, Attention (age 5–12), Delinquency (age 13–18), Anxiety,

Total scale -- An overall evaluation of the behaviors included in Externalizing, Internalizing, and Critical Pathology composites

Externalizing Composite -- Behaviors that involve conflicts between the individual and his or her environment

Conduct Scale -- Disruptive and hostile acts

Attention Scale -- Problems with concentration, distractibility, and motor excess (ages 5-12)

Delinquency Scale -- Acts that illustrate a failure to comply with societal rules and laws (ages 13-18)

Internalizing Composite -- Behaviors that reflect the individual's state of psychological well-being

Anxiety Scale -- Problems with worries, fears, low self-concept, and tension

Depression Scale -- Problems with withdrawal, few emotional reactions, lowered mood, and inability to experience pleasure

Critical Pathology Composite -- Behaviors that represent severe disturbances of childhood or adolescence

Autism Scale -- Problems of impaired social interactions and communication and unusual motor behaviors

Acute Problems Scale -- Behaviors that are hallucinatory, primitive, bizarre, self-injurious, or dangerous

FIG. 11.3. Description of the DSMD scales and composites.

Depression, Autism, and Acute Problem scales to determine if any one of these is significantly higher than the child's or adolescent's mean.

4. Analyze the items to determine which problem items were rated significantly high for the child and warrant consideration in treatment planning.
5. Compare ratings obtained from parents and teachers to determine if the child is rated differently in different environments or by different raters.
6. Compare pre- and posttest scores following treatment to determine effectiveness of interventions.

Step 1: Initial Examination of Total and Composite Scores. Step 1 is a descriptive one that involves examination of the *T*-scores on the broad scales. The cutoff score of 60 is suggested as a point to determine that significantly problems exist, but should not be used rigidly. Practitioners should consider the advantages and disadvantages of higher or lower values based on the aims of the evaluation and the specific populations of interest.

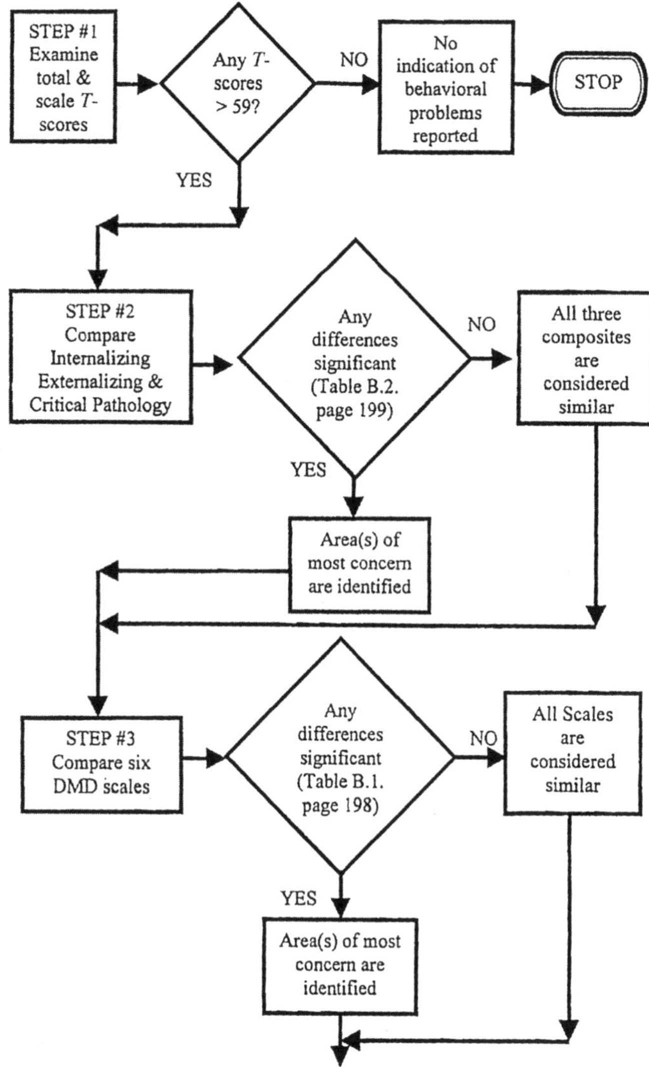

FIG. 11.4. Flow chart for interpretation of the DSMD.

Steps 2 and 3: Intraindividual Comparisons. Comparisons of the three composites as well as the six scales are accomplished using intraindividual comparisons. For example, comparing the six scale *T*-scores allows the clinician to determine if one or more of those scores are significantly elevated relative to the child's or adolescent's average of those scores. The purpose of such an analysis is the identification of any scale (or composite) score or scores that are significantly greater than the child's or adolescent's mean and thereby identify particular areas of concern. Because the *T*-scores for the six scales (or for the three composites) are compared for a individual for a single rating, this is an intraindividual approach to interpretation. This interpretive perspective, often used in interpreting intelligence test results (Naglieri, 1993; Sattler, 1988), is based on the comparison of each scale *T*-score to the individual's own mean *T*-score and was originally described by Davis (1959).

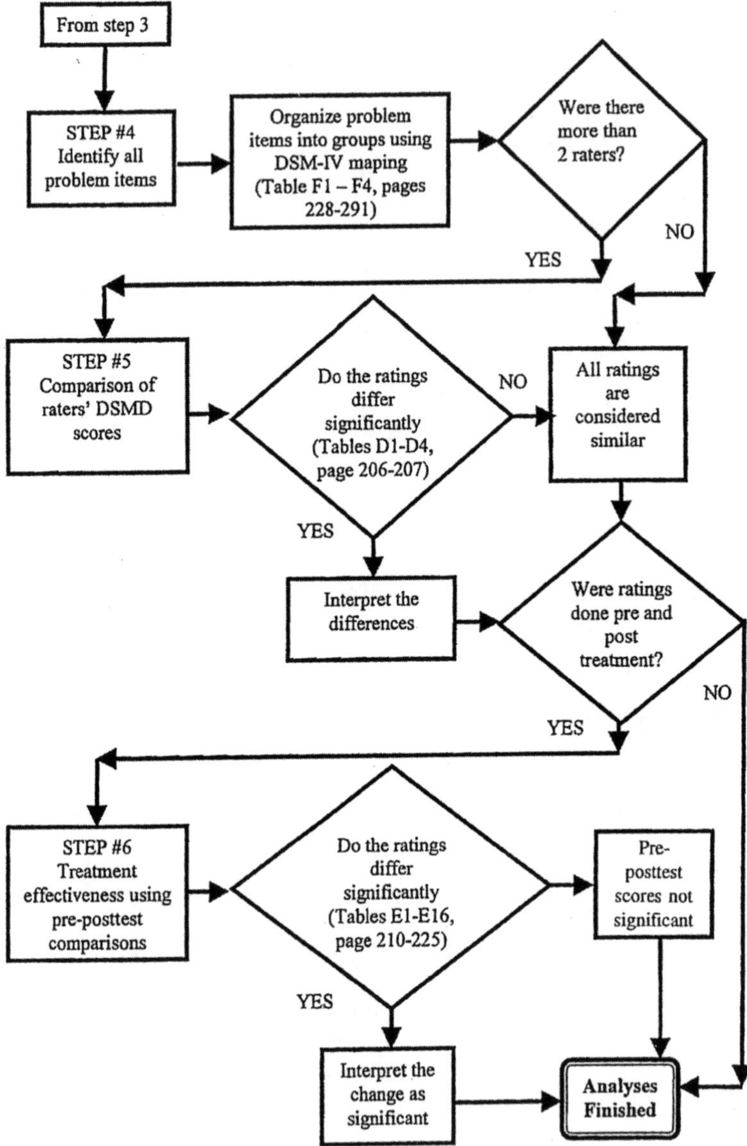

FIG. 11.5. Flow chart for interpretation of the DSMD.

The procedure for identifying significant differences between an individual's scale *T*-scores and the mean of scale *T*-scores or between composite *T*-scores and the mean of composite *T*-scores are basically the same. The following example illustrates the steps for scale *T*-scores using the data provided in Table 11.3. This illustration involves an 8-year-old female based on a rating by her mother (parent rater). To determine if any of the six *T*-scores is significantly greater than the girl's mean *T*-score, refer to the values in Table B.1 from the DSMD manual (Naglieri et al., 1994, pp. 198–199) and then:

1. Calculate the average of the six *T*-scores (in this case, 55.5). Subtract the mean from each of the scale *T*-scores to obtain the difference score (the difference

TABLE 11.3
Intraindividual Interpretative Example

Scale	*T-Score*	*Difference from Child's Mean*	*Difference Required at 90%*	*Result*
Conduct	58	2.5	6.1	Not Significant
Attention	68	12.5	9.9	Significant
Anxiety	55	−0.5	8.3	Not Significant
Depression	53	−2.5	8.7	Not Significant
Autism	54	−1.5	8.3	Not Significant
Acute Problems	45	−10.5	9.9	Not Significant
Child's Mean	55.5			

Note. Difference = *T*-score minus the child's average *T*-score. Negative difference scores are ignored because the goal of intraindividual comparisons is to identify high scores.

between each score and the child's average score). A positive sign indicates the scale *T*-score is above the child's mean; a negative sign indicates the scale *T*-score is below the mean. Ignore negative difference scores because the aim of the intraindividual comparisons is to identify high scores only.

2. Compare the difference scores to the values provided in Table B.1 of the DSMD manual. A difference score equal to or greater than the tabled value (and positive in sign) indicates that the scale *T*-score is significantly greater than the person's mean scale *T*-score. In this example, the Attention scale is an area of particular difficulty for this child, relative to her other scale *T*-scores.

Step 4: Problem Item Identification. Identification of specific problem items is the most detailed level of DSMD analysis. This level of analysis reflects specific behavioral difficulties that contribute to the overall *T*-scores for the scales and composites. The method of identifying specific problem items was developed following a similar approach to the one used by Naglieri, McNeish, and Bardos (1991). The method specifies that when an individual item score exceeds the normative mean item score plus one standard deviation it is considered significant. The values needed to identify a particular item as significant are provided in the DSMD manual (Tables C.1 and C.2) and noted on the DSMD record form. These scores indicate that the rater reported the child or adolescent is experiencing significant difficulty with a particular behavior to the extent that the item score is outside of the normal range.

Problem item identification provides important information for interpretation and intervention. First, problem item identification allows the practitioner to explain the nature of the behaviors that may contribute to a high score, for example, in the Conduct scale. The items rated at the problem item level are most important and specifically clarify the nature of the reported problem. Second, problem item analysis yields information that is very relevant for treatment planning. The items that were identified can be particularly useful for the development of behavioral goals and/or objectives in individual treatment or education plans.

Step 5: Comparison of Scores Across Raters. The standard error of the difference between scores must be taken into consideration when a practitioner compares DSMD scores obtained from different raters (Naglieri et al., 1994). Total scale *T*-scores based on ratings from a child's mother and father, for example, will differ as a function of measurement error. In order to account for measurement error, the DSMD manual provides the standard error of the difference between two scores as a method of determining when *T*-scores based on ratings by both parents, by two teachers, or by a parent and a teacher differ significantly.

Naglieri et al. (1994) provided the differences between *T*-scores needed for significance based on ratings obtained from two raters. Practitioners simply compare the two scores and contrast the result to tabled values (at the 90% level of significance). For example, if a 16-year-old female earned *T*-scores of 60 and 71 on the Anxiety scale, when rated by a parent and teacher, respectively. The 11-point difference is significant (the value reported in Table D.3. on page 207 of the DSMD manual is 10).

The next step in interpretation of the DSMD is conducted after treatment is provided. For this reason, the sixth step in interpretation is presented in the next section.

USE OF THE DSMD FOR TREATMENT MONITORING

The final step in the interpretation of the DSMD is the examination of change in scores over the course of treatment. This section, therefore, begins with the examination of pre- and posttest scores. The method described here is intended to provide a statistically supported evaluation of treatment effectiveness.

Step 6: Pretest–Posttest Comparisons

Continuing with the last step in Fig. 11.5, changes in a child's or adolescent's *T*-scores over the course of treatment can be evaluated using the DSMD. To do so, the statistical significance of the difference between pretest and posttest scores should be determined to account for psychometric issues. Naglieri et al. (1994) used a method described by Atkinson (1991), which requires the comparison of the pretest score with a range of scores that represents the variability expected by both regression to the mean and measurement error. The posttest score is compared to a range of scores provided in Appendix E of the DSMD manual. For example, if an 8-year-old male is initially rated by a teacher and earns a Conduct score of 76, a range of 72 to 79 provides the scores that can be expected due to measurement error and regression effects. If the boy was rated by the teacher after treatment and earned a score less than 72, then because posttest *T*-score would fall outside the range provided in the table, the change indicates a significant pre–post treatment effect.

The evaluation of the effectiveness of treatment outcomes based on the DSMD should also involve the dual criteria of statistically reliable and clinically meaningful change. Jacobsen and Truax (1991) recommended these two criteria. The first statistically reliable change is addressed through use of the standard error of prediction. The second is clinical meaningfulness of the change. That is, the closer the posttest score is to the normative mean, the more meaningful the change. Posttreatment scores are considered optimal if they fall below 60 (1 *SD* above the mean). Posttreatment scores that are significantly lower than the initial scores, but still above 60, indicate that improvement has been shown but behavioral problems are still present. For example, if a 10-year-old male obtains a pretreatment Total DSMD *T*-score of 70 as rated by his teacher and a posttreatment score of 64, the difference is significant (range = 65 – 74 for a pretest Total scale score of 70). Because the posttest score (64) falls below this range, there has been a significant change in behavior as reflected by the DSMD score. Because the posttreatment score is above 60, this means that problems are still indicated, but they are of a lesser severity than initially found.

DSMD and Treatment Monitoring: Conclusions

A crucial decision in the design and implementation of treatment monitoring and outcome efforts is the selection of appropriate dependent measures. To be maximally useful, the measures need to satisfy a variety of technical and practical criteria (Newman & Ciarlo, 1994). Perhaps most important, the measures need to be directly related to the goals of the treatment plan (i.e., have high content validity). The monitoring or outcome instrument should examine "the most important and frequently observed symptoms, problems, goals or other domains of change for the (individual or) group" (Ciarlo, Brown, Edwards, Kiresuk, & Newman, 1986, p. 26). In addition, the measures need to be standardized, well developed, and enjoy strong psychometric properties. Of special relevance is the need for the measures to be reliable and sensitive indices of changes in the child or adolescent's behavior over the course of treatment.

Treatment monitoring affords the client, the family, the therapist, and the funding source with reliable and clinically meaningful "real-time" data to gauge the ongoing success of the planned interventions. In this way, all parties are able to evaluate progress. Youngsters get feedback on the relative success of their efforts in working toward the agreed-on treatment goals. The parents similarly receive data on their youngsters' progress. Perhaps most important, the therapist is provided with reliable, timely feedback in the form of specific behavioral data on how well the treatment is progressing. The monitoring allows the therapist to make midcourse adjustments that reflects sound clinical practice and is the hallmark of a continuous quality improvement philosophy (Pfeiffer & Shott, 1996; Vermillion & Pfeiffer, 1993). The DSMD meets all these criteria and is therefore an excellent method for treatment monitoring.

USE OF THE DSMD FOR TREATMENT PLANNING

Until recently, the history of behavioral health care has been marked by a lack of attention to formalized treatment planning. Previously, most mental health providers offered at best only a sketchy and vague plan that did not include either a clinical formulation or implementation plan for the treatment, much less a set of measurable treatment goals. However, the health care field has entered an era of accountability (Linder, 1991). Governmental and private funders of mental health care are increasingly demanding outcome data to justify expenditures and select providers. Mirin and Namerow (1991) predicted that "reliable data about the outcomes of care will be essential in demonstrating that particular types of mental health care are worth paying for" (p. 1008).

Reliable outcome data necessitate a more carefully crafted treatment plan that meets the client's needs, is individualized and specific, and measurable in terms of setting goals and objectives that can be used to chart the client's ongoing progress and ultimate outcome. A detailed written treatment plan benefits not only the client, therapist, and insurance company, but also the psychotherapeutic process. The client is served by a written treatment plan in that it stipulates the focus of the treatment and the specific outcomes that the client and therapist are jointly and collaboratively working toward (Jongsman, Peterson, & McInnis, 1996). Therapists benefit because the plan serves as a road map that guides the treatment process and selection of therapeutic interventions, and keeps them on course working toward the resolution of the agreed on therapeutic goals.

The DSMD is only one important instrument used in the development of a treatment plan. The foundation of a well-conceived treatment plan includes a thorough biopsychosocial assessment, with particular attention to both historical and present factors that contribute to the client's presenting problem, as well as the anticipated resolution of the problem. In working with children and adolescents, in particular, the clinician will want to include pertinent information on family issues, medical and early developmental issues, school and academic concerns, current stressors and resources—both individual and within the family and community—current physical health, and a host of case-relevant psychosocial, emotional, behavioral, and interpersonal factors. The DSMD can be an important measure of a youngster's present psychiatric status that helps guide the development of the problem definition, case formulation, planned intervention, and anticipated treatment goals.

Treatment planning begins with the identification of a very select number of the most significant problems. The clinician benefits from identifying no more than one or two highest priority primary problems (see DSMD intraindividual method later), with perhaps an equally limited number of secondary significant problems (see DSMD scale and problem item analysis). This does not intimate that the client is not necessarily presenting with a multitude of significant behavioral concerns. Rather, it simply implies that the focus of treatment needs to start somewhere, and that it is best to begin with a prioritization of issues so that the youngster, family, and therapist can together work toward the resolution of a select number of specific issues.

The DSMD is very well suited to play a key role in this process. The DSMD provides the clinician with a methodology to identify specific symptoms that can guide the clinician in prioritizing behaviors rated as problematic by the youngster's parents and teachers. Additionally, the DSMD affords a linkage with the diagnostic criteria and codes found in the *Diagnostic and Statistical Manual of Mental Disorders* (APA, 1994), and behaviorally specific statements that can serve as a platform or starting point for personally crafted treatment goals and objectives.

Use of DSMD With Other Data

The DSMD, like any psychological test, is most appropriately used in treatment planning when incorporated with other diagnostic and clinical information. Although the DSMD is an instrument that provides ratings on descriptive behaviors of relatively low inference and high reliability, it is most useful when used in conjunction with other data to corroborate clinical hypotheses. Specifically, the DSMD should be used in concert with information obtained from a developmental, medical, and school history, behavioral observations (preferably conducted in a variety of settings), clinical interview with the child and parents, and other appropriate diagnostic information (e.g., self-report measure, personality test). Ultimately, the various sets of diagnostic information should complement the development of a detailed functional analysis of the youngster's behavior, with particular attention to both strengths and areas of concern, as well as a road map to guide intervention.

The DSMD affords the clinician a broad landscape of topographical descriptors of potential problem behaviors. In essence, the DSMD provides in an efficient and highly reliable fashion a focus on the "what" of problem behaviors. The clinician still needs to incorporate other information in developing a functional analysis of the problem behaviors—the "what for" that is driving or supporting the child's problems.

Potential Use or Limits for Treatment Planning in a Managed Care Setting

There is considerable utility and value in using the DSMD within a managed care environment, especially because the scale allows the clinician to efficiently assess, identify the problem, and formulating a reasonable (i.e., not costly, attainable) and measurable treatment plan. The DSMD is helpful to the clinician because the items readily translate into behaviorally measurable treatment goals. Items can easily be identified as high priority and therefore selected by the clinician, in collaboration with the youngster and parents, as most needing intervention. Additionally, the scale lends itself to evaluation of treatment effectiveness (see DSMD pre–post section).

USE OF DSMD FOR TREATMENT OUTCOMES ASSESSMENT

The DSMD is ideally suited for use in mental health treatment outcome assessment. As mentioned earlier, the content of the scale is derived primarily from the diagnostic criteria of the *Diagnostic and Statistical Manual of the American Psychiatric Association* (*DSM–IV*; American Psychiatric Association, 1994). In addition, it reflects the full range of psychopathology seen in childhood and adolescence, including the more severely disturbed disorders that are often missing from other scales. For instance, the DSMD includes items related to stereotypy, echolalia, fire setting, self-stimulatory and self-abusive behaviors, and hurting and torturing animals.

A unique feature of the DSMD regarding treatment outcome assessment is the pre–post comparison methodology. The dual criterion approach, which recognizes behavioral changes that are both statistically significant (i.e., reliable) and clinically meaningful (i.e., socially valid), provides practitioners with an effective treatment outcome methodology. The first aspect of this dual criterion addresses the issue of how large the change in *T*-scores must be to enable the therapist to conclude that there has been change in behavior, that is, that the pretest–posttest difference reflects "real differences as opposed to ones that are illusory, questionable or unreliable" (Jacobson & Truax, 1991, p. 12). The second aspect of the dual criterion addresses the social validity or real-life meaning of the noted changes in the youngster's behavior.

Newman and colleagues (Green & Newman, 1996; Newman & Ciarlo, 1994) provided a useful set of criteria for selecting psychological instruments for treatment outcome assessment. The criteria include relevance to the target group (standardization sample); a simple measure with good instructions and administration manual; a measure with objective referents (for which concrete examples are given at key points on the rating scale); use of multiple respondents; psychometric strength, including reliability, validity, and treatment sensitivity; low cost of the measure; readily understood by nonprofessional audiences; easy feedback and uncomplicated interpretation; useful in clinical services; and compatibility with clinical theories and practices. The DSMD meets all of these criteria and is therefore an excellent tool for treatment outcome assessment.

Potential Use for Service Report Cards

Governmental and private providers of mental health care are increasingly relying on monitoring and outcome data to justify expenditures, and to select and continue with providers. Reliable clinical data about the outcomes of mental health care is now essential in demonstrating that particular types of mental health services are worth paying for. Accrediting bodies such as the Joint Commission on the Accreditation of Health Care Organizations are systematizing the collection and reporting of outcome indicators, leading O'Leary (1993) to assert that report card day is coming for health care providers. Individual consumers of mental health services are becoming increasingly sophisticated with demonstrable value for their health care dollar. Because of the strengths of the DSMD already articulated, it can be considered an excellent outcome measure to include in a report card.

CASE STUDY

Selected Background Information

The case of Vincent is marked by considerable familial turmoil. Vincent, age 7, is a boy who has a history of behavior problems that have begun to have significant impact on his performance at school. His anxiety problems may be related to the marital discord of his parents, which has been present for at least the last 6 years, and the recent finalization of the divorce. He now resides with his father. Vincent's mother lives some distance away, in a different state.

DSMD Results

The DSMD Scoring Assistant provides scores based on ratings by Vincent's father. Vincent's overall patterns of behavior were not extreme enough to attain an elevated DSMD rating (see Fig. 11.6). His Total scale *T*-score of 57 (90% confidence interval = 54–60) is in the borderline range. A borderline score indicates that Vincent may be experiencing problems in certain areas or with specific behaviors. Vincent was rated as exhibiting a higher level of behavioral disturbance than 81% of children. Significant elevations were found on the Internalizing composite and on the Attention and Depression scales.

Vincent's highest rating was on the Internalizing composite, a measure of behaviors that reflects the individual's state of psychological well-being. Internalizing behaviors are those that include excessive worrying, social withdrawal, anxiety, and overcontrol or inhibition. On this composite Vincent received a *T*-score of 67 (90% confidence interval = 61–70), which falls in the elevated range. This score indicates that Vincent is experiencing more symptoms in this area than 93% of children. The Internalizing composite is comprised of the Anxiety and Depression scales on which Vincent obtained *T*-scores of 51 (90% confidence interval of 45–57) and 82 (90% confidence interval of 72–84), respectively. The Intraindividual Comparison, which compares individual scale and composite scores to Vincent's mean scale and composite scores, indicated significant elevations on the Internalizing Composite and the Depression scale (see Fig. 11.7).

It is apparent from these data that Vincent is experiencing attention problems as well as signs of depression. His DSMD Attention score of 65 is elevated, but his Depression score of 82 is significantly higher than the mean of all his six *T*-scores on the separate scales of the DSMD (see the section on Intraindividual Comparison). This means that the most severe area of concern is with signs of Depression, which should be the primary focus of intervention. Attention problems, although noted and important, are secondary to problems with Depression.

Further analysis of the DSMD Problem Items indicates that Vincent's depressed mood is apparent by high ratings on items involving Somatic Complaints (difficulty

Client Information
Name: Vincent
Gender: Male
Date of Rating: 10/3/97
Date of Birth: 10/3/90
Age: 7 years
Rater: Frank M.
Relationship to Child: Father
Norms Used: Parent
Scale Score Analyses
(significant findings are indicated by shaded areas)

DSMD Score Summary

Scale Composite	Raw Score	Vincent's *T* Score	90% Confidence Interval	Percentile
Conduct	29	44	41-48	30
Attention	13	65	56-69	93
Externalizing		55	51-58	72
Anxiety	16	51	45-57	62
Depression	37	82	72-84	99
Internalizing		67	61-70	93
Autism	8	50	45-55	64
Acute Problems	0	45	38-54	49
Critical Pathology		47	42-53	53
Total		57	54-60	81

*This table illustrates Vincent's functioning in comparison to a normative group. *T* scores have a mean of 50 and a standard deviation of 10; a score of 60 or higher indicates an area of concern.

FIG. 11.6. Devereux Scales of Mental Disorders: child form, ages 5–12.

sleeping and complaining of physical problems), lowered affect (appearing discouraged, unhappy, etc.), and interpersonal problems such as social isolation, emotional variability, poor self-esteem, and dependency. His high level of anxiety is apparent by his inattention (preoccupation by thoughts, trouble concentrating, and distorted thinking), overeating, and overactivity due to a high level of nervousness.

The DSMD Scoring Assistant also provides a listing of all problem items and the *DSM–IV* diagnostic categories with which they are associated. Although not presented in this chapter, this is intended to assist the practitioner with an initial examination of how the ratings of the child may be related to mental disorders included in the *DSM–IV*. They are not intended to be diagnostic, but rather to inform the practitioner of the degree to which the behaviors receiving high ratings might contribute to the criteria. Determination of specific diagnostic category should not be made solely on the basis of this, or any, rating scale. Examination of the results, like analysis of the problem items, brings out how Vincent's ratings suggest that he has earned scores that especially suggest separation anxiety disorder, major depressive episode, posttraumatic stress

	Vincent's *T* Score	Difference Score (*T* Score - Mean *T* Score)	Significant?* (p<.10)
Scale (Mean *T* Score=56.2)			
Conduct	44	-12.2	No
Attention	65	8.8	No
Anxiety	51	-5.2	No
Depression	82	25.8	Yes
Autism	50	-6.2	No
Acute Problems	45	-11.2	No
Composite (Mean *T* Score=56.3)			
Externalizing	55	-1.3	No
Internalizing	67	10.7	Yes
Critical Pathology	47	-9.3	No

FIG. 11.7. Intraindividual comparison. (Significant findings are indicated by shaded areas.) *Scale and composite scores that are significantly greater than Vincent's mean scale and composite scores are identified by "yes," indicating particular areas of concern (Devereux Scales of Mental Disorders Manual, p. 104).

disorder, acute stress disorder, and generalized anxiety disorder (all of which are consistent with the previous discussion). The additional areas provided by the DSMD Scoring Assistant would be considered less appropriate due to the smaller number of items included in each category and their inconsistency with the larger picture for this child.

DSMD Considerations

Vincent's behavior should be assessed by multiple raters in multiple environments to examine the consistency of behavioral ratings. These ratings should then be compared using the DSMD Interrater Comparison Procedure (Devereux Scales of Mental Disorders manual, p. 107) to assess the situational specificity or generality of Vincent's behavioral problems. Treatment planning should consider the reports of the following:

1. Somatic Complaints: A medical evaluation may be advisable to eliminate possible physiological determinants of Vincent's physical complaints.
2. Social Isolation: Frank M. reported Vincent to be socially withdrawn. Social

skills training may be an appropriate intervention to increase and encourage social contacts.

3. Depressed Affect: Vincent is reported to exhibit behaviors reflecting Depressed Affect, indicating that he may be suffering from a Mood Disorder. This possibility should be investigated using the *DSM–IV* Inquiry and other appropriate assessment techniques.
4. Vincent is at risk of truancy. Close contact should be maintained with his school.
5. A medical evaluation is recommended to rule out a physical cause for Vincent's somatic complaints.

Vincent's response to interventions should be measured using the DSMD Treatment Outcome Evaluation Procedure (Devereux Scales of Mental Disorders manual, p. 109). Because Vincent's Total scale *T*-score was not in the clinical range (60 or higher), the effectiveness of interventions should be assessed at the composite, scale, or item level. The following posttest *T*-scores would indicate reliable improvement: Internalizing composite, 59; Attention scale, 52; Depression scale, 69.

CONCLUSIONS

This chapter has provided a summary of information more fully discussed in the DSMD manual (Naglieri et al., 1994). Emphasis in this chapter, like in the DSMD manual, has been on illustrating how the rating scale can be used to assist in the identification of mental disorders. In addition, it is clear from the information presented that the DSMD gives practitioners and researchers a method that has high reliability, considerable validity support, and numerous interpretation methods. Most important are the psychometric methods for interpretation, including comparison of rater scores, comparisons of scores for an individual child, determination of specific behaviors to target in treatment, and determination of the effectiveness of treatment through examination of pre–post scores. The dual criterion of reliable and clinically meaningful change, in conjunction with other interpretive methods, provides clinicians with a tool to meet today's standards for identification, treatment monitoring, and determination of treatment effectiveness.

REFERENCES

Achenbach, T. M., McConaughy, S. H., & Howell, C. T. (1987). Child adolescent behavioral and emotional problems: Implications of cross informant correlations for situational specificity. *Psychological Bulletin, 101*, 213–232.

American Psychiatric Association. (1987). *Diagnostic and statistical manual of mental disorders* (3rd ed., rev.). Washington, DC: Author.

American Psychiatric Association. (1994). *Diagnostic and statistical manual of mental disorders* (4th ed.). Washington, DC: Author.

American Psychiatric Association Task Force on *DSM–IV*. (1991). *DSM–IV options book: Work in progress (7/1/91)*. Washington, DC: Author.

Anastasi, A. (1988). *Psychological testing* (6th ed.). New York: Macmillan.

Atkinson, L. (1991). Three standard errors of measurement and the Wechsler Memory Scale-Revised. *Psychological Assessment, 3*, 136–138.

Bentler, P. M. (1990). Comparative fit indices in structural models. *Psychological Bulletin, 107*, 238–246.

Ciarlo, J. A., Brown, T. R., Edwards, D. W., Kiresuk, T. J., & Newman, F. L. (1986). *Assessing mental health treatment outcome measurement techniques* (DHHS Publication No. ADM 86-1301). Washington, DC: U.S. Government Printing Office.

Crocker, L., & Algina, J. (1986). *Introduction to classical and modern test theory.* New York: Holt, Rinehart & Winston.

Dale, E., & O'Rourke, J. (1981). *The living word vocabulary.* Chicago: World Book Child-craft International.

Davis, F. B. (1959). Interpretation of differences among averages and individual test scores. *Journal of Educational Psychology, 50,* 162–170.

Dougherty, D. M., Saxe, L. M., Cross, T., & Silverman, N. (1987). *Children's mental health: Problems and services.* Durham, NC: Duke University Press.

Garfinkel, B. D., Carlson, G. A., & Weller, E. B. (Eds.). (1990). *Psychiatric disorders in children and adolescents.* Philadelphia: Saunders.

Green, R., & Newman, F. (1996). Criteria for selecting instruments to assess treatment outcomes. In S. I. Pfeiffer (Ed.), *Outcome assessment in residential treatment* (pp. 29–48). Binghamton, NY: Haworth Press.

Hooper, S. R., Hynd, G. W., & Mattison, R. E. (Eds.). (1992). *Child psychopathology: Diagnostic criteria and clinical assessment.* Hillsdale, NJ: Lawrence Erlbaum Associates.

Jacobsen, N. S., & Truax, P. (1991). Clinical significance: A statistical approach to defining meaningful change in psychotherapy research. *Journal of Consulting and Clinical Psychology, 59,* 12–19.

Jongsman, A. E., Peterson, L. M., & McInnis, W. P. (1996). *The child and adolescent psychotherapy treatment planner.* New York: Wiley.

Joreskog, K. G., & Sorbom, D. (1989). *LISREL 7: A guide to the program and applications* (2nd ed.). Chicago, IL: SPSS.

Lewis, M., & Miller, S. M. (Eds). (1990). *Handbook of developmental psychopathology.* New York: Plenum.

Linder, J. C. (1991). Outcomes measurement: Compliance tool or strategic initiative? *Health Care Management Review, 4,* 21–33.

Marsh, H. W., Balla, J. R., & McDonald, R. P. (1988). Goodness of fit indexes in confirmatory factor analysis: The effect of sample size. *Psychological Bulletin, 103,* 391–410.

Mirin, S. M., & Namerow, M. J. (1991). Why study treatment outcome? *Hospital and Community Psychiatry, 10,* 1007–1013.

Naglieri, J. A. (1993). Pairwise and ipsative comparisons for the WISC–III IQ and index scores. *Psychological Assessment, 5,* 113–116.

Naglieri, J. A., LeBuffe, P. A., & Pfeiffer, S. I. (1994). *Devereux Scales of Mental Disorders.* San Antonio, TX: The Psychological Corporation.

Naglieri, J. A., McNeish, T. J., & Bardos, A. N. (1991). *Draw a Person: Screening procedure for emotional disturbance.* Austin, TX: Pro-Ed.

Newman, F. L., & Ciarlo, J. A. (1994). Criteria for selecting psychological instruments for treatment outcome assessment. In M. E. Maruish (Ed.), *The use of psychological testing for treatment planning and outcome assessment* (pp. 98–110). Hillsdale, NJ: Lawrence Erlbaum Associates.

O'Leary, D. S. (1993). The measurement mandate: Report card day is coming. *Journal for Quality Improvement, 19,* 487–491.

Pfeiffer, S. I. (1989). Follow up of children and adolescents treated in psychiatric facilities: A methodology review. *The Psychiatric Hospital, 20,* 15–20.

Pfeiffer, S. I., & Shott, S. (1996). Treatment outcomes assessment: Conceptual, practical, and ethical considerations. In C. E. Stout (Ed.), *The complete guide to managed behavioral healthcare* (pp. 1–11). New York: Wiley.

Sattler, J. (1988). *Assessment of children* (3rd ed.). San Diego: J. M. Sattler.

Spivack, G., & Levine, M. (1964). The Devereux Child Behavior Rating Scales: A study of symptom behaviors in latency age atypical children. *American Journal of Mental Deficiency, 68,* 700–717.

Spivack, G., & Spotts, J. (1966). *Devereux Child Behavior Rating Scale.* Devon, PA: The Devereux Foundation.

Spivack, G., Spotts, J., & Haimes, P. E. (1967). *Devereux Adolescent Behavior Rating Scale.* Devon, PA: The Devereux Foundation.

Vermillion, J. M., & Pfeiffer, S. I. (1993). Treatment outcome and continuous quality improvement: Two aspects of program evaluation. *The Psychiatric Hospital, 24*(12), 9–14.

Wechsler, D. (1991). *Wechsler Intelligence Scale for Children* (3rd ed.). San Antonio, TX: The Psychological Corporation.

12

Treatment Planning and Evaluation With the Behavior Assessment System for Children (BASC)

R. W. Kamphaus
University of Georgia

Cecil R. Reynolds
Texas A&M University

Nancy M. Hatcher
University of Georgia

Sangwon Kim
University of Georgia

INTRODUCTION

The Behavior Assessment System of Children (BASC; Reynolds & Kamphaus, 1992) reflects two important characteristics of child assessment, multidimensions and multimethods. As a multidimensional measure, the BASC assesses thoroughly both positive and negative dimensions of child behavior. Information on the full range and degree of child behavior is vital in understanding child psychopathology. However, the importance of appreciating a child's adaptive skills in addition to maladaptive skills is often ignored, and only malfunctioning behaviors have been used to define child psychopathology. Also, the conceptions of child psychopathology have been based upon a categorical approach, which is best represented by the Diagnostic and Statistical Manual of Mental Disorders, Fourth Edition (DSM-IV; American Psychiatric Association, 1994). The limitation of this diagnostic system, however, is that it is not sensitive enough to identify children who do not meet the diagnostic criteria, but show subsyndromal symptoms and need some professional help.

In response to this problem, a dimensional approach has been suggested. This alternate system is promising in that it allows clinicians to assess adaptive behaviors as well as clinical symptoms, which eventually leads to a better understanding of child psychopathology. Behavior rating scales are thought of as a good candidate to accomplish the goals of a dimensional approach. Along with this, the BASC is a useful tool to fulfill the need of assessing the full range of child behavior.

The second feature of the BASC, multimethods, is closely related to practical considerations. Clinicians working with children tend to obtain information on a child by using multi informants, observations, and other data. There are some reasons for this practice: emotional behavioral difficulties typically have various facets so they need to be assessed from a number of different viewpoints, and children are less able to report their own problems than adults. The challenge that practitioners may face, however, is that it is difficult to integrate a variety of measures into the whole picture when these measures are inconsistent in purpose and construct. This is why the BASC is desirable. In fact, the scales of the BASC are consistent in purpose and construct so they allow clinicians to integrate information from various sources.

This chapter describes the BASC, which evaluates the behavior and self-perceptions of children aged 2½ to 18 years, and explains the following five components, which may be used individually or in any combinations:

- A self-report scale on which the child can describe his or her emotional and self-perceptions
- Two rating scales, one for teachers and one for parents, which gather descriptions of the child's observable behavior
- A structured developmental history
- A form for recording and classifying directly observed classroom behavior

Moreover, a new addition to the original BASC, the BASC ADHD Monitor (Kamphaus & Reynolds, 1998) is described in this chapter as well. It is designed to comprehensively assess the primary symptoms of ADHD for the purposes of treatment evaluation.

THE BASC COMPONENTS

Teacher Rating Scales

The Teacher Rating Scales (TRS) measures a child's adaptive and maladaptive behaviors in school. The TRS has three forms with items targeted at three age levels: preschool (age 2½–5), child (age 6–11), and adolescent (age 12 – 18). The forms contain descriptors of behaviors that the respondent rates on a 4-point scale of frequency, ranging from "Never" to "Almost always." The TRS takes 10 to 20 minutes to complete.

The TRS assesses clinical problems in the broad domains of Externalizing Problems, Internalizing Problems, and School Problems. It also measures adaptive skills. Table 12.1 shows the scales for all levels of the TRS. The slight differences between levels are because of developmental changes in the behavioral manifestations of child problems. Nevertheless, scales and composites with the same name contain essentially the same content at all age levels. In addition to scale and composite scores, the TRS provides a broad composite, the Behavioral Symptoms Index (BSI), that assesses the overall level of problem behaviors.

The TRS may be interpreted with reference to national age norms (general, female, or male) or to clinical norms. In addition, selected critical items may be interpreted individually. The TRS includes a validity check in the form of an *F* ("fake bad") index designed to detect a negative response set on the part of the teacher doing the rating.

Parent Rating Scale

The Parent Rating Scale (PRS) is a comprehensive measure of a child's adaptive and problem behaviors in community and home settings. The PRS shares several features with the TRS: It uses the four-choice response format; takes 10 to 20 minutes to complete; has three forms at three age levels composed of preschool, child, and adolescent. In addition, the PRS assesses almost all of the clinical problems and adaptive behavior domains that the TRS measures, producing the Behavioral Systems Index (BSI). However, the PRS does not have a School Problems composite, nor does it include the two TRS scales such as Learning Problems and Study Skills that are best observed by teachers. Table 12.2 shows the scale definitions of the PRS and TRS.

TABLE 12.1
Composites and Scales in the TRS and PRS

	Teacher Rating Scales			*Parent Rating Scales*		
Composite/Scale	*Preschool*	*Child*	*Adolescent*	*Preschool*	*Child*	*Adolescent*
Externalizing Problems	*	*	*	*	*	*
Aggression	*	*	*	*	*	*
Hyperactivity	*	*	*	*	*	*
Conduct Problems		*	*			
Internalizing Problems	*	*	*	*	*	*
Anxiety	*	*	*	*	*	*
Depression	*	*	*	*	*	*
Somatization	*	*	*	*	*	*
School Problem		*	*			
Attention Problems	*	*	*	*	*	*
Learning Problems		*	*			
Other problems						
Atypicality	*	*	*	*	*	*
Withdrawal	*	*	*	*	*	*
Adaptive Skills	*	*	*	*	*	*
Adaptability	*	*		*	*	
Leadership		*	*	*	*	*
Social Skills	*	*	*	*	*	*
Study Skills	*	*	*	*	*	*
Behavioral Symptoms Index	*	*	*	*	*	*

Note. Italicized scales compose the Behavioral Symptoms Index. Reprinted with permission from Reynolds and Kamphaus (1992, p. 3). Copyright 1992 by American Guidance Service, Inc.

In terms of interpretation, the commonalities existing between the PRS and the TRS can be identified as well. The PRS offers national age norms (general, female, and male) and clinical norms; critical items may be interpreted individually; an F index of the PRS provides information on the validity of the parent ratings.

Self-report of Personality

The Self-report of Personality (SRP) is an omnibus personality inventory consisting of statements that are responded to as true or false. The SRP, which takes about 30 minutes to complete, has forms at two age levels: child (age 8–11) and adolescent (age 12–18). These levels overlap considerably in scales, structure, and individual items. Both levels have identical composite scores: School Maladjustment, Clinical Maladjustment, Personal Adjustment, and an overall composite score, the Emotional Symptoms Index (ESI). The child level (SRP–C) has 12 scales, and the adolescent level (SRP–A) has 14 scales arranged into composites (see Table 12.3). Unlike the BSI for the rating scales, the ESI is composed of both negative (clinical) scales and positive (adaptive) scales whose scoring has been reversed, because these are the scales that load the highest on a general factor. SRP scale definitions are presented in Table 12.4.

Like the rating scales, the SRP may be interpreted with reference to national age norms (general, female, and male) or to clinical norms. Special indexes are incorporated to assess the validity of the child's responses: the *F* index, the *L* ("fake good") index for the SRP–A only, and the *V* index, designed to detect invalid responses

TABLE 12.2
Teacher and Parent Rating Scale Definitions

Scale	*Definition*
Adaptability	The ability to adapt readily to changes in the environment
Anxiety	The tendency to be nervous, fearful, or worried about real or imagined problems
Aggression	The tendency to act in a hostile manner (either verbal or physical) that is threatening to others
Attention Problems	The tendency to be easily distracted and unable to concentrate more than momentarily
Atypicality	The tendency to behave in ways that are immature, considered "odd," or commonly associated with psychosis (such as experiencing visual or auditory hallucinations)
Conduct Problems	The tendency to engage in antisocial and rule-breaking behavior, including destroying property
Depression	Feelings of unhappiness, sadness, and stress that may result in an inability to carry out everyday activities (neruovegetative symptoms) or may bring on thoughts of suicide
Hyperactivity	The tendency to be overly active, rush through work or activities, and act without thinking
Leadership	The skills associated with accomplishing academic, social, or community goals, including, in particular, the ability to work well with others
Learning Problems	The presence of academic difficulties, particularly in understanding or completing schoolwork
Social Skills	The skills necessary for interacting successfully with peers and adults in home, school, and community settings
Somatization	The tendency to be overly sensitive to and complain about relatively minor physical problems and discomforts
Study Skills	The skills that are conducive to strong academic performance, including organizational skills and good study habits
Withdrawal	The tendency to evade others to avoid social contact

Note. The PRS does not include TRS Learning Problems, Study Skills, or School Problems composite scales. Reprinted with permission from Reynolds and Kamphaus (1992, p. 48). Copyright 1992 by American Guidance Service, Inc.

because of poor reading comprehension, failure to follow directions, or poor contact with reality.

Structured Developmental History

The Structured Developmental History (SDH) is a comprehensive history survey that can be completed by adults who work with a child. A clinician may complete the SDH during an interview with a parent or guardian. Also, a parent may fill out this form either at home or in the clinic.

The SDH systematically gathers information on various areas that is crucial to the diagnosis and treatment process. Under the assumption that developmental events and medical problems in the family may have an impact on a child's current behavior, the SDH is designed to cover the child and family history, both social and medical. Because the content gathered through the SDH is extensive, the SDH should be an asset to any evaluation of a child, whether or not other BASC components are used.

TABLE 12.3
Composites and Scales in the SRP

Composite/Scale	*Child*	*Adolescent*
Clinical Maladjustment	*	*
Anxiety	*	*
Atypicality	*	*
Locus of Control	*	*
Social Stress	*	*
Somatization		*
School Maladjustment	*	*
Attitude to School	*	*
Attitude to Teachers	*	*
Sensation Seeking		*
Other Problems		
Depression	*	*
Sense of Inadequacy	*	*
Personal Adjustment	*	*
Relations With Parents	*	*
Interpersonal Relations	*	*
Self-esteem	*	*
Self-reliance	*	*
Emotional Symptoms Index	*	*

Note. Italicized scales compose the Emotional Symptoms Index. Reprinted with permission from Reynolds and Kamphaus (1992, p. 3). Copyright 1992 by American Guidance Service, Inc.

Student Observation System

The Student Observation System (SOS) is a form of recording a direct observation of the classroom behavior of a child. The SOS Part B uses the technique of momentary time sampling (i.e., systematic recording during 3-second intervals spaced 30 seconds apart over a 15-minute period) to record a wide range of children's behaviors, including positive (e.g., teacher–student interaction) and negative behaviors (e.g., inappropriate movement or inattention). SOS Part A is essentially a clinician's behavioral checklist that is completed after the Part B observation period. Although Parts A and B measure similar constructs to the PRS and TRS (e.g., aggression, inattention), it also measures constructs that are most relevant to the classroom milieu (e.g., working on school subjects, appropriate peer interaction).

The BASC SOS may be used appropriately in regular and special education classes. It can be used in the initial assessment as part of the diagnostic process. It can also be used repetitively to evaluate the effectiveness of educational, behavioral, psychopharmacological, or other treatments. The BASC SOS Parts A, B, and other components can contribute to the functional assessment of behavior from multiple perspectives:

Frequency: SOS Part A ratings of "Never observed," "Sometimes observed," and "Frequently observed." SOS Part B assesses frequencies by category of behavior problem, and PRS and TRS ratings tally the frequency of behavior problems.

Duration: SOS Part B ratings of percentage of time engaged in a particular behavior by category.

TABLE 12.4
Student Self-report of Personality Scale Definitions

Scale	*Definition*
Anxiety	Feelings of nervousness, worry, and fear; the tendency to be overwhelmed by problems
Attitude to School	Feelings of alienation, hostility, and dissatisfaction regarding school
Attitude to Teachers	Feelings of resentment and dislike of teachers; beliefs that teachers are unfair, uncaring, or overly demanding
Atypicality	The tendency toward gross mood swings, bizarre thoughts, subjective experiences, or obsessive-compulsive thoughts and behaviors often considered "odd"
Depression	Feelings of unhappiness, sadness, and dejection; a belief that nothing goes right
Interpersonal Relations	The perception of having good social relationships and friendships with peers
Locus of Control	The belief that rewards and punishments are controlled by external events or other people
Relations With Parents	A positive regard toward parents and a feeling of being esteemed by them
Self-esteem	Feelings of self-esteem, self-respect, and self-acceptance
Self-reliance	Confidence in one's ability to solve problems; a belief in one's personal dependability and decisiveness
Sensation Seeking	The tendency to take risks, to like noise, and to seek excitement
Sense of Inadequacy	Perceptions of being unsuccessful in school, unable to achieve one's goals, and generally inadequate
Social Stress	Feelings of stress and tension in personal relationships; a feeling of being excluded from social activities
Somatization	The tendency to be overly sensitive to, experience, or complain about relatively minor physical problems and discomforts

Note. Reprinted with permission from Reynolds and Kamphaus (1992, p. 58). Copyright 1992 by American Guidance Service, Inc.

Intensity: SOS Part A ratings of "disruptive"; SOS Part B ratings of frequency by category.

Antecedent events: SOS Part C descriptions of teacher position, behavior, and other variables that precede misbehavior.

Consequences: SOS Part C descriptions of teacher behavior, peer behavior, and other variables that follow a behavior.

Ecological analysis of settings: SOS observations made at various times of day and classroom setting. The PRS may be used for the assessment of behavior in the community and home environments.

DESCRIPTION OF BASC MATERIALS

Forms

The TRS, PRS, and SRP forms come in two formats: hand scoring or computer entry. The hand-scoring forms are printed in a convenient self-scoring format, allowing them to be scored rapidly without using templates or keys. Each form includes a profile of scale and composite scores. The computer entry forms, which are simpler one-part forms, are designed to allow the user to key item responses into a microcomputer in about 5 minutes or less.

Computer Software

A microcomputer program, BASC Plus, is available and offers online administration of the TRS, PRS, and SRP, and computer scoring of a completed computer-scored or hand-scoring form. The manual for BASC Plus explains how to use the program to administer, score, and report the TRS, PRS, and SRP (see sample BASC Plus printout in the Appendix). The BASC Enhanced ASSIST program offers users a simpler computer program that produces all possible scores, a graphical display of results, and item responses.

Spanish BASC

There are three Spanish BASC components available: the Spanish Parent Rating Scales, the Spanish Self-report of Personality, and the Spanish Structured Developmental History. Spanish editions of the PRS and the SRP are available in either hand-scoring or computer-entry format. These formats are scored in the same way as the English editions utilizing the same software.

CHOICE OF NORM SAMPLE

General Norms

The general norms are based on a large national sample that is representative of the general population of U.S. children with regard to sex, race and ethnicity, clinical or special education classification, and, for the PRS, parent education. These norms are subdivided by age and, therefore, indicate how the child compares with the general population of children that age. For many applications, these norms (combining females and males) will be the preferred norms and are recommended for general use.

Several of the scales of the TRS, PRS, and SRP show gender differences. Males tend to obtain higher raw scores on the Aggression, Conduct Problems, Hyperactivity, Attention Problems, and Learning Problems scales of the TRS and PRS, and on the Sensation Seeking, Attitude in School, Attitude to Teachers, and Self-esteem scales of the SRP. Females tend to score higher than males on the Social Skills, Study Skills, Leadership, and Depression scales of the SRP. These differences in scores likely reflect real differences between males and females in the incidence of the indicated behavioral or emotional problems.

Because diagnostic criteria do not differ by child sex, the general combined-sex norms should be used in most cases. General norms answer the question, "How commonly does this level of rated or self-reported behavior occur in the general population at this age?" Using general norms, more males than females will show high *T* scores on Aggression, for example, and more females than males will have high *T* scores on Social Skills. These norms preserved any observed gender difference in BASC standard scores. This is appropriate, and the general norms are used if the clinician believes that boys and girls are in fact different on various behavioral characteristics (i.e., observed differences are not because of psychometric artifacts). For example, girls score higher than boys on the SRP Anxiety scale (a common finding in research on anxiety; e.g., see Reynolds & Richmond, 1985). In determining which set of norms to use, the clinician must answer the question, "Are girls more anxious than boys, or are they simply more willing to admit to symptoms of anxiety?" If the former is true, then the general norms are more appropriate, but in the latter case, the gender-specific norms are the correct choice. Reynolds and Kamphaus (1992) recommended the use of the general norms, but the individual clinician may disagree and opt for the other norms. This allows the clinician more latitude than typically occurs on other behavioral and self-report scales.

Female and Male Norms

These norms are based on subsets of the general norm sample; each is representative of the general population of children of that age and gender. The effect of using these separate-sex norms is to eliminate differences between males and females in the distribution of *T* scores or percentiles. For example, although raw score ratings on the Aggression scale tend to be higher for males than females, use of separate-sex norms removes this difference and produces distributions of normative scores that are the same for both genders.

Clinical Norms

Clinical norms are most helpful when a clinician wants to compare a child to other children who are already in treatment. In practice, clinicians may want to know how a child functions compared to clinical populations as well as the normal population. The behavior ratings of children referred to clinical settings are more deviant than the ratings of nonreferred children. Consequently clinical norms have higher mean clinical scale raw scores than general norms. For example, an 8-year-old child who has a raw score of 18 on Attention Problems gets a T score of 69 with the general norm. But when the clinical norm is used, the child's T score becomes 60. Therefore, in this particular case, there is about one standard deviation difference between the general norm and clinical norm, which also significantly influences interpretations of the ratings. Clinical norms are only provided to children of four years and older.

INDEXES OF VALIDITY AND RESPONSE SET

Several indexes are provided to help the BASC user judge the quality of a completed form. Validity may be threatened by any of several factors, including failure to pay attention to item count, carelessness, an attempt to portray the child in a highly negative or positive light, lack of motivation to respond truthfully, or poor comprehension of the items. Information on the development of these indexes and the setting of cutoff scores is provided in Reynolds and Kamphaus (1992).

F Index

The *F* index, included on all of the BASC rating scales and self-report forms, is a measure of the respondent's tendency to be excessively negative about the child's behaviors or self-perceptions and emotions. The *F* scale was developed using traditional psychometric methods associated with Infrequency scales.

On the PRS and TRS, the *F* index is scored by counting the number of times the respondent answered "Almost always" to a description of the negative behavior or "Never" to a description of positive behavior. Because responses on the SRP are limited to true and false, items selected for that *F* index are either extremely negative items to which the child responded true or positive items to which the response was false. Items were selected for these scales that have a low probability of co-occurrence; that is, they are seldom endorsed in concert with one another.

The TRS, PRS, and SRP record forms show what levels of *F* index scores are high enough to be of concern. Detailed guidance to interpretation of the *F* index is given in Reynolds and Kamphaus (1992).

L Index

The *L* index, offered for the adolescent level of the SRP, measures adolescents' tendency to give an extremely positive picture of themselves—what might be called "faking good." The index consists of items that are unrealistically positive statements (e.g., "I like everyone I meet") or are mildly self-critical statements that most people would endorse (e.g., "I sometimes get mad"). Individuals scoring high on this scale may also be giving the most socially desirable response or possibly are psychologically naive relative to their peers. The SRP–A record form shows which *L* scores should be of concern.

V Index

Each level of the SRP includes a *V* index, made up of five or six nonsensical or highly implausible statements (e.g., "Superman is a real person"). The *V* index serves as a basic check on the validity of the SRP scores in general. If a respondent marks two or more of these statements as true, the SRP may be invalid.

BASC ADHD MONITOR

Nature and Purpose

The BASC ADHD Monitor fills a unique role in the assessment of children who are diagnosed with attention deficit hyperactivity disorder. The Monitor is the second step in an assessment regimen designed to enhance treatment planning and evaluation by more thoroughly assessing the primary symptoms of ADHD. Attention problems and hyperactivity constitute the core symptoms used by the *DSM-IV* to define the ADHD syndrome (Kamphaus & Frick, 2002). Problems in one or both of these areas are used to differentiate the three subtypes of ADHD: ADHD predominantly inattentive type, ADHD predominantly hyperactive-impulsive type, and ADHD combined type. Components of the original BASC system serve as the first step in the comprehensive assessment of children suspected of having ADHD. The BASC takes a broad sampling of child behavior to identify the full range of child problems. If the initial administration of the BASC reveals problems on the Attention Problems scales, Hyperactivity scale, or both, the diagnosis of ADHD becomes a possibility. Of greater importance, however, is the necessity to use the BASC teacher, parent, and self-report forms to rule out co-occurring problems, which can only be done with the initial use of a broad-based measure (Kamphaus & Frick, 2002). This is particularly important in diagnosis of ADHD, where so many comorbid disorders occur and where other disorders (e.g., use of narrow-band scales) may often result in overdiagnosis of ADHD.

The Monitor represents the second step in the comprehensive assessment of ADHD in that it is concerned with treatment design and evaluation. The narrowly focused

TABLE 12.5
BASC ADHD Monitor Constructs

Component	*Scales*
Parent Monitor	Attention Problems Hyperactivity Internalizing Problems Adaptive Skills
Teacher Monitor	Attention Problems Hyperactivity Internalizing Problems Adaptive Skills
BASC SOS	Response to Teacher/Lesson Peer Interaction Work on School Subjects Transition Movement Inappropriate Movement Inattention Inappropriate Vocalization Somatization Repetitive Motor Movements Aggression Self-injurious Behavior Inappropriate Sexual Behavior Bowel/Bladder Problems
ADHD Monitoring Plan	All monitor components and scales
ADHD Monitor ASSIST	All monitor components and scales

Monitor is designed to assess an expanded range of attention problems and hyperactivity symptoms in a practical, time-efficient manner. This additional detail allows the clinician to refine the diagnosis of ADHD and, of greater importance, to design a comprehensive treatment program aimed at reducing behavioral problems. The Monitor also provides Internalizing and Adaptive Skills scales that further encourage comprehensive treatment planning and evaluation of treatment effectiveness by allowing clinicians to include these important constructs easily in the treatment plan.

The BASC and BASC ADHD Monitor represent a coordinated multiple-step assessment system that allows the clinician to proceed from referral for ADHD to diagnosis, treatment design, and treatment evaluation with greater ease and precision. To achieve these assessment objectives, the Monitor utilizes information provided by parents, teachers, and a classroom observer to assess the constructs noted in Table 12.5.

Few child assessment measures are designed to meet the practical demands of treatment evaluation. In other words, few tests are constructed in a manner that facilitates the repeated collection and dissemination of child information. The Monitor is designed to meet the unusual practical demands dictated by the need for the repeated assessment of child behavior. The original BASC may be used repeatedly to evaluate treatment effects, particularly if a child is found to have multiple problems (e.g., ADHD, depression, anxiety, and conduct disorder) that cannot be fully assessed by the Monitor. In the case of ADHD and its subtypes, however, the Monitor is constructed so as to allow clinicians to evaluate treatment with greater efficiency.

The needs of child health care workers led to the development of the Monitor. Health care and related professionals in psychology, medicine, and education are all struggling to meet the needs of the child with ADHD. The epidemiological estimates of ADHD of 3% to 5% of the U.S. population are striking (Rapoport & Castellanos, 1996). Moreover, approximately 2% to 6% of elementary age schoolchildren may be receiving psychostimulant medication treatment at any given time, making this the most frequently used pharmacological treatment received by children (Bender, 1997). The problems of children with ADHD also put them at higher risk for a diverse array of other problems, including learning disabilities (Frick et al., 1991) and anxiety disorders (Last, 1993). A high comorbidity rate of this nature suggests that children with these problems are likely to receive a variety of medical and behavioral treatments at home, in school, and in other settings. These facts lead invariably to the conclusion that the population of children with ADHD present special assessment challenges as a result of the phenomenology of their problems, which dictates the creation of complex treatment strategies. One of the most significant challenges of ADHD treatment is the coordination of medical management and other treatment strategies. Consequently, assessment strategies have to be designed so as to enhance frequent and accurate communication among treatment providers, including parents, physicians, teachers, other clinicians, and the child.

The BASC ADHD Monitor is designed to enhance the work of all those individuals who provide services to children with ADHD. It has the following purposes:

1. *To provide accurate and frequent feedback to the prescribing physician.* The physician and other health care workers need accurate information to ensure that a child is receiving the most accurate psychotropic regimen and to adjust dosage. Information about the effects of medication on hyperactivity, attention problems, internalizing problems, and adaptive skills can aid the physician in making crucial medical treatment decisions.
2. *To ensure that the ongoing assessment of ADHJD problems is efficient, timely, and cost-effective.* Given the multiple time demands on parents, teachers, and others, little time remains to complete lengthy or unnecessarily complex rating scales that are not specifically targeted to the needs of the child with ADHD. On the other hand, the Monitor is designed to be adequately thorough to allow for the assessment of constructs in addition to the core dimensions of ADHD—internalizing problems and adaptive skills (Kamphaus & Frick, 2002). All of these assessment objectives must be achieved in an efficient way given the exigencies of health care. Accordingly, the Monitor is brief, yet it provides coverage of four important domains related to the functioning of the child with ADHD.
3. *To provide a system of devices that allows for input from multiple informants.* Teacher, parent, and clinician observations are all of potential importance for the treatment process, and communication among these individuals is crucial for effective treatment (Bender, 1997). Each Monitor form is designed to meet the specialized needs of each of these informants.
4. *To emphasize the assessment of specific behavioral outcomes to demonstrate accountability for services.* Increasingly, the effectiveness of child services is being challenged, thereby creating the need to assess outcomes. The Monitor assesses the *DSM–IV* criteria for ADHD and includes items that are written in clear behavioral terms. In addition, the monitor software is designed to produce output that gives providers and administrators a clear indication of response to the treatment. The Monitor is designed to provide clinicians with the information needed to adjust treatment whenever response to intervention is not optimal.

5. *To link assessment to treatment.* The Monitor is designed to be practical enough to be considered central to the treatment process. Heretofore, physicians and other clinicians have often had difficulty acquiring the feedback needed to adjust treatment. The test and software design of the Monitor was guided throughout by the need to provide information relevant to treatment. The selection of items and scales, test length, scoring and reporting systems, graphic output, and other Monitor characteristics were all guided by this central objective.
6. *To allow teachers to use a single form for evaluating treatment effects.* Teachers are often charged with evaluating the effects of medical and behavioral interventions, and they often have to review several behavioral charts, graphs, or other records to report on a child's progress (Bender, 1997). The BASC ADHD Monitor, because of its multiple components, is intended to assess a child's behavior both broadly and specifically to expedite the teacher's reporting duties.

Monitor Interpretation

ADHD Monitor interpretation can take several forms, depending on the instrument(s) used, theoretical orientation of the clinician, the nature of the evaluation questions posed, and other factors. Given space limitations, this chapter focuses on the "basics" of interpretation that are grounded in psychometric principles and customary practice. It is also important to keep in mind that the monitor is designed to create and evaluate treatment plans. Hence, interpretation of the scales as diagnostic devices is of considerably lesser importance.

In evaluating Monitor results, the individual clinician is asking whether or not significant change has occurred in response to treatment. For the parent and teacher Monitors, four questions are generally posed: Is treatment affecting symptoms of inattention? Is treatment affecting symptoms of hyperactivity? Is treatment affecting internalizing symptoms? Is treatment affecting adaptive skills? The questions related to change are multitudinous and parallel for the SOS, where clinicians may be assessing change at the item or scale level.

It appears, however, that the assessment of change is fraught with methodological and conceptual pitfalls (Jacobson & Truax, 1991). For instance, a high level of interference may be involved in the case where a child's hyperactivity has improved in response to the administration of methylphenidate. Certainly, an improvement in scores may indicate positive change, yet it is not possible to be certain that the medication was the cause. Placebo and other effects can only be ruled out in well-controlled studies. Hence, when it is said that a child has shown improvement in response to treatment, such a statement risks making an inappropriate interference. It merely makes the writing task easier.

It is common practice to use statistics to assess change. If, for example, it can be shown that a child's *T* score on the Hyperactivity scale went from 75 to 63 in response to treatment, then this may be a statistically significant improvement. Is this reduction in symptoms, however, clinically significant in the sense that the child, parents, teachers, and other are pleased with the child's progress in school and other spheres? Would this interpretation of this statistically significant amount of change be modified if the pre- and posttreatment scores were 85 and 74, respectively? The point is that it may be difficult to quantify change to the satisfaction of all stakeholders in a child's life.

The Monitor attempts to improve assessment of treatment effects by measuring multiple dimensions of behavior, as opposed to producing a single score. It is more likely that clinically significant change has occurred if a child shows improvement in hyperactivity, attention problems, internalizing, and adaptive skills.

Reynolds and Kamphaus (2002) provided the following guidelines for assessing change:

1. The level of functioning subsequent to behavioral intervention should fall outside the range of the dysfunctional population, where the range is defined as extending 2 *SD*s beyond (in the direction of functionality) the mean of the population.
2. The level of the functioning subsequent to behavioral intervention should fall within the range of the functional or normal population, where the range is defined as within 2 *SD*s of the mean of that population.
3. The level of the functioning subsequent to behavioral intervention places the client closer to the mean of the functional population than it does to the mean of the dysfunctional population.

To these, we would add an important fourth:

4. The response to treatment makes a positive difference in the day-to-day life of the patient.

Coordination With BASC Results

Use of the BASC will often precede administration of the ADHD Monitor. The use of an omnibus measure, such as the BASC, is crucial at the outset of the evaluation process (Kamphaus & Frick, 2002). Only a broad-based measure that assesses numerous constructs will allow the clinician to rule out comorbidities, alternative causes for the apparent symptomatology, and other diagnostic and treatment considerations.

Once diagnostic decisions are made, the ADHD Monitor can be used to develop and evaluate treatment plans. There is, however, one important area of interpretive overlap between the BASC and the BASC ADHD Monitor Parent and Teacher Forms. A *T*-score baseline for treatment evaluation can be obtained from either set of measures. There are two administration scenarios that are most likely.

First, a clinician may administer either or both of the BASC parent and teacher forms during the initial diagnostic evaluation. The obtained *T* scores for the Hyperactivity, Attention Problems, Internalizing Problems, and Adaptive Skills scales may be entered into the BASC ADHD software and be used as the baseline against which subsequent administrations of the ADHD Monitor will be compared.

Second, a clinician may administer either or both of the BASC ADHD Parent and Teacher Monitor Forms during the initial diagnostic evaluation. The obtained *T* scores for the Hyperactivity, Attention Problems, Internalizing Problems, and Adaptive Skills scales will then be used as the baseline against which the subsequent administrations of the ADHD Monitor Forms will be compared.

It is important to establish a *T*-score baseline in a timely fashion, regardless of the method used. In other words, a *T*-score baseline should be collected during the evaluation phase and prior to implementation of treatment. The ADHD Monitor *T* scores for parent and teacher rating scales serve as the most reliable indicator of behavioral change over time (see Kamphaus & Reynolds, 1998).

The SOS is designed specifically for classroom-based intervention. Accordingly, SOS results should not be considered when a clinician evaluates home-based intervention unless the home-based treatment is linked to a school-based one. For instance, a home-based reinforcement program may be utilized to improve behavior at school. Then, the SOS may be conducted to assess the effects of the home-based intervention.

Basically, the SOS assesses classroom behaviors by counting frequencies of maladaptive and adaptive behaviors. Consequently, SOS results from Parts A and B may be used to identify behaviors in need of intervention: any behavior problem exhibited or adaptive skill not exhibited becomes a potential candidate for intervention. Stated differently, problematic behaviors of high frequency can be targeted for decrease, and adaptive skills of low frequency also can be targeted for increase.

The SOS is unique among Monitor components in that it allows clinicians to prioritize behaviors for classroom-based intervention. The SOS also measures the "bothersomeness" of a child's behavior problems via the disruptive category of Part A. Often, children display a number of behavior problems, making it difficult to prioritize behaviors for intervention (Schwanz & Kamphaus, 1997). Therefore, the ratings of disruptiveness can be used to identify behaviors that should be targeted first for treatment.

BASC INTERPRETATIVE STEPS

BASC interpretation is described in detail in Reynolds and Kamphaus (1992; 2002). In abbreviated form, the following steps are advised by Reynolds and Kamphaus (2002). The experienced BASC user will find a fully developed interpretive system in that same source.

Step 1. Write down (or highlight, circle, or in some way mark) all scales with T scores at or above 60 for the clinical scales and at or below 40 for the adaptive scales. Scores in this range and more deviant ones are identified as either "at risk" or "clinically significant" on BASC printouts. By utilizing scores in this range, we are likely to reduce "false negatives" and error in the direction of "false positives" for screening, diagnostic and treatment purposes. In addition, utilization of scores in this range allows for the identification of subsyndromal problems that may require treatment, because they are associated with functional impairment (Cantwell, 1996).

Step 2. For each scale listed, identify supportive and nonsupportive evidence of a significant problem or competency. Clinicians may need to look over all the information available, including the child's history, other tests results, observations, and previous diagnosis. In this process, clinicians have to identify both evidence that supports a significant problem and evidence that is incompatible with the problem. For example, when a child is suspected as having depression, the fact that some family members have had depression and that the child's problems fit *DSM-IV* criteria for depression may support the consideration. However, if the child has been on medication for ADHD symptoms and the medicine has side effects such as depression, that information may be nonsupportive evidence.

Step 3. For each scale remaining, draw conclusions regarding diagnosis, subsyndromal problems, or competencies. Based on quantitative and qualitative information, diagnosis or problems can be identified.

CASE STUDY

The BASC was designed to aid the clinical diagnosis of disorders that are usually first apparent in childhood or adolescence. It is highly desirable that diagnosis be clearly linked to intervention. In this respect, treatment planning can also be facilitated by the BASC. Problem behaviors can be delineated and targeted in a program, leading to their reduction. Similarly, deficits in adaptive behaviors, such as study skills or social skills, can be identified and addressed in intervention designed to improve a child's overall adaptation (Reynolds & Kamphaus, 1992). The following case shows how the BASC plays a role in the process of diagnosis and treatment evaluation.

Stephen

Stephen is an 8-year-old third grader at a public school. He is referred to a community mental health center by his parents and his teacher because they are concerned about his high level of activity and inability to focus on academic tasks.

Regarding his family, Stephen lives with both biological parents. His father owns a small business and mother is a homemaker. A younger brother, Chris (age 7), is very different from Stephen in many ways, according to his parents: Chris is well behaved and shows excellent performance in school. The parents perceived that usually Stephen gets along with Chris, but sometimes feels embarrassed and jealous comparing himself to Chris. To help Stephen build self-esteem, his parents, particularly his mother, have been trying to praise him when he behaves well and to encourage him to do his best. However, they have found that it is hard to keep from getting angry at his "out of control" behaviors.

Stephen was a planned, full-term baby, and the delivery had no problems. However, his mother recalled Stephen was a difficult baby who frequently woke up at night, cried severely, etc. He was early to reach developmental milestones, crawling at 6 months old and walking at 10 months old.

His parents reported that some family members on his father's side have learning-related problems. Stephen's uncle, his father's brother, is diagnosed with mental retardation. In addition, Stephen's father had difficulty learning the alphabet in grade school and still has trouble concentrating, for example, when reading books. Based upon his own experiences, Stephen's father expressed his sympathy about Stephen's current difficulties and believed that he will "get over it."

Stephen is currently attending third grade. His teacher described him as being easily distracted, failing to complete work on time, bothering other peers when they are working, and making noises. Similar behavior problems were also reported by his preschool teacher. In preschool, Stephen had trouble sitting still during group activities and interrupted class activities.

Stephen has undergone numerous behavioral and educational treatments that have resulted in no noticeable improvement. Consequently, his parents and his teacher have requested a formal psychological evaluation. Stephen was administered an extensive battery of psychological tests, including intelligence tests, achievement measurements, classrooms observations, and a variety of parent and teacher rating scales. As part of the psychological assessment, the results of the BASC parent, teacher rating *T* scores, and SOS are shown in Tables 12.6 and 12.7.

The results of this initial evaluation were consistent with the diagnosis of ADHD combined type. The diagnosis was made, and related behavioral interventions were suggested. Further, Stephen's parents were admonished to seek a medical evaluation to determine the need for pharmacological intervention. Yet his parents did not seek pharmacological treatment, and some behavioral interventions were delivered—again, with little evidence of improvement.

His parents and teacher became concerned during his fourth-grade year about his lack of progress. One year later after the initial assessment, a second classroom

TABLE 12.6
Stephen's BASC Mother and Teacher Ratings t scores at Initial Evaluation

Scale	*Mother*	*Teacher*
Hyperactivity	65	70
Aggression	42	51
Conduct Problems	39	45
Anxiety	54	42
Depression	45	40
Somatization	50	37
Atypicality	54	60
Withdrawal	41	55
Attention Problems	63	68
Learning Problems	—	61
Adaptability	53	34
Social Skills	49	52
Leadership	35	40
Study Skills	—	51

observation (see Table 12.7) and other data were collected, suggesting that his ADHD symptomatology was not responding well to treatment. Consequently, his pediatrician placed him on a regimen of 5 mg of Ritalin twice a day during the academic year, to begin in November 2003. Follow-up SOS observations and teacher and parent interviews documented an extraordinarily positive response to intervention, including increasing schoolwork productivity and suppression of inappropriate movement and vocalizations and attention problems (see Table 12.7, December 2003 results).

BASC AS OUTCOME MEASURE

An evaluation of the BASC against the Newman and Ciarlo (1994) criteria for outcomes measures is presented in Table 12.8. The criteria included in Table 12.8 may be open

TABLE 12.7
SOS Results for Stephen at Initial Evaluation, Second Evaluation, and 1 Month After Initiation of Pharmacological Therapy

Scale	*October 2002*	*October 2003*	*December 2003*
Response to Teacher/Lesson	9	10	13
Peer Interaction	0	1	1
Work on School Subjects	7	4	15
Transition Movement	2	5	0
Inappropriate Movement	11	12	5
Inattention	8	6	3
Inappropriate Vocalization	3	2	0
Somatization	0	0	0
Repetitive Motor Movements	10	11	7
Aggression	0	0	0
Self-injurious Behavior	0	0	0
Inappropriate Sexual behavior	0	0	0
Bowel/Bladder Movements	0	0	0

TABLE 12.8
BASC Evaluation Against Criteria for Treatment Outcome Assessment

1. *Relevance to target group*
   "It is safe to assert that the BASC has been carefully developed and represents a synthesis of what is known about developmental psychopathology and personality development. The items for all of the components have been derived from a review of the relevant literature and collected clinical experience. All of the contents of the scales were selected from research findings, other measures, and clinical experience. The items were constructed with the help of professionals (including teachers) and students, and were carefully evaluated for readability, acceptability, and comprehensibility" (Sandoval & Echandia, 1994, p. 420).
   "Item content varies across levels to reflect developmental differences" (Flanagan, 1995, p. 179).

2. *Simple and teachable methods*
   "The record forms for the TRS, PRS, and SRP are clear and user-friendly. A true–false format was chosen for the SRP so that it would be more likely that children and adolescents would attend to the task sufficiently. The forms are completed quickly, are understandable to respondents, and are readily scored" (Flanagan, 1995, pp. 179, 180, 185).
   "Minimal self-instructional training is required in order to use the SOS appropriately, and hence it can be used by a wide variety of clinicians and educational professionals with varied training backgrounds" (Hoza, 1994, p. 9).
   "The test materials for the PRS and TRS are noteworthy for their convenient design. In contrast to other tests that require separate item booklets, answer sheets, scoring templates, and profile forms, all of these are combined into a single record form for both the PRS and TRS" (Kline, 1994, p. 291).

3. *Use of measures with objective referents*
   "The scale norms were constructed by using linear *T*-score scaling. This procedure is advisable because many of the constructs being measured are probably not normally distributed, and this metric preserves underlying distribution" (Sandoval & Echandia, 1994, p. 422).

4. *Use of multiple respondents*
   "The BASC is a multimethod test because information about a child's behavior is obtained from teacher(s) perspective, parent(s) perspective, and a student's perspective" (Miller, 1994, p. 24).
   "The BASC is a multimethod, multidimensional assessment system that measures both adaptive and problem behaviors as well as self-perceptions of school children both in school and in home settings" (Merenda, 1996, p. 232).

5. *More process-identifying outcome measures*
   "The BASC helps link dimensions of behavior and emotions to *DSM–III–R* criteria, treatment programming, and educational classifications" (Adams & Drabman, 1994).
   "For subtypes of ADHD, and specifically the ADHD:PI subtype, however, results would favor the use of the BASC PRS and TRS [over the Achenbach CBCL and TRF]" (Vaughn, Riccio, Hynd, & Hall, 1997, p. 355).

6. *Psychometirc strengths*
   "The BASC rating scales have strong psychometirc properties and useful scale content and structure" (Adams & Drabman, 1994, p. 4).
   "The BASC has several strengths, particularly with regard to the psychometrically well-developed TRS, PRS, and SRP scales" (Hoza, 1994, p. 9).
   Reliability: "Three types of reliability are reported for the general samples of the TRS and PRS: internal consistency, test–retest reliability, and interrater reliability. Internal consistency and test–retest reliability are reported for the SRP. The majority of BASC components have reliabilities greater than .80, which is psychometrically acceptable" (Flanagan, 1995, p. 181).

(Continued)

TABLE 12.8
(Continued)

Validity: Validity evidence reported by Reynolds and Kamphaus (1992) included the following:

CONFIRMATORY FACTOR ANALYSIS (CFA)
EXPLORATORY FACTOR ANALYSIS (EFA)

Teacher Rating Scale	*Parent Rating Scale*	*Self-report of Personality*
CFA	CFA	CFA
EFA	EFA	EFA

CRITERION-RELATED CORRELATION STUDIES

Teacher Rating Scale: Teacher's Report Form (two studies), Revised Behavior Problem Checklist, Conners Teacher Rating Scales, Burks Behavior Rating Scales, Behavior Rating Profile
Parent Rating Scale: Child Behavior Checklist (three studies), Personality Inventory for Children, Conners Parent Rating Scales, Behavior Rating Profile
Self-report of Personality: Minnesota Multiphasic Personality Inventory, Youth Self-report (two studies), Behavior Rating Profile, Children's Personality Questionnaire

7. *Relatively low cost*
Materials cost: Hard-score form: $1.20 each
OR Computer score form: $0.80 each
Enhanced ASSIST Software: $249.95 (unlimited uses)
OR BASC Plus software: $4.20 (per use)
Structured Observation System form: $1.32 each
Structured Developmental History form: $1.56 each

8. *Understanding by nonprofessional audiences*
"The parent rating scales can be readily understood and completed by parents with minimal assistance from the professional administering the scale. The protocols are efficiently arranged and attractive" (Sandoval & Echandia, 1994, p. 424).

9. *Easy feedback and uncomplicated interpretation*
"In practice, the BASC has been positively received by children, parents, teachers, and school psychologists. The data are easily interpreted and presented to parents and school personnel" (Flanagan, 1995, p. 185).

10. *Useful in clinical services*
"Integration of BASC data with other data obtained in a comprehensive assessment of a child is readily accomplished. Diagnosis of educational disabilities and descriptions of behavioral and emotional variables can be considerably simplified with the use of the BASC" (Flanagan, 1995, p. 185).
"The BASC assists with several assessment needs including the description of adaptive and maladaptive dimensions disorders, the decision for educational classification, the evaluation of treatment programs for behavior, and research regarding childhood emotional and behavioral disorders" (Adams & Drabman, 1994).

11. *Compatibility with clinical theories and practices*
"Samples for the general, male, and female norms were selected to be representative of the 1990 U.S. population aged 4 to 18 years, including exceptional children, for race and ethnicity. In addition, the goal was to have overlap of the samples across PRS, TRS, and SRP, to make the sets of norms comparable. Clinical samples were drawn from self-contained classrooms, community mental health centers, residential schools, juvenile detention centers, and university and hospital outpatient mental health clinics" (Flanagan, 1995, pp. 180–181).
"The BASC has unique potential to aid in diagnostic decision making, as it contains conceptually derived scales created for use in conjunction with psychiatric and educational classification systems" (Doyle, Ostrander, Skare, Crosby, & August, 1997, p. 281).

to interpretation, and new or different criteria may be of more value. Consequently, Table 12.8 was constructed to include the opinions of other scholars to the extent that is practicable.

EVALUATION STUDIES

As demonstrated previously, there are a number of advantages that the BASC has when used as an outcome measure. The following research findings show how the BASC has been effectively used in evaluation studies.

Williford, Woods, and Shelton (2000) designed a preliminary study to test the effects of individualized service plans, parent and teacher training, classroom management consultation, direct classroom intervention, and child social skills training on the externalizing problems of preschoolers. Head Start children with externalizing *T* scores in the 93rd percentile or beyond were assigned to *assessment only* and *intervention groups*. Intervention children received services over the course of one academic year. The results showed numerous differences between BASC TRS pre- and posttest ratings. Specifically, significant reductions were noted on the BSI, Externalizing composite, Hyperactivity, and Attention Problems scales; the greatest reduction was observed on the Aggression scale.

Merydith (2000) used the BASC TRS-A to assess the effects of violence prevention programs conducted in school. The researchers conducted small group training sessions for 50 minutes, once weekly, for 10 weeks. The results produced two significant findings. First, Externalizing Problems and School Problems on the TRS-A were reduced significantly. Second, adaptive skills increased. These improvements again suggest that the TRS-A is sensitive to the effects of even brief intervention programs, such as the one implemented in this study.

In addition, several dissertations designed to evaluate treatment effects used the BASC as an outcome measure. It is interesting that the BASC has been applied to various treatments that include behavior therapy, cognitive therapy, pharmacological treatment, neurofeedback, and an animal-assisted therapy (Drawe, 2001; Evans, 2000; Faubel, 1998; Hatcher, 2001; Moritz, 1998; O'Dell, 2001; Petra, 2001; Steve, 2001). This broad use of the BASC across treatments may imply its potential applicability for various intervention plans.

Although the BASC is a desirable evaluation measure, it does have some limitations for outcome assessment. For example, the BASC does not include enough items to assess change in patterns of illicit substance use. In addition, some severe behavior problems are not included (e.g., playing with feces). Hence, in every evaluation study, a satisfactory match between the BASC scales and treatment objectives should be assured.

CLINICAL RESEARCH

The BASC has been used in a variety of research studies. One of the main foci of the latest BASC research is the diagnosis of clinical populations such as ADHD. A number of studies have clarified the role that BASC parent and teacher ratings play in the diagnosis of ADHD (Doyle et al., 1997; Manning & Miller, 2001; Ostrander, Weinfurt, Yarnold, & August, 1998; Vaughn et al., 1997). Doyle et al. (1997) showed that the BASC PRS and The Child Behavior Checklist (CBCL; Achenbach, 1991) were roughly equivalent for the diagnosis of ADHD. In addition, the authors stated a preference for the use of the BASC because of the rational derivation of its scales. Vaughn et al. (1997) again noted equivalence between the two systems for the diagnosis of ADHD versus no ADHD. However, they found that for subtypes of ADHD, the BASC PRS and TRS were more accurate than the CBCL and TRF in detecting the presence of the ADHD Predominantly Inattentive subtype.

The BASC can be also used in evaluating children with Traumatic Brain Injury (TBI). The BASC rating scales contain a number of items that are strongly influenced by TBI, including problems in frontal lobe or executive functioning. In particular, the BASC Attention Problems, Learning Problems, and Conduct Problems scales have been demonstrated to correlate significantly with some neuropsychological performance measures. Riccio et al. (1994) examined correlations between the BASC rating scales and performance on the Wisconsin Card Sorting Test (WCST). The WCST is a cognitive measure requiring rule induction and set shifting on novel problem-solving tasks which are commonly considered to assess the integrity of frontal lobe functioning (Heaton, 1981), especially in children (Chelune & Thompson, 1987). The results indicated that the BASC Attention Problems scale was the most closely associated with the largest number of scoring alternatives on the WCST, including the perseverative errors score, often noted to be the best measure of frontal lobe functioning on the WCST. Also, the Conduct Problems scale and the Learning Problems scale showed good correlations with multiple scores on the WCST.

In addition to the empirical support described above, Barringer and Reynolds (1995) used an expert approach to identify the BASC rating scale items for a frontal lobe and executive functioning scale, followed by group comparisons. They surveyed editorial board members of the three leading clinical journals in neuropsychology, *Archives of Clinical Neuropsychology, Journal of Clinical and Experimental Neuropsychology*, and *The Clinical Neuropsychologist*. Each board member was asked to rate each BASC PRS item according to the strength of its perceived association with frontal lobe functioning. Based on the obtained ratings, the items were ranked and a series of item analyses were performed, using the BASC standardization and clinical norm groups. Then a set of 18 items with a high reliability (coefficient alpha of .84 on both the PRS–C and PRS–A) was identified, and seventeen of the 18 items are common to the PRS–C and the PRS–A. These items are listed in Table 12.9. The content of items is consistent with problems of attention and control as well as motivational issues. Dealing with motivation is important in treating patients with frontal lobe injuries because their lack of motivation (sometimes referred to as amotivational syndromes) is one of the major barriers to intervention. These items may be used as a measure of frontal lobe and executive functioning.

Children with TBI display changes in observable behavior, which can be rated objectively by knowledgeable observers. Moreover, changes in internal states are not uncommon on children with TBI. For example, depression may be induced as an organic problem following certain types and locations of TBI. In this case, the BASC SPR can be used as it covers the primary areas of interest thoroughly and contains measures of dissimulation to detect over- and underreporting of symptoms.

Besides the diagnostic utility of the BASC, studies have supported the effectiveness of the BASC in understanding the social and emotional functioning of various groups. Through the BASC SRP, De La Torre (1998) demonstrated that those with a history of sexual abuse had more difficulties in interpersonal relations and school adjustment. Further, with the BASC SRP, PRS, and TRS, Carter (1999) showed that significant psychopathology existed within adolescents with a history of school violence. Some researchers used the BASC for children with diseases, such as cancer or acquired brain

TABLE 12.9
BASC PRS Items Associated With Frontal Lobe and Executive Functioning

PRS–C ITEM NO.	*PRS–A ITEM NO.*	
8	51	Cannot wait to take turn
30	40	Throws tantrums
34	77	Hits other children
39	4	Forgets things
40	80	Repeats one activity over and over
41	70	Uses foul language
43	8	Needs too much supervision
44	115	Is a "self starter" (reversed scoring)
51	110	Is easily distracted
64	92	Is easily upset
67	55	Uses appropriate table manners (reversed scoring)
78	103	Interrupts others when they speak
86	99	Completes homework from start to finish without taking a break (reversed scoring)
89	71	Changes moods quickly
104	12	Begins conversations appropriately (reversed scoring)
108	47	Completes work on time (reversed scoring)
117	—	Adjusts well to changes in family plans (reversed scoring)
118	45	Argues when denied own way
—	67	Acts without thinking

injury, in an attempt to understand the disease's impact on psychosocial adjustment (Challinor, 1998; Shelby et al, 1998; Skinner, 2001). Shelby et al. (1998) investigated psychosocial behaviors in child survivors of acute lymphocytic leukemia by using the BASC PRS and found that the children had more difficulties in social competence and internalizing behavior compared to general norms. Consequently, it is important for professionals to understand the psychological challenges that those children may face in order to meet the needs.

Practitioners and researchers may use the BASC as part of family assessment. Because the BASC provides various views on a child's personality and behavior, it facilitates comparisons among child, parents, and teacher, and dyadic relationships in a family, such as a child and mother, and a child and stepfather, can be assessed (Nurse, 1999).

Research on predicting later behaviors of children demonstrated that the BASC is a useful measure of child outcomes. Nelson, Martin, Hodge, Havill, and Kamphaus (1999) used the BASC TRS and PRS as outcome criteria to assess the predictive validity of early temperament. They hypothesized that preschool temperament would predict later functional behavioral status: Parents rated child temperament when their children were 5, and parents and teachers rated child behaviors when the children were 8. The research findings indicated that three temperament constructs (i.e., negative emotionality, poor self-regulation of attention and motor behavior, and adaptability) were sometimes associated with the BASC TRS–C at age 8. Negative emotionality, the most meaningful predictor of all four TRS–C composites, was most highly related to the externalizing composite. Poor self-regulation of attention and motor control was related only to the school problems composite. Therefore, identification of problems early in development, via teacher ratings, may indicate early risk.

In addition, CHAMPUS, the U.S. military civilian and retiree health care system, began a longitudinal study of adolescents placed in residential treatment centers (RTCs) in 1997. The purpose of the study is to predict which adolescents referred for placement would actually benefit from the expensive RTC setting. Gaines (personal communication, 2001) reported that the BASC has been found to have "good predictive power" in this study, although details remain scant (cited in Reynolds & Kamphaus, 2002).

CHAMPUS, the U.S. military civilian and retiree health care system, began a longitudinal study of adolescents placed in residential treatment centers (RTCs) in 1997. The purpose of the study is to predict which adolescents referred for placement would actually benefit from the expensive RTC setting. Gaines (personal communication, 2001) reported that the BASC has been found to have "good predictive power" in this study, although details remain scant (cited in Reynolds & Kamphaus, 2002).

Several validity studies of other tests have been conducted using the BASC as a criterion measure (Locicero, 2001; Oehler-Stinnett & Boykin, 2001; Palmer, 2001; Smith & Reddy, 2002). A study by Oehler-Stinnett and Boykin (2001) examining the validity of the Teacher Rating of Academic Achievement Motivation (TRAAM) reported that the TRAAM was positively correlated with positive subscales of the BASC TRS, such as Adaptability, while negatively correlated with negative subscales of the BASC TRS, such as Learning Problems. In addition, Smith and Reddy (2002) assessed the concurrent validity of the Devereux Scales of Mental Disorders (DSMD; Naglieri et al., 1994) with the BASC. As shown in these research findings, the BASC can serve as a criterion measure, because it has sound psychometric properties and is widely used.

The BASC has also been used as an "advocate" of a dimensional approach discussed in introduction of this chapter. Kamphaus and his colleagues (1997; 1999; 2003) conducted a cluster analysis of the BASC rating scales norming sample. They aimed at developing a typology of child behavior from different perspectives of multi informants such as teacher, parents, and self. For example, for a typology of child classroom behavior rated by teacher (the BASC TRS–C), the seven clusters were identified: well adapted (34%), average (19%), disruptive behavior problems (8%), learning problems (12%), physical complaints/worry (11%), severe psychopathology (4%), and mildly disruptive (12%). It is important to notice that these clusters are distinguishable from one another not only in clinical symptoms but also in adaptive skills. Therefore, considering the full range of child behavior will improve the pitfalls of the current diagnostic system.

CONCLUSION

The BASC, like all psychological assessment tools, will be a work in progress for years to come. The accumulation of evidence has begun to reveal the worth of this set of instruments for a variety of purposes, including assessment and diagnosis, treatment evaluation, validity studies, and a research tool. Hopefully, this momentum will continue, as a vibrant research enterprise represents the field's greatest opportunity to produce new innovations in child personality and behavioral assessment.

REFERENCES

Achenbach, T. M. (1991). *Manual for the Child Behavior Checklist/4-18 and 1991 profile.* Burlington: University of Vermont, Department of Psychiatry.

Adams, C. D., & Drabman, R. S. (1994). BASC: A critical review. *Child Assessment, 4,* 1–5.

American Psychiatric Association. (1994). *Diagnostic and statistical manual of mental disorders* (4th ed.). Washington, DC: Author.

Barringer, M. S., & Reynolds, C. R. (1995, November). *Behavior ratings of frontal lobe dysfunctioning.* Paper presented at the annual meeting of the National Academy of Neuropsychology, Orlando, FL.

Bender, W. N. (1997). Medical interventions and school monitoring. In W. N. Bender (Ed.), *Understanding ADHD: A practical guide for teachers and parents* (pp. 107–122). Upper Saddle River, NJ: Merrill.

Cantwell, D. P. (1996). Classification of child and adolescent psychopathology. *Journal of Child Psychology and Psychiatry, 37,* 3–12.

Carter, S. P. (1999). The psychopathology of school violence. *Dissertation Abstracts International, 59* (7-A), 2339.

Challinor, J. M. (1998). Behavioral performance of children with cancer: Assessment using the Behavioral Assessment System for Children. *Dissertation Abstracts International, 58* (12-B), 6484.

Chelune, G., & Thompson, L. L. (1987). Evaluation of the general sensitivity of the Wisconsin Card Sorting Test among younger and older children. *Developmental Neuropsychology, 3,* 81–89.

De La Torre, R. (1998). The utility of the behavior assessment system for children with adolescent sexual offenders. *Dissertation Abstracts International, 59* (6-B), 3053.

Doyle, A., Ostrander, R., Skare, S., Crosby, R. D., & August, G. J. (1997). Convergent and criterion-related validity of the behavior assessment system for children-parent rating scale. *Journal of Clinical Child Psychology, 26,* 276–284.

Drawe, H. L. (2001). An animal-assisted therapy program for children and adolescents with emotional and behavioral disorders. *Dissertation Abstracts International, 61* (11-B), 6130.

Evans, C. M. G. (2000). The effects of writing about traumatic experiences on adolescents identified as Emotionally Disturbed (ED). *Dissertation Abstracts International, 60* (9-A), 3269.

Faubel, G. (1998). An efficacy assessment of a school-based intervention program for emotionally handicapped students. *Dissertation Abstracts International, 58* (11-A), 4183.

Flanagan, R. (1995). A review of the behavior assessment system for children (BASC): Assessment consistent with the requirements of the individuals with disabilities education act (IDEA). *Journal of School Psychology, 33,* 177–186.

Frick, P. J., Kamphaus, R. W., Lahey, B. B., Loeber, R., Christ, M. A. G., Hart, E. L., & Tannenbaum, L. E. (1991). Academic underachievement and the disruptive behavior disorders. *Journal of Consulting and Clinical Psychology, 59,* 289–294.

Hatcher, N. M. (2001). Moderators of change in attention-deficit/hyperactivity disorder symptomatology in a high-risk clinic sample. *Dissertation Abstracts International, 61* (11-A), 4284.

Heaton, R. H. (1981). *Wisconsin Card Sorting Test manual.* Odessa, FL: Psychological Assessment Resources.

Hoza, B. (1994). Review of the behavior assessment system for children. *Child Assessment, 4,* 5–10.

Jacobson, N. S., & Truax, P. (1991). Clinical significance: A statistical approach to defining meaningful change in psychotherapy research. *Journal of Consulting and Clinical Psychology, 59,* 12–19.

Kamphaus, R. W., DiStefano, C., & Lease, A. M. (2003). A self-report typology of behavioral adjustment for young children. *Psychological Assessment, 15,* 1–12.

Kamphaus, R. W., & Frick, P. J. (2002). *Clinical assessment of child and adolescent personality and behavior* (2nd ed.). Needham Heights, MA: Allyn & Bacon.

Kamphaus, R. W., Huberty, C. J., Distefano, C., & Petoskey, M. D. (1997). A typology of teacher rated child behavior for a national U.S. sample. *Journal of Abnormal Child Psychology, 25,* 453–463.

Kamphaus, R. W., Petoskey, M. D., Cody, A. H., Rowe, E. W., & Huberty, C. J. (1999). A typology of parent rated child behavior for a national U.S. sample. *Journal of Child Psychology and Psychiatry and Allied Disciplines, 40,* 607–616.

Kamphaus, R. W., & Reynolds, C. R. (1998). *BASC ADHD Monitor.* Circle Pines, MN: American Guidance Service.

Kline, R. B. (1994). New objective rating scales for child assessment: I. Parent and teacher informant inventories of the behavioral assessment system for children: The child behavior checklist, and the teacher report form. *Journal of Psychoeducational Assessment, 12,* 289–306.

Last, C. G. (1993). Introduction. In C. G. Last (Ed.), *Anxiety across the lifespan: A developmental perspective* (pp. 1–6). New York: Springer.

Locicero, K. A. (2001). The reliability, validity, and factor structure of the Almost Perfect Scale-Revised in a sample of middle school-aged adolescents. *Dissertation Abstracts International, 61*(10-B), 5617.

Manning, S. C., & Miller, D. C. (2001). Identifying ADHD subtypes using the Parent and Teacher Rating Scales of the Behavior Assessment Scale for Children. *Journal of Attention Disorders, 5,* 41–51.

Merenda, P. F. (1996). BASC: Behavioral assessment system for children. *Measurement and Evaluation in Counseling and Development, 28,* 229–232.

Merydith, S. P. (2000). Aggression intervention skill trainging: Moral reasoning and moral emotions. *NASP Communique, 28,* 6–8.

Miller, D. C. (1994). Behavior assessment system for children (BASC): Test critique. *Texas Association of School Psychologists Newsletter*, 23–29.
Moritz, E. K. (1998). Behavior therapy in game format for the treatment of childhood obsessive compulsive disorder. *Dissertation Abstracts International, 59* (1-B), 0423.
Naglieri, J. A., Pfeiffer, S. I., & LeBuffe, P. A. (1994). *Devereux Scales of Mental Disorders.* San Antonio, TX: The Psychological Corp.
Nelson, B., Martin, R. P., Hodge, S., Havill, V., & Kamphaus, R. (1999). Modeling the prediction of elementary school adjustment from preschool temperament. *Personality and Individual Differences, 26*, 687–700.
Newman, F. L., & Ciarlo, J. A. (1994). Criteria for selecting psychological instruments for treatment outcome assessment. In M. E. Maruish (Ed.), *The use of psychological testing for treatment planning and outcome assessment* (pp. 98–110). Hillsdale, NJ: Lawrence Erlbaum Associates.
Nurse, A. R. (1999). *Family assessment: Effective uses of personality tests with couples and families.* New York: Wiley.
Nurse, A. R. (1999). *Family assessment: Effective uses of personality tests with couples and families.* New York: Wiley.
O'Dell, B. D. (2001). The effects of neurofeedback on intelligence and behavior of children with attention deficit disorders. *Dissertation Abstracts International, 62* (2-B), 1093.
Oehler-Stinnett, J., & Boykin, C. (2001). Convergent, discriminant, and predictive validity of the Teacher Rating of Academic Achievement Motivation (TRAAM) with the ACTeRs-TF and the BASC-TRS. *Journal of Psychoeducational Assessment, 19*, 4–18.
Ostrander, R., Weinfurt, K. P., Yarnold, P. R., & August, G. J. (1998). Diagnosing attention deficit disorders with the Behavioral Assessment System for Children and the Child Behavior Checklist: Test and construct validity analyses using optimal discriminant classification trees. *Journal of Consulting & Clinical Psychology, 66*, 660–672.
Palmer, V. Y. (2001). A psychometric study of the Preschool Behavior Checklist with developmentally delayed preschool children. *Dissertation Abstracts International, 61* (12-A), 4745.
Petra, J. R. (2001). The effects of a choice theory and reality therapy parenting program on children's behavior. *Dissertation Abstracts International, 61* (9-B), 5001.
Rapoport, J. L., & Castellanos, F. X. (1996). Attention-deficit hyperactivity disorder. In J. M. Wiener (Ed.), *Diagnosis and psychopharmacology of childhood and adolescent disorders* (2nd ed., pp. 265–292). New York: Wiley.
Reynolds, C. R., & Richmond, B. O. (1985). *Revised Children's Manifest Anxiety Scale.* Los Angeles: Western Psychological Services.
Reynolds, C. R., & Kamphaus, R. W. (1992). *Behavior Assessment System for Children.* Circle Pines, MN: American Guidance Service.
Reynolds, C. R., & Kamphaus, R. W. (2002). *The clinician's guide to the Behavior Assessment System for Children (BASC).* New York: Guilford Press.
Riccio, C. A., Hall, J., Morgan, A., Hynd, G. W., Gonzalez, J. J., & Marshall, R. M. (1994). Executive function and the Wisconsin Card Sorting Test: Relationship with behavioral ratings and cognitive ability. *Developmental Neuropsychology, 10*, 215–229.
Sandoval, J., & Echandia, A. (1994). Behavior assessment system for children. *Journal of School Psychology, 32*, 419–425.
Schwanz, K. A., & Kamphaus, R. W. (1997). Assessment and diagnosis of ADHD. In W. N. Bender (Ed.), *Understanding ADHD: A practical guide for parents and teachers* (pp. 81–106). Upper Saddle River, NJ: Merrill/Prentice-Hall.
Shelby, M. D., Nagle, R. J., Barnett-Queen, L. L., Quattlebaum, P. D., & Wuori, D. F. (1998). Parental reports of psychosocial adjustment and social competence in child survivors of acute lymphocytic leukemia. *Children's Health Care, 27*, 113–129.
Skinner, C. L. (2001). Describing the cognitive, socioemotional, and academic sequalae of children with acquired brain injury. *Dissertation Abstracts International, 62* (2-B), 1137.
Smith, S. R., & Reddy, L. A. (2002). The concurrent validity of the Devereaux Scales of Mental Disorders. *Journal of Psychoeducational Assessment, 20*, 112–127.
Steve, P. K. (2001). A cognitive intervention for behaviorally disordered youth. *Dissertation Abstracts International, 62* (2-B), 1111.
Vaughn, M. L., Riccio, C. A., Hynd, G. W., & Hall, J. (1997). Diagnosing ADHD subtypes: Discriminant validity of the Behavior Assessment System for Children (BASC) and the Achenbach parent and teacher rating scales. *Journal of Clinical Child Psychology, 26*, 349–357.
Williford, A. P., Woods, J. E., & Shelton, T. L. (2000, August). *Project Mastery: A family-centered intervention for preschoolers with behavior problems.* Paper presented at the annual meeting of the American Psychological Association, Washington, DC.

13

The Adolescent Treatment Outcomes Module (ATOM)

Teresa L. Kramer and James M. Robbins
University of Arkansas for Medical Sciences

It is estimated that one out of five youth meet criteria for a mental disorder (Angold & Costello, 1995). Of these, only 5% to 7% receive some type of specialty mental health care (National Institute of Mental Health, 2001). Among children and adolescents who do access care, there is little evidence that they are provided empirically supported treatment or that their outcomes are improved as a result of obtaining services (Miller et al., 2002; U.S. Department of Health and Human Services, 2000; Weersing & Weisz, 2002). These data are critical when increasing expenditures for mental health care (National Institute of Mental Health, 2001) are requiring more cost-effective delivery of services.

Unfortunately, there are few valid, economical, easy-to-administer instruments that would provide information on multiple outcome domains for child and adolescent providers, clinical managers, and policy advocates (Robbins et al., 2001). These multiple domains would include (a) clinical status (diagnosis and symptom severity), (b) functional impairment across settings, and (c) consumer perspectives of changes in family impact and focal problems, as well as satisfaction with care (see Table 13.1 for a summary of instruments). Feedback in these domains at baseline could assist in treatment planning, whereas documented changes in symptoms, impairment, and family impact could be helpful in monitoring treatment progress and overall performance of a provider, treatment program, or health care system.

The Adolescent Treatment Outcomes Module (ATOM; Robbins et al., 1997; Robbins et al., 2001) was designed for use in routine care settings to assess multiple outcomes for youth ages 11 to 18 years. The ATOM also collects prognostic data that can be used for case-mix adjustment when comparing providers and programs (see Table 13.1). The ATOM consists of parallel versions of an adolescent and parent self-report instrument, which is completed at baseline and 6-month follow-up. The baseline report for parents also contains a family impact scale, whereas the parent follow-up assessment includes items omitted from the adolescent follow-up report to assess service use, types of care provided (e.g., medication, individual or family therapy, or 12-step program), family impact, and satisfaction with care.

The ATOM can be administered to adolescents 11 to 18 years of age presenting for treatment with emotional or behavioral problems. Adolescents who have borderline intelligence or lower, or who are currently psychotic, are not eligible for the ATOM. A parent or other caregiver who has had contact with the adolescent in the previous

TABLE 13.1
Domains Assessed by ATOM and Other Widely Used Instruments

	ATOM	CBCL	DISC	CAPA	CAS	DICA	DSADS	CAFAS	CIS	CGAS	VFI	BIS	BCQ	BAS	CABA	CSQ	VSS	CASA	CHIP	CHQ
No. of Items	*132*	*138*	*249*	*1401*	*56*	*715*	*820*	*7*	*18*	*1*	*24*	*27*	*21*	*19*	*13*	*8*	*351*	*176*	*219*	*57*
Focal Problems	X																			
Caseness	X		X	X	X	X	X													
Symptom Severity	X	X	X	X	X		X	X	X										X	X
Home Functioning	X			X	X			X	X	X	X	X							X	X
School Functioning	X	X		X	X			X	X	X	X	X							X	X
Legal Problems	X							X			X	X								
Friendships	X	X		X	X			X	X	X	X	X								
Dysfunctional Friends	X																			
Family Impact	X												X	X	X					X
Satisfaction	X															X	X			
Treatment	X																	X		
Prognostic	X																			

ATOM = Adolescent Treatment Outcomes Module, CBCL = Child Behavior Checklist, DISC = Diagnostic Interview Schedule for Children, CAPA = Children and Adolescent Psychiatric Assessment, CAS = Child Assessment Schedule, DICA = Diagnostic Interview for Children and Adolescents, DSADS = Schedule for Affective Disorders and Schizophrenia, CAFAS = Children and Adolescent Functional Assessment Scale, CIS = Columbia Impairment Scale, CGAS = Children's Global Assessment Scale, VFI = Vanderbilt Functioning Index, BIS = Brief Impairment Scale, BCQ = Burden of Care Questionnaire, BAS = Burden Assessment Scale, CABA = Child and Adolescent Burden Assessment, CSQ = Client Satisfaction Questionnaire, VSS = Vanderbilt Satisfaction Scales, CASA = Child and Adolescent Services Assessment, CHIP = Child Health and Illness Profile, CHQ = Child Health Questionnaire.

6 months must be available as an informant to complete the Parent Baseline Assessment. If an adolescent or parent has a reading level of fifth grade or below, they may need assistance in completing the instruments.

OVERVIEW OF THE INSTRUMENT

The ATOM was developed in collaboration with a group of 13 national experts in child and adolescent mental health services research and instrument development. Consistent with many of the guidelines outlined for children's behavioral health services (Substance Abuse Mental Health Services Administration, 2001), the experts concluded that a monitoring tool for adolescents should (a) obtain data from both the youth and his or her parent or legal guardian, (b) assess multiple clinical domains that might be targeted by interventions, and (c) include variables that would provide information about an individual patient's prognosis and facilitate case-mix adjustment of outcomes. The team then developed or identified items meeting these criteria, which were subsequently tested and validated.

The ATOM consists of six components: The 93-item Adolescent Baseline Assessment and the 150-item Parent Baseline Assessment, which take between 15 and 25 minutes to complete. These assessments should be complete within 1 to 3 days of the initial visit. The Clinician Baseline Assessment is comprised of 24 items and is used to collect data on the adolescent's diagnosis at baseline and treatments initiated. It requires approximately 1½ minutes to complete. The Adolescent and Parent Follow-up Assessments contain information similar to that obtained from the baseline assessments. The parent version also assesses service use, satisfaction with care, and family impact. These assessments take 15 to 25 minutes to complete. There is also a medical record review to document duration and type of treatment received. Components of the ATOM are described in the following section.

Clinical Status

The ATOM uses a set of symptom items that complement the primary diagnoses of youth (depression, anxiety, attention deficit disorder, conduct disorder, and oppositional defiant disorder). Possible scores range from 1 to 4 and are scored in the direction of increasing frequency, with symptom severity represented by an aggregate of all items. Questions on the current version were adapted from the Diagnostic Interview Schedule for Children (Shaffer, Fisher, Dulcan, & Schwab-Stone, 1996).

Test–retest showed the scale to be fairly stable over a 7-day period for parents ($r = 0.89$) compared to adolescents ($r = 0.53$, Robbins et al., 2001). The aggregate parent score was strongly associated with the Child Behavioral Checklist (CBCL; Achenbach, 1991a) Internalizing scale ($r = 0.65$) and the Child Health Questionnaire (CHQ; Landgraf, Abetz, & Ware, 1996) Mental Health (Emotional) Problems scale ($r = -0.71$) and Behavior Problems scale ($r = -0.72$). Parent reports on the ATOM were modestly correlated with the CBCL externalizing scale ($r = 0.40$). The Symptom Severity scale based on adolescent report was modestly related to adolescent reports on the Youth Self-report (YSR; Achenbach, 1991b) and CHQ.

Functioning

Items to assess functional impairment were adapted from the Brief Impairment Scale (Bird, 1995), which is an extension of the functioning domain of the Columbia

Impairment Scale (CIS; Bird et al., 1993) and the Family, Friendships and Self-Assessment Scale (Simpson, 1998; Simpson & McBride, 1992). Functioning during the prior 6 months is assessed using a 4-point scale (1 = never, 2 = rarely, 3 = often, 4 = always), with the exception of seven items that are dichotomous. Higher scores indicate greater impairment. Items were originally conceptualized to represent functional problems (a) in the home, (b) at school, (c) in the community (including trouble following rules and the law), (d) with friends, (e) with delinquent peers, and (f) in leisure activities (see Table 13.2). Two- to seven-item scales were constructed for each of the six domains.

Test–retest reliability for parent report was good for five of six functioning scales ($r > .78$), with high internal consistency (alpha = .71 to .81) (Robbins et al., 2001). The exceptions are a lower test–retest correlation for parent report of delinquent behaviors with peers ($r = .63$). Test–retest reliability and internal consistency for adolescents were lower for adolescents than parents ($r = .36$ to .71, alpha = .66 to .82). Scales were modestly correlated with the Columbia Impairment Scale ($r = .30$ to .48, $r = .33$ to .64 for parents and adolescents, respectively) and the CHQ scale assessing role limitations because of emotional or behavioral problems ($r = -.35$ to $-.45$ and $r = -.24$ to $-.54$ for parents and adolescents, respectively).

Results of a principal components analysis show that the functioning measures of the ATOM capture three broad areas of functioning (role performance, relationships, leisure activities) and sentinel events resulting from impaired functioning. The role performance domain was composed of a single factor, including items such as trouble following rules at home or school, problems with responsibilities at school, trouble getting involved in family activities, and trouble doing homework and schoolwork. The relationships domain was composed of three factors: trouble getting along with family members, difficulty making and keeping friends, and friendships with delinquent peers. Leisure activities was a single factor including items measuring lack of involvement in extracurricular activities such as clubs or hobbies, little or no participation in sports or physical activities, and few leisure time interests. Two sentinel events factors emerged from the principal components analysis: consequences for misconduct involving the legal system (arrests, incarceration, police contact) and consequences for misconduct at school (in-school suspension, suspension, and expulsion). The internal consistency (Cronbach's alpha) of these scales ranged from .70 to .86 for parent scales and from .57 to .83 for adolescent scales. The correlation between the ATOM role performance scale and the Columbia Impairment Scale school functioning scores was .67 for parents and .54 for adolescents. Parent responses to the ATOM Relationship scale, a combined measure of difficulties with family, friends, and delinquent peers, correlated .73 with the interpersonal scores of the Columbia Impairment Scale. Adolescent responses correlated .32. The ATOM Sentinel Events scale, a combined measure of legal and school consequences for misconduct, was correlated .52 with the CBCL Delinquency subscale.

Sentinel Indicators

The ATOM includes sentinel events that are indicative of high risk, for example, removal from the home, expulsion or suspension from school, and arrest or incarceration. Test–retest correlations for out-of-home placement and school expulsion or suspension, as reported by parent, were high ($r = .76$ and .83, respectively); adolescent reports of arrest or incarceration were more highly correlated over the 7-day test–retest period than parent reports ($r = .73$; Robbins et al., 2001).

TABLE 13.2
Parent–Adolescent Report of Impairment and Kappa Coefficients for Functioning Items
($N = 258$)

Variable	*Impairment by Respondent* Parent n (%)	Adolescent n (%)	*Kappa*
Role Performance			
Trouble with school work	162 (63%)	107 (41%)	.31*
Responsible at school	128 (49%)	79 (31%)	.24*
Trouble following rules at school	111 (43%)	61 (24%)	.06
Trouble getting along with teachers	109 (42%)	73 (28%)	.21*
Trouble doing chores	167 (65%)	102 (40%)	.13
Trouble following rules at home	165 (64%)	107 (41%)	.11
Trouble following rules and laws in the community	110 (43%)	65 (25%)	.18*
Relationships With Family			
Trouble getting along with father	96 (37%)	72 (28%)	.40*
Trouble getting along with mother	128 (50%)	100 (39%)	.28*
Trouble getting along with siblings	134 (52%)	116 (45%)	.22*
Family activities	74 (29%)	43 (17%)	.07
Relationships With Friends			
Trouble making friends	49 (19%)	31 (12%)	.24*
Trouble getting along with friends	33 (13%)	9 (3%)	−.01
Delinquent Peers			
Peers do things that could get them in trouble with the law	30 (12%)	49 (19%)	.13
Peers do things that could get them in trouble at school	44 (17%)	54 (21%)	.12
Peer use of weapons	14 (5%)	47 (18%)	.05
Leisure Activities			
Not involved in any sports	106 (42%)	67 (34%)	.26*
Not involved in any extracurricular activity	107 (42%)	88 (35%)	.24*
No hobbies	71 (28%)	31 (12%)	.03
No interests	50 (20%)	32 (13%)	.05
Sentinel Events			
In-school suspension	124 (48%)	131 (51%)	.52*
Expulsions	34 (13%)	29 (11%)	.29*
Out of school suspension	28 (11%)	16 (6%)	.21*
In or out of school suspension or expulsion	128 (50%)	134 (52%)	.53*
Arrest	67 (26%)	67 (26%)	.51*
Jail	39 (15%)	40 (16%)	.50*
Illegal activities	60 (23%)	72 (28%)	.39*
Talked to police	52 (20%)	66 (26%)	.34*
Arrest or jail	76 (29%)	81 (31%)	.46*

*$p < .05$. ** $p < .01$, Bonferroni corrected.

Consumer Perspectives

The ATOM assesses the impact that the adolescent's emotional or behavioral problems have on the family's functioning, using a modified version of a 19-item child and adolescent Burden Assessment Scale (BAS; Horwitz & Reinhard, 1995; Reinhard, 1994; Reinhard, Gubman, Horwitz, & Minsky, 1994). This scale inquires about the parent's objective burden (e.g., missing days at work, changing personal plans, cutting down on leisure time), subjective burden (e.g., worry about child's behavior, feeling guilty), and total burden on a scale of 0 to 3, with higher scores representing more impact. Internal consistency was acceptable: subjective burden (alpha = 82); objective burden (alpha = .87); and total burden (alpha = .90). The correlation between total burden assessment (BAS) and CHQ family impact was significant ($r = -.63$). Family impact, as assessed by the BAS, was also associated with higher scores on the ATOM Symptom Severity scale, the CBCL internalizing scale, and ATOM Role Performance and Relationship Functioning scales (Kramer, Robbins, Miller, Phillips, & Burns, 2002).

Parents are also asked at baseline to identify and rate on a 4-point scale the severity of the three primary problems that caused them to seek treatment for their son or daughter. Baseline severity scores were moderately correlated with the CBCL/YSR Internalizing scale ($r = .45$ and .50 for parents and adolescents) and Externalizing scale ($r = .42$ and .27 for parents and adolescents). At the 6-month follow-up, parents also complete a five-item Satisfaction scale, adapted from other widely used measures of patient satisfaction (Larsen, Attkisson, Hargreaves, & Nguyen, 1979; Lubalin et al., 1995). For example, the parent is asked, "How well did the program meet your child's needs?" and "Would you recommend this program to other family or friends?"

Prognostic Variables

A panel of experts in child and adolescent mental health services identified several factors that might influence the outcomes of adolescent mental health treatment, including (a) psychiatric and substance abuse comorbidity, (b) severity of baseline symptoms, (c) age of onset of emotional or behavioral problems, (d) prior psychiatric hospitalization, (e) gender, (f) parent history of behavioral health problems, (g) residential or academic instability, (h) family dysfunction, (i) poverty, (j) history of abuse, and (k) exposure to violence. Items to assess these factors were adapted from the Parent Data Form, developed by the American Academy of Child and Adolescent Psychiatry Task Force on Outcomes Research (Jensen et al., 1996). Test–retest correlations ranged from .31 for parent report of family substance abuse to 1.0 for parent report of residential instability (Robbins et al., 2001). In a recent study of case-mix models for adolescent mental health outcomes, Phillips and her colleagues (2003) found that early onset, family functioning, prior hospitalization, history of abuse and parent incarceration were independently correlated with symptom or functional outcomes ($r = .15$–$.41$), but had less impact when baseline clinical measures were simultaneously entered into logistic regressions.

USE OF THE ATOM IN TREATMENT PLANNING

Identification of Primary and Secondary Problems

The ATOM provides data on critical items that might influence the type and intensity of acute intervention: (a) suicidal ideation, (b) potential for harm to self because of impulsivity, (c) history of aggression and suicide attempt, (d) association with weapon-carrying peers, (e) risk of substance abuse, (f) possible safety concerns at home or at school, (g) possible history of abuse, and (h) comorbid medical conditions. The three sentinel indicators also provide information about an adolescent's level of risk, given that he or she has had a previous out-of-home placement because of emotional or behavioral problems, having been expelled or suspended from school, having been arrested or incarcerated, or all of these conditions.

In addition to the critical and sentinel items, the ATOM symptom items provide information about specific problems, as well as a barometer of the adolescent's clinical status. For example, an adolescent may be experiencing sadness and irritability (two common signs of depression) and problems in remembering and fidgeting (two common signs of attention deficit disorder). The items and scale can be hand scored, and individual patient reports are also available through NetOutcomes (2003), an Internet-based behavioral health outcomes management system developed and operated by the Center for Outcomes Research and Effectiveness at the University of Arkansas for Medical Sciences (2003). This service is free to individual practitioners. Because information obtained from both parent and adolescent is often discordant, it is recommended that the "or" rule be adopted, that is if either the parent or adolescent indicates a problem, then the provider should consider the possibility that a problem exists.

As seen in Figs. 13.1 and 13.2, the individual patient report provides baseline data on critical and sentinel items, symptoms, functional impairment, family impact, and case-mix measures. The report indicates areas for further assessment, as well as potential targets for clinical intervention. In the example, the patient, a 16-year-old African-American female, reports current suicidal ideation, potential for harm to self because of impulsivity, and several significant prognostic factors and sentinel events. Although she does not report previous suicide attempt, the provider should nonetheless more fully evaluate her potential for self-injury. In addition, the symptom report suggests difficulties in multiple areas, including the possibility of depression, attention problems, and conduct disorder. As a result, she and her parents are reporting functional impairment at school, at home, and in the community.

In addition to the parent and adolescent reports, the clinician completes a baseline assessment that includes information about diagnosis. The baseline ATOM also includes a 10-item, 4-point scale (1 = no problem, 2 = mild problem, 3 = moderate problems, 4 = serious problem) to capture the clinician's assessment of the adolescent's functional impairment. Internal consistency for the clinician scale is high (alpha = .70).

Appropriate Level of Care and Treatment Approach

The ATOM provides an extensive, broad-based report of an adolescent's level of distress, impairment, and prognostic indicators. It can be used in conjunction with a clinical interview to evaluate the most appropriate level and type of care. In the example provided, the adolescent is at high risk for self-harm, legal consequences, and potential out-of-home placement. A structured treatment setting, for example, inpatient or partial hospitalization, may be warranted until the adolescent can be stabilized, at which time she may benefit from an intensive, community-based intervention, such as multisystemic therapy (MST; Henggeler, Melton, Brondino, Scherer, & Hanley, 1997; Henggeler, Melton, Smith, 1992). Although the ATOM does not include specific treatment recommendations, because of the unique characteristics—history and prognosis of each adolescent—it can assist the provider in identifying problem areas and potential risk for harm and provide clinical documentation pertaining to medical necessity and need for treatment.

Prediction of Treatment Outcome

The prognostic characteristics may be used as a guide for predicting outcomes. Because they have not been validated on individual patients, however, interpretations of

NetOutcomes™

www.netoutcomes.net

Adolescent Treatment Outcomes Module

CLIENT ID: Patient One	PROGRAM: Demo Data PROVIDER: Provider A

AGE AT BL: **16**
GENDER: **Female**
RACE: **Black/African American**
DIAGNOSES: Primary, **major dep. Disorder**

Case-mix Factors—*factors often associated with the persistence or recurrence of emotional and behavioral problems*

Onset of aggression before age 6	no
Previous treatment	no
Poor family functioning	no
Parents with history of mental illness or substance abuse	no
Low family income	no
Multiple residences within past 5 years	no
Substance abuse	yes

Scores are based on the combined report or parent and adolescent using the most severe score for each item.

	Baseline	6-mo.
Clincian	1/1/01	N/A
Parent	1/1/01	7/1/01
Adolescent	1/1/01	7/1/01

Critical Items—*factors that may indicate a potential harm to self or others*

Suicidal ideation	yes	no
Suicide attempt	no	no
Potential for harm to self due to impulsivity	yes	yes
Aggression	yes	yes
Dangerous peers	yes	no
Possible safety concerns at home or school	no	no
Possible history of abuse or neglect	yes	N/A
Substance abuse	yes	yes
Number of comorbid medical conditions	1	N/A

Sentinel Indicators—*rare but significant events that provide information on seriousness of problems*

Out of home due to emotional or behavioral problems	yes	yes
Expelled or suspended from school	no	no
Arrested or incarcerated	yes	yes

FIG. 13.1. Sample Individual Patient Report for the ATOM.

these characteristics should be tentative. For example, the adolescent in Figs. 13.1 and 13.2 reports a fairly stable family environment and no previous history of treatment, which may serve to facilitate her recovery. These strengths, however, may be offset by her symptom severity, which should be considered in any clinical evaluation of an individual's overall prognosis.

NetOutcomes™

www.netoutcomes.net

Adolescent Treatment Outcomes Module	
CLIENT ID: Patient One	PROGRAM: Demo Data PROVIDER: Provider A

Emotional and Behavioral Problems

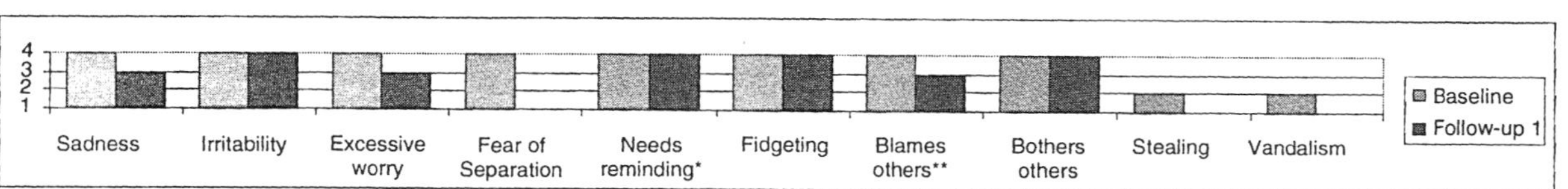

4 = problem occurs nearly every day, 3 = problem occurs a few days a week, 2 = problem occurs occasionally, 1 = problem does not occur at all
* Needs reminders to stay on task, **Blames others for own mistakes

Functional Impairment

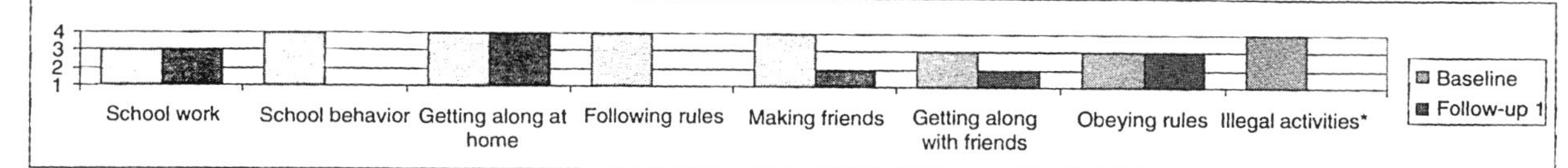

4 = problem occurs all the time, 3 = problem occurs often, 2 = problem occurs rarely, 1 = problem does not occur at all
*4 = illegal activities, 1 = no illegal activities

Family Impact—problems experienced by caregiver due to adolescent's emotional and behavioral problems

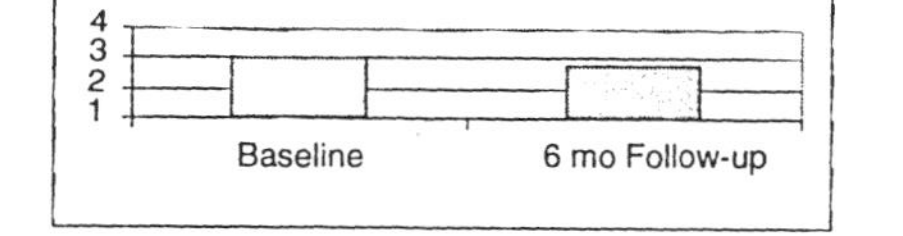

FIG. 13.2. Sample individual patient report for the ATOM, continued.

Concurrent Assessments

Research has shown that adolescents often present to treatment with multiple problems. For example, Miller and her colleagues (2002) found that 44% of 214 adolescents seeking mental health treatment in outpatient and inpatient settings were diagnosed by clinicians as having only one emotional or behavioral disorder. More than one third (34%) received two diagnoses, whereas 21.7% received three or more diagnoses. As mentioned previously, the ATOM screens for five disorders (depression, attention deficit, anxiety, oppositional defiant disorder, and conduct disorder). However, because the sensitivity of the items is variable (kappa = .35–.87), it is important to further assess these domains through clinical interview and/or administration of additional self-report instruments, including the Children's Depression Inventory (CDI; Kovacs, 1999) for internalizing disorders, or the Connors Parent Rating Scale (CPRS–R) or Connors Teacher Rating Scale (CTRS–R) (Conners, Sitarenios, Parker, & Epstein, 1998a, 1998b; Conners et al., 1997) for externalizing disorders.

Provision of Feedback

It is suggested that the ATOM be used as an adjunct to the treatment planning process, particularly when there are significant disagreements between parent and adolescent reports of problems. The NetOutcomes report can be particularly useful for comparing perceptions of acute problems and setting goals for treatment.

USE OF THE ATOM IN TREATMENT MONITORING

The ATOM monitors changes in symptoms, functioning, family impact, and critical and sentinel items over a 6-month period using the Parent and Adolescent Follow-up Assessments. No additional data are collected from the clinician. All ATOM symptom items are constructed using a 1-month frame of reference (e.g, How often in the past month were you sad for most of the day?), whereas all functioning items are assessed using a 6-month period (e.g., In the past 6 months, how often have you had trouble getting along with your father?) Sentinel and critical items are worded using a 6-month frame of reference (e.g., In the past 6 months, have you been expelled or told never to come back to school because of your behavior?) Because of the time frame of follow-up, the ATOM would be most applicable for treatment monitoring of 6 months or more, particularly in systems of care where it is critical to track the progress of patients over time. However, the ATOM may also be used in conjunction with short-term, evidence-based treatments, such as cognitive-behavioral therapy for depression, to assess the intervention's effectiveness in ameliorating global symptoms and functional impairment and the ability to sustain clinical improvements over time.

Change in ATOM outcomes has been associated with change in other outcome measures. Decreases in symptom severity were associated with decreases in the CBCL internalizing and externalizing scales (Spearman's rho = 0.65 and 0.40 for parents and 0.53 and 0.37 for adolescents, respectively) and the CHQ mental health and behavioral problems scales (Spearman's rho = −0.71 and −0.72 for parents and −0.44 and −0.43 for adolescents, respectively). Spearman's rho of greater than +/−0.24 is significant at the $p < .05$ level for a sample of $n = 70$ (Iman, 1978). These results suggest that the ATOM symptom scale may be more sensitive to changes in the internalizing domain, for example, anxiety and depression, than the externalizing domain, for example, oppositional behavior, particularly when using parent report. Changes in functional scales were also associated with changes in the CHQ scales on role limitations because of emotional problems and behavioral problems (Spearman's rho = −.35 to −.45 for parents and −.24 to −.51 for adolescents) and the CIS (Spearman's rho = .30 to .45 for parents and .41 to .45; Robbins et al., 2001). Changes in focal problem severity and family impact were correlated with the CBCL/YSR internalizing and externalizing scales and the CHQ family impact scale (Kramer et al., 2002; Robbins et al., 2001).

Follow-up data on the ATOM can be scored manually or entered into the NetOutcomes database to generate an individual report (see Figs. 13.1 & 13.2). As shown in the example, the female adolescent does exhibit improvement in suicidal ideation, association with dangerous peers, symptom severity, and functional impairment. Unfortunately, she still reports aggression and a potential for harm to self because of impulsivity. As a result, parent report on family impact remains at a high level; however, both parent and adolescent report satisfaction with services received.

The follow-up assessment also collects information on the type of services accessed and treatments received during the previous 6 months. These items were adapted from the Child and Adolescent Services Assessment (CASA; Ascher, Farmer, Burns, & Angold, 1996; Burns, Angold, & Magruder-Habib, 1990):

- Emergency room visit
- Inpatient hospitalization (psychiatric, general hospital or drug treatment unit), partial hospitalization
- Residential treatment
- Group home
- Therapeutic foster care
- Outpatient drug or alcohol services
- Home or school-based therapy
- Case management
- Outpatient individual, group, or family therapy from a psychiatrist, psychologist, or other mental health professional
- Other services (e.g., mentoring, calling a hot line, counseling from a minister or church member)

In addition to the service items, parents are also asked whether their son or daughter received any medication and, if so, the extent to which the adolescent adhered to the physician's instructions.

USE OF THE ATOM FOR TREATMENT OUTCOMES ASSESSMENT

The ATOM is a reliable and valid measure to monitor the outcomes of routine care for adolescents, meeting criteria established for the development, selection, and use of progress-outcome measures (Newman, Ciarlo, & Carpenter, 1999). The domains covered by the ATOM are relevant to adolescents regardless of their treatment status. In addition, the instrument is sensitive to change in clinical status, functioning, and family impact, and provides a limited amount of data on consumer perceptions of care. Initial pilot studies have shown that the measure is easy to administer, taking an average of 15 to 25 minutes to complete.

The paper-and-pencil version of the ATOM is available through the Internet and can be used by providers free of charge. For an additional expense, providers can use the NetOutcomes outcomes management system, which offers three types of aggregate reports (provider, program, and facility). Provider reports include quarterly summaries of baseline and follow-up data on all patients enrolled for the period and compare provider performance with national benchmarks. By comparison, program and facility reports present data on each provider in a program or facility and compare that information to national benchmarks for programs or facilities (see Fig. 13.3). In the example, Provider A's patients scored below program, facility, and benchmark averages at baseline on all clinical markers, with the exception of conduct disorder. Therefore, it would be anticipated that when the first follow-up is conducted, Provider A's patients would be less impaired in these areas when compared to other program, facility, and benchmark patients, with the exception of conduct disorder. The report indicates this has occurred, but not consistently in subsequent follow-ups.

The ATOM can be used to explore provider, practice, or program patterns of adolescent characteristics, treatment processes, and outcomes. Although it is an effective tool to use in individual treatment planning and monitoring, it was designed for use in routine clinical settings to systematically monitor the quality of care across patients.

Research Relevant to Using the ATOM as an Outcomes Measure

The ATOM has been used in several clinical settings to assess change over time in adolescents seeking treatment. However, there have been no systematic studies regarding the acceptability and effectiveness of using such tools in regular practice.

Research is currently under way to pilot the ATOM as a self-report instrument for children 9 to 11 years old and to develop a parent version of the instrument for children 5 to 9 years old. ATOM researchers are also testing a handheld computer version of the instrument.

Provision of Feedback

The format of the reports in NetOutcomes facilitates feedback to providers as well as clinical managers, medical directors, and other managers of a treatment facility or health plan. This feedback can be used to target quality improvement interventions that might enhance care for this population, particularly those adolescents identified as high risk because of suicidality, aggression, or potential for self-harm. Because research has demonstrated that clinicians need specific treatment recommendations rather than general feedback to change their practice patterns (Bero et al., 1998; Kanouse & Jacoby, 1988; Woolf, 1993), plans are under way to determine the most feasible and effective methods for incorporating such information into the NetOutcomes system.

The report generated from NetOutcomes can also be used to provide feedback to parents and adolescents as they initiate treatment. Discrepancies in scores between informants and mutual goals for treatment can be discussed in the initial treatment stages, whereas progress can be monitored through the follow-up process.

Limitations

There are several limitations to use of the ATOM in clinical practice. Administration and scoring of the instrument requires additional time, regardless of whether

NetOutcomes™

www.netoutcomes.net

Adolescent Treatment Outcomes Module

Provider Report for: Provider A

Emotional and Behavioral Problems—

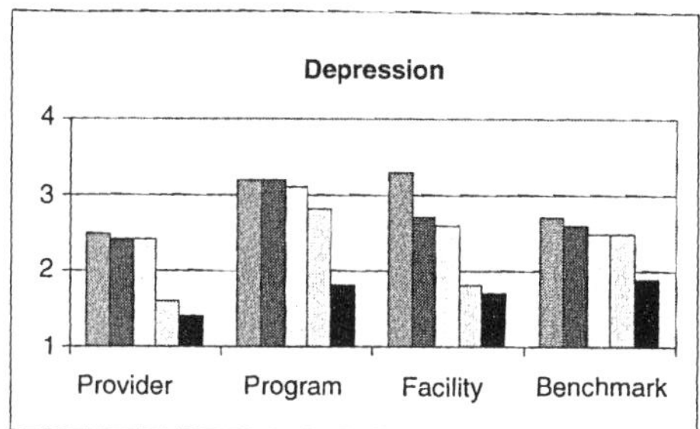

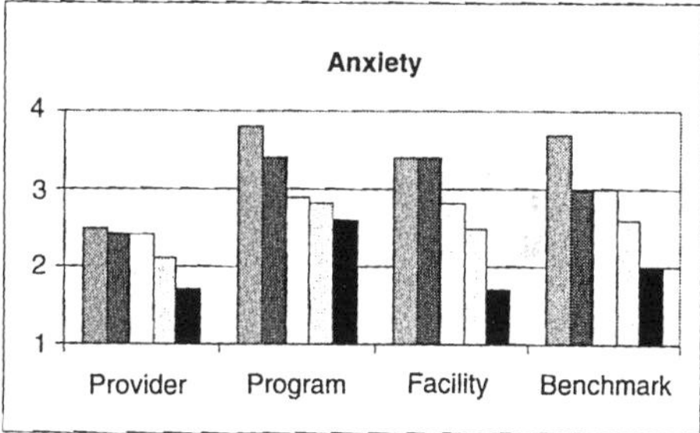

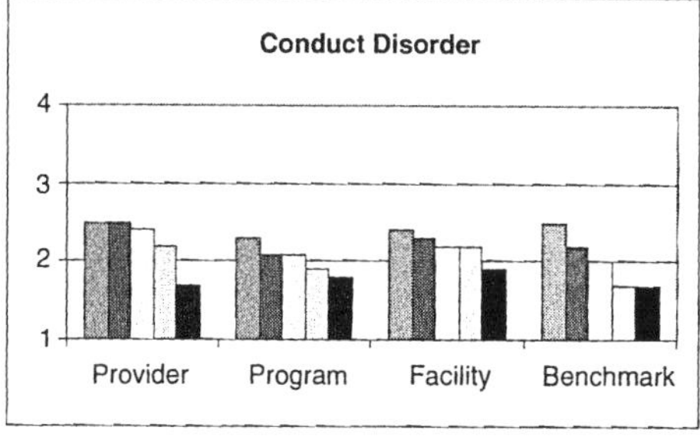

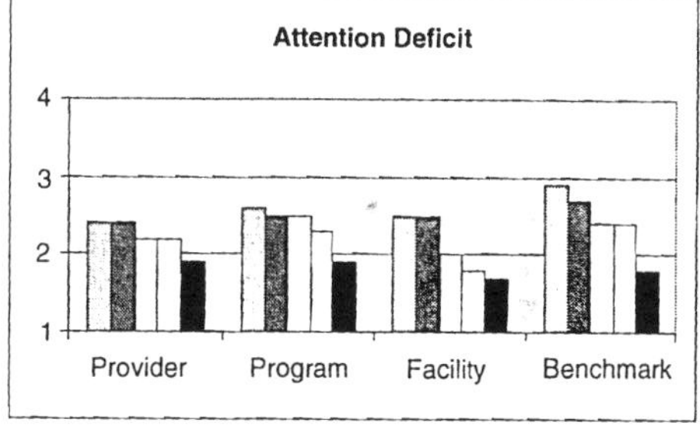

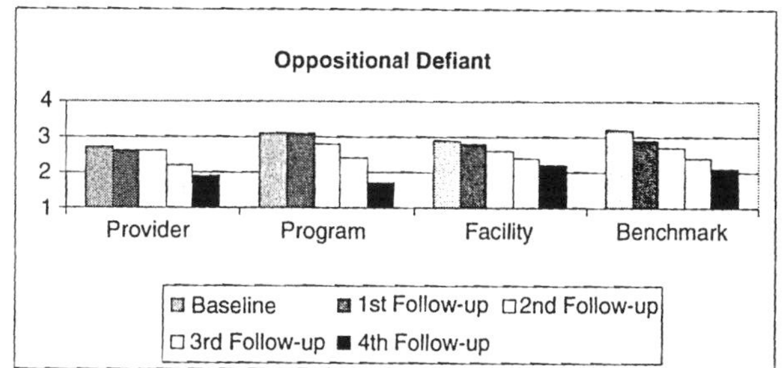

4 = problem occurs nearly every day, 3 = problem occurs a few days a week, 2 = problem occurs occasionally, 1 = problem does not occur at all

FIG. 13.3. Sample provider report for the ATOM.

the scoring is completed manually or data is entered into a newly created database or NetOutcomes. Second, each administration of the ATOM takes approximately 15 to 25 minutes to complete. Unless the clinical significance of the instrument is fully explained, adolescents and parents may perceive this as an undue burden, particularly when follow-up assessments are conducted through the mail. Obviously, low rates of follow-up would significantly bias the results of a larger outcomes management system. Third, validity studies on the ATOM were conducted in health care settings in a limited geographic region and may therefore not be representative of adolescents seeking treatment in other areas of the country. Additional normative data are needed for the instrument. In addition, although the ATOM was written at a fifth-grade reading level, there is concern that some adolescents and parents may not be able to comprehend items and respond accordingly. Therefore, a study is being conducted to assess the reliability of interviewer-assisted administration for individuals with less than a fifth-grade reading level. Fourth, as with any other outcome measure, the ATOM was designed to be an adjunct to the assessment process and should not be used as a sole source of information about the patient's diagnostic or clinical status. Finally, future research should be conducted to assess the effectiveness of the instrument in quality improvement monitoring and improvement processes.

Potential Use As a Data Source for Behavioral Health Service Report Cards

Results on the ATOM can be used as a data source for behavioral health service report cards. Specific performance indicators at the provider, program, or system level can be extracted from the data, including rates of symptom reduction, proportion of adolescents with improved functioning, number of emergency room visits or rehospitalizations for emotional or behavioral disorders since initiating treatment, and overall decrease in family impact.

SUMMARY

Behavioral and emotional disorders occur in one out of five adolescents, yet convincing data regarding the quality and outcomes of care are lacking. The ATOM can aid providers in assessing the multiple concerns of parents and adolescents presenting for treatment. The ATOM also provides data that are crucial for a provider's or system's quality improvement activities, program accountability, documentation of cost-effective services, compliance with accreditation standards, and effective decisions about care. Moreover, the Internet provides an easy and inexpensive alternative for analyzing and reviewing outcomes data for this population.

REFERENCES

Achenbach, T. M. (1991a). *Manual for the Child Behavior Checklist/4–18 and 1991 Profile.* Burlington: University of Vermont, Department of Psychiatry.

Achenbach, T. M. (1991b). *Manual for the Youth Self-Report and 1991 Profile.* Burlington: University of Vermont, Department of Psychiatry.

Angold, A., & Costello, E. J. (1995). Developmental epidemiology. *Epidemiological Review, 17,* 74–82.

Ascher, B. H., Farmer, E. M. Z., Burns, B. J., & Angold, A. (1996). The Child and Adolescent Services Assessment (CASA): Description and psychometrics. *Journal of Emotional & Behavioral Disorders, 4,* 12–20.

Bero, L. A., Grilli, R., Grimshaw, J. M., Harvey, E., Oxman, A. D., & Thomson, M. A. (1998). Closing the gap between research and practice: An overview of systemic reviews of interventions to promote the implementation of research findings. *British Medical Journal, 317,* 465–468.

Bird, H. R. (1995). *The Brief Impairment Scale.* New York: Columbia University, Department of Psychiatry.

Bird, H. R., Shaffer, D., Fisher, P., Gould, M. S., Staghezza, B., Chen, J. Y., & Hoven, C. (1993). The Columbia Impairment Scale (CIS): Pilot findings on a measure of global impairment for children and adolescents. *International Journal of Methods in Psychiatric Research, 3,* 167–176.

Burns, B. J., Angold, A., & Magruder-Habib, K. (1990). *Child and Adolescent Services Assessment (CASA): Parent Interview and Child Interview (Version 1.0).* Durham, NC: Duke University, Department of Psychiatry.

Conners, C. K., Sitarenios, G., Parker, J. D. A., & Epstein, J. N. (1998a). The revised Conner's Parent Rating Scale (CPRS–R): Factor structure, reliability, and criterion validity. *Journal of Abnormal Child Psychology, 26,* 257–268.

Conners, C. K., Sitarenios, G., Parker, J. D. A., & Epstein, J. N. (1998b). Revision and restandardization of the Conners' Teacher Rating Scale (CTRS–R): Factor structure, reliability, and criterion validity. *Journal of Abnormal Child Psychology, 26*, 279–291.

Conners, C. K., Wells, K. C., Parker, J. D. A., Sitarenios, G., Diamond, J. M., & Powell, J. W. (1997). A new self-report scale for assessment of adolescent psychopathology: Factor structure, reliability, validity, and diagnostic sensitivity. *Journal of Abnormal Child Psychology, 25*, 487–497.

Henggeler, S. W., Melton, G. B., Brondino, M. J., Scherer, D. O., & Hanley, J. H. (1997). Multisystemic therapy with violent and chronic juvenile offenders and their families: The role of treatment fidelity in successful dissemination. *Journal of Consulting and Clinical Psychology, 65*, 821–833.

Henggeler, S. W., Melton, G. B., & Smith, L A. (1992). Family preservation using multisystemic therapy: An effective alternative to incarcerating serious juvenile offenders. *Journal of Consulting and Clinical Psychology, 60*, 953–961.

Horwitz, A. V., & Reinhard, S. C. (1995). Ethnic differences in caregiving duties and burdens among parents and siblings of persons with severe mental illness. *Journal of Health and Social Behavior, 6*, 138–150.

Iman, R. L. (1978). Approximations of the critical region for Spearman's rho with and without ties present. *Communications in Statistics, B7*(3), 269–282.

Jensen, P. S., Irwin, R. A., Josephson, A. M., Davis, H., Venakis, S. N., Bloedau, L., et al. (1996). Data-gathering tools for "real world" clinical settings: A multisite feasibility study. *Journal of the American Academy of Child and Adolescent Psychiatry, 35*, 55–66.

Kanouse, D. E., & Jacoby, I. (1988). When does information change practitioner's behavior? *International Journal of Technology Assessment in Health Care, 4*, 27–33.

Kovacs, M. (1999). *Children's Depression Inventory.* North Tonawanda, NY: Multi-Health Systems.

Kramer, T. L., Robbins, J. M., Miller, T. L., Phillips, S. D., & Burns, B. J. (2002). *Family impact of emotional and behavioral disorders.* Unpublished manuscript.

Landgraf, J. M., Abetz, L., & Ware, J. E. (1996). *The CHQ user's manual.* Boston: New England Medical Center, Health Institute.

Larsen, D. L., Attkisson, C. C., Hargreaves, W. A., & Nguyen, T. D. (1979). Assessment of client/patient satisfaction: Development of a general scale. *Evaluation and Program Planning, 2*, 197–207.

Lubalin, J., Schnaier, J., Forsyth, B., Gibbs, D., McNeill, A., Lynch, J., & Ardini, M. A. (1995). *Design of a survey to monitor consumers' access to care, use of health services, health outcomes, and patient satisfaction.* Rockville, MD: Agency for Health Care Policy and Research.

Miller, T. L., Kramer, T. L., Robbins, J. M., Phillips, S. D., Wilson, C. E., Hargis, M. B., et al. (2002). *Measuring processes of mental health care for children: Development and testing of global and disorder-specific quality indicators.* Manuscript submitted for publication.

National Institute of Mental Health. (2001). *Blueprint for change: Research on child and adolescent mental health. Report on the National Advisory Mental Health Council's Workgroup on Child and Adolescent Mental Health Intervention Development and Deployment.* Washington, DC: U.S. Department of Health and Human Services, Public Health Service, National Institutes of Health.

NetOutcomes. (2003). *Individual patient and provider report samples.* Retrieved from http://www.netoutcomes.net/no_solutions/NO_Main/NO_ Home.asp?menu=nethome

Newman, F. L., Ciarlo, J. A., & Carpenter, D. (1999). Guidelines for selecting psychological instruments for treatment planning and outcome assessment. In M. E. Maruish (Ed.), *The use of psychological testing for treatment planning and outcomes assessment* (2nd ed., pp. 153–170). Mahwah, NJ: Lawrence Erlbaum Associates.

Phillips, S. D., Kramer, T. L., Compton, S. N., Burns, B. J., & Robbins, J. M. (2003). Case-mix adjustment of adolescent mental health treatment outcomes. *The Journal of Behavioral Health Services and Research, 30*(1), 125–136.

Reinhard, S. C. (1994). Living with mental illness: Effects of professional support and personal control on caregiver burden. *Research in Nursing and Health, 17*, 79–88.

Reinhard, S. C., Gubman, G. D., Horwitz, A., & Minsky, S. (1994). Burden Assessment Scale for families of the seriously mentally ill. *Evaluation and Program Planning, 17*, 261–269.

Robbins, J. M., Taylor, J. L., Burns, B. J., Rost, K. M., Kramer, T., & Smith, G. R. (1997). *Adolescent Treatment Outcomes Module (ATOM): User's manual.* Little Rock, AR: University of Arkansas for Medical Sciences.

Robbins, J. M., Taylor, J., L., Rost, K. M., Burns, B. J., Phillips, S. D., Burnam, M. A., et al. (2001). Measuring outcomes of care for adolescents with emotional and behavioral problems. *Journal of the American Academy of Child & Adolescent Psychiatry, 40*, 315–324.

Shaffer, D., Fisher, P., Dulcan, J. K., & Schwab-Stone, M. E. (1996). The NIMH Diagnostic Interview Schedule for Children Version 2.3 (DISC = 2.3): Description, acceptability, prevalence rates, and performance in the MECA study. *Journal of the American Academy of Child and Adolescent Psychiatry, 35,* 865–877.

Simpson, D. D. (1998). *Texas Christian University (TCU) data collection forms for adolescent programs.* Unpublished manuscript, Texas Christian University, Institute of Behavioral Research.

Simpson, D. D., & McBride, A. A. (1992). Family, Friends, and Self (FFS) assessment scales for Mexican American youth. *Hispanic Journal of Behavioral Science, 14,* 327–340.

Substance Abuse and Mental Health Services Administration. (2001). *Outcomes roundtable for children and Families.* Washington, DC: Author.

University of Arkansas for Medical Sciences, Center for Outcomes Research and Effectiveness. (2003). *NetOutcomes.* Retrieved January 22, 2002, from http://www.netcoutcomes.net

U.S. Department of Health and Human Services. (2000). *Report of the surgeon general's conference on children's mental health: A national action agenda.* Washington, DC: Author.

Weersing, V. R., & Weisz, J. R. (2002). Community clinic treatment of depressed youth: Benchmarking usual care against CBT clinical trials. *Journal of Consulting & Clinical Psychology, 70,* 299–310.

Woolf, S. H. (1993). Practice guidelines: A new reality in medicine, III: Impact on patient care. *Archives of Internal Medicine, 153,* 2646–2655.

14

Clinical Assessment of Adolescent Drug Abuse With the Personal Experience Inventory (PEI)

Ken C. Winters and Randy Stinchfield
University of Minnesota

William W. Latimer
Johns Hopkins University

OVERVIEW

Whereas drug use rates have remained relatively stable or even declined slightly among older age groups in recent years, illicit use among children and adolescents in the United States continues to rise. The first national drug use survey to include young people reported alarming levels of cigarette and marijuana smoking, alcohol consumption, and use of inhalants among children in Grades 4 through 6 (PRIDE, 2002). Indeed, among fourth graders, 4% reported past-year cigarette use and 8% reported past-year use of beer. These rates increased to 15% by Grade 6, and the frequency of drug use reported by high school students is still disturbingly high (Johnston, O'Malley, & Bachman, 2001). The drug-abuse treatment community has responded by continuing to develop age-appropriate services for drug-abusing youth (Winters, 1999; Williams & Chang, 2000). A cadre of screening and assessment tools to assist in the identification, referral, and treatment of drug-abusing adolescents has bolstered this trend (Winters, Latimer, & Stinchfield, 2002). This body of research has improved the assessment process by introducing more standardization to the field and permitting a wide network of professionals with diverse training and background to more objectively participate in the assessment process.

One tool in this group is the self-report questionnaire, Personal Experience Inventory (PEI; Winters & Henly, 1989). The PEI is listed as one of the suggested comprehensive assessment instruments in the National Institute on Drug Abuse *Adolescent Assessment and Referral Treatment System* (Rahdert, 1991). It has been reviewed in the 11th edition of the Mental Measurement Yearbook (Tucker, 1992), and its widespread use in research settings has been documented (Weinberg, Rahdert, Colliver, & Glantz, 1998).

RESEARCH GOALS AND APPLICATIONS

Research Goals

The development of the Personal Experience Inventory (PEI; Winters & Henly, 1989) was promoted by the view that assessment practices in the field in the 1980s were inadequate to meet the growing challenges in the service sector. Thus, we intended the PEI to provide clinicians and researchers with a comprehensive and standardized self-report inventory to assist in the identification, referral, and treatment of problems associated with teenage alcohol and drug abuse. To accomplish these goals, we set out to develop a norm-based instrument, consisting of scales reflecting multiple facets of adolescent substance use and related (coexisting) problems with sufficient reliability and validity.

The goal of measuring comorbid problems addressed an important instrumentation gap at the time of project inception. Teenage drug-use behaviors are complex: Their presence may cause other problems or may be a symptom of another primary behavioral or mental disorder (Clark & Winters, 2002). Such problems may require treatment in their own right, or they may appreciably change the focus and nature of recommended treatment. Psychosocial risk factors may serve as predisposing or precipitating variables that are important in the initiation of substance use, or these factors may contribute to continued use. Assessing these related factors should be a vital part of any substance-abuse assessment procedure. Thus, our position was to view adolescent drug abuse and related problems within the context of a broad array of psychological, social, and contextual behaviors, attitudes, consequences, and symptoms.

Applications

The PEI is intended to characterize the adolescent respondent according to the (a) severity of psychological and behavioral involvement with drugs, including alcohol; (b) nature and style of the drug use (e.g, consequences, personal effects, setting variables, polydrug use); (c) onset, duration, and frequency of use for 12 major psychoactive substance categories; (d) presence of psychosocial risk and protective factors, with a focus on variables thought to be risk or resiliency factors in adolescent drug-use severity; (e) existence of co-occurring behavioral and psychiatric problems that may accompany drug use; and (f) extent and nature of invalid response tendencies (e.g., faking bad, faking good).

Although the main purpose of the PEI is to address the clinical need related to treatment referral, the questionnaire also can be used as an evaluation tool in pre- and posttreatment assessment. We discuss the use of the PEI for these purposes later in the chapter.

SCALE DESCRIPTIONS

The PEI consists of two parts. The Problem Severity section (Part 1) consists of 153 questions that are organized into five Basic scales, five Clinical scales, three validity indexes, and a set of questions concerning drug-use frequency and duration, and age of onset. This section begins with 80 items that address drug-use experiences. Response options are formatted by either four points (never/once or twice/sometimes/often) or three points (never/once or twice/more than once or twice). A set of 16 yes–no items follow, 11 of which measure defensiveness. The next 14 items measure general frequency of drug use, which are followed by 37 items that address frequency and duration of drug use at 3 months, one year, and lifetime for 12 specific classes of drugs. The final six questions concern the onset of initial regular use of alcohol, marijuana, and other drugs. The Psychosocial section (part 2) consists of 147 items, which are divided into eight Personal Adjustment Scales, five Environment Scales, six Problem Screens, and two validity indexes. These items have either a four-point (strongly disagree/ disagree/agree/strongly agree or seldom or never/sometimes/often/almost always) response format, or a three-point response format (never/once or twice/more than once or twice). The reading level of the PEI is approximately sixth grade, based on the procedure developed by Fry (1977). An effort was made to construct items that have short sentences and that avoid complicated double negatives. Provided next are the definitions and number of items for each scale.

Part I—Problem Severity Sections

Basic Scales

1. *Personal Involvement With Chemicals* (29 items). This scale measures the degree of psychological involvement with drug use. High scores indicate frequent use at times and in settings that are inappropriate for drug use, use for psychological benefit or self-medication, and restructuring activities to accommodate use. Low scorers report relatively infrequent use and involvement limited primarily to social and recreational settings.

2. *Effects From Use* (10 items). The items of this set measure the immediate psychological, physiological, and behavioral effects of using alcohol and other drugs, most of which refer to negative or aversive states and feelings.

3. *Social Benefits of Use* (8 items). This scale reflects increase in perception of social affiliation and competence and peer acceptance as a result of drug use.

4. *Personal Consequence of Use* (11 items). Items in this set primarily focus on difficulties with friends, parents, school, and other social institutions resulting from substance use. Some items pertain to behavioral changes in the individual that may be related to these consequences.

5. *Polydrug Use* (8 items). The items defining this scale are all indicators of the use of drugs other than alcohol, including marijuana, stimulants, tranquilizers, cocaine, hallucinogens, heroin, or other opiates.

Clinical Scales

6. *Transsituational Use* (9 items). This set of items represents use in a variety of physical settings, particularly ones that are inappropriate for drug use (e.g., school) and use across a range of temporal settings (e.g., early morning).

7. *Psychological Benefits of Use* (7 items). These items suggest the use of drugs to reduce negative emotional states, such as loneliness, depression, boredom, anxiety, and use related to enhancing pleasurable affect.

8. *Social–Recreational of Use* (8 items). Items from this scale are associated with use of drugs to enhance social situations and peer interactions.

9. *Preoccupation* (8 items). High scorers report preplanning future use, restructuring activities to promote private or social use, and rumination about use.

10. *Loss of Control* (9 items). This set of items is associated with the inability to abstain from drug use or difficulty using in moderation when drugs are available.

Validity Indexes

11. *Infrequency* (7 items). These items refer to extremely unlikely drug use behavior and thus are expected to show very low rates of endorsement. High scorers may be "faking bad," displaying inattention, or randomly responding.

12. Defensiveness (15 items). The basis for this set of items was the 33-item Marlowe–Crowne Social Desirability Scale (Crowne & Marlowe, 1960), a frequently used measure of defensiveness or social desirability. The items were modified slightly to make them appropriate for an adolescent population.

13. Drug Use Frequency/Duration and Age of Onset. Items in this section summarize frequency of use of 12 categories of drugs during lifetime, the last 12 months, and the last 3 months. These items are similar to those used in recent national surveys of American high school seniors (Johnston et al., 2001). The final set of items in Part 1 inquire about the school grade at which the respondent first used and regularly used alcohol, marijuana, and other drugs.

Part II—Psychosocial Scales

Personal Adjustment Scales

1. Negative Self-image (10 items). This scale reflects lack of self-esteem and self-regard, personal dissatisfaction, and feelings of incompetence.

2. Psychological Disturbance (10 items). Items from this scale are associated with psychological problems and distress, such as difficulties with mood and thinking, and physical signs of distress.

3. Social Isolation (8 items). This scale taps perception of social discomfort and incompetence, and feelings of mistrust toward others.

4. Uncontrolled (12 items). These items focus on the tendency to act out, display anger and aggressiveness, and to defy authority figures and rules.

5. Rejecting Convention (11 items). The items in this set measure the extent to which the individual does not endorse traditional beliefs about right and wrong. Items ask about attitudes toward lying, breaking rules, stealing, and oppositional behavior.

6. Deviant Behavior (10 items). High scores on this scale suggest actual participation in unlawful, delinquent, or oppositional behavior (e.g., hitting a teacher, breaking into a home).

7. Absence of Goals (11 items). Elevated scores on this scale represent lack of planning or thinking about future plans, goals, and expectations, including finishing school and career attitudes.

8. Spiritual Isolation (7 items). High scores on this scale point to lack of belief in a spiritual life or force, few spiritual experiences, and little use of prayer.

Family and Peer Environment Scales

9. Peer Chemical Environment (8 items). The items defining this scale indicate involvement with drugs by one's peers.

10. Sibling Chemical Use (4 items). This set represents drug use by brothers or sisters.

11. Family Pathology (14 items). Items from this scale are associated with family problems of drug abuse, physical or sexual abuse, and severe family dysfunction.

12. Family Estrangement (9 items). This scale reflects lack of family solidarity and closeness, and the presence of parent–child conflict.

Screens for Other Problems

Brief screens are provided for the following problem areas:

13. Family Drug Abuse (parental and sibling drug abuse).

14. Physical Abuse (intrafamilial physical abuse).

15. Sexual Abuse (intrafamilial and other-source sexual abuse).
16. Eating Disorders (bulimia and anorexia nervosa).
17. Need for Psychiatric Referral (signs that suggest need for psychiatric evaluation).
18. Suicide Potential (indications of serious suicidality).

Validity Indexes

19. Infrequent Responses (11 items). These items have either very low or high rates of endorsement and may reflect "faking bad," inattention, or random responding (e.g., "I like sunny days," "I would rather lose a game than win").
20. Defensiveness (12 items). This is another subset of items from on the Marlowe–Crowne Social Desirability Scale and adapted for use with an adolescent population.

TEST ADMINISTRATION

Examinee Characteristics

The intended age range for the questionnaire is from 12 to 18 years. Although the test has been administered to older individuals, this is not generally recommended, because the test's development and validity data are based on adolescents. Some professionals may consider using the PEI with general population participants. In most cases, the low base rate of excessive drug involvement in a general adolescent population would argue against use of the Problem Severity section with this group. However, the instrument's Psychosocial scales may be relevant for general population administration, because clinical and nonclinical score distributions on many of these scales do not appear to be markedly different. Finally, great caution should be taken when the PEI is administered to populations whose demographic and background characteristics are largely different from those of the samples used in the validity analyses.

Materials and Scoring

The PEI can be administered in paper-and-pencil or computer formats (with materials marketed by Western Psychological Services). For paper-and-pencil administration, the six-page PEI test booklet is needed. Scoring requires either mailing or faxing the completed questionnaire to the publisher. Computer administration involves use of an IBM-compatible diskette. All score reports of the PEI are computer-generated and consist of standardized scores (based on both drug clinic and nonclinical standardization samples), narrative descriptions for each scale, and summaries of responses to the drug-use frequency and screening items. To assist with treatment referral decisions, an overview of residential treatment indicators are provided.

SCALE CONSTRUCTION

Problem Severity

Scale development efforts began by assembling a pool of 600 problem severity items from existing instruments that represented a broad range of drug-abuse problem indicators. In reviewing all the relevant literature, a diverse range of models and theoretical approaches to drug involvement were considered, including the Alcoholics Anonymous, learning, social-based, and the psychiatric model. This approach to defining the target constructs was oriented toward searching for characteristics and symptoms reflecting problems that precede or resulted from drug involvement.

The process of developing the problem severity scales employed both rational and empirical strategies (see Henly & Winters, 1988, for more details). Under the rational approach, items were assigned a priori to scales, and then reassigned or deleted based on their own-scale and other-scale correlations so that scale reliability and independence could be maximized. For the empirical approach, a variety of factor- and cluster-analytic procedures were employed in an effort to define relatively independent dimensions that emerged reliably across methods. Both procedures identified dimensions or constructs that were quite similar, and from the standpoint of psychometric adequacy, only modest differences in the two sets of scales existed. The relatively brief empirical scales had reliability estimates that approached or exceeded those of their longer rational counterparts, which is to be expected in view of empirical scale construction methods employed.

Psychosocial Scales

A great deal of research effort has been devoted to understanding the role of psychosocial factors in the etiology and maintenance of adolescent drug use (Glantz & Pickens, 1992; Hawkins, Catalano, & Miller, 1992). An extensive review of this research literature was conducted to identify an appropriate list of psychosocial risk factors. Studies reviewed included cross-sectional and longitudinal studies of high school samples, and adult retrospective and prospective studies of prealcoholic characteristics. The set of identified variables was supplemented by factors suggested by consultants and service providers. Over 200 new items were written to reflect the identified factors and formatted to have either three or four response options: never/once or twice/more than once or twice, strongly disagree/disagree/agree/strongly agree, or seldom or ever/sometimes/often/almost always. To these 232 items were added:

1. Thirty one items adapted from the Marlowe–Crowne Social Desirability Scale (Crowne & Marlowe, 1960);
2. Fourteen infrequency items expected to have rates of endorsement of less than 10% or greater than 90%
3. Eleven psychosocial stressor items reflecting life events that might be important contextual factors in interpreting questionnaire responses and that were viewed by the service providers as important clinical phenomenon in their own right (e.g., intrafamilial sexual abuse)
4. A 28-item drug use frequency checklist assessing frequency of use for nine classes of substances over lifetime, 12 months, and 3 months.

As detailed elsewhere (Henly & Winters, 1989), scale scores, reliability estimates (coefficient alpha), and item-scale correlations were computed for each a priori scale based on results from a drug clinic sample. Twelve scales having acceptable levels of reliability (alpha > .70) and independence (proportion of unique, reliable variance ≥ .25) emerged from the scale analyses.

Problem Screens

Specific criterion groups related to problem areas of interest were defined according to staff ratings on each client at the participating agencies. Ratings were recorded on a problem checklist and were based on interviews with the client, parents, and school informants, and on any in-house questionnaire administered routinely to adolescent clients. The specific criterion defined were (a) eating disorders, (b) intrafamilial physical abuse, (c) intrafamilial sexual abuse, (d) family (parent or siblings) history of substance abuse or dependence, (e) suicidal behavior, and (f) need for psychiatric referral. Psychosocial items relevant to each problem area were tested statistically for their discriminative value, and additive or configural decision rules were established that optimized the discrimination of the criterion groups identified from drug clinic samples.

Drug-Use Frequency Checklist

Included in the development of the PEI scales was the insertion of a drug-use frequency checklist adapted from survey instruments used in recent national surveys of high school seniors (e.g., Johnston et al., 2001). Frequency of drug use for 12 drug categories (from alcohol to inhalants) during lifetime, last 12 months, and last 3 months were included (the latter time frame was chosen rather than the more standard 1-month period as a clinical consideration).

RELIABILITY AND VALIDITY OF THE PEI

Samples and Procedures

Since the mid-1980s, the authors of the PEI have been collecting psychometric data from three types of sites: drug clinic, juvenile detention, and nonclinical (school). Participation in PEI research by an agency or program required an agreement from the administration that they (a) either allow research staff to collect the data or have their staff trained in PEI testing procedures; (b) collect additional data, such as concurrent measures; (c) follow informed consent and confidentiality procedures; and (d) provide all data to the research staff at the completion of their commitment. The drug clinic data have been collected from over 55 drug abuse evaluation or treatment programs across the United States and Canada, representing a range of service settings (residential and nonresidential, 30-day and longer term, short-stay evaluation, hospital based, and freestanding) and locales (rural and urban). The juvenile offender samples were obtained from nine sites: four residential, state-operated facilities that house adolescent felons and those in need of supervision, one drug education program for teenagers convicted of minor charges related to drug use, and four state drug evaluation programs that received referrals from the court. The school samples were collected from three school districts (two urban, one rural); here, participants were drawn from targeted classrooms believed to be representative of students within the participating school districts. Data collection for the drug clinic and juvenile offender samples has been an ongoing process since 1985; the school data were collected during a 12-month period (1986–1987).

The clinical samples were recruited by staff at the participating facilities. Adolescents who agreed to take the test were assured anonymity and confidentiality. For minors to participate, parental consent was also required. Test administrators (either facility employees or research staff) who administered the PEI received detailed and standard instructions, and they were responsible for collecting other data and questionnaires. Participants with obvious signs of intoxication, withdrawal, or other cognitive or learning impairments were screened from testing. If staff at the drug-clinic or juvenile-offender sites provided ratings and diagnoses, they were blind to PEI results. Drug-clinic participants were tested as soon as was practical after initial client contact, which was usually after 2 or 3 days from intake. Juvenile offender participants were tested prior to participation in any drug rehabilitation program.

The PEI and concurrent alternate drug-use questionnaires were administered either at agency intake or within 5 days after intake. The Minnesota Multiphosic Personality Inventory (MMPI) was administered independently of the PEI but usually within 2 to 3 days of PEI administration. A small sample of parents of adolescents who had completed the PEI were administered a questionnaire about their child's behavior and experiences. Staff at participating drug treatment programs provided client information (problem severity ratings, treatment history, referral recommendations, and discharge status) on a summary data form. Agency staff were blind to client PEI results.

Provided below is an overview of representative findings from these series of studies. Interested readers can turn to published manuscripts and reports for more complete descriptions of these PEI psychometric studies (Dembo, Schmeidler, Borden, Chin Sue, & Manning, 1997; Guthmann & Brenna, 1990; Henly & Winters, 1988; Henly & Winters, 1989; Winters, Latimer, Stinchfield, & Egan, 2003; Winters, Stinchfield, & Henly, 1993, 1996; Winters, Stinchfield, Henly, & Schwartz, 1991). For the sake of parsimony, psychometric findings for the Clinical Problem Severity scales are not reported. As described in an earlier section, these scales are redundant to the Basic Problem Severity scales, and their psychometric properties do not meaningfully differ from their companion scales.

Internal Consistency

Data on the internal consistency of the PEI scales are presented for the school sample and a combined "clinical" group consisting of the drug-clinic and juvenile-offender samples (the data between them are indistinguishable) as a function of gender and ethnic background. We also examined internal consistency for two age groups (young = 12–15 years; old = 16+ years); these data are quite similar to total group data, so we will not report them separately. The total internal consistency sample consisted of 7,181 participants (6,488 from drug-clinic and juvenile-offender sites, and 693 from school sites).

Table 14.1 provides a summary of composite reliability (coefficient alpha) data across sex and sites as a function of five ethnic groups. Good to excellent alpha coefficients were obtained across the ethnic samples. The range (and median) of alpha coefficients for the two main groups of PEI scales are as follows: Basic Problem Severity, .81 to .97 (m = .88); Psychosocial, .70 to .88 (m = .83). The internal consistency estimates for the Response Distortion scales (not shown in the table) are somewhat lower than the estimates for the substantive scales, but this is to be expected, because they have smaller standard deviations. The data also indicate that scale internal consistency estimates are quite consistent across subgroups defined by site (school, drug clinic, and offender), sex, and ethnicity (White, African American, American Indian, and Hispanic). In addition, these favorable results suggest that the PEI was

TABLE 14.1
Internal Consistency Coefficients for PEI Scales by Ethnic Groups

PEI Scale	*White (N = 4,501)*	*Hispanic (N = 1,263)*	*African American (N = 952)*	*American Indian (N = 335)*	*Asian American (N = 130)*
Basic Scales					
Personal Involvement With Chemicals	.97	.97	.96	.97	.97
Effects From Use	.90	.89	.89	.89	.89
Social Benefits	.88	.84	.86	.83	.86
Personal Consequences	.90	.85	.86	.87	.87
Polydrug Use	.88	.85	.76	.84	.80
Psychosocial Scales					
Negative Self-image	.84	.77	.71	.73	.70
Psychological Disturbance	.83	.81	.78	.83	.82
Social Isolation	.70	.73	.74	.77	.77
Uncontrolled	.88	.88	.85	.85	.84
Rejecting Convention	.75	.72	.70	.69	.70
Deviant Behavior	.85	.86	.83	.87	.87
Absence of Goals	.82	.81	.82	.82	.83
Spiritual Isolation	.87	.82	.78	.81	.78
Peer Chemical Environment	.83	.76	.73	.76	.79
Sibling Chemical Use	.85	.87	.81	.82	.86
Family Pathology	.83	.81	.82	.81	.78
Family Estrangement	.84	.80	.74	.79	.78

Note. Obtained results are based on composite data across sex and sites (drug clinic, juvenile offender, school).

developed by proper sampling of the content domains, and that the individual PEI scales are comprised of items that appear to be measuring a common attribute.

Test–Retest Reliability

A subset of drug clinic and school participants participated in a test–retest evaluation of the PEI. Because of second-testing refusal or absenteeism, or to errors in identification codes, participation rates at retest were less than 100%. Averaging across the test–retest samples, about 10% of the test cases could not be matched with retest data. Test–retest data was collected on two drug clinic samples (1-week interval, $n = 59$; 1-month interval, $n = 44$), a waiting list sample (1-month interval, $n = 46$), and a school sample (1-month interval, $n = 123$). The results suggest that temporal stability of the PEI scales varies as a function of the retest interval length and intervening experiences. In general, stability scores (intraclass correlations) were more stable for participants that did not receive formal drug-clinic services during the period between the two testings (i.e., the 1-month drug-clinic waiting list sample and the school sample). The range of stability coefficients for the 1-week drug-clinic waiting list for the Basic scales was .45 to .92 ($m = .71$); for the Psychosocial scales, the range was .38 to .88 ($m = .64$). The range of stability coefficients for the 1-month drug-clinic waiting list for the Basic scales was .80 to .87 ($m = .84$); for the Psychosocial scales, the range was .65 to .96 ($m = .77$). For the 1-month school sample, the range for the Basic scales was .42 to .83 ($m = .67$), and for the Psychosocial scales, the range was .65 to .91 ($m = .79$). Within the drug-clinic samples, greater score stability was observed in the 1-week retest group than in the 1-month retest group, which is to be expected from test–retest theory.

TABLE 14.2
Convergent Validity of the PEI Basic Scales

	Client Rating				*Research Staff Rating*		*Counselor Rating*			*Parent Rating*
PEI Basic Scale	*AAIS* (N = 224)	*ADS* (N = 83)	*DUF* (N = 140)	*Legal Problems* (N = 140)	*SUD* (N = 115)	*Referral* (N = 140)	*Consequences of Use* (N = 140)	*Symptoms* (N = 140)	*Global Rating* (N = 140)	*Consequences of Use* (N = 140)
Personal Involvement	.59	.59	.76	.43	.82	.88	.68	.74	.79	.26
Effects From Use	.56	.60	.63	.25	.65	.76	.55	.58	.68	.23
Social Benefits	.49	.53	.53	.28	.63	.66	.47	.57	.57	.13
Personal Consquences	.59	.60	.66	.58	.72	.80	.58	.60	.77	.19
Polydrug Use	.45	.35	.72	.44	.74	.81	.67	.70	.75	.20

Note. Questionnaire 1 Rating Description: AAIS = Adolescent Alcohol Involvement Scale; ADS = Alcohol Dependence Scale; DUF = drug-use frequency (aggregate across 12 drugs); SUD = substance-use diagnosis (1 = no diagnosis, 2 = abuse only, 3 = at least one dependence); Legal Problems, Consequences of Use, Symptoms, and Global Rating refer to rating forms described in Winters et al., 1996; Referral = recommended level of drug treatment (1 = no drug treatment, 2 = drug treatment). All correlations are significant at the $p < .01$ level, except those underlined.

Convergent Validity

Convergent validity evidence of the PEI scales will document the extent to which scale scores are associated with alternate measures of similar or related constructs. Data from the client and other informants (research staff, counselor, and parent or guardian) are presented in Table 14.2.

Correlation data were obtained between Basic Problem Severity Scales and the following self-report problem severity measures: Adolescent Alcohol Involvement Scale (AAIS; Mayer & Filstead, 1979); Alcohol Dependence Scale (ADS; Horn, Skinner, Wanberg, & Foster, 1982), a composite frequency score derived from the drug-use frequency (DUF) checklist included on the PEI; admitted legal problems; and substance-use disorder diagnoses (no diagnosis vs. abuse vs. dependence), based on results from a structured interview (Winters & Henly, 1993). The results indicate that the PEI Problem Severity scales are highly correlated with these related measures. The magnitude of these correlations (.25–.76, $m = .57$) indicates that the PEI Basic scales reflect, to a large degree, the same construct measured by these questionnaires.

Based on semistructured intake interviews, we identified ratings indicative of client drug involvement: global rating, consequences of drug use, drug-use symptoms (based on Heilman's [1973] signs of "chemical dependency"), substance-use diagnosis, and referral recommendation (no drug treatment vs. drug treatment). Also, the designated parent or guardian completed the same consequences checklist at intake. Counselor and research staff ratings converged highly with the PEI; all of these ratings had r's > .47 ($m = .68$). Perhaps not too surprising, the parent rating of consequences yielded a lower correlation (r's = .13–.26) Nevertheless, the significant and relatively large magnitude of the correlations between the PEI Basic scales and other informant ratings indicate that the PEI Problem Severity scales are not just congruent with other self-report measures.

Correlations between PEI Psychosocial scales and scales of the MMPI were computed. PEI scales that measure personal and interpersonal adjustment generally showed significant relationships with MMPI scales; those PEI scales reflecting values and characteristics of others showed little relationship to MMPI scales. To better define relationships between MMPI scales and relevant PEI scales, an interbattery factor analysis was conducted. As part of this analysis, a set of revised orthogonal scales was created for each inventory. Each of the orthogonal scales relates maximally to an existing scale but is statistically independent of the other orthogonal scales from its instrument. (Correlations of the original and corresponding PEI scales ranged from .87 to .98; those for the MMPI orthogonal ranged from .69 to .91.) Four statistically significant interbattery factors were extracted and rotated to a univocal varimax solution. Loadings of the orthogonalized scales on the interbattery factors are presented in Table 14.3.

Factor 1 may be hypothesized to represent tendencies toward acting-out behavior, given the salient positive loadings for orthogonalized Rejecting Convention (PEI), Deviant Behavior (PEI), and Hypomania (MMPI), and a negative loading for Hysteria (MMPI). Factor 2 may reflect global psychological distress, in view of the substantial loading of the Psychological Disturbance Scale (PEI), and moderate loadings for six of the nine MMPI scales. Factor 3 appears to be concerned with adolescent–parent conflict, based on salient loadings for Family Estrangement (PEI) and Psychopathic Deviate (MMPI) scales (which for adolescents often reflects family conflicts). Factor 4, on which Social Isolation (PEI) and Social Introversion (MMPI) scales load importantly, may be interpreted as reflecting feelings of loneliness or social inadequacy.

TABLE 14.3
Selected PEI Psychosocial Scales vs. MMPI Scales

	Interbattery Factor Loading			
	I	II	III	IV
Orthgonalized PEI Scale				
Negative Self-image		.32	.33	
Psychological Disturbance		.79		
Social Isolation				.79
Uncontrolled				
Rejecting Convention	.33			
Deviant Behavior	.66			
Absence of Goals			.33	
Family Estrangement			.68	
Orthogonalized MMPI Scale				
1. Hypochondriasis (Hs)	.30	.32		
2. Depression (D)		.34		
3. Hysteria (Hy)	−.40	.34		−.38
4. Psychopathic Deviate (Pd)			.79	
6. Paranoia (Pa)		.33		
7. Psychasthenia (Pt)		.45		
8. Schizophrenia (Sc)		.39		
9. Hypomania (Ma)	.57			
0. Social Introversion (Si)				.70

Note. Loadings < .30 in absolute value are omitted.

Criterion Validity

PEI scale scores have been examined as a function of setting (drug clinic, juvenile offender, and normal) and diagnosis. The analysis of variance (ANOVA) revealed three main results when PEI scales were compared on setting (see Table 14.4): (a) mean scores on the Problem Severity and Psychosocial scales were virtually identical for drug-clinic and juvenile-offender groups, except for a significantly higher Deviance mean score for the juvenile offender group; (b) the normal group had a significantly lower mean scores on all the Problem Severity scales compared to the drug clinic and juvenile offender groups; and (c) the normal group had mean scores on the Psychosocial scales that more closely resembled those of the other two groups, particular with respect to Social Isolation, Rejecting Convention, and Sibling Chemical Use.

The between-group analysis for diagnosis was performed on the Basic Problem Severity scales, because they were developed with the expectation of differentiating groups according to severity of substance-use diagnosis (see Table 14.5). The results of the ANOVA indicate that diagnosis group mean scores on each Basic scale differed significantly ($p < .01$), with mean differences ordered as expected (dependence > abuse > no diagnosis). Post hoc contrasts (Student–Newman–Keuls) yielded significant pairwise differences across all three groups on three of the five Basic scales. Scores on Effects from Use and Social Benefits for the abuse diagnosis group did not significantly differ from the no-diagnosis group (although the small sample size of the abuse group provided a less than optimal comparison to the other groups).

The previous findings offer evidence as to the criterion validity of the PEI. For the diagnostic comparisons, Problem Severity scale scores differed by virtue of diagnostic group, particularly between the abuse and dependence groups. Also, the widespread differences between the drug clinic and normal groups supports the PEI's validity.

TABLE 14.4
PEI Scale Standardized Scores as a Function of Group Membership

PEI Scale	School (N = 567) M	Juvenile Offenders (N = 160) M	Drug Clinic (N = 889) M
Basic Scales			
Personal Involvement With Chemicals	34.57	49.32	50.10
Effects From Use	38.36	50.09	50.22
Social Benefits	40.07	49.69	50.19
Personal Consquences	38.35	51.58	50.00
Polydrug Use	34.64	50.25	49.87
Psychosocial Scales			
Negative Self-image	42.12	51.11	49.95
Psychological Disturbance	45.96	50.88	49.81
Social Isolation	47.71	53.06	49.98
Uncontrolled	42.74	48.86	50.10
Rejecting Convention	48.00	49.79	49.85
Deviant Behavior	34.79	57.57	49.93
Absence of Goals	43.67	50.35	49.79
Spiritual Isolation	46.22	51.06	49.92
Peer Chemical Environment	39.03	49.91	50.00
Sibling Chemical Use	47.57	52.27	50.48
Family Pathology	41.99	52.57	49.81
Family Estrangement	40.63	47.11	49.95

Note. Due to group inequity in terms of sex and age distribution, PEI scale scores are reported in standardized form. All F ratios are significant at $p < .001$ level.

TABLE 14.5
Between-Group Analysis of PEI Basic Scales and Diagnostic Groups

PEI Basic Scale	Diagnostic Groups Scores (Mean ± SD)			F
	No Diagnosis (n = 48)	Abuse Diagnosis (n = 7)	Dependence Diagnosis (n = 60)	
Personal Involvement	35.9 ± 6.6	40.1 ± 4.2	51.3 ± 8.8	53.2
Effects From Use	39.8 ± 8.3	41.6 ± 7.0	52.4 ± 9.5	28.0
Social Benefits	39.7 ± 7.5	46.6 ± 4.4	50.2 ± 9.7	19.7
Personal Consequences	39.1 ± 5.9	43.6 ± 7.5	51.5 ± 9.3	32.8
Polydrug Use	38.3 ± 6.5	42.0 ± 4.9	51.9 ± 9.8	34.8

Note. All univariate F ratios reported are significant at $p < .001$ level.

Contrary to expectations, the drug-clinic and juvenile-offender groups had comparable mean scores. However, officials from the participating juvenile detention centers felt that the scores were not unexpected; they generally agreed that heavy drug use and personal and family problems are common to the juvenile offender population. Further, the literature offers similar conclusions. Studies have found that the causal relationships between various psychosocial variables and alcohol and marijuana abuse are similar to those associated with other forms of problem behavior (Jessor, Donovan, & Costa, 1991; Winters et al., 1996). Similarly, Kandel (1978), in a review of findings from eight major longitudinal studies of adolescent drug use, concluded that attitudes

TABLE 14.6
Association of Intake PEI Basic Scales With Treatment Involvement Variables

PEI Basic Scale	*Attended Drug Treatment (N = 140)*	*Frequency of Attendance at Drug Treatment (N = 140)*	*Attended Aftercare (N = 140)*	*Frequency of Attendance at Aftercare (N = 140)*
Personal Involvement	.39	.35	.31	.20
Effects From Use	.34	.27	.26	.17
Social Benefits	.26	.28	.26	.13
Personal Consequences	.26	.28	.29	.18
Polydrug Use	.40	.33	.36	.28

Note. All correlations (Pearson's R) are significant at the $p < .05$ level except those underlined. The categorical variables are coded as follows: counselor's treatment referral decision (1 = no treatment, 2 = drug education, 3 = outpatient treatment, and 4 = inpatient treatment); attended drug treatment (1 = no, 2 = yes).

and behavior associated with delinquent teenagers typically precede rather than result from drug involvement, and recent descriptive studies of youth in detention centers indicate that they report multiple problems and risk factors (Dembo et al., 1997; Zucker, Fitzgerald, & Moses, 1995).

Predictive Validity: Treatment Involvement

Research on the PEI's ability to predict future behavior has been directed at the Basic scales' association with treatment variables. The issue regarding the use of the PEI in predicting treatment outcome is complex enough that the topic will be addressed in a separate section. Next we discuss the association of PEI and treatment retention and participation variables.

The predictive validity results for the treatment involvement variables are summarized in Table 14.6. Moderately positive coefficients were obtained for the four treatment involvement variables (mean $r = .28$, range $r = .13–.40$), suggesting that as drug-use problem severity increases, client involvement in treatment tends to increase somewhat as well. The results also indicated a slight tendency for the magnitude of the associations to correspond to the temporal distance between the intake measure and the predicted treatment variable. The size of the validity coefficients tended to decrease as the predicted variable represented further temporal distance from the intake PEI measures. For example, the PEI scales had a mean r of .33 with drug treatment involvement, in contrast to a mean r of .19 with frequency of attendance to aftercare.

Based on the limited literature in this area, one should not expect to find sizeable correlations between client report of problem severity and treatment involvement variables. Engagement in treatment is likely affected by a variety of factors (Weinberg et al., 1998; Winters, 1999). However, the modest correlations obtained suggest a tendency among youth who acknowledge more severe problems to attend treatment compared to those who report less severe problem severity. The extent to which adolescent drug treatment participation variance is mediated by other factors is an important line of research that has received a great deal more attention in the adult literature. A potentially fruitful research direction is to understand the role of motivational factors and stages (e.g., Prochaska & DiClemente, 1992) as they pertain to seeking and attending drug treatment. There have been some recent efforts to develop treatment readiness measures for adolescent drug abusers that incorporate motivational constructs (e.g., Cady, Winters, Jordan, Solberg, & Stinchfield, 1996; DeLeon, Melnick, Kressel, & Jainchill, 1994).

USE OF THE PEI FOR TREATMENT REFERRAL

Overview of Treatment Planning Issues

The primary aim of an effective treatment plan is to develop a set of interrelated treatment strategies tailored to the unique assets and problems of the client. Such plans are thus best considered within a larger context defined by ongoing relationships between assessment, treatment planning, and treatment outcome. This section will describe how clinicians may use the PEI as one source of information to assist with the development of an individualized treatment plan. Theoretical issues central to treatment planning, as well as current research in this area, will be presented to provide a context for how to use the PEI as a treatment planning tool.

Determining the Appropriate Treatment Across a Continuum of Care

Descriptions of the continuum of care available to treat adolescent drug abusers typically describe four basic levels: outpatient, partial hospitalization, residential, and inpatient treatment programs (Center for Substance Abuse Treatment, 1999; Margolis, 1995; Muisener, 1994). The primary determinants of placement within a given level of care are (a) the nature and severity of the adolescent's drug use and related problems, and (b) the degree and quality of support present in the his or her environment. The former dimension concerns the adolescent's drug-use problem severity, medical status, and psychosocial (including psychiatric) functioning. The environmental dimension concerns the behaviors, attitudes, and psychiatric status of family members, and the quality of interpersonal relationships with other adults and peers who play key roles in the adolescent's life.

Outpatient Treatment

Outpatient treatment may include a range of services and levels of intensity that do not provide overnight stay. One primary indication for outpatient treatment is the presence of a stable interpersonal environment. Outpatient treatment may also be indicated when the adolescent presents with no significant psychiatric or medical problems while possessing sufficient resources to take advantage of services that have inherently less structure when compared to residential treatment. Outpatient treatment for adolescent substance abuse is likely to be more effective by coordinating individual and family sessions that address both the adolescent's substance use, as well as family issues underlying maladaptive behaviors (Minuchin, 1974).

Partial Hospitalization Program

Partial hospitalization programs, or day treatment, is the highest outpatient intensity level and has been defined as providing 20 or more hours of structured programming weekly (Center for Substance Abuse Treatment, 1999). Several indicators for partial hospitalization include (a) continued substance abuse despite outpatient treatment, (b) substantial relapse following abstinence achieved during residential care, or (c) continuation of care following successful completion of residential treatment (Muisener, 1994). In addition, interpersonal support must be sufficient to promote abstinence, and the adolescent should not present with significant psychiatric or medical problems.

Residential Treatment

Residential treatment generally provides a range of interrelated individual, group, and family services applied within a setting where patients remain overnight (Center for Substance Abuse Treatment, 1999). Length of treatment has declined substantially during recent years such that the average length of stay for residential patients is approximately 30 days (Latimer, Newcomb, Winters, & Stinchfield, 2000). Residential treatment is indicated for youth with significant substance-abuse problems. In addition, residential treatment indicators include: (a) continued substance abuse despite partial hospitalization treatment, (b) significant environmental distress that greatly heightens continued substance abuse or relapse risk by an adolescent currently in outpatient or partial hospitalization treatment, or (c) significant medical or psychiatric problems exhibited by the adolescent that require acute or ongoing management (Muisener, 1994).

Inpatient Treatment

Inpatient treatment provides the most intensive residential treatment experience and is housed in a medical unit where constant patient supervision is available, when indicated (Center for Substance Abuse Treatment, 1999). Inpatient and residential treatment options have much in common. Given changes following the advent of managed care, the degree of problem severity required to obtain inpatient treatment is extreme; that is, the immediate safety of the adolescent patient or others is in question. Thus, the primary difference between residential and inpatient programs is that the latter generally serve adolescents who present with severe psychiatric or medical problems that threaten the immediate safety of the substance-abusing adolescent.

Treatment Placement

The use of the PEI to inform treatment placement decisions must be made with a wide range of information sources and assessment strategies (Tarter, 1990). The PEI is intended to serve as one source of information within the clinical process of determining intervention or treatment placement. Table 14.7 suggests PEI-based guidelines for placing drug-abusing youth in programs along a continuum of care. Obviously, these guidelines should not be the sole source for decision making but should be used in conjunction with other reports and clinical judgement. PEI dimensions utilized in the placement guidelines include signs of (a) psychological dependence, (b) loss of control or excessive preoccupation with drugs, (c) family problems, and (d) psychiatric problems that may coexist with a substance use disorder.

Theoretical Models of Treatment Planning

Our conceptualization of adolescent drug-abuse treatment planning incorporates knowledge from two general research areas: adolescent development and biopsychosocial factors associated with substance abuse vulnerability (Glantz & Pickens, 1992; Margolis, 1995; Weinberg et al., 1998).

TABLE 14.7
Guidelines for Substance Abuse Treatment Placement Along a Continuum of Care

PEI-Related Characteristic	*Outpatient or Partial Hospitalization*
Depth of psychological dependence	>40*T* & <60*T* on most or all Problem Severity Basic scales
Signs of loss of control of drug use or excessive preoccupation with drug use	>40*T* & <60*T* on Loss of Control OR Preoccupation With Drugs scales
Signs of family dysfunction	>40*T* & <60*T* on Family Pathology OR Family Estrangement OR Sibling Chemical Use scales AND Sexual and Physical Abuse Problem Screens are negative
Signs of psychiatric problems	>40*T* & <60*T* on Psychological Disturbance scale OR Psychiatric Referral Problem Screen is positive AND Suicide Potential Problem Screen is negative
PEI-Related Characteristic	*Residential or Inpatient Treatment*
Depth of psychological dependence	$T > 60$ on most or all Basic scales
Signs of loss of control of drug use or excessive preoccupation with drug use	$T > 60$ on Loss of Control scale OR Drug use $T > 60$ on Preoccupation With Drugs scale
Signs of family dysfunction	$T > 60$ on Family Pathology scale OR $T > 60$ on Family Estrangement scale OR $T > 60$ on Sibling Chemical Use scale OR Sexual Abuse Problem Screen is positive OR Physical Abuse Problem Screen is positive
Signs of psychiatric problems	$T > 60$ on Psychological Disturbance scale OR Psychiatric Referral Problem Screen is positive OR Suicide Potential Problem Screen is positive

Adolescent Development and Treatment Planning

Understanding developmental issues of adolescence is central to the formulation of effective substance-abuse treatment plans for youth (Dawes et al., 2000; Tarter, 2002; Trad, 1993). Perhaps paramount in the adolescent assessment process is to distinguish normative and developmental roles played by drug use in this age group. In a strict sense, normal trajectory for adolescents is to experiment with a wide range of substances for a while and then abandon their use as one matures out of adolescence (Shedler & Block, 1990). Characterization of the development of a substance-use disorder has multiple facets, including identification of relevant substances, determination of consumption histories, and description of substance-specific problems. Further, drug-use changes over time need to be depicted.

TABLE 14.8
Use of PEI to Address Unique Adolescent Characteristics Pertinent to Treatment Planning[a]

Adolescent Characteristic	*Use of PEI*
"Adolescent drug abuse manifests itself through problem behaviors rather than overt signs of drug abuse."	The Personal Involvement With Chemicals scale is an effective measure of psychological dependence and consequences of use for adolescents. The Uncontrolled and Deviant Behavior scales address problem behaviors associated with drug abuse. *T* scores based on drug clinic norms between 40 and 60 reflect medium to high risk. *T* scores above 60 reflect very high risk.
"The disorder progresses more rapidly in adolescents than it does in adults."	The PEI assesses 3-month, 6-month, and 12-month use frequencies for alcohol and other drugs prior to intake assessment. Differences in frequency levels between these time points for each substance may be used to examine recent progression of use patterns. In addition, school grade of initial use is assessed for alcohol, marijuana, and other drugs.
"Adolescents abuse more than one drug; they may have a 'drug of choice,' but they almost always use several drugs."	The PEI assesses use frequency levels across alcohol, marijuana, and 10 additional drug categories.
"Adolescents experience strong denial; they have not yet experienced the negative consequences that an adult has experienced."	The PEI contains school and drug-based norms, providing adolescents in apparent denial (e.g., years of "everyone uses drugs") with information that their use is drastically elevated compared to typical adolescents (i.e., school-based norms), and equivalent to youth in drug-abuse treatment (i.e., drug-clinic norms).
"The enabling system surrounding adolescents is stronger than is usually found with adults. Usually, drug use is accepted in their peer group."	Elevated Drug Clinic *T* scores on the the following scales reflect an interpersonal system that likely promotes universal adolescent substance use: Peer Chemical Environment, Sibling Chemical Use, and Family Pathology.
"Adolescents experience developmental delays directly caused by drug use."	Elevated *T* based on school norms on the following scales reflect possible delays on key psychosocial dimensions under development during adolescence: Negative Self-image, Psychological Disturbance, Social Isolation, Absence of Goals, Spiritual Isolation.

[a] Quotations from Margolis (1995).

Beyond developmental considerations of drug use, there are several general developmental issues of adolescence that are relevant to treatment. These include: (a) negotiating levels of individuation and separation in relation to parents and families, (b) identity formation, (c) adjusting to physical changes, (e) sexuality, (f) academic functioning, and (g) peer relationships (Alexander, 2000; Erikson, 1963; Parrish, 1994; Schulenberg, Maggs, Steinman, & Zucker, 2001; Wagner, Waldron, & Feder, 2001). Awareness of developmental issues underscores, for example, the need for appropriate levels of self-determination during adolescence to develop self-esteem and psychosocial competencies, and sensitivity that the adolescent client may perceive treatment as an impediment to achieving individuation. Such awareness has informed modifications in traditional 12-step approaches to treatment, as well as the use of cognitive-behavioral and relapse prevention models when treating substance-abusing youth. Table 14.8 illustrates how the PEI may be used to measure characteristics unique to adolescents that also may importantly influence treatment planning (Margolis, 1995).

Adolescent Substance Abuse Determinants and Treatment Planning

Theoretical conceptualizations of adolescent treatment planning have also relied heavily on research on biopsychosocial factors associated with the onset and severity of substance abuse. Major assessment dimensions used to determine a treatment planning include: (a) drug-abuse problem severity; (b) areas of psychosocial strength and weakness, including comorbid psychiatric status; and (c) available resources in the community (Friedman & Utada, 1989; Rahdert, 1991; Tarter, 1990; Trad, 1993; Winters, 1999). Rather than viewing drug use as a disease, current research and treatment programs tend to view adolescent drug involvement in terms of interactions between individual, interpersonal, and contextual factors that together heighten vulnerability (Glantz & Pickens, 1992; Hawkins, Doueck, & Lishner, 1992; Weinberg et al., 1998).

The PEI is based on research and theory consistent with this view that adolescent drug abuse should be described according to problem severity and psychosocial dimensions. Within this framework, the following section provides suggestions on how PEI score profiles might inform specific treatment strategies for individual patients organized by these two central dimensions. Given the lack of definitive research regarding the effectiveness of different treatment strategies for adolescent drug abusers (Williams & Chang, 2000), our suggestions should be viewed as clinical starting points rather than as empirically derived findings.

DEFINING LOW, MEDIUM, AND HIGH RISK ON THE PEI PROBLEM SEVERITY AND PSYCHOSOCIAL SCALES

Cut points defining low, medium, and high risk on PEI scales were based on extant research findings (e.g., Winters et al., 1993), clinical judgment, and a desire to make the standard PEI score report user-friendly as a treatment planning tool. As background, PEI scales are coded so that higher scores always reflect risk status. Thus, *T* scores below 40 based on drug clinic norms (i.e., approximately 16% of drug treatment youth in the "drug clinic" standardization sample) indicate low risk. Psychosocial dimensions on which adolescent drug abusers exhibit low risk generally represent either (a) issues that require no specialized treatment or (b) personal assets or protective factors that may be utilized within treatment to promote self-esteem and improve coping in areas of weakness. *T* scores between 40 and 60 reflect medium to high risk on the given scale and likely indicate a need for specialized services. Finally, *T* scores above 60 reflect high to very high-risk. A lack of specialized services addressing high-risk issues indicated by this drug clinic *T* score cut score will likely compromise treatment effectiveness substantially.

Drug-Abuse Problem Severity

The PEI focuses on drug-use history (limited primarily to frequency) and several behavioral dimensions associated with problem severity. The drug-use frequency dimension is defined in terms of "how often" the individual has used drugs for three time periods across the twelve categories. The PEI's Basic Problem Severity scales assess psychological dependence, consequences of use, and reasons for use (as noted in an earlier section, the Clinical Problem Severity scales are redundant to the Basic scales). The probability of referral to drug treatment increases in a linear fashion as scores on the Basic scales increase (Winters et al., 1993). No such direct relationship exists when aggregate drug-use frequency scores are compared to drug treatment referral decisions. In this light, we consider the Basic scales as primarily useful for assisting with the referral decision point of drug treatment versus no drug treatment.

Psychosocial Functioning

Individual, group, and family substance-abuse treatment approaches are available for youth that incorporate a range of 12-step, behavioral, cognitive, and family systems. The 12 PEI psychosocial scales can be heuristically organized according to five domains derived from a combination of factor analytic and rational decision-making strategies (Henly & Winters, 1989). In the absence of empirical-based models, we offer a rational strategy for linking treatment and psychosocial scale elevations.

Attitudes and Beliefs

Studies examining the impact of attitudes have indicated that irrational beliefs (Binion, Miller, Beauvais, & Oetting, 1988; Denhoff, 1987), false perceptions of peer drug use (Bauman & Ennett, 1994), deviant attitudes (Newcomb & Bentler, 1988; Willis & Clearly, 1999), and expectations that drug use will produce favorable social and personal effects (Berdiansky, 1991; Brown, Christiansen, & Goldman, 1987) predict both adolescent drug abuse and relapse following treatment. Modifying maladaptive beliefs is critical to attaining abstinence according to social learning conceptions of drug-use determinants (Marlatt, 1979).

Elevated *T* scores on the Rejecting Convention scale indicates the rejection of traditional beliefs about right and wrong. Although adolescent substance-abuse studies are lacking in this area, preliminary findings from the adult literature support the use of cognitive therapies to alter irrational beliefs. Adult alcoholics receiving Rational–Emotive Therapy exhibited significant increases in rational thinking following treatment (Mathews & Parker, 1987; Ray, Freidlander, & Solomon, 1984). Rational–Emotive Therapy has also been applied effectively within therapeutic communities (Ferstein & Whiston, 1991; Yeager, DiGiuseppe, Olsen, & Lewis, 1988) and with alcoholic offenders (Cox, 1979; Rosenberg & Brian, 1986).

Coping Skills

Problem-solving and coping skill deficits among adolescents also predict substance-use problem severity and relapse following treatment (Brown, Stetson, & Beatty, 1989; Kaplow, Curran, & Dodge, 2002; Labouvie, 1986; McCormick, Dowd, Quirk, & Zegarra, 2002; Myers & Brown, 1990). Deficits in coping are also associated with HIV-risk among drug-abusing youth with cognitive-behavioral programs being implemented to reduce risk (St. Lawrence, Jefferson, Alleyne, & Brasfield, 1995). The importance of coping skills for relapse prevention is supported by an adult literature that has identified high-risk situations for relapse (Curry & Marlatt, 1987). Among adolescents, peer pressure to use drugs appears to be the predominant relapse precipitant (Brown, Vik, & Creamer, 1989).

Although the PEI does not directly assess the adolescent's perceived ability to cope with substance-use risk situations, elevated *T* scores on the Social Isolation scale reflects, in part, poor coping skills pertinent to making prosocial friends. Developing skills for communication, adult connectedness, and prosocial peer relationships will likely provide a critical buffer against stressors that typically operate when youth exhibit elevated *T* scores on the Social Isolation scale (Hawkins et al., 1992). Cognitive therapies such as Problem Solving Therapy (D'Zurilla & Goldfried, 1971) may be utilized for this deficit. Also related to coping skills problems are elevated *T* scores on the Absence of Goals scale. This scale reflects coping deficits related to school functioning that are common among the one-in-two drug-abusing adolescents who ultimately drop out (Friedman, Glickman, & Utada, 1985). Cognitive interventions with drug-abusing (Palmer & Paisley, 1991) and low-achieving (Hawkins et al., 1988) adolescents have produced increases in school performance while also reducing rates of school expulsion and suspension (e.g., Eggert, Seyl, & Nicholas, 1990; Eggert, Thompson, Herting, & Nicholas, 1994).

Disruptive Behavioral Problems

Behavioral and impulse-control problems are common among drug-abusing youth (DeMilio, 1989). Elevated rates of conduct disorder have been reported among youth with a substance-use disorder in community and clinical samples (Armstrong & Costello, 2002; Azrin et al., 2002; Bukstein, Glancy, & Kaminer, 1992; Latimer, Stone, Voight, Winters, & August, 2002; Monopolis, Brooner, Jadwisiak, Marsh, & Schmidt, 1991; Rohde, Lewinsohn, & Seeley, 1996). Prospective research reveals that antisocial behaviors in late childhood and the initiation of substance use in early adolescence predict later substance involvement (Armstong & Costello, 2002; Boyle et al., 1992; Clark, Parker, & Lynch, 1999; Windle, 1990). Although dual diagnosis studies have generally found higher rates of conduct disorder among boys than girls, the rate among girls treated for substance abuse is still high, with several studies suggesting that at least one in three exhibit significant conduct disturbance (Brown, Gleghorn, Schuckit, Myers, & Mott, 1996; Bukstein et al., 1992; Latimer et al., 2002; McKay & Buka, 1994).

Elevated *T* scores on the Deviant Behavior, Uncontrolled, and Peer Chemical Environment scales are indicative of serious behavioral disturbance. Research with adults suggests that sociopathic clients characterized by behavioral and impulse-control problems respond more favorably to behavioral interventions that focus on coping-skill development (Allen & Kadden, 1995). Thus, anger management, stimulus control, and reinforcement management techniques that utilize behavioral strategies to increase self-regulation may be used to reduce deviance among substance-abusing youth. In addition, given that adolescents with more severe behavioral problems and insufficient family support are likely to be referred to treatment settings with greater restrictions, it is imperative that the application of new self-regulation skills are first practiced in a safe environment where success is likely. Ultimately, however, it is equally important to provide opportunities for youth to apply skills in real-life settings comparable to those encountered following treatment (Marlatt & Gordon, 1985).

Psychiatric Disorders

A growing base of research suggests that an estimated 75% of youth treated for a substance-use disorder have at least one comorbid psychiatric disorder (Armstrong

TABLE 14.9
Estimated Rates of Comorbid Disorders Among Adolescents in Treatment for Psychoactive Substance Use Disorders (PSUD)[a]

Disorder Comorbid With PSUD	*Estimated Percentage*
No comorbid condition	25%
Attention deficit hyperactivity disorder	30%
Oppositional defiant disorder	30%
Conduct disorder	50%
Learning disorders	50%
Communication disorders	NR[b]
Mood disorders	40%
Anxiety disorders	40%

[a]Estimated rates are based on several references from the literature (Bukstein et al., 1992; Horner & Scheibe, 1997; Stowell, 1991; Weinberg et al., 1998).
[b]No adequate research available on which to base estimate.

& Costello, 2002; Regier, Boyd, & Burke, 1988; Stowell, 1991). Table 14.9 illustrates estimated rates of comorbidity based on a review of the literature (Bukstein, Glancy, & Kaminer, 1992; Horner & Scheibe, 1997; Stowell, 1991; Weinberg et al., 1998). In addition, comorbidity status among youth treated for substance abuse is associated with less favorable treatment experiences and poorer outcomes, including shorter length of stay, earlier and more severe relapse episodes, school failure, and HIV exposure (Adams & Wallace, 1994; Bryan & Stallings, 2002; Clark & Scheid, 2001; Kaminer, Burleson, & Goldberger, 2002; Moss, Kirisci, & Mezzich, 1994). Although further research is critically needed in this area, extant findings suggest that treatment plans focusing on reducing or eliminating substance use will be compromised substantially if comorbid disorders are left undetected and not addressed.

The PEI provides information pertinent to the assessment of emotional and behavioral problems among substance-abusing youth. Although not designed as a diagnostic tool, elevated *T* scores on the Psychological Disturbance and, to a lesser degree, Negative Self-Image and Social Isolation scales, reflect disturbances in mood, anxiety, and self-esteem. Psychosocial treatments for psychiatric disorders among youth include a broad range of behavioral, cognitive-behavioral, family systems, and psychodynamic approaches (Walker & Roberts, 1992). Unfortunately, little is known from systematic research about pharmacological treatment of psychiatric disorders among drug-abusing youths, despite the possibility that psychiatric disorders may underlie a secondary problem with drugs (Klorman, Coons, Brumaghim, Borgstedt, & Fitzpatrick, 1988; Pelham et al., 1990). Similarly, few studies have compared the effectiveness of different psychosocial treatments designed to address comorbid disorders among substance-abusing youth (Azrin et al., 2002; Catalano, Hawkins, Wells, Miller, & Brewer, 1991; Williams & Chang, 2000; Winters, 1999). Nonetheless, the assessment of comorbid psychiatric disorders among substance-abusing youth is essential to planning effective treatment.

Family Problems

Alcohol and drug abuse, as well as chaotic home environments, is common among family members of substance-abusing youth (Hawkins et al., 1992; Grant, Martinez, & White, 1998; Shek, 1998). Not surprisingly, inclusion of a family treatment component for substance abuse has rapidly become a norm in adolescent settings (Liddle & Dakof, 1995; Liddle et al., 2002; Risberg & Funk, 2000; Wagner, Waldron, & Feder, 2001).

Elevations on the following family-based scales of the PEI are relevant to such family problems: The Family Pathology scale reflects serious dysfunction, including parental substance abuse, sexual abuse, and physical abuse; the Family Estrangement scale indicates inconsistent or poor communication patterns between family members; and the Sibling Chemical Use scale indicates significant sibling substance use.

A fundamental assumption of family therapy models is that individual pathology, including substance abuse, is largely a reflection of a dysfunctional family system (Nichols, 1987). Although this assertion may be less applicable to the chronic adult alcoholic, environmental determinants such as the family system likely play an even greater role in adolescent when compared to adult substance abuse. Elevated *T* scores on the Family Pathology, Family Estrangement, and Sibling Chemical Use scales reflect family systems with problems associated with substance abuse, including (a) the absence of adaptive communication patterns between parent–child and spousal subsystems, (b) blaming and labeling of the substance abusing adolescent as the "bad seed," (c) parents using the identified problem of their child's substance abuse to avoid marital conflicts, and (d) active modeling of substance abuse by a parent or sibling. In addition, our research suggests that sibling substance use represents an underresearched yet highly potent predictor of adolescent substance abuse (Latimer, Winters, Stinchfield, & Traver, 2000; Windle, 2000). Thus, scores in the abnormal range on the Family Pathology, Family Estrangement, and Sibling Chemical Use scales call attention to the need for a thorough family assessment to identify problematic subsystems and communication patterns. Family therapy may represent the most potent aspect of treatment for substance-abusing youth with significant family dysfunction, particularly given the substantive role of the family following treatment.

LIMITATIONS OF THE PEI AS A TREATMENT PLANNING TOOL

A single instrument generally does not capture every dimension of interest pertinent to its assessment domain. The PEI was intended to assist with referral decisions across a range of options, from brief interventions (which may be brief conversations between an adolescent and a concerned adult) to more formalized treatment conducted in outpatient or residential settings. In this light, the PEI provides detailed information pertaining to problem severity and psychosocial characteristics to inform treatment planning, yet the tool does not address pharmacological history, academic achievement, physical health status, and other areas undoubtedly relevant to substance-abuse treatment and outcome. In addition, the PEI is not designed to directly assess key resources available in the adolescent's community, such as school-based programs that foster abstinence through extracurricular activities. Finally, the PEI does not directly assess the client's readiness to change; success with drug treatment may be importantly linked to the youth's motivational state (Prochaska & DiClemente, 1992). In sum, the PEI can serve as a useful, but not exclusive, component of an adolescent assessment system for informing treatment planning.

USE OF THE PEI IN TREATMENT EVALUATION

Overview of Measuring Treatment Outcome

Drug treatment programs have generally received intensive scrutiny, perhaps more so than other health care services, because of the nature of addiction and the visibility of its effects. Adolescent drug treatment programs and models have recently been subject to similar scrutiny (Williams & Chang, 2000; Winters, 1999). Treatment outcome information is thus invaluable to the field; such documentation provides a clearer picture of the types of clients served and helps programs determine the effectiveness and cost offsets of different strategies and improve program performance. Although the PEI was not developed specifically for the purpose of measuring treatment outcome, it is relevant to consider its role in this capacity. To determine the effectiveness of the PEI as an outcome measure, it is important to outline the parameters of a an effective tool that accurately assesses outcome. Newman, Ciarlo, and Carpenter (1999) enumerate guidelines for instrument selection. These guidelines were originally developed by the National Institute of Health (Ciarlo, Brown, Edwards, Kiresuk, & Newman, 1986) and have been updated to reflect the demands of managed care and consumer choice in the clinical community. Of the 11 guidelines delineated, the PEI clearly meets 10 of them. The PEI is a self-report measure and does not allow for multiple respondents.

The value of any standardized questionnaire as a measure of change is an important statistical and clinical question (Collins & Horn, 1991). Some investigators use difference scores, but they tend to be less reliable than the scores used to compute them, and the value of the Time 1 score introduces a bias into the difference score calculation (Allen & Yen, 1979). Dividing the simple difference score by the Time 1 score provides a partial correction for this bias. From a clinical standpoint, the important question is how many clients got better, how many got worse, and how many did not change. Along these lines, Jacobson and Truax (1991) have proposed using the concept of "clinically significant change," which refers to a score change from the abnormal to the normal range. They have statistically operationalized this concept with the Reliable Change Index (RCI). The RCI yields a change score that is corrected for the amount of measurement error inherent in the instrument. This is done by computing the difference between pretest and posttest scores and dividing by the standard error of difference for the measure (which is estimated from the measure's temporal stability). We regard the RCI analysis as quite appealing, because it addresses the practical needs of the treatment service provider while still maintaining statistical standards of significance. Thus, it can be argued that for an instrument to have utility as an outcome measure, it must demonstrate satisfactory measurement error and provide meaningful information to treatment providers and researchers.

THE PEI AS AN OUTCOME EVALUATION TOOL

How does the PEI measure up to the two standards described? The PEI authors took great care toward developing highly meaningful scales with high utility for problem description. It stands to reason that the scales should also be relevant to the measurement of treatment outcome. The Problem Severity scales, by measuring extent of involvement with drugs, are appropriate for evaluating level of change in drug-use behaviors. The Drug Use Frequency Checklist provides a measure of posttreatment abstinence and levels of nonabstinence for specific drugs. Further, the Psychosocial Risk scales provide measures of change for important areas of personal functioning and environmental status that are highly relevant to evaluating the client's outcome within the broader context of life functioning, as well as the specific context of reaching and maintaining abstinence or, at minimum, harm reduction.

In terms of the PEI's measurement error, its temporal stability has been examined over a time interval that is more in line with treatment outcome designs, such as

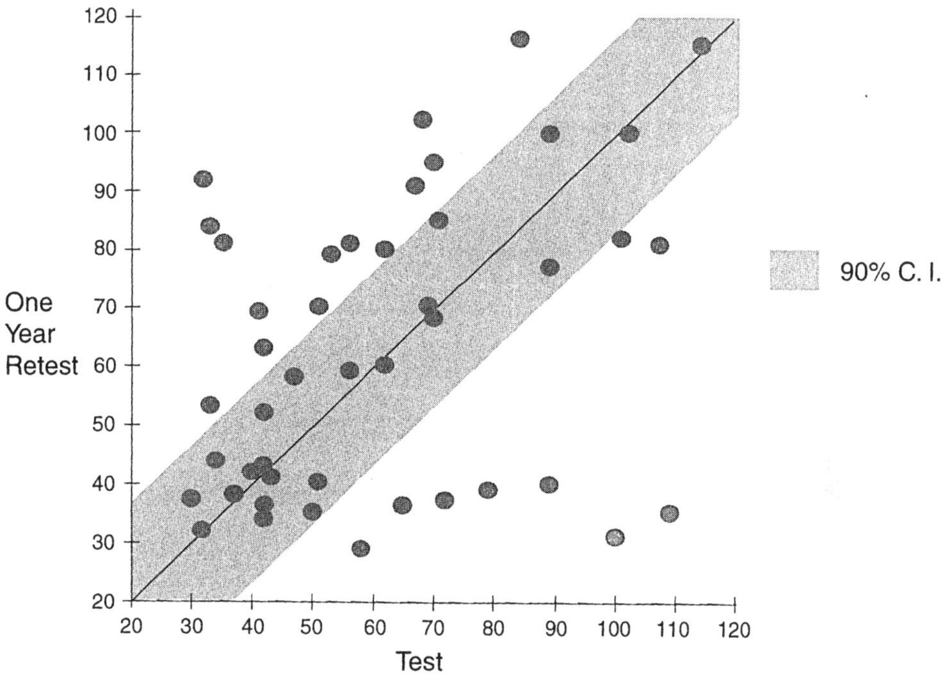

FIG. 14.1. The PIC's raw score at initial assessment and 1-year retest.

1-year time interval (Stinchfield & Winters, 1997). We found that all five PEI Basic scales exhibited satisfactory 1-year test–retest reliability in a clinical sample ($n = 37$) that did not receive treatment over the test–retest interval. Test–retest correlation coefficients ranged from $r = .86$ to $r = .89$. Retest scores were generally higher than initial test scores in this untreated clinical sample. This increase in involvement with drugs is not surprising given that these adolescents did not receive treatment during the 1-year time interval. This evidence of satisfactory 1-year temporal stability is necessary for using these scales as a measure of change over a 1-year interval, the magnitude of the stability coefficients exceeding Nunnally's (1978) standard of at least .70 or higher.

This PEI 1-year temporal stability information was then used to measure the significance of PEI change scores in a separate adolescent drug treatment sample ($n = 45$) using the RCI analysis. For the sake of brevity, we focused the analysis on the primary Basic scale, the Personal Involvement with Chemicals Scale (PICS). Difference scores were computed for each participants by subtracting the intake PICS raw score from the 1-year follow-up PICS raw score and then dividing by the standard error of difference for the PICS (which was 10.4).

Figure 14.1 shows a scatter plot of admission assessment and 1-year follow-up PICS raw score retest data for the treatment sample. The shaded diagonal illustrates a 90% confidence interval of plus or minus 1.65 standard error of difference (i.e., + or −1.65 multiplied times 10.4, or + or −17 points). A confidence interval around the RCI is computed to indicate three types of outcome: statistically significant improvement, statistically significant deterioration, and no change or unreliable change. In Fig. 14.1, points in the shaded diagonal indicate no change or unreliable change. Points above the shaded diagonal represent a statistically significant increase in PICS raw score (i.e., deterioration), and points below the shaded diagonal indicate a statistically significant decrease in PICS raw score (i.e., improvement). Figure 14.1 shows that 14 participants

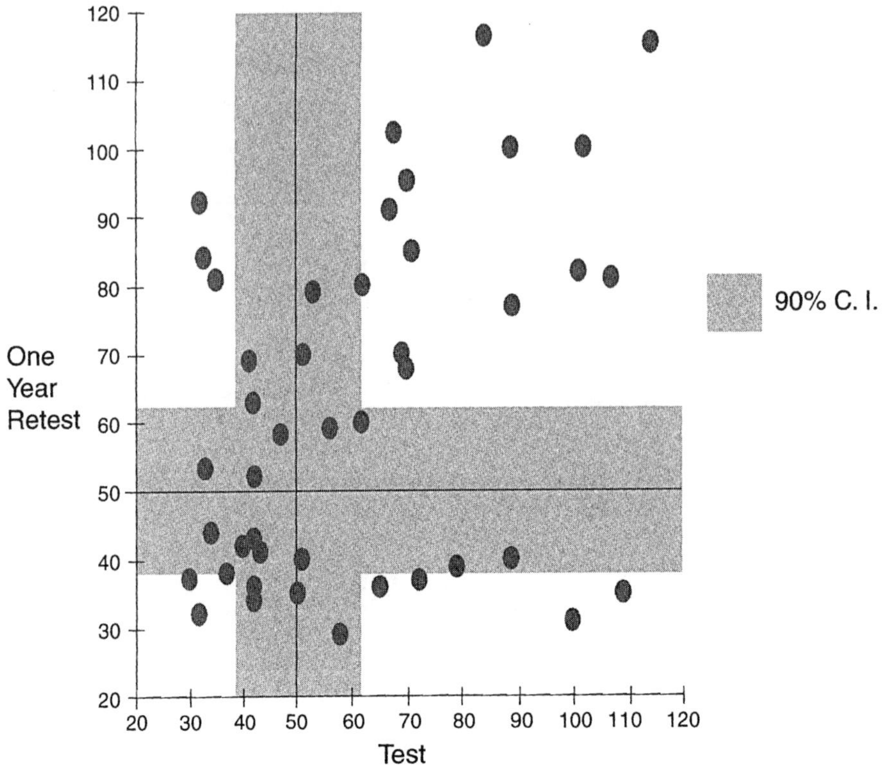

FIG. 14.2. Functional and dysfunctional ranges of the PIC's raw score at initial and 1-year retest.

(31%) obtained significantly higher scores at 1-year follow-up assessment (i.e., deteriorated), 22 (49%) exhibited no significant change, and 9 (20%) obtained significantly lower scores at 1-year follow-up assessment (i.e., improved).

For assessing clinical significance of change, Jacobson and Truax (1991) recommended using a cut score that provides optimal discrimination between functional and dysfunctional groups. Given that the PEI was standardized on a school sample ($N = 693$) and a drug clinic sample ($N = 1,120$, Winters & Henly, 1989), these samples may be considered to represent functional and dysfunctional groups. The optimal cut score between these two groups was determined by computing a discriminant function analysis using the PICS score to predict group membership in either the school or drug clinic sample. A PICS raw cut score of ≥ 50 provided optimal discrimination with a hit rate of 90%.

Figure 14.2 shows a scatter plot of the same test and 1-year follow-up PICS raw score retest data that was shown in Fig. 14.1 for the treatment sample ($n = 45$). The shaded vertical and horizontal lines split the sample into functional and dysfunctional ranges at intake and 1-year retest. The shaded lines represent a cut score of ≥ 50, with a 90% confidence interval of plus or minus 1.65 standard error of measurement (i.e., $+$ or $-$ 1.65×7.4, or $+$ or $-$ 12). Points within the shaded lines indicate classification uncertainty; that is, there is a greater chance of misclassification of participants in this score range.

A clinically significant improvement is represented by a participant's score that moves from the dysfunctional range at admission assessment to the functional range at 1-year follow-up. For this sample, clinically significant improvement was exhibited by 4 participants (9%) who moved from the dysfunctional range at admission to the functional range at 1 year follow-up (i.e., the 4 participants in the lower right-hand quadrant).

SUMMARY AND LIMITATIONS

We have demonstrated how the PEI can be used as a measure of treatment outcome in the context of a RCI analysis. The model of treatment outcome methodology described here has several advantages, including the (a) focus on measuring change from pretreatment to posttreatment, which is superior to reporting posttreatment abstinence rates alone (Stinchfield, Owen, & Winters, 1994; Winters, Stinchfield, Opland, Weller, & Latimer, 2000); (b) consideration of the instrument's measurement error in the change analysis; and (c) sensitivity of the statistical approach toward providing outcome results for individual clients. If we had analyzed change more traditionally, such as with a pretest–posttest design, our ability to identify that some clients may have improved meaningfully would have been hampered. In fact, the prepost analysis (paired t test) for this particular treatment sample was not statistically significant ($t = -.38$, $df = 44$, $p = .71$). Of course, even the most powerful statistical evaluation analysis has its limitations. One has to consider the measurement error inherent to the instrument, as well as the problem of unreliable self-report. It is worth reiterating the often-cited dictum that a comprehensive follow-up evaluation requires the integration of several lines of evidence.

CASE STUDY OF DAVID: "DISRUPT THIS"

A PEI case study is presented as an example of how the instrument can support the clinician in describing client problems and referring for treatment. The case of David ("Disrupt This") reinforces the significance of assessing psychiatric concomitant problems that often coexist with adolescent drug involvement. The PEI findings discussed here are from the intake assessment.

David

The case highlights the complications of drug abuse in the context of an existing psychiatric illness. David is a diagnostic challenge because of his coexisting drug abuse and attentional problems. This 17-year-old boy was seen for an evaluation at a local community mental health center. The discovery by his parents of marijuana in his bedroom triggered the evaluation.

David had been a challenge to his parents since he was a toddler. Aggressive, overactive, always on the go, David pushed his parents' patience and disciplining skills to the limits. When David was not making commotion on his own, he often created turmoil by teasing his older sister. And David's life at school was equally chaotic. He was routinely a challenge for his teachers. Parent–teacher conferences regarding David's behavior and poor school performance were commonplace.

David's parents are highly educated and financially comfortable. But several years of parenting classes and family therapy did little to improve their ability to handle David. It was not until their son was evaluated for stimulant medication and began a regular regimen of Ritalin that the Wilson household finally experienced more orderliness than chaos.

David started experimenting with tobacco at age 11 and alcohol at age 12. Later in adolescence, he began using alcohol two or three times a week, always to intoxication. Marijuana was commonly used on days when he did not drink. His use pattern accelerated when he stopped taking Ritalin at age 13. David later admitted in the clinical interview that he experienced a mild therapeutic effect from the street drugs that mimicked the clinical effects of Ritalin.

Generally, David had difficulty with schoolwork and did not fit in socially with his peers. He did have one friend with whom he got high a lot. They would spend hours together drinking or smoking and playing their guitars. When David's parents discovered the marijuana in his bedroom, he openly admitted to frequent use. He minimized the use as "no big deal" and rationalized it as a "hobby."

David's Problem Severity scale *T* scores, presented in Table 14.10, depict his comorbid clinical picture. All his drug clinic standardized scores on the Basic and Clinical Problem Severity scales were above 50*T*, the mean of the drug clinic standardization sample. Because it appears that David uses drugs to self-medicate, it is not surprising

TABLE 14.10
PEI Scores for Case Study of David

Scale	*Drug Clinic T—Other Score*
Problem Severity Scales	
Personal Involvement With Chemicals	59
Effects From Use	52
Social Benefits	60
Personal Consequences	51
Polydrug Use	58
Social–Recreational Use	52
Psychological Benefits	65
Transsituational Use	55
Preoccupation With Drugs	60
Loss of Control	64
Psychosocial Risk Scales	
Negative Self-image	52
Psychological Disturbance	60
Social Isolation	65
Uncontrolled	67
Rejecting Convention	63
Deviant Behavior	63
Absence of Goals	51
Spiritual Isolation	58
Peer Chemical Environment	71
Sibling Chemical Use	45
Family Pathology	53
Family Estrangement	62
Problem Screens	
Need for Psychiatric Referral	positive
Eating Disorder	negative
Sexual Abuse	negative
Physical Abuse (intrafamilial)	negative
Family Chemical Dependency History	negative
Suicide Potential	negative

that his score on the Psychological Benefits of Use scale was very elevated (65*T*). His elevated *T* score on the Preoccupation and Loss of Control scales reflect his severe involvement with drugs and indicate that he likely met a substance-use dependence disorder.

David's responses to the drug consumption items (not shown in Table 14.10) are congruent with the information obtained by the counselor during the assessment interview. David reports that he is a heavy user of alcohol and a regular user of marijuana.

The pattern of scores on David's Problem Severity scales and his drug-use history are consistent with a decision to refer for drug treatment. Scale scores on Part 2 of his PEI report, particularly scores on the Personal Adjustment scales, indicate that David's treatment needs are complex. His attentional problems are reflected in scale elevations on Uncontrolled; his tendency toward aggressiveness is consistent with elevations on the Rejecting Convention and Deviant Behavior scales; and his difficulty in making friends is seen with the high scale score on Social Isolation. His drug-using environment is reflected in the elevation on the Peer Chemical Environment scale.

Among the Problem Screens, only the Need for Psychiatric Referral was positive. An inspection of the items on this screen indicated that David endorsed these items: "My mind doesn't seem to work quite right" (sometimes); "My thoughts are confused or go too fast" (often); and "I have trouble sleeping" (often). David also endorsed two miscellaneous items related to his history with attentional problems: "A doctor has told my parents that I'm hyperactive or something like that" (more than once or twice); "A doctor has prescribed medicine, like Ritalin, to help me control my behavior at school" (more than once or twice).

All four of David's response distortion scale scores are within normal limits (not shown in Table 14.10). But as is often the case with a heavy drug user who completes the PEI, David's Infrequency–I and Infrequency–II scale scores were at the high end of the normal range (59*T* and 61*T*, respectively).

Given these PEI results and David's clinical history, and information from interviews with David's parents, the clinical staff referred him to a residential treatment program that specialized in youth with coexisting psychiatric problems.

FUTURE DIRECTIONS AND SUMMARY

The PEI is intended to serve as a clinically oriented assessment instrument for use in problem identification and treatment referral for youth suspected of problems associated with drug involvement. Current data on its psychometric properties, particularly the Problem Severity scales, generally offer favorable evidence that the PEI is a reliable and valid instrument of its intended purposes. Nonetheless, more research on the PEI is needed on several fronts. There is still a paucity of data on the PEI's ability to predict treatment outcome and the role it may have in matching clients to optimal treatment approaches. Work is continuing on its psychometric properties in ethnically diverse youth; recent work has focused on boys only (Winters et al., 2003). Also, the authors are updating the content coverage of the PEI. A scale to measure problem recognition is being field-tested, and a parallel parent version is being developed (Winters, Anderson, Bengston, & Stinchfield, 2000). Finally, there are several research challenges related to factors that affect accuracy and degree of disclosure of self-report, including method factors (Aquilino, 1994).

ACKNOWLEDGMENTS

Parital support for this chapter provided by NIDA Grant Nos. DA05104 (Winters) and DA10777 (Latimer). The authors extend a thanks to Tamara Fahnhorst for assisting with the manuscript.

REFERENCES

Adams, L., & Wallace, J. L. (1994). Residential treatment for the ADHD adolescent substance abuser. *Journal of Child and Adolescent Substance Abuse, 4*, 35–44.

Alexander, C. J. (2000). Gay youth: More visible but fewer problems? *Journal of Gay and Lesbian Social Services: Issues in Practice, Policy and Research, 11*, 113–117.

Allen, J. P., & Kadden, R. M. (1995). Matching clients to alcohol treatments. In R. K. Hester & W. R. Miller (Eds.), *Handbook of alcoholism treatment approaches* (2nd ed., pp. 278–291). Needham Heights, MA: Allyn & Bacon.

Allen, M. J., & Yen, W. M. (1979). *Introduction to measurement theory*. Monterey, CA: Brooks/Cole.

Aquilino, P. (1994). Interview mode effect. *Public Opinion Quarterly, 58*, 210–240.

Armstrong, T. D., & Costello, E. J. (2002). Community studies on adolescent substance use, abuse or dependence and psychiatric comorbidity. *Journal of Consulting and Clinical Psychology, 70*, 1224–1239.

Azrin, N. H., Donohue, B., Teichner, G. A., Crum, T., Howell, J., & DeCato, L. A. (2002). A controlled evaluation and description of individual cognitive problem solving and family-behavior therapies in dually-diagnosed conduct-disordered and substance-dependent youth. *Journal of Child and Adolescent Substance Abuse, 11*, 1–43.

Bauman, K. E., & Ennett, S. T. (1994). Peer influence and adolescent drug use. *American Psychologist, 49*, 820–822.

Berdiansky, H. (1991). Beliefs about drugs and use among early adolescents. *Journal of Alcohol and Drug Education, 36*, 26–35.

Binion, A., Miller, C. D., Beauvais, F., & Oetting, E. R. (1988). Rationales for the use of alcohol, marijuana, and other drugs by eighth-grade Native American and Anglo youth. *International Journal of the Addictions, 23*, 47–64.

Boyle, M. H., Offord, D. R., Racine, Y. A., Szatmari, P., Fleming, J. E., & Links, P. (1992). Predicting substance use in late adolescence: Results of the Ontario Child Health Study follow-up. *The American Journal of Psychiatry, 149*, 761–767.

Brown, S. A., Christiansen, B. A., & Goldman, M. S. (1987). The Alcohol Expectancies Questionnaire: An instrument for the assessment of adolescent and adult alcohol expectancies. *Journal of Studies on Alcohol, 48*, 483–491.

Brown, S. A., Gleghorn, A., Schuckit, M. A., Myers, M. G., & Mott, M. A. (1996). Conduct disorder among adolescent alcohol and drug abusers. *Journal of Studies on Alcohol, 57*, 314–324.

Brown, S. A., Stetson, B. A., & Beatty, P. A. (1989). Cognitive and behavioral features of adolescent coping in high risk drinking situation. *Addictive Behaviors, 14*, 43–52.

Brown, S. A., Vik, P. W., & Creamer, V. A. (1989). Characteristics of relapse following adolescent substance abuse treatment. *Addictive Behaviors, 14*, 291–300.

Bryan A., & Stallings, M. C. (2002). Case control study of adolescent risky sexual behavior and its relationship to personality dimensions, conduct disorder, and substance use. *Journal of Youth and Adolescence, 31*, 387–396.

Bukstein, O. G., Glancy, L. J., & Kaminer, Y. (1992). Patterns of affective comorbidity in a clinical population of dually diagnosed adolescent substance abusers [Special section: Substance abuse]. *Journal of the American Academy of Child and Adolescent Psychiatry, 31*, 1041–1045.

Cady, M., Winters, K. C., Jordan, D. A., Solberg, K. B., & Stinchfield, R. D. (1996). Motivation to change as a predictor of treatment outcome for adolescent substance abusers. *Journal of Child and Adolescent Substance Abuse, 5*, 73–91.

Catalano, R. F., Hawkins, J. D., Wells, E. A., Miller, J., & Brewer, D. (1991). Evaluation of the effectiveness of adolescent drug abuse treatment, assessment of risks for relapse, and promising approaches for relapse prevention. *The International Journal of the Addictions, 25*, 1085–1140.

Center for Substance Abuse Treatment. (1999). Screening and assessing adolescents for substance use disorders. (Treatment Improvement Protocol Series No. 31). Rockville, MD: Substance Abuse Mental Health Services Administration.

Ciarlo, J. A., Brown, T. R., Edwards, D. W., Kiresuk, T. J., & Newman, F. L. (1986). *Assessing mental health treatment outcome measurement techniques*, DHHS Publication No. (ADM) 86-1301, Rockville, MD: National Institute on Mental Health.

Clark, D. B., Parker, A., & Lynch, K. (1999). Psychopathology and substance-related problems during early adolescence: A survival analysis. *Journal of Clinical Child Psychology, 28*, 333–341.

Clark, D. B., & Scheid, J. (2001). Comorbid mental disorders in adolescents with substance use disorders. In J. R. Hubbard & P. R. Martin (Eds.), *Substance abuse in the mentally and physically disabled* (pp. 133–167). New York: Dekker.

Clark, D. B., & Winters, K. C. (2002). Measuring risks and outcomes in substance use disorders prevention research. *Journal of Consulting and Clinical Psychology, 70*(6), 1207–1223.

Collins, L. M., & Horn, J. L. (Eds.). (1991). *Best methods for the analysis of change*. Washington, DC: American Psychological Association.

Cox, S. G. (1979). Rational behavior training as a rehabilitative program for alcoholic offenders. *Offender Rehabilitation, 3*, 245–256.

Crowne, D. P., & Marlowe, D. (1960). A new scale of social desirability independent of psychopathology. *Journal of Consulting Psychology, 24*, 349–354.

Curry, S., & Marlatt, G. A. (1987). Building self-confidence, self-efficacy, and self-control. In W. M. Cox (Ed.), *Treatment and prevention of alcohol problems* (pp. 117–135). New York: Academic Press.

Dawes, M. A., Antelman, S. M., Vanyukov, M. M., Giancola, P., Tarter, R. E., Susman, E. J., Mezzich, A., & Clark, D. B. (2000). Developmental sources of variation in liability to adolescent substance use disorders. *Drug and Alcohol Dependence, 61*, 3–14.

DeLeon, G., Melnick, G., Kressel, D., & Jainchill, N. (1994). Circumstances, motivation, readiness and suitability (the CMRS Scales): Predicting retention in therapeutic community treatment. *American Journal of Drug and Alcohol Abuse, 20*, 495–515.

Dembo, R., Schmeidler, J., Borden, P., Chin Sue, C., & Manning, D. (1997). Use of the POSIT among arrested youths entering a juvenile assessment center: A replication and update. *Journal of Child and Adolescent Substance Abuse, 6*, 19–42.

DeMilio, L. (1989). Psychiatric syndromes in adolescent substance abusers. *American Journal of Psychiatry, 146*, 1212–1214.

Denhoff, M. S. (1987). Irrational beliefs as predictors of adolescent drug abuse and running away. *Journal of Clinical Psychology, 43*, 412–423.

D'Zurilla, T. J., & Goldfried, M. R. (1971). Problem solving and behavior modification. *Journal of Abnormal Psychology, 78*, 197–126.

Eggert, L. L., Seyl, C. D., & Nicholas, L. J. (1990). Effects of a school-based prevention program for potential high school dropouts and drug abusers. *International Journal of the Addictions, 25*, 773–801.

Eggert, L. L., Thompson, E. A., Herting, J. R., & Nicholas, L. J. (1994). Preventing adolescent drug abuse and high school dropout through an intensive school-based social network development program. *American Journal of Health Promotion, 8*, 202–215.

Erikson, E. H. (1963). *Childhood and society*. New York: Norton.

Ferstein, M. E., & Whiston, S. S. (1991). Utilizing RET for effective treatment of adult children of alcoholics. *Journal of Rational Emotive and Cognitive Behavior Therapy, 9*, 39–49.

Friedman, A. S., Glickman, N., & Utada, A. (1985). Does drug and alcohol use lead to failure to graduate from high school? *Journal of Drug Education, 15*, 353–364.

Friedman, A. S., & Utada, A. (1989). A method for diagnosing and planning the treatment of adolescent drug users--The Adolescent Drug Abuse Diagnosis Instrument (ADAD). *Journal of Drug Education, 19*, 285–312.

Fry, E. (1977). Fry's readability graph: Clarification, validity, and extension to Level 17. *Journal of Reading, 21*, 242–253.

Glantz, M., & Pickens, R. (Eds.). (1992). *Vulnerability to drug abuse*. Washington, DC: American Psychological Association.

Grant, D., Martinez, D. G., & White, B. W. (1998). Substance abuse among African American children: A developmental framework for identifying intervention strategies. *Journal of Human Behavior in the Social Environment, 1*, 137–163.

Guthmann, D. R., & Brenna, D. C. (1990). The Personal Experience Inventory: An Assessment of the instrument's validity among a delinquent population in Washington State. *Journal of Adolescent Chemical Dependency, 1*, 15–24.

Hawkins, J. D., Catalano, R. F., & Miller, J. Y. (1992). Risk and protective factors for alcohol and other drug problems in adolescence and early adulthood: Implications for substance abuse prevention. *Psychological Bulletin, 112*(1), 64–105.

Hawkins, J. D., Doueck, H. J., & Lishner, D. M. (1988). Changing teaching practices in mainstream classrooms to improve bonding and behavior of low achievers. *American Educational Research Journal, 25,* 31–50.

Heilman, R. O. (1973). *Early recognition of alcoholism and other drug dependencies.* Center City, MN: Hazelden Foundation.

Henly, G. A., & Winters, K. C. (1988). Development of problem severity scales for the assessment of adolescent alcohol and drug abuse. *International Journal of the Addictions, 23,* 65–85.

Henly, G. A., & Winters, K. C. (1989). Development of psychosocial scales for the assessment of adolescent alcohol and drug involvement. *International Journal of the Addictions, 24,* 973–1001.

Horn, J. L., Skinner, H. A., Wanberg, K., & Foster, F. M. (1982). *Alcohol Use Questionnaire (ADS).* Toronto, Ontorio, Canada: Addiction Research Foundation.

Horner, B. R., & Scheibe, K. E. (1997). Prevalence and implications of attention-deficit hyperactivity disorder among adolescents in treatment for substance abuse. *Journal of the American Academy of Child and Adolescent Psychiatry, 36,* 30–36.

Jacobson, N. S., & Truax, P. (1991). Clinical significance: A statistical approach to defining meaningful change in psychotherapy research. *Journal of Consulting and Clinical Psychology, 59,* 12–19.

Jessor, R., Donovan, J. E., & Costa, F. M. (1991). *Beyond adolescence: Problem behavior and young adult development.* Cambridge, England: Cambridge University Press.

Johnston, L. D., O'Malley, P. M., & Bachman, J. G. (2001). *National survey results on drug use from the monitoring the future study. 1975–2000.* Rockville, MD: U.S. Dept. of Health and Human Services, Public Health Service, National Institute of Health, National Institute on Drug Abuse.

Kaminer, Y., Burleson, J. A., & Goldberger, R. (2002). Cognitive-behavioral coping skills and psychoeducation therapies for adolescent substance abuse. *Journal of Nervous and Mental Disease, 190,* 737–745.

Kandel, D. B. (Ed.). (1978). *Longitudinal research on drug use: Empirical findings and methodologies issues.* Washington, DC: Hemisphere.

Kaplow, J. B., Curran, P. J., & Dodge, K. A. (2002). Child, parent, and peer predictors of early-onset substance use: A multisite longitudinal study. *Journal of Abnormal Child Psychology, 30,* 199–216.

Klorman, R., Coons, H. W., Brumaghim, J. T., Borgstedt, A. D., & Fitzpatrick, P. (1988). Stimulant treatment for adolescents with attention deficit disorder. *Psychopharmacology Bulletin, 24,* 88–92.

Labouvie, E. W. (1986). Alcohol and marijuana use in relation to adolescent stress. *International Journal of the Addictions, 21,* 333–345.

Latimer, W. W., Newcomb, M., Winters, K. C., & Stinchfield, R. D. (2000). Adolescent substance abuse treatment outcome: The role of substance abuse problem severity, psychosocial, and treatment factors. *Journal of Consulting and Clinical Psychology, 68,* 684–696.

Latimer, W. W., Stone, A. L., Voight, A., Winters, K. C., & August, G. J. (2002). Gender differences in psychiatric comorbidity among adolescents with substance use disorders. *Experimental and Clinical Psychopharmacology, 10,* 310–315.

Latimer, W. W., Winters, K. C., & Stinchfield, R. D., & Traver, R. (2000). Demographic, individual and interpersonal predictors of adolescent alcohol and marijuana use following treatment. *Psychology of Addictive Behaviors, 14,* 162–173.

Liddle, H. A., & Dakof, G. A. (1995). Family-based treatment for adolescent drug use: State of the science. In E. Rahdert & D. Czechowicz (Eds.), *Adolescent drug abuse: Clinical assessment and therapeutic interventions* (pp. 218–254). Rockville, MD: National Institute on Drug Abuse.

Liddle, H. A., Rowe, C. L., Quille, T. J., Dakof, G. A., Mills, D. S., Sakran, E., & Biaggi, H. (2002). Transporting a research-based adolescent drug treatment into practice. *Journal of Substance Abuse Treatment, 22,* 231–243.

Margolis, R. (1995). Adolescent chemical dependence: Assessment, treatment, and management. *Psychotherapy, 32,* 172–179.

Marlatt, A. G. (1979). Alcohol use and problem drinking: A cognitive-behavioral analysis. In P. C. Kendall & S. D. Hollon (Eds.), *Cognitive-behavioral interventions: Theory research and practice* (pp. 199–152). New York: Academic Press.

Marlatt, G. A., & Gordon, J. R. (1985). *Relapse prevention: Maintenance strategies in the treatment of addictive behaviors.* New York: Guilford.

Mathews, L. J., & Parker, R. A. (1987). Alcoholism treatment with biochemical restoration as a major component. *International Journal of Biosocial Research, 9,* 92–104.

Mayer, J., & Filstead, W. J. (1979). The Adolescent Alcohol Involvement Scale: An instrument for measuring adolescents' use and misuse of alcohol. *Journal of Studies on Alcohol, 40,* 291–300.

McCormick, R. A., Dowd, E. T., Quirk, S., & Zegarra, J. H. (2002). The relationship of NEO–PI performance to coping styles, patterns of use, and triggers for use among substance abusers. *Addictive Behaviors, 23,* 497–507.

McKay, J. R., & Buka, S. L. (1994). Issues in the treatment of antisocial adolescent substance abusers. *Journal of Child and Adolescent Substance Abuse, 3*, 59–81.

Moss, H. B., Kirisci, L., & Mezzich, A. C. (1994). Psychiatric comorbidity and self-efficacy to resist heavy drinking in alcoholic and nonalcoholic adolescents. *American Journal on Addictions, 3*, 204–212.

Myers, M. G., & Brown, S. A. (1990). Coping responses and relapse among adolescent substance abusers. *Journal of Substance Abuse, 2*, 177–189.

Minuchin, S. (1974). *Families and family therapy.* Cambridge, MA: Harvard University Press.

Monopolis, S. J., Brooner, R. K., Jadwisiak, R. M., Marsh, E., & Schmidt, C. W. (1991). Preliminary report on psychiatric comorbidity in adolescent substance abusers. *NIDA Research Monograph 105*, DHHS Publication No. (ADM) 91-1753, Washington, DC: Govt. Printing Office, 293–294.

Muisener, P. P. (1994). *Understanding and treating adolescent substance abuse.* Thousand Oaks, CA: Sage.

Newcomb, M. D., & Bentler, P. M. (1988). The impact of family context, deviant attitudes, and emotional distress on adolescent drug use: Longitudinal latent-variable analyses of mothers and their children. *Journal of Research in Personality, 22*, 154–176.

Newman, F. L., Ciarlo, J. A., & Carpenter, D. (1999). Guidelines for selecting psychological instruments for treatment planning and outcome. In M. E. Maruish (Ed.), *The use of psychological testing and treatment planning for outcomes and assessment, second edition* (pp. 153–170). Mahwah, NJ: Lawrence Erlbaum Associates.

Nichols, M. P. (1987). *The self in the system.* New York: Brunner/Mazel.

Nunnally, J. C. (1978). *Psychometric theory* (2nd ed.). New York: McGraw-Hill.

Palmer, J. H., & Paisley, P. O. (1991). Student assistance programs: A response to substance abuse. *School Counselor, 38*, 287–293.

Parrish, S. L., Jr. (1994). Adolescent substance abuse: The challenge for clinicians. *Alcohol, 11*(6), 453–455.

Pelham, W. E., Jr., Greenslade, K. E., & Vodde-Hamilton, M., Murphy, D. A., Greenstein, J. J., Gnagy, E. M., Guthrie, K. J., Hoover, M. D., & Dahl, R. E. (1990). Relative efficacy of long-acting stimulants on children with attention deficit-hyperactivity disorder: A comparison of standard methylphenidate, sustained-release methylphenidate, sustained-release dextroamphetamine, and pemoline. *Pediatrics, 86*, 226–237.

PRIDE. (2002). Retrieved January 27, 2003 from PRIDE internet site. http://www.pridesurveys.com/main/

Prochaska, J. O., & DiClemente, C. C. (1992). Stages of change in the modification of problem behaviors. In M. Hersen, R. M. Eisler, & P. M. Miller (Eds.), *Progress in behavior modification* (pp. 184–214). Sycamore, IL: Sycamore.

Rahdert, E. (Ed.). (1991). *The Adolescent Assessment/Referral System manual* (DHHS Publication No. ADM 91-1735). Rockville, MD: National Institute on Drug Abuse.

Ray, J. B., Freidlander, R. B., & Solomon, G. S. (1984). Changes in rational beliefs among treated alcoholics. *Psychological Reports, 55*, 883–886.

Regier, D. A., Boyd, J. H., & Burke, J. D. (1988). One-month prevalence of mental disorders in United States. *Archives of General Psychiatry, 45*, 977–986.

Risberg, R. A., & Funk, R. R. (2000). Evaluating the perceived helpfulness of a family night program for adolescent substance abusers. *Journal of Child and Adolescent Substance Abuse, 10*, 51–67.

Rohde, P., Lewinsohn, P. M., & Seeley, J. R. (1996). Psychiatric comorbidity with problematic alcohol use in high school students. *Journal of the American Academy of Child and Adolescent Psychiatry, 35*, 101–109.

Rosenberg, H., & Brian, T. (1986). Cognitive-behavioral group therapy for multiple-DUI offenders [Special issue: Drunk driving in America: Strategies and approaches to treatment]. *Alcoholism Treatment Quarterly, 3*, 47–65.

St. Lawrence, J. S., Jefferson, K. W., Alleyne, E., & Brasfield, T. L. (1995). Comparison of education versus behavioral skills training interventions in lowering sexual HIV-risk behavior of substance-dependent adolescents. *Journal of Consulting and Clinical Psychology, 63*, 154–157.

Schulenberg, J., Maggs, J. L., Steinman, K. J. & Zucker, R. A. (2001). Developmental matters: Taking the long view on substance abuse etiology and intervention during adolescence. In P. M. Monti, S. M. Colby, & T. A. O'Leary (Eds.) *Adolescents, alcohol, and substance abuse: Reaching teens through brief interventions* (pp. 19–57). New York: Guilford.

Shedler, J., & Block, J. (1990). Adolescent drug use and psychological health. *American Psychologist, 45*, 612–630.

Shek, D. T. L. (1998). A longitudinal study of the relation of family factors to adolescent psychological symptoms, coping resources, school behavior and substance abuse. *International Journal of Adolescent Medicine and Health, 10*, 155–184.

Stinchfield, R. D., Owen, P., & Winters, K. C. (1994). Group therapy for substance abuse: A review of the empirical research. In A. Fuhriman & G. Burlingame (Eds.), *Handbook of group psychotherapy* (pp. 458–488). New York: Wiley.

Stinchfield, R., & Winters, K. C. (1997). Measuring change in adolescent drug misuse with the Personal Experience Inventory (PEI). *Substance Use and Misuse, 32*, 63–76.

Stowell, R. (1991). Dual diagnosis issues. *Psychiatric Annals, 21*, 98–104.

Tarter, R. E. (1990). Evaluation and treatment of adolescent substance abuse: A decision tree method. *American Journal of Drug and Alcohol Abuse, 16*, 1–46.

Tarter, R. E. (2002). Etiology of adolescent substance abuse: A developmental perspective. *American Journal on Addiction, 11*, 171–191.

Trad. P. V. (1993). Substance abuse in adolescent mothers: Strategies for diagnosis, treatment and prevention. *Journal of Substance Abuse Treatment, 10*, 421–431.

Tucker, J. A. (1992). Review of the Personal experience Inventory. In J. J. Kramer & J. C. Conoley (Eds.), *The eleventh mental measurements yearbook* (pp. 661–663). Lincoln, NE: Buros Institute of Mental Measurements.

Wagner, E. F., Waldron, H. B., & Feder, A. B. (2001). Alcohol and drug abuse. In H. Orvaschel & J. Faust (Eds.) *Handbook on conceptualization and treatment of child psychopathology* (pp. 329–352). Amsterdam: Pergamon/Elsevier.

Walker, C. E., & Roberts, M. C. (Eds.). (1992). *Handbook of clinical child psychology* (2nd ed.). New York: Wiley.

Weidman, A. A. (1985). Engaging family of substance abusing adolescents in family therapy. *Journal of Substance Abuse Treatment, 2*, 97–105.

Weinberg, N. Z., Rahdert, E., Colliver, J. D., & Glantz, M. D. (1998). Adolescent substance abuse: A review of the past 10 years. *Journal of the American Academy of Child and Adolescent Psychiatry, 37*, 252–261.

Williams, R. J., & Chang, S. Y. (2000). Comprehensive and comparative review of adolescent substance abuse treatment outcome. *Clinical Psychology: Science and Practice, 7*, 138–166.

Willis, T. A., & Clearly, S. D. (1999). Peer and adolescent substance use among 6th–9th graders: Latent growth analyses of influences versus selection mechanisms. *Health Psychology, 18*, 453–463.

Windle, M. (1990). A longitudinal study of antisocial behaviors in early adolescence as predictors of late adolescent substance use: Gender and ethnic group differences. *Journal of Abnormal Psychology, 99*, 86–91.

Windle, M. (2000). Parental, sibling, and peer influences on adolescent substance use and alcohol problems. *Applied Developmental Science, 4*, 98–110.

Winters, K. C. (1999). Treating adolescents with substance use disorders: An overview of practice issues and treatment outcomes. *Substance Abuse, 20*, 203–225.

Winters, K. C., Anderson, N., Bengston, P., & Stinchfield, R. D. (2000). Development of a parent questionnaire for the assessment of adolescent drug abuse. *Journal of Psychoactive Drugs, 32*, 3–13.

Winters, K. C., & Henly, G. A. (1989). *Personal Experience Inventory test and manual*. Los Angeles: Western Psychological Services.

Winters, K. C., & Henly, G. A. (1993). *Adolescent Diagnostic Interview and manual*. Los Angeles: Western Psychological Services.

Winters, K. C., Latimer, W. W., & Stinchfield, R. (2002). Clinical issues in the assessment of adolescent alcohol or other drug use. *Behavior Research and Therapy, 40*(12), 1443–1456.

Winters, K. C., Latimer, W. W., Stinchfield, R. D., & Egan, E. (2003). Measuring drug abuse scales in four ethnic groups of adolescent boys. Submitted for publication.

Winters, K. C., & Stinchfield, R. D., & Henly, G. A. (1993). Further validation of new scales measuring adolescent alcohol and other drug abuse. *Journal of Studies on Alcohol, 54*, 534–541.

Winters, K. C., & Stinchfield, R. D., & Henly, G. A. (1996). Convergent and predictive validity of scales measuring adolescent substance abuse. *Journal of Child & Adolescent Substance Abuse, 5*, 37–55.

Winters, K. C., Stinchfield, R., Henly, G., & Schwartz, R. (1991). Validity of adolescent self-report of alcohol and other drug involvement. *International Journal of the Addictions, 25*, 1379–1395.

Winters, K. C., Stinchfield, R. D., Opland, E., Weller, C., & Latimer, W. W. (2000). The effectiveness of the Minnesota Model for treating adolescent drug abusers. *Addiction, 95*, 601–612.

Yeager, R. L., DiGiuseppe, R., Olsen, J. T., & Lewis, L. (1988). Rational-emotive therapy in the therapeutic community. *Journal of Rational-Emotive and Cognitive Behavior Therapy, 6*, 211–235.

Zucker, R. A., Fitzgerald, H. E., & Moses, H. D. (1995). Emergence of alcohol problems and the several alcoholisms: A developmental perspective on etiologic theory and life course trajectory. In D. Cicchetti & D. J. Cohen (Eds.), *Developmental psychopathology 8 Vol. 2. Risk, disorder and adaptation* (pp. 677–711). New York: Wiley.

15

The Child and Adolescent Functional Assessment Scale (CAFAS)

Kay Hodges
Eastern Michigan University

INTRODUCTION

Symptoms and diagnoses have been the traditional cornerstone of clinical assessments. Over the past decade, a second concept, impairment, has come to be regarded as important in making treatment decisions. Impairment reflects the consequences or effects of symptoms or problems on functioning. In fact, epidemiological research over the past decade demonstrated clearly that presence of a diagnosis is not comparable to impairment or need for treatment (Bird et al., 1990, 2000). These findings have, in part, been responsible for the inclusion of the concept of impairment in the most recent edition of the *Diagnostic and Statistical Manual of Mental Disorders* (*DSM–IV*; American Psychiatric Association, 1994). Although impairment in functioning is stipulated as a criterion for receiving a diagnosis, impairment is not defined in most of the diagnostic criteria. For some diagnoses, a vague statement is included about the disturbance causing clinically significant impairment in social, academic, or occupational functioning.

The last decade has also given rise to an increasing expectation that treatment research should include outcome measures that assess everyday functioning in real-world contexts to provide some assurance that the change is clinically significant, as opposed to just statistically significant (Kazdin & Kendall, 1998; Kazdin & Weisz, 1998). This emphasis is consistent with the views of consumer advocates. Speaking from a family perspective, Osher (1998) succinctly stated that parents want their children to function better in the natural settings of their communities, which is translated into: living at home, going to school and getting good grades, enjoying friends and activities, and becoming responsible adults living independently.

When the Center for Mental Health Services (CMHS) of the Substance Abuse and Mental Health Services Administration operationalized the definition of Serious Emotional Disturbance (SED), it required the presence of a functional impairment, which substantially interferes with or limits the child's role or functioning in family, school, or community activities (Substance Abuse and Mental Health Administration, 1993). This operationalized definition of SED is used to determine prevalence rates for the purpose of identifying the mental health needs of children at a national and state level (Friedman, Katz-Leavy, Manderscheid, & Sondheimer, 1996). In applying for federal block grant funds from CMHS, the states must demonstrate that they are giving priority to meeting the needs of youths with SED.

Most states have, or are in the process of developing, eligibility criteria for levels of intensity of services, as well as procedures requiring providers to report on treatment outcome. More than two dozen states use the Child and Adolescent Functional Assessment Scale (CAFAS; Hodges, 2000a) as one component in determining whether a child is eligible for SED services, to assess outcome for youth receiving services, or both (Georgetown University National Technical Assistance Center for Children's Mental Health, 2002). In addition, a number of states currently use the CAFAS to track youths in state custody, because of involvement with child protection or juvenile justice. Also, because the CMHS uses the CAFAS as an outcome measure for the national evaluation of the System of Care Initiative, 67 grantees that provide services to high-risk youths with SED utilize the CAFAS (Holden, Friedman, & Santiago, 2001).

These activities at the state and federal level parallel changes that are taking place in the private sector. Increasingly, third-party payers are expecting mental health providers to document severity of impairment for the client to qualify for more intensive or costly treatments. In addition, third-party payers are requiring continual monitoring of the client's level of functioning, with an expectation that intensity of treatment will be reduced as impairment lessens. The term *outcome monitoring* differs from outcome evaluation in that the information obtained as treatment progresses may be used to modify the ongoing treatment plan. Outcome monitoring is a dynamic process, whereas outcome evaluation could be restricted to pre- and posttreatment events.

In this chapter, the psychometric data on the CAFAS, as well as current uses of the CAFAS instrument for treatment planning, treatment monitoring, and outcome assessment, will be reviewed. The CAFAS is used for a variety of purposes. It provides a means for (a) actively managing cases by periodically assessing progress toward specified goals(s), (b) classifying cases for use with specific treatment protocols, (c) designing treatment plans which link problematic behavior with a target goal and related strengths, (d) determining intensity of services or appropriate level of care, (e) assessing (pre- and post-) outcome for program evaluation, (f) organizing case conferences, supervision, and discussions with the caregiver about the youth's needs or ongoing program, (g) documenting clinical decisions that can withstand audits, and (h) generating objective data for clinical, administrative, and research use.

OVERVIEW OF THE INSTRUMENT

Description of the CAFAS

The CAFAS measures impairment in day-to-day functioning in children and adolescents who have, or may be at risk for developing, emotional, behavioral, substance use, psychiatric, or psychological problems. The CAFAS is used by agencies providing behavioral health services, as well as by various child-serving agencies. The CAFAS can be used for youth in a full-day school program in elementary school (i.e., kindergarten, 1st grade) through 12th grade. When the CAFAS was developed in 1989, it consisted of only five subscales. When it was revised in 1994, it was expanded to its current eight subscales. In 2000, the rules for scoring the CAFAS and some of the CAFAS items were modified primarily for the purpose of clarifying how to rate youths not living in their homes. A list of changes made in the CAFAS items in the 2000 version is contained in the *CAFAS Self-Training Manual* (Hodges, 2000b).

The CAFAS is a menu of behavioral descriptors that are organized around domains of functioning, which comprise subscales. Eight subscales assess the youth, and two additional scales assess the caregivers' ability to provide for the youth adequately. Each of the subscales consists of a set of behavioral descriptors grouped into levels of impairment: severe impairment (severe disruption or incapacitation), moderate impairment (persistent disruption or major occasional disruption in functioning), mild impairment (significant problems or distress), and minimal or no impairment (no disruptions of functioning). The level of impairment is determined by the behavioral descriptors that the rater indicates were true for the youth during the rating period. The subscales assessing the youth are School/Work (i.e., ability to function satisfactorily in a group educational environment), Home (i.e., extent to which the youth observes reasonable rules and performs age-appropriate tasks), Community (i.e., respect for the rights of others and their property and conformity to laws), Behavior Toward Others (i.e., appropriateness of youth's daily behavior), Moods/Emotions (i.e., modulation of the youth's emotional life; reflects anxiety and depression), Self-harmful Behavior (i.e., extent to which the youth can cope without resorting to self-harmful behavior or verbalizations), Substance Use (i.e., youth's substance use and the extent to which it is inappropriate or disruptive), and Thinking (i.e., ability of youth to use rational thought process).

For each subscale and each severity level, there is a set of items describing behavior. To rate a youth, the rater reviews the items in the severe impairment category first. If any item describes the youth's functioning, the youth's level of impairment for the subscale is "severe." If none of the items in the severe category characterize the youth, the rater continues to the moderate category, progressing through the remainder of the categories as needed until the youth's level of functioning can be described. The time period considered when rating the CAFAS is defined by the user. Typically, it is the last month or the last 3 months. The rater chooses items that describe the youth's most impaired functioning during the time period.

Each subscale is accompanied by a list of positive characteristics relevant to the subscale's domain. Two examples for the School/Work subscale are "attends regularly" and "gets along okay with teachers." These positive behavioral descriptions can be coded as strengths for youths who have the characteristic, or as goals for youths who lack the behavior but for whom achieving it is realistic. Thus, for each domain (i.e., subscale), the rater can select one or more problem behaviors (from the CAFAS items), as well as strengths and goals. Although the endorsement of goals and strengths is optional, most raters use them because they are helpful in developing an outcomes-driven, strengths-based treatment plan.

Typically, the youth is rated by a practitioner or case manager based on information collected as part of routine services. The actual rating takes about 10 minutes. The CAFAS is not "administered." The CAFAS ratings are based on what the rater has observed or on what has been reported by the youth, the caregivers, or other informants.

What if a youth's behavior is not fully described in the CAFAS items? To accommodate this situation, an item referred to as Exception is provided for each subscale at each severity level. The rater can circle the item number corresponding to Exception and explain the reason in a designated space below each subscale.

There are two scales for rating the youth's caregivers: Material Needs (i.e., extent to which the youth's functioning may be affected by lack of resources, such as food, clothing, housing, medical attention, or neighborhood safety) and Family/Social Support (i.e., extent to which the youth's functioning may be disrupted because of limitations in the family's psychosocial resources relative to the youth's needs). In the event that a youth has more than one caregiver, each may be rated. The caregiver scales also have an accompanying list of strengths and goals.

The intent of the caregiver scales is to provide information about the context in which the youth functions. They provide a means of rating environmental factors, which, if present, are important to consider in designing an effective treatment plan.

CAFAS Scoring

For the purposes of generating quantitative scores, a level of impairment is assigned a score: severe, 30; moderate, 20; mild, 10; and minimal or no impairment, 0. A total score is generated for the youth by totaling the eight subscales. The caregiver scores are not combined with the youth's subscales. Strength and goal items are also not included in the CAFAS total score. A higher score indicates greater impairment, with a range from 0 to 240.

A total score of 0 means that the youth has no impairment when compared to a nondeviant youth functioning in the natural environment. The "minimal or no impairment" category anchors the evaluation of the youth to a criterion that represents a minimal standard of functioning if the youth is to develop unimpeded. A youth with no or minimal impairment on all of the eight CAFAS subscales would have the following characteristics: (a) attends school regularly (or, if 16 years or older and not in school, has a job or is receiving vocational training), (b) has at least a C average (or if not, the youth's work is commensurate with abilities), (c) is not disruptive to others in the classroom (because of behavioral or emotional problems), (d) behaves well enough to be taught in a regular classroom in a community school, (e) performs satisfactorily at the work setting (if working), (f) typically follows reasonable rules, routines, and curfew in the home setting, (g) poses no threat to others or property in the home, (h) follows laws and is considered trustworthy to follow laws (i.e., no special circumstances, such as court supervision, are needed to maintain lawful behavior), (i) uses socially acceptable, nonaggressive means of resolving conflicts with others, (j) can manage feelings of depression and anxiety so that they do not interfere with school or work duties, with relationships with others, or result in often feeling distressed, (k) copes with problems without having serious self-harmful thoughts or actions, (l) does not use alcohol or other drugs or, if the youth does use, does not do so excessively and there is no negative impact on self or others, and (m) does not talk or act in such a way that other people think the youth is "crazy" or "weird" (i.e., communication is not disordered or eccentric).

A calibration of clinical significance is inherent in the CAFAS, because normative behavior is defined by the "no or minimal impairment" behaviors and because the behaviors assessed on the CAFAS relate to day-to-day functioning in the real world. Both the CAFAS total score and the scores on individual subscales gauge how far the youth is from this standard.

Developing Local Norms

Each locality using the CAFAS should generate local norms for CAFAS total scores. Any given youth can then be compared to other youth from the same cultural context. This is consistent with the recommendation by Newman, Ciarlo, and Carpenter (1999), who stated that development of local norms is preferred and should become standard practice for any measure used for setting funding guidelines or for setting standards for treatment review. State governmental entities that collect quality assurance data and state associations that pool their data provide an opportunity to generate local norms. Typical ranges for children with specific problems or challenges (e.g., substance users, youths in foster care) have been generated by organizations serving these youths and by research samples. In addition, the *CAFAS Manual for Training Coordinators, Clinical Administrators, and Data Managers* (Hodges, 2002) provides data showing the percentile of youths associated with various CAFAS total scores for a state sample of children referred to public mental health. Percentile scores from this same sample are also provided for youths presenting with various problems at intake (e.g., thought disorder, substance use, depression, delinquency, etc.).

Ancillary Materials for Parents, Other Informants, and Preschoolers

Interview for Parents. An optional 30- to 40-minute structured interview for parents (CAFAS Parent Report) has been developed, which obtains all of the information needed to rate the CAFAS (Hodges, 1994). The interview can be administered via phone or in person (Hodges, 1995e). The interview is particularly useful for training new staff, for collecting follow-up data after services have been terminated, and for ensuring comprehensive collection of information if routine procedures do not result in obtaining sufficient information.

Checklist for Other Informants. The information needed to rate the CAFAS can also be obtained via use of the CAFAS Checklist for Adult Informant (Hodges, 1995a). The Checklist consists of a series of statements that are scored as yes (true) or no (false). Adult informants include professional caregivers (e.g., foster parents) and any other practitioners or persons providing services to the youth (e.g., teachers, social service or juvenile justice workers). Items relevant to each CAFAS subscale appear on a separate page, so any given informant can complete one or more subscales. There is also a Checklist for Youths (Hodges, 1995b), which obtains information about problems that may not be known to the caregiver and consists of four subscales: Community (i.e., delinquency), Substance Use, Mood, and Self-harmful Behavior.

Parents Choosing Goals for Their Children. The goals and strengths for each subscale also appear on two forms that were developed for parents, to ensure that parents formally participate in choosing the goals for their child (Hodges, 1998a) and their family (Hodges, 1998b). The parent is asked to choose goals, prioritize them in order of importance, and identify strengths that the practitioner may not know. The practitioner can go over this form with the parents and use it as the basis for the goals that the practitioner endorses on the CAFAS form.

The PECFAS for Preschoolers. There is a downward extension of the CAFAS for children from ages 3 to 7 years old, which is referred to as the Preschool and Early Childhood Functional Assessment Scale (PECFAS; Hodges, 1995d). Generally, if a child is attending a full-day school program in elementary school (e.g., kindergarten, first grade), the CAFAS is appropriate. The user should consider the child's developmental age, rather than chronological age, in deciding whether to rate him or her using the CAFAS or PECFAS. The PECFAS has the same subscales as the CAFAS, with the exception of the omission of the Substance Use subscale. The content of the items on the PECFAS refers to behaviors that are more typical of younger children (e.g., temper tantrums, finicky eater).

Similar to the CAFAS, for the PECFAS, there are strengths and goals accompanying each subscale and an interview for caregivers (referred to as PECFAS Parent Report; Hodges, 1995c). In addition, items have been selected from the PECFAS interview to generate the PECFAS Parent Report Screener (Hodges, 1997). The Screener is a 10-minute interview that is used to identify potential problems for children in preschool (e.g., Head Start) or children registering for kindergarten. If the Screener identifies any problems, then the entire PECFAS interview is administered to confirm whether there are problems and, if so, to consider referral for services as needed (Loseth, Carlson, Lucht, & Schmid, 2003). Psychometric properties of the PECFAS have been described in Murphy et al. (1999) and Binck (1997).

The Computer CAFAS

This system allows the clinician to rate the youth, including strengths and goals, on a computer and generate a clinical interpretive report and a treatment plan for each CAFAS administration. In addition, the CAFAS computer system generates two administrative reports that collapse data across clients for a time period specified by the user. One report describes the severity of impairment of all youth at intake and the other describes the pre- to posttreatment outcome results.

The computer program generates the SPSS syntax and data files needed for direct use in SPSS. The export facility also permits exporting all of the collected information into other formats, for example, for inputting into Excel and ACCESS. The generation of the SPSS and ACCESS data files greatly facilitates aggregating large databases for the purpose of producing local norms, as had been done in some states (e.g., Hodges, Xue, & Wotring, in press b; Hodges & Wotring, 2002). For the purpose of answering substantive questions (e.g., Does resource allocation correspond to youth impairment?), other information is collected in the computer program besides the CAFAS, including: (a) at intake, demographic information, multiaxial diagnoses, and presence of current and past risk factors, (b) at subsequent CAFAS ratings (e.g., every 3 months), services and interventions rendered and extent of interagency collaboration, and (c) at termination, the circumstances of termination of services.

Reliability and Validity Data

The psychometric properties of the CAFAS have been investigated extensively, using large data sets generated by two evaluation studies: the Fort Bragg Evaluation Project (Breda, 1996) and the national evaluation of the demonstration service grants, which were federally funded by the CMHS branch of the Substance Abuse and Mental Health Services Administration (Holden et al., 2001; Manteuffel, Stephens, & Santiago, 2002). The CMHS has funded 67 sites in 43 states to assist communities in developing systems of care for providing services to youth with serious emotional disturbance. In 1993 and 1994, 22 communities were awarded 5-year grants; in 1997, 9 communities were funded; in 1998, 14 communities were funded; and in 1999 and 2000, 22 communities received awards.

The two studies had quite different samples, permitting an opportunity to examine the CAFAS in varying contexts. In the Fort Bragg Evaluation Project, the youth were dependents of Army personnel, lived mostly in middle income family settings, had generous mental health benefits, and were referred for mental health problems, with no requirement that they be impaired or SED (Hodges, Wong, & Latessa, 1998). In the CMHS-funded evaluation, the youth were SED, from mostly impoverished families, a diverse group in terms of sociodemographic characteristics and involvement with multiple agencies serving children and families, and received mental health services within developing systems of care that were sponsored with the grant awards.

Data on the CAFAS is also available from a statewide database consisting of youths referred to publicly funded community mental health services providers (Hodges & Wotring, 2002). This data set has been used to describe children who receive services, the outcome for various types of clients, and the relationship between youth impairment and allocation of services. Data from each of these three large data sets have provided evidence of the validity of the CAFAS.

Reliability. Coefficient alpha values were calculated to determine internal consistency, which reflects on the homogeneity of the measure. For the CAFAS, this reflects on whether the various subscales of the CAFAS measure the same construct. Given that the subscales are intended to measure different aspects of impairment, moderate values would be expected. The values for the CAFAS at intake, 6 months, 12 months, and 18 months were .63, .68, .67, and .67, respectfully, in the Fort Bragg Evaluation Project (Hodges & Wong, 1996). In the CMHS study, alpha values for the CAFAS were .73 at intake and .78 at 6 months (Hodges, Doucette-Gates, & Liao, 1999). In addition, the results indicated that the reliability for the entire scale would be lower if any of the individual subscales were omitted from the CAFAS. These alpha values were supportive of the reliability of the CAFAS, given that the separate subscales were intended to assess different domains of impairment.

Interrater reliability of the CAFAS has been assessed with lay raters (i.e., undergraduate and graduate college students) and with front-line staff (Hodges & Wong, 1996). Pearson correlations between the trainees and the criterion score (i.e., the "gold standard") were calculated. With both types of raters, high correlations (ranging from .92 to .96) were observed for the total CAFAS score. For the individual subscales, the reliability ranged from .73 to .99, depending on the subscale. Comparable results were observed when intraclass correlations were determined to examine consistency across raters, ignoring the criterion answers (Hodges & Wong, 1996).

A second interrater reliability study (Pernice, Gust, & Hodges, 1997) used lay raters (undergraduate and first-year graduate students) who conducted telephone interviews with parents of children referred to a public mental health clinic, using the CAFAS interview. The parents were interviewed by two different raters, on separate occasions, with an interinterview time period ranging from 3 to 14 days. The Pearson correlation for the total score between raters using the 1994 version of the CAFAS interview was .91, with the correlations for the individual subscales ranging from .79 to 1.00.

Content and Face Validity. Content validity depends on the extent to which an empirical measurement reflects a specific domain of content, whereas face validity is concerned with the extent to which a measure looks like it measures what it is intended to measure (Nunnally, 1978). In the construction of the CAFAS, the various domains of functioning were identified, and items were selected that reflected impairment in the specific domain. For example, for the School subscale, items were developed for describing the problems related to attendance, disobedience in the classroom, unsafe behavior in the classroom, poor attention or overactivity, and below average academic achievement.

In applied settings, face validity can play an important role if data will be used to try to influence decision making by lay persons, such as legislators and policy makers (Nunnally, 1978). The CAFAS has strong face validity, because CAFAS scores can always be translated into specific problematic behaviors. All ratings on the CAFAS must be supported by endorsement of specific items that are objective and behavioral, such as "expelled from school." Also, improvement over time can be described by the changes in domain and global scores, as well as by observable changes in specific behaviors, as reflected by the specific items endorsed. For example, a child suspended from school for aggressive behavior at intake may be described as having behavioral problems that can be handled by the classroom teacher, with no intervention by disciplinarians needed, at 6-months follow-up. Such concrete evidence of improvement, which is verifiable by examining specific item endorsements, is more persuasive than abstract scores not directly related to behavior for the specific youth.

Concurrent Criterion-Related Validity. Validity has also been examined by determining whether CAFAS scores were different for subgroups of youths who should presumably differ in extent of impairment. Results from both the Fort Bragg Evaluation Project and the CMHS studies have provided evidence of concurrent criterion-related validity. Studies have been conducted to determine whether CAFAS scores differed for youth: (a) being served at different levels of intensity of care, (b) living in settings that differ in restrictiveness and in use of staff with specialized skills at handling problem behaviors, (c) severity of psychiatric diagnosis, and (d) specific problematic behaviors and risk factors. Inpatients scored significantly higher on the CAFAS, indicating greater impairment, than youths receiving home-based services, day treatment, etc., who in turn scored significantly higher than youths in outpatient care (Hodges & Wong, 1996). Children living with their parents or in regular foster care were significantly less impaired than youths in various residential placements, with youths in therapeutic foster care scoring in between these two groups (Hodges et al., 1999). Youths with more serious psychiatric disorders were more impaired than youths diagnosed with less serious disorders (e.g., adjustment, anxiety; Hodges et al., 1999). Higher impairment scores on the CAFAS have been associated with problems in social relationships (Hodges & Wong, 1996), involvement with juvenile justice (Doucette-Gates, Hodges, & Liao, 1998; Hodges et al., 1999; Hodges & Wong, 1996), school-related problems (Doucette-Gates et al., 1998; Hodges et al., 1999; Hodges & Wong, 1996), and child and family risk factors (Manteuffel et al., 2002; Walrath, Mandell, Liao, et al., 2001).

Predictive Validity. CAFAS score at intake has been compared to subsequent services utilization and cost for services in both the Fort Bragg and CMHS studies. In the Fort Bragg Evaluation Project, the CAFAS total score at intake predicted, at 6 and 12 months postintake, restrictiveness of care, total cost of all services received, number of bed days, and number of days of services (Hodges & Wong, 1997). Higher impairment was significantly related to more restrictive care, higher cost, more bed days, and more days of services. Additional simultaneous multiple regressions were conducted to compare the predictive power of the CAFAS to other measures, including the Child Behavior Checklist (CBCL; Achenbach, 1991). The CAFAS total score was a significant predictor of all four utilization indicators at both 6 and 12 months, whereas number of problems endorsed on the CBCL was not predictive of any of the utilization indicators (Hodges & Wong, 1997).

Simultaneous multiple regressions were also conducted to compare the predictive power of the CAFAS to the presence or absence of common diagnoses. At intake, diagnoses were determined via computer algorithm scoring, based on answers given in a structured diagnostic interview administered to the parent about their child's behavior, the parent version of the Child Assessment Schedule (PCAS; Hodges, 1990, 1993). Even when compared to diagnosis, the CAFAS at intake was the strongest predictor of subsequent cost, restrictiveness of services, number of bed days, and number of services at both 6 and 12 months. The only diagnosis, which was significant at both 6 and 12 months, was conduct disorder. Even so, the CAFAS was a more powerful predictor (Hodges & Wong, 1997).

In the evaluation study of the CMHS-funded sites, the CAFAS predicted restrictiveness of living arrangement and number of days in out-of-family care (Hodges, Doucette-Gates, & Kim, 2000). In addition, the CAFAS score at intake predicted subsequent contact with the law and school attendance. Youths with higher impairment at intake were significantly more likely to have contact with the law or the court and to have poor school attendance at 6 months postintake (Hodges & Kim, 2000). In a study conducted for one of the CMHS sites, the CAFAS at intake was found to be a significant predictor of subsequent number of service episodes and service cost (Doucette-Gates et al., 1998). A study by Quist and Matshazi (2000) found that a higher CAFAS at discharge from a juvenile justice residential center predicted recidivism during the year after discharge.

These findings provide considerable evidence of the reliability and validity of the CAFAS. The measure has demonstrated both concurrent and predictive validity in studies operating in applied clinical settings. In addition, the CAFAS performed better than other measures in predicting subsequent clinical sequelae that have important real-life implications, such as costs spent and restrictiveness of setting in which the child can be served.

Generalizability

Generalizability refers to whether the measure performs as expected when applied to various subgroups of youths. Findings from the CMHS studies revealed that the CAFAS was useful in describing the needs of children with various demographic profiles who were referred from a wide variety of agencies, including mental health, schools, juvenile justice, and child welfare (Walrath, dosReis, et al., 2001; Walrath, Nickerson, Crowel, & Leaf, 1998; Walrath, Sharp, Zuber, & Leaf, 2001). Studies by other researchers have also demonstrated the usefulness of the CAFAS in describing impairment in children served by juvenile justice (Quist & Matshazi, 2000; Rosenblatt, Rosenblatt, & Biggs, 2000), child welfare (Zima, Bussing, Crecelius, Kaufman, & Berlin, 1999), and educational programs (Rosenblatt & Rosenblatt, 1999).

Basic Interpretive Strategy

Before interpreting the CAFAS, it is first important to determine whether the information on which the CAFAS ratings were based was adequate in terms of comprehensiveness. To ensure adequate collection of information from important informants, the rater is asked to document sources of information, including the method of obtaining information (i.e., in-person, telephone, written documentation) and relationship of the informant to the youth. Interpretation of the CAFAS can be approached from three vantage points: total score, individual subscale scores, and specific item endorsements.

Interpretation of the CAFAS Total Score. The CAFAS total score is the sum of the individual youth subscales, using the values assigned to the four levels of impairment. There are no cutoff scores for the CAFAS that dictate treatment decisions. Treatment decisions consider many variables, and, in optimal situations, they evolve from collaboration among the professionals, the youth's caregivers, the youth, and other important persons in the youth's life. Although research has shown that the impairment level of the youth may be a cornerstone (Hodges & Wong, 1997), other variables that are considered important in making treatment decisions include: whether the youth demonstrates behaviors that put himself/herself or others at risk and the degree of judged risk (see individual item endorsements); the youth's awareness of the problems and willingness to work on them constructively; the resources available in the family and community for managing the youth's behaviors; the ability of professionals to work in a model aimed at providing the least restrictive care; existing economic incentives; and whether there is a consensus in the clinical literature on the recommended treatment protocol.

Although there are no cutoff scores, a general framework for putting the CAFAS total score into context for the lay person (e.g., parent) is referred to as Overall Level of Dysfunction and is presented on the first page of the CAFAS form. These guidelines, which were developed based on the validity studies previously described, are intentionally general, because other variables besides the CAFAS total score will determine disposition. They are as follows: total score of 0 to 10, youth exhibits no noteworthy impairment; 20 to 40, youth likely can be treated on an outpatient basis, provided that risk behaviors are not present; 50 to 90, youth may need additional services beyond outpatient care; 100 to 130, youth likely needs care that is more intensive than outpatient, includes multiple sources of supportive care, or both; 140 and higher, youth likely needs intensive treatment, the form of which would be shaped by the presence of risk factors and the resources available within the family and the community. These general guidelines can be augmented if local entities have a data set available that can be used to generate benchmarks or typical treatment arrays associated with ranges on the CAFAS total score.

Interpretation of the Individual Subscale Scores. The CAFAS Profile is the cornerstone in interpreting the CAFAS results. Figure 15.1 shows the Profile for the youth subscales, which appears on the second page of the CAFAS form. Figure 15.2 presents the Profile for the caregiver subscales. The horizontal axis contains the names of the individual CAFAS subscales, and the vertical axis, the levels of impairment. The numbers in the body of the table refer to the item numbers in the CAFAS. For example, 2 under the School/Work subscale for severe impairment, refers to item number 002, which is "Expelled or equivalent from school" on the CAFAS form. The rater circles the item numbers that correspond to those items endorsed on the CAFAS. Then the rater fills in the circles indicating the severity level for each subscale. When the circles are connected, a profile appears. In Fig. 15.3, two profile lines are presented for the case example presented at the end of this chapter; the solid line reflects the youth's profile at intake, and the dotted line, at 6 months postintake.

The Profile provides an easy format for focusing discussions about the client's needs and progress, whether it be with the youth, the caregivers, or other professionals. Over time, staff may want to establish clinical care protocols for specific profile patterns. High endorsements on specific subscales may be seen as indicators for evaluative consults, particular treatment protocols, or a specific plan for prioritizing the progression of treatment goals to be addressed. In fact, the CAFAS Profile results can be used to identify subgroups of youths served by the agency. Then it can be determined whether there are evidence-supported treatments available for each of the subgroups and whether the agency offers these treatments. (Burns, Hoagwood, & Mrazek, 1999; Hoagwood, Burns, Kiser, Ringeisen, & Schoenwald, 2001). An example of how this has been done in one statewide system will be presented later.

Interpretation of Specific Item Endorsements. Specific items on the CAFAS inquire about behaviors that pose a risk to the youth or others. These items, referred to as Risk

Level of Impairment	School/Work Role Performance	Home Role Performance	Community Role Performance	Behavior Toward Others	Moods/ Emotions	Self-Harmful Behavior	Substance Use	Thinking
SEVERE 30	1 2 3 4 5 6 7 8 9 10 11 ○	41 42 43 44 45 46 47 48 49 50 ○	66 67 68 69 70 71 72 ○	88 89 90 91 92 ○	116 117 118 119 120 ○	142 143 144 145 ○	154 155 156 157 158 159 160 161 162 163 164 ○	182 183 184 185 186 ○
MODERATE 20	12 13 14 15 16 17 18 19 20 21 ○	51 52 53 54 55 56 ○	73 74 75 76 77 78 79 ○	93 94 95 96 97 98 99 100 101 102 ○	121 122 123 124 125 126 127 ○	146 147 148 ○	165 166 167 168 169 170 171 ○	187 188 189 190 191 192 ○
MILD 10	22 23 24 25 26 27 ○	57 58 59 60 61 ○	80 81 82 83 ○	103 104 105 106 107 108 109 110 ○	128 129 130 131 132 133 134 135 ○	149 150 ○	172 173 174 175 ○	193 194 195 196 197 ○
MINIMAL/NO 0	28 29 30 31 32 33 34 35 36 37 38 39 ○	62 63 64 ○	84 85 86 ○	111 112 113 114 ○	136 137 138 139 140 ○	151 152 ○	176 177 178 179 180 ○	198 199 ○
COULD NOT SCORE	40 ○	65 ○	87 ○	115 ○	141 ○	153 ○	181 ○	200 ○

FIG. 15.1. CAFAS Profile: Youth's functioning.

Level of Impairment	Name:____ Relationship:____		Name:____ Relationship:____		Name:____ Relationship:____	
	Primary Family: Material Needs	Primary Family: Family/Social Support	Non-Custodial Family: Material Needs	Non-Custodial Family: Family/Social Support	Surrogate Caregiver: Material Needs	Surrogate Caregiver: Family/Social Support
SEVERE 30	201 202 ○	211 212 213 214 215 216 217 218 219 220 221 ○	240 241 ○	250 251 252 253 254 255 256 257 258 259 260 ○	279 280 ○	289 290 291 292 293 294 295 296 297 298 299 ○
MODERATE 20	203 204 ○	222 223 224 225 226 227 228 229 ○	242 243 ○	261 262 263 264 265 266 267 268 ○	281 282 ○	300 301 302 303 304 305 306 307 ○
MILD 10	205 206 ○	230 231 232 233 234 ○	244 245 ○	269 270 271 272 273 ○	283 284 ○	308 309 310 311 312 ○
MINIMAL/NO 0	207 208 209 ○	235 236 237 238 ○	246 247 248 ○	274 275 276 277 ○	285 286 287 ○	313 314 315 316 ○
COULD NOT SCORE	210 ○	239 ○	249 ○	278 ○	288 ○	317 ○

SAMPLE

FIG. 15.2. CAFAS Profile: Caregiver resources.

Behaviors, are listed on the first page of the CAFAS and are flagged on the client report generated by the CAFAS computer system if any are endorsed for the youth. They include: suicidal, aggressive, sexual, fire setting, runaway, dangerous substance use, and psychotic behaviors. These identified behaviors allow the team to consider: (a) whether immediate action is needed to prevent harm to the youth or others; (b) whether the youth's school setting and living environment are appropriate, given the perceived risks; and (c) how treatment will address these risk behaviors.

Interpretation of Goals and Strengths. The endorsed goals and strengths, done in collaboration with the parent, are used to design the individualized treatment plan.

USE OF THE CAFAS FOR TREATMENT PLANNING

The CAFAS provides and organizes information vital to treatment planning. It readily ties goals to be accomplished in treatment to outcome evaluation. The treatment goals selected are guided by the problems that are interfering with the youth's development,

Level of Impairment	School/Work Role Performance	Home Role Performance	Community Role Performance	Behavior Toward Others	Moods/ Emotions	Self-Harmful Behavior	Substance Use	Thinking
SEVERE 30	1 2 3 4 5 6 7 8 9 10 11	41 42 43 44 45 46 47 48 49 50	66 67 68 69 70 71 72	88 89 90 91 92	116 117 118 119 120	142 143 144 145	154 155 156 157 158 159 160 161 162 163 164	182 183 184 185 186
MODERATE 20	12 13 14 15 16 17 18 19 20 21	51 52 53 54 55 56	73 74 75 76 77 78 79	93 94 95 96 97 98 99 100 101 102	121 122 123 124 125 126 127	146 147 148	165 166 167 168 169 170 171	187 188 189 190 191 192
MILD 10	22 23 24 25 26 27	57 58 59 60 61	80 81 82 83	103 104 105 106 107 108 109 110	128 129 130 131 132 133 134 135	149 150	172 173 174 175	193 194 195 196 197
MINIMAL/NO 0	28 29 30 31 32 33 34 35 36 37 38 39	62 63 64	84 85 86	111 112 113 114	136 137 138 139 140	151 152	176 177 178 179 180	198 199
COULD NOT SCORE	40	65	87	115	141	153	181	200

FIG. 15.3. CAFAS Profile comparing intake and 3 months evaluation for Jamie (case example). Intake scores are solid; 3 months scores have dashes.

TABLE 15.1
Treatment Plan Generated by CAFAS

	School/Work	*Home*	*Behavior Toward Others*
Problems	Grade average is lower than C.	Persistent failure to comply with reasonable rules and expectations within the home (e.g., bedtime, curfew)	Persistent problems or difficulties in relating to peers because of antagonizing behaviors
Goals	School grades are average or above.	Obeys curfew	Expresses anger through appropriate verbalizations or healthy physical outlets. Is aware of problems related to social skills and is working on improving them. Participates in positive peer activities (e.g., sports).
Strengths	Attends regularly, likes going to school	Behavior at home is devoid of aggressive acts or threats. Respectful of property in the home. Takes pride in being able to do some activities independently.	Can be fun to be with (e.g., jokes, is witty, has a sense of humor).
Plan	(1) Establish a behavioral plan in which Jamie takes home a chart everyday indicating whether she did C work or above that day (indicated by a "smiley" face). Any unfinished work is sent home to complete in the evening. A "smiley" face will be rewarded by allowing her to watch her favorite TV show (after she completes all of her homework) with her foster mom and other kids in the home. If she gets 3 out of 5 "smiley" faces for the week, she gets a trip with her foster mom to the used clothes and toys shop on Saturday, where she can choose an item of her choice up to $3.00. (2) Teacher will continue to structure her activities (e.g., have her sit next to the teacher) and to reinforce good behavior (e.g., place a check on a card on Jamie's desk; Jamie can use checks to obtain rewards).	(1) Install a motion detector so that Jamie's attempts to sneak out past bedtime to old neighborhood will be detected. (2) On-call crisis intervention is available through case manager. (3) In-home counseling twice a week. Any behavior or family problems are discussed, and specific behavior plans are developed as needed.	(1) Enroll her in after-school activities (drama club) where she will learn appropriate ways of handling disagreements and hopefully make prosocial friends. (2) In foster home, "catch her" when she appropriately (verbally) expresses disagreement. Reward with a compliment or hug.

Computer System for Jamie Foster

Moods/Emotions	*Substance Use*	*Thinking*	*Primary Caregiver*
Sad or anhedonic in at least one setting for up to a few days	For 12 years or younger, occasional use without intoxication and without becoming obviously high	Unusual perceptual experiences not qualifying as pathological hallucinations	Gross impairment in parental judgment or functioning (may be related to substance abuse)
Has self-awareness of emotional state/emotions. Has an appropriate understanding of "blame" (does not blame self too much).	No use of substances. Is involved in alternative prosocial activities.	No hallucinations or delusions.	Substance-using caregiver is seeking services to deal with his or her own substance use.
Shows a range of emotions	Acknowledges substance use	Can express self adequately and clearly. Thinks logically.	Caregiver cooperates with agencies providing services to youth.
(1) Foster mom will read a book to her about how children feel when they have substance-abusing parents. Encourage her to not blame herself if parents cannot kick their habit. (2) Foster mom will tolerate her feeling sad. (3) Foster mom will try to provide opportunities for Jamie to talk with her (e.g., ask her to help with a chore where pleasant conversation is possible, accompany foster mom in the car to run errands).	(1) Get Jamie involved with incompatible prosocial activities (e.g., after-school programs and Saturday YMCA athletic programs). (2) Foster parents and therapist educate her about effects of alcohol. (3) Limit contact with friends from old neighborhood. (4) Prevent "sneaking out" (see plan for motion detector). (5) Attend Alateen.	(1) Foster parents observe her closely and keep diary of any possible episodes of hallucinations. (2) Reduce anxiety and concern about her safety. (3) Consider psychiatric consult if symptoms continue.	(1) Continue Jamie's placement in foster care. (2) Social services will assist mother in trying to secure an apartment in a safer neighborhood. (3) Compliment and recognize that mother is cooperating with agencies working with Jamie. (4) Communicate to mother that she and stepdad must seek treatment (e.g., AA) and consistently participate. As needed, provide treatment to mother about the issue of how to manage if stepdad will not participate in substance abuse treatment or abandons the family. (5) Weekly session on improving caregiving skills, to be initiated by social service worker.

because most funding in behavioral health services is based on this paradigm. Recognition of the strengths of the youth and the family allows for a contextual understanding of the problem behaviors and the design of an effective intervention. For this reason, each CAFAS subscale contains target behaviors, strengths, and goals. For each subscale, the practitioner can indicate specific steps to be undertaken to achieve the goal and remedy the target problem. Alternately, one can indicate that no steps are planned, because either there is no problem to remedy or the problems are not a priority at present and will be deferred. The CAFAS form contains a treatment plan that can be completed by the rater, and the CAFAS software generates this form based on the endorsements for problem behaviors, strengths, and goals. The example provided in Table 15.1 is the intake treatment plan for the case example presented at the end of the chapter. In this section, clinical issues and research findings relevant to treatment planning are described.

Identifying Areas of Severe Impairments

Areas of severe impairment are easily identified by examining the CAFAS Profile. The association of each problem with an impairment level helps to identify the most critical issues to address. Problems indicating severe impairment typically have the most pernicious effect on the youth's development and, thus, are normally given priority. The presence of severe impairment in any of the eight domains measured by the CAFAS jeopardizes the youth's development. For example, school nonattendance, which would be scored as severe impairment on the School/Work subscale, jeopardizes the youth's subsequent academic achievement (and subsequent job opportunities and earning power as an adult) and continued development of social skills and a prosocial network of friends (and increases the subsequent risk for delinquency and teenage pregnancy). In addition, natural helpers in the community (e.g., teachers, ministers, coaches, relatives, neighbors) are less likely to assist a needy youth who is severely impaired. Sometimes it is tempting to work on less intimidating goals; however, the practitioner needs to be attentive to whether the treatment plan will eventually lead to an improvement in the youth's most impaired functioning. The CAFAS Profile and individual items provide a built-in focus on the most severe areas of impaired functioning.

Differentiating Subgroups of Youths Based on CAFAS Tiers

Cluster analysis and other related analytic procedures can be used to identify groupings of youths on the basis of their CAFAS Profile (i.e., the youth's scores on the individual CAFAS subscales). Five clusters of youth were identified by Lemoine and McDermott (1997) with a Louisiana sample, and a relatively similar set of clusters was found by Hodges and Wotring (2000) with a Michigan sample. These cluster analyses were useful in identifying subgroups of youths; however, they had limited utility because cluster analysis cannot be used to classify youths at the time that they present at intake. Thus, an algorithm was derived for classifying the youths into subgroups such that the clusters were approximated, yet the practitioner could do the classification by visually inspecting the CAFAS Profile for a few minutes. The scoring algorithm for this rationally derived method, referred to as CAFAS Tiers, is presented in the *CAFAS Manual for Training Coordinators, Clinical Administrators, and Data Managers* (Hodges, 2002). The youth's profile of subscale scores determines to which of the following categories the youth is assigned: thought problems, maladaptive substance use, self-harmful behavior, delinquency (refers to the Community subscale), severe mood disturbance (depression, anxiety), problematic behaviors (in school, at home, or in interactions with others) with moderate mood disturbance, problematic behaviors (without moderate mood disturbance), moderate mood, and adjustment problems with impairment. The classification is hierarchically arranged, such that qualifying for a condition higher up in the list (e.g., thought problems) excludes the youth for a category appearing lower (e.g., delinquency), even if the youth has both types of problems. Conditions higher up in the list are more complex and often require further investigation before treatment can be planned. Thus, the categories high in the hierarchical ordering can have co-occurrences for the conditions below them (e.g. youths assigned to the maladaptive substance use grouping could also have suicidal and delinquent behavior). In particular, notice that the youths in the delinquency grouping do not have co-occurring thought problems, maladaptive substance use, suicidal behavior, severe depression, or severe anxiety, because these problems appear higher up in the hierarchy.

Research with the classification system has demonstrated that it is clinically useful and has empirical support. Hodges and Xue (2002) confirmed that the categories form a continuum in terms of overall severity of impairment at intake, as indicated by total score on the CAFAS, as well as by number of subscales rated as severely impaired. Youths in categories placed higher in the hierarchy (e.g., thought problems) were more impaired than youths assigned to categories lower in the hierarchy, with the scores corresponding to the order in the hierarchy. Hodges, Xue, and Wotring (2001) also found a correspondence between order in the hierarchy and presence of risk factors, such as previous hospitalization for psychiatric or substance use problems. In addition, Hodges et al. (in press b) demonstrated that the categories formed a continuum in terms of end-of-treatment level of functioning. There was an inverse relationship between ordinal position in the hierarchy and likelihood of having nonclinical status at the end of treatment. For example, far fewer youths in the thought-problem and maladaptive-substance-use categories had a nonclinical status at the end of treatment, compared to delinquent youths, who in turn were less likely to have a nonclinical status compared to youths assigned to the problematic behaviors categories. These findings support the use of this classification system in clinical application, because it helps identify youths who are the most impaired, have a greater likelihood of having associated risk factors, and have a much poorer prognosis in terms of clinical outcome. CAFAS Tiers offers a very quick means of organizing youths into subgroups for the purposes of triaging cases, providing managerial or administrative supervision of the flow of cases through agency services, and for research or continuous quality improvement activities.

Identifying Co-occurrence of Problems

Co-occurrence, or comorbidity, refers to having more than one diagnosis or condition (Hodges, Xue, & Wotring, 2002). The CAFAS Profile helps identify two important types of comorbidity: co-occurrence of a behavioral and emotional problems and co-occurrence of maladaptive substance use and another psychiatric condition. Disorders reflecting behavioral problems (e.g., conduct disorder) are also described as externalizing (Achenbach, 1991), and emotional problems (e.g., anxiety or depression) as internalizing. Elevations on the Moods/Emotions and Self-harmful Behavior subscales would reflect internalizing symptoms, whereas elevations on the first four subscales on the Profile (i.e., School/Work, Home, Community, Behavior Toward Others) typically reflect externalizing problems, although for any given youth can reflect either externalizing or internalizing problems. Examination of the specific items would be needed to confirm whether they appear to reflect internalizing or externalizing problems for any given youth. Another important type of comorbidity is the presence of both a substance use problem and another psychiatric condition. This pattern is easily identified by a profile that peaks on the Substance Use subscale and any other subscale.

A study of 5,638 youths with SED who were served by community mental health service providers in Michigan revealed considerable comorbidity among the sample, using the CAFAS Tiers classification system (Hodges et al., 2002). Considering only maladaptive substance use, self-harmful behavior, delinquency, and severe or moderate mood disturbance, the rates of co-occurring problems were as follows: 77% for maladaptive substance use, 32% for self-harmful behavior, 33% for delinquency, and 35% for severe or moderate mood disturbance. Further, youths with co-occurring delinquency or co-occurring maladaptive substance use were significantly less likely to make therapeutic progress, defined as the proportion of youths whose CAFAS score changed from severe or moderate impairment to mild or no/minimal impairment on the various CAFAS subscales from their intake to last CAFAS evaluation (Hodges et al., 2002).

More detailed analyses using logistic regression were conducted to examine outcomes for youths rated as severely or moderately impaired on the Moods/Emotions subscale at intake (Xue, Hodges, & Wotring, in press). The results revealed that the presence of a co-occurring problem was a stronger predictor of reduction in impairment on the Moods/Emotions subscale than other predictors, including: sex, age, previous juvenile justice involvement, previous psychiatric hospitalization, and previous out-of-home placement. Presence of co-occurring problems, particularly delinquency and substance use, was a poor prognostic indicator for improvement in mood. Thus, the CAFAS Tiers categorization system has proved to be useful in identifying patterns of co-occurrence of problems and in linking specific comorbidities to the likelihood of successful outcome.

Identifying Pervasiveness of Problems

Pervasiveness refers to the extent to which the youth has problems across different settings. Three of the subscales are associated with specific settings (i.e., School/Work, Home, and Community). A fourth reflects on the youth's interpersonal relationships across settings (i.e., Behavior Toward Others). Research on co-occurrence of problems conducted with the Michigan sample of youths with SED revealed that youths with pervasive problems across settings (i.e., school, home, and social interactions) had a much poorer prognosis, compared to youths with problems across fewer domains of functioning (Hodges et al., in press a). To further examine this, analysis were conducted on a less impaired sample from the Michigan database (i.e., included all referred youths rather than restricted to youths with SED). To focus on youths who did not have severe diagnoses more typically observed in adolescents, the sample excluded youths who qualified for any of the following client types, based on the CAFAS Tiers: thought problems, maladaptive substance use, self-harmful behavior, delinquency, or severe mood disturbance. A cluster analysis on the remaining 4,777 youths revealed five clusters: Pervasive Problems (i.e., on the School/Work, Home, Behavior Toward Others subscales), School With Mood, Home With Mood, School and Home, and Mood Only. Youths from the Pervasive Problems cluster, which composed

23% of the sample, were significantly more likely to have been previously psychiatrically hospitalized and to have an impaired caregiving environment. Outcome was measured by reduction in CAFAS total score from intake to last CAFAS evaluation and by the proportion of youths whose impairment on the CAFAS subscales was reduced from severe or moderate to mild or no/minimal impairment. Although the results revealed that the youths in the Pervasive Problems cluster made significant improvement, their gains were substantially less than observed for the other clusters (Hodges, Xue, & Wotring, in press a).

To further investigate the importance of pervasive impairment in predicting successful outcome, logistic regressions were conducted to compare this variable to: various demographic characteristics, risk factors (i.e., prior hospitalization, prior juvenile justice involvement, prior out-of-home placement), and caregiver resourcefulness (Xue, Hodges, & Wotring, in press). Being a member of the Pervasive Problems cluster was the strongest predictor of poor outcome for all of the relevant subscales: School/Work, Home, Behavior Toward Others, and Moods/Emotions. Being male was also a strong predictor for poorer outcome on the School/Work subscale, as would be expected given the higher referral rates for school problems for boys. These research findings demonstrate that severe or moderate impairment on all three of the School/Work, Home, and Behavior Toward Others subscales of the CAFAS is a poor prognostic indicator. These results would argue for identification of these youths at intake for the purposes of offering a more potent intervention, and for following these youths until a reduction is seen in severity across more than one setting. These findings would also make a case for earlier intervention before pervasive impairment is observed, especially in light of the known stability of externalizing disorders (Hodges et al., in press a).

Treatment Planning During Crisis Intervention

Evaluation of youths in the emergency room, or in other crisis intervention settings, requires that the practitioner quickly assess the situation and the youth's status, make a recommendation for the immediate future and justify the recommendations to the consumers (i.e., the youth, caregivers, and referring physician). This situation also provides an opportunity for providing a provisional treatment plan that can help the caregivers as they continue to cope with the evolving situation in their family. Wale, Barckholtz, and Denter (in press) found that using the CAFAS for crisis assessment in an emergency room proved satisfactory for meeting the Medicaid guidelines for determining severity of illness and intensity of intervention. Further, using the CAFAS also resulted in a 29% reduction in total clinician time spent on each crisis contact, more timely reports, and a better understanding of the rationale for the dispositions by consumers.

Considering Impairment in the Youth's Caregiving Environment

The caregiver scales provide information on the extent to which the youth's functioning is negatively affected by the caregiver's difficulty in providing for the youth's material needs (i.e., Material Needs scale) and in providing the youth with emotional support and guidance (i.e., Family/Social Support scale). The latter scale includes items that describe caregiver behaviors and characteristics that can have a pernicious effect on a child's development, including: substance abuse, serious psychiatric illness, inadequate supervision of the youth, domestic abuse, abusive or neglectful behavior, and inadequate care of a child who was previously abused. The scale also addresses situations where the youth's needs may exceed the family's resources (i.e., single parent with an autistic child). This scale helps identify issues that need to be addressed for progress to be made in the youth's condition and, thus, need to be considered in planning interventions. For example, a caregiver who feels rejecting of the youth may benefit from respite care until the youth's behavior becomes less burdensome on the family, or an alcoholic caregiver may need to lessen his or her addiction before being able to responsibly parent the youth. A high score on the Material Needs subscale may mean that interventions other than psychological may be needed, including collaboration with other agencies that provide needed assistance.

In the two studies that were previously described as using logistic regression to examine predictors of poor outcome (Xue et al., 2002a, 2002b), one of the predictors assessed was impaired caregiving environment (i.e., severe or moderate impairment on the Caregiver: Family/Social Support scale at intake). In both studies, an impaired caregiving environment was a significant prognostic indicator of poor outcome. These results underscore that severe or moderate impairment in caregivers at intake may require a special focus, or set of interventions, to avert treatment failure.

An appreciation of the caregiver's positive resources is also important in trying to design a plan that provides services in the least restrictive environment. The list of strengths, which accompany the caregiver scales (e.g., caregiver exercises good control when provoked), helps identify behaviors that can be used to foster change in the family and can serve to remind clinicians of the family's positive characteristics.

Sharing the CAFAS Reliability Results With the Family

During the treatment planning process, the caregivers should be actively involved in choosing goals and strengths for the youth and should be given an opportunity to review the CAFAS Profile and endorsed items. In fact, the client report produced by the CAFAS computer system lists all of the items endorsed and shows the Profile in a graph format. On the report, there is a place for both the caregiver and, if appropriate, the youth to write comments and to sign. This gives the therapist an opportunity to ask the caregiver whether his or her assessment was correct. Disagreements that arise in the discussion could potentially lead the therapist to change the endorsements, because misunderstandings were clarified. Alternately, the discussion may lead caregivers to revise their perceptions of their youths' difficulties or their perceptions of the extent to which these difficulties place the youths' future at risk. In fact, caregivers appear to benefit from the way the CAFAS depicts problems, because it provides an objective, visually oriented approach to labeling behaviors according to the likelihood of interfering with the youth's future development. In any case, a productive and important exchange will likely occur. This is important if the resulting treatment plan is to be viable.

Selecting an Appropriate Treatment Array

The results of the CAFAS assessment can be used to help determine whether the youth has a condition that may warrant implementation of an evidence-supported treatment, and, if so, which one. On the other hand, if there is no apparent evidence-supported treatment appropriate for the youth's constellation of problems, then the CAFAS can be used to guide the selection of clinical care practices to be employed. This can be done at the level of the individual practitioner working with a case or at the managerial level, in which supervisors or groups of practitioners establish treatment protocols. When a practitioner is working with a caregiver regarding recommendations, reference can be made to the clinic treatment protocol, to the research literature that justifies it as the treatment of choice, and, if the clinic has studied its own outcome, to the evidence that its agency has good results with the approach. For example, research with the statewide database in Michigan revealed the frequency of conditions categorized by the CAFAS Tiers (Hodges et al., in press b) and the frequency of co-occurrence of problems (Hodges et al., 2002). With this information, it was possible to develop a flowchart that links the CAFAS Tiers conditions (distinguishing between conditions with no co-occurring conditions and combinations of co-occurring conditions) to treatments, with preference given to evidence-supported treatments if they are available for the condition. This type of flowchart can be constructed for specific populations, as, for example, has been done for children in foster care (Hodges & Chamberlain, 2002). A detailed mapping of evidence-supported treatments to specific CAFAS Profiles and CAFAS Tiers subgroupings is provided in the *Manual for Training Coordinators, Clinical Administrators, and Data Managers* (Hodges, 2002).

Potential Limitations of the CAFAS for Treatment Planning

The CAFAS is helpful in determining what behaviors the youth must abandon, as well as the skills that the youth must develop to improve the likelihood of functioning in a nonclinical range. In regards to the caregiver, the CAFAS is helpful in identifying the behaviors that the caregiver needs to abandon, but much less helpful in regard to the skills that the caregiver would be wise to develop. To remedy this deficiency, additional caregiver scales have been developed that focus on caregiver skills. These scales, which were based on the research evidence present in the literature, focus on four skills: giving directives (requests), reinforcing desirable behavior, ignoring or disciplining undesirable behavior, and monitoring the youth while the youth is away from home or while the youth is at home with no adult present. These additional caregiver skills scales have been piloted, along with an adherence scale for therapy to determine whether the practitioner focused on teaching them during the session.

Sometimes, practitioners object to measures like the CAFAS, because they assume that the list of problems or goals generated dictates the content of therapy. That is not the case; any therapeutic approach that is an ethical and effective way to achieve the goals and reduce the problem behaviors is legitimate. For example, a youth may be brought for treatment for excessive disruptive behavior, and there may be no reports of depressive symptoms from the youth or the parents. The practitioner may infer that there is underlying depression, based on the youth's situation. If there is no documentable depression present at intake, the Moods/Emotions subscale will not be scored as impaired. However, the intervention could focus on hypothesized underlying depression. Irrespective of the treatment approach, the treatment outcome will be judged on whether the disruptive behavior documented on the School/Work and Home subscales decreased.

In summary, the CAFAS Profile and the CAFAS treatment plan provide a means of organizing the target behaviors, resources, and goals for both the youth and the caregiver. It provides a concrete representation that helps focus treatment team discussions, supervision issues, and collaborative sessions with caregivers. The CAFAS total score, the Profile pattern, and the CAFAS Tiers category assignment all provide a rough gauge of expected treatment intensity, likely treatment approaches, and general costliness.

USE OF THE CAFAS FOR TREATMENT MONITORING

Overview

The CAFAS can be administered at the beginning of treatment and at the end, even if the therapy is relatively short-term (e.g., 2 months). For situations in which longer term interventions are applied, or the youth is in custodial care of a therapeutic nature, progress over time can be monitored via multiple CAFAS evaluations. An important characteristic of the CAFAS is that it can be used to actively manage treatment so as to maximize outcome. In most clinical settings, the ratings for the CAFAS are done at intake, every 3 months thereafter, and at exit from service. The time frame rated is typically the last 30 days. By reviewing the Profile over time, objective assessment can be used to influence future treatment decisions. For example, if a youth's targeted behavior is not changing, then an alternative strategy should be entertained. The purpose of treatment monitoring is to get a reading on how the youth's behaviors and the caregiver's resourcefulness are progressing. If there is a stalemate, then the treatment plan needs to be reevaluated. This could take many forms: concretely showing the CAFAS Profile to the family and seeking their input, consulting with colleagues, or progressing to a different protocol that has been developed for these situations. In fact, the CAFAS allows programs to empirically study the effectiveness of various strategies for difficult situations.

Change over time can be reflected on the Profile, as demonstrated in Fig. 15.3. In the CAFAS computer system, the client report provides a listing of all previous CAFAS ratings for the client and produces a graph, illustrating the first and current ratings. This comparison can be instructive for staff and families. On the hopeful side, the family members can see that, despite the work that remains to be done, much has been accomplished. In contrast, when there has been a lack of progress, the graph provides an objective basis for a discussion about realistic treatment options. By using a concrete representation, as depicted in the CAFAS Profile and the computer-generated graph, the failure to make progress or the worsening situation is undeniable. Staff can no longer assume that more of the same is better. The family members are also faced with generating a realistic plan.

How often should the youth be rated? What should be the duration of the time period being rated? These decisions can be tailored to the individual setting or program and are related to the anticipated length of treatment. The most common scenario is rating on a quarterly basis (i.e., every 3 months), with the duration rated being 30 days. Because the rating is of the youth's severest functioning, rating the last 30 days provides an opportunity for the therapeutic interventions to have some effect. Rating less frequently (e.g., every 6 months) is certainly acceptable, but likely unwise if the funder desires progress toward achieving goals or lessening problematic behavior. Unless the youth's progress is monitored, it will not be possible to detect failure to respond or deterioration in the youth's functioning, which should result in a revised treatment plan. At the very minimum, the youth should be evaluated at intake, at 3 months postintake, and periodically until exiting services. The rationale for always evaluating youths at 3 months is that the existing literature suggests that most treatment gains are made early in the intervention (Kazdin, Mazurick, & Siegal, 1994).

The CAFAS can also be used to monitor therapeutic progress during treatment at the managerial or supervisory level. Hodges and Wotring (2002) described a statewide endeavor, called the Level of Functioning Project, which focuses on assisting providers in learning to continuously monitoring their outcomes. Using the computer CAFAS, providers submit outcome data monthly and receive immediate feedback on the cases that are currently in treatment. This monthly feedback arrives as reports, which are actually Excel files, in which the level of analysis is the individual client. The reports provide information on type and extent of impairment at intake, CAFAS total score for all evaluations, interventions and collaborative services received, caregiver resource level, and, if relevant, risk characteristics of the child and the family. The reports are organized around the following questions: Is every youth getting a quarterly outcome evaluation in a timely fashion? Which clients are currently making poor progress? Which clients are at high risk for poor response to treatment, out-of-home placement, high service utilization, or high service cost? What are the needs of clients who recently entered services? Using these types of reports for managerial oversight has resulted in fewer incidences of poor match between the youth's needs and the resources allocated. These reports help the providers accomplish several goals: prevent unnecessary restrictive placements, maximize benefits to clients, provide targeted supervision and support to staff, manage responsibly agency resources, and hold staff accountable for records compliance.

Potential Limitations of the CAFAS for Treatment Monitoring in a Managed Care Setting

The CAFAS was not designed to assess change over very short time spans, such as 2 weeks. Other measures designed for daily ratings would be preferable. However, sometimes a 2-week stay in a residential program is part of a continuum of care. Thus, the youth could still be assessed with the CAFAS over time as he or she progresses from more to less restrictive treatment settings. This is fine for assessing the youth, but what if one objective of the evaluation is to assess the program? In the situation of a short-term hospitalization, the unit could rate the youth on all eight subscales before and after the short hospitalization. In addition, at intake, the staff could stipulate which individual subscale of the CAFAS they plan to impact during the short-term hospitalization. Examples would be: the Self-Harmful Behavior subscale for suicidal youths, the Moods/Emotions subscale for depressed youths, the Thinking subscale for psychotic youths, and the Behavior Toward Others subscale for youths with a variety of other presenting problems. Provided that the unit chooses the outcome criteria ahead of time by stipulating the subscales on which they will be assessed, this is an appropriate option. Rating the entire CAFAS provides a picture of how the youth looks as he or she progresses through each stage of the continuum of care. In fact, the CAFAS Profile, the item endorsements, and the CAFAS treatment plan can be forwarded with the youth as he or she progresses through the continuum of care. For example, when the youth exits from a service, the staff can indicate how the CAFAS Profile and item endorsements have changed from admission to discharge and prepare a plan for the step-down program to which the youth is transferring.

USE OF THE CAFAS FOR TREATMENT OUTCOMES ASSESSMENT

This section will address the following topics: (a) evaluation of the CAFAS on the NIMH criteria for outcome measures (Newman et al., 1999), (b) research findings on the sensitivity of the CAFAS to assessing change, (c) CAFAS outcome indicators, (d) use of outcome data at the agency and state level, (e) precautions in using the CAFAS as an outcome measure, and (f) potential use as a data source for behavioral health service report cards.

Evaluation on NIMH Criteria for Outcome Measures

Relevance to Target Group. The target group for the CAFAS is youth referred for behavioral health problems or at risk for behavioral health problems. It is appropriate for children ranging from minimal to high impairment. It has been successfully used to assess outcome in children referred from a variety of child service agencies, including schools, social services, and juvenile justice. (See section on validity of the CAFAS).

Simple, Teachable Methodology. The CAFAS has straightforward and easily understandable instructions that can be implemented by staff who are professionally charged with caring for youth. The measure has objective referents in that the items on the CAFAS are mostly behavioral descriptions. There are extensive training and support materials. The *CAFAS Self-training Manual* (Hodges, 2000b) is used to train raters to be reliable. It contains instructions for scoring, demonstration vignettes with answers, and vignettes to use for the purpose of establishing reliability. New employees can work through the manual on their own. It is helpful to assign one staff member to ensure that the training is satisfactorily accomplished. This training coordinator scores new employees' reliability vignettes using the answer key provided. Simple criteria for judging reliability are given in the *Manual for Training Coordinators, Clinical Administrators, and Data Managers* (Hodges, 2002). There are additional vignettes that can be used if the trainee does not achieve reliability with the *CAFAS Self-training Manual*. To address possible rater drift, vignettes, referred to as Booster Vignettes, have also been developed to reassess reliability annually.

Use of Objective Referents. Newman et al. (1999) defined an objective referent as one for which concrete examples are given for each level of a measure. They describe this as a critical quality for managed care eligibility and level of care decisions, and, in fact, cite the CAFAS as one of the best examples of a scale with objective referents. The CAFAS has 200 concrete descriptions of youth behaviors grouped by level of impairment, from which the rater chooses those that apply to the youth. The items are specific, for example, "chronic truancy resulting in negative consequences" [e.g., loss of course credit, failing courses or tests, parents notified]. The items are written in common everyday terms. They are verifiable, resulting in the CAFAS holding up well under audits. In fact, specific supporting comments can be written on the CAFAS form to reduce redundancy in the case record and to provide clear justification for audit purposes. A detailed set of instructions that provide the rationale underlying the scoring, definitions, and examples are contained in the *CAFAS Self-training Manual* (Hodges, 2000b).

Use of Multiple Respondents. The CAFAS is completed by the practitioner who has interviewed the family. To rate the CAFAS, information must be obtained about all major aspects of the youth's life. The rater is instructed to seek information from all important informants and is required to indicate the type of informants and the modes of communication. To assist in obtaining information from informants outside the immediate family, the Checklist for Adult Informant was developed so that questions about various subscales could be sent to the most appropriate reporters.

More Process-Identifying Outcome Measures. The criterion states that it is preferable to use measures that provide a means for regularly collecting information on the client's progress, which is precisely how the CAFAS is used. The specific items endorsed on the CAFAS provide a map of what needs to be addressed, while periodic ratings of the CAFAS provide an ongoing progress report.

Low-Cost Relative to Its Uses. The CAFAS is very cost-effective, because it can be the main vehicle for determining level of care and treatment recommendations at intake and for client tracking after intake. The CAFAS can assist in achieving numerous tasks at different levels of the agency. The CAFAS helps the practitioner organize the treatment plan so that it is integrated with outcome assessment. This encourages an outcomes-driven approach to treatment. In addition, assessing the client quarterly on the CAFAS helps the practitioner actively manage treatment, by using an empirical orientation, and maximizes good outcomes. The clinical supervisor or manager can use the database on the CAFAS (or the individual written CAFAS forms completed by staff) to identify cases that are not progressing well or are at risk for poor outcome so that targeted support can be offered to staff and families. In addition, the agency staff can link profiles on the CAFAS to preferred treatment protocols. In some agencies, the CAFAS provides the cornerstone for utilization review activities, which focus on treating the youth in the least restrictive environment, as well as on responsibly managing the limited resources available. At the level of the agency, the database on the CAFAS can be used to achieve various tasks related to quality assurance, including genuine continuous quality improvement activities, as well as documentation for accreditation. The CAFAS database can be used for program evaluation, to study factors related to cost effectiveness, to reexamine guidelines regarding levels of care, and to maintain or seek new funding.

Understanding by Nonprofessional Audiences. The CAFAS is easily understood by nonprofessional parties, including caregivers, other professionals, and administrative or bureaucratic personnel concerned with fiscal or public policy issues. The CAFAS requires no interpretation. The arenas assessed are straightforward and meaningful in real life (e.g., school, home, etc.). Impairment is described primarily in terms of impact on everyday behavior (e.g., sent to a school authority figure because of failure to follow school rules, depression accompanied by refusal to go to school). Indicators of change over time can be qualitatively described for the individual youth and for groups of clients. Both consumers and other stakeholders can easily visualize how the youth is functioning and whether he or she has improved. Further, if treatment goals have not been successfully achieved, the CAFAS also provides the consumer, and others helping the consumer, with information on what behaviors still need to be changed.

Data on the CAFAS can be aggregated across clients to answer questions posed by administrative and legislative policy makers. Statistical tests can be performed on the quantitative scores generated by the CAFAS to help evaluate program effectiveness. The use of the CAFAS by policy makers in Michigan provides an example of how it can be used to study effectiveness of services, to generate an empirical basis for state-mandated guidelines (e.g., level of care criteria), to determine training needs, to encourage implementation of evidence-supported treatments at the state level, and to identify local programs that could potentially be developed as evidence-supported treatments to be disseminated statewide (Hodges & Wotring, 2002).

Easy Feedback and Uncomplicated Interpretation. The scores from the CAFAS are not derived or based on any scoring key or algorithm. When the rater identifies the items that are true for the youth, the score is determined for that subscale. The results are easily interpreted and require no further explanation than what is contained on the CAFAS form itself.

Usefulness in Clinical Services. This criterion is defined as the usefulness of the measure in describing the likelihood that the client needs services, helping in planning the array and levels of services, providing justification for the services for third-party payers, and helping to assess whether the client is responding to the treatment, and, if not, delineating the areas of functioning for which the treatment appears to be unsuccessful. The CAFAS is useful in accomplishing each of these clinically relevant tasks. The CAFAS can be useful in a variety of clinical functions, including documenting need for services, determining eligibility for levels of care, treatment planning, and treatment monitoring.

Compatibility With Clinical Theories and Practices. The CAFAS is not dependent on any given theory or view of child psychopathology. The CAFAS has been used to evaluate a variety of interventions; it is not dependent on a particular orientation. It assesses the positive effects of interventions. Irrespective of the intervention used, functioning will be measured in terms of how the youth performs at various age-appropriate life tasks. The spectrum of subscales covering various arenas of functioning also demonstrates improvement in specific areas, even if other areas have not changed.

Research Findings on Sensitivity to Assessing Change

The CAFAS consistently shows change as treatment progresses and the youth improves. In the Fort Bragg Evaluation Project, repeated-measures analysis of variance was conducted to determine whether impairment scores became lower over time. There was a significant main effect for time. From intake to 12 months, youth who were in residential care at intake had a drop in CAFAS total score from 64 to 34; for youth in alternative care at intake, the reduction was 54 to 29; and for the youth in outpatient care at intake, the reduction was from 41 to 23. At 18 months, the means for all three groups were within three points of one another (i.e., 22–25) (Hodges & Wong, 1996). Analyses collapsing across all groups also found the CAFAS to be sensitive to change. There was significant reduction in total CAFAS score from intake to 6 months ($d = .51$), from intake to 12 months ($d = .67$), and for intake to 18 months ($d = .78$). These effect sizes represent moderate to large effect sizes (Hodges et al., 1998).

An analysis of the national evaluation of the CMHS-funded grantees revealed a significant decrease in impairment from intake to 6 months (Hodges et al., 1999). Further, this study addressed the important question of whether the CAFAS is appropriate for assessing change for the variety of youths who may present with behavioral health problems. A series of repeated-measures analysis of variance was conducted to determine whether the CAFAS was affected by demographic group membership, nature of the child's problems, or risk factors. The dependent variable was total CAFAS score, with two levels (intake and 6 months postintake). A significant interaction would mean that some youth improved at a more rapid rate than others. All of the interactions for time by the various youth characteristics were nonsignificant. This means that although some youths were more impaired at intake than other youths, all of them improved. There were no interactions for demographic variables, including age, gender, race, family income, or custodial caregiver. Children referred from various agencies (e.g., mental health, social services, juvenile justice, school) improved at similar rates, as did youth with varying diagnoses. Youth with a history of difficulties in school, with the law, or with past mental health or substance use problems improved at a rate similar to that of children without those risk factors. Thus, the CAFAS was successful at documenting outcome along the entire spectrum of clinical need, from mild to severe impairment.

An outcome study conducted by one of the CMHS sites confirmed the same finding (Walrath, Mandell, & Leaf, 2001). Children demonstrated significant functional improvement from baseline to 6 months, regardless of referral source (i.e., school system, social services, juvenile justice, mental health), presenting problem, risk factors, age, or gender. The proportion of change did not differ significantly as a function of these demographic and risk factors.

Subsequent analyses of the CMHS national sample (Manteuffel et al., 2002) examined change from intake to 2 years for children enrolled in systems of care. A statistically significant improvement in functioning, as evidenced by a reduction in the CAFAS total score, was observed. In addition, the authors determined the proportion of youth who exhibited a clinically significant change, defined as a 20-point change in the total CAFAS score, because it approximated the Reliable Change Index (Jacobson & Truax, 1991). On the CAFAS, 49.5% met this criterion for successful outcome, compared to 44.8% for the CBCL (Achenbach, 1991). Outcome results for individual CMHS-funded sites have also been reported, revealing significant reduction in youth impairment (Resendez, Quist, & Matshazi, 2000; Rosenblatt & Furlong, 1998; Walrath, Mandell, & Leaf, 2001). Results for a large outcome study conducted for the state of Michigan revealed a significant reduction in impairment, with mostly moderate to large effects (Hodges et al., in press b).

CAFAS Outcome Indicators

Illustrations of various outcome indicators and how to derive them are available in the *Manual for Training Coordinators, Clinical Administrators, and Data Managers* (Hodges, 2002). Examples of various outcome indicators applied to actual clinical data are available in Hodges et al. (1998), Manteuffel et al. (2000), and Hodges et al. (2002, in press b, in press a). The indicators chosen for any given study would depend on the types of youths served and the primary goal of the intervention. A brief description of a selection of these indicators is provided here. Note that for the indicators that are proportions of youths who meet a specific criterion, the indicators can also be used to evaluate individual clients during treatment.

Change in Mean CAFAS Total Score. For aggregated data, the difference in the pre- and posttreatment scores for the sum of the eight youth subscales can be analyzed with paired *t* tests.

CAFAS Individual Subscale Scores. Paired *t* tests can also be used to assess change in each of the eight youth subscales and the caregiver scales. Figure 15.4 presents an illustration of the decrease in impairment scores observed from pre- to posttreatment.

Proportion of Youth With a Reduction in CAFAS Total Score. This indicator is scored as successfully achieved if the CAFAS total score from intake to exit (or last CAFAS evaluation) is reduced by 20 or more points. This represents a change equivalent to approximately a one half standard deviation in the total CAFAS score (Hodges &

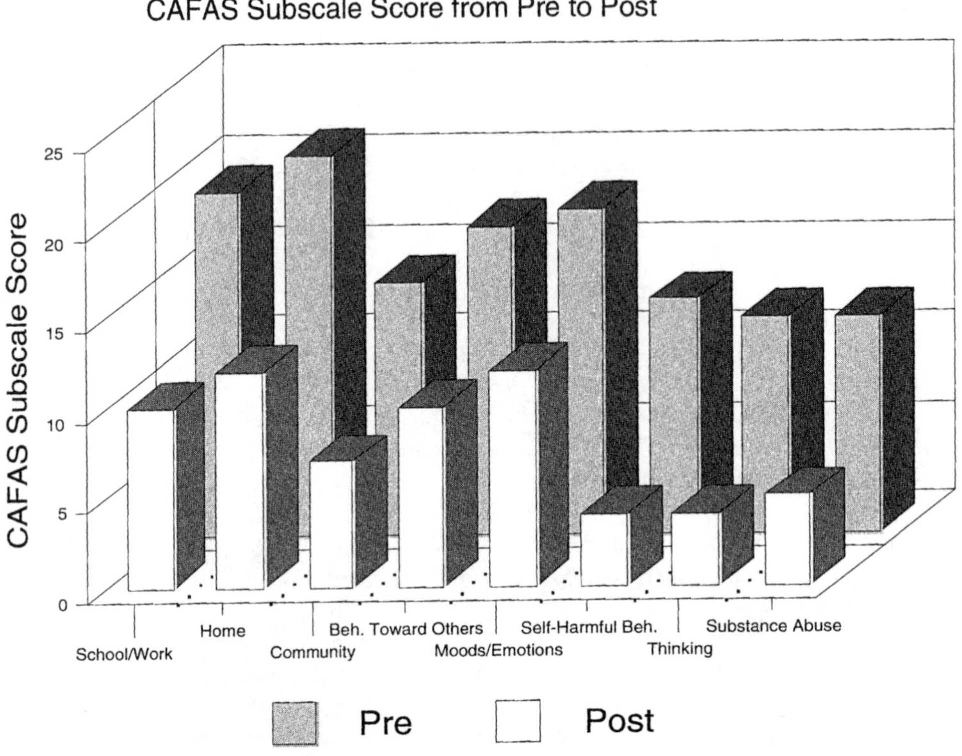

FIG. 15.4. Example graph showing pre- and postscores for the CAFAS subscales.

Xue, 2002; Hodges et al., in press b). Requiring a change of one-half standard deviation corresponds to a moderate effect size, as defined by Cohen (1988). A 20-point reduction was also used as a criterion of clinical significance by Manteuffel et al. (2002).

Proportion of Youth With No Severe Impairments at Exit. This indicator is applied to the subset of youths who were rated as severely impaired on one or more CAFAS subscales at intake. Youths meet this criterion if on their exit CAFAS they had no subscales rated as severely impaired.

Proportion of Youth With an Exit CAFAS ≤ 40. This indicator is the proportion of youths who, on their exit CAFAS, had a total CAFAS score of 40 or lower. This represents a target end-of-services functioning that most likely means that the youth is functioning well enough to be living in the community with a family and going to school or working.

Proportion of Youth With a Reduction in Impairment on Selected CAFAS Subscales. The outcome indicator is the proportion of youths whose CAFAS score decreased on selected subscales.

Proportion of Youths With a Reduction in Impairment on the CAFAS Target Subscale as Defined by CAFAS Tiers. This outcome indicator assumes that the highest priority of treatment is to effect a change in the behaviors that are the most problematic for the youth's development. For the purpose of this outcome indicator, the subscale(s) that resulted in the youth's assignment to the specific CAFAS Tiers category that he or she qualified for is considered the targeted subscale. For example, for youths in the thought problems subgroup, the Thinking subscale is considered the target scale. The criterion for improvement is reduction in impairment from the severe or moderate level to the mild or no/minimal impairment level. This indicator reflects a high level of success in reducing impairment in a domain of functioning that is likely the most critical for the youth. Youths in the mild impairment category are generally manageable in their natural environment (e.g., mainstream classroom in public school).

Elimination of Youth Risk Behaviors. Pre- and postcomparisons can be made on specific risk behaviors that can be measured by the presence or absence of each behavior or by the total number of risk behaviors present for a youth. The behaviors of the youth, which can put the youth or others at risk, are defined as: physical aggression in any setting, sexual inappropriateness in any setting, fire setting, runaway behavior, dangerous substance use, and suicidal talk or acts.

Use of Outcome Data at the Agency and State Level

CAFAS scores, combined with the other information obtained via the CAFAS Computer System, can be aggregated across clients to provide agency and state-level data for the purposes of: encouraging continuous quality improvement, informing system change and policy development, identifying training needs, and stimulating interest in evidence-supported treatments. The statewide data set collected by the state of Michigan has been used for these purposes (see Hodges & Wotring, 2002). Quarterly data reports are generated for each provider, and a state database is generated annually. The provider-specific reports are only shared with the concerned provider, whereas statewide data are shared with all providers. This report answers the following questions: Whom do we serve (i.e., demographic characteristics and risk factors present at intake)? What are the types and extent of youths' impairments at intake? What are the outcomes for youths (i.e., evaluates outcome for each of the CAFAS Tiers subgroupings and includes outcome to-date for long-term ongoing cases)? Are the client records up-to-date so that outcome can be continuously evaluated? Is the agency serving targeted youths? What types of services are being delivered? What are the treatment dropout rates and outcomes for closed cases (i.e., client has exited services)?

Because there are case-mix differences among the providers, direct comparison to the state database is not necessarily appropriate, although it can be informative. For example, the provider can determine whether other providers are also obtaining poorer outcome for specific client types. In the Michigan example (Hodges & Wotring, 2002), each provider received Excel graphs that displayed the data for each of these questions by fiscal year. This permitted each provider to determine whether they were making improvements in their own programs. This graphic presentation of outcome for different types of clients has stimulated interest among front-line practitioners in learning about evidence-based training, because their relative effectiveness is readily apparent. Because some providers use the data for advocating for services (e.g., press releases, accreditation, applying for grants), having the data available in graph form is helpful.

Precautions in Using the CAFAS as an Outcome Measure

For any assessment or outcome measure, it is important to try to ensure the integrity of data collected. The issue of maintaining integrity of data is similar to maintaining fidelity in clinical practice for evidence based treatments. For the CAFAS, it is critical to ensure that the CAFAS subscale scores are based on item endorsements, as specified by the directions. Thus, data should always be collected at the level of the individual item endorsements (which determine the score), rather than at the level of the subscale scores or total score. Global scores generally do not perform well as measures of outcome, most likely because of vulnerability to respondent bias (Hodges & Gust, 1995). Also, a record of these item endorsements should be kept in the youth's record to ensure that the rater had a basis for the scores, and the rater's signature should be placed on the form (in the place specified).

A second important issue in assessing change over time is to try to reduce information variance as a cause of differences in the youths' scores over time. Information variance can result from either differences in comprehensiveness of the information collected (e.g., that can arise from different interviewing styles) or from differences in the informants from whom information was sought (e.g., parent and youth only versus family members, school, and juvenile justice). Any means can be used to gather the information needed to rate the CAFAS (e.g., typical clinical interview in routine practice), as long as sufficient information to rate all items on the CAFAS is obtained. If needed, the structured interview and checklist designed for the CAFAS can be used.

Potential Use as a Data Source for Behavioral Health Service Report Cards

The CAFAS can be used as an outcome measure for behavioral health service report cards. The CAFAS was recommended by the Task Force convened by the Mental Health Statistics Improvement Program (MHSIP) of the Center for Mental Health Services to develop a consumer-oriented mental health report card (Mental Health Statistics Improvement Program Task Force, 1996). The CAFAS was recommended as a measure for evaluating children and adolescents with SED and for non-SED youth. The outcome indicators and the CAFAS scores selected by the MHSIP Task Force are as follows: (a) reduced psychological distress, (i.e., proportion of youth with a decreased level on the Moods/Emotions subscale), (b) reduced impairment from substance abuse, (i.e., proportion of youth with a decreased level on the Substance Use subscale), (c) improvement in school performance, (i.e., proportion of youth with decreased score on the School subscale), (d) reduced involvement in the criminal justice system, (i.e., proportion of youth with a decreased level on the Community subscale), (e) increased social integration, (i.e., proportion of youth with a decreased level on the Behavior Toward Others subscale), and (f) increased overall level of functioning, (i.e., proportion of youth with an decreased score for the CAFAS total scale).

CASE EXAMPLE

In this section, a case example is presented. It includes a summary of the information learned at intake, interpretation of the CAFAS scores based on the intake information, and a subsequent assessment made 6 months later.

Summary of Case at Intake

Jamie Foster is a 11-year-old girl who was placed in foster care approximately 2 weeks ago. The schoolteacher had reported that Jamie often came to school looking disheveled, and on two occasions recently smelled of alcohol. Jamie has never appeared to be intoxicated or high. Jamie had bragged to her classmates that she drank alcohol at home. Jamie's parents have never attended a parent conference at the school even though the teacher requested it. The teacher reported the alcohol incidents to social services, who documented that both Jamie's mother and stepfather are unemployed alcoholics who live on disability. Jamie's mother asserts that Jamie did not get the alcohol at home, but probably from the "bad kids" in the neighborhood. Jamie likes to "hang around" outside, where she watches older kids in the street. The mother reports that Jamie does not obey curfew because she likes to watch the "action." The parents were unresponsive to the concerns brought by up social services. They stated that they were unable to control Jamie around the issue of curfew and were unwilling to make a commitment to seek treatment for themselves. It did not appear that they could effectively keep Jamie from sneaking alcohol at home. Jamie has had no record with the juvenile justice; nor was there any evidence that Jamie has engaged in delinquent activities. The school reported that Jamie is quite smart but does not apply herself. She has a D average overall. She is somewhat of a management problem in the classroom, but the teacher feels that she can manage her as long as she "stays ahead of her" by managing Jamie's activities and opportunities. She thinks Jamie actually likes praise from adults. At school, Jamie has appeared sad or "down" for several days, but then she seems to "bounce back." The teacher says that Jamie has considerable difficulty in getting along with other youths. The teacher thinks this mainly results from poor social skills and a learned "bully" attitude she has picked up from older kids. Other kids either ignore or reject her because she acts this way. At her foster home, Jamie is still able to attend the same school, but is removed from the immediate neighborhood in which her parents live. Jamie can get to her old neighborhood by taking the city bus. The foster mom is concerned about Jamie sneaking out to her old neighborhood, especially after everyone goes to bed. The foster mother would also like help with managing Jamie's behavior at home, which she finds difficult because Jamie is as likely to disobey as obey when it comes to following rules and regulations. She would like to have on-call consultation available in case Jamie "runs" or becomes difficult when caught "running." Also, the foster mother reported that Jamie told her that she did not like to go to bed because sometimes she see figures changing in colors and shapes.

CAFAS Items Endorsed at Intake

The endorsed items by subscale (presented in abbreviated format) were as follows:

School: Grade average is lower than C (no. 19)

Home: Persistent failure to comply with reasonable rules and expectations within the home (no. 51)

Community: Youth does not negatively impact on the community (no. 84)

Behavior Toward Others: Persistent problems / difficulties in relating to peers (no. 101)

Moods/Emotions: Sad / anhedonic in at least one setting for up to a few days at a time (no. 133)

Self-harmful Behavior: Behavior is not indicative of tendencies toward self-harm (no. 151)

Substance Use: For ≤ 12 years, occasional use without intoxication or becoming high (no. 170)

Thinking: Unusual perceptual experiences not qualifying as pathological hallucinations (no. 196)

CAFAS Scores and Profile at Intake

Jamie's total score at intake is 100, placing her in the overall level of dysfunction category, indicating that services more intensive or supportive than outpatient may be needed. Jamie's profile at intake is represented by the solid line on Fig. 15.3. The subscale scores and impairment levels by subscale are as follows:

School: Moderate Impairment (20)

Home: Moderate Impairment (20)

Community: No Impairment (0)

Behavior Toward Others: Moderate Impairment (20)

Moods/Emotions: Mild Impairment (10)

Self-harmful Behavior: No Impairment (0)

Substance Use: Moderate Impairment (20)

Thinking: Mild Impairment (10)

CAFAS Youth Risk Behaviors at Intake

No items suggesting risk behaviors (e.g., suicidal/ideation behavior, aggression, sexual behavior, fire setting, runaway behavior, psychotic or organic symptoms, or severe substance use) were identified.

Treatment Plan at Intake

A treatment plan is designed, based on the behavioral items endorsed on the CAFAS, and the goals and strengths endorsed for each subscale. In Fig. 15.4, an example treatment plan is presented for Jamie Foster. When using the CAFAS software, the rater simply writes in the specifics under the heading "Plan," because the remainder of the Treatment Plan is automatically set up by the software. Because there was no impairment for two of the subscales, Community and Self-harmful Behavior, they do not appear in Fig. 15.4.

Subsequent Evaluation at 3 Months Postintake

At 3 months postintake, Jamie was reassessed, using the last 30 days as the time period being rated. Jamie's functioning has improved considerably. When she first moved to the foster home, Jamie's behavior was similar to what it had been at home. She continued to engage in verbal fights and bullying other kids. She attempted to leave the foster home presumably to visit her old neighborhood or to make contact with "street youth" in her new neighborhood. She also stayed out passed curfew until stronger controls were established. Much of Jamie's behavior has improved, but she still has problems getting along with other kids, quarreling with them or picking on them. She is still showing poor effort at school, although she is no longer doing below average overall. In the foster home, she needs to be watched to be sure she does her assigned chores. Jamie expresses worry about her parents' chances of accepting the need for services and whether the treatment will be successful. Her stepfather disappeared when pressed to go for treatment. Her mother was resistant for 3 months, but has recently indicated willingness to initiate inpatient treatment. Jamie also worries that her mother does not love her anymore. Although she is sad about her mother and stepfather, she is able to sleep at night. She reports feeling much safer now that she is not around her former friends as much. However, she stills gets stomachaches when she thinks about her parents. The unusual perceptual experiences have disappeared with the reduction in the anxiety level. Although Jamie no longer has access to, or drinks, alcohol regularly, there were two instances when her breath smelled like alcohol. Jamie is proud of her progress and her accomplishments. She is beginning to see the benefits of active, positive coping strategies. She is understandably sad about her parents' impairments but has come to appreciate the attentive and caring attitude of her foster parents. The CAFAS items endorsed at 3 months were as follows:

School: School productivity is less than expected for abilities (no. 26)

Home: Has to be watched or prodded to get her to do chores or comply with requests (no. 58)

Community: Does not negatively impact on the community (no. 84)

Behavior Toward Others: Unusually quarrelsome, argumentative, or annoying to others (no. 103)

Moods/Emotions: Often anxious or sad, with related symptom (e.g., stomachaches) (no. 128)

Self-harmful Behavior: Not indicative of tendencies toward self-harm (no. 151)

Substance Use: For $\leq$ 12 years, used substances more than once in the rating period (no. 174)

Thinking: Thought as reflected by communication is not disordered or eccentric (no. 198)

The above item endorsements would result in a total score of 50, which is a reduction of 50 points from her total score of 100 at intake. On the CAFAS Profile in Fig. 15.3 the dotted line depicts her scores at 3 months. For the sake of brevity, the revised treatment plan done at 3 months is not presented. However, it is noteworthy that an item that was a problem at intake (i.e., below-average grade average) becomes a strength at 3 months (i.e., average or above-average grades). Over time, specific functioning in various domains can be tracked so that any failure to make progress or slippage into poorer performance will not be missed and can be attended to as soon as it is observed. Also, tracking both the youth's and caregiver's behaviors permits looking at the relationship of the two, to see if deterioration or improvement in the youth appears to be related to the youth's environment.

SUMMARY

Extensive evidence of reliability, validity, and sensitivity to assessing change has been generated for the CAFAS since its development in 1989. The CAFAS permits integrating intake assessment, treatment planning, treatment monitoring, and outcome evaluation. It works equally well for youth with behavioral or emotional problems who are served by juvenile justice, child welfare, education, or mental health. There are numerous examples of states and agencies using outcome results generated by the CAFAS to impact services and policies. Quantitative changes on the CAFAS reflect meaningful qualitative changes in day-to-day functioning that have wide appeal (e.g., keep kids in school, in their own home, out of trouble). Further, the CAFAS can be used not only for assessing outcome but also as one of the criteria for demonstrating need for services and for qualifying for specific levels of care. The youth's pattern of scores across the eight domain areas can be used to guide protocols for interventions, including evidence-based treatments. Even more important, the CAFAS can be readily understood by families who are entitled to influence and understand decisions that affect the services their children receive.

Typically, outcome measures have been offensive to practitioners, who view them as increasing paperwork yet adding little value to planning or actual treatment. This is exacerbated when the outcome results are turned over to an oversight authority before the staff have any information on how the data reflect on their program. The CAFAS minimizes these negative elements. The practitioner can use the CAFAS to monitor the progress of treatment for the purpose of maximizing therapeutic gains. The CAFAS is also intended to be an aid to treatment planning, as it links problem behaviors to related strengths and goals. The graphic depiction of the CAFAS scores on both the CAFAS Profile and on the computerized CAFAS client report helps all persons involved in the youth's care, including the family, focus on extent of improvement in the most important domains of functioning. In this respect, the CAFAS is the practitioner's ally.

The increasing requirements for collecting outcome data and for matching client needs to resource allocation are onerous, yet they provide an opportunity for practitioners to become actively involved in generating ideas for increasing clinical effectiveness, based on empirical data. Rather than being a burden, this leads to increased morale if the practitioner is centrally involved, rather than simply being judged after the fact (Hodges & Wotring, 2002). To the extent that practitioners and clinical managers engage in ongoing efforts to examine outcome and improve services, it is potentially a win–win situation for all stakeholders. These activities will provide insight into the types of services and programs that are most effective for different types of clients.

REFERENCES

Achenbach, T. M. (1991). *Manual for the Child Behavior Checklist/4–18 and 1991 Profile.* Burlington: University of Vermont Department of Psychiatry.

American Psychiatric Association. (1994). *Diagnostic and statistical manual of mental disorders* (4th ed.). Washington, DC: Author.

Binck, D. (1997). *Reliability and validity of a multidimensional measure of functioning: The Preschool and Early Childhood Functional Assessment Scale (PECFAS).* Unpublished master's thesis, Eastern Michigan University, Ypsilanti.

Bird, H., Davies, M., Fisher, P., Narrow, W., Jensen, P., Hoven, C., et al. (2000). How specific is specific impairment? *Journal of the American Child and Adolescent Psychiatry, 39,* 1182–1189.

Bird, H. R., Yager, T. J., Staghezza, B., Gould, M. S., Canino, G., & Rubio-Stipec, M. (1990). Impairment in the epidemiological measurement of childhood psychopathology in the community. *Journal of the American Academy of Child and Adolescent Psychiatry, 29,* 796–803.

Breda, C. S. (1996). Methodological issues in evaluating mental health outcomes of a children's mental health managed care demonstration. *The Journal of Mental Health Administration,* 23(1), 40–50.

Burns, B. J., Hoagwood, K., & Mrazek, P. J. (1999). Effective treatment for mental disorders in children and adolescents. *Clinical Child and Family Psychology Review, 2*, 199–254.

Cohen, J. (1988). *Statistical power analysis for the behavioral sciences* (2nd ed.). Hillsdale, NJ: Lawrence Erlbaum Associates.

Doucette-Gates, A., Hodges, K., & Liao, Q. (1998). Using the Child and Adolescent Functional Assessment Scale: Examining child outcomes and service use patterns. In J. Willis, C. Liberton, K. Kutash, & R. M. Friedman (Eds.), *Proceeding of the 11th Annual Research Conferences: A System of Care for Children's Mental Health: Expanding the Research Base* (pp. 333–340), Tampa, FL: Research & Training Center for Children's Mental Health.

Freidman, R. M., Katz-Leavy, J. W., Manderscheid, R. W., & Sondheimer, D. L. (1996). Prevalence of serious emotional disturbance in children and adolescents. In R. W. Manderscheid & M.A. Sonnerschein (Eds.), *SAMHSA, Center for Mental Health Services Mental Health, United States*, 1996 (pp. 71–89). Tiburon, CA: Centralink Publications, Washington, DC.

Georgetown University National Technical Assistance Center for Children's Mental Health. (2002). *Evaluation initiative*. Retrieved December 13, 2002, from http://www.georgetown.edu/research/gucdc/eval.html

Hoagwood, K., Burns, B. J., Kiser, L., Ringeisen, H., & Schoenwald, S. K. (2001). Evidence-based practice in child and adolescent mental health services. *Psychiatric Services, 52*, 1179–1189.

Hodges, K. (1990). *Child Assessment Schedule–Parent Form* (3rd ed.) Ypsilanti: Eastern Michigan University.

Hodges, K. (1993). Structured interviews for assessing children. *Journal of Child Psychology and Psychiatry, 34*, 49–68.

Hodges, K. (1994). *CAFAS parent report*. Ypsilanti: Eastern Michigan University.

Hodges, K. (1995a). *CAFAS checklist for adult informant*. Ypsilanti: Eastern Michigan University.

Hodges, K. (1995b). *CAFAS checklist for youths*. Ypsilanti: Eastern Michigan University.

Hodges, K. (1995c). *PECFAS parent report*. Ypsilanti: Eastern Michigan University.

Hodges, K. (1995d). *Preschool and Early Childhood Functional Assessment Scale* (3rd ed.). Ypsilanti: Eastern Michigan University.

Hodges, K. (1995e, March). *Psychometric study of a telephone interview for the CAFAS using an expanded version of the scale*. Paper presented at the eighth annual research conference: A System of Care for Children's Mental Health: Expanding the Research Base, University of South Florida, Florida Mental Health Institute, Research and Training Center for Children's Mental Health, Tampa, FL.

Hodges, K. (1997). *PECFAS parent report screener*. Ypsilanti: Eastern Michigan University.

Hodges, K. (1998a). *CAFAS parents' goals for their child*. Ypsilanti: Eastern Michigan University.

Hodges, K. (1998b). *CAFAS parents' goals for their family*. Ypsilanti: Eastern Michigan University.

Hodges, K. (2000a). *Child and Adolescent Functional Assessment Scale* (3rd ed.). Ypsilanti: Eastern Michigan University.

Hodges, K. (2000b). *Child and Adolescent Functional Assessment Scale Self-training Manual* (3rd ed.). Ypsilanti: Eastern Michigan University.

Hodges, K. (2002). *Manual for training coordinators, clinical administrators, and data managers* (2nd ed.). Ypsilanti: Eastern Michigan University.

Hodges, K., & Chamberlain, J. (2002, July). *Using CAFAS to identify empirically-based treatments and level of care needed for youths in foster care*. Paper presented at the Foster Family–Based Treatment Association 16th Annual Conference on Treatment Foster Care, Chicago.

Hodges, K., Doucette-Gates, A., & Kim, C. S. (2000). Predicting service utilization with the Child and Adolescent Functional Assessment Scale in a sample of youths with serious emotional disturbance served by Center for Mental Health Services–funded demonstrations. *The Journal of Behavioral Health Services & Research, 27*, 47–59.

Hodges, K., Doucette-Gates, A., & Liao, Q. (1999). The relationship between the Child and Adolescent Functional Assessment Scale (CAFAS) and indicators of functioning. *Journal of Child and Family Studies, 8*(1), 109–122.

Hodges, K., & Gust, J. (1995). Measures of impairment for children and adolescents. *Journal of Mental Health Administration, 22*, 403–413.

Hodges, K., & Kim, C. S. (2000). Psychometric study of the Child and Adolescent Functional Assessment Scale: Prediction of contact with the law and poor school attendance. *Journal of Abnormal Child Psychology, 28*, 287–297.

Hodges, K., & Wong, M. M. (1996). Psychometric characteristics of a multidimensional measure to assess impairment: The Child and Adolescent Functional Assessment Scale (CAFAS). *Journal of Child and Family Studies, 5*, 445–467.

Hodges, K., & Wong, M. M. (1997). Use of the Child and Adolescent Functional Assessment Scale to predict service utilization and cost. *Journal of Mental Health Administration, 24*, 278–290.

Hodges, K., Wong, M. M., & Latessa, M. (1998). Use of the Child and Adolescent Functional Assessment Scale (CAFAS) as an outcome measure in clinical settings. *The Journal of Behavioral Health Services and Research, 25*, 325–336.

Hodges, K., & Wotring, J. (2000). Client typology based on functioning across domains using the CAFAS: Implications for service planning. *The Journal of Behavioral Health Services & Research, 27*, 257–270.

Hodges, K., & Wotring, J. (2002). *Role of monitoring quality of care in initiating implementation of evidence-based treatments at a state level.* Manuscript submitted for publication.

Hodges, K., & Xue, Y. (2002). *CAFAS outcome indicators using data from the CMHS-funded comparison study.* Manuscript submitted for publication.

Hodges, K., Xue, Y., & Wotring, J. (2001, February). *Relationship between rate of improvement on the CAFAS and youth, family, and treatment characteristics.* Paper presented at the 14th annual research conference, A System of Care for Children's Mental Health: Expanding the Research Base, Tampa, FL: University of South Florida, the Louis de la Parte Florida Mental Health Institute, Research and Training Center for Children's Mental Health.

Hodges, K., Xue, Y., & Wotring, J. (2002). Presence of multiple and pervasive problems as prognostic indicators of outcome for youth with SED. Manuscript submitted for publication.

Hodges, K., Xue, Y., & Wotring, J. (in press a). Outcomes for children with problematic behavior in school and at home served by public mental health. *Journal of Emotional and Behavioral Disorders.*

Hodges, K., Xue, Y., & Wotring, J. (in press b). Use of the CAFAS to evaluate outcome for youths with SED served by public mental health. *Journal of Child and Family Studies.*

Holden, E. W., Friedman, R. M., & Santiago, R. L. (2001). Overview of the national evaluation of the Comprehensive Community Mental Health Services for Children and Their Families Program. *Journal of Emotional and Behavioral Disorders, 9*(1), 4–12.

Jacobson, N. S., & Truax, P. (1991). Clinical significance: A statistical approach to defining meaningful change in psychotherapy research. *Journal of Consulting and Clinical Psychology, 59*, 12–19.

Kazdin, A. E., & Kendall, P. C. (1998). Current progress and future plans for developing effective treatments: Comments and perspectives. *Journal of Clinical Child Psychology, 27*(2), 217–226.

Kazdin, A. E., Mazurick, J. L., & Siegel, T. C. (1994). Treatment outcome among children with externalizing disorder who terminate prematurely versus those who complete psychotherapy. *Journal of the American Academy of Child Adolescent Psychiatry, 33*, 549–557.

Kazdin, A. E., & Weisz, J. R. (1998). Identifying and developing empirically supported child and adolescent treatments. *Journal of Consulting and Clinical Psychology, 66*(1), 19–36.

Lemoine, R. L., & McDermott, B. E. (1997). Assessing levels and profiles of service need using the CAFAS. In: C. J. Liberton, K. Kutash, & R. M. Friedman (Eds.), *Proceedings of the 10th Annual Research Conference: A system of care for children's mental health: Expanding the Research Base* (pp. 371–375). Tampa, FL: Research & Training Center for Children's Mental Health.

Loseth, R., Carlson, S., Lucht, J., & Schmid, C. O. (2003). Addressing mental health concerns in early childhood: A system for early identification and evaluating effectiveness. In C. Newman, C. J. Liberton, K. Kutash, & R. M. Friedman (Eds.), *Proceedings of the 15th Annual Research Conference: A System of Care for Children's Mental Health: Expanding the Research Base* (pp. 410–412). Tampa, FL: University of South Florida, The Louis de la Parte Florida Mental Health Institute, Research and Training Center for Children's Mental Health.

Manteuffel, B., Stephens, R., & Santiago, R. (2002). Overview of the national evaluation of the Comprehensive Community Mental Health Services for Children and Their Families Program and summary of current findings. *Children's Services: Social Policy, Research, and Practice, 5*(1), 3–20.

Mental Health Statistics Improvement Program Task Force. (1996, April). The MHSIP Consumer-Oriented Mental Health Report Card. *Substance Abuse and Mental Health Services Administration: Center for Mental Health Services.* Washington, DC: U.S. Department of Health & Human Services.

Murphy, J. M., Pagano, M. E., Ramirez, A., Anaya, Y., Nowlin, C., & Jellinek, M. S. (1999). Validation of the Preschool and Early Childhood Functional Assessment Scale (PECFAS). *Journal of Child and Family Studies, 8*, 343–356.

Newman, F. L., Ciarlo, J. A., & Carpenter, D. (1999). Guidelines for selecting psychological instruments for treatment planning and outcome assessment. In. M. E. Maruish, *The use of psychological testing for treatment planning and outcomes assessment* (pp. 153–170). Mahwah, NJ: Lawrence Erlbaum Associates.

Nunnally, J. C. (1978). *Psychometric theory* (2nd ed.). New York: McGraw-Hill.

Osher, T. (1998). Outcomes and accountability from a family perspective. *The Journal of Behavioral Health Services & Research, 25*(2), 230–232.

Pernice, F., Gust, J., & Hodges, K. (1997). *A structured interview for collecting objective outcome data in clinical settings.* Paper presented at the 10th Annual Research Conference: A System of Care for Children's

Mental Health, the Research and Training Center for Children's Mental Health, Tampa, FL: University of South Florida, The Louis de la Parte Florida Mental Health Institute, Research and Training Center for Children's Mental Health.

Quist, R., & Matshazi, D. (2000). The Child and Adolescent Functional Assessment Scale (CAFAS): A dynamic predictor of juvenile recidivism. *Adolescence, 35*(137), 181–192.

Resendez, M. G., Quist, R. M., & Matshazi, D. G. M. (2000). A longitudinal analysis of family empowerment of families and client outcomes. *Journal of Child and Family Studies, 9*, 449–460.

Rosenblatt, J., & Furlong, M. (1998). Outcomes in a system of care for youths with emotional and behavioral disorders: An examination of differential change across clinical profiles. *Journal of Child and Family Studies, 7*, 217–232.

Rosenblatt, J. A., & Rosenblatt, A. (1999). Youth functional status and academic achievement in collaborative mental health and education programs: Two California care systems. *The Journal of Emotional and Behavioral Disorders, 7*(1), 21–30, 53.

Rosenblatt, J. A., Rosenblatt, A., & Biggs, E. E. (2000). Criminal behavior and emotional disorder: Comparing youth served by the mental health and juvenile justice systems. *The Journal of Behavioral Health Services & Research, 27*, 227–237.

Substance Abuse and Mental Health Services Administration. (1993). Final notice establishing definitions for (1) Children with a serious emotional disturbance, and (2) adults with a serious mental illness. *Federal Register, 58*, 29422–29425.

Wale, H., Barckholtz, P., & Denter, L. (in press). *Evidence for standardizing and tracking evaluations for hospitalization in a crisis intervention program.* In C. Newman, C. J. Liberton, K. Kutash, & R. M. Friedman (Eds.), *Proceedings of the 16th Annual Research Conference on a System of Care for Children's Mental Health: Expanding the Research Base*, Tampa, FL: University of South Florida, The Louis de la Parte Florida Mental Health Institute, Research and Training Center for Children's Mental Health.

Walrath, C., dosReis, S., Miech, R., Liao, Q., Holden, W., DeCarolis, G., et al. (2001). Referral source differences in functional impairment levels for children served in the Comprehensive Community Mental Health Services for Children and Their Families Program. *Journal of Child & Family Studies, 10*, 385–397.

Walrath, C., Mandell, D., & Leaf, P. (2001). Responses of children with different intake profiles to mental health treatment. *Psychiatric Services, 52*(2), 196–201.

Walrath, C. M., Mandell, D. S., Liao, Q., Holden, E. W., DeCarolis, G., Santiago, R. L., et al. (2001). Suicide attempts in the "comprehensive community mental health services for children and their families" program. *Journal of the American Academy of Child and Adolescent Psychiatry, 40*, 1197–1205.

Walrath, C. M., Nickerson, K. J., Crowel, R. L., & Leaf, P. J. (1998). Serving children with serious emotional disturbance in a system of care: Do mental health and non-mental health agency referrals look the same? *The Journal of Emotional and Behavioral Disorders, 6*(4), 205–213.

Walrath, C. M., Sharp, M. J., Zuber, M., & Leaf, P. (2001). Serving children with SED in urban systems of care: Referral agency differences in child characteristics in Baltimore and the Bronx. *The Journal of Emotional and Behavioral Disorders, 9*(2), 94–105.

Xue, Y., Hodges, K., & Wotring, J. (in press). *Extra strength treatment needed: Predictors of poor outcome for children with behavioral problems.* In C. Newman, C. J. Liberton, K. Kutash, & R. M. Friedman (Eds.), *Proceedings of the 16th Annual Research Conference Proceedings: On a System of Care for Children's Mental Health: Expanding the Research Base*, Tampa, FL: University of South Florida, The Louis de la Parte Florida Mental Health Institute, Research and Training Center for Children's Mental Health.

Xue, Y., Hodges, K., & Wotring, J. (in press). *Implementing evidence-based treatments for mood-impaired youths: The need for considering co-occurring problems.* In C. Newman, C. J. Liberton, K. Kutash, & R. M. Friedman (Eds.), *Proceedings of the 16th Annual Research Conference on a System of Care for Children's Mental Health: Expanding the Research Base*, Tampa, FL: University of South Florida, The Louis de la Parte Florida Mental Health Institute, Research and Training Center for Children's Mental Health.

Zima, B. T., Bussing, R., Crecelius, G. M., Kaufman, A., & Belin, T. R. (1999). Psychotropic medication treatment patterns among school-aged children in foster care. *Journal of Child and Adolescent Psychopharmacology, 9*(3), 135–147.

16

The Child Health Questionnaire (CHQ) and Psychological Assessments: A Brief Update

Jeanne M. Landgraf
HealthAct

INTRODUCTION

Until the mid–late 1990s, few measures were available for assessing the general health-related quality of life in children and adolescents. Their application was often limited to use within well-controlled clinical trials. Today, however, quality of life has become increasingly prominent in practice-based research, and there are a number of scholarly publications that provide comprehensive overviews and summaries of both generic and condition-specific measures for children and adolescents and their use across a variety of settings (Bullinger, Mackensen, & Landgraf, 1994; Drotar, 1998; Eiser & Morse, 2001; Koot & Wallander, 2001; Landgraf, 1999, 2001; Landgraf, Ravens-Sierber, & Bullinger, 1997; Lollar, Simeonsson, & Nanda, 2000; Rodrigue, Geffken, & Streisand, 2000). The increase in the use of quality-of-life measures for children and adolescents may be in part because of the changing dynamic in the health care environment, an increased awareness that health is multidimensional (i.e., both physical and psychosocial), an increased understanding of different assessment methods (such as Likert, Guttman, Item Response Theory, Utility Indices, Standard Gamble) and refinements to quality-of-life measures themselves.

To be truly useful as an evaluative tool for practitioners and clinical decision-makers, pediatric instruments must reflect the cultural uniqueness of this population, be developmentally sensitive and multidimensional in scope—capturing both the physical and psychosocial well-being of children and adolescents (Landgraf & Abetz, 1996). An assessment tool must not only measure a child's capacity to engage in physical activities, but provide evidence concerning the degree of limitation he or she may experience in accomplishing different tasks that involve dexterity, motor skill, and exertion, (Landgraf, Abetz, & Ware, 1996, 1999). To be considered conceptually robust, both a child's internal health—emotional status and self-esteem—and his or her external or observable well-being, such as behavioral problems or social limitations, must be captured. Finally, because children live within a family structure, however uniquely this unit may be defined, understanding the impact or outcome of therapeutic interventions on the family should be an essential component of the assessment process. (Landgraf & Abetz, 1996; Landgraf et al., 1996, 1999).

OVERVIEW

The Child Health Questionnaire (CHQ) is a general quality-of-life instrument that can be used irrespective of a child's age or gender. It was designed for use with children or adolescents with or without a physical or psychological health issue. The CHQ provides the clinical practitioner with insights into parental perceptions concerning their child's emotional, physical, and social well-being. The CHQ also measures the impact that the child's health and well-being has on the parent and family.

The name CHQ actually refers to a family of instruments; there are complementary versions for self-completion by parents and children themselves. The parent-completed version is available in two lengths—50 items (CHQ–PF50) and 28 items (CHQ–PF28). The PF28 captures the same concepts as the PF50, but with fewer items. Standard Flesch–Kincaid reading estimates (Lapp & Flood, 1978) as computed in Microsoft Word suggest that the parent forms are understandable for 80% of English-speakers with a fourth-grade reading level. The parent versions have been normed in a general U.S. population for children 5 years of age and older. The CHQ–PF28 may be more appropriate for large samples and population-based studies.

The child self-report version is 87 items (CHQ–CF87) and captures the same general concepts as the parent report. Standard Flesch–Kincaid reading estimates (Lapp & Flood, 1978) as computed in Microsoft Word suggest that the self-report version is understandable for 85% of children in the third grade. It is recommended for completion by children at least 10 years of age or older. Development of a shorter more practical length version and age and gender-specific norms are planned for the CHQ–CF87.

Table 16.1 identifies the concepts and corresponding number of items found in the CHQ–PF50, –PF28, and –CF87. The majority of the concepts are captured using multiple items and a graduated response continuum (e.g., All of the time–None of the time). The standard 4-week time recall is also used. Concepts common to the parent and child self-report version include the following: physical functioning; general health; pain; mental health; self-esteem; behavior; role/social limitations—physical, emotional, or behavioral; family limitations; family cohesion; and change in health. The parent form also includes two additional scales: emotional impact and time impact.

Table 16.2 provides the item content and response options for scales and items in the CHQ–PF50. To briefly summarize, the Physical Functioning scale measures the presence and extent of physical limitations because of health problems. General Health is a subjective assessment of overall health, illness, and resilience. Bodily Pain measures intensity and frequency of general pain and discomfort. Mental Health measures frequency of both negative and positive emotional states. Self-Esteem measures satisfaction with school and athletic ability, looks and appearance, ability to get along with others and family, and life overall. Behavior measures overt behavior as a component of mental health by assessing the frequency of behavior problems such as aggression, delinquency, hyperactivity and impulsivity, and social withdrawal. Role/Social limitations measure limitations in the kind, amount, and performance of schoolwork and activities with friends because of emotional, behavioral, or physical difficulties. Family Activities measures the frequency of disruption in usual family activities, such as eating meals or watching television. Family Cohesion is a single item that provides an overall perception of family relationships. Parental Impact—Emotional captures the degree of anxiety and concern the parent feels with regard to his or her child's emotional, behavioral, or physical well-being. Parent Impact—Time assesses the degree to which the parent's time to attend to personal needs is impacted by his or her child's emotional, behavioral, or physical well-being. Change in health is a single item that

TABLE 16.1
Number of Items in Different Lengths of the Child Health Questionnaire

Scales[a]	Parent Completed PF50	Parent Completed PF28	Child Completed CF87
Physical Functioning	6	3	9
Role/Social–Emotional	} 3	} 1	3
Role/Social–Behavioral			3
Role/Social–Physical	2	1	3
Bodily Pain	2	1	2
General Behavior	6	4	17
Mental Health	5	3	16
Self-esteem	6	3	14
General Health Perceptions	6	4	12
Change in Health	1	1	1
Parental Impact—Emotional	3	2	—[b]
Parental Impact—Time	3	2	—[b]
Family Activities	6	2	6
Family Cohesion	1	1	1
Number of concepts	14[c]	14	12
Number of items	50	28	87

[a] Scales are listed in the order they appear in all versions of the CHQ.
[b] These scales are not included in the child-competed version of the CHQ.
[c] Role/Social–Emotional and Role/Social–Behavioral count as two separate concepts, though the items are combined.
Table reproduced in part with permission (Landgraf et al., 1999, p. 32).

measures improvement, stability, or decline in the child's health during the previous year.

Each concept measured in the CHQ yields an independent scale score. For ease of interpretation, raw scale scores are transformed on a 0 to 100 continuum, with 0 representing the lowest score possible and 100 representing the highest possible score. Table 16.3 presents a brief explanation for interpreting CHQ scores. In general, a score of 100 indicates excellent health overall, optimal physical functioning, a high sense of self and emotional well-being, the ability to get along with others, and very little negative impact on the parent and family. Conversely, a low score suggests that the child is in poor overall health, is limited in daily physical activities, does not get along well with others or exhibits negative behaviors, and that the family is negatively impacted by the child's health and psychosocial well-being. The scale scores are often referred to as the CHQ profile, because they provide information across all the individual concepts—14 for the parent forms and 12 for the child self-report.

To be more useful to providers and make it easier to interpret findings, it is also possible to derive an overall "summary" of the concepts for the parent forms only. Figure 16.1 provides a graphic illustration of the measurement model underlying the summary scoring method. Summary scoring is currently only available for the parent-completed from. Development of summary scoring for the self-report version will commence once a short form has been derived and thoroughly tested.

There are actually two summary components—physical and psychosocial health. These component scores have been shown to account for 59.2 percent of the total measured variance in a general sample of 914 children in the United States (Landgraf et al., 1996, 1999). The mean summary score for either component is set to 50,

TABLE 16.2
List of Items[a] and Response Options[b] Found on the CHQ–PF50

1. In general, would you say your child's health is:
2. Has your child been limited in any of the following activities due to health problems?
   a. Doing things that take a lot of energy, such as playing soccer or running?
   b. Doing things that take some energy, such as riding a bike or skating?
   c. Ability (physically) to get around the neighborhood, playground, or school?
   d. Walking one block or climbing one flight of stairs?
   e. Bending, lifting, or stooping?
   f. Taking care of him/herself, that is, eating, dressing, bathing, or going to the toilet?
3. Has your child's school work or activities with friends been limited in any of the following ways due to EMOTIONAL difficulties or problems with his/her BEHAVIOR?
   a. Limited in the KIND of schoolwork or activities with friends he/she could do
   b. Limited in the AMOUNT of time he/she could spend on schoolwork or activities with friends
   c. Limited in PERFORMING schoolwork or activities with friends (it took extra effort)
4. Has your child's school work or activities with friends been limited in any of the following ways due to problems with his/her PHYSICAL health?
   a. Limited in the KIND of schoolwork or activities with friends he/she could do
   b. Limited in the AMOUNT of time he/she could spend on schoolwork or activities with friends

5a. How much bodily pain or discomfort has your child had?
5b. How often has your child had bodily pain or discomfort?

6. How often has each of the following statements described your child?
   a. Argued a lot
   b. Had difficulty concentrating or paying attention
   c. Lied or cheated
   d. Stole things inside or outside the home
   e. Had tantrums or a hot temper
   f. Compared to other children your child's age, in general would you say his/her behavior is:
7. How much of the time do you think your child:
   a. Felt like crying?
   b. Felt lonely?
   c. Acted nervous?
   d. Acted bothered or upset?
   e. Acted cheerful?
8. How satisfied do you think your child has felt about:
   a. His/her school ability?
   b. His/her athletic ability?
   c. His/her friendships?
   d. His/her looks/appearance?
   e. His/her family relationships?
   f. His/her life overall?
9. How true or false is each of these statements for your child?
   a. My child seems to be less healthy than other children I know.
   b. My child has never been seriously ill.
   c. When there is something going around, my child usually catches it.
   d. I expect my child will have a very healthy life.
   e. I worry more about my child's health than other people worry about their children's health.
   f. Compared to one year ago, how would you rate your child's health now:
10. How much emotional worry or concern did each of the following cause you?
    a. Your child's physical health
    b. Your child's emotional well-being or behavior
    c. Your child's attention or learning abilities

(Continued)

TABLE 16.2
(*Continued*)

11. Were you limited in the amount of time you had for your own needs because of:
    a. Your child's physical health
    b. Your child's emotional well-being or behavior
    c. Your child's attention or learning abilities
12. How often has your child's health or behavior:
    a. limited the types of activities you could do as a family?
    b. interrupted various everyday family activities (eating meals, watching TV)?
    c. limited your ability as a family to "pick up and go" on a moment's notice?
    d. caused tension or conflict in your home?
    e. been a source of disagreements or arguments in your family?
    f. caused you to cancel or change plans (personal or work) at the last minute?
13. Sometimes families may have difficulty getting along with one another. They do not always agree and they may get angry. In general, how would you rate your family's ability to get along with one another?

Note: Reproduced with permission from Landgraf, 2003, content taken from CHQ user manual 1996, pp. 364–369.

[a] A 4-week recall period is used for all scales except for the Change in Health (CH) and Family Cohesion (FC) items and the General Health (GH) scale. The recall stem for Change in Health is "compared to last year."

[b] Options include the following: Excellent, Very good, Good, Fair, Poor • Yes, limited a lot; Yes, limited some; Yes, limited a little; No, not limited • None, Very mild, Mild, Moderate, Severe, Very severe • None of the time, Once or twice, A few times, Fairly often, Very often, Every/Almost every day • Very often, Fairly often, Sometimes, Almost never, Never • All of the time, Most of the time, Some of the time, A little of the time, None of the time • Very satisfied, Somewhat satisfied, Neither satisfied nor dissatisfied, Somewhat dissatisfied, Very dissatisfied • Definitely true, Mostly true, Don't know, Mostly false, Definitely false • Much better now than 1 year ago, Somewhat better now than 1 year ago, About the same now as 1 year ago, Somewhat worse now than 1 year ago, Much worse now than 1 year ago • None at all, A little bit, Some, Quite a bit, A lot.

with a standard deviation of 10. In general, scores at or above 50 are good. Scores below 50 suggest that the parent perceives the child to have some limitations or difficulties.

The CHQ Manual provides sample-size estimates needed to achieve statistically significant differences of 2 to 20 points for both the CHQ scales and the Summary Components. The estimates are based on the U.S. representative sample of children using formulas published by Cohen (1988). The sample size needed depends on the type of design and the particular scale or summary. Scales with fewer items often require a greater sample size. The summaries, however, are calculated using factorial weights for 10 of the scales; thus, in general, their use requires a smaller sample size to achieve a statistical difference.

Further work is needed to determine what constitutes a clinically meaningful change across different condition groups and applications. In general, however, it is possible to compare a patient's score relative to the means derived for the U.S. representative sample using confidence intervals published in the CHQ Manual. For example, a 12-year-old female scores 52.00 on the Mental Health scale. The observed score for the U.S. sample of boys and girls of the same age is 77.4. The difference between the two scores is 25.4. Because 25.4 is greater than 14 points, which, as published in the manual, represents two standard errors of measurement below the published norm for this scale, one would be correct 95% of the time in concluding that a score of 52.00 is statistically below the norm. The next step might be to talk further with the family and administer standardized depression screeners or other instruments to

TABLE 16.3
Summary of Concepts in the CHQ Parent (PF) and Child (CF) Completed Forms:
Interpretation of Low and High Scores

Concepts[a]	*Form*	*No. of Items*	*No. of Levels*	*Low Score*	*High Score*
Physical Functioning	PF50 PF28 CF87	6 3 9	19 10 28	Child is limited a lot in performing all physical activities, including self-care, because of health.	Child performs all types of physical activities, including the most vigorous, without limitations because of health.
Role/Social–Physical	PF50 PF28 CF87	2 1 3	7 4 10	Child is limited a lot in schoolwork or activities with friends as a result of physical health.	Child has no limitations in schoolwork or activities with friends as a result of physical health.
General Health Perceptions[b]	PF50 PF28 CF87	6 4 12	25 17 49	Parent believes child's health is poor and likely to get worse.	Parent believes child's health is excellent and will continue to be so.
Bodily Pain	PF50 PF28 CF87	2 1 2	11 6 11	Child has extremely severe, frequent, and limiting bodily pain.	Child has no pain or limitations because of pain.
Parental Impact—Time	PF50 PF28	3 2	10 7	Parent experiences a lot of limitations in time available for personal needs because of child's physical and/or psychosocial health.	Parent doesn't experience limitations in time available for personal needs because of child's physical and/or psychosocial health.
Parental Impact—Emotional	PF50 PF28	3 2	13 9	Parent experiences a great deal of emotional worry/concern as a result of child's physical and/or psychosocial health.	Parent doesn't experience feelings of emotional worry/concern as a result of child's physical and/or psychosocial health.
Role/Social–Emotional[c]	PF50[c] PF28[c] CF87	[c] [c] 3	[c] [c] 10	Child is limited a lot in school work or activities with friends as a result of emotional problems.	Child has no limitations in schoolwork or activities with friends as a result of emotional problems.
Role/Social–Behavior	PF50[c] PF28[c] CF87	3[c] 1[c] 3	10[c] 4[c] 10	Child is limited a lot in school work or activities with friends as a result of behavior problems.	Child has no limitations in school work or activities with friends as a result of behavior problems.
Self-esteem	PF50 PF28 CF87	6 3 14	25 17 57	Child is very dissatisfied with abilities, looks, family/peer relationships, and life overall.	Child is very satisfied with abilities, looks, family/peer relationships, and life overall.
Mental Health	PF50 PF28 CF87	5 3 16	21 13 65	Child has feelings of anxiety and depression all of the time.	Child feels peaceful, happy, and calm all of the time.
General Behavior[b]	PF50 PF28 CF87	6 4 17	25 17 69	Child very often exhibits aggressive, immature, delinquent behavior.	Child never exhibits aggressive, immature, delinquent behavior.

(Continued)

TABLE 16.3
(Continued)

Concepts[a]	*Form*	*No. of Items*	*No. of Levels*	*Low Score*	*High Score*
Family Activities	PF50	6	25	The child's health very often limits and interrupts family activities or is a source of family tension.	The child's health never limits or interrupts family activities nor is a source of family tension.
	PF28	2	9		
	CF87	6	25		
Family Cohesion[b]	PF50	1	5	Family's ability to get along is rated "poor."	Family's ability to get along is rated "excellent."
	PF28	1	5		
	CF87	1	5		
Change in Health	PF50	1	5	Child's health is much worse now than 1 year ago.	Child's health is much better now than 1 year ago.
	PF28	1	5		
	CF87	1	5		

[a] A 4-week recall period is used for all scales except for the Change in Health (CH) and Family Cohesion (FC) items and the General Health (GH) scale. The recall stem for Change in Health is "compared to last year."

[b] Includes a stand-alone global item that measures along a five-level response continuum from "excellent" to "poor."

[c] Role/Social–Emotional and Role/Social–Behavior are combined into one scale in the PF50 and PF28.

Table reproduced in part with permission from Landgraf et al., 1999, pp. 38–39.

further assess the problem and develop a treatment plan. An example of this scenario is presented in the hypothetical case study later in this chapter.

To further assist interpretation, preliminary normative data and clinical benchmarks have been collected in a general sample of children in the United States (Landgraf et al., 1996, 1999) and Australia (Waters, Salmon, & Wake, 2000; Waters, Salmon, Wake, Hesketh, & Wright, 2000; Waters, Wright, Wake, Landgraf, & Salmon, 1999). Potential projects are currently being discussed for Scotland and the Netherlands.

Item scaling results, and the reliability and validity of the CHQ, are thoroughly documented in the User Manual (Landgraf et al., 1996, 1999) and are readdressed in many of the studies to date. To briefly summarize, the minimum criteria for item internal consistency ($\geq .70$) was exceeded on average by 91% of all item tests performed in the representative U.S. sample and 16 subgroups (based on child age, gender, condition, parent gender, educational status, marital status, working status, and ethnicity), and by 84% of all item tests in the clinical samples. This finding means that items correlated with their hypothesized scale. The average success rate for tests of item discriminant validity across all subgroup tests was 94%. This finding indicates that items not only correlate highly with their hypothesized scale, but that the correlations were at least one to two standard errors higher than correlations with all other items in the measure. Overall, these robust findings replicated across the 16 subgroups support the hypothesized groupings used to score the CHQ scales and justify the use of summated ratings to compute CHQ scores.

Based on the success of meeting and in most cases exceeding tests of scaling assumptions, one would expect the CHQ scales to demonstrate a satisfactory level of internal consistency reliability and to show a distinct pattern of empirical results in validity tests. These expectations were confirmed. Alpha coefficients greater than or equal to .80 were observed across most of the scales. Test–retest reliability has not been

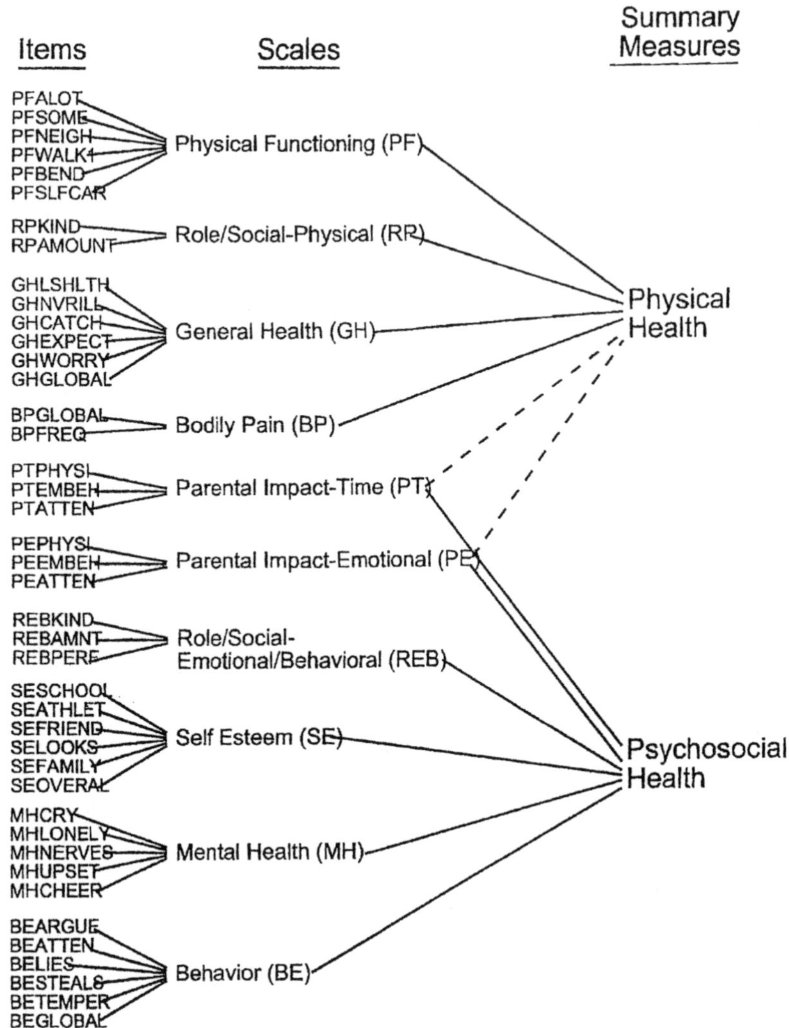

FIG. 16.1. CHQ Measurement Model. Reprinted with permission from Landgraf et al., 1996, p. 285.

performed on the CHQ. Early work by experts have shown that the alpha coefficient represents the average of all possible split-half reliability estimates adjusting for scale length and has been shown to approximate test–retest estimates when scaling assumptions are met (Ware, Davies-Avery, & Donald, 1978; Ware, Johnston, & Davies-Avery, 1979; Ware & Karmos, 1976). Further, Nunnally and Bernstein (1994) recommended that the retest method generally not be used to estimate reliability because of inherent weaknesses that could cause spuriously high correlations.

The CHQ has been shown to discriminate across and within groups varying in severity of asthma, juvenile rheumatoid arthritis, and attention deficit hyperactivity disorder (Landgraf, Abetz, DeNardo, & Tucker, 1995; Landgraf et al., 1996, 1999; McGrath et al., 1999).

Using emergent international guidelines, the CHQ has been rigorously translated or adapted for use in more than 38 languages. There are numerous publications concerning psychometric findings for the translations. Further background information, a list of languages, and a complete bibliography of the CHQ is now available online (at www.healthact.com).

Of note since the initial release of the CHQ in 1996 is the number of investigations that extended beyond traditional psychometric evaluations to assess the health-related quality of life for many common conditions and diseases, and in some instances, the outcome of treatment. The CHQ is often selected for use because it provides a rich understanding of the psychological burden of different conditions. Collectively, these studies present a compelling profile of the relative burden of health issues on children and their families. There are now studies in children with attention deficit hyperactivity disorder (DeVeaugh-Geiss et al., 2002; Michelson et al., 2001), arthritis (Paediatric Rheumatology International Trials Organisation, 2001), asthma (Asmussen et al., 2000; Kanter, et al., 2002; Sawyer et al., 2000), bacterial meningitis (Koomen, 2003), cancer (Bhatia et al., 2002; Rodary et al., 2001; Rodary, Landgraf, Kalifa, Lerveger, & Gentet, 2000; Waters, Wake, Hesketh, Ashley & Smibert, 2003), cerebral palsy (Houlihan et al., 1999; Liptak et al., 2001; McCarthy et al., 2002; Schneider, Gurucharri, Gutierrez, & Gaebler-Spira, 2001; Vitale et al., 2000, 2001a), cystic fibrosis (Epker & Maddrey, 1998), diabetes (Cameron et al., 2002; Perwein, Bennett-Johnson, & Silverstein, 2000; Wake, Hesketh, & Cameron, 2000), D-Transposition (Dunbar-Masterson et al., 2001); epilepsy (Gilliam et al., 1997); food allergy (Sicherer, Noone, & Munoz-Furlong, 2001), germ cell tumors (Sands et al., 2001), head injury (Aitken et al., 2002), hemophilia (Shapiro et al., 2001), Kawasaki disease (Baker, Gauvreau, Newburger, & Jenkins, 1999, 2001), obesity (Wake, Salmon, Waters, Wright, & Hesketh, 2002), renal failure (Kurtin, Landgraf, & Abetz, 1994), sleep-disordered breathing (Rosen, Palermo, Larkin, & Redline, 2002), spinal deformity (Vitale et al., 2000, 2001b), and tonsil and adenoid disease (Stewart et al., 2000).

Further information is now available about the performance of the CHQ relative to the use of other quality-of-life tools and standardized instruments. For example, potential tradeoffs in using the CHQ and the Health Utilities Index have been assessed (Nixon Speechly et al., 1999; Raat, Bonsel, Essink-Bot, Landgraf, & Gemke, 2002). The HUI is complementary in its focus but was developed using a different measurement design model (utility theory). The CHQ and its performance relative to the Wee–Functional Independence Measure, Youth Risk Behavior Questionnaire, Diagnostic Interview Schedule for Children, and the Child Behavior Checklist are also available (Rey, Sawyer, Raphael, Patton, & Lynskey, 2002). Other studies have looked at academic performance measures (Koomen, 2003; Shapiro et al., 2001).

Several studies have been conducted to assess the relative precision of the CHQ as compared to disease and condition-specific instruments in asthma (McGrath et al., 1999), arthritis (Landgraf, Abetz, DeNardo, & Tucker, 1995; Paediatric Rheumatology International Trials Organisation, 2001), cancer (Bhatia et al., 2002; Sawyer, Antoniou, Toogood, & Rice, 1999), cerebral palsy (Schneider, Gurucharri, Gutierrez, & Gaebler-Spira, 2001), diabetes (Perwein, Bennett-Johnson, & Silverstein, 2000), children with limitations to gross motor functioning (McCarthy et al., 2002) and musculoskeletal functioning (Daltroy, Liang, Fossel, Goldberg, & Pediatrics Outcomes Instrument Development Group, 1998).

USE OF THE CHQ IN TREATMENT PLANNING

The CHQ was designed to be used as a common yardstick to gauge the relative burden of disease in children and the relative benefit of treatment irrespective of the child's age, gender, or the nature of the condition (physical, behavioral, social). As a self-completed health assessment tool, the CHQ is designed to provide the clinical practitioner with further insight into parental perceptions concerning children's emotional health, their self-esteem, behavior, school performance, and social limitations, and a brief assessment of the state of family relationships. It was not designed for use as a diagnostic tool, nor was it intentionally designed for use in assessing the outcome of treatment for psychological conditions. However, because it is a generic instrument and can be used across a wide spectrum of conditions, the CHQ may be useful in identifying key areas to target and planning different treatment options. It has become a standard practice to administer the CHQ prior to intervention as a baseline assessment tool and again postintervention as an objective measure of the potential outcome of care and treatment.

USE OF THE CHQ FOR TREATMENT MONITORING

Many scales within the CHQ utilize a standard 4-week recall period. Combined with the robust alpha coefficients observed across most scales ($\geq .80$), it is therefore quite appropriate for use as an instrument to monitor change at the individual patient level. Nunnally and Bernstein (1994) recommended alpha coefficients of at least .80 or higher for individual patient-level analyses. However, there are several constraints that must be noted. The most noteworthy point is that the CHQ was normed using 4 weeks as the standard time referent.

If the objective of a study is to assess the efficacy of a treatment that lasts only a few days (e.g., administration of an antibiotic) or an intervention that happens quickly (e.g., short-term psychotherapy), the time referent of many instruments like the CHQ (i.e., past 4 weeks, past month, etc.) may not be appropriate for assessing potential change. From a psychometric perspective, any modification to a standardized instrument—no matter how minor—may impact psychometric findings and the underlying integrity of the measure. Therefore, instruments must always be used according to the specifications of the developer. Acute versions (i.e., 1-week recall or less) may exist for some quality-of-life instruments. Evaluation of these instruments will have undergone the same rigorous testing and evaluation as the original measure. An acute version of the CHQ is not available at this time. As is the case with all aspects of validity, providing evidence of an instrument's sensitivity to change is an iterative process. Each application adds to a rich database of information concerning the use or limitation of a given instrument.

USE OF THE CHQ TO ASSESS THE OUTCOME OF TREATMENT

Newman, Ciarlo, and Carpenter (1999) identified five broad categories against which to assess the quality of instruments designed to measure the outcome of care and treatment—application and relevance to target population, methods and procedures, psychometric features, cost, and utility considerations. Each of these issues, as they relate to the CHQ, have been carefully identified and thoroughly discussed in the CHQ User's Manual (Landgraf et al., 1996, 1999). The psychometric strengths of the CHQ were summarized earlier in this chapter. The remaining quality characteristics are briefly readdressed now for the convenience of the reader.

Application/Relevance

The cultural diversity of children and adolescents in the United States is being dramatically redefined (Lewit & Baker, 1994). Given this, it has been argued that the standard criteria used to evaluate state-of the-art health assessment tools should be expanded to include evidence of their appropriateness in groups differing in cultural orientation, ethnicity, and race (Landgraf & Abetz, 1996). Thus, an important hallmark of the CHQ development was a thorough evaluation and documentation of the relevance of both items and concepts that constitute its architectural framework in 16 different subgroups derived from the U.S. sample and clinical conditions (Landgraf & Abetz, 1997, 1998; Landgraf et al., 1996, 1999). Other studies have also assessed the potential influence of ethnicity and culture on health-reported quality of life for children in the United States (Asmussen et al., 2000; Hepner & Sechrest, 2002; Legett et al., 2001).

Methods and Procedures

The CHQ was designed and validated as a self-completed instrument. However, because certain study designs necessitate the use of trained interviewers, the content of the CHQ was scripted to facilitate its use in settings that require either phone or face-to-face interviews. However, normative data was collected using a mail-out–mail-back methodology. Based on evidence with adult assessment tools (McHorney, Kosinski, & Ware, 1994), differences in mean scores for the CHQ scales can be expected, depending on the chosen mode of administration. It is hypothesized that scores will be inflated if an interviewer administers the CHQ; that is, individuals will report more favorable scores indicating better functioning and well-being. To date, however, no studies have been conducted to confirm this position. Regardless, users are strongly encouraged to consult the CHQ User's Manual (Landgraf et al., 1996, 1999) for specific guidelines on administering the form.

Briefly, the CHQ should be completed independent of guidance from others, including family members or clinical, administrative, or study personnel. Using general conventions, (6 items/minute), the parent-completed CHQ can be completed by most people in approximately 10 to 12 minutes. Given its length, the self-report will take considerably longer.

At the commencement of work on the parent form, the goal was to develop a tool that could be administered across a broad age spectrum (5–18 years). Given the complexities of establishing validity in children under age 12, work initiated with the development and validation of the parent-completed instrument. About a year into the program, however, it became obvious that a complementary child-completed version would greatly facilitate our understanding of salient measurement issues—most notably, the potential tradeoffs in using multiple reporters within a family.

Work on a child report version of the CHQ began as a direct result of an incident with my then 9-year-old daughter. She had observed the CHQ on our dining room table and began answering the questions concerning limitations in her physical well-being. We were in agreement for all but one of the items—limitations in strenuous activities. Having seen her excel on the soccer field, I scored her as having no limitations; however, she reported herself to be quite limited. After further inquiry and clarification, I learned that she was having considerable difficulty breathing but had thought that such problems were "normal." She was eventually diagnosed with asthma. Her condition is currently managed with several therapeutics, and she is completing her 2nd year of collegiate lacrosse. The experience convinced me that development of a parent-completed tool was insufficient and that to be truly useful, parallel development and validation of a self-report tool would be essential to the success of our measurement program.

As argued elsewhere (Landgraf & Abetz, 1996), the objective in using multiple reporters is not to establish concordance or evaluate interrater agreement of the form. Rather, it is to provide a standard platform so that each voice can be heard and the best possible treatment plan can be devised. In addition, a better understanding of the perceptions of both parents and their children will facilitate practitioners in establishing realistic expectations for all involved—often an essential ingredient to the success of any family-centered intervention, especially for children receiving treatment for psychiatric or behavioral problems.

Psychometric findings for the child self-report version (Kurtin, Landgraf, & Abetz, 1994; Landgraf & Abetz, 1997) have also been examined outside the United States Countries include Australia (Waters et al., 2001), France (Rodary, LePlege, Kalifka, & Bernard, 1997; Rodary et al., 2000, 2001), the Netherlands (Raat, Landgraf, Bonsel, Gemke, & Essink-Bot; 2002), Sweden (Landgraf, Erling, Wilkund, Abetz, & Ware, 1995; Norrby & Nordholm, 2001), and Yugoslavia (Kvrgic, Niciforovic-Surkovic, Ukropina, & Potic, 2001a, 2001b). Robust findings from these investigations using multitrait analysis and other traditional methods of questionnaire evaluation (reliability, validity) are favorable and support use of the CHQ–CF.

Presently, the length of the self-report version (87 items) may make it prohibitive for use outside of the research arena. Concurrent with writing the CHQ User's Manual, empirical tests were conducted to derive a more practical, short-form alternative for the CHQ–CF. It quickly became apparent, however, that to apply the same rigorous and thorough evaluation that is the hallmark of the parent forms would require additional time and result in publication delays. Thus, the development work was temporarily suspended, but a short form has always been targeted as an important next step, and work is again proceeding in tandem with ongoing translation work and other projects.

Recent studies have also examined differences in scores among parents and children (Choe, Soo, Vitale, Spellman, & Roye, 2001; Cunningham, Chiu, Landgraf, & Glicklich, 2000; Epker & Maddrey, 1998; Kvrgic et al., 2001b; Levi & Drotar, 1999; Rodary et al., 2001; Sawyer et al., 1999; Wake, Hesketh, & Cameron, 2000), parents, and clinicians (Waters et al., 2003).

Cost and Utility Considerations

Despite considerable advances concerning the interpretation of health outcomes data, relatively little attention has been given to the presentation of results to the lay medical community, including clinicians, administrators, and payers. Historically, software developers have taken the lead in designing the standardized reports generated by patient-based assessment tools, and outcomes service organizations have developed systems to expedite the process by which data is collected (i.e., touch-screen programs, computer-adaptive testing, voice-simulated technology). Because many of these efforts are adjunct activities designed to increase market share, there exists tremendous variability in the way data is collected, processed, analyzed, and ultimately presented.

Scoring, analysis, and interpretation of the CHQ require a strong understanding of statistical software traditionally used by the scientific community (e.g., SAS, SPSS). To facilitate analysis and interpretation and meet the burgeoning demands of a diverse group of users, scoring and reporting services are now available at the secure, password protected CHQ Web site (www.healthact.com). Reports are available at the patient and aggregated group level, and include both CHQ Summary Scores and CHQ Profile Scale Scores. Scores are compared over time periods and to the national sample.

HYPOTHETICAL CASE STUDY USING THE CHQ

Considerable time and effort was spent on evaluating the relevance and conceptual framework of the CHQ items and scales in an effort to construct a practical and useful instrument for both research and clinical care (Landgraf et al., 1996, 1999). To optimize its development, access to the prestandardized CHQ was limited to carefully designed studies that provided opportunities to evaluate its clinical relevance across an array of conditions. As a result, data accrued from case-specific situations is limited. However, the availability of normative data allows us to create a hypothetical case study to illustrate the potential utility of the CHQ for mental health providers. This illustration is based in part on information provided in early application studies.

Sean, an active 11-year-old, was brought to the clinic for observation and testing. During in-depth interviews his parents revealed that he was generally aggressive and argumentative. He had difficulty paying attention in school and following through with tasks at home. He often exhibited outbursts of anger and frustration if requests were not granted. He appeared to be extremely bright, but despite this, achieved low academic marks. His parents reported that he appeared relatively disinterested in activities at home and on occasion had expressed strong negative feelings towards his siblings. There were considerable conflicts at home.

As part of the diagnostic process, Sean's parents were asked to complete several standardized screening and diagnostic instruments. It is strongly recommended that condition-specific instruments also be used if feasible and available, as these may be more sensitive and provide even greater insight into the specific impact of a condition and allow providers to more finely tune treatment. Thus, in this instance, based on initial discussions, it would be strongly recommended that Sean's parents complete both the CHQ and the ADHD Impact Module—a tool specifically designed to assess the quality of life for children with ADHD and their families (Landgraf, Rich, & Rappaport, 2002). In this hypothetical illustration about the CHQ, differences in scores are provided for that measure only.

Comments obtained during the interview were reflected in low scores for seven of the CHQ scales—Role-Emotional/Behavioral (limitations in schoolwork), Behavior, Mental Health, Self-esteem, Parent Impact—Emotional (emotional concern/worry for the parent, and Family Activities (limitations on family). As displayed in Table 16.4, baseline mean scores were 67.8, 55.6, 62.8, 61.3, 49.2, and 63.5, respectively. Each of these scores is lower than those published (Landgraf et al., 1996, 1999) for the U.S. sample of boys (91.4, 74.1, 79.6, 79.6, 78.0; and 88.9) and comparable to the sample of 83 children with attention problems (68.7, 54.5, 66.8, 62.6, 58.5, and 62.1).

Not surprising, scores obtained for the other standardized tools supported a diagnosis of attention deficit hyperactivity disorder and borderline depression, and findings on the AIM correlated with scores on the self-esteem scale and the parent emotional impact scale from the CHQ. Based on these findings, the team designed a comprehensive treatment program that included behavior modification techniques, medication, and family therapy. After 6 months of treatment, the CHQ was

TABLE 16.4
Selected Mean CHQ–PF50 Scale Scores[a] Hypothetical Case Study Example

CHQ Scale	*Baseline Scores*	*Posttreatment Scores*
Role–Emotional/Behavioral[b]	67.8	97.8
Behavior[c]	55.6	68.3
Mental Health[c]	62.8	72.8
Self-esteem	61.3	64.5
Parental Impact—Emotional[d]	49.2	68.3
Family Activities	63.5	67.3

[a] Scores range 0–100; a higher score is better.
[b] $p < .03$, [c] $p < .04$, [d] $p < .02$.

readministered to monitor progress of treatment. Although scores on the school limitations, behavior, and parental anxiety scales were higher relative to baseline, differences in scores between baseline and the 6-month assessment were not significant. However, at the end of the 12-month program, t test results indicate a significant difference for four of the scales—school limitations, behavior, mental health, and parent emotional anxiety (+30.0, +12.7, +10.0, +19.1). These findings, presented in Table 16.4 as posttreatment scores, indicated a noticeable improvement in Sean's school performance. In addition, he seemed less depressed, and some of the anxiety previously reported by his parents had been alleviated.

CONCLUSION

Clearly, a single instrument will not be appropriate for all applications. Empirical evidence supports the use of the CHQ as a viable instrument to assess the health-related quality of life of children and their families. Its potential as a tool to measure the outcome of care and treatment continues to be investigated. It is important to underscore that the CHQ was not designed as a diagnostic tool, although the presence of normative data and benchmarks for some conditions may facilitate its use in this regard.

The motivation behind the construction and validation of the CHQ was to create a robust tool that was comprehensive in scope and applicable to children and adolescents with and without health issues. The CHQ, like other quality-of-life instruments that are now available, has undergone careful scientific study, and it is anticipated that work in this regard will continue. Underlying the motivations for development of the CHQ was a broader intent—to give voice to "those often unknown unremembered . . . half-heard between two waves of the sea" (Landgraf et al., 1999, p. 19). As evidenced by its increased widespread use in the United States and elsewhere, the broader and more compelling objective of the program continues to be achieved.

REFERENCES

Aitken, M. E., Tilford, J. M., Barrett, K. W., Parker, J. G., Simpson, P., Landgraf, J., et al. (2002). Health status of children after admission for injury. *Pediatrics, 110,* 337–342.

Asmussen, L., Olson, L. M., Grant, E. N., Landgraf, J. M., Fagan, J., & Weiss, K. B. (2000). Use of the Child Health Questionnaire in a sample of moderate and low-income inner-city children with asthma. *American Journal of Respiratory and Critical Care Medicine, 162,* 1215–1221.

Baker, A. L., Gauvreau, K., Newburger, J., & Jenkins, K. (1999, February). *Late impact of Kawasaki disease on physical and psychosocial health in children*. Abstract presentation at the sixth International Kawasaki Disease Symposium, Waikoloa, HI.

Baker, A. L., Gauvreau, K., Newburger, J., & Jenkins, K. (2001, May). *Physical and psychosocial health in patients who have had Kawasaki disease*. Abstract presentation at the World Congress of Pediatric Cardiology, Toronto, Ontorio Canada.

Bhatia, S., Jenney, M. E., Bogue, M. K., Rockwood, T. H., Feusner, J. H., Friedman, D. L., Robison, L. L., & Kane, R. L. (2002). The Minneapolis–Manchester Quality of Life instrument: Reliability and validity of the Adolescent Form. *Journal of Clinical Oncology, 20*, 4692–4698.

Bullinger, M., Mackensen, S., & Landgraf, J. M. (1994). Assessing the quality of life of children. *Quality of Life Research, 3*(1), 41.

Cameron, F. J., Clarke, C., Hesketh, K., White, E. L., Boyce, D. F., Dalton, V. L., et al. (2002). Regional and urban Victorian diabetic youth: Clinical and quality-of-life outcomes. *Journal of Paediatrics and Child Health, 38*, 593–596.

Choe, J., Soo, J. I., Vitale, M. G., Spellman, M. E., & Roye, D. P. (2001). Perspectives on pediatric outcomes: A comparison of parents' and patients' rating of quality of life following orthopaedic intervention. *Quality of Life Research, 10*(3), 218. Abstract obtained from Abstract No. 103.

Cohen, J. (1988). *Statistical power analysis for the behavioral science* (2nd ed.). Hillsdale, NJ: Lawrence Erlbaum Associates.

Cunningham, M. J., Chiu, E. J., Landgraf, J. M., & Glicklich, R. E. (2000). The health impact of chronic recurrent rhinosinusitis in children. *Archives of Otolaryngology—Head & Neck Surgery, 126*, 1363–1368.

Daltroy, L. H., Liang, M. H., Fossel, A. H., Goldberg, M. J., & Pediatric Outcomes Instrument Development Group. (1998). The POSNA Pediatric Musculoskeletal Functional Health Questionnaire: Report on reliability, validity, and sensitivity to change. *Journal of Pediatric Orthopedics, 18*, 561–571.

DeVeaugh-Geiss, J., Conners, C. K., Sarkis, E. H., Winner, P. K., Ginsberg, L. D., Hemphill, J. M., et al. (2002). GW320659 for the treatment of attention-deficit/hyperactivity disorder in children. *Journal of the American Acadamy of Child and Adolescent Psychiatry, 41*, 914–920.

Drotar, D. (Ed.). (1998). *Measuring health-related quality of life in children and adolescents: Implications for research and practice*. Mahwah, NJ: Lawrence Erlbaum Associates.

Dunbar-Masterson, C., Wypij, D., Bellinger, D. C., Rappaport, L. A., Baker, A. L., Jonas, R. A., et al. (2001). General health status of children with D-Transposition of the great arteries after the arterial switch operation. *Circulation, 104*(Suppl. I), 138–142.

Eiser, C., & Morse, R. (2001). Quality-of-life measures in chronic diseases of childhood. *Health Technology Assessment, 5*(4).

Epker, J. V., & Maddrey, A. M. (1998). Quality of life in pediatric patients with cystic fibrosis. *International Journal of Rehabilitation and Health, 4*(4), 215–222.

Gilliam, F., Wyllie, E., Kashden, J., Faught, E., Kotagal, P., Bebin, M., et al. (1997). Epilepsy surgery outcome: Comprehensive assessment in children. *Neurology, 48*, 1368–1374.

Hepner, K. A., & Sechrest, L. (2002). Confirmatory factor analysis of the Child Health Questionnaire—Parent Form 50 in a predominantly minority sample. *Quality of Life Research, 11*, 763–773.

Houlihan, C. M., Conway, M., Stallings, V., Chumlea, W., Worley, G., Henderson, R., et al. (1999, September). Growth in children with cerebral palsy: A population-based survey. *Developmental Medicine and Child Neurology, 12*, 32. Abstract presented at the annual meeting of the American Academy for Cerebral Palsy and Developmental Medicine. Washington, DC.

Kanter, L. J., Siegel, C. J., Snyder, C. F., Pelletier, E. M., Buchner, D. A., & Goss, T. F. (2002). Impact of respiratory symptoms on health-related quality of life and medical resource utilization of patients treated by allergy specialists and primary care providers. *Annals of Allergy, Asthma & Immunology, 89*(2), 139–147.

Koomen, I. (2003). *Prognosis of bacterial meningitis in childhood*. Unpublished master's thesis, Utrecht University Medical Center.

Koot, H. M., & Wallander, J. L. (Eds.). (2001). *Quality-of-life in children and adolescent illness: concepts, methods, and findings*. East Sussex, England: Brunner-Routledge.

Kurtin, P., Landgraf, J. M., & Abetz, L. (1994). Patient-based health status measures in pediatric dialysis: Expanding the assessment of outcomes. *American Journal of Kidney Diseases, 24*, 376–382.

Kvrgic, S., Niciforovic-Surkovic, O., Ukropina, S., & Potic, M. (2001a). Effect of sociodemographic characteristics on health status and quality of life in schoolchildren and adolescents in Yugoslavia. *Medicinski Pregled, 54*, 229–233.

Kvrgic, S., Niciforovic-Surkovic, O., Ukropina, S., & Potic, M. (2001b). Quality of life assessment in school-age children and adolescents in Yugoslavia from the viewpoint of the children and their parents. *Medicinski Pregled, 54*, 323–326.

Landgraf, J. M. (1999). Issues in measuring and monitoring the health-related quality of life of children surviving cancer. *International Journal of Cancer, 12*, 147–150.

Landgraf, J. M. (2001). Measuring and monitoring quality of life in children and youth: A brief commentary. *Sozial und Praventivmedizin, 46*, 281–282.

Landgraf, J. M., & Abetz, L. (1996). Measuring health outcomes in pediatric populations: Issues in psychometrics and application. In B. Spilker (Ed.), *Quality of life and pharmacoeconomics in clinical trials* (2nd ed., pp. 793–802). Philadelphia: Lippincott-Raven.

Landgraf, J. M., & Abetz, L. (1997). Functional status and well-being of children representing three cultural groups: Initial self-reports using the CHQ–CF87. *Psychology and Health, 12*, 839–854.

Landgraf, J. M., & Abetz, L. (1998). Influences of sociodemographic characteristics on parental reports of children's physical and psychosocial well-being: Early experiences with the Child Health Questionnaire. In D. Drotar (Ed.), *Measuring health-related quality of life in children and adolescents* (pp. 105–126). Mahwah, NJ: Lawrence Erlbaum Associates.

Landgraf, J. M., Abetz, L., DeNardo, B. A., & Tucker, L. B. (1995, October). *Clinical validity of the Child Health Questionnaire—Parent Form in children with rheumatoid arthritis.* Poster presented at the 1995 National Scientific Meeting of the American College of Rheumatology, San Francisco.

Landgraf, J. M., Abetz, L., & Ware, J. E. (1996). *The CHQ: A user's manual* (1st ed.). Boston: The Health Institute.

Landgraf, J. M., Abetz, L., & Ware, J. E. (1999). *The CHQ: A user's manual* (2nd ed.). Boston: HealthAct.

Landgraf, J. M., Erling, A., Wilkund, I., Abetz, L., & Ware, J. E. (1995, October). *The Child Health Questionnaire: Issues in translation, language, and culture for Swedish children and their parents.* Poster presentation at the Second Annual Meeting of the International Society for Quality of Life Research, Montreal, Quebec, Canada.

Landgraf, J. M., Ravens-Sieberer, U., & Bullinger, M. (1997). Quality of life research in children: Methods and instruments. *Dialogues in Pediatric Urology, 20*(11), 5–7.

Landgraf, J. M., Rich, M., & Rappaport, L. (2002). Measuring quality of life in children with Attention-deficit/Hyperactivity Disorder and their families: Development and evaluation of a new tool. *Arch. Pediatr. Adolesc. Med., 156*, 384–391.

Lapp, D., & Flood, J. (1978). *Teaching reading to every child.* New York: McMillan.

Legett, S., Karahodzic, H. K., Klie, M., Klepper, M., Klutho, R., Homan, S., et al. (2001, April). *Health status of Bosnian children in St. Louis, Missouri.* Poster presented at the 2001 Pediatric Academic Societies Annual Meeting, Baltimore.

Levi, R. B., & Drotar, D. (1999). Health-related quality of life in childhood cancer: Discrepancy in parent–child reports. *International Journal of Cancer Supplement, 12*, 58–64.

Lewit, E. G., & Baker, L. G. (1994). Race and ethnicity changes for children. In *The future of children: Critical health issues for children and youth, 4*(3), 134–44. Los Angeles: Center for the Future of Children, the David and Lucile Packard Foundation.

Liptak, G. S., O'Donnell, M., Conaway, M., Chumlea, W. C., Wolrey, G., Henderson, R. C., et al. (2001). The health status of children with moderate to severe cerebral palsy. *Developmental Medicine and Child Neurology, 43*, 364–370.

Lollar, D. J., Simeonsson, R. J., & Nanda, U. (2000). Measures of outcomes for children and youth. *Archives of Physical Medicine and Rehabilitation, 81*(Suppl. 2), S46–S51.

McCarthy, M. L., Silberstein, C. E., Atkins, E. A., Harryman, S. E., Sponseller, P. D., & Hadley-Miller, N. A. (2002). Comparing reliability and validity of pediatric instruments for measuring health and well-being of children with spastic cerebral palsy. *Developmental Medicine and Child Neurology, 44*, 468–476.

McGrath, M., Bukstein, D. A., Buchner, D. A., Guzman, G. L., Landgraf, J. M., & Goss, T. (1999). Assessment of the relationship between disease severity and general and disease specific health-related quality of life in pediatric asthma patients. *Ambulatory Child Health, 5*, 249–261.

McHorney, C., Kosinski, M., & Ware, J. E. (1994). Comparisons of the costs and quality of norms for the SF–36 Health Survey collected by mail versus telephone interview: Results from a national survey. *Medical Care, 33*, 15–28.

Michelson, D., Faries, D., Wernicke, J., Kelsey, D., Kendrick, K., Sallee, F. R., et al. (2001). Atomoxetine in the treatment of children and adolescents with attention-deficit/hyperactivity disorder: A randomized, placebo-controlled, dose-response study. *Pediatrics, 108*(5), 1–9.

Newman, F. L., Ciarlo, J. A., & Carpenter, D. (1999). Criteria for selecting psychological instruments for treatment outcome assessment. In M. E. Maruish (Ed.), *The use of psychological testing for treatment planning and outcome assessment* (pp. 153–170). Mahwah, NJ: Lawrence Erlbaum Associates.

Nixon Speechley, K., Maunsell, E., Desmeules, M., Schanzer, D., Landgraf, J. M., Feeny, D. H., et al. (1999). Mutual concurrent validity of the Child Health Questionnaire and the Health Utilities Index: An exploratory analysis using survivors of childhood cancer. *International Journal of Cancer Supplement, 12*. 95–105.

Norrby, U., & Nordholm, L. A. (2001). Reliability and validity of a Swedish version of Child Health Questionnaire (CHQ). *Quality of Life Research, 10*(3), 287. Abstract obtained from Abstract No. 377.

Nunnally, J. C., & Bernstein, I. R. (1994). *Psychometric theory* (3rd ed.). New York: McGraw-Hill.

Paediatric Rheumatology International Trials Organisation. (2001). Quality of life in juvenile rheumatoid arthritis patients compared to healthy children. *Clinical and Experimental Rheumatology, 19*(4), S23.

Perwein, A. R., Bennett-Johnson, S., & Silverstein, J. H. (2000). Quality of life assessment in youth with Type 1 diabetes: Use of a brief generic measure. *Quality of Life Research, 9*(3), 281 (Abstract No. 1584).

Raat, H., Bonsel, G.J., Essink-Bot, M. L., Landgraf, J. M., & Gemke, R. J. (2002). Reliability and validity of comprehensive health status measures in children; The Child Health Questionnaire in relation to the Health Utilities Index. *Journal of Clinical Epidemiology, 55*(1), 67–76.

Raat, H., Landgraf, J. M., Bonsel, G. J., Gemke, R. J., & Essink-Bot, M. L. (2002). Reliability and validity of the Child Health Questionnaire–Child Form (CHQ–CF87) in a Dutch adolescent population. *Quality of Life Research, 11*, 575–581.

Rey, J. M., Sawyer, M. G., Raphael, B., Patton, G. C., & Lynskey, M. (2002). Mental health of teenagers who use cannabis: Results of an Australian survey. *British Journal of Psychiatry, 180*(3), 216–221.

Rodary, C., Bellon, N., Landgraf, J. M., Kalifa, C., Baruchel, & Qunintana, E. (2001). The Child Health Questionnaire (CHQ): Comparison of the quality of life (qol) scores obtained by the parent report (PF50) and the self-report (CF87). *Quality of Life Research, 10*(3), 216. Abstract obtained from Abstract No. 93.

Rodary, C., Bellon, N., Landgraf, J. M., Kalifa, C., Chastagner, P., & Vannier, J. P. (2001). Validation in French of the Child Health Questionnaire Parent Form (CHQ–PF50) in children aged 9–19 years suffering from cancer. *Quality of Life Research, 10*(3), 268 (Abstract No. 300).

Rodary, C., Landgraf, J. M., Kalifa, C., Lerveger, G., & Gentet, J. C. (2000). Ability of the Child Health Questionnaire (CHQ–CF87) to detect differences in quality of life (QOL) between children according to type of cancer. *Quality of Life Research, 9*(3), 266 (Abstract No. 1509).

Rodary, C., LePlege, A., Kalifka, C., & Bernard, J. L. (1997). *Adaptation in French of the Child Health Questionnaire (CHQ) and validation in children 10–18 years of age.* Paper presented at the Ninth Annual Meeting of the International Association for Quality of Life Research, Vienna, Austria.

Rodrigue, J. R., Geffken, G. R., & Streisand, R. M. (Eds.) (2000). *Child health assessment: A handbook of measurement techniques.* Needham Heights, MA: Allyn & Bacon.

Rosen, C.L., Palermo, T. M., Larkin, E. K., & Redline, S. (2002). Health-related quality of life and sleep-disordered breathing in children. *Sleep, 25*(6), 657–666.

Sands, S. A., Kellie, S. J., Davidow, A. L., Diez, B., Villablanca, J., Weiner, H., et al. (2001). Long-term quality of life and neuropsychologic functioning for patients with CNS germ-cell tumors: From the First International CNS Germ-Cell Tumor Study. *Neuro-Oncology, 3*, 174–183.

Sawyer, M., Antoniou, G., Toogood, I., & Rice, M. (1999). A comparison of parent and adolescent reports describing the health-related quality of life of adolescents treated for cancer. *International Journal of Cancer Supplement, 12*, 39–45.

Sawyer, M., Spurrier, N., Whaites, L., Kennedy, D., Martin, A. J., & Baghurst, P. (2000). The relationship between asthma severity, family functioning and health-related quality of life of children with asthma. *Quality of Life Research, 9*(10), 1105–1115.

Schneider, J. W., Gurucharri, L. M., Gutierrez, A. L., & Gaebler-Spira, D. J. (2001). Health-related quality of life and functional outcome measures for children with cerebral palsy. *Developmental Medicine and Child Neurology, 43*, 601–608.

Shapiro, A., Donfield, S. M., Lynn, H. S., Cool, V. A., Stehbens, J. A., Hunsberger, S. L., et al. (2001). Defining the impact of hemophilia: The academic achievement in children with hemophilia study. *Pediatrics, 108*(6), 1–6.

Sicherer, S. H., Noone, S. A., & Munoz-Furlong, A. (2001). The impact of childhood food allergy on quality of life. *Annals of Allergy, Asthma & Immunology, 87*, 461–464.

Stewart, M. G., Friedman, E. M., Sulek, M., Hulka, G. F., Kuppersmith, R. B., Harrill, W. C., et al. (2000). Quality of life and health status in pediatric tonsil and adenoid disease. *Archives of Otolaryngology—Head & Neck Surgery, 126*(1), 45–48.

Vitale, M. G., Choe, J., Levy, D. E., Gelijns, A. C., Moskowitz, A. J., Hyman, J. E., et al. (2001a). Assessment of health status in patients with cerebral palsy: What is the role of quality of life measures. *Quality of Life Research, 10*(3), 238 (Abstract No. 181).

Vitale, M. G., Choe, J., Levy, D. E., Gelijns, A. C., Moskowitz, A. J., Hyman, J. E., et al. (2001b). Pediatric spine deformity: Assessing patient outcomes and quality of life. *Quality of Life Research, 10*(3), 201 (Abstract No. 34).

Vitale, M. G., Roye, D. P., Levy, D. E., Gelijns, A. C., Moskowitz, A. J., & Puffingbarger, W. R. (2000). An exploration of quality of life outcomes measurement in scoliosis and cerebral palsy. *Pediatrics, 104*, 716.

Wake, M., Hesketh, K., & Cameron, F. (2000). The Child Health Questionnaire in children with diabetes: Cross-sectional survey of parent and adolescent-reported functional health status. *Diabetic Medicine, 17*, 700–707.

Wake, M., Salmon, L., Waters, E., Wright, M., & Hesketh, K. (2002). Parent-reported health status of overweight and obese Australian primary school children: A cross-sectional population survey. *International Journal of Obesity and Related Metabolic Disorders, 26*, 717–724.

Ware, J. E., Davies-Avery, A., & Donald, C. A. (1978). *Conceptualization and measurement of health for adults in the Health Insurance Study: Vol. 5. General health perceptions* (Corp. Publication No. R-1987/5-HEW). Santa Monica, CA: RAND.

Ware, J. E., & Karmos, A. H. (1976). *Development and validation of scales to measure perceived health and patient role propensity* (Vol. 2). Carbondale, IL: Southern Illinois University School of Medicine.

Ware, J. E., Johnston, S. A., & Davies-Avery, A. (1979). *Conceptualization and measurement of health for adults in the Health Insurance Study: Vol. 3. Mental health* (Corp. Publication No. R-1987/3-HEW). Santa Monica, CA: RAND.

Waters, E., Salmon, L., & Wake, M. (2000). The parent-form Child Health Questionnaire in Australia: Comparison of reliability, validity, structure, and norms. *Journal of Pediatric Psychology, 25*, 381–391.

Waters, E., Salmon, L., Wake, M., Hesketh, K., & Wright, M. (2000). The Child Health Questionnaire in Australia: Reliability, validity, and population means. *Australian and New Zealand Journal of Public Health, 24*(2), 207–210.

Waters, E. B., Salmon, L. A., Wake, M., Wright, M., & Hesketh, K. D. (2001). The health and well-being of adolescents: A school-based population study of the self-report Child Health Questionnaire. *The Journal of Adolescent Health, 29*(2), 140–149.

Waters, E. B., Wake, M. A., Hesketh, K. D., Ashley, D. M., & Smibert, E. (2003). Health-related quality of life of children with acute lymphoblastic leukaemia: Comparisons and correlations between parent and clinician reports. *International Journal of Cancer, 103*, 514–518.

Waters, E., Wright, M., Wake, M., Landgraf, J., & Salmon, L. (1999). Measuring the health and well-being of children and adolescents: A preliminary comparative evaluation of the Child Health Questionnaire in Australia. *Ambulatory Child Health, 5*, 131–141.

17

Measurement as Communication in Outcomes Management: The Child and Adolescent Needs and Strengths (CANS)

John S. Lyons and Dana Aron Weiner
Northwestern University

Melanie Buddin Lyons
Buddin Praed Foundation

INTRODUCTION

The children's mental health services system has fallen short of the ideal. This is especially true in the public sector, where children often receive inadequate or inappropriate treatment. Several large-scale research projects have found that improving access and coordination within these service systems does not necessarily result in improved outcomes for children (Bickman, Lambert Andrade, & Penaloza, 2000). These findings call into question the effectiveness of existing services (Bickman, Noser, & Summerfelt, 1999; Bickman, Lambert, Andrade, & Penaloza, 2000; Weiss, Catron, Harris, & Phung, 1999).

To address this shortcoming, there is growing interest in evidence-based treatment planning (Hoagwood, Burns, Kiser, Ringeisen, & Schoenwald, 2001). However, such treatment planning is predicated on reliable, valid, and feasible outcome measurement methods. Flawed measures implemented within complex systems along with inconsistent involvement of stakeholders have impeded the outcomes measurement process (Lambert, Ogles, & Masters, 2000; Lyons, Howard, O'Mahoney, & Lish, 1997).

Outcome measures should be able to assess clinical status, well-being, level of functioning, and quality of life (Lambert, Hansen, & Finch, 2001; Sederer, Dickey, & Hermann, 1996; Steinwachs, Flynn, Norquist, & Skinner, 1996). To be applicable in real-world service settings, measures must balance the need for comprehensiveness with the need for efficiency and brevity. Although the standard goals for children's services can be quite simple (e.g., at home, in school, out of trouble; Rosenblatt, 1993), the full range of outcomes requires more sophisticated measurement to support decision making and quality management. At the same time, measures must be brief and easy to use to facilitate their use by busy providers.

Stakeholders in the children's mental health services system (e.g., child and family, providers, administrators, evaluators) have different priorities for target outcomes and for methods of measurement (Fischer, Shumway, & Owen, 2002). Ideally, the selection of target outcomes for measurement should be a collaborative process involving representatives of various perspectives. Evaluators are likely to advocate for use of the most reliable and empirically valid measures, but translating these from research into clinical practice can be problematic. Administrators might emphasize the cost and utility of measures for quality improvement and accountability. Service providers might stress meaningfulness and ease of use. Service recipients might advocate for measures with relevance and respect for consumers. Selected outcome measures should honor all of these perspectives.

In response to these complexities, we have evolved an approach to the design of outcome measures that is distinct from psychometric approaches. This paper will briefly review these traditional approaches to outcomes measurement and present the communication model of measurement. The Child and Adolescent Need and Strengths (CANS) measure will be used to illustrate the development and applications of a measure developed from a communication perspective.

APPROACHES TO OUTCOMES MEASUREMENT

Although psychometric theory has resulted in significant contributions in measurement for research in behavioral health, the application of these approaches to the development of measures for outcomes management has some notable drawbacks. They may lack one or more of the prerequisites of comprehensiveness, brevity, relevance, and real-world validity needed to apply findings in meaningful ways in a service delivery environment. In this section, we review psychometric and clinimetric approaches to measurement development and present an alternative approach: a communication model.

Psychometric Approaches

Most of the currently available outcome measures have been developed from either classical test theory (Anastasi, 1968; Nunally, 1976) or item response theory (Rost & Langeheine, 1997). Although the theoretical assumptions and statistical approaches of item response theory are dramatically different from those of classical test theory (Drasgow & Schmitt, 2002), both require multiple items to measure a single construct. Also, both implicitly value precision in measurement over brevity, although item response theory does offer strategies for identifying the most efficient number of items to accurately assess a construct. Multi-item measures can be an implementation challenge in the mental health services context, where multiple dimensions must be assessed in a brief time.

The majority of mental health services aim to impact multiple dimensions of an individual's functioning. For example, crisis intervention may reduce suicide risk and the likelihood of violence, improve self-care, mobilize resources, and stabilize symptoms. Outpatient therapy is seen as having a potential impact on symptoms, subjective well-being, and functioning. Thus, regardless of the specific intervention, comprehensive mental health outcomes measurement requires a multidimensional approach to capture the complexity of the impact of services (Lambert, Ogles, & Masters, 2000).

Outcome measures often must be completed within a brief time frame, as neither clinicians nor service recipients are inclined or able to spend a great deal of time completing measures. Long measures with overlapping or redundant items, such as those valued by classical test theory (i.e., high internal consistency reliability), can be too time-consuming for respondents to complete. This can result in missing data that threaten the validity and utility of outcomes assessment for services, programs, or systems.

The absence of clear relevance to treatment planning can be problematic for the use of a measure. A clinician who does not see the relevance of a measure for his or her work is unlikely to devote time and attention to completing it. Service recipients have the same perspective. Both perspectives demand that a measure have face validity, which is less valued by both classical test theory and item response theory.

Clinimetrics

In response to the problems with psychometric approaches previously identified, measurement developers in medicine have utilized a theoretical approach referred to as clinimetrics (Feinstein, 1986). The stated goal of clinimetrics is to convert "intangible clinical phenomenon into formal specified measurement" (Apgar, 1966, p. 125). Virginia Apgar is generally credited with developing the first measure from this perspective (Apgar, 1966). First introduced in 1953, the "Apgar" is routinely utilized as a health status measure at birth. Clinimetric tools are now quite common in medicine (e.g., Bloem, Beckley, van Hilten, & Roos, 1998; Stone, Salonen, Lax, Payne, Lapp, & Inman, 2001; Gates, 2000; Hoff, van Hilten, & Roos, 1999).

Feinstein (1999) has enumerated six principles that speak to the differences between clinimetrics and psychometrics:

1. Selection of items is based on clinical rather than statistical criteria.
2. Factors need not be weighted.
3. Scoring is simple and readily interpretable.
4. Variables are selected to be heterogeneous rather than homogeneous.
5. Measures must be easy for clinicians to use.
6. Face validity is required and subjective states are not measured because of limited sources of observation.

Current applications of clinimetrics have some notable limitations (Marx, Bombardier, Hogg-Johnson, & Wright, 2000; Zyzanski & Perloff, 1999). Many clinimetric scales consist of a single item. When complex phenomena are described, a single item fails to communicate complexity. For example, a Childhood Global Assessment Scale (Endicott, Spitzer, Fleiss, & Cohen, 1976) that ranges from 0 to 100 can provide a general sense of how a child is doing, but it cannot capture individual dimensions of functioning that are useful to clinicians. In addition, single-item measures are not particularly sensitive to change. For these reasons, Zyzanski and Perloff (1999) and others have called for an integration of clinimetric and psychometric approaches to measurement.

Service delivery settings have very different priorities than do research settings. Accommodating these technical and contextual requirements requires a broad scope for models of measurement. This model must include guidelines for utility in clinical operations as well as reliability and validity. Measures intended for the evaluation of treatment outcomes should be easy to use and brief. Their output should be clear, unambiguous, relevant, easy to translate into service planning recommendations, and accessible to providers, consumers, and policy makers. Neither classical test theory nor item response theory fully informs the development of measures meeting these requirements in outcome management applications.

A Communication Model

Measures used within service delivery operations must be able to easily and accurately communicate relevant results. Feedback about performance is central to quality improvement and outcomes management (Clark, Schyve, Lepoff, & Ruess, 1994; Koike, Unutzer, & Wells, 2002; Krulish, 2002; Schiff & Goldfield, 1994). This feedback requires the integration of measurement into the information feedback loop (Lichtman & Appleman, 1995). Thus, it can be argued that communication is a primary goal of measurement in clinical settings (Howard, Moras, Brill, Martinovich, & Lutz, 1996; Lueger, Howard, Martinovich, Lutz, Anderson, & Grissom, 2001). This includes communication between recipients and providers about perceptions of clients' needs; communication between providers, program administrators, and evaluators about clinical status; communication between providers and payers about medical necessity for and benefits from services; and communication among providers and other partners about the goals and outcomes of an integrated children's system of care.

Communication theory is a broad and diverse field that informs improvements in outcomes management strategies. Although this chapter does not present a comprehensive review of the communication theory literature, there are three areas within communication theory that have particularly influenced the development of our approach to measurement development. The first construct is the theory of communicative action. Simply stated, communicative action is a consensus-based approach that relies on mutual definitions of how to reach a goal (Habermas & Seidman, 1989). Kihlstroem and Israel (2002) found that group leadership actions based on communicative action theory lead to greater openness to diversity and individual experiences. Friedland (2001) posited that communication forms the primary ecology of postindustrial communities; this logic is relevant for the children's system of care. According to this theory, the foundation for a system of care would be effective action-oriented communication based on consensus among the partners in that system.

Second, White (2001) highlighted communication as the basis for innovation in science. Within this context, the dissemination of evidence-based practices into the field requires consensus across the field that new practices are better than current practices. This kind of consensus cannot be reached by the publication of randomized clinical trials alone, but by ongoing interaction among service delivery, evaluation, and research (Drake, 2002).

Finally, Harris's work in organizational communication has laid out the importance of communication within business environments (Harris, 2002). He conceptualized communication as a nonlinear process that plays a central role in effective leadership, organizational development, and establishing an organization's culture. This is especially important within the children's mental health service system. Given the organizational complexity of most children's systems of care, the system is in need of communication tools to serve these functions.

Application of the communication model within the children's services system will require the establishment of a common ground, and common language, among mental health, child welfare, juvenile justice, and school systems. With these goals in mind, we have worked to develop a communication model of measurement. The model builds on some of the tenets of psychometric theory (high face and content validity, high interrater reliability, high concurrent and predictive validity) and the six principles of clinimetrics, adding three additional requirements:

1. All partners in the service delivery system of care should participate in the development and uses of the measure.

2. The goal of item selection is to include single items that represent each of the key constructs, identified by consensus, that inform good decision making and service planning in the service delivery operation.
3. The levels of each item should be directly translatable into action steps for treatment planning.

From the communication perspective, a good measure should be clear, concise, relevant, and comprehensive without being redundant. It should use common, understandable language and be easy to use. Most important, a measure should be useful for the three primary purposes for which one requires these tools in clinical practice: decision support, quality improvement, and outcomes monitoring.

Decision support strategies help ensure that clinically appropriate decisions are made consistently at key points in the service delivery process. Quality improvement activities ensure that potentially effective interventions are provided when needed and that needs are assessed accurately and in a timely fashion. Outcome monitoring efforts inform clinicians, administrators, and evaluators about the impact of an intervention or program. The measurement approach should allow for all three of these tasks to be accomplished for every case, program, and system. For the past decade, we have been working to develop outcomes management tools using a communication model that blends the strengths of psychometric and clinimetric strategies to measurement development. Perhaps the most widely used tool of this type is the Child and Adolescent Needs and Strengths (Lyons, 1999). Versions of the CANS have been developed to guide service delivery for children with mental health needs, developmental disabilities, child welfare, and juvenile justice involvement. In addition, a specific version for children 3 years old and younger has been developed. Development of the CANS is grounded, in part, in our prior work modeling decision making for hospital and residential services for children and adolescents (Lyons, Mintzer, Kisiel, & Shallcross, 1998).

CANS: DEVELOPMENT, STRUCTURE, AND FUNCTION

Development

As part of a major reform of the child welfare service system in Illinois, we assessed the extent to which psychiatric hospitalization and residential treatment services were used appropriately. For this purpose, we developed the Childhood Severity of Psychiatric Illness (CSPI). This measure was designed to assess the dimensions important to good clinical decision-making for intensive and expensive mental health service interventions. We have demonstrated the utility of the CSPI for reforming decision making for residential treatment (Lyons et al., 1998) and for quality improvement in crisis assessment services (Leon, Uziel-Miller, Lyons, & Tracy, 1999; Lyons, Kisiel, Dulcan, Cohen, & Chesler, 1997). The strength of the measure has been that it has face validity and is easy to use, yet reliably provides sufficiently comprehensive information regarding the clinical status of the child or youth that can be translated into policy and treatment recommendations.

The Child and Adolescent Needs and Strengths builds on the conceptual approach of the CSPI but expands the assessment to include additional areas of needs and the assessment of strengths. The CANS was developed using focus groups with a variety of participants, including families, representatives of the provider community, case managers, and staff. Each focus group was charged with answering the question: "What do we need to know about children and their families to effectively plan and monitor services?" Items were then developed and sent back to focus group participants, who gave feedback on the wording and the levels of each item. The item selection process used a clinimetric approach to begin building a common assessment language. Thus, consensus of those using the tool on the inclusion of an item was more important than intercorrelations among items. This process places measure construction decisions in the hands of the people who will be utilizing the tool.

Structure

The CANS consists of dimensions that are either areas of need or areas of strength. Anchors, standard across these dimensions, are used to rate the level of each need or strength. The anchors are worded in terms of the level of intervention needed, which enables the CANS to produce information that is instantly relevant for service planning. A rating of 2 or 3 on a need indicates that this need should be addressed in service planning.

Table 17.1 provides a summary of the dimensions of the CANS–MH. Unless otherwise specified, each rating is based on the child's functioning in the last 30 days. Each of the dimensions is rated on a 4-point scale after routine service contact, a semistructured interview, or a review of notes from case files. Raters are encouraged to use corresponding "action levels" to help make the determination between two adjacent ratings. For example, a rater torn between a rating of 1 or 2 should consider whether the need requires action or continued observation.

Table 17.2 illustrates the CANS–MH using two items, Psychosis and Danger to Self, from the CANS–MH. For the Psychosis item, "No evidence" indicates the absence of any signs of thought disorder (e.g., hallucinations, delusions, bizarre behavior, or

TABLE 17.1
Domains and Individual Items of the CANS–MH

- Problem Presentation: Psychosis
  - Attention deficit/impulse control
  - Depression/anxiety
  - Oppositional behavior
  - Antisocial behavior
  - Substance abuse
  - Adjustment to trauma
  - Situational consistency of problems
  - Temporal consistency of problems
- Risk Behaviors: Danger to Self
  - Danger to other
  - Elopement
  - Sexually abusive behavior
  - Social behavior
  - Crime/delinquency
- Functioning: Intellectual Developmental
  - Physical/medical
  - Family
  - School/day care
- Care Intensity & Organization
  - Monitoring
  - Treatment
  - Transportation
  - Service permanence
- Caregiver Needs & Strengths
  - Physical/behavioral
  - Supervision
  - Involvement with care
  - Knowledge
  - Organization
  - Residential stability
  - Resources
  - Safety
- Strengths: Family
  - Interpersonal
  - Relationship permanence
  - Education
  - Vocational
  - Well-being
  - Spiritual/religious
  - Talents/interests
  - Inclusion

TABLE 17.2
Two Example Items From the Child and Adolescent Needs and Strengths

Psychotic Symptoms
This rating is used to describe symptoms of psychiatric disorders with a known neurological base. *DSM–IV* disorders included on this dimension are schizophrenia and psychotic disorders (unipolar, bipolar, NOS). The common symptoms of these disorders include hallucinations, delusions, unusual thought processes, strange speech, and bizarre or idiosyncratic behavior.

0 This rating indicates a child with no evidence of thought disturbances. Both thought processes and content are within normal range.
1 This rating indicates a child with evidence of mild disruption in thought processes or content. The child may be somewhat tangential in speech or evidence somewhat illogical thinking (e.g., age inappropriate). This also includes children with a history of hallucinations but none currently. The category would be used for children who are below the threshold for one of the *DSM–IV* diagnoses previously listed.
2 This rating indicates a child with evidence of moderate disturbance in thought process or content. The child may be somewhat delusional or have brief intermittent hallucinations. The child's speech may be at times quite tangential or illogical. This level would be used for children who meet the diagnostic criteria for one of the disorders previously listed.
3 This rating indicates a child with a severe psychotic disorder. Symptoms are dangerous to the child or others.

Danger to Self
This rating describes both suicidal and significant self-injurious behavior. A rating of 2 or 3 would indicate the need for a safety plan.

0 Child has no evidence or history of suicidal or self-injurious behaviors.
1 History of suicidal or self-injurious behaviors but no self-injurious behavior during the past 30 days.
2 Recent (last 30 days) but not acute (today) suicidal ideation or gesture. Self-injurious in the past 30 days (including today) without suicidal ideation or intent.
3 Current suicidal ideation and intent in the past 24 hours.

bizarre thinking). A 1 could be used either where there is suspicion of these symptoms or after a youth who was actively psychotic has been stabilized for some time through medications. A 2 indicates that a youth has clear evidence of these problems and requires active treatment. A 3 indicates a level of these symptoms that requires immediate intervention to prevent harm. The CANS–MH is not a diagnostic tool, but because diagnoses also play a role in communicating a child's needs, the CANS is designed to be consistent with the Diagnostic and Statistical Manual of Mental Disorders (*DSM–IV*, 1994). Thus, for Psychosis, a 2 or 3 is consistent with the presence of one of the disorders whose symptoms are covered by this item.

In the second item in Table 17.2, Danger to Self, no evidence or history of suicidal behavior means that no action is required in this regard. Because we know that children who have attempted suicide in the past are more likely to repeat this behavior, a history of suicide requires monitoring and prevention. A lifetime history of significant suicidality is included within the watchful waiting/prevention level (1). This helps clinicians remain aware of the potential risk. Recent suicidal ideation or behavior requires intervention. Acute suicidal ideation and intent requires immediate action. Psychiatric hospitalization is likely a consideration for children scoring a 3 on this item. As we have shown elsewhere, this level of this item is strongly related to inpatient admissions (Leon et al., 1999).

One of the implications of this item structure is that it is unnecessary to score the CANS in order to understand and apply its results for an individual child and family. Whereas scoring is recommended for purposes of outcome monitoring, service planning comes directly from level of rated needs and strengths. For needs, 2 and 3 indicate areas that require inclusion in the service plan, whereas 1 suggests a need for monitoring or preventive activities.

For strengths, 0 indicates a strength that could be the centerpiece of a strength-based plan; a 1 indicates a strength that can be utilized in strength-based planning; a 2 indicates an area where a strength has been identified but must be developed; and a 3 indicates areas where no strength is currently identified that require strength identification and building efforts. The individual strengths included in the CANS–MH were derived from focus groups with system partners that were used to develop the Child and Adolescent Strengths Assessment (CASA; Lyons, Kisiel, Sokol, & Reyes, 2000). In this study, which used the CSPI and the CASA, we found that strengths and problems were significantly but independently correlated with level of functioning and the probability of high-risk behavior, suggesting that optimal child outcomes would result from both addressing needs and identifying and building strengths. This finding stimulated the integration of the two tools into the CANS.

Function

The CANS functions as an information integration tool. Whoever completes the CANS must take all the information available (e.g., observation, documentation, or both) and integrate it into his or her best estimate of the level of need or strength.

Family-friendly interview prompts have been developed for the CANS in collaboration with parents of children with serious emotional and behavioral items. However, parent interviews are not always feasible (e.g., some child-welfare applications). The sources of information may vary from child to child; therefore, the CANS method allows the rater to take the information available from all sources and integrate it into the rater's best estimate of the level of needs and strengths.

The CANS is designed to be used either as a prospective assessment tool for decision support during the process of planning services, or as a retrospective assessment tool based on the review of existing information for use in the design of service systems. This flexibility allows for a variety of innovative applications. For example, the CANS can be used to conduct retrospective file reviews for planning purposes. Then, based on the result of the planning study, CANS data can be used prospectively to direct efforts at system evolution (Lyons et al., 1997).

The flexibility of this measurement approach in either clinical operations or records review facilitates measurement audits (Anderson, Lyons, Giles, Jensen, & Estles, 2003; Lyons, Rawal, Yeh, Leon, & Tracy, 2001). By reviewing a randomly selected set of records, one can easily monitor the reliability with which the CANS is completed prospectively. This is an important method for use in situations where there is concern about the over- or underreporting of clinical needs or when there is interest in monitoring the success of ongoing training efforts.

The modular design of the CANS–MH allows the tool to be adapted for local applications without jeopardizing its measurement properties. By *modular*, we mean that because each item can stand alone, consensus process allow partners to decide which items should or should not be included or whether a new item should be created for a local application. For example, in the Alaskan Youth Initiative application, partners in this program expressed a need to include an item called Cycling of Symptoms.

This item was designed for children with episodic symptom presentation to reflect whether the child's current symptom level reflected the best or worst of the cycle. Children whose symptoms do not cycle are rated as 0. For the New Jersey version, Fire Setting was separated out of Danger to Others; however, the logic of Danger to Others was maintained, leaving it comparable to the same item used in other venues.

The CANS also can be used to monitor outcomes. This can be accomplished in one of two ways. First, the proportion of cases that move from ratings of 2 or 3 to 1 or 0 can be studied to identify the proportion of cases with resolved needs or bolstered strengths. However, to enhance the measure's sensitivity to change, it is also possible to combine items within dimensions (e.g., Problems) to obtain a dimension score. Changes in dimension scores can then be studied over time. In studies across a range of program and service settings, we have found that the dimension scores of the CANS are sensitive to change after a minimum of 3 months of service delivery. Thus, the CANS is not ideal for measuring the effect of short-term service interventions (e.g., crisis stabilization). It has worked well for monitoring outcomes of intensive community services, intensive outpatient services, treatment foster care, and residential treatment services.

Training

The CANS can only be utilized by individuals who have participated in our sequenced training model. The first phase of the training involves "remoralization." This phase emphasizes the potential importance of outcomes management to the trainee and the system. The goal of this phase of training is to help trainees realize that the CANS is a different type of assessment. The second phase of training is an explanation of the communication model. The third phase involves a detailed review of the manual with case examples for each dimension. In addition, a supplementary glossary is provided with additional helpful information, such as symptoms of major *DSM–IV* (1994) disorders. In the fourth stage, a practice vignette is distributed, and small groups complete the CANS for the sample case. Working through a case example with others crystallizes the use of CANS for trainees. After feedback and discussion of the group exercise, a practice vignette is completed by each individual trainee. Following feedback and discussion of this vignette, each trainee completes a test vignette to establish reliability.

Only trainees who are reliable at .70 (intraclass correlation) or more are considered trained. Remedial training is provided to individuals who are not reliable. In our experience of training more than 5,000 individual on this model, we have found that about 90% of trainees are reliable at the end of the standard training.

PROPERTIES OF THE CANS MEASURE: RELIABILITY, VALIDITY, AND SENSITIVITY TO CHANGE

Reliability

The following describes a series of reliability studies for the CANS–MH. Two primary methods are used. In one method, a standard vignette is given to a group of individuals who had completed the training protocol previously described. They then completed the CANS–MH based on the case description in a test vignette. In the second method, case records are reviewed independently by two or more reviewers, each of whom complete the CANS–MH based on the information available in the record. In each case, reliability more than .70 using item-level intraclass correlation coefficients (mixed model) is considered adequate.

Case Vignettes. As a part of standard training in the use of the CANS–MH (as previously described) in five different states, all training participants completed the CANS–MH for a reliability test case vignette. Across these trainings, a total sample of 188 CANS–MH trainees turned in a CANS–MH. Comparisons were made between the CANS–MH ratings by the trainees and those of the first author. Average reliability, using intraclass correlation, was .76. One hundred fifty-two (86.7%) of these trainees had reliabilities above .70; 67 (35.6%) had reliabilities above .80. Nineteen (10%) had reliabilities between .63 and .69. Only five trainees (2.7%) had reliabilities below .60.

Case Records. In two record review studies, 19 reviewers were trained to complete the CANS–MH on medical records. Following training, each of these reviewers completed the CANS–MH on a randomly selected record that was independently reviewed by the first author. Average reliability for all 19 reviewers was .83. Intraclass correlations were calculated for each reviewer. Seventeen of the 19 reviewers (89%) had reliabilities more than .70, with two reviewers (11%) having reliabilities of .69. Four reviewers (21%) had reliabilities more than .90. Eight reviewers (42%) had reliabilities between .80 and .89.

Anderson et al. (2003) have recently published a reliability study of the CANS–MH in which two case-record reviews of 60 cases were compared and each was compared to a prospectively completed CANS–MH used in ongoing service delivery, completed by the treating clinician. The results of this study suggest that the CANS is reliable at the individual-item level even in ongoing use in clinical service delivery.

Validity

Concurrent and Discriminant Validity: Comparison With the CAFAS. One of the most commonly used measures in the children's mental health service system is the Child and Adolescent Functional Assessment Survey (CAFAS; Hodges, McKnew, Cytryn, Stern, & Klein, 1982; Hodges & Wotring, 2000). The CAFAS provides ratings on five or eight dimensions that are combined into a single score that represents the child's overall level of functioning across major life domains.

A validity study was conducted using the CANS–MH and the CAFAS, administered with 249 youth served through the Mental Health Juvenile Justice (MH–JJ) Initiative. One of the goals of the study was to demonstrate discriminant validity, that the CANS and the CAFAS measured different facets of the same construct (child functioning) in different ways. Ideally, we hoped to find moderate correlations between CANS–MH and CAFAS scores. Both tools were completed by the MH–JJ liaison at the initiation of service planning.

The correlation between the CAFAS and CANS–MH total score was .63 ($df = 247$, $p < .001$). Next, we correlated the CAFAS subscales that had a parallel single CANS–MH item. The correlation between the CAFAS School/Work subscale and the CANS–MH school functioning item was .59 ($df = 247$, $p < .001$); between CAFAS Self-harm and CANS–MH Danger to Self item was .61 ($df = 247$, $p < .001$); between the CAFAS Substance Abuse and the CANS–MH Substance Use item was .73 ($df = 247$, $p < .001$); and between the CAFAS Thinking subscale and the CANS–MH Psychosis item the correlation was .54 ($df = 247$, $p < .001$). Thus, these individual

TABLE 17.3
Correlations Between the CANS and CAFAS at Enrollment Into the Illinois Mental Health Juvenile Justice Initiative for 249 Youths

CAFAS	*Problems*	*Risks*	*Functioning*	*Caregiver*	*Strengths*	*Total*
School role	.08	.09	.37**	.10	.28**	.31**
Home role	.18**	.24**	.21**	.04	.27**	.37**
Community role	.27**	.31**	.15	.08	.15*	.32**
Moods/behavior	.21**	.24**	.25**	.14*	.15*	.31**
Moods/emotions	.05	.19**	.13	.16**	.26**	.24**
Self-harmful behavior	.07	.26**	.09	.11	.23**	.25**
Substance use	.17**	.10	.03	.03	.22**	.21**
Thinking	.17**	.06	.02	.06	.00	.10
Total	.29*	.33**	.25**	.23**	.42**	.63**

items of the CANS–MH which could be tested with reasonable comparisons to the CAFAS appear to be valid indicators.

Table 17.3 presents the correlations between the CAFAS subscales and the CANS dimension scales. Review of this table and the correlations previously presented suggest that there is a significant measurement overlap between the two tools but that they also appear to assess somewhat different aspects of child and family functioning.

Predictive Validity: Prediction of Level of Care. In a planning study undertaken for a large northeastern state, 1,592 records were reviewed. The sampling was a stratified random sample in which a set of 20 randomly selected cases from the prior year of service were selected from randomly selected programs within each of the five regions of the state. Reviews were completed by independent reviewers with an average reliability of .86, weighted by the numbers of cases reviewed. Of these cases, 772 were selected, representing three distinct levels of care: residential treatment, intensive community-based treatment (i.e., intensive case management and a Medicaid waiver program that followed a wraparound model), and outpatient treatment.

A discriminant function analysis was used to predict group membership in the three levels of care using the five domain scores of the CANS–MH. With three groups, two discriminant functions were created, and both were statistically significant ($\chi^2 = 352.9$, $df = 10$, $p < .001$ and $X^2 = 43.0$, $df = 4$, $p < .001$, respectively). The CANS–MH accurately classified 63% of all cases into their actual level of care. This prediction model represents a statistically significant improvement above chance ($\chi^2 = 450{,}6$, $df = 12$, $p < .001$). Based on the structure matrix, the first discriminant function was a linear combination of Care Intensity (.847), Risk Behaviors (.750), Problems (.707), and Functioning (.493). The second discriminant function was a linear combination of Caregiver Capacity (.529) and Strengths (−.471).

Table 17.4 presents the predicted and actual level of care for the full sample. All five domains of the CANS provided independent and statistically significant contributions to this prediction model. The significant relationship of strengths to level of care replicates findings from a study in another state using the CSPI and Behavioral and Emotional Rating Scale (Epstein, 1998; Oswald, Cohen, Best, Jensen, & Lyons, 2001).

The data presented in Table 17.4 demonstrate that the CANS is most accurate in identifying children at the highest level of care. They also suggests that decision making on admission in these services is consistent with the original program designs, in that more challenging youth are served in more intensive and expensive programs.

TABLE 17.4
Classification of Cases Into Three Levels of Care Using the Domain Scores of the CANS–MH

	Predicted		
Actual	*Low*	*Intermediate*	*High*
Low	206 (65%)	72 (23%)	37 (12%)
Intermediate	86 (30%)	138 (48%)	66 (22%)
High	14 (7%)	28 (13%)	173 (80%)

Note. Row percents are included to represent the accuracy with which actual LOC is predicted.

Not surprisingly, the accuracy is lowest for the intermediate level of care; it appears that a significant number of children are served at this level that are more similar to children served at either a lower or higher level of care. Thus, opportunities for step-down (e.g., the 20% of cases in residential treatment who look more like outpatient or intensive outpatient) can be identified. Likewise, the need for more intensive community treatment slots is represented by the fact that 23% of children served in the lowest level of care had needs consistent with children served in higher levels of care. Consistent with this finding (and others in the overall study), a primary result of this planning study was to increase investment in developing more intensive community services (Lyons, Carpinella, Rosenberg, Zuber, Fazio, & MacIntyre, in press). This illustrates the immediate applicability of CANS data for policy change.

Sensitivity to Change: The CANS as an Outcome-Monitoring Tool

Because of its design (a recommended 30-day window for most ratings), the CANS has limited applicability for the monitoring of change over a short period of time. It could not be expected to be useful for assessing change in an acute care setting, for example. However, it is designed to allow for the monitoring of change over a longer period of time. To allow the items of the CANS to detect reliable change for interventions that extend 3 months or longer, it is possible to move to a psychometric strategy. Because the Cronbach alphas within dimensions (e.g., Problems) are generally above .70, one can add the items within dimension to calculate a score. Calculating dimension scores enhances the statistical power by increasing the variability of the measure.

Table 17.5 presents data studying change over time with two different types of treatment. One hundred randomly selected recipients of Intensive Treatment Services (community-based wraparound model) were assessed at admission and discharge. One hundred twenty-six youth who were arrested and detained and found to have either a psychotic or affective disorder were assessed at enrollment and after 6 months of referral to community treatment and case monitoring activity. With the exception of caregiver capacity and strengths in the MH–JJ cohort, all other CANS dimensions demonstrated reliable improvement over the full samples. The effect sizes ranged from small to moderate to large depending on the dimension and the treatment group. Thus, it appears that the CANS dimension scores are sensitive to change and can be used for monitoring outcomes (i.e., change in status) in a variety of service settings.

LIMITATIONS

Although the CANS offers a number of unique advantages relative to other available measures, it does have some limitations. First, training and ongoing monitoring of

TABLE 17.5
Comparison of Means and Standard Deviations of Admission and Discharge CANS–MH Domain Scores for a Random Sample of Children Served in Intensive Community Treatment Programs or Residential Treatment Centers

	Intensive Community			*Mental Health Juvenile Justice*		
CANS Domain	*Admit*	*Discharge*	*Effect Size*	*Admission*	*Discharge*	*Effect Size*
Problems	8.0 (2.5)	5.8 (3.5)	0.79	8.6 (2.5)	6.9 (3.1)	0.59
Risk behaviors	3.4 (2.5)	2.5 (2.6)	0.33	7.0 (2.9)	5.8 (3.0)	0.39
Functioning	5.3 (1.7)	4.8 (1.9)	0.26	2.9 (2.4)	0.9 (1.7)	0.82
Caregiver	5.1 (4.6)	3.8 (4.7)	0.35	5.9 (3.9)	6.5 (4.4)	0.15
Strengths	18.6 (4.3)	17.4 (4.4)	0.42	16.5 (4.3)	14.4 (4.9)	0.49

$^{*}p < .01$. $^{**}p < .001$.

reliability is important. It is likely not possible for most individuals to become reliable in the use of the CANS by simply reading and studying the manual. With training, it is clearly possible to use the CANS reliably in the field. Second, because of the item construction, the CANS is likely less sensitive to change, particularly over short periods of time, than other measures. However, particularly when dimension scores are used, the CANS appears to capture meaningful change across a number of program types. Finally, given its modular design, different locales can use different versions with different items. The granting of local control over measurement design can complicate cross-system comparisons. Although it is possible to manage these comparisons given the use of identical items, care must be taken to ensure appropriate cross-site comparisons are made (Rawal, Lyons, MacIntyre, & Hunter, in press).

CONCLUSION

By focusing on the communication role of measurement in outcomes management, the CANS–MH illustrates a novel approach that integrates psychometric and clinimetric approaches to measurement within the children's service delivery system. Although classical test theory and item response theory continue to play an important role in measurement development, additional considerations beyond the psychometric properties of a tool should influence the development, design, and use of outcomes measures.

Evidence from reliability studies indicates that the CANS can be completed reliably by individuals working with children and families. The CANS demonstrates both concurrent validity and predictive validity in initial studies. In addition, effect sizes from two outcomes studies support the use of the CANS for monitoring outcomes. Thus, it appears that the CANS is a reliable and valid tool for use within children's services.

Various versions of the CANS are used currently in at least twenty-one different states. The applications include decision support, quality improvement, and outcomes monitoring. Decision support applications include both establishing appropriate level of care and assisting service planning. Quality improvement activities involve monitoring the match between identified needs and services provided, and the extent to which strengths are identified and included in service plans. Outcomes monitoring applications involve monitoring the effectiveness of services over 3- to 6-month intervals.

It has become increasingly apparent that in order to effectively manage and evolve systems of care for children and families, it is necessary to ensure that service recipients are represented in all aspects of the process. One means of ensuring representation is to consistently collect information on the needs and strengths of children and families who are served using a measure that takes all perspectives into account. In this way, services can be understood from the perspective of their overarching purpose—to help children and families. The CANS is one tool that can facilitate this process. The CANS allows for the reliable and valid communication of needs and strengths to inform decision making at the individual child and family level while enabling administrators to monitor the quality and effectives of services at the program and system level.

ACKNOWLEDGMENTS

A large number of individuals have participated in the development of the CANS tools over the past 5 years, and it is impossible to name everyone. However, the following individuals have made particularly notable contributions to the development of the CANS: M. Connie Almeida, Rachel L. Anderson, Mina Dulcan, M.D., Ardas Khalsa, Cassandra Kisiel, John Lavigne, Michael Lee, Mary Beth Rautkis, Harry Shallcross, and Patricia Sokol. The CANS tools are open-domain tools that are free for anyone to use. They be obtain from the authors or by visiting www.buddinpraed.org.

REFERENCES

American Psychological Association. (1994). *Diagnostic and statistical manual of mental disorders*. Washington, DC: Author.

Anastasi, A. (1968). *Psychological Testing*, 3rd ed. Toronto, Ontario, Canada: Macmillan.

Anderson, R. L., Lyons, J. S., Giles, D. M., Price, J. A., Estes, G. (2003). Examining the reliability of the Child and Adolescent Needs and Strengths-Mental Health (CANS-MH) Scale from two perspectives: A comparison of clinician and researcher ratings. *Journal of Child and Family Studies, 12*, 279–289.

Apgar, V. (1966). The newborn (Apgar) scoring system. Reflections and advice. *Pediatric Clinics of North America, 13*, 645–650.

Beardslee, W. R., Wright, E., Rothbertg, P. C., Salt, P., BVersage, E. (1996). Response of families to two preventive intervention strategies: Long-term differences in behavior and attitude change *JAACAP, 35*, 774–782.

Bickman, L. (1996). Implications of a children's mental health managed care demonstration evaluation. *Journal of Mental Health Administration, 23*, 107–117.

Bickman, L., Lambert, E. W., Andrade, A. R., & Penaloza, R. V. (2000). The Fort Bragg continuum of care for children and adolescents: Mental health outcomes over 5 years. *Journal of Consulting and Clinical Psychology, 68*, 710-716.

Bickman, L., Noser, K., & Summerfelt, W. T. (1999). Long-term effects of a system of care on children and adolescents. *Journal of Behavioral Health Services & Research, 26*, 185–202.

Bloem, R. B., Beckley, D. J., van Hilten, B. J., & Roos, R. A. (1998). Clinimetrics of postural instability in Parkinson's disease. *Journal of Neurology, 245*, 669–673.

Clark, G. B., Schyve, P. M., Lepoff, R. B., & Ruess, D. T. (1994). Will quality management paradigms of the 1990s survive into the next century? *Clinical Laboratory Management Review, 8*, 426–428, 430–434.

Drake, R. (2002, November). *Psychiatric rehabilitation and evidence-based medicine.* Carl Taube Award lecture to the American Public Health Association, Philadelphia.

Drasgow, F., & Schmitt, N. (Eds.). (2002). *Measuring and analyzing behavior in organizations: Advances in measurement and data analysis.* San Fransisco: Jossey Bass.

Endicott, J., Spitzer, R. L., Fleiss, J. L., & Cohen, J. (1976). The global assessment scale. A procedure for measuring overall severity of psychiatric disturbance. *Archives of General Psychiatry, 33*, 766–771.

Epstein, M. H. (1998). Strength-based assessment: the Behavioral and Emotional Rating Scale. *Behavioral Healthcare Tomorrow, 7*, 46–48.

Epstein, M. H., & McGee, J. L. (1996). Roles of federal and state governments in outcomes assessment. *American Journal of Medial Quality, 11*, 18–21.

Feinstein, A. R. (1999). Multi-item "instruments" vs. Virginia Apgar's principles of clinimetrics. *Archives of Internal Medicine, 159*, 125–128.

Fischer, E. P., Shumway, M., & Owen, R. R. (2002). Priorities of consumers, providers, and family members in the treatment of schizophrenia. *Psychiatric Services, 53*, 724–729.

Friedland, L. A. (2001). Communication, community, and democracy: Toward a theory of communicatively integrated community. *Communication Research, 28*, 358–391.

Gager, P. J., & Elias, M. J. (1977). Implementing prevention programs in high-risk environments: Application of the resiliency paradigm. *American Journal of Orthopsychiatry, 67*, 363–373. 1977.

Gates, G. A. (2000). Clinimetrics of Meniere's disease. *Laryngoscope, 110*, 8–11.

Habermas, J., & Seidman, S. (1989). Juergen Habermas on society and politics: A reader. Frankfurt, Germany: University of Frankfurt.

Hammer, K. M., Lambert, E. W., & Bickman, L. (1997). Children's mental health in a continuum of care: Clinical outcomes at 18 months for the Fort Bragg demonstration. *Journal of Mental Health Administration, 24*, 465–471.

Harris, T. E. (2002). *Applied organizational communication: Principles and pragmatics for future practice*. Mahwah, NJ: Lawrence Erlbaum Associates.

Hoagwood, K., Burns, B. J., Kiser, L., Ringeisen, H., & Schoenwald, S. K. (2001). Evidence-based practice in child and adolescent mental health services. *Psychiatric Services, 52*, 1179–1189.

Hodges, K., McKnew, D., Cytryn, L., Stern, L., & Klein, J. (1982). The Child Assessment Schedule (CAS) diagnostic interview: A report on reliability and validity. *Journal of the American Academy of Child and Adolescent Psychiatry, 21*, 468–473.

Hodges, K., & Wotring, J. (2000). Client typology based on functioning across domains using the CAFAS: Implications for service planning. *Journal of Behavioral Health Services & Research, 27*, 257–270.

Hoff, J. I., van Hilten, B. J., & Roos, R. A. (1999). A review of the assessment of dyskinesias. *Movement Disorders, 14*, 737–743.

Howard, K. I., Moras, K., Brill, P. L., Martinovich, Z., & Lutz, W. (1996). Evaluation of psychotherapy. Efficacy, effectiveness, and patient progress. *American Psychologist, 51*, 1059–1064.

Kihlstroem, A., & Israel, J. (2002). Communicative or strategic action—An examination of fundamental issues in the theory of communicative action. International *Journal of Social Welfare, 11*, 210–218.

Koike, A. K., Unutzer, J., & Wells, K. B. (2002). Improving the care for depression in patients with comorbid medical illness. *American Journal of Psychiatry, 158*, 1738–1745.

Krulish, L. H. (2002). A basic and practical overview of the six steps of outcome-based quality improvement: Part 2. *Home Healthcare Nurse, 20*, 585–586.

Lambert, M. J., Hansen, N. B., & Finch, A. E. (2001). Patient-focused research: Using patient outcome data to enhance treatment effects. *Journal of Consulting and Clinical Psychology, 69*, 159–172.

Lambert, M. J., Ogles, B. M., & Masters, K. S. (2000). Choosing outcome assessment devices: An organizational and conceptual scheme. *Journal of Counseling & Development, 70*, 527–532.

Leon, S. C., Uziel-Miller, N. D., Lyons, J. S., & Tracy, P. (1999). Psychiatric hospital utilization of children and adolescents in state custody. *Journal of the American Academy of Child and Adolescent Psychiatry, 38*, 305–310.

Lichtman, D. M., & Appleman, K. A. (1995). Measures of effectiveness: A methodology of integrating planning, measurement, and continuous improvement. *Military Medicine, 160*, 189–193.

Lueger, R. J., Howard, K. I., Martinovich, Z., Lutz, W., Anderson, E. E., & Grissom, G. (2001). Assessing treatment progress of individual patients using expected treatment response models. *Journal of Consulting & Clinical Psychology, 69*, 150–158.

Lyons J. S. (1999). *The Child and Adolescent Needs and Strengths for children with mental health challenges*. Winnetka, IL: Buddin Praed Foundation. Also retrieved from www.buddinpraed.org

Lyons, J. S., Carpinella, S., Rosenberg, L., Zuber, M., Fazio, M., & MacIntyre, J. (in press). *Needs-based planning for the children's mental health service system in New York*. Psychiatric Services.

Lyons, J. S., Howard, K. I., O'Mahoney, M. T., & Lish, J. (1997). *The measurement and management of clinical outcomes in mental health*. New York: Wiley.

Lyons, J. S., Kisiel, C. L., Dulcan, M., Cohen, R., & Chesler, P. (1997). Crisis assessment and psychiatric hospitalization of children and adolescents in state custody. *Journal of Child and Family Studies, 6*, 311–320.

Lyons, J. S., Mintzer, L. L., Kisiel, C. L., & Shallcross, H. (1998). Understanding the mental health needs of children and adolescents in residential treatment. *Professional Psychology: Research and Practice, 29*, 582–587.

Lyons, J. S., Rawal, P., Yeh, I., Leon, S., & Tracy, P. (2001). Use of measurement audit in outcomes management. *Journal of Behavioral Health Services & Research 29*, 75–80.

Marx, R. G., Bombardier, C., Hogg-Johnson, S., & Wright, J. G. (2000). Clinimetric and psychometric strategies for development of a health measurement scale. *Journal of Clinical Epidemiology, 52*, 105–111.

Nunnally, J. (1976). *Psychometric theory*. New York: Wiley.

Ogles, B. M., Lambert, M. J., & Masters, K. S. (1996). *Assessing outcome in clinical practice*. Needham Heights, MA: Allyn & Bacon.

Orlikoff, J. E. (1994). CQI trends and transitions. *Healthcare Executive, 9*, 12–15.

Oswald, D. P., Cohen, R., Best, A. M., Jensen, C. E., & Lyons, J. S. (2001). Child strengths and level of care for children with emotional and behavioral disorders. *Journal of Emotional and Behavioral Disorders, 9*, 192–199.

Rawal, P., Lyons, J. S., MacIntyre, J., & Hunter, J. C. (in press). Regional variations and clinical indicators of antipsychotic use in residential treatment: A four-state comparison. *Journal of Behavioral Health Services and Research.*

Rosenblatt, A. (1993). In home, in school, and out of trouble. *Journal of Child and Family Studies, 2*, 275–282.

Rost, J., & Langeheine, R. (1997). *Applications of latent train and latent class models in the social sciences*. New York: Waxmann.

Schiff, G. D., & Goldfield, N. I. (1994). Deming meets Braverman: toward a progressive analysis of the continuous quality improvement paradigm. *International Journal of Health Services, 24*, 655–673.

Sederer, L. I., Dickey, B., & Hermann, R. C. (1996). The imperative of outcomes assessments in psychiatry. In L. I. Sederer & B. Dickey (Eds.), *Outcomes Assessment in Clinical Practice*. Baltimore: Williams & Wilkins.

Sheasby, J. E., Barlow, J. H., Cullen, L. A., & Wright, C. C. (2000). Psychometric properties of the Rosenberg self-esteem scale among people with arthritis. *Psychological Reports, 86*, 1139–1146.

Steinwachs, D. M., Flynn, L. M., Norquist, G., & Skinner, E. A. (Eds). (1996). *Using client outcomes information to improve mental health and substance abuse treatment*. San Fransisco: Jossey-Bass.

Stone, M., Salonen, D., Lax, M., Payne, U., Lapp, V., & Inman, R. (2001). Clinical and imaging correlates of response to treatment with infliximab in patients with anklylosing spondylitis. *Journal of Rheumatology, 28*, 1605–1614.

Stroul, B. A. (1993). *Systems of care for children and adolescents with severe emotional disturbances: What are the results?* Washington, DC: CASSP Technical Assistance Center, Center for Child Health and Mental Health Policy Center, Georgetown University Child Development Center.

Weiss, B., Catron, T., Harris, V., Phung, T. M. (1999). The effectiveness of traditional child psychotherapy. *Journal of Consulting & Clinical Psychology, 67*, 82–94.

White, W. J. (2001). A communication model of conceptual innovation in science. *Communication Theory, 11*, 290–314.

Zyzanski, S. J., & Perloff, E. (1999). Clinimetrics and psychometrics work hand in hand. *Archives of Internal Medicine, 159*, 1816–1817.

18

Quality of Life of Children: Toward Conceptual Clarity

Ross B. Andelman
Contra Costa Children's Mental Health Services

C. Clifford Attkisson and Abram B. Rosenblatt
University of California, San Francisco

> When it comes to saying in what happiness consists, opinions differ, and the account given by the generality of mankind is not at all like that of the wise. The former take it to be something obvious and familiar, like pleasure or money or eminence, and there are various other views, and often the same person actually changes his opinion. When he falls ill he says that it is his health, and when he is hard up he says it is money.... Happiness demands not only complete goodness but a complete life.
>
> (Aristotle, *Ethics*, quoted in Calman, 1987, p. 1).

Quality of life (QOL), like "happiness," is a familiar yet elusive concept. It is a malleable, multifaceted, and all-encompassing construct that belongs to a family of similarly broad abstractions—happiness, life satisfaction, the good life, and subjective well-being are related, if not synonymous, concepts (Calman, 1987; Campbell, Converse, & Rodgers, 1976; Diener, 1984).

Since Aristotle first pondered the indeterminate nature of happiness, philosophers, social scientists, and the generality of mankind have pondered the general themes, attributes, and constituents of these interrelated constructs. Few, however, attend, or wish to attend, to all the facets of happiness, choosing instead to mold QOL to suit their particular purpose. This tendency to restrict the conceptual scope of QOL investigations and the generally unsettled nature of the construct hinders research and limits the value of findings for health policy formulation.

QOL emerged over the last quarter century as a widely endorsed index of outcome in health services research and is now an established determinant in health policy formulation. For many researchers, however, the meaning of QOL has been assumed to be self-evident. Investigators have used a wide variety of definitions of QOL, and great inconsistency has characterized the use of the term. Consequently, there is little consensus regarding how to best conceptualize and operationalize this construct. This is especially the case in efforts to measure the QOL of children for whom QOL is likely to have unique attributes. The absence of a clear conceptual understanding of QOL in children hampers the development of specific measures and indicators that can be used to assess the QOL of children.

There are numerous potential advantages of the development of consistent, accepted, and widely utilized measures of QOL of children. Such measures can be essential for treatment planning, especially given the emphasis in many contemporary service systems and treatment models on providing more integrated and coordinated care for youth with emotional and behavioral disorders. Popular systemic and programmatic reforms in service delivery such as the Systems of Care philosophy (Stroul & Friedman, 1996) and the Wraparound process (Burchard & Clark, 1990) emphasize holistic assessments that incorporate not only psychiatric symptomatology but also functioning and well-being. Similarly, current empirically based treatments in mental health such as multisystemic therapy (MST, Henggeler & Borduin, 1990) also call for a broad-based assessment process. QOL is highly consistent with many of the goals of contemporary service systems and empirically based treatments.

QOL can also constitute an essential component of outcomes assessment in children's services. There is currently no clear or standard metric for determining the effectiveness of children's mental health services. Although there are a number of commonly used measures in children's mental health, most emphasize functioning and symptomatology, and researchers commonly assemble a battery of measures to tap a range of domains (Rosenblatt, 1998; Rosenblatt & Rosenblatt, 2002). However, such measurement strategies can produce results that are difficult to interpret from a policy and a scientific perspective (Rosenblatt & Woodbridge, 2003). Further, many existing measures remain inconsistent with the systemic, programmatic, and policy-related goals. QOL has the potential to serve as a common metric that can address the interests of knowledge generation and policy formulation.

The goal of our review is both comprehensive and synthetic. We extensively review more than 30 years of research studies. The studies represent work in a broad range of conditions and populations reviewed using explicit inclusion criteria. The literature is examined in several dimensions to provide a comprehensive overview of the context in which the conceptualization of QOL as applied to children has evolved. Integral to this task is an examination of the nature and adequacy of existing assessment methodology, as well as a distillation of the explicit and implied conceptualization. We aim to summarize advances made by those working in this field and note the limitations imposed by the field. Finally, we provide a framework for development of a conceptual theory of childhood QOL and outline directions for further research. We think that a better understanding of the construct and its measurement in children will guide the development of valid, reliable, and more comprehensive methods for assessing childhood QOL. The development of such measures is essential if QOL is to be incorporated effectively into the evaluation of the efficacy and the quality of health care for children.

The impetus for this review derives from a desire to stimulate development of QOL instruments sensitive to the specific life circumstances and problems of children with emotional and behavioral disorders. At the end of the chapter, we present one approach to improving the theoretical conceptualization of childhood QOL. We hope that this chapter will be helpful to other investigators in this field, both those involved in empirical studies using the QOL construct and those engaged in QOL instrument development. By contributing to a clearer conceptualization of QOL and working toward an effective measure of QOL in children, we emphasize our basic belief in the importance of well-being as a factor in the health of a child.

MODERN HISTORICAL CONTEXT

During the first half of the 20th century, social scientists sought to delineate QOL by measuring a set of objective social indicators, including wealth, security, and employment status (Campbell et al., 1976). Beginning with the work of Bradburn (1969) and Cantril (1965) in the 1960s and culminating in the population surveys of Campbell et al. (1976) and Andrews and Withey (1976), social scientists moved from equating QOL with material welfare toward a more psychological conceptualization—deflecting the emphasis from being "well off" toward a concern with a sense of well-being (Campbell et al., 1976; Hanestad, 1996). Andrews and Withey (1976) conducted an extensive population survey and found three independent components of global subjective well-being: cognitive judgment of satisfaction, positive affective responses, and negative affective responses. Although acceptance of these three factors is not universal, they remain the cornerstone findings from the social science studies of subjective well-being and QOL (Diener, 1984).

Even before the publication of landmark works on QOL in the social sciences, such as *The Quality of American Life* (Campbell et al., 1976) and *Social Indicators of Well-being* (Andrews & Withey, 1976), the construct had already entered the medical lexicon. The appropriation of QOL by the health sciences is generally appreciated to have its inception in the 1958 constitution of the World Health Organization (WHO). In its constitution, WHO defined health "as a state of complete physical, mental, and social well-being, and not merely the absence of disease and infirmity" (Hanestad, 1996). Although they cite this comprehensive definition, health researchers have, in fact, employed a more limited definition of QOL. Designated as health-related quality of life (H-R QOL), this more limited construct emphasizes aspects of personal experience related specifically to health care or health status (Hanestad, 1996).

Over the past decade, a host of social, political, economic, and technological forces have transformed the structure of health care provision. These forces have brought the construct of QOL to the forefront of health care research. Rapid advances in medical knowledge and surgical procedures have made possible a progressive decline in the mortality rate of previously fatal conditions such that survival statistics no longer provide a complete or sufficient accounting of the benefits of a given technology (Hollandsworth, 1988). Some of these new technologies, organ transplant and cancer chemotherapy, for example, while providing potential for cure or improved life expectancy, involve significant risk of failure and in some cases considerable morbidity (Cella & Bonomi, 1995; Gerhardt, 1990; Najman & Levine, 1981). Other contemporary medical interventions, or example, nonsteroidal anti-inflammatory agents for arthritis and so-called novel antipsychotic medications for schizophrenia, offer neither cure nor increased longevity but are aimed at alleviating pain and improving functioning, previously elusive goals in the history of medicine (Thomas, 1974). Outcomes research, then, has evolved to take into account the long-term consequences, both positive and negative, of medical interventions and the life course of those living longer with chronic conditions. In this context, the measure of QOL, with its emphasis on well-being and functional status, has held out the promise of encompassing the best aggregate of data pertinent to evaluating treatments that increase longevity or improve function.

In the early 1990s, increasing dissatisfaction with health services, coupled with rapidly growing costs created a major political movement to reform health care (Hargreaves, Shumway, Hu, & Cuffel, 1998; Starr, 1992). These reform efforts were intended to increase the quality of care, especially the effectiveness of services, but control costs and manage access. The recognition that the rate of increase in health care expenditures is not sustainable has made the prospect of limited and more intensively managed health care resources inescapable (Kaplan, 1989). It has intensified the need to balance the costs against the outcomes of care. Although far from simple, determining the cost side of this equation may be easier than quantifying the benefits of health care. The measure of QOL, with the possibility of translating qualitative perceptions into quantitative data, has proven to be an invaluable component of the benefit side of this analysis.

Finally, partly in reaction to the changes accompanying health care reform and partly a consequence of the changing social reality of medicine, the health care industry has seen the emergence of a more informed and sophisticated consumer and a diminution of the aura once surrounding the physician's judgments and recommendations (Fairhurst & May, 1995; Laine & Davidoff, 1996; Rapp, Shera, & Kisthardt, 1993). The consequence of these changes in the culture of medicine is an increase in the demand by patients and their families for more objective and clinically relevant information with which to evaluate medical options and outcomes. Thus, QOL, often described as a consumer-centered construct, has gained legitimacy with researchers and physicians sensitive to this change in culture.

These same factors have contributed to the growing interest in QOL research in the field of children's health. Like adults, children have benefited from medical advances, especially in the fields of oncology, neonatology, and organ transplantation (Goodwin, Boggs, & Graham-Pole, 1994; Holmes & Holmes, 1975; Jenney, Kane, & Lurie, 1994; Reynolds, Garralda, Postlethwaite, & Goh, 1990; Saigal et al., 1996; Sokal, 1995; Wray, Radley-Smith, & Yacoub, 1992). As a result of these advances, there is a growing population of children with once fatal, now chronic, illnesses whose current life quality and future prospects are unclear (Hinds, 1990; Jenney et al., 1994; McGee, 1994; Pal, 1996; Parsons & Brown, 1998; Rosenbaum, Cadman, & Kirpalani, 1990; Spieth & Harris, 1996; Stein & Jessop, 1982). It is estimated, for example, that there are now more than 200,000 survivors of childhood cancer (Parsons & Brown, 1998). The advances in pediatric medicine, including the care of chronically ill children, have been costly, and the resources required to provide state of the art treatment to children has not escaped the scrutiny of those developing health policy (Orenstein & Kaplan, 1991). Although children remain in a relatively powerless role as patients, increasing numbers of parents are becoming sophisticated and aggressive guardians of their children's interests and have a vested interest in the impact of medical intervention (Kirschbaum, 1996).

REVIEW OF THE RESEARCH LITERATURE

Since gaining the attention of health science researchers, the field of QOL research, as reflected in peer-reviewed journal articles, has grown enormously. From 1966 through 1974, a total of 83 articles were identified in a MEDLINE literature search using the Medical Subject Headings (MeSH Term) quality of life. During the following 20 years, there was a marked increase in the number of quality of life citations with 125 for the year 1975, 402 for 1985, 1907 for 1995, and 3744 for 2001. Since 1992, QOL has had its own peer reviewed journal, *Quality of Life Research*, and a less formal publication, *Quality of Life Newsletter*, as well as an international organization, *The International Society for Quality of Life Research*, which has held annual conferences since 1994.

The research interest in QOL of children is distinguished by its somewhat tardy and limited appearance in peer-reviewed journals. Only 16 articles on quality of life in children were identified between 1966 and 1974, using the MEDLINE database and adding the search term exact subject child (birth through age 18) to MeSH Term quality of life. Although the absolute number of articles on children's QOL remains low, this

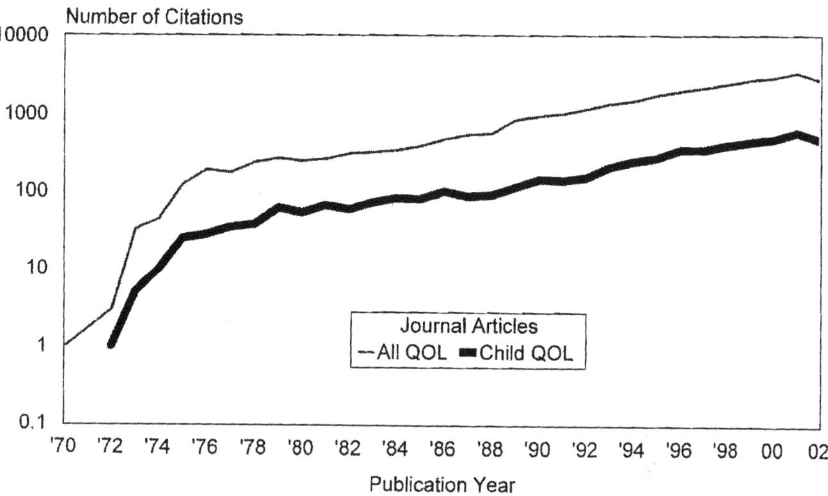

FIG. 18.1. Number of QOL literature citations per year as a function of publication year.

should not obscure the rapid rate of increase in the number of articles published, which parallels the rate of increase in the QOL field as a whole. In the years 1975, 1985, 1995, and 2001, there were 25, 82, 283, and 625 citations, respectively—constituting annually from 16 to 20% of the total QOL literature. Figure 1 demonstrates the parallel progression on a logarithmic scale from 1970 through 2002.

Previous reviews of the literature on childhood QOL focus primarily on specific medical conditions (Badia Llach, Benavides Ruiz, & Rajmil Rajmil, 2001; Baker, Hesdon, & Marson, 2000; Bandell-Hoekstra, Abu-Saad, Passchier, & Knipschild, 2000; Bender, 1996; Blaiss, 1999; Bradlyn, Harris, & Spieth, 1995; Bradlyn & Pollock, 1996; Broughton & Broughton, 1994; Carpay & Arts, 1996; Cella & Tulsky, 1993; Chang, 1991; Colver & Jessen, 2000; Dodson, 1994; Duffy & Duffy, 1997; Ferrell, 1995; Finlay, 1998; Jenney et al., 1995; Juniper, 1997a, 1997b; King et al., 1997; Mattejat & Remschmidt, 1998; Meyers & Weitzner, 1995; Mulhern et al., 1989; Murray & Passo, 1995; Osman & Silverman, 1996; Quittner, 1998; Rutishauser, Sawyer, & Bowes, 1998; Sloan, Khakoo, Cluff, & Waldman, 1979). Other reviews focus on available instruments or methodological issues (Eiser & Morse, 2001a; Connolly & Johnson, 1999; Erling, 1999; Hughes & Hwang, 1996; Kind, 1994; Kozinetz et al., 1999; Marra, Levine, McKerrow, & Carleton, 1996; Pal, 1996; Richards & Hemstreet, 1994; Rosenbaum et al., 1990; Spieth & Harris, 1996). Vivier, Bernier, and Starfield (1994) provide an excellent overview of the broader field of pediatric health outcomes.

Few reviews assess the literature on empirical studies of childhood QOL (Bullinger & Ravens-Sieberer, 1995; Eiser & Morse, 2001b, 2001c; Najman & Levine, 1981; Schmidt, Garratt, & Fitzpatrick, 2002). Najman and Levine (1981) included three pediatric studies in a review of 23 research studies. Bullinger and Ravens-Sieberer (1995) reviewed 320 articles identified in the English and German literature. In their comprehensive review, four aspects of the literature are described: condition of study populations, age range, article type, and assessment informant. Bullinger and Ravens-Sieberer (1995) found that: (1) the literature is dominated by theoretical work with a paucity of empirical studies, (2) the majority of publications focus on two conditions–children with cancer and children who have undergone organ transplant, and (3) the research participants are predominantly adolescents followed by elementary age children with few studies of preschool age children. Bullinger and Ravens-Sieberer (1995) found assessment strategies to be dominated by parent report with a small minority taking into account the child's perspective. In further analysis of the 53 empirical studies published in 1993 and 1994, few meet Bullinger's and Ravens-Sieberer's criteria for research significance as determined by (a) the use of a multidimensional assessment instrument, (b) the presence of a control, and (c) a sample size over 100. Eiser and Morse (2001b, 2001c) reviewed 137 articles and identify 43 instruments, 19 generic and 24 disease-specific, that they felt were potentially useful in clinical trials or following interventions. They found "no distinctions made in the literature between measures of QOL, health, or functional status" (2001b). In a more in-depth investigation, they found 16 instruments that utilized the report of both the child and the parent, 7 that elicited information only from the parent, and 17 instruments completed solely by the child (2001b). Eiser and Morse also reported on the use in childhood studies of measures designed for adult populations, and on the concordance of child and parental report (2001b). Schmidt, Garratt, and Fitzpatrick (2002) identified 16 generic pediatric QOL instruments, meeting predefined research and psychometric criteria. They highlight two instruments as particularly promising, the Child Health Questionnaire (Landgraf, Abetz, & Ware, 1996) and the Child Health and Illness Profile (Schmidt et al., 2002; Starfield et al., 1993).

Earlier reviews, then, bear witness to the pediatric populations in which QOL has been studied most extensively and at the same time document the limitations of published research.

Literature Selection

A computer-assisted search of the medical literature using MEDLINE and of the psychological literature using PsycINFO, from 1967 through 1996, was conducted using the key word and exact subject combinations, quality of life and child (birth through age 18). A follow-up search of the medical literature using MEDLINE, from 1997 to 2002, was conducted using the MeSH Term *quality of life* and exact subject *child*. More than 5,524 citations were thereby identified. Additional articles were found in the bibliographies of selected articles and reviews and from a bibliography compiled by Tamburini (1996) that is available on CD-ROM. Article titles and abstracts were screened and selected for further inspection using a "broad net" approach. Articles were selected for inclusion in this review if the following criteria were satisfied: (1) the population addressed includes children or adolescents; (2) QOL is a central focus of the article; (3) the conceptualization or assessment of QOL involves more than purely medical or physiological criteria; and (4) the article includes at least an English language abstract with sufficient data to answer some if not all of the research questions.

The articles are coded along six broad dimensions. The first two dimensions provide an overview of the literature. *Article type* stratifies the literature into three categories: (1) theory or literature review, (2) instrument development or pilot study, and (3) empirical study. *Study populations* examines the characteristics of the study samples, including age, sample size, and defining condition or context. Only the defining characteristic is considered in theoretical or review articles. In the instance of duplicate reporting on the same study sample, characteristics of a single sample are described only once.

The third and fourth dimensions examine methodological issues. *Measurement method* examines the type of strategy adopted by the article for evaluating QOL. Four common strategies for evaluating QOL are distinguished on the basis of their utilization of (a) social indicators, (b) indices, utilities or classifications, (c) batteries of proxy measures, and (d) multidimensional profiles. The first of these strategies is typically employed in population-based studies, whereas the latter three are employed in studies of individuals. These latter three strategies are not mutually exclusive, as some studies utilized more than one approach. *Source of information* explores a critical aspect of methodology. It is a common, if not universal, practice to gather data about a child's behavior, cognitive abilities, and emotional state from multiple perspectives. In this review of QOL assessment, four potential informants are identified, including the child participant, the parent, the clinician or researcher, and the teacher. In this regard, data obtained by physiological examination or formal cognitive testing are distinguished from the subjective report of the child.

The last two dimensions explore the status of conceptualization. *QOL defined* quantifies the presence or absence of an explicit definition of QOL. We accepted as a "definition" any general statement describing the author's understanding of the construct or discussion of the complexity of the construct. In the final dimension, *domains* are explored as an implicit indicator of QOL conceptualization. QOL is commonly described and measured across several dimensions or domains, each domain typically represented by one or more questions or items. A domain is a hypothetical construct and an object of measurement or empirical study. Patrick and Erickson (1993) define *QOL domain* as a "state, attitude, perception, behavior or other sphere of action or thought related to health or quality of life. All the entities [items] in a single domain have some property in common" (p. 417). Domains can be identified statistically using factor analysis to identify themes or questionnaire items that empirically sort together. More typically, domains are identified a priori as areas of interest and provide the basis of initial item development and selection. Subsequently, empirical studies yield data that are used to evaluate a priori choices and to refine or extend item development.

In an attempt to capture broad dimensional themes while preserving the scope of the instruments described, 24 domains were identified as sufficiently prevalent, descriptive, and discrete to organize the less-than-perfectly delineated domains found in the literature. There were some especially broad domains that we expanded to account for a richer variety. For example, we divided the domain of "physical health" into "general physical health," "mobility or motor functioning," "disease or treatment specific symptoms" (in which we included "pain"), and "physiologic status as measured by physical exam (signs) or laboratory test." On the other hand, we collapsed "parent-child relations" and "sibling relations" into "familial relationships." Despite the recognition that the domain described variably as social functioning or peer or social relationships differed in significant ways from a domain typically described as social support, it was often difficult to discriminate between the two and reluctantly we collapsed these into a broad domain of social relations or social functioning.

Our review of these final two dimensions provides the springboard for further exploration of the problem of how to conceptualize QOL. In this section of the chapter, the construct of QOL of children is considered from five prominent frames of reference, including dimensionality, boundaries, descriptive terminology, relativity, and development.

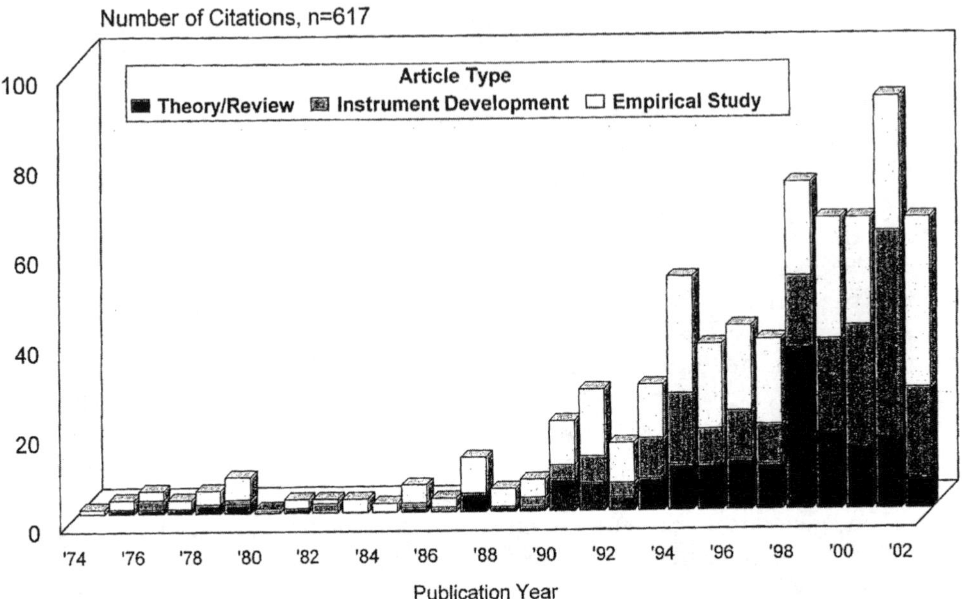

FIG. 18.2. Number of child QOL literature citations, by article type, as a function of publication year.

Overview of the Literature Reviewed

Of more than 5,524 citations identified, 648 articles and 41 chapters, drawn from more than 200 different journals and 10 books met inclusion criteria and were reviewed. Journal articles and book chapters were drawn from the years 1973 (the earliest year in which an article met inclusion criteria) through 2002, with 619 (90%) published since January 1990.

Allowing for some categorical overlap, there were 171 conceptual or review articles, 206 articles describing some phase of instrument development or pilot studies, and 336 articles reporting the results of empirical studies. Figure 2 shows the number of each type of article as a function of publication year, providing an overview of the literature over nearly 30 years. Included in the instrument development category are 49 articles describing the translation of one or more previously validated instruments into another language or for a particular culture. Ruperto et al. (2001) described a very ambitious project to adapt and translate two measures, the Child Health Questionnaire (Landgraf et al., 1996) and the Childhood Health Assessment Questionnaire (Singh, Athreya, Fries, & Goldsmith, 1994), for use in 32 countries. The empirical studies included 254 cross-sectional observational studies, 42 prospective cohort studies, 5 studies positing hypothetical situations, 22 clinical trials or cross-sectional intervention studies, four population based cross-sectional studies, four case-control studies, two retrospective cohort study, and two meta-analyses.

Evolution of the Child QOL Literature

Evident in the progression presented in Figures 1 and 2 is the considerable and evolving interest in QOL in general and specifically in QOL of children. The childhood QOL literature is less impressive for its magnitude than its breadth, dispersed among a wide range of journals and books. There is not a cooperative or orchestrated investigation but a multitude of individual efforts. The sharp increase in published articles beginning about 1990 is coincident with major shifts in health care, most notably the proliferation of managed care mechanisms across all provider types (Starr, 1992) and may reflect a marketplace influence on the application of the construct. Figure 2 also demonstrates the relative growth of articles within each of the three categories: theory, development, and empirical study. Along with the growing number of empirical studies, it is encouraging to note that a comparable increase can be seen in theoretical articles and papers describing instrument development. Although there is little evidence of the "classic" scientific pattern of an evolution from theoretical to empirical work, the commingling of theoretical and empirical work probably reflects more closely how science actually progresses in applied fields. Optimistically, this suggests that the urgency to assess the QOL in various pediatric populations is stimulating heuristic exploration of the construct and the methodology for its measurement. Given such a short history of interest from such a diverse field of investigators, conceptual heterogeneity can be expected. The conceptual heterogeneity of this field, however, could prove difficult to understand without periodic synthesis and review.

Study Populations

Figure 3 shows the number and types of articles addressing specific populations. The vast majority of the 688 articles and chapters reviewed focus on children with chronic medical conditions, including 277 (40%) with one of only five types of disorders-cancer, asthma or allergic rhinitis, rheumatic disease, or epilepsy. About 12 % ($n = 83$) focus on non-clinical populations. There are few studies (2%, $n = 14$) of psychologically vulnerable populations and, through 2002, only 12 articles (< 2%) related to children with emotional or behavioral problems, the first appearing in 1996 (Clark & Kirisci, 1996).[1]

Study populations are quite variable. Through 1996, about half of the studies (106 of 202 for which data are available, 52%) present data on fewer than 100 participants.

[1] Between 1996 and 2002, 14 articles have been published that address aspects of the QOL of children with mental disorders or disabilities (Brantley, Huebner, & Nagle, 2002; Clark & Kirisci, 1996; Dazord et al., 2000; DeVeaugh-Geiss et al., 2002; Flechtner, Moller, Kranendonk, Luther, & Lehmkuhl, 2002; Gilmore & Milne, 2001; Landgraf, Rich, and Rappaport, 2002; Mattejat & Remschmidt, 1998; Mattejat et al., 1998; Patrick, Edwards, & Topolski, 2002; Sawyer et al., 2002; Stein & Kean, 2000; Wurst et al., 2002; Zullig, Valois, Huebner, Oeltmann, & Drane, 2001). Mattejat and Remschmidt (1998) reviewed the concept and brief literature. Seven articles report on studies of specific populations, using existing instruments or methodologies. Clark and Kirisci (1996) reported the impact of posttraumatic stress disorder, depression, and alcohol use disorders on QOL in adolescents. Brantley et al. (2002) studied adolescents with mild mental disabilities using the MSLSS (Huebner, 1994). Dazord et al. (2000) compared children in good health with those with somatic, social, and psychological difficulties. DeVeaugh-Geiss et al. (2002) studied children with attention deficit hyperactivity disorder (ADHD) using the CHQ (Landgraf et al., 1996). Gilmore and Milne (2001) applied the concept of Quality Adjusted Life Years (QALYs; Torrance, 1987) to children with ADHD. Sawyer et al. (2002) used the CHQ in a large population-based study, focusing on youth with ADHD, major depressive disorder, and conduct disorder. Stein and Kean (2000) analyzed epidemiological data from the Ontario Health Survey, including the Quality of Well-Being Scale, and reported on the QOL of adolescents and adults with social phobia. Zullig et al. (2001) compared the QOL of substance-abusing adolescents with nonabusing adolescents, using the MSLSS. Five articles (three in the German literature) describe the development and piloting of instruments targeting children and adolescents with mental disorders (Flechtner et al., 2002; Landgraf et al., 2002; Mattejat et al., 1998; Patrick et al., 2002; Wurst et al., 2002).

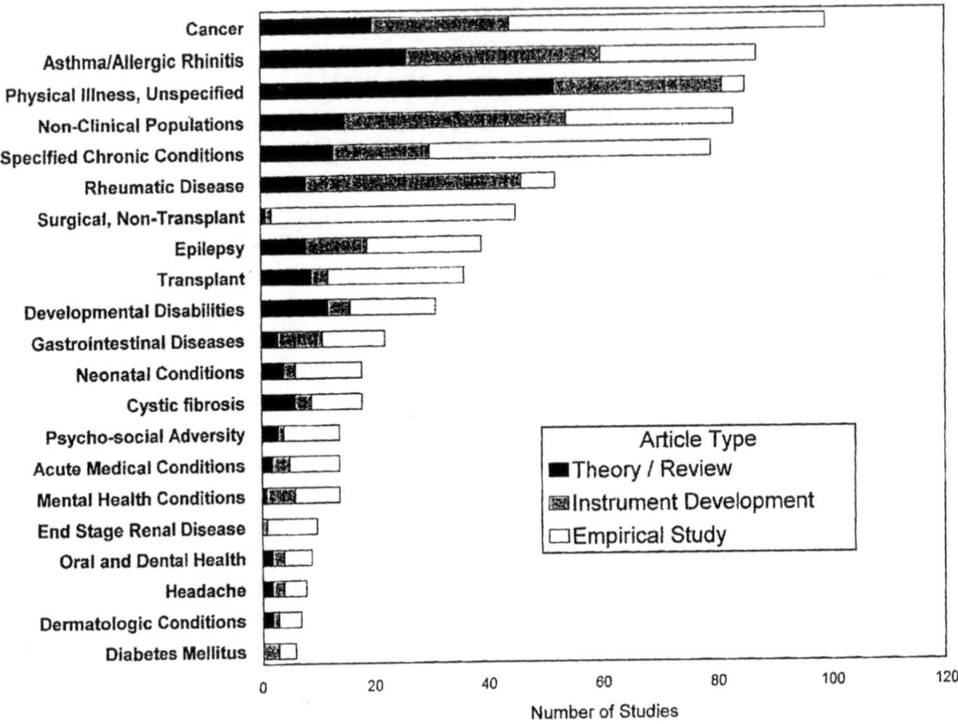

FIG. 18.3. Number of child QOL studies as a function of participant characteristic or condition.

Between 1997 and 2002, although just over half of the empirical studies report on samples larger than 100 participants (72 of 136, 53%), more than three fourths of instrument development studies report on samples larger than 100 (87 of 113, 77%). 40 (9%) of the studies reviewed gathered data on more than 1,000 participants.

An equal number of studies included children between the ages of 5 and 12 years and adolescents, 263 (72%) of the 363 studies for which age data are available. Children under 5 years are least frequently sampled and are represented in only 30% ($n = 109$) of studies. Although more than one third (29%, $n = 122$) of the studies restricted sampling to a single age group, it was not uncommon to find sampling across a wide range in age. Many of the studies reviewed include adults ($n = 76$, 21%), as well as children and adolescents, in their sample, and 17 studies (5%) sampled across the entire life span.

Conceptual Implications of Populations Studied

For the most part, QOL has been used to study children with a variety of chronic, often devastating medical conditions. Especially in the fields of pediatric cancer, asthma, and epilepsy, the literature is more substantial, coherent, and conceptually advanced. For example, Christie and French (1994) constructed three age-delineated and developmentally sensitive instruments to assess QOL of children with asthma. In a large number of empirical studies, especially before 1996, the samples size is small and the age range of participants varies widely, reflecting the ready availability of participants with particular chronic conditions in single clinical settings, and reflecting a field characterized by multiple small efforts. Because sample sizes are typically small, it is not surprising to find samples representing a wide range of ages, suggesting a tendency to sacrifice developmental homogeneity to maximize sample size. An alternative approach can be found in the work of Apajasalo et al. (1996a, 1996b), who cast a wide net in developing QOL instruments, targeting children with nonspecific medical conditions, but in so doing focus on more narrow age ranges.

To study the QOL of children with chronic medical conditions, investigators may place an emphasis on aspects of physical health and individual functioning typically impaired by illness, medication side effects, and time-consumed by involvement in ongoing medical care. In such studies, the ultimate benchmark of the quality of a child's life is to be without pain, without medication, and without the need for more than routine well-child care. Measures developed specifically for chronically ill populations tend to have little capacity to detect variance in the QOL of the healthiest subpopulations. Such measures tend to preclude conceptual consideration of the nature of QOL for those without chronic illness. In addition, some important populations are barely present in the literature to date, leaving significant gaps in our understanding of the concept. Of special note is the paucity of studies of childhood psychiatric populations for whom the nature of QOL may have unique characteristics. The growing number of studies of childhood QOL in nonclinical populations provides an important counterbalance to the otherwise pervasive emphasis on chronic disease. This work, however, is typically not published in the medical literature, limiting its accessibility to health science researchers.

Measurement Methods

The literature reviewed demonstrates a variety of methodological approaches to measurement of the QOL of children. Data on measurement methodology are available in 499 studies. More than three fourths ($n = 411$, 82%) of these studies describe or utilize a multi-item questionnaire or interview protocol. Of these, about half (50%, $n = 205$) utilize a condition-specific instrument.[2] Almost one third ($n = 158$, 32%) of the 499 studies examined use a battery of inventories, tests, and questionnaires in assessing QOL. Standardized tests of development, intelligence, and achievement are employed

---

[2] Condition-specific instruments described in the literature reviewed include the Childhood Asthma Questionnaire (Christie, French, Sowden, & West, 1993), the Childhood Epilepsy Quality of Life Scale (CAVE-Spanish; Herranz & Casas, 1996), the Childhood Health Assessment Questionnaire (rheumatoid arthritis; Singh et al., 1994), the Children's Dermatology Life Quality Index (Lewis-Jones & Finlay, 1995), the Diabetes Life Satisfaction Scale (Ingersoll & Marrero, 1991), the PAQLQ (Juniper et al., 1996), the PCQL (Varni et al., 1998), the Pediatric Oncology Quality of Life Scale (Goodwin et al., 1994), the Quality of Life Headache in Youth Scale (Langeveld et al., 1996), the Quality of Life in Epilepsy (Wildrick, Parker-Fisher, & Morales, 1996), and the Zamberlan Quality of Life Questionnaire (liver transplant; Zamberlan, 1992).

Generic questionnaires described in the literature reviewed include the Child Health and Illness Profile (Starfield et al., 1993), the Functional Status Questionnaire (Jette et al., 1986; Stein & Jessop, 1982), the CHQ (Landgraf et al., 1996), the COOP Charts (Wasson, Kairys, Nelson, Kalishman, & Baribeau, 1994), the Health Insurance Study Health Status Questionnaire (Eisen, Ware, Donald, & Brook, 1979), The MSLSS (Huebner, 1994), the Nordic Quality of Life Index (Lindstrom & Eriksson, 1993), the Nottingham Health Profile (Jones, Bolyard, & Dale, 1993), the Perceived Life Satisfaction Scale (Adelman, Taylor, & Nelson, 1989), the Quality of School Life Questionnaire (Epstein, & McParland, 1976), the Sickness Impact Profile (Hulsebos, Beltman, dos Reis Miranda, & Spangenberg, 1991), the Students' Life Satisfaction Scale (Huebner, 1991), and the TNO AZL Children's Quality of Life Questionnaire (Vogels et al., 1998).

in 17% ($n = 26$) of those studies utilizing a battery of instruments.[3] In addition, measures of self-esteem, psychiatric symptoms, and behavior are commonly used as part of measurement batteries. The Child Behavior Checklist, a common measure of behavioral and emotional symptoms, is used in about 10% ($n = 16$) of the studies using a battery of measures. Sixty-nine articles (14%) employ a clinician-assigned global health status rating or index, often based on data obtained from the parent, child, or both (e.g., Barr et al., 1999; Trudel, Rivard, Dobkin, Leclerc, & Robaey, 1998) Two studies (Juniper, Guyatt, Feeny, Griffith, & Ferrie, 1997; Nixon Speechley et al., 1999) compare multidimensional questionnaires to indexes. Three of the studies reviewed (Garbarino & Crouter, 1978; Jordan, 1983, 1992) use social indicators to assess the status of children in well-circumscribed contexts. Aside from the methodology used in these three studies, there is considerable overlap in the methodology used by investigators. Construct-specific multidimensional profiles are used as part of a battery of measures in 123 (78%) of these 158 studies. Global indexes are incorporated in measurement batteries in 18 (11%) studies.

Conceptual Implications of Measurement Methods

Social Indicators. Reverting to a conceptualization of QOL prominent prior to the 1970s surge of interest in QOL, the social indicator method makes use of available ecological data. The data are selected in part by virtue of availability and in part as a function of the author's conceptualization. Whereas the selection of indicator variables may appear arbitrary and the method itself indirect, the use of social indicators allows for the use of a QOL construct on a grand geographic and historical scale. In one study (1983), Jordan devised an index to compare the QOL of the children of the world by national characteristics and, in the other (1992), the tracking of the QOL of British children from 1815 to 1914. Garbarino and Crouter (1978) used social indicators to investigate the social context of child maltreatment, demonstrating that environmental and material factors are not irrelevant to the construct.

Such studies remain removed from the QOL of individuals and provide no insight into the subjective response of individuals to the conditions described. In fact, it was the discovery that the reported subjective well-being of individuals was not a function of status as reflected by various social indicators that stimulated the development of more direct survey approaches to the measurement of QOL (Andrews & Withey, 1976; Campbell et al., 1976). However, the kind of objective characteristics explored through this method may prove to be more conceptually significant in the treatment of QOL for children than our literature review reveals given the potentially heightened impact of environmental and other objective conditions on the lives of children. Social problems such as a lack of adequate educational resources, poverty and poor nutrition, and victimization and violence may have more profound impact on childhood QOL, especially when they occur during critical developmental stages.

Batteries of Measures. The majority of studies focus on the QOL of individual children, using individually administered questionnaires, interviews, or batteries of instruments, and reporting the findings either as profiles or in terms of utilities. The

[3] Among the standardized tests used in QOL batteries are the Bayley Scale of Infant Development, the Denver Developmental Scale, the Griffiths Mental Development Scale, the Wechsler Intelligence Scale, and the Wide Range Achievement Test.

employment of a battery of instruments in measuring children's QOL is borrowed from prevalent practice in the psychological evaluation of children and is not common in the study of adult QOL. In fact, all of the studies in this category utilize instruments originally designed to measure other psychological constructs. Though prior to 1996, less than half of the studies using a battery of instruments include any instrument specific to the QOL construct, more recent batteries typically include one or more QOL instrument. The battery approach is the most labor intensive and information rich method for determining QOL. It can be argued that this approach makes up for its inelegance in potential comprehensiveness, established psychometrics, and better fit to a specific study. However, batteries are expensive to administer, time-consuming, and best for very small studies. The most critical problem inherent in the battery approach is the use of measures that are not specific to the QOL construct. When a QOL-specific instrument is missing from the battery, QOL must be extrapolated from measures initially developed and intended for other purposes or for more limited purposes. Investigators using the battery approach might argue that they have captured the QOL of their participants. The indirect nature of their investigation, however, leaves the actual construct of what they have measured imprecise.

Global Indexes and Utility Scales. If the battery approach overwhelms with data, the approach using indices, classifications, or utilities is reductionistic—reducing an array of data to a single number. Based either on clinical judgment or on data obtained through interviews, health or functional status is reported on a single scale with four to seven levels or on a linear scale, numerically anchored1 to 100 or 0 to 1.00.[4] Two of these assessment instruments, Bloom's Functional Classification Scales and the Play-Performance Scale for Children are broad-based functional classifications assigned by the clinician. The latter is modeled directly on the earliest example of a functional classification system, the Karnofsky Scale (Lansky, List, Lansky, Cohen, & Sinks, 1985). Such scales provide very broad objective indexes on the participant's functional status at the expense of detail. Classification scales provide no data from the participant's perspective or about the participant's psycho-social-material condition. On the other hand, two other scales in this category, the Quality of Well-Being Scale (QWB) and the Multi-attribute Health Status Classification System (MHSCS), are the bases for utility indices, which are constructed to reflect the participant's perspective, in a quantitative form.

Utility scales allow for the quantification of otherwise qualitative data and allow for the use of H-R QOL data in cost-benefit analysis. Quality of life is described in terms of quality adjusted life years, or QALYs (Torrance, 1987), or as *Well Years* (Kaplan & Anderson, 1988). "The utility approach can be used to measure a single cardinal value, usually between 0 and 1, that reflects the H-R quality of life of the individual at a particular point in time" (Torrance, 1987, p. 594). Torrance defined QALY as the product of a quantity, the number of years of life remaining, and a numeric qualifier or utility between 0 and 1, the latter described as a measure of the strength of one's preference of one health state relative to another (Torrance, 1987). Different health states are assigned utilities using one of several methods, including rating scales,

[4] Among the frequently used classification systems are Bloom's Functional Classification Scales (Bloom, Wallace, & Henk, 1969), the Play-Performance Scale for Children (Lansky, List, Lansky, Cohen, & Sinks, 1985), the Quality of Well-Being Scale (Kaplan & Anderson, 1988), the Multiattribute Health Status Classification System (Feeny et al., 1992), and the utility scale derived from it, the HUI (Torrance et al., 1996).

standard gamble, and time trade-off (Torrance, 1987). Using the utility approach, quantified comparisons can be made across disease states and across age ranges. The real strength of this approach is in its potential usefulness to health economists who must approach health care costs globally.

Unfortunately, there are two problems posed by this method. The methodology for weighting various health states demands a cognitive capacity that may be beyond the functional limits of young children, and therefore weighting may only reflect parental or other expert opinion. Second, both classification systems and utilities are based on deficit states, leaving the absence of infirmity as the optimum state, a retreat from the WHO definition of health. Despite these drawbacks, this approach has proven valuable as reported in the adult literature and may have considerable promise for use with children.

Multidimensional Profiles. The QOL of children is most frequently assessed using a single multidimensional questionnaire or interview specific to this construct. The majority of the studies reviewed employ new instruments designed for a particular study or in development for a particular population. The preponderance of multidimensional instruments used in the assessment of QOL tends to reify QOL as a multidimensional construct, a proposition that is discussed in more detail in a subsequent section of this chapter. That a core set of QOL domains seems to have emerged neither implies that the existence of such a set nor the nature of this set has empirical construct validity, especially when the construct is applied to children. Few of these studies describe how domains or individual questions were selected. French, Christie, and West (1994) provided a notable exception to this predicament, devising a systematic empirical approach to determining what aspects of life to include in their asthma-specific instruments.

Much discussion in the QOL literature has focused on the relative benefits of condition-specific versus generic instruments (Kaplan & Anderson, 1988; Patrick & Erickson, 1993). Condition or disease-specific measures focus on symptoms and side effects characteristic of a population having a specific disease or disorder with the hope that the measure will be sensitive to subtle changes over time. Generic measures, however, allow for cross-population comparison and are viewed as more powerful health policy tools. Kaplan and Anderson (1988) argued that generic measures are more sensitive to unanticipated symptoms and side effects and are no less sensitive to change than condition-specific measures. It should be pointed out that the debate resides wholly within a health care framework. Lehman (1996) proposed an expanded construct hierarchy for QOL, ranging from disease-specific to generic health-related to global QOL. Unfortunately, others in the health research field rarely consider this more comprehensive framework.

Source of Information

In 477 of the studies reviewed, the source of information (informant) is identified. The choice of informant and the number of informants varies considerably in this literature. Figure 4 demonstrates the choice of informant grouped by number of informants. In the majority of the studies ($n = 331$, 69%), data are obtained from a single informant. For single informant studies, the child participant and the parent are equally likely to chosen (child $n = 165$, parent $n = 163$). One fourth of the studies ($n = 118$) elicit the perspective of two informants; most of these ($n = 83$, 70%) involve the parent and child participant. In very few ($n = 26$, 5%) of the studies, data are gathered from

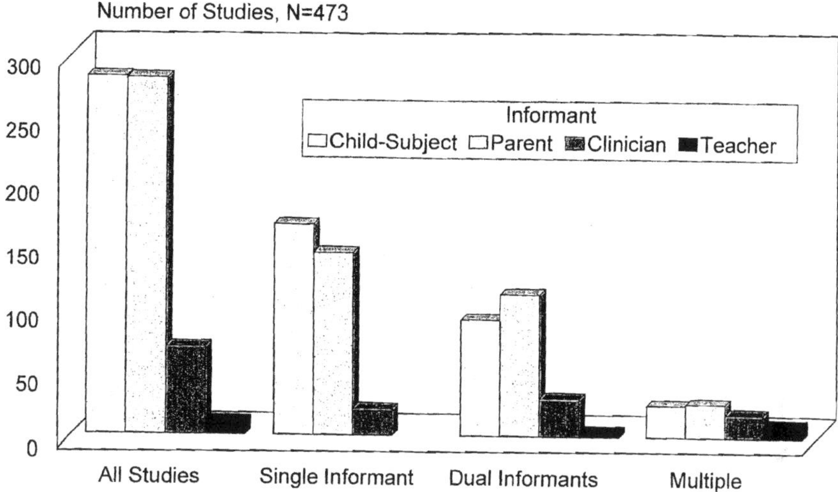

FIG. 18.4. Number of child QOL studies as a function of informant, grouped by number of informants.

three or more sources. Of the 477 studies for which the informants are identified, 59% ($n = 281$) elicit information from the child participant, 59% ($n = 281$) do so from the parent, 14% ($n = 69$) from the clinician, and 3% ($n = 13$) from the teacher. Breaking down the number of informants and specific sources by participant age group reveals that younger children are rarely asked directly about their QOL. As children get older, they are more likely to be a source of information.

Conceptual Implications of Information Sources

Despite considerable, ongoing debate regarding the reliability and validity of self-report data, researchers generally depend on self-report of adults in the assessment of functional status, emotional state, and subjective sense of well-being. On the other hand, a child's self-report has been generally viewed with greater skepticism, and child-focused data are typically elicited from proxies either in lieu of the child's report or as corroboration.

The prominent use of multiple informants in the assessment of the QOL of children allows for a greater range of information about the child, as well as a broader, more comprehensive conceptualization. At the same time, the fact that QOL data are obtained from the child participant directly in more than half of the studies suggests that the child's perspective is viewed as important to the construct. The challenges for investigators then include (a) how to obtain valid and reliable information from the child and (b) what information is best obtained from whom.

The capacity of the child to provide reliable and valid information depends on the child's understanding of the area of interest and the child's ability, cognitively and developmentally, to collaborate in a self-report rating design. Zeltzer et al. (1988) found that children as young as 5 years could understand and use a visual analogue scale to rate somatic symptoms based on vignettes. Harter and Whitesell (1989) demonstrated that a child first appreciates simultaneous experience of two emotions at about 7 years but cannot fully appreciate the simultaneous experience of opposing emotions evoked by a single source until about 11 years. West (1994) described the use of a "smiley" face scale, coloring, and age-appropriate phrasing to facilitate the use of attitude questionnaires with children between the ages of 8 and 11 years. These findings suggest that within a developmentally informed study, the prospects for obtaining reliable and valid information from a child may not be so bleak. Although a child's limited ability to comprehend certain questions or complex Likert-type response scales may limit the scope and utility of self-report QOL data, the alternative use of proxy informants is no less problematic.

Several authors (Achenbach, McConaughy, & Howell, 1987; Edelbrock, Costello, Dulcan, Conover, & Kala, 1986; Eiser & Morse, 2001a; Herjanic, Herjanic, Brown, & Wheatt, 1975; Offord et al., 1996; Stanger & Lewis, 1993; Weissman, Orvaschel, & Padian, 1980) have investigated multiple informant correlation. Herjanic et al. (1975) found very high agreement between the reports of children, 6 to 16 years and their parents on factual information. In response to emotional and behavioral questions, however, agreement between various informants—children, parents, and teachers—has been found to be modest at best (Achenbach et al., 1987; Edelbrock et al., 1986; Herjanic et al., 1975; Offord et al., 1996; Stanger & Lewis, 1993; Weissman et al., 1980). In their review of 14 QOL dual informant studies, Eiser and Morse (2001a) found higher correlation between parent and child report for observable behavior than nonobservable (emotional and social) functioning. The perspectives of proxies, especially on emotional or internal matters, may suffer from lack of information and are certain to be colored by the proxies' relationship to the child. Some suggest that only the child can provide a subjective view of their QOL (Erling, 1999). Alternately, the parents' or teachers' perceptions may serve to counterbalance a child's variance in awareness of or reluctance to report on internal processes and behaviors. These findings suggest that the full spectrum of information may not be available from a single source and support the importance of collecting information about emotional and behavioral status from multiple perspectives (Burns, 1996; Eiser & Morse, 2001a; Hoagwood, Jensen, Petti, & Burns, 1996; Rosenblatt & Attkisson, 1993).

DEFINING QUALITY OF LIFE

From the data presented thus far, it is clear that the conceptual nature of childhood QOL is far from certain. It is surprising, then, to find that authors of the research literature reviewed rarely define QOL explicitly. We reviewed the full text of 270 articles published through 1996 and found that only one third ($n = 91$, 34%) offer an explicit definition of QOL. Of this more limited review, the theoretical papers and review articles do provide a stronger conceptual contribution. More than two thirds ($n = 45$, 69%) of the 65 review and theory articles reviewed define QOL whereas 48% ($n = 29$) of the 60 articles describing instrument development do so. Of the 147 articles reporting on empirical studies, only 14% ($n = 20$) offer an explicit definition of QOL. The paucity of definitions represented in these articles illustrates both the assumption of a common ground, that is, no need to define the obvious, and the evasion of a philosophical quagmire. The definitions that are offered in the literature ranged from impressionistic to the systematic, indicative of the complex nature of QOL and the lack of theoretical cohesiveness.

In lieu of explicit definition, evidence of conceptual thought may be found elsewhere. Bergner (1989) suggested that when an explicit definition is not provided, the reader is expected to deduce one from the dimensions assessed. Confirming Bergner's assertion, data on the domains assessed are far more common. Domains are identified in 211 (85%) of the 249 empirical or instrument development studies published through 1996. This finding seems to reify a commonly accepted characteristic of the QOL construct, that it is multidimensional. We will explore this proposition in more depth in the next section of this chapter. Although considerable variation is found in the domains assessed, of 24 we identified, 6 domains, including (1) functional status or activity limitation, (2) role performance, (3) social functioning, (4) emotional well-being, (5) symptoms associated with physical illness or treatment, and (6) physical health in general are each assessed in more than half of the studies reviewed. This finding suggests a significant and promising degree of implicit conceptual common ground. At the same time, the emphasis on physical symptoms and physical health may reflect the nature of the populations under consideration. In contrast to the above six domains, relatively neglected domains of potential importance include resilience and self-efficacy (McGee, 1994; Starfield, 1987) and environmental conditions, including home, school, and community (Bullinger & Ravens-Sieberer, 1995; Lindstrom, 1994). Figure 5 demonstrates the frequency with which each of the 24 most prevalent domains is assessed in studies through 1996.

We compared the domains assessed by five diverse validated QOL instruments: the Multidimensional Student's Life Satisfaction Questionnaire (MSLSS; Huebner, 1994), a generic questionnaire developed for assessment of nonclinical populations; the Child Health Questionnaire (CHQ; Landgraf et al., 1996), a generic health-related QOL instrument developed for studies of clinical populations; the Health Utilities

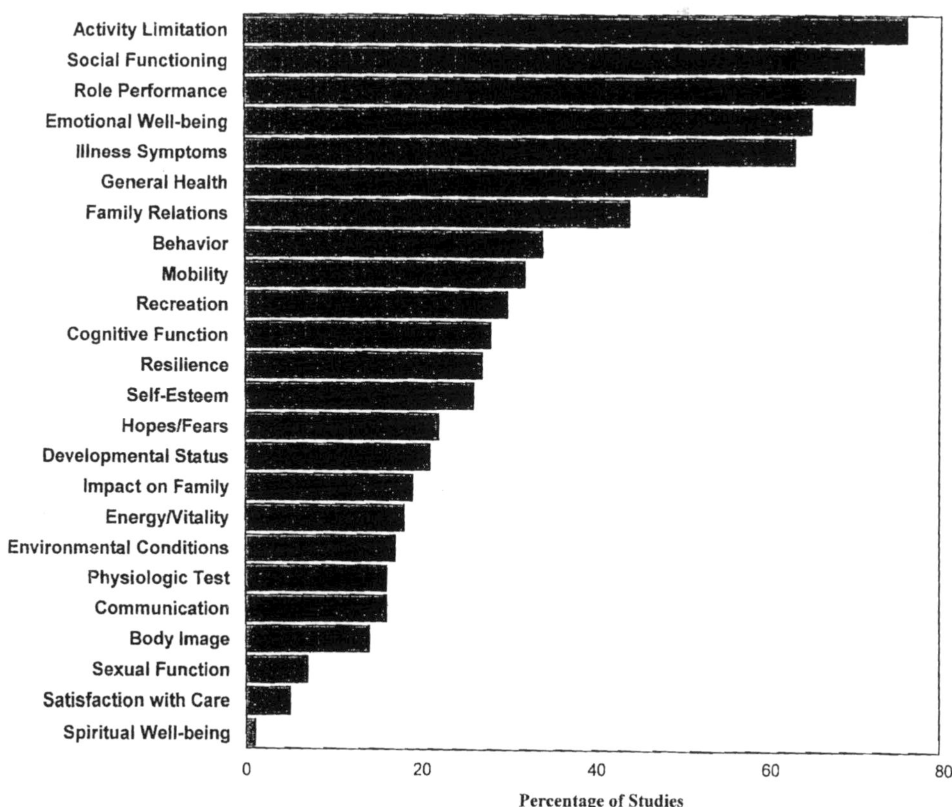

FIG. 18.5. Percentage of child QOL studies assessing specific QOL domains.

Index Mark 2 Classifications (HUI; Torrance et al., 1996), a generic health status classification system; and two disease-specific QOL questionnaires-the Pediatric Asthma Quality of Life Questionnaire (PAQLQ; Juniper et al., 1996) and the Pediatric Cancer Quality of Life Inventory (PCQL; Varni et al., 1998). As might be expected, there were areas of consensus and divergence. The CHQ, HUI, PAQLQ, and PCQL all assess physical function and emotional function; the CHQ, HUI, and PAQLQ all assess activity restrictions; the CHQ, HUI, and PCQL assess symptoms and pain; the CHQ and PAQLQ both assess worries, energy and vitality, and self-esteem, the last also assessed by the MSLSS. The HUI and PCQL assess cognitive functioning, whereas the CHQ and MSLSS assess aspects of academic or school performance and family functioning. Social functioning is assessed by the CHQ, PCQL, and MSLSS. Of these five instruments, only the CHQ assesses behavior, wishes, and health perception, and only the MSLSS assesses the living environment.

CONCEPTUALIZING QUALITY OF LIFE OF CHILDREN

The QOL construct, specifically as it relates to children, can be explored in a variety of ways. Implicitly or explicitly, the literature highlights several critical conceptual aspects of QOL, among which are the following:

1. *Dimensionality*: Is QOL a multidimensional construct or a super-ordinate, global judgment?
2. *Boundaries*: In the fields of health and behavioral science, is it more appropriate to delineate health-related quality of life as the proper area of study?
3. *Descriptive terminology*: What words are used to describe QOL?
4. *Relativity*: Against what standard of comparison or from whose perspective is a QOL appraisal made?
5. *Developmental context*: Does the conceptualization of QOL of children demand any special consideration? Below, each of these constructs is more fully described.

Dimensionality

A common assertion is that QOL is a multidimensional construct. In one of the earliest attempts to examine the QOL of children, Eisen, Ware, Donald, and Brook (1979) cited the WHO definition of health as the basis for a multicomponent conceptual framework. Several authors (Austin, Smith, Risinger, & McNelis, 1994; Bradlyn et al., 1995; Farmer & Michener, 1979; French et al., 1994; Hoare & Russell, 1995; Langeveld, Koot, Loonen, Hazebroek-Kampschreur, & Passchier, 1996; Neff & Dale, 1990; Nespoli et al., 1995; Schmidt et al., 1993; Sloan, Khakoo, Cluff, & Waldman, 1979; Starfield et al., 1995) propose a list of dimensions or domains in lieu of a formal or integrated definition of QOL. Conversely, Zamberlan (1992) defined QOL as "a subjective global characterization made by the child about physical and emotional functioning, symptoms of disease and treatment, peer and family relationships and interactions, and the child's current overall assessment of well-being according to stated life-satisfaction" (p. 172). Huebner (1994) proposed the measurement of global life satisfaction as a summary assessment or a "general evaluation of the quality of a person's life that is over and above evaluation of specific domains" (p. 149).

The debate on the dimensionality of QOL has its roots in the formative studies in the field. Campbell et al. (1976), in an adult survey using a multidimensional approach, concluded that such an approach would provide a more detailed and comprehensive picture of an individual's life experience than a single measure:

> The utility of global assessments is somewhat limited, unless they are fleshed out with more detailed information about reactions to more specific domains of life. Common sense would suggest that if a person feels disappointed with his current life situation, it is because certain features of his life—a marriage turned sour, a job below expectations—are particularly dissatisfying. More generally, we might expect that whatever global report an individual gives as to his overall sense of well-being should be some compound of his gratification's and disappointments with more specific features of life. (p. 61)

Andrews and Withey (1976), by contrast, proposed a global approach to the measure of QOL, believing that the individual's evaluation of life quality has more to do with a personal system of values than with particular life dimensions. Although more elegant, one-dimensional approaches to life satisfaction have been criticized on the basis of reliability (Diener, 1984). The only parameter of reliability that can be analyzed for a one-dimensional scale is temporal, and one-dimensional scales have been found to be less reliable over time (Diener, 1984). This leaves the investigator with the difficult task of distinguishing true change from measurement error. In the adult health literature, multidimensional models of QOL have long been favored, based on the belief that they provide greater research utility and richer conceptual value (Aaronson, Bullinger, & Ahmedzai, 1988; Cella & Bonomi, 1995; Hughes & Hwang, 1996; Patrick & Ericksson, 1993). From a practical perspective, we agree with the reasoning of many contributors to the adult QOL field that a multidimensional approach may offer greater opportunity for advances in scientific knowledge and greater capacity to influence improvements in quality of care.

Boundaries

Attendant to the selection of QOL domains is a consideration of the context of study and the delineation of boundaries or framework of the construct. Several authors in the pediatric medical field embrace the more restrictive concept of H-R QOL (Dodson, 1994; Jenney et al., 1995; Schipper, Clinch, & Powell, 1990; Vickrey, Hays, Brook, & Rausch, 1992). Kind (1994) stated that H-R QOL is specific to the health care context and referred to "those aspects of life which are affected by the provision or withholding of health care" (p. 108).

The delineation H-R QOL places emphasis on the impact of illness symptoms and treatment side effects, typically focusing on more objective domains of role performance and functional status. Dodson (1994) drew a distinction between health status and H-R QOL, the latter characterized by subjective perception of health-related domains and sense of well-being. Although they embraced the more restricted concept of H-R QOL, Jenney et al. (1995) acknowledged part of the problem inherent in its adoption: "The term implies that illness can have consequences in almost every domain of life" (p. 146). McDowell and Newell (1996) acknowledged the diffuse boundaries of the QOL construct:

> These [instruments] are variously termed "general health status measures" or "measures of health-related quality of life." Although the trend has been toward calling these

> instruments quality of life measures, the term is rarely defined and there is no clear distinction between quality of life measures and methods.... It seems idle to dispute whether a given instrument measures functional status, health status, or quality of life, so we will use the labels interchangeably. (p. 380)

Not only is the selection of health-related domains problematic, but also the scope of health care interventions is not always easily discerned. From our perspective, the HR-QOL approach has limited conceptual and practical usefulness. Its greatest contribution has been in the area of severe chronic illness, where the overriding concern is the impact of physical impairment on selected aspects of life and social adaptation. In the realm of child mental health, however, interventions often address the home, family, and educational environments, as well as functioning within those environments, challenging the presumption that the boundaries of H-R QOL are purely medical.

Inevitably, a formal theory of QOL must encompass all significant dimensions of individual life, including those now considered "health related" and those that extend to family, work, school, and the broader social environment. In the future, it will be understood that health care impacts aspects of life not currently considered to be within the boundaries of "health related."

Descriptive Terminology

Whether a one-dimensional or multidimensional approach is preferred, whether a restrictive or comprehensive concept of QOL is adopted, the questions still must be posed in descriptive terms, such as "how happy are you with..."or "how satisfied are you with..." Integral to an understanding of the various interpretations of QOL, then, is an appreciation of the subjectivity of the terms used to describe QOL. Maeland provided a useful inventory of such terms, including proposed definitions (Hanestad, 1996):

- *Happiness*—reflecting the affective component of the individual's experience
- *Satisfaction*—reflecting the cognitive component of the individual's experience
- *Functional ability* (or the closely related *capacity*)—in relation to physical, social, cognitive, and psychological aspects of life
- *Need fulfillment*—relating to the different needs that have to be satisfied
- *Self-realization*—emphasizing personal growth and development.

Happiness and satisfaction represent alternative modes of subjective appraisal, complementary though not mutually exclusive. The distinction between these two was the basis of considerable debate in the formative QOL literature, with Cantril and Campbell emphasizing *satisfaction*, Bradburn adopting the term happiness (Campbell et al., 1976), and Andrews and Withey (1976) choosing to anchor their scales with the terms *delighted* and *terrible*. McDowell and Newell (1996) suggested that happiness represents a transient response to immediate events, whereas satisfaction indicates a comparison of current circumstances to an external or temporally removed standard. Although the distinction between happiness and satisfaction is largely lost in the child literature, subjective appraisal is often cited as a cardinal feature of QOL (Dodson, 1994; French et al., 1994; Hinds, 1990; Lash & Sigal, 1976; McGee, 1994; Reid & Renwick, 1994; Richards & Hemstreet, 1994; Schmidt et al., 1993).

Some contributors to the child literature are troubled by the subjective and therefore inherently unscientific nature of QOL, turning instead to an aggregate of more objective indicators of functional ability, including cognition, behavior, return to school, and self-esteem (Gemke & Bonsel, 1996; Wray, Radley-Smith, & Yacoub, 1992).

Opportunity for need fulfillment is less prominent in the conceptualization of QOL of children, but can be inferred in the inclusion of objective environmental conditions in the QOL equation as advocated by several authors (Bullock, Little, & Millham, 1994; Felce & Perry, 1996; Jordan, 1992; Lindstrom, 1994). For example, Jordan (1992) proposed an index of QOL based on available assets, "conducive to health and harmony" (p. 257). Similarly, Lindstrom (1994) defined QOL in terms of "essential population resources" and proposed a model in four spheres, with "the global sphere representing society and the macro environment, the external sphere representing socioeconomic conditions, the interpersonal sphere representing the structure and function of social support, and the personal sphere representing physical, mental, and spiritual conditions" (p. 529).

The connection between need fulfillment and well-being can be traced to Maslow, who identified a hierarchy of need domains-such as physiological, safety, love, esteem, and self-actualization as the basis for well-being (Patrick & Erickson, 1993).

Like need-fulfillment, *self-realization* is a term rarely encountered explicitly in the child QOL literature. Self-realization is more complex, involving the interspace between the subjective and objective, environmental opportunities and constraints, and a developmental progression.

McGee (1994) proposed alternate terminology, *perception* in lieu of *happiness* or *satisfaction*; *resources* to capture much of what might otherwise fall under the rubric of *functional ability*; and a middle term, *integration*, a category in which she includes *self-esteem*, *security*, and *competence*. In delineating the subjective, *perception*, and the objective, *resources*, McGee was again left with a more difficult set of terms that may be related to both Maeland's *need fulfillment* and *self-realization*.

The evaluative terms chosen to capture QOL indicate conceptual orientation, whether subjective, objective, or integrative. They provide a template for measurement, as in *"how happy are you with . . ."* and alert one to the potential scope of the field to be measured, whether subjective appraisal or functional domains, environmental conditions or personality attributes.

A comprehensive theory of QOL must encompass the full spectrum of evaluative terms: subjective states of being, relative satisfaction of need, external resources viewed in tandem with internal capacities, and observable functional and adaptive status. QOL, understood as a complex interactive composite of all these aspects, would offer the most comprehensive conceptualization. As the basis for a measure, however, such a conceptualization may prove to be unwieldy. In developing an instrument to measure QOL, authors must acknowledge their particular choices in limiting comprehensive conceptualization in the service of scientific progress.

Relativity

The standard against which QOL is measured is rarely considered. Relative to *what* does one gauge satisfaction with life? Calman (1987) described the evaluative process as a function of the gap between current reality and aspiration: "Quality of life measures the difference, at a particular period of time, between the hopes and expectations of the individual and the individual's present experience" (p. 7).

Several authors (Berardo & Berardo, 1992; Cella & Bonomi, 1995; Cella & Tulsky, 1993; Hinds, 1990; Najman & Levine, 1981; Schalock, 1996) have adopted the notion of a relativity "gap" between current experience and expectation in their conceptual discussions of QOL. Dennis, Williams, Giangreco, and Cloninger (1993), in a complex model, proposed the convergence of three spheres of values and needs—those of the individual, those held in common by all people, and those specific to the individual's culture—as the basis of comparison in the evaluation of an individual's QOL. Andrews and Withey (1976) outlined eight possible standards of comparison, including:

- Change in one's life over time ("better off today than yesterday")
- Relative to an ideal (culturally based)
- Relative to "good enough" (the car still runs; the roof doesn't leak; still employed)
- Comparison to a personal swing point or threshold (an internal barometer of well being)
- Rate of change (frequency of pay increase versus the actual increment)
- Relative to norm (how one ought to feel about a specific attribute/domain)
- Self-oriented (not influenced by objective condition, idiosyncratic)
- Relative to the "other guy" (how some one else in your situation feels).

The evaluative process is inherently dynamic and idiosyncratic, adjusting to changes in the individual's circumstances and to the acquisition of new information, insight, aptitude, or experience. The capacity to engage in such a process requires a certain degree of cognitive skill and a body of experience on which to draw comparisons, two elements assumed to be present in healthy adults but only emergent in children. A challenge, then, to the assessment of childhood QOL is the orientation of the child participant to the psychological task of comparison.

Developmental Context

Children are described as "moving targets" (French et al., 1994), propelled along an intricate developmental trajectory, complicating and challenging a singular or uniform conceptualization of QOL across the life cycle. Several authors (Bradlyn & Pollock, 1996; French et al., 1994; Goodwin, Boggs, & Graham-Pole, 1994; Kurtin, Landgraf, & Abetz, 1994; Mulhern, Fairclough, Friedman, & Leigh, 1990; Mulhern et al., 1989; Pantell & Lewis, 1987; Schalock, 1996; Schalock & Begab, 1990; Stark & Faulkner, 1996; Stein & Jessop, 1992) incorporated the idea of a developmental framework in their definition of QOL. Kaplan and Anderson (1988) took another approach, arguing against a separate conceptual framework for QOL (health status) in children, suggesting that such an approach unnecessarily complicates the application of QOL data in the policy arena.

When development is considered, two aspects are typically emphasized, cognitive capacity and role elaboration. The level of cognitive development has implications for method of assessment. Cognitive aspects of development include not only language acquisition and reading comprehension but also the ability to understand and evaluate subtleties of emotions, self-worth, and etiologies of illness (Bird & Podmore, 1990; Eiser & Havermans, 1994; Harter, 1989; Harter & Whitesell, 1989; Lewis & Lewis, 1982). Role elaboration involves age-appropriate behaviors and the recognition that the range of interests and activities vary considerably as a function of age throughout the life span including, but not limited to, childhood and adolescence.

Stark and Faulkner (1996), in their three-dimensional model of QOL, adopted Erikson's psychosocial stage theory of development. Erikson's epigenetic theory distinguishes eight stages of ego development, each characterized by developmental tasks and core conflicts, and resolution of each stage's core conflict culminates in a decisive shift in the basic orientation of the individual to himself and society at large (Erikson, 1964). Common dimensions of popular adult measures of QOL[5] are intimacy and vocational productivity, key characteristics, according to Erikson, of young and middle adulthood. Implicitly, these adult instruments may be seen as developmentally sensitive, a characteristic inconsistently present in the child QOL measures. Given the greater range of psychosocial development from birth through adolescence and then from adolescence through mature adulthood, the measurement of QOL in youth must accommodate a developmental perspective and directly assess QOL for a particular age group based on appropriate developmental tasks and developmental norms.

Comprehensive Conceptual Models

Whereas some authors have focused on one or more conceptual issue, others have attempted to provide a more comprehensive definition of QOL for children. For example, Stark and Faulkner (1996) conceptualized QOL graphically across three dimensions. Along one dimension are seven life domains–health care, living environment, family, social and emotional relationships, education, work, and leisure. The second dimension is characterized by Eriksonian developmental stages—early childhood, late childhood, adolescence, adulthood, and late adulthood. The third domain is reflective of the specific population in question, those with mental retardation, and represents four levels of support—intermittent, limited, extensive, and pervasive. Felce and Perry (1996), borrowing from Campbell et al. (1976), proposed a different three-dimensional model of QOL that incorporates an interplay between objective life conditions, subjective appraisal of those objective conditions, the mediating influence of personal values, and aspirations. Nichols (1978) focused on two other constructs as central to that of QOL: self-respect and freedom of choice. Schalock (1996) brought together many of the components discussed above in his commentary on the subject:

> QOL should be viewed as an organizing concept... best understood from the perspective of the individual... QOL embodies general feelings of well-being, opportunities to fulfill one's hopes and dreams, and positive social interactions... QOL cannot be separated from an individual's developmental stage, support network, and relevant life domains. (p. 123-125)

Similarly, Bradlyn and Pollock (1996) offered a succinct definition that provides structure for the construction or evaluation of an instrument: "Quality of life is a multidimensional construct, incorporating both objective and subjective data, including (but not limited to) the social, physical, and emotional functioning of the child and, when indicated, his/her family. QOL measurement must be sensitive to changes that occur throughout development" (p. 49).

Development of a comprehensive conceptual model is essential to an understanding of the construct. Such a model must at least address each of the five dimensions discussed and at the same time provide sufficient direction for the development of measures to assess the construct.

---

[5] Sickness Impact Profile (Bergner et al., 1976), Index of Well-Being (Campbell et al., 1976), McMaster Health Index (Chambers et al., 1976), EuroQol Quality of Life Scale (EuroQol Group, 1990; Nord, 1991), Nottingham Health Profile (Hunt, McKenna, McEwen, Williams, & Papp, 1981); Functional Status Questionnaire (Jette et al., 1986), Quality of Life Interview (Lehman, 1988; Lehman, Ward, & Linn, 1982), and Short Form-36 Health Survey (Ware & Sherbourne, 1990).

DIRECTIONS FOR FURTHER STUDY: A RESEARCH AGENDA

The child QOL literature is characterized by a broad range of study populations, considerable variation in measurement method, inconsistent definition, and idiosyncratic application of the term *QOL*. The literature may be seen, then, as a reflection of both the fundamental challenges of measuring QOL, the historical and contemporary uncertainty regarding the basic nature of the construct, the burgeoning demand of the outcomes field for QOL data, and the specific challenges posed by the context of childhood.

The rapid growth of interest in childhood QOL poses further challenges to the development of the field. The literature is approaching a complexity and size that makes it difficult to understand the knowledge base. There appears to be considerable diversity but some consensus within the field, with a host of external pressures stimulating rapid development, selection, and use of QOL measures. Still, the existing literature shows unmistakable promise. The importance of the construct is demonstrated by its ubiquitous proliferation. The hope for utility of QOL as a descriptive mechanism and as a measure of health care outcome for children is revealed in the efforts of many of the investigators.

What direction might research take in the future? This review suggests that the agenda should include (a) inclusion of a broader diversity of study populations, (b) improvement of measurement methods and more sophisticated use of psychometrics, and (c) investment in conceptual development and the shoring up of theoretical structure.

Study Populations. To achieve conceptual cohesiveness, empirical research must cut across study populations and extend further into others yet to be studied. The vast majority of QOL studies have focused on a range of specific chronic medical conditions. Although some community studies have been conducted, there is no consensus regarding the normative level of quality of life in children. Specifically, more research is needed employing diverse community samples and populations of children with emotional or behavioral problems. These needed studies will not only broaden the base of normative data but will also prevent the definition of QOL from becoming myopically determined by its focus on children with chronic medical conditions. This is especially important given the developmental progression of childhood and the likelihood that measures of QOL in this population will require age, gender, and socioeconomic norms. Without more work on QOL in community samples of children, it is difficult to assess whether the QOL of youth receiving care for specific illnesses is relatively high, relatively low, or about the same as most children. The inclusion of QOL measures in community studies, consequently, is important, especially if these measures can also be used within clinical populations.

Younger children have received relatively less attention than older children in research studies, perhaps because of the difficulty of formulating the construct for those with a more limited range of social, cognitive, and communicative experiences, or perhaps because of the overriding importance of basic biological needs and parental attachment for the very young. Similarly, much more needs to be understood about the QOL of "transitional"-aged children who are about to enter adulthood, whose QOL is typically now assessed using adult QOL measures. In the broadest sense, more research is needed on how QOL changes across the developmental process, from childhood to adulthood. More longitudinal work on the long-term course of QOL in community samples, treated and untreated clinical samples, is also warranted. Somewhat surprisingly, there is even a paucity of research on the shorter term QOL-related outcomes of medical interventions in children. In the long run, many medical interventions with children are presumed to allow for full and productive lives. Yet, relatively few studies use either cross sectional or (preferably) longitudinal designs to assess QOL at multiple points across the life span.

Measurement Methods and Information Sources. A great deal more fundamental research is needed regarding the procedural ("practical") aspects of QOL assessment, including the relative merits of various measurement methods, choice and range of informants, reconciliation of discordance between informants, domain selection and emphasis, and question construction. The challenges related to instrumentation are relatively more complicated in the research of child populations. Questions of vocabulary and concept comprehension, the constriction of time, scale comprehension, and use of words versus pictographs are a few of these challenges. We have already discussed the challenges posed by the need to use multiple informants to gather self-reported and other-reported information regarding child QOL. In addition, the rapid rate of developmental change in youth may require the use of normative data to gauge progress over time.

Children perceive time differently than adults and may have difficulty understanding questions that begin with phrases such as "over the last 6 months." Adults are usually capable of knowing that a bad day does not necessarily impact on various aspects of their quality of life in general, a capacity not clearly possessed by younger children. The problem children have in understanding time frames impacts on the reliability and on sensitivity to change.

Given the tremendous challenges to the development of child QOL measures, it is not surprising that we call for more research in this area. The importance of such research cannot be understated, given the prevailing pressures to measure QOL that is found in many contemporary medical studies and settings. The utility of QOL data for medical practice and health policy dictates systematic, conceptually driven research programs to produce reliable, valid measures. At best, the use of unreliable, invalid QOL measures will produce data that are difficult to interpret. At worst, the use of such measures can lead decision makers to change care patterns based on spurious or unreliable findings.

Conceptual Development. Further conceptual work is needed to sharpen and enhance the theoretical base underpinning the science and application of the QOL construct for children. The constructs underlying QOL need to be conceptually delineated so that instruments can be assessed for their underlying validity. On the conceptual end of the dialogue between theory and practice, broad all-encompassing formulations need to be weighed against methodological limitations and practical considerations. A working definition must fully encompass the construct but should be capable of guiding instrument development. Such a dynamic between working definition and measurement might best be approached from multiple frames of reference, such as the five we have discussed.

How might this work? If the QOL of children is defined as multidimensional, then the selection of appropriate domains becomes an important research agenda. If the QOL construct chosen is restricted to health-related boundaries, the determination of what is and what is not a health-related domain must be addressed. Choice of terminology might either precede or follow selection of relevant domains. Question formulation and functional content must be guided by developmental consideration. Most critically, a developmental frame might allow the psychosocial context of the child to be the subtext for integrative assessment beyond the child's immediate physical, emotional, and social reality.

If this process did, indeed, work, service providers and researchers would find themselves with a new and unique tool for treatment planning and assessment. QOL can serve as an integrative concept, focusing on those domains that most appeal to many practitioners, administrators, and even policy makers. A QOL measure could conceivably replace the current "battery of measurement tools" approach to assessment and outcomes measurement that can lead to duplication, excess paperwork, and contradictory results (Rosenblatt & Rosenblatt, 2002). Such a process builds in relevance, assuring that QOL measures will address those domains and populations essential to the goals of current behavioral health service delivery systems.

CONCLUSION

For many chronic medical conditions, QOL has become a core measure of clinical outcome, joining morbidity and mortality as a cardinal index of health care efficacy and effectiveness. For serious medical conditions of childhood, much of the pioneering work on QOL has been done with children suffering from cancer and asthma, and with recipients of organ transplants. Concurrent with these established research directions, our review demonstrates a welcome increase in the emphasis on theory and measurement development. To date, however, no unifying QOL theory has emerged. The field remains fragmented by ad hoc measurement strategies and a tendency to focus narrowly on QOL dimensions specific to a given condition or, more generally, on criteria of physical health. There has been little attention to many other important QOL dimensions, most notably environmental conditions and social support.

Progress in the childhood QOL field is currently propelled by increasing interest in outcomes measures within the health policy arena and by the emergence of efficacious treatments for severe childhood disorders. Progress will be enhanced by investigations of important new research populations, including vulnerable populations, children and youth with emotional and behavioral disorders, and community samples, as well as clinical populations from diverse socioeconomic and ethnic populations. It is essential that QOL be studied in diverse community samples so that results from clinical samples can be compared with children in general and with specific subsamples of interest from the general population of children. It is important for the field to move beyond narrow band measurement strategies and to investigate a broader range of QOL dimensions. To accomplish this goal, there is need for a formal theory of the quality-of-life construct. Such a theory must integrate the many concepts that comprise the construct and allow operationalization so that assessment measures can be designed and implemented for use in health policy research and in the evaluation of health care efficacy and effectiveness.

Progress in this arena can impact directly on how service providers and administrators view treatment planning and the assessment of outcomes. Many current assessment and outcomes tools derived from a tradition of clinical efficacy research, where treatments are developed and tested in controlled conditions and with circumscribed populations that may not translate to "real world" practice settings and populations. Similarly, many existing measures do not translate, either psychometrically or conceptually, to current service delivery settings (Rosenblatt & Rosenblatt, 2002). QOL measures developed in the context of diverse community samples and broad-based measurement strategies can, by purpose and design, address the needs of contemporary delivery systems. Such measures can, consequently, address some of the challenges raised in recent initiatives (e.g., Hoagwood, Hibbs, Brent & Jensen, 1995) calling for the development of more relevant and applicable empirically based treatments in behavioral health.

Some may be skeptical about the theoretical integrity of a broad-based QOL construct, believing instead that the essence and substance of QOL is physical health and resiliency expressed in terms of functional status. We believe that other life dimensions must be explored, and where appropriate, incorporated into a more comprehensive conceptual model. Measurement instruments can then be developed based on the theoretical model and validated through empirical research. In addition, we think that an essential subjective component is embedded in the QOL construct requiring accurate and reliable assessment of the unique perspective of the individual—a proposition that may be difficult if not impossible to achieve with children. It is our firm belief that achievement of theoretical cohesion and broadband measurement of childhood QOL will promote critical advances in the provision of health care to children.

ACKNOWLEDGMENTS

Preparation of this chapter was supported in part by research and training grants from the National Institute of Mental Health (MH46122 and MH18261) and by support from an NIMH Research Center Grant (Center for Mental Health Services Research, MH43694) to the University of California San Francisco and the University of California Berkeley. The authors wish to thank the following individuals for their help and assistance in the completion of the manuscript: Hannah Dresner and Joel Yager. The views expressed in this chapter represent those of the authors only.

REFERENCES

Aaronson, N. K., Bullinger, M., & Ahmedzai, S. (1988). A modular approach to quality-of-life assessment in cancer clinical trials. *Recent Results in Cancer Research, 111*, 231–249.

Achenbach, T. M., McConaughy S. H., & Howell, C. T. (1987). Child/adolescent behavioral and emotional problems, implications of cross-informant correlation for situational specificity. *Psychological Bulletin, 101*, 213–232.

Adelman, H. S., Taylor, L., & Nelson, P. (1989). Minors' dissatisfaction with their life circumstances. *Child Psychiatry & Human Development, 20*, 135–147.

Andrews, F. M., & Withey, S. B. (1976). *Social indicators of well-being: Americans' perceptions of life quality*. New York: Plenum.

Apajasalo, M., Rautonen, J. Holmberg, C., Sinkkonen, J., Aalberg, V., Pihko, H., et al. (1996). Quality of life in pre-adolescence: A 17-dimensional health-related measure (17D). *Quality of Life Research, 5*, 532–538.

Apajasalo, M., Sintonen, H., Holmberg, C., Sinkkonen, J., Aalberg, V., Pihko, H., et al. (1996). Quality of life in early adolescence: A sixteen-dimensional health-related measure (16D). *Quality of Life Research, 5*, 205–211.

Austin, J. K., Smith, M. S., Risinger, M. W., & McNelis, A. M. (1994). Childhood epilepsy and asthma: Comparison of quality of life. *Epilepsia, 35*, 608–615.

Badia Llach, X., Benavides Ruiz, A., & Rajmil Rajmil, L. (2001). Instrumentos de evaluación de la calidad de vida relacionada con la salud en niños y adolescentes con asma. [Instruments for measuring health-related quality of life in children and adolescents with asthma]. *Anales Espanoles de Pediatria, 54*, 213–221.

Baker, G. A., Hesdon, B., & Marson, A. G. (2000). Quality-of-life and behavioral outcome measures in randomized controlled trials of antiepileptic drugs: a systematic review of methodology and reporting standards. *Epilepsia, 41*, 1357–1363.

Bandell-Hoekstra, I., Abu-Saad, H. H., Passchier, J., & Knipschild, P. (2000). Recurrent headache, coping, and quality of life in children: a review. *Headache, 40*, 357–370.

Barr, R. D., Simpson, T., Whitton, A., Rush, B., Furlong, W., & Feeny, D. H. (1999). Health-related quality of life in survivors of tumours of the central nervous system in childhood-A preference-based approach to measurement in a cross-sectional study. *European Journal of Cancer, 35*, 248–255.

Bender, B. G. (1996). Measurement of quality of life in pediatric asthma clinical trials. *Annals of Allergy, Asthma, and Immunology, 77*, 438–445.

Berardo, D. H., & Berardo, F. M. (1992). Quality of life across age and family stage. *Journal of Palliative Care, 8*(3), 52–55.

Bergner, M. (1989). Quality of life, health status, and clinical research. *Medical Care, 27(Suppl. 3)*, S148–S156.

Bergner, M., Bobbitt, R. A., Pollard, W. E., Martin, D. P., & Gilson, B. S. (1976). The sickness impact profile: validation of a health status measure. *Medical Care, 14*, 57–67.

Bird, J. E., & Podmore, V. N. (1990). Children's understanding of health and illness. *Psychology & Health, 4*, 175–185.

Blaiss, M. S. (1999). Quality of life in allergic rhinitis. *Annals of Allergy, Asthma, and Immunology, 83*, 449–454.

Bloom, H. J. G., Wallace, E. N. K., & Henk, J. M. (1969). The treatment and prognosis of medulloblastoma in children: A study of 82 verified cases. *American Journal of Roentgenology, 105*, 43–62.

Bradburn, N. M. (1969). *The structure of psychological well-being*. Chicago: Aldine.

Bradlyn, A. S., Harris, C. V., & Spieth, L. E. (1995). Quality of life assessment in pediatric oncology: A retrospective review of phase III reports. *Social Science and Medicine, 41*, 1463–1465.

Bradlyn, A. S., & Pollock, B. H. (1996). Quality-of-life research in the Pediatric Oncology Group: 1991–1995. *Journal of the National Cancer Institute Monographs, 20*, 49–53.

Brantley, A., Huebner, E. S., & Nagle, R. J. (2002). Multidimensional life satisfaction reports of adolescents with mild mental disabilities. *Mental Retardation, 40*, 321–329.

Broughton, W. A., & Broughton, R. J. (1994). Psychosocial impact of narcolepsy. *Sleep, 17(Suppl. 8)*, S45–S49.

Bullinger, M., & Ravens-Sieberer, U. (1995). Health related quality of life assessment in children: A review of the literature. *Revue Europeenne de Psychologie Appliquee, 45*, 245–254.

Bullock, R., Little, M., & Millham, S. (1994). Assessing the quality of life for children in local authority care or accommodation. *Journal of Adolescence, 17*, 29–40.

Burchard, J. D., & Clark, R. T. (1990). The role of individualized care in a service delivery system for children and adolescents with severely maladjusted behavior. *Journal of Mental Health Administration, 17*, 48–98.

Burns, B. J. (1996). What drives outcomes for emotional and behavioral disorders in children and adolescents? In D. M. Steinwachs, L. M. Flynn, G. S. Norquist, & E. A. Skinner (Eds.), *Using client outcomes information to improve mental health and substance abuse treatment. New directions for mental health services, No. 71*. (pp. 89–102). San Francisco: Jossey-Bass.

Calman, K. C. (1987). Definitions and dimensions of quality of life. In N. K. Aaronson & J. H. Beckmann (Chief Eds.), J. L. Bernheim, & R. Zittoun (Assoc. Eds.), *Quality of life of cancer patients: Vol. 17. Monograph series of the European Organization for Research and Treatment of Cancer* (pp. 1–9). New York: Raven.

Campbell, A., Converse, P. E., & Rodgers, W. L. (1976). *The quality of American life: Perceptions, evaluations, and satisfactions*. New York: Russell Sage.

Cantril, H. (1965). *The pattern of human concerns*. New Brunswick, NJ: Rutgers University Press.

Carpay, H. A., & Arts, W. F. (1996). Outcome assessment in epilepsy: Available rating scales for adults and methodological issues pertaining to the development of scales for childhood epilepsy. *Epilepsy Research, 24*(3), 127–136.

Cella, D. F., & Bonomi, A. E. (1995). Measuring quality of life: 1995 update. *Oncology, 9(Suppl. 11)*, 47–60.

Cella, D. F., & Tulsky, D. S. (1993). Quality of life in cancer: Definition, purpose, and method of measurement. *Cancer Investigation, 11*, 327–336.

Chambers, L. W., Sackett, D. L., Goldsmith, C. H., McPherson, A. S., & McAuley, R. G. (1976). Development and application of an index of social function. *Health Services Research, 11*, 430–441.

Chang, P. N. (1991). Psychosocial needs of long-term childhood cancer survivors: A review of literature. *Pediatrician, 18*, 20–24.

Christie, M. J., & French, D. J. (Eds.). (1994). *Assessment of quality of life in childhood asthma*. Langhorne, PA: Harwood.

Christie, M. J., French, D. J., Sowden, A., & West, A. (1993). Development of child-centered disease-specific questionnaires for living with asthma. *Psychosomatic Medicine, 55*, 541–548.

Clark, D. B., & Kirisci, L. (1996). Posttraumatic stress disorder, depression, alcohol use disorders and quality of life in adolescents. *Anxiety, 2*(5), 226–233.

Colver, A., & Jessen, C. (2000) Measurement of health status and quality of life in neonatal follow-up studies. *Seminars in Neonatology, 5*, 149–157.

Connolly, M. A., & Johnson, J. A. (1999). Measuring quality of life in paediatric patients. *Pharmacoeconomics, 16*, 605–625.

Dazord, A., Manificat, S., Escoffier, C., Kadour, J. L., Bobes, J., Gonzales, M. P., Nicolas, J., & Cochat, P. (2000). Qualité de vie des enfants: intérêt de son évaluation. Comparaison d'enfants en bonne santé et dans des situations de vulnérabilité (psychologique, sociale, somatique). [Quality of life of children: importance of its evaluation. Comparison of children in good health with those at risk (psychological, social, somatic)]. *Encephale, 26*(5), 46–55.

Dennis, R. E., Williams, W., Giangreco, M. F., & Cloninger, C. J. (1993). Quality of life as context for planning and evaluation of services for people with disabilities. *Exceptional Child, 59*, 499–512.

DeVeaugh-Geiss, J., Conners, C. K., Sarkis, E. H., Winner, P. K., Ginsberg, L. D., Hemphill, J. M., et al. (2002). GW320659 for the treatment of attention-deficit/hyperactivity disorder in children. *Journal of the American Academy of Child and Adolescent Psychiatry, 41*, 914–920.

Diener, E. (1984). Subjective well-being. *Psychological Bulletin, 95*, 542–575.

Dodson, W. E. (1994). Quality of life measurements in children with epilepsy. In M. R. Trimble & W. E. Dodson (Eds.), *Epilepsy and quality of life* (pp. 217–226). New York: Raven.

Duffy, C. M., & Duffy, K. N. (1997). Health assessment in the rheumatic diseases of childhood. *Current Opinion in Rheumatology, 9*, 440–447.

Edelbrock, C., Costello, A. J., Dulcan, M. K., Conover, N. C., & Kala, R. (1986). Parent-child agreement on child psychiatric symptoms assessed via structured interview. *Journal of Child Psychology and Psychiatry and Allied Disciplines, 27*, 181–190.

Eisen, M., Ware, J. E. Jr., Donald, C. A., & Brook, R. H. (1979). Measuring components of children's health status. *Medical Care, 17*, 902–921.

Eiser, C., & Havermans, T. (1994). Knowledge and attitudes as determinants of "quality of life" in children with asthma. In M. J. Christie & D. J. French (Eds.), *Assessment of quality of life in childhood asthma* (pp. 99–106). Langhorne, PA: Harwood.

Eiser, C., & Morse, R. (2001a). Can parents rate their child's health-related quality of life? Results of a systematic review. *Quality of Life Research, 10*, 347–357.

Eiser, C., & Morse, R. (2001b). Quality-of-life measures in chronic diseases of childhood. *Health Technology Assessment, 5*(4), 1–157.

Eiser, C., & Morse, R. (2001c). A review of measures of quality of life for children with chronic illness. *Archives of Disease in Childhood, 84*, 205–211.

Epstein, J. L., & McParland, J. M. (1976). The concept and measurement of the quality of school life. *American Educational Research Journal, 13*, 15–30.

Erikson, E. H. (1964). *Childhood and society*. New York: Norton.

Erling, A. (1999). Methodological considerations in the assessment of health-related quality of life in children. *Acta Paediatrica (Suppl. 88)* 106–107.

EuroQol Group. (1990). EuroQol-A new facility for the measurement of health-related quality of life. *Health Policy, 16*, 199–208.

Fairhurst, K., & May, C. (1995). Consumerism and the consultation: The doctor's view. *Family Practice, 12*, 389–391.

Farmer, R. G., & Michener, W. M. (1979). Prognosis of Crohn's disease with onset in childhood or adolescence. *Digestive Diseases and Sciences, 24*, 752–757.

Feeny, D., Furlong, W., Barr, R. D., Torrance, G. W., Rosenbaum, P., & Weitzman, S. (1992). A comprehensive multiattribute system for classifying the health status of survivors of childhood cancer. *Journal of Clinical Oncology, 10*, 923–928.

Felce, D., & Perry, J. (1996). Assessment of quality of life. In R. L. Schalock & G. N. Siperstein (Eds.), *Quality of life: Conceptualization and measurement* (pp. 63–72). Washington, DC: American Association on Mental Retardation.

Ferrell, B. R. (1995). The impact of pain on quality of life. A decade of research. *Nursing Clinics of North America, 30*, 609–624.

Finlay, A. Y. (1998). Quality of life assessments in dermatology. *Seminars in Cutaneous Medicine and Surgery, 17*, 291–296.

Flechtner, H., Moller, K., Kranendonk, S., Luther, S., & Lehmkuhl, G. (2002). Subjective quality of life of children and adolescents with psychiatric disorders: development and validation of a new assessment scale. *Praxis der Kinderpsychologie und Kinderpsychiatrie, 51*(2), 77–91.

French, D. J., Christie, M. J., & West, A. (1994). Quality of life in childhood asthma: Development of the Childhood Asthma Questionnaires. In M. J. Christie & D. J. French (Eds.), *Assessment of quality of life in childhood asthma* (pp. 157–180). Langhorne, PA: Harwood.

Garbarino, J., & Crouter, A. (1978). Defining the community context for parent-child relations: The correlates of child maltreatment. *Child Development, 49*, 604–616.

Gemke, R. J., & Bonsel, G. J. (1996). Reliability and validity of a comprehensive health status measure in a heterogeneous population of children admitted to intensive care. *Journal of Clinical Epidemiology, 49*, 327–333.

Gerhardt, U. (1990). Qualitative research on chronic illness: The issue and the story. *Social Science and Medicine, 30*, 1149–1159.

Gilmore, A., & Milne, R. (2001). Methylphenidate in children with hyperactivity: review and cost-utility analysis. *Pharmacoepidemiology and Drug Safety, 10*(2), 85–94.

Goodwin, D. A., Boggs, S. R., & Graham-Pole, J. (1994). Development and validation of the Pediatric Oncology Quality of Life Scale. *Psychology Assessment, 6*, 321–328.

Hanestad, B. R. (1996). Whose life is it anyway? In A. Hutchinson, E. McColl, M. Christie, & C. Riccalton (Eds.), *Health outcome measures in primary and out-patient care.* (pp. 187–198). Amsterdam, The Netherlands: Harwood Academic Publishers.

Hargreaves, W. A., Shumway, M., Hu, T., & Cuffel, B. (1998). *Cost-outcome methods for mental health.* San Diego, CA: Academic Press.

Harter, S. (1989). Causes, correlates, and the functional role of global self-worth: A life-span perspective. In J. Kolligan & R. Sternberg (Eds.). *Perceptions of competence and incompetence across the life span* (pp. 67–97). New Haven, CT: Yale University Press.

Harter, S., & Whitesell, N. R. (1989). Developmental changes in children's understanding of single, multiple, and blended emotion concepts. In C. Saarni & P. L. Harris (Eds.), *Children's understanding of emotion* (pp. 81–116). New York: Cambridge University Press.

Henggeler, S. W., & Borduin, C. M. (1990). *Family therapy and beyond: A multisystemic approach to treating the behavior problems of children and adolescents.* Pacific Grove, CA: Brooks/Cole.

Herjanic, B., Herjanic, M., Brown, R., & Wheatt, T. (1975). Are children reliable reporters? *Journal of Abnormal and Child Psychology, 3*, 41–48.

Herranz, J. L., & Casas, C. (1996). Escala de calidad de vida del nino con epilepsia [Quality of life in childhood epilepsy]. *Revista de Neurologia, 24*, 28–30.

Hinds, P. S. (1990). Quality of life in children and adolescents with cancer. *Seminars in Oncology Nursing, 6*, 285–291.

Hoagwood, K., Hibbs, E., Brent, D., & Jensen, P. (1995). Efficacy and effectiveness studies of child and adolescent psychotherapy. *Journal of Consulting and Clinical Psychology, 63*, 683–687.

Hoagwood, K., Jensen, P. S., Petti, T., & Burns, B. J. (1996). Outcomes of mental health care for children and adolescents: I. A comprehensive conceptual model. *Journal of the American Academy of Child and Adolescent Psychiatry, 35*, 1055–1063.

Hoare, P., & Russell, M. (1995). The quality of life of children with chronic epilepsy and their families: Preliminary findings with a new assessment measure. *Developmental Medicine and Child Neurology, 37*, 689–696.

Hollandsworth, J. G. (1988). Evaluating the impact of medical treatment on the quality of life: A 5-year update. *Social Science and Medicine, 26*, 425–434.

Holmes, H. A., & Holmes, F. F. (1975). After ten years, what are the handicaps and life styles of children treated for cancer? An examination of the present status of 124 such survivors. *Clinical Pediatrics, 14*, 819–823.

Huebner, E. S. (1991). Initial development of the Student's Life Satisfaction Scale. *School Psychology International, 12*(3), 231–240.

Huebner, E. S. (1994). Preliminary development and validation of a multidimensional life satisfaction scale for children. *Psychological Assessment, 6*, 149–158.

Hughes, C., Hwang, B. (1996). Attempts to conceptualize and measure quality of life. In R. L. Schalock & G. N. Siperstein (Eds.), *Quality of life: Conceptualization and measurement* (pp. 51–62). Washington, DC: American Association on Mental Retardation.

Hulsebos, R. G., Beltman, F. W., dos Reis Miranda, D., & Spangenberg, J. F. (1991). Measuring quality of life with the sickness impact profile: A pilot study. *Intensive Care Medicine, 17*, 285–288.

Hunt, S. M., McKenna, S. P., McEwen, J., Williams, J., & Papp, E. (1981). The Nottingham Health Profile: subjective health status and medical consultations. *Social Science and Medicine. Part A, Medical Sociology, 15(3 Pt 1)*, 221–229.

Ingersoll, G. M., & Marrero, D. G. (1991). A modified quality-of-life measure for youths: Psychometric properties. *Diabetes Educator, 17*, 114–118.

Jenney, M. E., Kane, R. L., & Lurie, N. (1995). Developing a measure of health outcomes in survivors of childhood cancer: A review of the issues. *Medical and Pediatric Oncology, 24*(3), 145–153.

Jette, A. M., Davies, A. R., Cleary, P. D., Calkins, D. R., Rubenstein, L. V., Fink, A., et al. (1986). The Functional Status Questionnaire: Reliability and validity when used in primary care. *Journal of General Internal Medicine, 1*(3), 143–149.

Jones, E. A., Bolyard, A. A., & Dale, D. C. (1993). Quality of life of patients with severe chronic neutropenia receiving long-term treatment with granulocyte colony-stimulating factor. *Journal of the American Medical Association, 270*, 1132–1133.

Jordan, T. E. (1983). Developing an international index of quality of life for children: The NICQL Index. *Journal of the Royal Society of Health, 103*, 127–30.

Jordan, T. E. (1992). An index of the quality of life for Victorian children and youth: The VICY Index. *Social Indicators Research, 27*, 257–277.

Juniper, E. F. (1997a). How important is quality of life in pediatric asthma? *Pediatric Pulmonology* (Suppl. 15), 17–21.

Juniper, E. F. (1997b). Quality of life in adults and children with asthma and rhinitis. *Allergy, 52*, 971–977.

Juniper, E. F., Guyatt, G. H., Feeny, D. H., Ferrie, P. J., Griffith, L. E., & Townsend, M. (1996). Measuring quality of life in children with asthma. *Quality of Life Research, 5*, 35–46.

Juniper, E. F., Guyatt, G. H., Feeny, D. H., Griffith, L. E., & Ferrie, P. J. (1997). Minimum skills required by children to complete health-related quality of life instruments for asthma: comparison of measurement properties. *European Respiratory Journal, 10*, 2285–2294.

Kaplan, R. M. (1989). Health outcome models for policy analysis. *Health Psychology, 8*, 723–735.

Kaplan, R. M., & Anderson, J. P. (1988). A general health policy model: Update and applications. *Health Services Research, 23*, 203–235.

Kind, P. (1994). Measuring quality of life in children. In M. J. Christie & D. J. French (Eds.), *Assessment of quality of life in childhood asthma* (pp. 107–117). Langhorne, PA: Harwood.

King, C. R., Haberman, M., Berry, D. L., Bush, N., Butler, L., Dow, K. H., et al. (1997). Quality of life and the cancer experience: the state-of-the-knowledge. *Oncology Nursing Forum, 24*, 27–41.

Kirschbaum, M. S. (1996). Life support decisions for children: What do parents value? *ANS. Advances in Nursing Science, 19*, 51–71.

Kozinetz, C. A., Warren, R. W., Berseth, C. L., Aday, L. A., Sachdeva, R., & Kirkland, R. T. (1999). Health status of children with special health care needs: measurement issues and instruments. *Clinical Pediatrics, 38*, 525–533.

Kurtin, P. S., Landgraf, J. M., & Abetz, L. (1994). Patient-based health status measurements in pediatric dialysis: Expanding the assessment of outcome. *American Journal of Kidney Diseases, 24*, 376–382.

Laine, C., & Davidoff, F. (1996). Patient-centered medicine: A professional evolution. *Journal of the American Medical Association, 275*, 152–156.

Landgraf, J. M., Abetz, L., & Ware, J. (1996). *The CHQ user's manual*. Boston: New England Medical Center, Health Institute.

Landgraf, J. M., Rich, M., & Rappaport, L. (2002). Measuring quality of life in children with attention-deficit/hyperactivity disorder and their families: development and evaluation of a new tool. *Archives of Pediatrics & Adolescent Medicine, 156*, 384–391.

Langeveld, J. H., Koot, H. M., Loonen, M. C., Hazebroek-Kampschreur, A. A., & Passchier, J. (1996). A quality of life instrument for adolescents with chronic headache. *Cephalalgia, 16*(3), 183–196.

Lansky, L. L., List, M. A., Lansky, S. B., Cohen, M. E., & Sinks, L. F. (1985). Toward the development of a play performance scale for children (PPSC). *Cancer, 56*, 1837–1840.

Lash, T., & Sigal, H. (1976). *State of the child: New York City*. New York: Foundation for Child Development.

Lehman, A. F. (1988). A quality of life interview for the chronically mentally ill. *Evaluation and Program Planning, 11*, 51–62.

Lehman, A. F. (1996). Measures of quality of life among persons with severe and persistent mental disorders. *Social Psychiatry and Psychiatric Epidemiology, 31*, 78–88.

Lehman, A. F., Ward, N. C., & Linn, L. S. (1982). Chronic mental patients: The quality of life issue. *American Journal of Psychiatry, 139*, 1271–1276.

Lewis, C. E., & Lewis, M. A. (1982). Determinants of children's health-related beliefs and behaviors. *Family and Community Health, 4*, 85–97.

Lewis-Jones, M. S., & Finlay, A. Y. (1995). The Children's Dermatology Life Quality Index (CDLQI): Initial validation and practical use. *British Journal of Dermatology, 132*, 942–949.

Lindstrom, B. (1994). Quality of life for children and disabled children based on health as a resource concept. *Journal of Epidemiology & Community Health, 48*, 529–530.

Lindstrom, B., & Eriksson, B. (1993). Quality of life among children in the Nordic countries. *Quality of Life Research, 2*, 23–32.

Marra, C. A., Levine, M., McKerrow, R., & Carleton, B. C. (1996). Overview of health-related quality-of-life measures for pediatric patients: Application in the assessment of pharmacotherapeutic and pharmacoeconomic outcomes. *Pharmacotherapy, 16*, 879–888.

Mattejat, F., Jungmann, J., Meusers, M., Moik, C., Nolkel, P., Schaff, C., et al. (1998). An inventory for assessing the quality of life of children and adolescents–a pilot study. *Zeitschrift fur Kinder- und Jugendpsychiatrie und Psychotherapie, 26*(3), 174–182.

Mattejat, F., & Remschmidt, H. (1998). Assessing the quality of life of children and adolescents with psychiatric disorders-A review. *Zeitschrift fur Kinder und Jugendpsychiatrie und Psychotherapie, 26*(3), 183–196.

McDowell, I., & Newell, C. (1996). *Measuring health: A guide to rating scales and questionnaires* (2nd ed.). New York: Oxford University Press.

McGee, H. M. (1994). Quality of life: Assessment issues for children with chronic illness and their families. In M. J. Christie & D. J. French (Eds.), *Assessment of quality of life in childhood asthma* (pp. 83–97). Langhorne, PA: Harwood.

Meyers, C. A., & Weitzner, M. A. (1995). Neurobehavioral functioning and quality of life in patients treated for cancer of the central nervous system. *Current Opinion in Oncology, 7*, 197–200.

Mulhern, R. K., Fairclough, D. L., Friedman, A. G., & Leigh, L. D. (1990). Play performance scale as an index of quality of life of children with cancer. *Psychological Assessment, 2*, 149–155.

Mulhern, R. K., Horowitz, M. E., Ochs, J., Friedman, A. G., Armstrong, F. D., & Copeland, D. (1989). Assessment of quality of life among pediatric patients with cancer. *Psychological Assessment, 1*, 130–138.

Murray, K. J., Passo, M. H. (1995). Functional measures in children with rheumatic diseases. *Pediatric Clinics of North America, 42*, 1127–1154.

Najman, J. M., & Levine, S. (1981). Evaluating the impact of medical care and technologies on the quality of life: A review and critique. *Social Science and Medicine. Part F, Medical and Social Ethics, 15*(2-3), 107–115.

Neff, E. J., & Dale, J. C. (1990). Assessment of quality of life in school-aged children: A method-Phase I. *Maternal-Child Nursing Journal, 19*, 313–320.

Nespoli, L., Verri, A. P., Locatelli, F., Bertuggia, L., Taibi, R. M., & Burgio, G. R. (1995). The impact of pediatric bone marrow transplantation on quality of life. *Quality of Life Research, 4*, 233–240.

Nichols, P. J. (1978). General management of the young chronic sick. *Journal of the Royal Society of Medicine, 71*, 442–447.

Nixon Speechley, K., Maunsell, E., Desmeules, M., Schanzer, D., Landgraf, J. M., Feeny, D. H., et al. (1999). Mutual concurrent validity of the child health questionnaire and the health utilities index: an exploratory analysis using survivors of childhood cancer. *International Journal of Cancer* (Suppl. 12), 95–105.

Nord, E. (1991). EuroQol: health-related quality of life measurement. Valuations of health states by the general public in Norway. *Health Policy, 18*, 25–36.

Offord, D. R., Boyle, M. H., Racine, Y., Szatmari, P., Fleming, J. E., Sanford, M., et al. (1996). Integrating assessment data from multiple informants. *Journal of the American Academy of Child and Adolescent Psychiatry, 35*, 1078–1085.

Orenstein, D. M., & Kaplan, R. M. (1991). Measuring the quality of well-being in cystic fibrosis and lung transplantation. The importance of the area under the curve. *Chest, 100*, 1016–1018.

Osman, L., & Silverman, M. (1996). Measuring quality of life for young children with asthma and their families. *European Respiratory Journal* (Suppl. 21), 35s–41s.

Pal, D. K. (1996). Quality of life assessment in children: A review of conceptual and methodological issues in multidimensional health status measures. *Journal of Epidemiology and Community Health, 50*, 391–396.

Pantell, R. H., & Lewis, C. C. (1987). Measuring the impact of medical care on children. *Journal of Chronic Diseases, 40* (Suppl. 1), 99S–115S.

Parsons, S. K., & Brown, A. P. (1998). Evaluation of quality of life of childhood cancer survivors: A methodological conundrum. *Medical and Pediatric Oncology* (Suppl. 1), 46–53.

Patrick, D. L., Edwards, T. C., & Topolski, T. D. (2002, June). Adolescent quality of life, Part II: Initial validation of a new instrument. *Journal of Adolescence, 25*, 287–300.

Patrick, D. L., & Erickson, P. (1993). *Health status and health policy: Quality of life in health care evaluation and resource allocation*. New York: Oxford University Press.

Quittner, A. L. (1998). Measurement of quality of life in cystic fibrosis. *Current Opinion in Pulmonary Medicine, 4*, 326–331.

Rapp, C. A., Shera, W., & Kisthardt, W. (1993). Research strategies for consumer empowerment of people with severe mental illness. *Social Work, 38*, 727–735.

Reid, D. T., & Renwick, R. M. (1994). Preliminary validation of a new instrument to measure life satisfaction in adolescents with neuromuscular disorders. *International Journal of Rehabilitation Research, 17*, 184–188.

Reynolds, J. M., Garralda, M. E., Postlethwaite, R. J., & Goh, D. (1991). Changes in psychosocial adjustment after renal transplantation. *Archives of Disease in Childhood, 66*, 508–513.

Richards, J. M. Jr., & Hemstreet, M. P. (1994). Measures of life quality, role performance, and functional status in asthma research. *American Journal of Respiratory and Critical Care Medicine, 149*(2 Pt. 2), S31–S39.

Rosenbaum, P., Cadman, D., & Kirpalani, H. (1990). Pediatrics: Assessing quality of life, In B. Spilker (Ed.), *Quality of life assessment in clinical trials* (pp. 205–215). New York: Raven.

Rosenblatt, A. (1998). Assessing the child and family outcomes of systems of care for youth with severe emotional disturbance. In M. H. Epstein, K. Kutash, & A. Duchnowski (Eds.), *Outcomes for children and youth with emotional and behavioral disorders and their families: Programs and evaluation best practices*. Austin, TX: PRO-ED.

Rosenblatt, A., & Attkisson, C. C. (1993). The assessment of outcomes for sufferers of severe mental disorders: A conceptual framework and review. *Evaluation and Program Planning, 16*, 347–363.

Rosenblatt, A., & Rosenblatt, J. A. (2002). Assessing the effectiveness of care for youth with severe emotional disturbances: Is there agreement between popular outcome measures? *Journal of Behavioral Health Services and Research, 29*, 259–273.

Rosenblatt, A., & Woodbridge, M. (2003). Deconstructing research on systems of care for youth with EBD: Frameworks for policy research. *Journal of Emotional and Behavioral Disorders, 11*(1), 27–38.

Ruperto, N., Ravelli, A., Pistorio, A., Malattia, C., Cavuto, S., Gado-West, L., et al. (2001). Cross-cultural adaptation and psychometric evaluation of the Childhood Health Assessment Questionnaire (CHAQ) and the Child Health Questionnaire (CHQ) in 32 countries. Review of the general methodology. *Clinical and Experimental Rheumatology, 19*(4 Suppl. 23), S1–S9.

Rutishauser, C., Sawyer, S. M., & Bowes, G. (1998). Quality-of-life assessment in children and adolescents with asthma. *European Respiratory Journal, 12*, 486–494.

Saigal, S., Feeny, D., Rosenbaum, P., Furlong, W., Burrows, E., & Stoskopf, B. (1996). Self-perceived health status and health-related quality of life of extremely low-birth-weight infants at adolescence. *Journal of the American Medical Association, 14*, 453–459.

Sawyer, M. G., Whaites, L., Rey, J. M., Hazell, P. L., Graetz, B. W., & Baghurst, P. (2002). Health-related quality of life of children and adolescents with mental disorders. *Journal of the American Academy of Child and Adolescent Psychiatry, 41*, 530–537.

Schalock, R. L. (1996). Reconsidering the conceptualization and measurement of quality of life. In R. L. Schalock & G. N. Siperstein (Eds.), *Quality of life: Conceptualization and measurement* (pp. 123–139). Washington, DC: American Association on Mental Retardation.

Schalock, R. L., & Begab, M. J. (Eds.). (1990). *Quality of life: Perspectives and issues*. Washington, DC: American Association on Mental Retardation.

Schipper, H., Clinch, J., & Powell, V. (1990). Definitions and conceptual issues. In B. Spilker (Ed.), *Quality of life assessment in clinical trials* (pp. 11–24). New York: Raven.

Schmidt, G. M., Niland, J. C., Forman, S. J., Fonbuena, P. P., Dagis, A. C., Grant, M. M., et al. (1993). Extended follow-up in 212 long-term allogeneic bone marrow transplant survivors. Issues of quality of life. *Transplantation, 55*, 551–557.

Schmidt, L. J., Garratt, A. M., & Fitzpatrick, R. (2002). Child/parent-assessed population health outcome measures: A structured review. *Child: Care, Health, and Development, 28*, 227–237.

Singh, G., Athreya, B. H., Fries, J. F., & Goldsmith, D. P. (1994). Measurement of health status in children with juvenile rheumatoid arthritis. *Arthritis and Rheumatism, 37*, 1761–1769.

Sloan, F. A., Khakoo, R., Cluff, L. E., & Waldman, R. H. (1979). The impact of infectious and allergic diseases on the quality of life. *Social Science and Medicine, 13A*, 473–482.

Sokal, E. M. (1995). Quality of life after orthotopic liver transplantation in children. An overview of physical, psychological and social outcome. *European Journal of Pediatrics, 154*(3), 171–175.

Spieth, L. E., & Harris, C. V. (1996). Assessment of health-related quality of life in children and adolescents: An integrative review. *Journal of Pediatric Psychology, 21*, 175–193.

Stanger, C., & Lewis, M. (1993). Agreement among parents, teachers, and children on internalizing and externalizing behavior problems. *Journal of Clinical Child Psychology, 22*, 107–115.

Starfield, B. (1987). Child health status and outcome of care: a commentary on measuring the impact of medical care on children. *Journal of Chronic Diseases* (Suppl. 40) 99S–115S.

Starfield, B., Bergner, M., Ensminger, M., Riley, A., Ryan, S., Green, B., et al. (1993). Adolescent health status measurement: Development of the Child Health and Illness Profile. *Pediatrics, 91*, 430–435.

Starfield, B., Riley, A. W., Green, B. F., Ensminger, M. E., Ryan, S. A., Kelleher, K., et al. (1995). The Adolescent Child Health and Illness Profile: A population-based measure of health. *Medical Care, 33*, 553–566.

Stark, J. A., & Faulkner, E. (1996). Quality of life across the life span. In R. L. Schalock & G. N. Siperstein (Eds.), *Quality of life: Conceptualization and measurement* (pp. 23–32). Washington, DC: American Association on Mental Retardation.

Starr, P. (1992). *The logic of health-care reform*. Knoxville, TN: Whittle Direct Books.

Stein, M. B., & Kean, Y. M. (2000). Disability and quality of life in social phobia: Epidemiologic findings. *American Journal of Psychiatry, 157*, 1606–1613.

Stein, R. E. K., & Jessop, D. J. (1982). A noncatagorical approach to chronic childhood illness. *Public Health Report, 97*, 354–362.

Stroul, B. A. & Friedman, R. M. (1996). The system of care concept and philosophy. In B. A. Stroul, (Ed.), *Children's mental health: Creating systems of care in a changing society* (pp. 1–22). Baltimore: Brookes.

Tamburini, M. (Ed.). (1996). *Quality of life assessment in medicine* [CD-ROM]. Milan: Glamm Interactive.

Thomas, L. (1974). *The lives of a cell: Notes of a biology watcher.* New York: Viking.

Torrance, G. W. (1987). Utility approach to measuring health-related quality of life. *Journal of Chronic Diseases, 40*, 593–603.

Torrance, G. W., Feeny, D. H., Furlong, W. J., Barr, R. D., Zhang, Y., & Wang, Q. (1996). Multiattribute utility function for a comprehensive health status classification system. Health Utilities Index Mark 2. *Medical Care, 34,* 702–722.

Trudel, J. G., Rivard, M., Dobkin, P. L., Leclerc, J. M., & Robaey, P. (1998). Psychometric properties of the Health Utilities Index Mark 2 system in paediatric oncology patients. *Quality of Life Research, 7,* 421–432.

Varni, J. W., Katz, E. R., Seid, M., Quiggins, D. J., Friedman-Bender, A., & Castro, C. M. (1998). The Pediatric Cancer Quality of Life Inventory (PCQL). I. Instrument development, descriptive statistics, and cross-informant variance. *Journal of Behavioral Medicine, 21*(2), 179–204.

Vickrey, B. G., Hays, R. D., Brook, R. H., & Rausch, R. (1992). Reliability and validity of the Katz Adjustment Scales in an epilepsy sample. *Quality of Life Research, 1,* 63–72.

Vivier, P. M., Bernier, J. A., & Starfield, B. (1994). Current approaches to measuring health outcomes in pediatric research. *Current Opinion in Pediatrics, 6,* 530–537.

Vogels, T., Verrips, G. H., Verloove-Vanhorick, S. P., Fekkes, M., Kamphuis, R. P., Koopman, H. M., et al. (1998). Measuring health-related quality of life in children: The development of the TACQOL parent form. *Quality of Life Research, 7,* 457–465.

Ware, J. E., Jr., & Sherbourne, C. D. (1992). The MOS 36-item short-form health survey (SF-36). I. Conceptual framework and item selection. *Medical Care, 30,* 473–483.

Wasson, J. H., Kairys, S. W., Nelson, E. C., Kalishman, N., & Baribeau, P. (1994). A short survey for assessing health and social problems of adolescents. Dartmouth Primary Care Cooperative Information Project (The COOP). *Journal of Family Practice, 38,* 489–494.

Weissman, M. M., Orvaschel, H., & Padian, N. (1980). Children's symptom and social functioning self-report scales. Comparison of mothers' and children's reports. *Journal of Nervous and Mental Disease, 168,* 736–740.

West, A. (1994). Methodological issues in the assessment of quality of life in childhood asthma: What educational research has to offer. In M. J. Christie & D. J. French (Eds.), *Assessment of quality of life in childhood asthma* (pp. 121–130). Langhorne, PA: Harwood.

Wildrick, D., Parker-Fisher, S., & Morales, A. (1996). Quality of life in children with well-controlled epilepsy. *Journal of Neuroscience Nursing, 28,* 192–198.

Wray, J., Radley-Smith, R., & Yacoub, M. (1992). Effect of cardiac or heart-lung transplantation on the quality of life of the paediatric patient. *Quality of Life Research, 1,* 41–46.

Wurst, E., Herle, M., Fuiko, R., Hajszan, M., Katkhouda, C., Kieboom, A., et al. (2002). The quality of life of chronically ill and psychiatrically disturbed children. Initial experiences with an inventory for assessing quality of life in children and adolescents. *Zeitschrift fur Kinder und Jugendpsychiatrie und Psychotherapie, 30*(1), 21–28.

Zamberlan, K. E. (1992). Quality of life in school-age children following liver transplantation. *Maternal-Child Nursing Journal, 20,* 167–229.

Zeltzer, L. K., LeBaron, S., Richie, D. M., Reed, D., Schoolfield, J., & Prihoda, T. J. (1988). Can children understand and use a rating scale to quantify somatic symptoms: Assessment of nausea and vomiting as a model. *Journal of Consultation and Clinical Psychology, 56,* 567–572.

Zullig, K. J., Valois, R. F., Huebner, E. S., Oeltmann, J. E., & Drane, J. W. (2001). Relationship between perceived life satisfaction and adolescents' substance abuse. *The Journal of Adolescent Health, 29,* 279–288.

Author Index

Note: **I** denotes Volume 1, **II** denotes Volume 2, **III** denotes Volume 3. Numbers in *italics* indicate the page where the complete reference is given.

A

B

C

D

E

F

G

H

I

J

M

N

P

T

U

V

W

X

Y

Z

Subject Index

Note: **I** denotes Volume 1, **II** denotes Volume 2, **III** denotes Volume 3. Numbers in *italics* indicate the page where the complete reference is given.

B

E

F

G

I

J

K

L

M

N

P

Q

R

S

T

U

W

X

Y

Z

Printed and bound by PG in the USA